DATE DUE

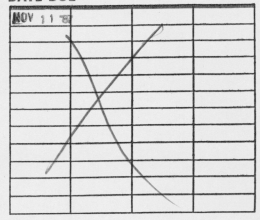

NOV 11 '87			

The Music of
Benjamin Britten

Peter Evans

The Music of
Benjamin Britten

Illustrated with over 300 music examples
and diagrams

University of Minnesota Press

Minneapolis

First published in the United States of America in 1979
by the University of Minnesota Press, 2037 University
Avenue Southeast, Minneapolis, Minnesota 55455

Printed in Great Britain

Library of Congress Cataloging in Publication Data

Evans, Peter Angus, 1929–
  The music of Benjamin Britten.
  Bibliography: p.
  Includes index.
  1. Britten, Benjamin, 1913–1976. Works. I. Title.
ML410.B853E9   780'.92'4   78-31606
ISBN 0-8166-0836-9

Acknowledgments

Several sections of this book reproduce, adapt or expand articles and review articles contributed to various musical journals. I am grateful to the editors of *Tempo*, *Faber Music News*, *The Musical Times* and *Opera* for permission to use such material in this new form. To Dr Donald Mitchell I owe the original impetus towards writing the book and subsequently much help in making scores available, often in advance of publication. I am also grateful to Tabitha Collingbourne, who set the music examples, and to Janet Harrison, who typed considerable stretches of the manuscript; while my wife's part in so protracted an enterprise reached far beyond the chores of typing and proof-reading she undertook.

The music examples are reproduced by kind permission of the following publishers.

Boosey & Hawkes: Chap. 1, nos 1–3a, 4 and 6–16. Chap. 2, nos 2–13. Chap. 3, nos 4–18. Chaps 5–12, all exx. Chap. 13, nos 1–13. Chap. 14, nos 1–14. Chap. 15, nos 1ai and bi and 2–16. Chap. 16, nos 1–3. Chap. 18, all exx.

Faber Music: Chap. 4, all exx. Chap. 13, nos 14–17. Chap. 14, nos 11–25. Chap. 15, nos 17–28. Chap. 17, nos 12–14. Chaps 19–21, all exx.

Oxford University Press: Chap. 3, nos 1–3.

Stainer & Bell Ltd (for U.K. market) and *Galaxy Music Corporation* New York (for U.S.A. market): Chap. 1, no. 5. Chap. 2, no. 1.

Universal Edition: Chap. 1, no. 3b (copyright 1922, renewed 1950).

PETER EVANS

Contents

Preface and Biographical Note

Britten's death on 4 December 1976, at the age of sixty-three, brought tributes from many parts of the world. The recognition that a unique creative spirit had been lost to the music of our time was painfully strong in the country whose musical life he had enriched so signally and so diversely for four decades, but it was clearly shared far more widely. *The Times*' obituary summarized Britten's significance aptly: 'He was the first British composer to capture and hold the attention of musicians and their audiences the world over, as well as at home; he was the first British composer to centre his mature work prolifically on the musical theatre—grand opera, chamber opera, sacred music-drama.'[1] A saddening circumstance of his last years, more immediately obvious to the general public than the necessarily great reduction in his activity as a composer brought about by his illness, was his withdrawal from all practical participation in music. Any biographical study which seeks to present Britten as he was known to his contemporaries will be at least as much concerned with the pianist, the conductor, the festival director, the instigator of musical experience at all kinds of level, as with the composer. Most happily, future generations will find some clue to the mixture of respect and affection which Britten the practitioner inspired in performers and audiences in the series of recordings he made of his own works and a remarkably wide range of other music. Yet ultimately his reputation will remain alive solely for the qualities that continue to be found within that central part of his life's work, the compositions.

The present study is an attempt to review Britten's entire creative output as it is received by one pair of ears and one set of analytical faculties. It is not the first analytical companion to his music, for at an unusually early stage in his career he was paid the compliment of a comprehensive symposium.[2] This appeared in 1952, one year before the composer's fortieth birthday, and an impressively catholic team of writers discussed almost every work written in the twenty years since the Opus 1 *Sinfonietta* had appeared. During the

---

[1] *The Times*, December 6, 1976.
[2] D. Mitchell and H. Keller (eds), *Benjamin Britten: a commentary on his works from a group of specialists*, London 1952. (Hereafter 'Mitchell-Keller')

1

remaining twenty-four years of his life, while never again matching the extraordinary speed with which he produced large-scale compositions during the late 1940s, Britten continued steadily to build on that early achievement with works in most of the standard media—as well as in some that were more or less his own invention. The symposium stopped at Opus 50, a notable point indeed, for it was marked by *Billy Budd*. My own original intention was to end with Opus 88, a less round number but a no less notable opera—*Death in Venice*. Britten's death, after he had triumphed over the crippling disability of his illness by producing seven further scores, took away the hope that another extensive, and probably significantly different, period of composing activity might lie beyond the opera, and it became logical to survey the completed work.

In general, I have tended to give rather fuller treatment to its second half, partly because of material already available in the symposium, but also because there exists in addition to that volume a considerable body of writing, whether analytical, critical or anecdotal, about Britten's earlier compositions, but much less about his more recent work. This reflects accurately enough his decline as a controversial figure, but has scant relation either to the quality of the later music or to the stylistic development it reveals. *Curlew River* (to take an obvious example), which has been found a powerfully affecting experience by countless audiences, marked changes in the composer's conception of both texture and time that are relevant to all his subsequent work, yet the body of critical writing it has attracted is very slight by comparison with the shoals of articles which attended the first operas in their early years.

The reasons for this are evident enough, but they still merit a closer scrutiny. Thirty years ago, British musicians remained amazed, if not disconcerted, by the imaginative precision with which Britten deployed a fluent technique, amazed too that native opera could succeed, here and abroad, for the somewhat insular policy British music had pursued since the early years of the century still had wide currency. Of course, in a survey of Western musical styles conducted in those post-war years Britten could have been said to be a pronouncedly conservative figure, even while he was still confirming his reputation. 'Conservative' need not be considered a particularly loaded term; but nor need 'iconoclastic', which is perhaps the nearest it has to an opposite. Different artists must react differently, even to a common inheritance, and historical inevitability is a particularly hazardous doctrine in the arts. Measured against, say, the French *Six* or Stravinsky in his more suavely neo-classical contexts, Britten appears fairly near a norm of indebtedness to past practice. Measured against the linguistic innovations of Schoenberg and his pupils, or even of the Bartók of the twenties and thirties, the music that brought Britten to the widest notice—the Serenade and *Peter Grimes*, for instance—may appear unadventurous in its reliance on traditional vocabulary and resources. But a composer is bound to no absolute

2

criteria of topicality. Provided that the language he uses suggests to him still hidden creative potentialities, an urge to set out, perhaps from known premises but towards new destinations, then, should his essential creativity be sufficient to the task, he may produce work that will continue to command a hearing, because it offers an enlargement of our experience too.

Though we easily enough take up an international vantage-point today, one of Britten's own signal achievements in the years around *Grimes* was to demonstrate to his countrymen that musical insularity was no longer a necessary policy of self-defence. Not only did he show that an Englishman's music could be taken up without a patronizing air by the rest of the Western musical world. In assimilating certain continental influences into his own work (Mahler, Berg and Stravinsky were the most obvious at this stage), he had also pointed towards some degree of *rapprochement* with the principal forces of European music. It was for a new generation of British composers, men like Fricker and Hamilton, to take as their linguistic starting-point the achievements of Schoenberg, Stravinsky and Bartók, while still younger generations were to profit from the excitingly, at times confusingly, diverse examples of Europe and America in the fifties and sixties—from Darmstadt, from Messiaen's Conservatoire classes, from Boulez, Stockhausen and Babbitt, from Kagel and Cage. No longer need the typical British composer feel deprived of stimuli from beyond his immediate environment.

Meanwhile, Britten was a witness to this profound transformation of his native musical scene. That he should appear at times to be relegated to the status of an ancient monument by some of his younger colleagues never seemed to depress him unduly. Iconoclasm can be a necessary as well as an exhilarating spur to more creative attitudes, and in any event, as the obituary tributes confirmed, the finer talents recognized both the superb craftsman-ship and the rich creative harvest of Britten's work. But critical attention in his later years was almost inevitably focused upon those figures and developments that represented the aspirations of a new race of musicians. Yet the composers of Britten's generation had to go on finding a way forward, steering perilously between the Scylla of letting an achieved stylis-tic balance freeze into a gesture of calculated defiance, and the Charybdis of seizing desperately upon every innovation of younger colleagues that might plausibly invest their work with some semblance of topicality. I have tried in these pages to show the slow, organic process by which Britten came to terms (his own terms) with various aspects of twentieth-century musical thought; that his works continued to sound like no one but Britten's need not astonish us. Indeed, such evidence as I offer of technical change is not directly relevant to an aesthetic evaluation of the music in question, for the work of art is judged by the conviction and beauty with which it establishes relations within itself. I find Britten's later output to be impressively satisfying by such a criterion, able to create and re-create in the listener an experience that the composer has exactly encompassed in musical processes. Criticism intent principally on the *dernier cri* may overlook such music altogether, and even those critics who were maturing when Britten's work was our nearest approach to that ideal may see their prime obligation as keeping abreast, wherever their intuitive sympathies may have lodged *en route*. So it is that, in his later years, apart from those curious outbursts of interest which mark the passing of each decade in a prominent artist's career, Britten was not very searchingly discussed in print; some of the obituary notices sought to make amends, some were equivocal. The present study seeks to fill some gaps in the investigation of Britten's music, but to say no last words; I do not doubt that a younger generation of musical scholars and commentators will make his music their concern some day, and enjoy a perspective longer than my own.

Of course, extended studies of Britten and some notable articles have appeared since the symposium. Pride of place here must go to Eric Walter White's book, for it is the third version of what was in 1948 a pioneer study. In its current form[3] it provides a biography rich in illuminating detail, and an account of the operas that is particularly interesting for its discussion of their literary background. My own book offers no biographical material beyond the summary appended to this preface and the details most relevant to each piece discussed. Patricia Howard's thoughtful study of the operas[4] includes analysis of musical procedures, but her concern is chiefly to test the validity and consistency of each opera as a musico-dramatic entity. Though I have sometimes differed from their findings, I have not sought to challenge or to supplant either of these commentators, but rather to offer a more detailed account than was relevant to their purposes of those musical techniques on which all Britten's dramatic (and in the instrumental works, quasi-dramatic) situations depend.

My principal intention has been to study the musical processes of each of Britten's works and to offer the results in the form of a commentary. The treatment of a given work is commonly chronological, but with most of the operas it has seemed to me less unwieldy to discuss specific aspects in turn. Inevitably such a study must appear irritatingly repetitive in some respects, particularly if read in straight sequence, but I have thought it more useful to plan the book so that it can be consulted as a reference to any individual work. I hope that, in pursuing this aim, I have not buried too deeply that investigation of Britten's developing style and changing methods which sustained my own interest in so extensive a project. I recognize that the kind of analysis I have favoured is viewed with suspicion in some quarters today: the term 'descriptive' would be applied to it with pejorative intent. I own therefore that my investigations set out from a strong, but essentially intuitive, response to this music, and are directed towards identifying the compositional grounds for the nature of the response, the causes that have ensured

[3] E. W. White, *Benjamin Britten: his life and operas*, London 1970. (Hereafter 'White')
[4] P. Howard, *The Operas of Benjamin Britten*, London 1969. (Hereafter 'Howard')

the composer's effects. The partisanship or element of pre-judgment that this may imply is in fact common to many analysts who would pride themselves on a greater degree of objectivity than mine, since their very choice of material (how many Hummel analyses have been published, to how many of Mozart?) involves a judgment that is initially intuitive. In writing a book that will no doubt be read chiefly by those to whom Britten's music already makes some kind of an appeal, I have borne in mind that for many of them an entirely dispassionate dissection (perhaps in purely diagrammatic terms) of the compositional process, even if it were possible, might be alienating rather than illuminating. But I hope that my commentary proceeds consistently from demonstrable musical facts, so that it will have some validity even for the reader who offers no guarantees of warm emotional response to the music under discussion.

I have written, then, for the listener who may not be professionally concerned in the mechanics of music, but I have assumed him to have some technical knowledge. Unless our aim is to provide an imaginative analogue to the experience afforded by a piece of music (which is often to say more about ourselves than about it), we can only convey any certain meaning about the piece by determining what *happens* within it; and to ensure that we take each other's meaning aright, we have no alternative to the use of technical terms of a reasonably unambiguous nature. Most readers are likely to accept that in the discussion of instrumental works I have justifiably assumed some understanding of the ways in which tonal and motivic relationships have structural consequences. If our hope is to follow more clearly the composer's thought processes and to find some reason for what may strike us, taking no thought at all, as the right (or, indeed, an entirely unpredictable) next move, then we must be prepared to attach importance to matters he can be shown to have regarded as important. As far as possible I have tried to demonstrate thematic and otherwise local phenomena of particular interest by the use of music type, but the reader who is to follow the workings of Britten's structural designs must be prepared to consult the scores. It is in extending this analytical approach to the vocal, and especially the dramatic, works that I may be thought by some to have investigated compositional means at the expense of musico-dramatic ends. Yet Britten's mastery of the art of composition remains, in his operas as elsewhere, a mastery of tonal and harmonic structures, of thematic cast, cross-reference and transformation, of resourceful textural variety and of imaginative deployment of voices and instruments—though it would be futile indeed not to show the uniquely fitting relationship of each of these to verbal and dramatic contingencies. Furthermore, to have given another account of the operas threaded chiefly on their plots (which I take to be familiar, at least in outline, to my readers) would have duplicated information that is readily available elsewhere.

Long though the book is, I have had to be selective, especially in my discussion of the major dramatic works. In rejecting any rigid consistency of approach to the study of works so varied in scope and emphasis, it may be that I have too artlessly revealed by my choice of topics a succession of predilections and blind spots. A statement of musical facts is my central submission; but to relate these back to the experience which stimulated the enquiry is an exercise in their interpretation, and I have not suppressed the tendency to undertake this. None the less, I hope that I have indicated in my treatment of each major score its cardinal compositional principles, those which quite different forms of analysis would confirm to have been guiding the composer's decisions.

Some explanation is owed the reader for my omissions. Though Britten's early development, before and during his studies with Frank Bridge, must some day offer a fascinating field of enquiry (for the composer who leaps into prominence with the *Sinfonietta* clearly already has a long and eventful history to be unearthed), the only material available at present is that which the composer published in his last years. Almost invariably he added the touching-up strokes he must have found irresistible, but the Britten student will need to erase these before venturing a reliable historical reading. Meanwhile, though such pieces as the de la Mare songs, *Tit for Tat*, and the *Walztes* for piano afford charming glimpses into Britten's musical *boyhood*, they are disregarded in this study; on the verge of the official *oeuvre*, the 1931 quartet is included, as the relatively minor revision is known. Excluded too are the hundreds of pages of mature Britten which make up his incidental music to stage and broadcast plays and his film music. This far weightier omission can be justified only on the grounds that none of this material is published, and that the reader is unlikely to find an opportunity to hear any of it, except perhaps one or two radio scores that have become classic items in the BBC archives. But I do not doubt that the orderly documentation of this corpus of unknown Britten (begun by Eric Walter White in his book, and in a subsequent *Tempo* article)[5] and its critical appraisal are important tasks that await their researcher. An even more demanding task begins to show itself with the welcome news that the vast body of the composer's sketch and autograph material is likely to be preserved intact in the archives now being set up at Aldeburgh. Finally, I have excluded Britten's arrangements, whether of folk-songs or the National Anthem, Bach or Mahler, and his realizations of Purcell and of *The Beggar's Opera*. This will appear to some readers an omission bordering on the perverse, but my concern has been to show the rich amalgam of the composer's own style, whereas the predetermination of melodic line and of structure (in folksong and in the ballad opera) reduces his rôle, however deftly executed and however witty or affecting the outcome, to that of a commentator; the given nature of infinitely more in the major Purcell scores converts his rôle to that of an

---

[5] E. W. White, 'Britten in the Theatre: a provisional catalogue', *Tempo* 107, 1973, p. 2.

editor. Of course, the relevance of Britten's continued, and typically practical, interest in Purcell to his own creative achievement is not overlooked at the appropriate points in the book.

I have retained the practice followed in the Mitchell-Keller symposium of grouping together the smaller works according to *genre*, but of devoting a separate chapter to each opera. However, to have maintained this pattern exactly would have resulted in some chapters of quite unwieldy size (on the songs, for instance), and would have blurred too severely the book's picture of chronological stylistic development. The compromise I have adopted is to survey all the music preceding *Peter Grimes* (1945) in three genre chapters, then to look at the big line of operas that extends (taking in, rather illogically, a ballet) to *A Midsummer-Night's Dream* (1960). At this central point, I have grouped together all Britten's music for performance by children, since in this way its remarkable variety of types and approaches becomes clear. Then I have reverted to a treatment by *genre*, only separating the Canticles from the other songs, and the *War Requiem* from the other choral music; these chapters cover therefore the entire span from immediately after *Grimes* to the very last works. One consequence is that in some contexts I refer to the influence of the church parables style before I have discussed those works; a few moments' cross-reference may become necessary at such points. Finally I have followed the parables with the two works in which Britten returned to more conventional operatic resources—*Owen Wingrave* and *Death in Venice*. As was my original intention, that last magnificent opera provides me with a *terminus ad quem* as fitting as *Billy Budd* was for the symposium: both works crown the achievements of the periods leading up to them.

While such a book cannot fail to provide evidence of the impressive bulk and the catholic range of Britten's music, I hope that my commentary demonstrates some of the means by which it has enriched the lives of listeners and of performers wherever the Western musical tradition is prized.

Edward Benjamin Britten was born at Lowestoft, Suffolk, on 22 November 1913, a happy chance that was later to allow musicians to celebrate St Cecilia's Day and his birthday together. Music formed an important part of his early experience, for his mother was an amateur singer, and he was encouraged to explore, and even to compose, before formal tuition on piano and viola began. Opportunities for hearing music at a less homely level were rare, however, and his attendance at the Norwich Festivals of 1924 and 1927 opened new horizons. At the second of these the boy, by now composing prolifically, attracted the interest of Frank Bridge, whose pupil he became. It is difficult to imagine a more fortunate encounter of talents, for Bridge was in these very years turning away from the manner of his earlier music, admirably competent within eclectically Romantic conventions, towards a style which was highly unusual in England then (and has only received any measure of appreciation very recently) in that it sought to draw on the study Bridge had made of developments in Central Europe—of Bartók, Schoenberg and Berg.

Britten was always at pains to acknowledge the debt he owed Bridge for these decisive years of tuition.[6] He had already demonstrated precocious powers of musical invention, but these had now to be justified in the face of a constant rigorous scrutiny, to be measured against exacting technical criteria. While still in his mid-teens, Britten was required to develop a professional control of his musical material, yet he was encouraged to approach the task less through traditional academic disciplines than through the refining of his inner and outer ear and the exploration of some of the most adventurous music being written at that time. Even though this tuition could be carried on only during school holidays, the evidence is clear (for example, from the early quartet discussed in Chapter 1) that by the time of his entry to the Royal College of Music in 1930, he already had a technical virtuosity which must have appeared alarming in an environment where basic contrapuntal skills were regarded as a compulsory preamble to composition, and the approved twentieth-century exemplars were essentially nationalist, if not parochial. Not surprisingly, Britten found some aspects of the course frustratingly elementary,[7] and even his composition lessons with John Ireland do not seem to have deposed Bridge from the rôle of chief critic and adviser he was to play until the end of his life in 1941. The difficulty of finding a platform for his music (or even performers capable of doing it justice) was another disappointment to Britten, and incidents like the failure of the college library to obtain a score of *Pierrot Lunaire* were cumulatively disenchanting. It is as a pianist that he seems to have gained most from his RCM years, studying with Arthur Benjamin. Benjamin's own composing style can be detected in Britten's only early piano composition, *Holiday Diary*, and the lucid detail of Britten's piano playing, whether as a song accompanist (one of the greatest of his time), in chamber music or (all too rarely after the early years) as a soloist, is impressive testimony to Benjamin's teaching.

The Macnaghten-Lemare concerts gave Britten his first London hearing in December 1932, and included a performance of the Op. 1 *Sinfonietta* one month later. The interest that work declares, albeit with most recognizably English phraseology, in Schoenberg's musical thought was sharpened by hearing *Wozzeck* in 1934, from which experience Britten conceived the idea of studying with Berg when he left college in the summer. It appears that this use of the travelling scholarship he had been awarded was officially considered unsuitable, but he did visit Vienna, where part of the Op. 6 violin

[6] Cf. B. Britten, 'Frank Bridge (1879–1941)', *Faber Music News*, Autumn 1966, p. 17.
[7] Cf. his comments in M. Schafer, *British Composers in Interview*, London 1963, p. 114.

suite was written. The International Society for Contemporary Music festivals provided a chance for the young Britten to be heard in Europe: the oboe quartet was given at Florence in 1934, the violin suite at Barcelona two years later, while the Frank Bridge variations scored a decisive success at Salzburg in 1937. But it was at home that the composer needed to find work, and in those years large-scale commissions were not easily come by. Britten found congenial tasks in writing music for plays and for documentary films made by the G.P.O. Though the slight and unconventional resources at his disposal might appear restrictive, in fact the flair he revealed for satisfying highly specific yet diverse demands with them was an invaluable addition to his technical armoury. And in the films' script-writer, W. H. Auden, he discovered a collaborator with whom he was to undertake far less ephemeral projects.

It was through the promptings of Auden's example that Britten first tested his music's ability to carry a powerfully-committed social, even political, message, and sowed the seeds from which so much of his later music was to spring. At this stage, in works like the orchestrally accompanied song-cycle, *Our Hunting Fathers* (1936), and the choral *Ballad of Heroes* (1939), the tone is sometimes more shrill and the mood more bitterly ironic than in the succession of more generalized statements and commentaries begun by *Peter Grimes*. Yet the self-conscious technical *élan* of this music of the thirties and the barbed tongue do not give the whole story: in Messalina's lament or in the Nocturne from Britten's first song-cycle with piano, *On this Island* (1937), a compassionate lyricism can be heard that is less qualified by irony than the texts which prompt it. Even so, audiences, and especially critics, were uncomfortable before a brilliance almost suspect in a country that still took a perverse pride in amateurish cultivation of the arts. Britten's personal discontent was intensified by the general political climate in Europe as, with the Spanish cause already lost, temporizing in the face of Nazi aggression seemed to betoken a spiritual malaise. Auden's belief that America offered a chance to escape the taint led to his emigration; Britten decided to follow him there during 1939.

By the time of his departure from England, Britten had made a mark at least as incisively with instrumental scores as with vocal, and during his brief American period the balance remained unchanged: between the violin concerto (1939) and the first quartet (1941) came the *Sinfonia da Requiem*, three works which are now securely in the repertory. But in the light of later developments still more significance attaches to the other American works. He had been accompanied to the United States by the tenor, Peter Pears, and with two song-cycles, *Les Illuminations* (1939) and the Michelangelo Sonnets (1940), he responded to Pears's individual artistry and penetrating musical intelligence, inaugurating a creative partnership that was to be the foundation on which most of his finest achievements in both opera and song would be based. The Auden collaboration bore one further fruit in the

9

operetta, *Paul Bunyan,* produced at Columbia University, New York, in 1941. It shows a determined attempt on the part of poet and composer to identify themselves not only with the American folklore from which the plot is drawn, but with American ways of thinking and feeling.

For Britten, however, such identification proved impossible to sustain. Whatever the dissatisfactions that had clouded his view of life in England, it now became clear to him how deeply rooted was his affection for his native heritage: the decisive moment came with his reading an article by E. M. Forster on the poet of Britten's native Suffolk, George Crabbe. Having resolved to return home, he immediately turned his attention to setting English verse again: Auden's *Hymn to Saint Cecilia* was perhaps a farewell offering, but *A Ceremony of Carols* suggests a conscious *rapprochement* with English musical traditions; both were written in 1942 during the voyage. At much the same time he began the series of British folk-song arrangements that was to be continued intermittently for the rest of his life, while his recognition of Purcell's crucial place in English music was creatively reflected in *Rejoice in the Lamb* (1943). Britten's pacifist convictions made him a conscientious objector, but he was happy to help in keeping civilized values alive by giving recitals, often with Peter Pears, to the most diverse audiences, an experience which seems to have intensified his search for a direct, widely comprehensible idiom. Certainly with the Serenade for tenor, horn and strings of 1943 he demonstrated a new stylistic assurance and a new mastery of the penetratingly simple idea. It is this work which most clearly declares his readiness to embark on the broad, richly-varied canvas of true opera, and his chance came when Joan Cross, Director of the Sadler's Wells Company, entrusted to him the work that should mark the reopening of the company's theatre on 7 June 1945. Following up the enthusiasm for Crabbe kindled in America, Britten had been working since early 1944 on *Peter Grimes*, and the opera's generosity of musical ideas, deftness of characterization and underlying compassion brought it a resounding success; this quickly proved to be far more than local, as many of the world's greatest opera houses added the work to their repertories.

Even before the full extent of this success was evident, Britten had drawn from the achievement of so ambitious an undertaking a confidence which was to carry him through the most amazingly prolific years of his career. The Donne Sonnets, the second quartet and the *Young Person's Guide to the Orchestra*, three works indebted, in quite different ways, to Henry Purcell, were all completed in the same year as *Grimes*. Yet in the following year Britten produced a further opera, *The Rape of Lucretia*, and in 1947, *Albert Herring*. In these scores he set about the task of providing a native repertory for a country which had but two established opera houses and no tradition of continuing support for opera. The largest scale of enterprise could rarely be indulged, but by drastically reducing musical demands to a small number of solo singers and an orchestra of solo colours, a composer could hope to make

10

his works available in quite modest provincial theatres. Britten's form of chamber opera was effectively tested in the contrasted worlds of *Lucretia* and *Herring*, their success being great enough to justify the formation of a special company, the English Opera Group, to tour such works. In 1948 the group played an important rôle in the establishment of the Aldeburgh Festival, an annual event held in and around the small Suffolk coastal town where Britten had now made his home. For the rest of his life the composer's work schedule was chiefly regulated by the festival's needs: as well as writing the majority of his works for performance there, he sustained a huge burden of conducting, piano-playing and organizational activities for twenty-five years, until illness compelled his withdrawal. Aldeburgh typifies Britten's preferred working conditions in that it required him to write with highly specific, and usually very familiar, performers and surroundings in mind. While Pears's cardinal rôle remained, regular visitors to the festivals like the Soviet cellist Mstislav Rostropovich, and his wife, the soprano Galina Vishnevskaya, the baritone Dietrich Fischer-Dieskau, the guitarist Julian Bream and the harpist Osian Ellis, all helped to give new slants to Britten's imagination in the works he wrote for them. The church 'parables' written during the 1960s were also brought into being by the special circumstances of a festival where a fine church was more easily available than a fine concert hall or opera house.

Perhaps the single work that best demonstrates the spirit of the Aldeburgh enterprise is *Noyes Fludde* (1957), for this mystery play drew on large numbers of Suffolk children as singers, actors and players to create music of a kind that is altogether *sui generis* (and deeply moving), not adult music patronizingly watered down. Something of this remarkable ability to combine amateur and professional resources had been seen in the cantata, *Saint Nicolas*, as early as 1948, while in the following year the Spring Symphony had used the traditional English large-scale choir as a virtuoso instrument, and *The Little Sweep* had given children an operatic entertainment of their own. In all such undertakings Britten was concerned to inculcate a professional degree of application, if not always a professional degree of complexity. And he did not forsake composition at the most taxing professional level when the opportunity presented itself. For the Festival of Britain in 1951 he was commissioned to write another large-scale opera, *Billy Budd*, and for the Coronation celebrations of Queen Elizabeth II in 1953 he wrote an operatic study of Elizabeth I, *Gloriana*. Both were given at Covent Garden, the latter with a success much qualified by the unfortunate transformation of a musical occasion into a society function. Its reputation has been salvaged in later productions, but its appeal seems more nationally delimited than that of Britten's other operas. *Budd*, on the other hand, has been recognized widely as a dramatic achievement at least on the level of *Grimes* (and musically a good deal more concentrated), while the opera written for the Venice Biennale of 1954, *The Turn of the Screw*, is generally

11

held to be Britten's most intense work in the medium of chamber opera. Its construction around a set of orchestral variations on a twelve-note theme signals the beginning of an interest, wholly non-doctrinaire yet far from casual, in the unifying properties of melodic and harmonic twelve-note contexts and other quasi-serial devices, which was to prompt the composer's invention in innumerable later works.

Britten and Pears continued to travel regularly on recital tours, such cycles as the Hardy and Hölderlin settings with piano, the *Songs from the Chinese* with guitar and the Nocturne with orchestra being written for Pears. On their tour of the Far East in 1955, Britten heard Balinese music and saw Japanese Noh-plays, two exotic art forms which made a profound impression and were to affect his own music. The first showed itself in the subject and the sonorities of a full-length ballet, *The Prince of the Pagodas*, written during 1956, while the more pervasive influence of the second brought about the pronounced modification of his idiom that distinguished the trilogy of church parables begun with *Curlew River* in 1964. The intervening years included the production at the 1960 Aldeburgh Festival of an opera which enlarged the 'chamber' concept, *A Midsummer-Night's Dream*, to a text ingeniously adapted from Shakespeare by Britten and Pears, and for the consecration of the new Coventry Cathedral in May 1962 Britten wrote a *War Requiem*, interleaving the liturgical text with poems of a First War victim, Wilfred Owen. The two works, so contrasted in spirit, invite comparison for the manner in which they operate on several musical planes that remain distinct yet interactive, and for the broad review they offer of the composer's stylistic horizons during the previous two decades. The *Requiem* in particular appears consciously to draw to a common focus the most diverse elements, as though striving to give a universal currency to its impassioned condemnation of war. The first performance was soon and widely followed up, marking a peak in Britten's standing with a quite general musical public comparable to that achieved by *Grimes*.

But whereas *Grimes* appeared as a harbinger of the palmy days in which Britten consolidated its stylistic traits, the *War Requiem* came to appear a retrospective survey of an amplitude he was increasingly to spurn. The revival of his interest in purely instrumental writing, sparked off by Rostropovich, seems to have intensified his research into the material of music at a minute, cellular level: already in the cello sonata of 1961 there is to be traced a new economy of motivic working. Yet here the movements retain the boldly 'characteristic' contrasts implied by their titles, whereas the Cello Symphony of two years later is Britten's supreme achievement in musical thinking that calls on no references outside itself: as the unusual title suggests, it even renounces much of the dramaticism latent in the 'concerto' principle. However, it is in the starkly reduced textures of the church parables that renunciation and reassessment most obviously become pre-occupations in his music of the sixties. The flexibility of temporal relations

12

(and consequent dismantling of harmonic mechanisms) that the Japanese models inspired brought Britten's music unexpectedly close to the spirit, however remote from the letter, of that being developed by much younger contemporaries. Works such as the song-cycle, *The Poet's Echo*, show that his own concern was not to pursue a 'modernity' that could well have been factitious but to find a means of assimilating this freer musical discourse into the amalgam of his earlier style. It was written in 1965, during a visit Britten and Pears paid to a Composers' House in Armenia. They had first visited Russia two years earlier when a representative sample of Britten's music had been warmly received. The year 1963 was no less notable for the affectionate recognition at home of the composer's fiftieth birthday by innumerable celebratory performances and the publication of a *Festschrift*.[8]

After almost twenty years of successful adaptation of whatever resources were to hand, the Aldeburgh Festival acquired in 1967, with the opening of the Maltings at Snape, its own concert hall—again an adaptation, one which delightfully retains its regional character but is admirably suited, above all in its magnificent acoustics, to its new, permanent purpose. It also proved to have excellent 'atmosphere' as a recording studio, and in the years following its opening Britten was very active as a conductor both at concerts and in recordings. A grievous blow to the 1969 Festival, a fire which gutted the Maltings after the first performance that year, made further inroads on his energies, for he and his colleagues resolved that its rebuilding should be completed for the following year's festival; incredibly, this was achieved. Though the Maltings made possible a larger scale of operatic presentation than the festival had previously been able to contemplate, it was not until 1973 that Britten completed an opera specifically for this stage, *Death in Venice*. Two years earlier, *Owen Wingrave* had been transmitted on BBC Television, by which it was commissioned. In fact the television opera was later transplanted to the stage (Covent Garden, 1973) and *Death in Venice*, a work which gave Peter Pears his most searching rôle of the many he had created, enjoyed a success marked by the tour abroad of the original production and new productions overseas.

Even though the subject of that opera was one on which the composer had been pondering for long, it encourages the view that this last opera was quite consciously a swan-song in that medium. Yet Britten was evidently at the height of his creative powers in writing it, even while he was aware that an ailing heart condition demanded treatment. Only when the opera was finished did he enter hospital, for an operation that proved no more than partially successful. He could take no part in the musical shaping of the *Death in Venice* première, and it became clear that all practical music must now be denied him. But he gradually picked up compositional threads, first in revising two early scores, *Paul Bunyan* and the 1931 quartet, then in new

---

[8] A. Gishford (ed.), *Tribute to Benjamin Britten on his Fiftieth Birthday*, London 1963.

works, most notably the solo cantata *Phaedra*, written for Janet Baker, and in the third string quartet, which draws from the searing experience of *Death in Venice* (and, no doubt, that of its personal aftermath) a sublimity that is intensely affecting. The quartet was first performed on 19 December 1976, fifteen days after the composer's death. His funeral at Aldeburgh was a reminder of all he had done to celebrate the regional inspiration of his talents; the subsequent memorial service in Westminster Abbey confirmed that the fruits of those talents were national and international in their powerful appeal.

The Westminster order of service listed the many formal tributes to his achievement which had been paid to Britten, the university doctorates, orders, medals and prizes. From his own country he had received the supreme honour for artistic and intellectual distinction, membership of the Order of Merit, in 1965, following that of the Companionship of Honour in 1952, but he had, it was widely assumed, declined those honours that measure success in the worlds of politics and business. In the June preceding his death, however, he became a Life Peer, the first composer to be honoured in this way. Among the many distinctions awarded him from abroad, the Aspen Award of 1964 takes pride of place, for it elicited in his speech of acceptance an important summary of his artistic beliefs, his aspirations and his fears.[9]

No less well known is the composer's declaration on another occasion that it was not for him to know whether he would come to represent in the music of his time 'a wave or a ripple'.[10] Allied to this unaffected concentration on the immediate task rather than the judgments of posterity was a marked lack of enthusiasm for discussing the technical aspects of his own music: a comment made on the appearance of the pioneer analytical studies in the Mitchell-Keller symposium sought almost to disown findings that, while no doubt scarcely revelatory to him, concerned incontrovertible enough aspects of his work.[11] The present study again attempts to demonstrate that, whatever the moments of piercingly simple and spontaneous invention that continue to arrest the listener to Britten's music, his stature ultimately depends on an ability to sustain their vision across the broad spans, in other words the ability to compose prodigiously well.

[9] B. Britten, *On Receiving the first Aspen Award*, London 1964.
[10] Cf. C. Mason, 'Britten at 50', *Tempo* 66/67, 1963, p. 1.
[11] Cf. I. Holst, 'Working for Benjamin Britten', *Musical Times* cxviii, March 1977, p. 202.

1 Early Chamber and Piano Music

The first span of Britten's activity, up to his return from America, is bounded by two chamber works, the *Sinfonietta* and the first string quartet, both of which demand examination in some detail if the composer's precocious command of structural thinking is to be made clear. What happens in the nine years between them is partly a strengthening of faith in tonal mechanisms and partly a development of idiosyncratic melodic and harmonic procedures; sometimes a big step comes in a slight work, and at this formative stage it is worth while to look carefully at even those scores which may seem peripheral.

SINFONIETTA, OP. 1

Erwin Stein's suggestion that Schoenberg's first Chamber Symphony formed part of the background of Britten's Op. 1 is entirely convincing,[1] even though in scale and sonorities the two scores are so unlike. In 1932, other models could have been found for this deployment of a rich mixture of solo colours in the formerly neglected territory between orthodox chamber and orchestral styles, but most of them, notably the Hindemith sets of *Kammermusiken*, Op. 24 and Op. 36, amplified industriously contrapuntal textures into mechanized structures redolent of the Baroque concerto. It is part of Britten's debt to Bridge, and indeed to that whole tradition of belated English Romanticism which was summed up in the 'phantasy' production stimulated by W. W. Cobbett, that, whatever his impatience with parochial decorum, he found still less to attract him in the brisk propulsion and ritornello symmetries of the Hindemithian manner. His ambition was to find new potentialities in that subtler, truly symphonic thematicism which is concerned less with unequivocal definitions than with releasing the musical energy stored in smaller motivic units. The closely-argued procedures of Schoenberg's early chamber works, their hard-won lyricism and their dramaticism that is inherent in the thematic life, all seem to have made a strong appeal to Britten as he sought to fashion an instrumental language

[1] E. Stein, 'The Symphonies', in Mitchell-Keller, p. 247.

tenser than the self-indulgent 'tunefulness' of a debilitated English chamber tradition and yet more subject to the fantasy than the undemanding rigidity of the pseudo-Baroque. It is still too little recognized how consistent has been Britten's reliance on the unifying power of intricate motivic derivation even during the period of his most open-handed melodic invention; the *Sinfonietta* provides grounds, as clearly as does *The Turn of the Screw*, for identifying Schoenberg's lasting relevance to this preoccupation.

There are many quite direct signs of Schoenberg's influence in the *Sinfonietta*. The most obvious, the horn call (see Ex. 1), is also instructive in what it does *not* borrow from its model in the Chamber Symphony: in place of Schoenberg's series of perfect fourths, imperiously pointing beyond accepted tonal restrictions (in fact, rather further than the rest of the work is prepared to go), Britten substitutes a pentatonic fanfare followed by a

Ex. 1. 1

Cf. Ex. 2
for bracketed
shapes

Mixolydian descending scale. If its phrasing were more suavely aspiring, this line could wander unobserved into one of those English works that coloured their Brahmsian lyrical periods with folky inflexions. However, the acute tension that this outburst momentarily relieves, the unyielding confrontation of B flat and A across a wide compass, ensures that we hear no pastoral tones in the horn theme. These absolute sevenths, that play so important a part in the *Sinfonietta*, also take us back to Schoenberg. The route might be traced through Frank Bridge (see the first bar of Ex. 5 below); their inversions as seconds are, as we shall see, closer to an English appoggiatura practice. Yet even at its most involved, Bridge's late style required a wealth of subsidiary detail—accompaniment patterns, parallel strands and harmonic reinforcements. For the cogent economy of Britten's first movement, in which long paragraphs often contain no element that is not palpably motivic, we must look either to some twelve-note contexts or to the Schoenberg of the first two quartets and the Chamber Symphony. It is the tenuity of Britten's textures and his avoidance of chromatic relationships that ensure so contrasted a quality of sound.

Analysis demonstrates how the opening span expounds most of the germinal shapes of the work (see Ex. 2), but these are so securely bound into one unfolding line that we isolate none of those portentous 'mottoes' which, from Liszt onwards, have tended to inhibit the flow of such structures. Even the horn-call (Ex. 1) is a logical extension of the earlier melodic motion which, by phrase overlaps and the total avoidance of all harmonic and tonal (as opposed to intervallic and modal) definition, drives on the paragraph for

16

Ex. 1.2

thirty-nine bars; its interruption is caused by an F sharp (fig. 4) that swerves decisively out of the established modality (scale of F with natural or flat seventh). The process by which a first subject shape (from bars 5–6) is transformed into that of the second subject invites comparison with Schoenberg's characteristic blurring process (see, for example, the Second Quartet) that makes of transition a gradual metamorphosis. The imitative extension of this aspiring second subject (Ex. 3a) strengthens the echo we may hear in it of the Chamber Symphony (Ex. 3b). If the sonata thesis is to retain its validity, then it is the contrast of such unified themes that must make a stronger impression than the converse, and here, with the cello's falling phrase (fig. 9, bar 3), we feel a clear sonata duality to have been expounded. But instead of the conventional tonal dichotomy there have been only suggestive parallels: an opening modality in which D seems the most likely

Ex. 1.3 (a)

17

Ex.1.3 (b)

final, then a second group that explores sharper regions (e.g., between figs 6 and 7, approximately E major) before moving to a close in F delicately implied by the dominant pedal of fig. 9.

The development's juxtaposition and assimilation of phrases from the two groups serves to emphasize their kinship, but it is also dramatic in the direct opposition of modes: whereas the ubiquitous seventh began as a tense interval within a single field, it now often represents two poles of tonal attraction. Indeed, clearer tonal implications can be found here than in the exposition, and Britten ironically contrives that the most obstinate assertion (by the pizzicato double-bass) is of the D minor which, *faute de mieux*, we shall have assumed to be the movement's tonic key. The scalic motion that was the basic stuff of the first subject connects long stretches of otherwise fragmentary texture before it is systematized as a pizzicato ostinato built from tetrachords (from fig. 15, bar 4), superimposed so as to yield constant seventh and ninth relationships. The static quality of this background prevents our feeling that the returning first group motives on the wind are coalescing into restatement. Only with the return of the second subject, nobly delivered in three octaves by the strings, does the first achieve its greatest eloquence, as a countering wind line. And the tensions of this epitomizing confrontation are still softened by no harmonic padding: restatement is far from synonymous with relaxation. Apart from the two competing elements, there is only a vast pedal on A (i.e., the classically hallowed *preparation* for restatement), clearly a dominant in its use of the fifth-motive (from bars 4–5), yet constantly challenged by B flats in the upper parts. Instead of achieving cadential resolution, this interval manages only to contract to its inversion, so that the music collapses on to the seventh from which it began.

The allusive technique of this movement, by which freely superimposed melodic activity in broadly contrasted modal areas takes the place of harmonically confirmed tonal areas, is far from a renunciation of tonality's

18

structural propensities, but shows a mastery of their adaptation that is a more remarkable achievement in an Op. 1 than would be many more iconoclastic procedures. In particular, the conventional view of the sonata's dramatic potentialities has been rejected. The middle section is climactic neither in thematic behaviour nor in tonal crisis, and even the conflated restatement appears to be no more than *en route* for a destination that, for the moment, it fails to reach. Instead of an arch, Britten has drawn a line that continues to rise after the mid-point; and this revaluation of the formula is to become his preferred solution to the sonata problem.

The destination is to be reached, of course, at the end of the whole work, but the slow movement postpones the issue while still drawing on familiar thematic shapes. In its use of cushions of harmony, much of it triadic, this is a more conventional piece, but its variation procedures are a long way from the soft option of the apprentice composer. The nostalgic melisma to which the first movement's second subject is transformed in the opening bars suggests a pastoral rhapsody, but what follows is a re-creation of all the chief melodic shapes, with *e* (see Ex. 1) as an elaborate anacrusis and with ninths replacing sevenths as the underpinning interval. When the variation theme and its sinuous counterpoint emerge on high violins (Ex. 4), the characteriz-

Ex. 1.4

ing interval has become the second; Stein usefully draws attention to this early appearance of a Britten fingerprint.[2] Yet it could be added that the 'sonority of the second' had already won a fair measure of acceptance in that English tradition towards which Britten momentarily glances in this movement. Beginning with the nineteenth-century organists' love of the poignant suspension, we can trace the expressive second through the gesturing appoggiaturas of Parry's and Elgar's middle strands (already fairly close to Britten's appoggiatura usage) to more 'absolute' seconds in the pentatonic harmony of folk-influenced composers, to Delius's or Ireland's added notes, and, most significantly in this work dedicated to Britten's teacher, to Frank Bridge's bold use of the interval (see Ex. 5, written in 1926).

Britten's theme is formed by the organic development of its opening interval across a wide span, and with adroit rhythmic adjustment; the

---

[2] Ibid., p. 249.

Ex. 1.5

patently constructed character is appropriate enough to a scaffolding for variations. Yet these prove to be far from rigidly schematic, and the horn's initial bold transformation is abandoned dramatically for a new lyrical treatment by the oboe, with viola arpeggios. As in the first movement, modes are easier to define than their finals, but if we take Ex. 4 to centre on C, then the subsequent progress has been through B natural (horn) to B flat at this oboe statement. In a paragraph that amounts to two variations, the new texture is expanded and the statements move through A natural to G, a soaring climactic version in canon at two bars' distance. Sustained drone fifths that maintain ninth or seventh relationships with thematic notes have persisted throughout this build-up, and the climax dissolves to isolate two stark ninths, widely separated in register. A transitional variation (around F) leads back to restatement at the original pitch by horn with bassoon counterpoint, and the framing ninths contract in a mirrored formation which confirms their essentially inert, non-progressive quality—a usage that is difficult to parallel in British music of this date.

The final Tarantella, into which the viola leads (by a neat metrical modulation), also uses mirror techniques—diverging streams of fifths in its accompaniment, two-part counterpoint inverted in two further parts and fanfare-like successions of thirds with their reflections. This is the first of Britten's *moto perpetuo* movements and a *tour de force* in its control of slowly unwinding paragraphs of genuinely fast music. It is also a highly classical sonata derivative in its use of patently 'episodic' subsidiary sections; seamless transition has rarely been regarded as a virtue in finale structures. Though the main theme's use of first movement shapes is clear enough, the tutti chords flung into its initial statement are taken literally from the point at which the first movement was abandoned, a necessary reminder, after the variation interlude in E flat, that their resolution remains to be accomplished. Even so, D can be accepted as central less equivocally than in the first movement exposition, and the more declamatory second subject (with ostinato accompaniment—from fig. 8) twice sets out around C sharp, but tumbles through a great circle of thirds into a development that works out fragments of the *moto perpetuo* theme at length, above a succession of pedals. This rather dry treatment of his 'tarantella' material serves a far

20

more conventional purpose than did the first movement development, but interest quickens when Britten once more refuses to view restatement as the recovery of an even keel: while the strings are still busy with their imitative development of the first subject, the double bass reiterates a pedal that is now recognizably on the dominant, pointing forward with classical urgency, but a stentorian horn solo is already under way with the second subject, approximately in the tonic. The melodramatic collapse which ensues shows the best kind of musical wit—one which depends on the actions, not the demeanour, of themes. And the sequel is no less piquant. After a furtive chain of thirds has suddenly explained itself as a great superimposition of the crucial sevenths, the bassoon reverts to a more orthodox statement of the second subject. With that disposed of, a final section brings back the first subject. But again limp restatement is avoided, for it appears as perpetual background motion to a recall of all the earlier material of the work. The chief motivic source, the opening theme (Ex. 2), emerges first in mere outline, as a pizzicato fugato, then the first movement's second subject (see Ex. 3a), the slow movement theme (Ex. 4) and finally a broad restatement of the opening theme, far more literal than was achieved in the first movement. The horn-call is in evidence too, and its last ascent salutes the achievement of D as an unequivocal centre, a tonic that releases the tension of the opening interval some fifteen minutes later.

Thus a long span in its wealth of incident and cumulative power occupies a fairly short duration. Yet it is worth examining this first Britten score in detail, for it affirms a precocious command of structural thought—a far more surprising gift to detect in a young Englishman of the thirties than, say, melodic charm or rhythmic enterprise; and many of its procedures were to become typical of the composer's mature practice. Of his lyrical power there are few traces here, of his clear, warm harmonic sonority there is as yet a rather Spartan denial, and of his mastery of orchestral resource only that part to be exploited in the edgier contexts of the chamber operas is fore-shadowed here. But of the idiosyncratic reappraisal of the classical thesis that was to make possible a work like the Cello Symphony, Op. 68, all the signs may be found in Britten's Op. 1.

STRING QUARTET IN D MAJOR (1931)

Before considering the Op. 2 oboe quartet, it is interesting to glance, if only parenthetically, at the string quartet Britten had written in 1931, shortly before the *Sinfonietta*, for even though it bears no opus number, it was eventually published in 1975, and it seems that the retouchings were sufficiently slight[3] (regrettably no mention is made of them in the score) for us to regard this work, written while the composer was still in his first year at the RCM, as an immediate background to the writing of the *Sinfonietta*.

[3] Cf. C. Matthews, 'Britten's Indian Summer', *Soundings* vi, 1977, p. 44.

In a note on the score, Britten mentions that he showed this quartet to Frank Bridge, who pronounced its counterpoint to be 'too vocal', but Ireland, by now his official teacher, did not agree. Certainly the counterpoint appears too ostentatious at times, as in the elaborate working-out of second-group ideas against first in the development of the first movement, but this is because the harmonic product is rather casually directed. More idiomatic textural interest grows as a tonal goal, E flat, is sighted, while the opening of the restatement, in abandoning 'counterpoint' entirely for a misty superimposition of ostinato versions of the opening motive, sounds a prophetic note (echoed very clearly, we shall find, in the official first quartet). The tonal ambiguity created at this point, E flat persisting as no less valid than the returning D tonic of the cello's augmented theme, is of a kind that was to be incorporated more systematically into later structural plans. Here it marks the single crisis within a sonata allegro surprisingly little concerned with tonal arguments—or even unequivocal definitions: the second group is actually recapitulated briefly at the original pitch, though its essential relations to the tonic are a flexibly modal supertonic minor, restated as mediant minor. As at moments in both Op. 1 and Op. 2 we hear in this theme something of the wayward 'rhapsody' of so much contemporary English music, but a laconic accompaniment disowns its ardour. It is the first subject, however, which emphasizes Britten's receptivity to less parochial influences: its opening statement in octaves provides a repertory of four contrasted, though related, motivic shapes which subsequently function independently in textures that are as single-mindedly thematic as anything in the Schoenberg quartets. From such passages to the still more Schoenbergian movement of the *Sinfonietta* was a short step.

In other ways too Op. 1 is strongly foreshadowed by this quartet. The slow movement is a ternary piece, less imaginative in sonority than the *Sinfonietta*'s variations, but its deviation from the central D to C minor suggests the D–E flat of Op. 1, while the finale ends by bringing back first movement material. The quartet's return is more or less literal, and so less subtly integrated than the *Sinfonietta*'s, but both feel like necessary summings-up of earlier uncompleted discussions. For in both works each movement gives way to the next, and there are obvious links in thematic material. Beyond these, a network of far less obvious links can be traced in the quartet, the scherzo-like finale deriving every shape from the earlier movements, often by synthesis. Its pizzicato fugato centrepiece perhaps lacks the witty economy Britten would have brought to it a few years later, but the fleet textures of this movement are far more evidently his alone than are the more stolid preceding movements. It is slightly disappointing to find that so characteristic a device as the return of the main theme superimposed upon this pizzicato idea is a product of the 1974 revision.[4] Even so, the quartet as a

---

[4]   Ibid.

whole serves to remind us that the sublimely simple idea was not an unsol-
icited gift of the gods; a formidable technical armoury had to be assembled
before renunciation could become an artistic stimulus.

PHANTASY, QUARTET FOR OBOE AND STRINGS, OP. 2

In the same year as he wrote the *Sinfonietta*, Britten attempted a still more
ambitious structural fusion. The *Phantasy* oboe quartet forms a single arch
in which the germinal theme, a lyrical impulse neutralized by cryptic march
accompaniments (see Ex. 6), frames an epic sonata design, but also flowers

Ex. 1.6

into an eloquent slow movement between the sonata's development and
restatement. Britten's title acknowledges the currency given in England to
composite forms of this kind by Cobbett's vision of a synthesis of the proud
native traditions of the consort Fancy and the Romantics' cyclic modifications and conflations of sonata practice. Too often the twentieth-century
Fantasy became a repository of ideas attractive enough in themselves but
underdeveloped and set into too casual a relationship. Far more than in even
the slow movement of the *Sinfonietta*, Britten is prepared to recognize his
English environment, both by relaxing at the mid-point into such pastoral
strains as Ex. 7, with its floating sixths and easy-going sequence, and by
allowing the oboe to indulge its penchant for rhapsodic melisma. Yet he has
again learnt something from Schoenberg's example (who in turn had looked
to Liszt) in the articulation of the structure; and, indeed, in so short a work
he has needed to ensure that unification more stringent than that of Schoenberg's early composite designs shall be sensed below the diversity of surface
incident.

23

Ex. 1.7

The thematic primacy of the oboe's introduction theme and the subtle derivations by which the other shapes stem from this are admirably demonstrated in Paul Hamburger's analysis.[5] Relations between the derivatives too (other than through their common source) have independent meanings: for example, the sonata's second subject is sufficiently close in contour to the first (see Ex. 8a and b) to permit its being omitted entirely in Britten's

Ex. 1.8 (d)

Ex. 1.8 (b)

typically abridged restatement. The use of one preferred solo colour against a family of three like colours naturally prompts far more harmonic textures than those of Op. 1. Britten sometimes draws on the ready-made added-note style that was still enjoying a vogue in English music, but even when his chords are formed from a single mode, they are nearly always placed in contexts that imply conflicting tonal pulls. When the work becomes audible (its opening silent bar has a place in the quasi-programmatic scheme, as a

[5] P. Hamburger, 'The Chamber Music', in Mitchell-Keller, p. 215.

24

straining of the ears), its snatches of march rhythm, on the cello's F sharp and A, are opposed by the viola drum rhythm on E inflected by F natural, representing a V versus IV that is explained in the I of the oboe's G-centred tune; but this too is modally equivocal, with the flat seventh and sharp fourth of so much later Britten as alternatives to an orthodox 'major' pattern. The sonata first subject (Ex. 8a) is around C, but its underlying ostinato D flat is more than a protracted Neapolitan, while the second subject (Ex. 8b) uses an uncommitted pentatonic accompaniment figure to hover somewhere between a Dorian B, a Lydian D and A major. The structural point is made, however, in that the two themes stand clearly to flat and sharp sides of the introduction's tonal norm; again, broad areas, not established points, provide the exposition's contrast. A doubly dramatic effect is therefore achieved (at fig. 12) when, following Schoenberg's use of introductory motives to point up significant structural divisions, Britten brings back the march in the bright key area of the second subject, and then deflects it into the C minor of the first subject for the development of that theme. With the relation of its tune to its bass ostinato twisted (D, not C, now opposes D flat, the G drone remains constant; cf. Ex. 8a), this goes in the baldest of sequences round a circle of major thirds to a further statement on D. But the theme's scalic figure (cf. bar 8 in Ex. 8a) is thus of E minor, and it is this tonal area which has remained intact after the strings have thrust into the new andante section. The slow movement retains the unrest of development at first, incisive reminders of the first subject on the oboe punctuating the violin's passionate elaboration of the basic shape of the introduction (cf. Ex. 6). After the texture has simplified and the oboe withdrawn, the viola repeats the violin theme to open the long centrepiece for strings alone; the placid subsidiary idea shown above at Ex. 7, one more reminder that Britten emerged from the world of John Ireland as well as that of late Bridge, plays a bigger part than its originally episodic nature would suggest. The oboe's reappearance, with the arabesques proper to 'fantasy', brings the work nearest to self-indulgent reverie, though the semitonal opposition of tonal fields preserves some tension. Carrying on from where it left off, the oboe develops the first subject's pentatonic fall before turning to the Ex. 6 theme and in due course to the theme that has emerged during its absence (Ex. 7). This it plays in C against the return in E of the ostinato bass of the first subject. And so the way is prepared for another compressed restatement: the first subject (at fig. 30) is on C sharp and its bass on C (i.e., rôles are reversed), the drone now undulates around F sharp, while on top the oboe continues to elaborate the slow movement theme on B. Tonality begins to coalesce around C as restatement becomes more exact, but instead of the second subject, the oboe cadenza figure that has twice already marked structural divisions diverts the course back to its source in the march, the events of which appear in reverse order until the cello's F sharp–A reiterations fade into the distance from which they emerged. The quasi-programmatic note thus confirmed has also been discernible in the course of the work so that its thematic artifice, though scarcely less cunning than that of the *Sinfonietta*, is concealed by a far more wayward air. That the *Phantasy* is the less satisfactory work results from its more comprehensive textural premises: Britten's harmonic language is not yet developed enough to prevent his falling back on a bland, rather impersonal pastoral manner (see Ex. 7), while sprawling rhapsodic lines honour a convention more than they meet an expressive need of so clear-sighted a composer.

HOLIDAY DIARY, OP. 5

In Britten's first published work for the piano, he deliberately exploits a wide range of instrumental sonorities without undue concern for consistency in what is no more than a loosely connected series of character-pieces. The character is not always his own: the knockabout stuff that opens 'Early morning bathe' owes something to the neatly effective pianism of the dedicatee, Arthur Benjamin, whose own piano suite had appeared in 1927, seven years before *Holiday Diary*. It is significant that Britten hits on a more original texture when he settles down to depict the swimmer's regular motion, and is able to sustain it through a long paragraph by occasional modulatory twists. Even so, the second piece, 'Sailing', emphasizes the anonymity of the first, for it achieves a wholly personal sonority for the first time in Britten's work. In doing so it abandons the tonal ambiguities of the early chamber works, even the mercurial shifts of the previous piece, in favour of an unclouded D major melody, secured by a fifth drone and with an accompaniment figure that rocks gently between mildly dissonant intervals—seconds, fourths, sevenths and ninths—all within the single mode (see Ex. 9). The method seems simple to the point of vacuity if we compare

Ex. 1.9

the more clangorous diatonic formulations of contemporary Stravinsky works—and, of course, consider their rhythmic tension. But the strength of this music is no less real for resting in highly refined techniques—in the shaping of a line so that a rising figure countering a slow descent becomes a momentous expressive event, and in the independent variation of phrase length in melody and accompaniment so that their encounters are unpre-

26

dictable. After the music has drifted into F and back again, the luminous D major is coloured with a Lydian fourth that intensifies its prophetic sound; indeed, there are pre-echoes in this piece of innumerable more mature Britten contexts, from *Lucretia* to the Cello Symphony's variations. The squall that blows up in the middle section underlines with more astringent dissonance the theme's distortion, but the effect is petulant rather than graphic; beautifully modified textures justify an otherwise almost literal *da capo*.

The mechanized gaiety of 'Funfair' is conveyed by a refrain that in its neo-Baroque cut for once betrays Stravinsky's influence fairly directly, though of that composer's disjunct phrasing there is no sign in this onward-spinning piece; the episodic side-shows are too diverse a collection for musical comfort, whatever the verve of their musical depiction. In the last piece, 'Night', he works out at far greater length the texture of intervals strictly mirrored across a vast space that had provided an arresting passage in the *Sinfonietta*'s slow movement. It may not be coincidental that Britten chose to emulate Bartók's obsessive plotting of symmetries (see, for example, the second piano concerto, of 1931) in a nocturnal piece. Neither the nature mysticism of Bartók's night-pictures nor their intense melancholy, qualities that reflect centuries of Hungarian peasant life, are recalled in this momentary gravity of a young man, but the snatches of melody on another tonal plane, that drift into the textural void, function like the strains of song which provide the human note in Bartók (see 'The night's music', from *Out of Doors*, of 1927); here the transformed shapes of movements 1, 3 and 2 represent the dreamer's recollections of the day's activities. Though these are all centred on A (with a typical alternative implication of F sharp), the surrounding breathing of the night avoids the harmonic monotony of consistent mirrored movement about its initial C–G correspondence by short stretches of freer movement that permit the unobtrusive adoption of a new axis. The rapidity with which these pieces were written, in a few days of October 1934, suggests that the composer did not attach undue importance to this first piano score, but its discovery of a quite personal tone is the more notable for occurring in the middle of some rather heterogeneous, if deft, adaptations of contemporary idioms.

SUITE FOR VIOLIN AND PIANO, OP. 6

One month after writing his piano suite, Britten was in Vienna, setting to work on another, for violin and piano. Like the oboe quartet, it achieved an ISCM performance (at Barcelona in 1936), but at home it must have offered much less reassurance than did the *Phantasy* to lovers of newly-found English 'traditions'. Whereas the piano suite was thrown off by a high-spirited youth, this strives towards an altogether more sophisticated musical wit: the result is exhilarating, because the treatment is always inventive, but much of the material is too dry to leave any deep impression.

Ex.1.10 (a)

Ex.1.10 (b)

Andante maestoso

Ex.1.10 (c) *ff*

Ex.1.10 (d)

Ex.1.10 (e)

Sempre molto mosso

Ex.1.10 (f)

Lento tranquillo

Ex.1.10 (g)

Alla Valse – Vivace e rubato

The musical motto on the title page is given as E–F–B–C, but these precise intervals play less part in the work than does the general shape of this motive and its inversion, which can be traced in every section. Some acquaintance with serial ways of thinking may account for this single generating cell of notes, and would also explain the persistent use of scales displaced by octave-transposition, a practice that gives the work a more wilfully 'modern' sound than is to be heard elsewhere in Britten's early chamber music. But the free widening and contracting of interval in a motive that remains recognizable is a classical technique that was being given new currency by Bartók; some of Britten's derived shapes are shown in Ex. 10. The opening of the Introduction, Ex. 10b, presents a curious juxtaposition: an octave-transposed whole-tone scale that leads us to wonder what music of Schoenberg's school Britten was able to see (if not hear) in Vienna, and a Lydian fanfare in Lombard rhythm that could recur in almost any of the composer's later scores. The march is a determinedly cryptic music, of nervous rhythms, discontinuous textures and melodic lines that are displaced by octave transposition, but Britten's experiments stop short almost ostentatiously in one field: the first thirty-three bars do not belie their key signatures by a single accidental (which does not mean that harmonic relations are entirely conventional).

Cross-rhythms in the main idea and asymmetrical phrasing in its *cantabile* foil keep the Moto perpetuo urgent rather than exhibitionist. Its structure is adventurous too, for while the wide range of textural variants Britten deploys and the increases of speed convey the sensation of a constantly unfolding movement, the thematic paragraphs and their key areas are operating with the logic of a sonata. However, as in so much early Britten, 'key' is an allusive rather than definitive term: though we may take the exposition of the Moto perpetuo's first idea to be roughly in D Aeolian (violin) followed by D Lydian (piano), we cannot assign the second (tenth bar of fig. 9) to G on any evidence more substantial than its initial pedal, yet its 'flat-side' function remains unmistakable. Momentum never flags throughout an eventful development, and the way to restatement is doubly pointed (*animando* after fig. 15) by a pedal that ingeniously conflates the dominant and the flat supertonic. The modal variants of the main idea are reversed on restatement, D 'major' preceding 'minor', the latter section typically adding the *cantabile* second subject's return in augmentation as its counterpoint. A bass ostinato persisting throughout this final synthesis (see Ex. 10e) seems to confirm that A is a dominant, but the movement fades out enigmatically on its opening chord (a derivation from the motto) without cadential outcome.

The 'Lullaby', like 'Sailing' in the piano suite, has some diatonic harmonies of prophetic simplicity (see Ex. 10f), to which the violin's impassioned *coloratura* flight provides an almost extravagant response; the growth by sequence remains too evident, even though the two-bar unit is sometimes elongated. In the 'Waltz' (see Ex. 10g) Britten turns from idiosyncratic treatment of familiar genres towards a blatant parody that must retain in some sense the essence of the clichés it derides. In a ternary arrangement of ternary waltzes the middle section is loosely bitonal, but the outer sections depend on slight dislocations of truculently orthodox progressions. Paul Hamburger has pointed out[6] how deftly Britten juxtaposes here two mutually exclusive conceptions of the waltz—Viennese and French. The eleventh-hour intrusion of the suite's opening figure (cf. Ex. 10b) and the basic motive (Ex. 10a) contrives a specious rather than inevitable symmetry across the whole work.

INTRODUCTION AND RONDO BURLESCA FOR TWO PIANOS, OP. 23, NO. 1

During the next five years Britten undertook the series of ambitious orchestral scores discussed in Chapter 2, including the Bridge Variations, the two concertos and the *Diversions*, and the *Sinfonia da Requiem*, but all his work in smaller media was vocal. Much of this involved the piano, however, and his writing for that instrument in such works as the Auden and the Michelangelo cycles had, under the stimulus of specific verbal moods and images, made decisive progress towards a wholly personal tone, needing none of the defensive urbanity of pastiche. The two pieces for two pianos, Op. 23, with which Britten returned to instrumental writing, lack this sense of style as a spontaneous expressive focus. Of course, as Stravinsky spent years in demonstrating, style may also be a matter of innumerable telling deviations from a stylistic model, which thus assumes the rôle of the composer's subject-matter. But the first of these pieces, Op. 23, no. 1 (written in November, 1940) never makes very clear the object of its mockery. The heavy French overture style of the introduction, the chattering rhythms and successive perfect fourths of the refrain, and the long canon in which this is worked out all suggest a *Gebrauchsmusik* order of neo-classicism, yet they may represent nothing more than another look at the mechanistic (and fourth-obsessed) manner of the *Diversions*, written a few months earlier. And Britten's use of boldly juxtaposed triads and melodic chains of thirds similarly recalls devices he had made distinctively his own in the Michelangelo Sonnets, just completed. Its splendid pianistic sonorities should have assured this rondo some foothold in a meagre repertory, but a parody of a garrulous manner succeeds too well if it also is garrulous.

MAZURKA ELEGIACA FOR TWO PIANOS, OP. 23, NO. 2

Eight months later Britten wrote a companion piece. This is dedicated to the memory of Paderewski, and is far more defined in its subject-matter, which embraces not only a musical type but a great artist's style of playing. How

---

[6] Ibid., p. 219.

Ex.1.11 (a)

fruitful such a stimulus can be has been shown more profoundly in the works called forth by Rostropovich's artistry; just as those works contain reflections of the music the cellist interprets supremely well, of Bach and of his Soviet contemporaries, so this elegy dwells on Paderewski the Chopin interpreter (rather than on the insignificant figure of Paderewski the composer). The opening shape stirs memories of the Op. 7, no. 2 mazurka so potently that we take this solo line (a in Ex. 11) to revolve round the dominant of F minor until two countering ideas (b and c) imply A flat. Belatedly a stock left-hand accompaniment joins in, momentarily suggesting another alternative, B flat minor, and only towards the end of the paragraph is F (Aeolian) minor agreed on—by a cadential process differently timed in each of the strata. After a development that merges tonal areas in a series of heroic gestures, the *da capo* is too elegantly ornamented to recover the original 'evocative and obsessional' quality[7] (and it omits c). The alternative mazurka, in the major, is the more ardent for having to pit its lines against an elaborate drone, but its climactic exchanges of material lean so far towards a bombastic tradition of nineteenth-century pianism that a dramatic reversal is needed, in the course of which the drone's obsessions find a natural consequence in those of the returning first mazurka. A new sequel fashions from elements b and c (Ex. 11) a pointedly elegiac block harmony; these two shapes also survive the trickling-out of the main theme (a) with a poignant effect that may translate a memory of Chopin's Op. 17, no. 4.

These pieces provided fairly simple *ad hoc* solutions to the problem of relating form to content. The earliest chamber works, Opp. 1 and 2, had been the work of a far more ambitious researcher into the possible further consequences of classical structural principles, but one who was content to allow (in the *Sinfonietta*) a somewhat faceless or (in the *Phantasy*) a texturally diffuse music to complete some stages of the design. Britten's first string quartet therefore came as a parallel in the smaller media to the *Sinfonia da Requiem* in its demonstration that he could now conceive extensive structures of an originality that sprang directly from that of the material itself.

[7] A. Dickinson, 'The Piano Music', in Mitchell-Keller, p. 273.

31

STRING QUARTET NO. 1, OP. 25

The quartet was written one year after the symphony, in 1941, and was the last important score of Britten's American period; like Bartók's fifth and Schoenberg's fourth, it is dedicated to Elizabeth Sprague Coolidge, the patron who did so much to preserve for the twentieth-century string quartet its classical predominance among chamber media. This elevated position has implied the corollary that the challenge of the great tradition cannot lightly be shrugged off, and, although Britten's essay is short by classical standards, its four-movement pattern constitutes the most literal acknowledgment of the exemplars in all his instrumental works; bearing in mind the composer's earlier feats of structural virtuosity, we need not expect this disarming deference to extend far into the detailed argument.

The articulation of a sonata allegro by two further appearances of a spacious introductory theme, before the development and in the coda, also has fairly exact classical precedents, not only in the 'Pathétique' sonata but in the Beethoven Quartet in B flat, Op. 130. But the respective ratios of slow to quick music make clear that Britten has not chosen to read a new significance into a borrowed procedure: in his quartet the andante sections play for almost precisely the same duration as the allegro sections. And since the listener forms his impressions of a movement's balance from this rather than from counting bars, his experience is likely to be that between these two types of motion (and the radically differentiated sonorities they propel) exists the fundamental contrast on which the structure depends. Of course, the *grave* sections of the 'Pathétique' provide drastic contrast, but they are felt to be fateful intrusions upon, not participants in, the sonata dialectic conducted in the main sections. Though a vestigial dualism persists in Britten's expository allegro, the first and second subjects (see Ex. 12b and c) are so patently fashioned of the same stuff that no dramatic consequences arise from their fusion in the development and no sense of thwarted expectations from the almost total elimination of the second from the restatement. Even the tonal displacement which is a traditional second-group function serves another purpose in this exposition: it defines no single opposed area, but acts as a transition to the andante's return in a clear F major. Thus, the scheme of the three slow sections, in D–F–D, more palpably marks out the movement's tonal design than does the sonata-allegro chain of events.

Ex. 1.12 (a)

Ex. 1.12 (b)

Ex. 1.12 (c)

Britten's 'sonority of the second' and the limpid D major first discovered in 'Sailing' had already joined company in the flutes' refrain of 'Requiem aeternam' in the *Sinfonia da Requiem*. In the andante of the quartet (Ex. 12a) the diatonic clusters are tighter but much higher, a strangely penetrating sound that quivers in nervous rhythms before it achieves the momentum for each change of position. This is music about to unfold, not the serene progress towards cadence of the symphony; and the confident tread of the wide-ranging bass there (Bergian in its doubling of clarinet and harp) is replaced here by the cello's fitful but static arpeggios (Stravinskyan in their omission of the fifth). In fact, however, it is the cello's failure to comply with the upper strings when their melodic arch is closed at bar 22 that triggers off the allegro: its C natural is an irritant which cannot be shaken off throughout the whole of the first subject (Ex. 12b), a paragraph that in consequence grows more and more vehement, eventually involving the other three strings in a drivingly cross-accented canonic statement of the basic seven-crotchet shape. Only after this has collapsed on to a despairingly flat chord (at bar 54) does the cello propose a route to the first unanimous tonic D, celebrated with the percussively syncopated rhythmic figure of the allegro opening, *x*. Thus, what sounds like a transition makes secure the tonal areas from which, traditionally, it might be expected to lead. So this D is reinterpreted as a mediant and the second subject (Ex. 12c) sets out at bar 61 in B flat (Mixolydian-cum-Dorian). Apart from its preference for flat tonal areas, this contains no feature that has not been adumbrated already; its syncopated scale-figures and legato semiquavers have been gradually derived from the opening rhythm *x*, and the canto fermo that joins these augments the melodic motive of bar 28 (hereafter *y*). The tonal outcome of this 'transitional' second subject, the F in which the andante is to return, is achieved by the cello, and with some justice since it has spent the entire first

33

subject reiterating a preparatory dominant pedal; this long-term explanation confirms the view that the crucial key relations of this movement are those of the andante sections.

The second allegro brings back the *x* rhythm in a homophonic form nearer the original, and its canto fermo lines take the augmentation (sometimes inverted) of the first subject beyond the *y* group, but otherwise it is at first scarcely more developmental than was the second subject. At bar 119 sharp keys are suddenly reinstated (indeed, essentially the tonic) but a quite new texture in the violins (Ex. 13), though much quieter than the lower strings,

Ex. 1.13

prevents their attempts to initiate a restatement. These violin parts are not merely ornamental postponements of the return: the second violin, as well as developing the scalic idea further, sustains a (nominally) dominant pedal that for twenty-five bars remains a fixed point in a paragraph intent on compensating for earlier flat tendencies by moving sharp. Meanwhile the first violin has begun by spinning into a revolving triplet figure the three high notes which formed the andante's first chord (cf. Exx. 12a and 13) and it continues to sketch in a misty variation of that music. A unanimous outcome for these conflicting strands appears possible when the scalic movement becomes general, and a determined move is made towards a climactic restatement in A. The violins achieve this, but the lower strings reinstate the C natural that characterized the first subject's exposition (cf. Ex. 12b); its purpose now is quite different, for its flat seventh against the sharp fourths of the violins produces Britten's favourite mixed mode (Lydian/Mixolydian), its opposed pulls neutralizing in a reinforced D tonic. Restatement is abridged, and far from literal, the close imitation of *y* being its chief concern. Some reminder of the second subject is provided by the augmentation (from bar 160) of this imitative texture; its wealth of contradictory tonal pulls is kept in check by a tonic pedal inflected with the legato (i.e., second group) form of *x*. As this texture rises up to be assimilated into the andante's tonic restatement, the cello moves through its D harmonic series, revealing at the seventh harmonic the most natural explanation of all for the ubiquitous C natural. Its original intrusion in the cello is recalled as the andante fades, provoking a belated restatement of the allegro's opening *x* rhythms. But the cycle is not to be repeated, and a simple resolution of the tension is offered in the final juxtaposition of slow and fast fragments.

The extremely subtle relationship between inherent characteristics of the material and its structural working-out showed Britten at twenty-seven to be a master of tonal architecture with scarcely a rival on the English scene, yet the first quartet has still to achieve the recognition of an assured place in the repertoire. The second quartet's greater appeal presumably stems from its more immediately engaging melodic lines, its more leisurely time-scale and the *tour de force* quality of its first movement and its Chacony. And it must be owned that the scherzo of the 1941 quartet lacks the strongly-characterized tone of its successor; it is very deft, but a certain dryness is not dispelled by the mannered humour of its second theme. Its key of F refers back to the first movement's argument, but its further tonal wanderings seem more wayward. Thematically all three ideas (arranged ABCBABA) stem from the triplet anacrusis rhythm that gradually (but at metrically unpredictable points) invades the opening arpeggio texture. A drone offers the second theme fixed moorings which it prefers to ignore, and the developmental episode C is notable for one of the rare suggestions in this work that Britten had considered Bartók's solutions of quartet problems when devising his own. The Andante calmo brings us back to a world that is wholly Britten's, and one for which we have been prepared by the first movement: the work's opening is echoed, but as a relaxed open third (see Ex. 14a), and the motive *y* gradually gives way to a scalic norm of melodic movement. As the harmonic thirds persist, this key of B flat, like the cello's original (Ex. 12a) delineation of D, is established without the help of a fifth degree, and D is its crucial related key, even the brief dominant visits that herald the restatement being reached through the mediant major.

Ex. 1.14 (a)

Ex. 1.14 (b)

Ex.1.14 (c)

After the exploratory stages of a and b in Ex. 14, the main theme proper (c), on an immobile tonal basis, can range widely in mode; its vast melodic range too, and its phrase structure (9–10–8) contribute to the spacious arc. The last phrase is a beautifully prepared move away from B flat to the C in which the middle section begins. This juxtaposes declamatory arpeggios with snatches of the main theme, still flowing on in its almost isorhythmic scansion of the 5/4 metre. At the evocative brightness of D major the music seems to be becalmed, and even *en route* from the dominant to the tonic, D creeps in again. Before this tonic (bar 418) is firm enough to bear the restatement of the main theme (c), a dramatic review of the whole route is undertaken, b in B flat, C and D being interrupted by the arpeggio figure, and F insisted on so vehemently that it is accepted in a double dominant preparation for c's return (typically, Britten avoids platitude by anticipating the bass's move in the progression). Restatement is literal though with delicate new accompaniment (all based on b and its inversion) until the last phrase. This again gravitates to C, halfway-house between B flat and D, and in a most poetic coda these two keys are held in perfect equipoise through imitative entries of c, bars 3–4, so that only the final chord confirms that the tonic (in its weakest, 6/4 position) is to prevail.

The finale neatly conflates the melodic thirds and the Lydian tendency of the quartet's opening into a Haydnish quip (*a* in Ex. 15) which, with its

Ex.1.15

consequent, *b*, is promptly flung into a welter of apparently random (but remarkably consonant) imitative encounters. This invigorating activity, in constant crescendo, reaches a climax when the semiquaver thirds tumble down four octaves to relegate this theme to the rôle of a busy counterpoint to a new theme (Ex. 16a). Its bold fanfares contain the essential shape of the work's opening andante, and flat sevenths provide another link with the first movement's preoccupations. A new derivative of *a* in Ex. 15 (bar 530), inverting its thirds, seems to be establishing itself as a second subject in F, but it proves transitory, leading to the sharp side before fading out on an

Ex.1.16 (a)

Ex.1.16 (b)

uncommitted A. What follows wittily summarizes the tonal tendencies of the whole work in juxtaposing F and B flat in a new, and in sonata terms 'second' subject (Ex. 16b). This is promptly developed, as are the first subject's quip and its transitional derivative. After a preparatory pedal containing almost as much IV as V (from bar 601) the fanfare theme is restated below the imitative working of the quip, then in its original form. Its peroration merges into a brief return of the second subject (Ex. 16b), now juxtaposing all three keys, F, D and B flat, and a forceful passage of accelerating harmonies extends the theme's scalic opening into a reminder of the first and third movements while underneath the cello arpeggios look back to the scherzo. The upward-leaping form of the quip, omitted from the earlier stage of this pithy restatement, reappears now (another Haydnish touch) to decorate the final tonic in the pure Lydian modality from which the quartet set out.

37

2 Early Orchestral Music

Despite the extreme sensitivity Britten had revealed in setting texts as unexpected and heterogeneous as those of Auden, Rimbaud and Michelangelo, until he returned from America it would have seemed reasonable to assume that instrumental composition was to form the core of his work. Of a slightly older British generation, William Walton had shown this emphasis still more pronouncedly, and Alan Rawsthorne was setting out on a comparable course. Before them both Elgar and Vaughan Williams had gone far towards transferring the focus of English musical aspirations from the chorus to the orchestra. Not only they, but composers as unlike as Bax and Rubbra shared with other belated nationalist schools (in Finland and America, for example) the belief that the symphonic form which had once symbolized a peculiarly German concentration of musical thought could answer the needs of those who had won their independence of German idioms. Yet Britten, like Walton, made his mark first in the chamber media, for opportunities of orchestral performance did not easily come the way of an unknown young composer. The first sounds which he heard of his own full scoring were of a major work, the symphonic cycle, *Our Hunting Fathers*, and here the 'symphonic' qualities were those which could control, not determine the nature of, material conceived in response to potent verbal stimuli. The Bridge Variations were individually brilliant character pieces and together a virtuoso display of thematic derivation, and Britten's command of such techniques proved no less apt when he was faced with the challenge of a restricted pianism in the *Diversions*. But the piano concerto had also drawn characters more effectively than consequences, and only with the violin concerto and the *Sinfonia da Requiem* did Britten undertake in orchestral textures such problems of complex musical organization as he had tackled in the two early chamber scores.

SIMPLE SYMPHONY, OP. 4
Given those works and their immediate successor, *A Boy was Born*, as evidence of Britten's bold command of texture and structure, we may find opus 4, the Simple Symphony for strings (orchestra or quartet) disappoint-

ingly unadventurous. To examine the original piano pieces and songs, written when the composer was no more than twelve, that provided the material for this suite would be of the greatest interest to any student of style. And at many later stages of Britten's development it is instructive to note how he sought to present wholly characteristic ideas in drastically simplified terms. Here, however, ideas that have the simplicity of a highly musical child, that is, which give neat shape and the occasional deft twist to clichés remembered from here and there, have been juxtaposed to form symmetrical classicist structures. In the process, one suspects, they may have lost something of their innocence: the twenty-year-old composer seems to have been unable to resist a few touching-up strokes of sophistication, so that elsewhere the child's unabashed delight in entirely conventional moves can sound affected. But the great merit of the work lies in its range of idiomatic string textures, achieved without stretching the technical capacities of quite modest amateur players.

The 'Boisterous Bourrée' takes the cliché V–I cadence to punctuate some pleasantly bizarre counterpoint exercises (complete even to a long-note *canto fermo* of descending scales the second time round) and to provide an ostinato below or around the innocuous, yet cunningly phrased, second subject. 'Playful Pizzicato' also makes great play with an arpeggiated V–I ostinato, though with some rather crude harmonic workmanship; the trio is more characteristic both in the witty silent bars of the tune and (especially on its second, tonic, statement) its use of open strings to petrify diatonic progression. The 'Sentimental Saraband' sounds rather too like the bogus-Baroque popular in songs by such forgotten composers as H. Lane Wilson, but the expressiveness gained from pressing orthodox progressions against a pedal is pure enough Britten; the diminished seventh before figure 3 is a solecism and the cadence at 3 stems from Edward German. The abandoning in the middle section of conventional textural fullness for tune (sometimes paralleled) plus transparent accompaniment figures gives a pleasantly cooler ring to the sentiment, even though the tune is banal enough; the subsequent rhetoric is absurd but oddly affecting. After a grandiose initial switch of key, the 'Frolicsome Finale' builds up excitement with a theme that a cinema pianist would have cherished—even though he might not have foreseen its 'learned' development. Yet it is the more 'English' second idea that produces the climactic effects, particularly in the swinging manipulation of its syncopes.

VARIATIONS ON A THEME OF FRANK BRIDGE, OP. 10
Britten often showed his ability to respond to a commission with a work not merely well finished but conceived in musical terms that reflect directly, yet not restrictively, the circumstances of its first performance. Among his early scores the Bridge Variations represent his most adventurous response to such a challenge: this showpiece for an English string orchestra (the Boyd

Neel) was to be heard by a foreign audience (at the 1937 Salzburg Festival), and it was written as a tribute to a composer who, for so long a polished craftsman in a delicate but somewhat isolated tradition of English lyricism, had latterly developed a boldly exploratory idiom (see, for example, the quotation from Bridge's third quartet given on page 20) much affected by what he had found in the work of Alban Berg. In fact, Bridge's theme, taken from a work of his earlier period, the Idylls for String Quartet of 1906, has just that faintly wistful air which his pupil was helping to blow out of English music with the brash sonorities of his variations. But this is not to imply that youthful iconoclasm dictated this treatment; on the contrary, when Britten's essays in a host of European manners have drawn on the theme more and more cryptically, it is finally reinstated in an ardent harmonization that is the composer's most personal utterance in the work, and is thus, if only in retrospect, recognizable as the recovery of an English tone of voice. When Hindemith told Walton that his viola concerto was very English in its employment of tunes rather than themes, he voiced a common criticism of our twentieth-century revival of composition (whether it is just is another matter). Britten answers it with a formidable display of thematic research, but ends by savouring the tune a good deal more indulgently than Bridge had done.

For, whatever its curiously mingled echoes, of Franck as well as Elgar, Bridge's theme is already a tightly organized span (see Ex. 1). Essentially it has only three shapes, the falling fifth *a*, the curving two-bar phrase *b* (in itself an *a* variant) and the cadential semitone *c*; the paragraph is assembled from simple variations and transpositions of these and is then repeated in a more elaborate guise. Though its harmonic vocabulary of sevenths and

Ex. 2.1

thirteenths has too strong a period flavour to offer much to Britten's variation procedures, Bridge's tonal scheme is full of ambiguous allusions: E minor (or A minor?), E flat, E minor V, E flat (or E flat minor) V, C sharp minor (or F sharp minor?), C (via B flat V⁷?) – E minor. For Britten tonal ambiguity had already proved in Opp. 1 and 2 a means of bracing structures, and it was to prove his most powerful means of creating ambivalence of mood; but instead of the rapidly shifting centres of Ex. 1, with their chromatically slipping progressions, he has usually preferred to compress the contradictory implications from the successive into the simultaneous. So the theme's first chord, an augmented triad with major seventh, suggested the bristling opposition of Britten's introductory flourishes; to describe this as E major versus C is to oversimplify, for the arpeggio and scale figures are of a mixed scale, and their superimposition (from bar 5) produces F chords as the urge away from E. Thus the vast sustained bass C is not so much a would-be tonic as a would-be dominant to the first chord of the work, and the tonal friction is of Britten's favourite semitonal variety. A highly-charged state induced by eleven vigorous bars of this deadlock is thus resolved when Bridge's second chord (bar 2 of Ex. 1) emerges: what Britten borrowed was a fragile lyrical wisp, but to reveal its fitness for the cardinal rôle it is to play in his own design, he introduces it as a dramatically potent liberating force.

The repercussions are strongly felt in the Adagio first variation, in which the impassioned violin phrases develop the decorative contours of Bridge's second version (i.e., Ex. 1 from bar 19) into a memory of the introduction's interval shapes (especially its C–B–G sharp). The lower strings' slow harmonies incorporate reiterations of *a*, now as a diminished fifth, and the semitonal *c* in brusquely juxtaposed triads, usually with a conflicting bass. Tensions are finely controlled, the climactic chord provoking an incandescent outburst from the violins before a purposeful route back to the initial C major is found. The movements that follow substitute for this glimpse of the dramaticist some agreeable studies by the *pasticheur* and the satirist. The bizarre martinet of the quick March seems to be a German, but the commentary of violin shakes and fanfares is entirely Britten's; *ai*, *aii* and their inversion are the motivating shapes of the busily sequential dotted rhythms. From this self-importance the Gallic insouciance of the Romance brings

41

Ex.2.2

relief, but its relationship to the theme is far from casual. As Ex. 2 shows, the urbane violin line synthesizes *aii* and *b*, while the pizzicato bass (in quasi 6/8 throughout) elevates *ai* + *aii* + *b* almost to the status of a ground. The dissociation of melody from accompanying harmony that gives this piece its Boulangerish (rather than Stravinskyan) sound is more apparent than real: almost every one of these elegantly dissonant downbeats turns out to be an appoggiatura. A fierier Latin music is guyed in the strumming guitars and the obligatory melodic *brio* of the 'Aria Italiana', but only in the middle section is there enough harmonic piquancy to give much edge to the taste of ebullient vulgarity; again the span *ai* + *aii* + *b* is transformed to form the basic pattern (bars 8 and 9). A better musical joke is the 'Bourrée Classique' with its open-string drones (the fifths of *a*) that signally fail to follow the harmonic argument; an unusually direct Stravinskyan echo comes in the solo violin writing (compare *L'Histoire du Soldat* and that recurrent Britten model, *Apollon*), but the complacent circle of fifths (from bar 44) and the rudimentary tonal (not harmonic) structure approach far closer to historical exemplars than do any of Stravinsky's neo-Baroque essays.

The fifth of *ai* stands as a ludicrously extravagant preparatory gesture to the 'Wiener Walzer', while *b* is drawn out into the importunate blandishments of the second theme. In accompanying this Britten rises to feats of ecstatic harmonic displacement that give this piece a far more pungent wit than the waltz of Op. 6. But the 'Moto Perpetuo', though no less bold in its single-line 'texture' than was that of the Suite, is too determined an orchestral *tour de force* to achieve the structural subtlety of the earlier example; its only explicit thematic reference is to *ai* and *aii* in the coda. In the 'Funeral March' *ai* becomes a thudding drum rhythm, and its fifth is filled out in the melodic descent from the tense opening supertonic; the less compliant third phrase (bar 8, related to *b*) has already been heard in conflation in the opening chords. The opulent anguish of the whole piece stems from the inability of chromatically straining chords (many of them prophetic of the *Grimes* style) to break from the moorings of the elemental scheme dictated by the bass; little reading between the lines is needed to sense the symbolism of the central dominant pedal (another drumbeat in its thrumming across the

42

double basses' open strings), challenged by ever more distant tonalities in the block harmony above but always forcing these inexorably back. Yet the pathos of the recessional phrases ends in exhaustion rather than resignation: the bass ostinato ends on the dominant, against an unresolved subdominant above. Mahler's influence on this expressive pattern has often been remarked, and it is easy to assume that this cortège was as much the simulation as the distillation of emotion in a young man of twenty-five (just as the so-called *Sturm und Drang* of Mozart's early G minor symphony can seem a pose); but the sonorities are newly-imagined, and all that seems lacking is a more comprehensive emotional context from which this somewhat dissociated threnody can spring. Certainly it leaves its mark on the 'Chant' which follows: broken phrases, reproducing the scansion of the theme but in a far more restricted melodic span, are set within the frame of an impassive pedal (inflected by *c*'s semitones).

The fugue subject incorporates *ai* and *aii*, together with the rising tritone of the theme's bass. Its exposition goes athletically through all the motions of introducing new voices and countering rhythms while remaining imperturbably monophonic. A second subject (from fig. 31) converts a Mahlerian impulse (cf., e.g., 'Der Trunkene im Frühling' in *Das Lied von der Erde*) into Stravinskyan terms; its exposition collects two countersubjects before stretti begin, but all these fugal drives are neutralized by the mechanistic bass which rises to the surface (at fig. 33) in an episode. On its return the first subject compensates for its earlier economy by proliferating in endless stretti, and against this flickering background a *canto fermo* unwinds developments of Bridge's theme, leading through a Bergian unison into its restatement in Britten's richest D major. Rich but not complacent, for when the line admits of an obvious D major harmonization, the accompaniment moves away to preserve the taut relationship: typically the climax of opposition is semitonal (D Lydian against dominant seventh of D flat). After a coda that draws out *b* in ethereal threads, the final bars settle on a more relaxed juxtaposition—Bridge's E as added-note in Britten's D.

SOIRÉES MUSICALES, OP. 9, AND MONT JUIC, OP. 12

One year before the Bridge variations, Britten had handled, in *Our Hunting Fathers*, the full orchestral palette with a virtuosity that was to seem scarcely less astonishing when the work was revived after almost thirty years. Yet he chose, or was encouraged by circumstances, to restrict his further exploration of orchestral finesse to arrangements, of Rossini in the suite *Soirées Musicales* (1936), and of Catalan dances in *Mont Juic* (1937). The orchestration of material conceived for the piano (even when the piano style is as unidiomatic as Rossini's) presents problems so different from the conception of orchestral ideas that it is misleading to suggest that these arrangements provide any rules of thumb to Britten's orchestral method. They surmount the textbook's favourite sustaining-pedal problems with ridiculous

43

ease (see, for example, the 'Canzonetta') but never attempt to produce opulent sound in the process; this wiry score, retaining Rossini's harmonies even when they amount to no more than two parts, achieves an even cleaner sonority than the Italian opera orchestra, for the padding of accompaniment rhythms is ruthlessly abandoned in favour of their selective instrumentation. The greater agility of the modern brass section is fully utilized, melodic lines being rapidly distributed among all the orchestral colours, even within the phrase. A minor but characteristic ingenuity may be noted in Britten's employment here of '*ad lib.*' instruments: this never reduces the scoring to a cautious grey, and the dispensable parts contribute some neat additional points. Five years later, for a ballet by Balanchine, Britten provided a companion suite, *Matinées Musicales*.

Mont Juic, written in collaboration with Lennox Berkeley, bears the shadow of contemporary events in its Lament, subtitled 'Barcelona, 1936', but there is little that is mordant in the irony of the other movements. The nonchalant delicacy with which tunes part company with their accompaniments is an art of the thirties which both composers had mastered, and there is no strain in their alliance. Berkeley's comments in the Britten symposium[1] give no hint of their respective shares in the work; if we may believe that Britten contributed the second and fourth movements, they provide a delightful footnote to a study of his resourcefulness in discovering simple but telling orchestral effects.

PIANO CONCERTO, OP. 13

Britten's only piano concerto (for such it is, despite the optimistic label 'No. 1' under which it was published) was written to introduce him to a Promenade Concert audience in 1938. In this first instrumental work to bear a title inviting direct comparison with classical models, he did much to invalidate the comparison by adding movement titles, Toccata, Waltz, Recitative and Aria and March, which put the concerto into a less onerous category, that of the suite of genre pieces. The recurrence of favourite types like the march and the waltz suggests that the line to which this work belongs is that begun by the Violin Suite, and extended in the Bridge Variations and (later) the *Diversions*; even in setting a text, the *Ballad of Heroes* of the following year, Britten identified the movements as essays in received manners. Such music is expected to be apt and decorative rather than unique and organic; yet there will remain room for the display of an original wit in the twists given to the familiar phrase and progression, the new colouring with which old subjects are decked out. At this stage of his development Britten rarely chose to commit himself to an instrumental music in which he could not accept a subject (i.e., a highly circumscribed musical convention) to canalize his invention, and from which he could not, by the very nature of the task,

[1] L. Berkeley, 'The Light Music', in Mitchell-Keller, p. 288.

44

appear to disengage himself emotionally. Much has been made of this by critics determined to see in these early activities the opera composer in search of his *métier* and, since it is easier (and certainly quicker) to read titles than to investigate musical procedures, a legend has been perpetuated that Britten preferred to avoid, or cultivated at the expense of his most individual voice, an intra-musical structural logic.

Of course, the piano concerto's first movement *is* a toccata, a piece calculated to show off the soloist's skill in maintaining a brittle clangour through patterned figurations. But the orchestra is not, like the piano, a vast percussion instrument: its many sustaining instruments demand material of quite another cast, and so there arises very naturally the kind of dichotomy that has customarily been explored by sonata methods. This movement remains one of Britten's longest sonata essays; that it is not his most

Ex.2.3

engaging stems as much from the textural rigidity of the toccata convention as from stiffness in the structure. The first subject's major seventh (*a* in Ex. 3) is rarely absent for long, since it provides accompaniment patterns elsewhere, and its influence is to persist in the chief shapes of the Waltz and the March. As well as this pervasive unifying element there is a more local one in the brass fanfare of alternating chords which appears in the orchestral counterstatement of the first subject. Sideslipping 6/4s, sevenths and ninths form the modish but limited harmonic equipment, though a central D is affirmed clearly enough. The orchestra's *cantabile* theme takes much longer to define a distinctive second tonal area, and still longer to suppress the piano's intrusions with toccata material, including a flippant diminution of the new theme. It achieves a broad statement in E major, to which the augmented shapes of the first subject act as bass, and a pedal sustains this centre through the codetta. As Walton had done four years earlier in his symphony, Britten encompasses long spans by pedals, giving to the development a dual time scale: the two subjects (later joined by the subsidiary fanfare idea) are briskly worked out in opposition, but a single harmonic unit (the augmented triad on B flat) persists for many bars and static basses mark out a leisurely progress through flat areas that compensate for the exposition's swing. The contrapuntal conflation of the piano's first subject and the orchestral second (augmented) which opens the restatement is characteristic of the composer but, regrettably, it is denied the force of epigram: the second subject is represented again at the orthodox moment by its diminution, and makes a literal return after the cadenza. This implies even more than a classical measure of 'reconciliation' since not only is D retained (as the last great pedal) but the piano finally consents to essay this *cantabile* line. The fanfare theme, having articulated the cadenza dramatically, is restored to its original thematic context in a coda, and the reiterated cadence moves are all made through the inversion of *a*.

So the waltz theme's relation to that major seventh (see Ex. 3) is plain, while the piano's entry is a still more evident derivation from the fanfare theme. The horn's preparatory fourth (cf. the opening gambit of the Bridge Variations waltz) becomes a characteristic middle harmony, accommodated equally well whether the bass leans towards the tune's D or towards a contradictory B flat; exactly this bass oscillation was to recur one year later in the *Sinfonia da Requiem*'s finale. But the present context is at Britten's furthest remove from that drained beauty of sonority: the mordant quality of this waltz pastiche is pointed up by bizarre scoring, decorously inapposite progressions and fatuous little imitative phrases. The trio is a piano *moto perpetuo* on orchestral drones, and preparation for the return is neatly poised as a dominant of both D and B flat; in the coda, every element of the movement is fused, revealing the opening fourth to be another offshoot of the fanfare theme.

In place of the 1939 slow movement, a Recitative and Aria, Britten substituted in his revision of 1945 an Impromptu. The title is borne out by the passages in which, having completed one variation, the piano remains within its tonal area to muse freely over a new figurative idea, then transfers to a new tonality to work this out in the following variation over the orchestra's rigidly preserved statement of the theme. This ground is isorhythmic and highly repetitive melodically (see Ex. 4) but its apparently

Ex.2.4

monotonous successions of minor thirds and semitones can adapt themselves to innumerable harmonic and tonal readings. As we should expect from a piece contemporary with *Peter Grimes*, these variations provide a fine collection of Britten's typical harmonic configurations, much influenced by the initial false relations, but more warmly triadic than were the first two movements. And in the year of homage to Purcell (in the Donne Sonnets as well as the second quartet), Britten was alive to the possibilities of cross-phrasing that a ground presents, even if his canon 2 in 1 on the ground (variation V) is not pursued with Purcellian rigour. After a climactic variation in which triads collide head-on, the piano retraces in reverse its figurative patterns against a limpid final statement of the orchestral theme; the ability to keep still was one that Britten had mastered since the concerto's first appearance.

As we are reminded forcibly by the irritatingly smart vulgarity of the final march. But further adroit motivic transformation, of the major seventh and of the fanfare theme (which now is expanded into a second theme) establishes palpable relations with the first two movements, and the reliance on protracted pedals revives their air of decorative busyness. A sonata scheme (with reversed restatement broken up by the cadenza) is almost completed on the basis of a central A before a blatant swing to D (Schubertian in its relation to the exposition procedure, cf. figs 52 and 64), a key emphatically reinstated by a coda that brings back first movement shapes in somewhat specious clinching gestures.

VIOLIN CONCERTO, OP. 15

The piano concerto's D major is that key in which the Britten of this early period discovered some of his most characteristic sounds. From 'Sailing' in

Holiday Diary to the 'Requiem aeternam' in the *Sinfonia da Requiem* and the first quartet, D appears in association with a luminous harmony of gentle diatonic dissonance. Yet the piano concerto pointedly rejects such ideals. Even the first movement's *cantabile* theme is accompanied by a chromatic stream of mechanically reiterated thirds, ensuring that we hear in its simple aspirations more than a touch of the banal. If a defensive irony persists in the violin concerto, written one year later, in 1939, it now takes a far more urbane form. The bright D major towards which both first and last movements strive can never be beyond dispute when their starting points have been respectively F major and a succession of rapidly shifting tonal areas, but the most memorable writing in the work comes at the points where D sustains itself against flattening tendencies.

Though the solo violin proposes both melodic ideas in the first movement, the orchestra sheds a wry light on them by its accompaniment rhythms and by the chromatic progression that ushers in first subject and coda. This tension between themes and accompaniments is less than an elemental opposition of forces, and so the piano concerto's simple relationship between medium and structure is not repeated. But the argument conducted in terms of tonality is far more original than that of the earlier concerto, utilizing the sonata principle to arrive at a structure which in some respects is not a sonata at all. Eric Walter White's description of this concerto as 'in D minor'[2] may point an appropriate moral but it is certainly not applicable to the opening of the story. This exposition is more 'against F' than for anything in particular. Though the blatant definition of a root position is never

Ex. 2.5 (a)

Ex. 2.5 (b)

[2] White, p. 31.

admitted, the violin's broad opening melody, of a rather studied lyricism, is evidently centred on F (see Ex. 5a). Only at fig. 3 are there second thoughts, when the violin brusquely attempts to replace this with D, only to find that its sharp ventures conflict with orchestral excursions to the flat side. These transitional upheavals gradually drain away the lyrical impulse, and their bitonal friction is embodied in the second subject (Ex. 5b); by this time the violin is trying to impose A (dominant of the key it thought of too late) while the importunate rhythms of the transition persist in the bass on F. (In its mock-military flavour and bitonal irony this second subject brings a reminder of the character-piece style Britten was still prone to fall back on; but in the coexistence of A and F it may be considered a precursor of the Cello Symphony's second group.) Occasionally a unified key area is touched on, but honours remain more or less even: for example, the F minor of fig. 4, bar 9 yields to the D major 6/4 of bar 13. At fig. 7 the dominant preparation of the preceding bars seems about to produce an outcome in F, to gestures that (since fig. 6) have become more developmental than expository. But the dominant is dramatically thwarted of its goal when, in a sudden stillness, the F appears, overlaid by B minor. Obviously enough, this is the turning-point of the movement's tonal argument, but only through harmonic movements of great subtlety does Britten allow D to gain the ascendancy from this point to fig. 8. No less refined are the beautiful melodic synthesis by which the militant second subject is assimilated into the lyrical flow of the first (from fig. 7, bar 10) and the slow chromatic descent that guides the way to a luxuriously protracted (3/2 instead of 4/4 bars) D major restatement of the opening theme. Its mood has already prevailed, and indeed, with the achievement of the new key area all the second subject's frictions are made redundant. So restatement is restricted to the first subject, in a D that fluctuates between major and Aeolian minor (i.e., F natural can be admitted, on new terms); only with the long final tonic major, in which the violin ascends in a glow of harmonics, do the second subject's accompaniment rhythms make a delicately ironic reappearance. Thus, in totally eliminating the second group from his restatement Britten has broken more radically than before with traditional sonata practice, but he has again produced a design in which restatement is the emotional peak: indeed, here 'restatement' is a misnomer, for this is the achievement towards which both exposition and development have been striving, not a rosier vision of the *status quo*.

Key seems just as elusive in the scherzo, though the signature confirms the E minor above which the soloist first states the refrain (Ex. 6). Before this he has paraded the stamping accompaniment figure *a* through a variety of tonal areas, while the orchestra has established the scalic movement carried on by the *c* figure. Scales, whether chromatic (and *b* is the cue for these) or juxtaposing conflicting diatonic segments as in *c*, are the vital stuff of this whole movement, the simplicity of contour (and of underlying harmonic

Ex.2.6

units such as *a*) preserving intelligibility at a fast tempo. There is a subsidiary theme (at fig. 15) and a working out of Ex. 6 before a trio, rooted by musette-like pedals but with a prominent diminished fifth. Britten's orchestration, dry and incisive in its punctuation of the violin's formidable *bravura*, turns to the fantastic when the scherzo is resumed as a tuba solo (developing *b*) with an ostinato for two piccolos. A final E is achieved, but the strings unexpectedly introduce above it reiterations of the trio motive—five quavers long, and therefore a powerful propulsion across the bars. Against these two fixed elements the wind force a rising chromatic scale, inducing a tension that is dramatically resolved when the soloist imperiously takes over the strings' tongue-tied figure and launches it into the cadenza.

These first two movements were played without a break, yet their material had no palpable relationship. The cadenza, as well as elaborating brilliantly the accompanying rhythms of the first movement, demonstrates an affinity between its opening theme and the scherzo's scalic preoccupation, from which we naturally move into a still simpler scale; the process is shown at Ex. 7a, b, c and d. The trombones make an impressive first entry in the concerto when they accept this suggestion, developing it with oracular solemnity into the ground of the passacaglia finale. As the soloist carries on with the falling patterns of the first movement, a potent link is forged with the ground's descending element. We have seen that the piano concerto concealed some

Ex.2.7 (a)

Ex.2.7 (b)

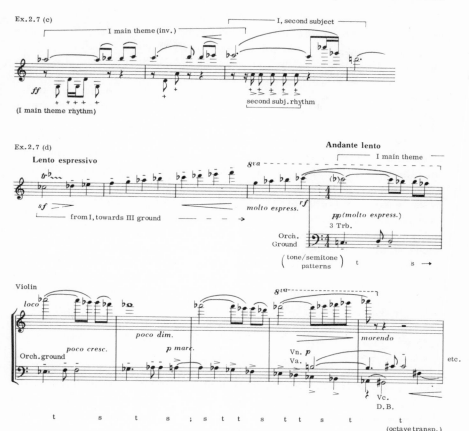

tight motivic organization under its 'characteristic' trimmings, but in the violin concerto Britten moves decisively towards the open acceptance of formula as a basis for, rather than a discipline upon, invention. In the later period of instrumental composition that begins with the cello sonata, this was to become still more evident. With the later works in mind, it cannot seem fortuitous that the scales of Britten's ground are so patterned in their alternation of tone and semitone, even though subsequent variations do not preserve the pattern. This was Britten's first passacaglia, and his determination to give it the continuity that will amass the weight of a movement, not a succession of genre pieces, is declared in the opening fugato exposition of the ground. Each entry, of a tonally unstable subject, begins a semitone lower, so that definitions are even further away than in the earlier movements, but successive variations gradually establish centres more certainly and more lastingly, often by the use of pedals. And it is significant that this elucidating process is part of a wider development, the emergence of a highly

51

personal tone. Already at fig. 38, the bland violin line against ostinato accompaniment has more than the thirties insouciance of the Bridge Variations Romance, and the following march, with its Lydian fourth and muscular scalic movements, has lost all suspicion of pastiche. But it is with the emergence at the quasi-restatement of an unequivocal D centre that Britten leaps forward to a bold simplicity foreshadowing the *Grimes* style in the Lydian-cum-Mixolydian form of the ground and the eloquent counterpoint to it.

In the closing section the ground is represented by chant-like phrases, harmonized merely in common chords and dominant sevenths but in newly-imagined contexts; these turn more and more on the recovery of D from flattening counter attractions, and they therefore sum up the tonal argument of the two main movements. The soloist's impassioned fantasy at the close of each phrase is concerned less with tonality than with modality: its semitonal inflexions achieve their fullest significance in the final shake between F and F sharp, so that the orchestra's open fifth on D is finally committed to neither major nor minor. With these closing pages, at once ardent and epitomizing, Britten gave impressive evidence of a command of absolute expressive forms that was not to be fully realized until the Cello Symphony, twenty-four years later.

DIVERSIONS, OP. 21, FOR PIANO (LEFT HAND) AND ORCHESTRA

One of the scores withdrawn by the composer, of a work for piano and strings, *Young Apollo*, Op. 16, dates from August 1939, immediately before the Violin Concerto. It is impossible to know how much this depended on a programmatic continuity, but its rejection of the concerto's connotations provides a precedent of some sort for the next work for piano and orchestra. It will be convenient to consider this work, the *Diversions*, immediately after the two concertos even though strict chronology would require us to consider first the *Sinfonia da Requiem*. In the concertos Britten's exploitation of the solo instrument's nature had produced such elegantly appropriate structures as a toccata dominated by the piano's percussive small-talk and an opening movement sustained by the violin's *cantabile* eloquence. The second of these virtually abandoned the sonata argument (though not its typical processes of thought) while the first somewhat over-simplified the problem of the sonata-concerto by associating the fundamental duality of material quite rigidly with the duality of forces. When the composer at last returned to the problem, in 1963, he found a solution of greater subtlety, but one so much more bound up with inter-thematic issues than with any conflict of forces that he chose to view the result as a 'symphony' rather than a concerto. In 1940, however, when Britten conceived his fourth work for soloist and orchestra, the lesson that seems to have emerged most clearly from the two concertos was that he had struck his richest vein of invention in turning from the prodigality of the sonata to the restrictive (and on the face of it not inherently dualistic) mould of the passacaglia. We may feel that, just because the ground's progressive mechanism is so assured, Britten could spurn too abject a reliance on literal rotation and could allow his fancy to make of the limitation a stimulus.

The decision to write a solo work, with orchestra, for the one-armed pianist, Paul Wittgenstein, brought restrictions of another kind. The piano, that 'universal instrument' which the nineteenth century had developed for supermen, able to simulate—and directly to challenge—the power and textural opulence of the full symphony orchestra, had to be shorn of some stock associations. Given a total span no greater than that of a violin's triple stopping, a soloist can no longer command the platitude of exact antiphony, and even the simultaneous provision of tune and accompaniment is only to be secured by an athletic *style brisé*. Commonly, then, he will provide either line or patterned texture, but, on an instrument of so vast a range, either function divorced from the other will tend to arrogate to itself an unusually wide *tessitura*. Britten foresaw this when establishing a basis for the work that should serve well in both functions: a magisterial circle of fifths in the orchestra's opening statement spans more than five octaves (see Ex. 8). As

Ex. 2.8

Joan Chissell has pointed out,[3] this is not so much a theme as raw material, and the succession of different articles into which the following 'diversions' fashion it seems calculated ostentatiously to disprove hasty theories about the limitations of the medium. Equally, of course, such variety prevents the sense of inadequacy that might result from pursuing a sonata argument in persistently idiosyncratic textures.

[3] J. Chissell, 'The Concertos', in Mitchell-Keller, p. 264.

This statement (Ex. 8) establishes a principle, of movement by fifths and fourths, that will need supplementation if melodic shapes of any subtlety or charm are to emerge. As a basis for chord construction, too, it seems rather mannered, though it encourages the kind of added- (and subtracted-) note diatonic formations that Britten had already learnt to use with versatility. But as a basis of progression (i.e., as a succession of chord roots) it has a long and honourable history, one which had been gently mocked in the Bourrée of the Bridge Variations. In its heyday, the Late Baroque period, it was used equally for sequential circuits within a static tonality and for the more adventurous movements of endless dominants that could lead to new tonal areas. Pursued to a logical (albeit equal-tempered) conclusion, the circle of fifths touches on all twelve classes of pitch and offers twelve tonal centres. Britten presents his statement above a stubbornly reiterated C pedal, and after F sharp is reached (i.e., the half-circle) he returns by the same route—though by substituting fourths for fifths at this point he maintains the upward movement. The variations are equally firmly anchored to tonal bases, so that not even constant excursions through twelve-note successions (see, e.g., Variation 2) endanger a traditional structural coherence. The relevance of this method to the variations of *The Turn of the Screw* is as obvious as is the kinship of the two themes.

The ten variations and tarantella finale are belated, and very polished, examples of those 'characteristic' styles Britten was to abandon soon. In turning to the stimulus of text instead of genre he hastened the discovery of a musical character that needed none of the disclaimers of pastiche. Already in *Les Illuminations* the transmutation of moods first aroused by a poetic medium had ousted the representation of *Affekte*, and this clarifying process is reflected to some degree in the *Diversions*. The suavity of the Romance lacks the harmonic nonchalance of its opposite number in the Bridge set; whatever the debt in method to Fauré in this and the Nocturne (as also in the Rimbaud cycle), such carefully-timed achievements of new tonal resting-points are expressive events of just that precision which the song-writer needs. Another gain can be heard in the bright expanding diatonic sounds of the Arabesque, capturing an atmosphere without recourse to melodic definition, foreshadowing the manner of some operatic preludes. Though the 'Chant' explores further than ever before the effect of moving triads against an independent bass, it is too studied to bear comparison with that of the Bridge set. The facetious 'Badinerie', too, lacks the earlier spontaneity, while the Adagio is only saved from platitude by the powerful use of internal pedals in the middle section. Appropriate audience response to an astonishing pianistic *tour de force* is worked up in a long finale that wittily uses the fifths as counterpoint or harmony to a determinedly scalic tarantella. Their reappearance in so crude a form emphasizes the adroitness with which Britten has elsewhere converted them into other contours: the two patterns in Ex. 9 show how he avoids the cliché while preserving the circle intact.

Ex.2.9 (a)

Ex.2.9 (b)

SCOTTISH BALLAD, OP. 26, FOR TWO PIANOS AND ORCHESTRA

The last American score raised problems of another kind: four hands at two pianos encourage obese sonorities even before a rôle is found for the orchestra. If we exclude Mozart's concerto (and, with all its witty repartee, this does not approach the perfection of his solo concertos), the two-keyboard concerto, whether Bach's in C major or Bartók's reworking of his great sonata, seems to find in the orchestra a liability; Stravinsky's decision to cast his Concerto without an orchestra is persuasive, if not apparently logical. Britten avoids the principal structural issue, of how to find a dramatic relationship between the two soloists and another between them and the orchestra while preserving a deployment of thematic material that justifies itself in 'absolute' terms, by avoiding altogether the lofty associations of *concerto*. His *Scottish Ballad*, Op. 26 (1941; written, like the Op. 23 pieces, for Ethel Bartlett and Rae Robertson) is given a licence by its title to string together a succession of 'characteristic' musics; the dramatic effects of their juxtaposition need have no long-term implications, while their superimposition will offer soloists and orchestra piquantly contrasted rôles.

In his Soutar settings of 1969 Britten was to furnish pithily apt music for some quintessentially Scottish aphorisms without sporting a bogus tartan. But in the Ballad he seizes on every popular conception of Scottish music and magnifies it to a point which a Scotsman might find nearer caricature than affectionate overstatement. He begins with the most noble of psalm-tunes, *Dundee*, melodically in C but harmonized from a stentorian A minor opening, through huge contrary movements of the two pianos (each terminated by an orchestral explosion) that lead to a tonal chaos in which the last line is never completed; instead the pianos dissolve into cadenza. This includes the funereal rhythm that is to dominate the first of the two main movements, which follows after a whole-tone protraction of the psalm-tune's last line and its eventual achievement of cadence in the violas. The funeral march rhythm, with its prominent 'Scotch snap', has a melodic form in C Aeolian, worked out in a solemn undertone by the pianos. But the tonal situation is complicated by the entry (in the soft but incisive piping of oboes

55

and clarinets) of the lament, 'Turn ye to me', in B flat minor and repeated in F sharp minor. When C is recovered for the second strain (violins, bar 65), it acquires a deflection, C major–D flat minor, the first of many bases for those sequences on adjacent degrees and back that characterize so much Scottish music. As Trio of the March, a pentatonic tune appears in the piano (bar 83), paralleled at the fifth below so that its C major is converted into an F context; a scalic third part diversifies the harmonic situations and the texture is expanded by octave doublings. With the return of the march rhythm, 'Turn ye to me' is now a penetrating wail of woodwind and muted trumpet in (roughly) F minor, while the pianos and lower strings add to the C major/D flat minor juxtaposition a 'subdominant' of F major/F sharp minor. This thunderous lament at last burns itself out with a statement of its germinating rhythm (brass and side-drum) on the closing C, and *Dundee* is recalled in the woodwind; its cadences are now marked by shimmering chords in which the semitonal frictions persist. The last phrase is withheld altogether this time, and the shimmer is converted into a drone on the fifth A–E which is to be heard throughout the greater part of the quick finale, a reel, that now begins.

Its tonal centre is A, its mode usually Mixolydian, and its adjacent-degree sequences are a tone apart. The frenetic emphasis on the initial motive, E–G–A, and the innumerable repetitions as the dance becomes more abandoned remain entertaining because of the spiritedly varied disposition of the tune in the pianos (in competitive alternation now) and of the drone in the orchestra. After some eighty bars of that inescapable A bass, the music is suddenly catapulted into an orchestral episode (bar 236) that exploits shifts of a tone so vigorously as to tempt the pianos to retaliate with complete whole-tone scale movements (the earlier whole-tone activity comes into focus here). At the peak of this episode a new reel tune is produced by the pianos (at 272), in F though above a B flat accompaniment (cf. the treatment of the tune at bar 83). Its modulatory development fades to form an ostinato-like background for a quiet return of 'Turn ye to me' in an elaborately bitonal situation, quoted at Ex. 10, if only because no allocation of its strands to precise centres would give an accurate impression of its equivocal nature. The A–E drone returns, to be sustained for 36 bars by the same wind players, saved, if scarcely cheered, by the escape clause, '*respirare ad lib.*'. Below them, double bassoon, timpani and harp add a low Mixolydian G natural, while the Highland dance that the strings in turn throw off includes a Lydian D sharp; a further element in this Rossini-ish build-up is the repeated brass interpolation of the first line of *Dundee* (also with Lydian fourth). The strings then attempt more of the psalm-tune as stabbing punctuation of the reel (the possible programmatic implications of this confrontation defy conjecture), but a coda brings back the E–G–A motive that began the finale, now in an A Aeolian on F context. After further witticisms created by the whole-tone shifts of phrases, A becomes Mixolydian again and the E–G–A

Ex. 2.10

is played off against itself in a dizzying number of different temporal ratios. The pianos' brilliant dash for home is delayed by the brass, whose sobering first line of *Dundee* is supported on a whole-tone scale that leads down to an unequivocally final A.

CANADIAN CARNIVAL, OP. 19

In the purely orchestral medium the Ballad had precedent of a kind in the one work of Britten's American period that borrows local colour from his environment. Written in 1939 and first performed in the following year (in England, ironically enough), *Canadian Carnival* is little more than a sophisticated pot-pourri of folky song and dance, arranged inside a quasiprogrammatic frame. It is surprising to find how sympathetically, and promptly, the composer responded to that nostalgic evocation of the lonely prairie that Copland had introduced into his music only one year earlier (*Billy the Kid*; *Outdoor Overture*). The debt of Britten's opening and closing trumpet calls is unmistakable but, typically, his fanfares become involved in a maze of conflicting tonalities. More systematized bitonality in the breezy *alla danza* movement is between D major tune and B flat accompaniment, a deliberately unsubtle use of a relationship that had already underlain the wry waltz of the piano concerto, and was to find its most rarefied form in the finale of the *Sinfonia da Requiem*.

SINFONIA DA REQUIEM, OP. 20

Though the *Diversions* are slightly later, among Britten's orchestral works the Sinfonia marks the peak of his first period as indisputably as does the Op.

25 Quartet in his chamber music. It has escaped from the neglect that once was common to the two works, but less certainly from misreadings of its nature. Given some familiarity with the two concertos discussed above, we need not suspect a sense of unpreparedness to have prompted his avoidance of the bald title, 'symphony'. The claims on the listener's attention of a programme that had fired the composer's imagination could not be ignored, but its declaration does not imply the renunciation of truly symphonic processes of expansion. When Scott Goddard saw the influence of Verdian operatic accompaniments in 'a succession of reiterated patterns, rhythmic or melodic',[4] he was not only bolstering up a curious explanation of Britten's Italian title, but enlarging on a point he had made earlier, that reiterative patterns may betray the composer 'who never develops into a symphonic thinker'. One suspects that the patterns he had in mind were those of the first two movements, yet in fact it is the last movement which depends for its mood of drained calm on the static quality of a hymnic refrain. Only in its trio does the central movement juxtapose ideas inertly, those of the scherzo being projected dynamically across broad spans. Even if we limit our view of 'symphonic thinking' by linking it with the sonata principle, Britten's first movement must appear a modification that intensifies the sonata's forward surge, once again reserving the most dramatic confrontation for the stage traditionally concerned with recapitulatory consolidation.

More to the point is Erwin Stein's description of this 'Lacrymosa' movement as being 'conceived as an integral unit'.[5] For it is true that on one level, that of programmatic suggestibility, we hear it as an unbroken procession of mourners. On another level, too, the near-ubiquity of certain figures may seem to resemble a Baroque homogeneity of content. Yet, as Haydn tirelessly demonstrated, distinctions of function, pointed up by changes in attendant detail and tonal orientation, can allow one basic shape to take on that otherness from which the sonata drama springs. Indeed, Britten's climax (which is thus in a direct line between those of the sonata movements in Op. 1 and the second quartet) turns on the assimilation into a single texture of two ideas that, whatever they may have in common, have formerly constituted contrasting elements.

At Ex. 11 are shown three stages of the exposition. The first is a melodic curve that acquires momentum from its syncopations against the marching pulse of the bass, a background so potent after its explosive opening Ds that no other accompaniment is needed. The germinal cell is the semitone, x, and semitonal relationships of another kind contribute to this uneasy yet aspiring line, in the ambivalent Bs and Fs. Though the marching bass climbs chromatically to the subdominant for the violas' repetition of the cello theme, D is

[4] S. Goddard, 'Benjamin Britten', in A. Bacharach (ed.), *British Music of our Time*, Harmondsworth 1946, p. 214.
[5] E. Stein, 'The Symphonies', in Mitchell-Keller, p. 249.

Ex.2.11 (a)

Ex.2.11 (b)

Ex.2.11 (c)

regained for Ex. 11b. Here the figure in minor sixths is a pendant to (a), though without its developing curve; it merely marks time (the marching bass having disappeared) and movement passes to the saxophone's slowly expanding line of sevenths. With the march's disappearance, tonal definitions become meaningless, making the more arresting a return of (a)

59

on full strings with wind counterpoint (adapting the slower rhythms of (b) to the crucial semitone x) that reinstates D. Thus far the shape, enclosing a subsidiary idea of the first group within lightly and heavily scored versions of the main idea, is entirely classical. Again the march tread is abandoned, and tonal security goes out with it, but the sequel, shown at (c), is now of a fundamentally different order. The syncopations of (a) persist (on muted trumpets) but with no pulse on which to engage they cling limply to an enigmatic E flat. Around this, major and minor triads alternate between trombones and flutes, in search of a key but also striving through semitonal inflexions (the ubiquitous x) to generate motion. Interpolations from the first group (mainly of y) merely underline the immobility of the chordal idea, and its tonal anguish can achieve no relief greater than the major-plus-minor 6/4 (with another semitonal irritant in the sharpened fourth) on which it fades out.

Development as a middle section prerogative is not pursued far, and its effect is the opposite of the traditional acceleration of the eventful. The saxophone theme of (b) briefly proliferates in stretti of superimposed sevenths until the minor seventh becomes a vast pendulum on the brass. Meanwhile, y has continued to mark, rather than to use, time in mournful repetitions. This recourse to Goddard's 'repetitive patterns' is, however, far from decorative: it induces a need for decisive action which explodes with a cymbal clash as the seventh C–B flat is recognized to be also an augmented sixth that can cadentially *achieve* a B natural. Here for the first time we seem to have escaped both from the fateful gloom of the opening D minor and from the subsequent gropings through a tonal mist. So there is high tragedy in the immediate reassertion against this B of D minor, as unequivocal centre of the chordal second subject, which now begins (fig. 13) a reversed 'restatement', though the vehemence with which the brass fling this theme against the dissonant syncopations of the rest continues to project the action forward to a climax.

The first subject's return is obviously to be involved in this climax, but the thunderous marching bass that heralds it is on a dominant pedal (the first appearance of this degree in the movement) and remains there when the theme begins to accumulate momentum (cf. the procedures of the *Sinfonietta*; see p. 18). The great potential of so belated a dominant is realized when, at the melodic peak, the brass bring back the second subject as a gargantuan opposition of minor and major triads to the major and minor thirds of the first subject. Resolution of so elemental a conflict seems inconceivable: the two ideas simply batter against each other in short bursts, separated by strange lulls in which the drum beat falters and the brass fade to a bright echo. Semitonal frictions persist as the movement fades into the 'Dies irae' scherzo (which immediately sets up another such relationship). The opulence of gesture in this first movement tempts the listener to read into it a far more ramified programme than the composer's title warrants. So

it is salutary to observe that its growth as a sonata organism, though unorthodox in timing (118 bars of exposition to 40-plus-55 of development-
cum-restatement) has been controlled by an intra-musical logic.

The scherzo accommodates a wealth of macabre details within the simple
structural plan AB(A)CA-coda, which, despite the elimination of B,
amounts to a *da capo* form, with C set apart as a trio. The figures reiterated
obsessively as the main idea are shown in Ex. 12, but nothing less than the
full span would show how, on a much slower time-scale, *a* is woven into an

Ex.2.12

extensive line, most of it conjunct if we ignore octave transpositions. Of
course, we do nothing of the kind: our first (and most important) impression
is of disjointed fragments that appear from all corners of the orchestra, but
the suspicion that this activity, far from being random, betrays an ominous
certainty of direction, can be rationalized by tracing the lines blurred by
changes of register. It will be seen that in the opening bars the tritone
relationship E flat–A is more prominent (largely because of the E flat triads
of *b*) than is the semitone or major seventh, and the effect of this persists
throughout the movement—in the trio's ostinato and the tritonal transposition of the *da capo*'s opening; the significance of these contexts for the *War
Requiem* needs little emphasis. The empty fourth of the trumpets looks back
to that of the horns in the piano concerto's waltz; both stand in a semitonal
relation to a D tonic, and in another respect, the co-existence of D and B flat
which is approached in 'Dies irae' and achieved in 'Requiem aeternam', the
waltz appears to have proved a model worth refining. The *brio* of the second
theme's tarantella rhythms momentarily gives some point to Scott Goddard's Italianate reading. Certainly this Last Trump is a far cry from the
deathly solemn sound, but the vision of the whole scherzo is of a headlong
career towards an ultimate chaos rather than the Judgment Seat. The
interruption of the trio proves in retrospect to have given us our bearings in
this ride to Hell, for it looks back to the mourners' burden of 'Lacrymosa'
(i.e., Ex. 11a, now reduced to a maudlin futility by the saxophone and an
accompanying ostinato) and forward to the refrain of 'Requiem aeternam',
here still a biting mockery (fig. 27 trumpets). A further irony comes in the *da
capo* of Ex. 12, which achieves an overpoweringly sonorous rooted D minor
(with the E flat abandoned for an added E natural) before splitting up into
the lurid depictions of the coda.

Erwin Stein doubted whether 'disorder has ever before been conveyed in so convincing a musical form',[6] but it may be that such splintered textures have in themselves little power to shock by now. As before, the outrage with which we hear this furious breakdown of musical sanity is prompted by the remarkable proximity to a conventional ordering that lies beneath it: reduced to a single octave register, it proves to be a series of patterned routes to emphatic perfect cadences. From its expiring twitchings the harp and bass clarinet pick up the last three-note figure, A–B flat–D and reverse it to set in motion the fluid bitonal bass of 'Requiem aeternam' (Ex. 13). Thus the shadow of catastrophe persists in the undertow of the finale.

Ex. 2.13

Mahler and Stravinsky are the names that crop up in discussion of this symphony's sonorities. Mahlerian though the doubling of bass clarinet and harp is, the exposed arpeggios suggest still more strongly the Mahler disciple, Alban Berg; and it may not be irrelevant to add that for another example of a slow movement derived from material announced in the trio section of the previous movement we can look to Berg's *Lyric Suite*. The limpid diatonicism of the three flutes may loosely be called Stravinskyan, though it belongs to a Britten line we have traced from 'Sailing', and the responsorial structure of their dialogue with the horns has parallels in Stravinsky's elegiac music. This reminds us that 'Requiem aeternam' remains a prayer for, not the achievement of, a beatific (or perhaps, indeed, a nescient) peace. And so the mourners' burden (Ex. 11a) is still relevant, though it can now exchange the saxophone's distortion for intimations of

<hr />

[6] Ibid., p. 251.

ecstasy. The rhythm of Ex. 13 bar 3 and its consonant second (also in the horns' response) persist in the accompaniment of this central paragraph, the seconds being piled up in a piercingly bright harmony at the climax—an incandescent passage approached through a Mahlerian string canon. As in the previous movements, Britten relies here on stepwise basses for an underlying continuity, intermediary between the indifferent ostinato and the developing melodic impulse. In such strongly tonal contexts the conjunct bass also has great articulative powers: with the completion of the second descent from D to D, we pass inevitably, *via* the major second common to both themes, to restatement of the first. Thus, despite the prolongation of some intermediate steps as pedals, there has been in this ABA piece neither a second-key affirmation nor any determined negation of the first, no 'action' from which to recover a poise, and so the hymnic flute theme placidly runs its course. Such key dichotomy as the movement has revealed has been fused in the accompaniment pattern (which rises to a brief eloquence at the horns' final response). More than two decades later, Britten was to turn once more to a fusion of third-related keys in a comparable context—'Dormi nunc' from the *Cantata Misericordium*. That visionary moment in the cantata fades to a return of the opening, but the extremely moving sound of the Sinfonia's conflated majors springs from our recognition that their brightness has been filtered from the constituents of that D minor which brooded darkly over the first two movements.

PRELUDE AND FUGUE FOR 18-PART STRING ORCHESTRA, OP. 29

Britten's only instrumental score between his return from America and the composition of the second quartet was a Prelude and Fugue for string orchestra divided into 18 parts, written in 1943. It has less claim on our affection than on our admiration: the technique which Bach devised to give nine players independent parts in the *concertino* sections of the third Brandenburg Concerto is here extended to twice that number and is maintained throughout the greater part of the fugue. This must have provided a welcome review of the individual talents normally submerged in a corporate body—the Boyd Neel Orchestra, for whose tenth anniversary the piece was written. But, given so workaday a subject, proliferation so indefatigable may try the listener's patience. Certainly the simpler textures of the *grave* frame, with their pungent tonal pulls and rich modality, give a much more vivid picture of the creative personality that was developing so rapidly in the contemporary vocal works.

3 Early Vocal and Choral Music

A BOY WAS BORN, OP. 3

If the last few instrumental scores before Britten emerged as an opera
composer betrayed the effect of his recent experience of word-setting in
their unequivocal re-creation of definable emotional states, his earliest
large-scale work for voices was evidently fashioned according to structural
and textural procedures commonly thought proper to 'absolute' instrumental composition. How consciously the nineteen-year-old Britten conceived
the choral variations as a *tour de force* is already to be seen in the theme (see
Ex. 1). Its initial four notes are made, by repetition, transposition, inversion

Ex.3.1

of strands and re-harmonization, to yield a chorale with alleluya refrains,
totalling forty-six bars. As there is clearly little else here to be varied, the
entire work springs from, or around, this four-note motive (*x* in Ex. 1), and
as it is first heard coupled to the words of the title, all that follows can be
regarded, verbally and musically, as exegesis of that one pithy text.

64

If we detach the fourth note from *x* (a repetition of the second), we are left with one of the most fruitful shapes in the history of Western music (to look no further). Added to its own transposition a fourth or a fifth up, it produces a pentatonic scale of strong contour but no fixed centre. Despite Britten's key signature, D is here no more than the initial note, and E the first of several degrees on which phrases close, commonly on an open fifth. There is no revival of strict modality, but neither is there much reliance on the progressive harmonic apparatus of major-minor tonality. Chords are the product of firm line-drawing: the triad is nowhere to be found and the sevenths that feature so prominently are allowed neither the indulgence nor the implication of orthodox resolution. The superficial impression may be that Britten has profited from the modality of Vaughan Williams and/or from the rich added-note harmonies of such English composers as John Ireland, but this is a drier, more ascetic sound than either; if the rhetoric of its refrain owes a slight debt to Walton (*Belshazzar's Feast* had appeared in the year before the variations were begun; compare bars 8–10 in Ex. 1 and the bars around fig. 77 in the Walton), it is one to which the rest of the work adds nothing.

The variations are a richly differentiated series yet they remain faithful to principles, as well as to the motive, established by the theme. In 'Lullay, Jesu' the open fifth is converted into constant rocking 'Lullay's while 'Jesu' is inevitably reiterated to the 'Boy' motive, *x*; an elaborate background texture is woven from the two ideas. The trebles' descant and the choir's harmonic textures, which carry the dialogue between Jesus and his mother, are freer but entirely congruous; word-painting can therefore be vividly conveyed in the slightest deviations—see the expansion from two to four parts at 'your grievance' and the flattening, with consequent false relation, at 'woe'. This second example is the peak of a phrase that shows Britten already highly sensitive to rhythmic subtleties of declamation. Though the movement's broad tonal span may be charted from a presumptive D Aeolian, even the final drooping 'Lullay' fifths (A-D) are neutralized by the trebles' close on B flat.

Just as these fifths, while derived from the theme's harmony, have become a motive characteristic of the first variation, so in the second, 'Herod',

Ex.3.2

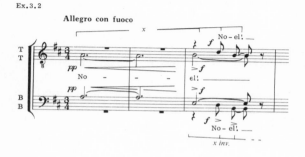

Britten devises new shapes by dividing and re-timing the ubiquitous x (see Ex. 2), and makes of these unifying elements peculiar to this scherzo. The narrative is carried along by men's voices, often in a unison line braced by tense, asymmetric rhythms. Harmony is still further from the triadic, preferring the hard sound of superimposed perfect fourths, and the B minor we may assume from the signature is, as so often in Britten from this early period onwards, no more than a background against which we hear consistent or fluctuating deviations from major/minor norms. A 'centre' or 'final' is less important here than a basic modal repertoire; granted that there has been in use more or less the selection of notes implied by a signature of two sharps, the effect of the swing at figure 25 through a 'six flats' (or sharps) area to 'three flats' is powerful whether or not we feel E flat to be central; it coincides with the entry of the women's voices and the supplication to Christ (yet another x form). The following variation, 'Jesu, as Thou art our Saviour', reinforces the prayer in the simplest movement of the cycle. A solo treble weaves x into a pentatonic melisma on the name 'Jesu' to round off the framing refrain and the two intervening verses, all of which are in choral homophony. The method obviously owes much to contexts in Vaughan Williams that suggest mystical rhapsody, but the mood Britten induces is very different: the soprano chorus line, transfixed throughout on one imploring note (the note is B—that of Berg's one-note fantasy in *Wozzeck* rather than of Purcell's), throws into high relief the attendant harmonies. These therefore become quite precise emotional counters, fluctuating between awestruck open fifth and yearning minor third, tense superimposition of fourths, sharp dissonance of seventh and ninth (at 'dolour') and the near-repose of the rooted diatonic seventh; the pure triad is almost wholly eliminated.

Variation 4, 'The Three Kings', further explores the pentatonic implications of x, taking for its characteristic (and, of course, illustrative) pattern an endless wandering of vocalized quavers. Though these are usually organized as an eight-bar ground, they are passed between vocal sub-sections in two-bar stretches; the resulting fluidity is orchestral in effect and to find the most exact parallel we might look to Mahler's (rather than any more folky) pentatonicism, as in parts of *Das Lied von der Erde*. The superstructure is also 'scored' so that verbal continuity is achieved only in the total effect. Key centres are now far less equivocal, and the third-related scheme, E flat–C–A, patently a symbol of the three kings, is reversed in a dramatically compressed form as they offer their gifts. Though Britten uses Christina Rossetti's title for his fifth variation, 'In the bleak midwinter', her poem is one part of a diptych, snow piling on snow in a cool, iridescent harmony of women's voices (concealing an inversion of x), and soon the words are being used chiefly for their sonorous qualities. Against this impressionistic backcloth the boys' chorus sings the Corpus Christi Carol in regular, etched strophes that are Britten's nearest approach to folksong pastiche. Then the background texture gently contracts again to the vibrant minor second which is the true 'centre' of this piece. The visionary quality which we discern in this co-existence of two musics so unlike (these faithfully mirroring the bizarre juxtaposition of cryptic medieval imagery and chaste pre-Raphaelite wonder) remains an astonishing achievement in a composer so young: this ability to connect was not to be employed so searchingly again until the *War Requiem*.

The huge finale is an elaborate rondo, incorporating more carols as its episodes and in a coda drawing threads together from the whole work. Its refrain (see Ex. 3) uses both the fifth, now rising (contrast 'Lullay'), and *x*,

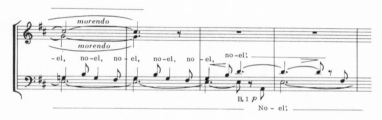

now the generating shape of lilting iambic phrases and a 'Wassail' figure that gradually ousts these; the mounting excitement of this long section arises from its being constantly poised on an E (of the basses' 'Noel'; see Ex. 3) while its lines suggest a D centre. This admirably exploits the ambivalence of the theme's first line and its predilection for seventh chords. The first episode, 'Good day, Sir Christmas', set in harmony of fourths and fifths and with its own motto phrase, turns about F sharp, and by an enharmonic swing the Noel refrain returns a semitone lower than at first (i.e., around D flat), later modulating to E flat. Another move brings something like D Dorian for 'Get ivy and hull', delivered in a monotonous sing-song that is appropriate to this collection of old saws. The refrain's next appearance around G is joined by the bell-like scales in canon of 'Welcome be Thou, heaven king', before a climactic return to D. In the first stage of the coda, stentorian unison statements of *x* deliver the message of the angels in phrases that articulate quieter textures—of unison Ds endlessly overlapping in the choral parts, while the boys recall the earlier variations, 4, 6 ('Wassail'), 5, 2, 1 and 3.

Finally, 'This night a child is born', briefly introduced into the Ivy and Hull episode, is now given its head in hymnic phrases that expand the x shape. 'Sing Hosanna' provides an obvious route back to the theme's 'alleluya' phrase (see Ex. 1), while the tonal scheme reiterates that of the finale proper, F sharp–D flat–E flat and a D now Aeolian rather than Dorian. A vast inversion of x projects into the final D major triad, a startlingly bright conclusion when it has been withheld in all the previous movements.

The motivic economy of the whole cycle and the large-scale organization of thematic material in this finale seem to be the work of a composer remarkably well versed in a structural logic owing nothing to verbal directives. By comparison with most later Britten word-setting, there is unusually little attempt to find telling images for specific words or momentary inflexions of mood, but the new musical means devised for each variation create moods (of some subtlety, notably in Variation 5) that give an incisive edge to those of the poems. We may well find a cosier response to the traditional joys of Christmas in *A Ceremony of Carols*, but *A Boy was Born* presents the greater challenge to the musicianship of choirs and audiences.

TE DEUM IN C MAJOR (1935) AND JUBILATE (1961)
For a composer who has enriched the music of Christianity with such inspired commentaries on unconventional texts (*Rejoice in the Lamb, Noyes Fludde* and so on), Britten has shown remarkably little enthusiasm for enlarging the standard repertoire of the cathedral service and its imitation in the major parish churches. Of his two Te Deum settings the earlier, written in 1935 for Maurice Vinden and the choir of St Mark's, North Audley Street, was described as 'drab and penitential' by Constant Lambert[1]. Certainly its initial protraction of a C major triad and the ostentatious motivic working of the organ bass do seem self-consciously economical; though the sonata-like shape of the whole balances well, even tonally the piece is oddly lacking in those unexpected perspectives that enliven many a page of merely 'occasional' Britten. More than twenty-five years later, the composer added a Jubilate setting to this at the request of the Duke of Edinburgh. Here the unifying organ figure is far more fruitful, the heterophonic relationship between upper (decorated) and lower (plain) forms of the lines piquant, and the return from the tonal detours characteristically inventive.

OUR HUNTING FATHERS, SYMPHONIC CYCLE FOR HIGH VOICE AND ORCHESTRA, OP. 8
The key position of *Our Hunting Fathers* in Britten's early development might almost be inferred even before the music was known. This was his first song-cycle, his first score for full orchestra and his first collaboration (outside the documentary film studio) with Auden; what must have seemed still

---

[1] Quoted in White, p. 28.

more auspicious to the young composer, this was his first important commission. Though the Norwich Festival did not lack enterprise (Vaughan Williams's *Five Tudor Portraits* also had their performance at the 1936 festival, and *Job* had been introduced at Norwich six years earlier), the native East Anglian must have had a clear view of the limits within which his music and its literary subject matter should be confined if the work was to meet with a ready understanding. In fact Britten never wrote a less circumspect piece, yet his refusal to ingratiate was more than a move in the game of *épater le bourgeois*. The opportunity of writing for a large and expert orchestra was too precious to be wasted on either the decorously festive or the pertly iconoclastic; the great range of adventurous orchestral dispositions shows how eagerly the technical challenge was seized. Yet Auden's compilation of texts was not only the stimulus to virtuosity but a prickly goad to a tender social conscience. For this commentary on man's relations with the animals who share his world tells us much about man, and little of it is reassuring.

Auden's anthology, demanding a response both ironic and compassionate, was welded together by the poet's own didactic prologue and epilogue. The composer, sure enough of his ability to match each mood in turn, felt that some more essentially musical means was needed of drawing them all to a focus. The cycle therefore includes much thematic cross-reference, most obviously in the persistence of a motive presented in the opening recitative (*x* in Ex. 4). This is more than a motto and less than a germ cell

Ex.3.4

for the whole work, and the way in which structural procedures are affected by its transformations and developments makes the use of the epithet 'symphonic' as convincing as in many a symphonic poem; a more obvious justification is to be found in the correspondence of its four movements (after the prologue) to the classical plan. As in the choral variations, we may observe the determination of a composer whose first extended works had been instrumental to brace his word-settings by some 'absolute' principle.

69

To preserve for the motive the appropriate flexibility, it must be given no cut-and-dried symbolic intent. Even so, it is far from the neutral four-note shape of *A Boy was Born*. This major arpeggio descending to the tonic and then climbing to the minor third is already an expressive event: the sensation of affirmation suddenly negated is reinforced by dynamics, scoring and harmony/tonality. It is probably more to the point to see in this an intensification of Schubertian major/minor inflexions than to make much of its close resemblance to a familiar shape from *Mathis der Maler*; nor are we yet approaching the consistent use of alternative readings of degrees which in later Britten can lead to a tortuously introverted line that is his chief debt to Bartók.

The key to which Ex. 4 relapses to end the opening recitative, C minor, is that from which the movement set out. Indeed, much of the strength of Britten's recitative style (as of Purcell's) lies in the highly organized harmonic plan of the accompaniment; here the key motive is at once the climax and the resolution of the whole pattern. Any truly 'symphonic' cycle is likely to concern a revolution of tonalities, but Peter Pears's description[2] of a progress from this initial C minor, *via* movements in D major, D minor, D major, to an epilogue in C minor, makes a more symmetrical and less dramatic design than the listener senses. For as in many of Britten's early scores (the *Sinfonietta* and Violin Concerto are two examples that have been discussed in this light), the classical antithesis of key tends to be replaced by one between definable tonal area and indefinable or overlapping areas. The prominence of D in both second and third movements already places the supremacy of C in jeopardy. The fourth movement can scarcely be assigned a tonal centre at all, though the key signature bears out a reading against an E minor background; however, the orchestral interlude to which it leads confirms that in the whole span this is the developmental peak. Inevitably, therefore, it poses the question of a return—whether to the assertive D or the distant C. This interlude is arrestingly punctuated by the trombones' reiteration of x, now beginning as a B flat *minor* triad, but always stopping short of the motive's final note until at last this is achieved explosively with the major third, D natural. This D is accepted in both epilogue and funeral march (most prominently in a relation of x first heard in the prologue at 'O pride, so hostile to our charity'; cf. Ex. 4) but is placed in constant opposition to the xylophone's dry-bones figure (a derivative from the Dance of Death) in C, and the tonal friction persists to the end (see Ex. 6 below).

After the beautiful moulding of rhythm and line in the prologue's recitative, 'Rats Away' strikes a harsh, brazen note in its concerto-like bravura, pseudo-Gregorian incantations and wiry orchestral textures. Britten could scarcely have demonstrated more ruthlessly his severance from the pallid tastefulness of contemporary English song than in this coruscating piece.

---

[2] P. Pears, 'The Vocal Music', in Mitchell-Keller, p. 61.

Yet its lack of decorum, achieving a mordant peak in an 'In nomine' invocation punctuated by shrieks of 'Rats!', never threatens formal coherence. The structure is arched (abcba), with a sonata-like tonal unity in the restatement; *x* assumes many derivative forms, some of them pointedly Stravinskyan, except in their long-term harmonic function (see, e.g., from the fourth bar of fig. 13).

In 'Messalina', *x* takes on a complementary phrase (the source of its interlude form mentioned above); see Ex. 5. The lament, from fig. 21, is an

early example of Britten's penetrating use of even, mainly conjunct, line: vapidity is averted by the placing of the big intervals (mostly cadential fifths), the plangent harmonic seconds, the undertow of the orchestral counterpoint (perhaps excessively addicted to 'expressive' appoggiatura) and the simple tonal circuit. The original form of *x* provides a fine sweep of impassioned line at the climax, obsessive in its reiterations yet roaming wildly in its tonal course. The orchestral coda that sublimates this cry (the last 'fie, fie' of which sounds on in the unbroken tonic pedal) also uses the *x* derivative of the opening (see Ex. 5); like Mahler, Britten here produces some of his most luminous effects from what appears to be a chamber orchestra of soloists, but in fact is dependent for all its subtler shadings on the resources of a full orchestra.

It is no more absurd that Messalina's grief on the death of her monkey should have inspired Britten to this wholly committed pathos than that the threnody for Albert, assumed dead rather than dissolute, should have produced the most powerful music in *Herring*. Perhaps the lamentation is somewhat overdrawn, but it is not satirized, for it springs from the human capacity for love. It is the capacity for wanton cruelty on to which Britten turns his angry scorn in the scherzo, 'Dance of Death', a *tour de force* for singer and orchestra that Pears aptly compares to 'the final rattle of the

"Dies Irae" movement of the *Sinfonia da Requiem*.[3] Written long before
the exploitation of consonants as percussion instruments had become
schematic, this piece uses the violently rolled *r* and the reiteration of the
dogs' names to create the taut rhythmic excitement of a hawking scene; the
conjunct first motive suggests furious energy held in check. The ugliness of
the scene is implied by the chromatically distorted halloos into which the
second motive (up a fourth, down a seventh) grows. The *x* motive appears
only as an ecstatic shout at the kill, and leads to more overt derision of the
huntsman's pleasures. In the interlude, a truly symphonic working-out of all
the scherzo motives (articulated by *x*—see above), the implicit violence is
given its head in a way that recalls Berg's use of interludes in *Wozzeck*.

Ex.3.6

And the Epilogue and Funeral March represent still more evidently the
young Britten's determination to come to grips with music of a complexity,
emotional as well as textural, that had become current in Central Europe.
This is self-consciously 'modern' music, a little crude in its dissonant harmonic relations (see the accompaniment to the opening narration), and too
stuffed with superimposed details in the climactic march texture (from fig.
66). The chief motives at work, shown above in Ex. 6, contrast strikingly: the
xylophone's banal little figure, *a*, and its tonally opposed accompaniment
recur unchanged and so with an increasingly chilling vacuity, while the
chromatic figure, *b* (recalling 'O pride so hostile to our charity'; cf. Ex. 4), is
constantly reworked into harmonic textures. We might see here an attempt

3 Ibid., p. 62.

to give fruitful co-existence to the Stravinskyan and the Schoenbergian. Both elements are denied expansion, being used in alternation as background detail to the vocal line. But this too is fitful, after the manner of the prologue's recitative, yet without the earlier binding harmonic scheme. Only with the simpler texture of the middle section ('Who nurtured in that fine tradition') does the music begin to breathe easily, with a sustained violin line and a harmonic scheme that clarifies, even to a modal B flat (near-Phrygian) and a momentous swing back into C at the key words, 'and be anonymous'. The rhapsodic yet systematic shaping of the high violin line (derived from *b*) looks forward to many later Britten passages. So, too, does the final statement of *x*, which emerges on flutes and oboes to introduce to the funeral march an expressive canto fermo against the insensate twitchings of *a* and a welter of distorted motives in the brass. More directly even than Berg in his D minor interlude, Britten draws on a broad lyricism to assert human compassion in a context of chaotic violence.

ON THIS ISLAND, OP. 11

Our Hunting Fathers was an attempt to apply to word-settings something of the comprehensive structural logic Britten had shown in his first two instrumental scores, though in place of Schoenberg's influence the disruptive Expressionist fantasy of Berg was a dominant force. The second Auden cycle, *On this Island*, five songs for high voice and piano written in 1937, reflects the intervening experience of writing an elaborate set of *genre* pieces, each self-contained and texturally immaculate, the Frank Bridge Variations. 'Symphonic' was an accurate description of the orchestral cycle's processes, but Britten's first cycle with piano is made up, not of movements, but of songs, each neatly realized within a simple structural frame. And this disarming neatness characterizes other features of the music—its melodic lines (often sequential), its patterned piano textures and its near-orthodox harmony. Neither satire nor protest is excluded, but they give no more than a cryptic edge to an urbane mode of speech: the one song in which they set the tone, 'As it is, plenty', is markedly the weakest in the set.

Peter Pears identifies Stravinsky as the chief influence at work, and singles out *Apollon* as the key score.[4] Reference to that serenely beautiful work gives a telling impression of Britten's reorientation in the later cycle, though any comparison of precise contexts demonstrates how much closer to traditional harmonic movement is the younger composer's practice. In Ex. 7a, the semiquaver figuration may be compared with Polymnie's variation (e.g., fig. 47 in the Stravinsky score) and the falsely related Cs with those shown in Ex. 7b, from 'The Birth of Apollo'. But whereas Britten's chromatic appoggiatura on a dominant seventh is entirely classical, the Stravinsky context presents a dominant cadence superimposed on a tonic cadence. Only the

[4] Ibid., p. 64.

Ex.3.7 (a)

Ex.3.7 (b)

retention of the high D as a pedal in the first bar of Ex. 7a shows any approach to Stravinskyan bi-functional harmony, and the voice's resolving E flat explains this away. In the following line of the song, Britten makes more prolonged use of a pedal that modifies the quality of his chords, but essentially they function round a pure circle of fifths—as does much of the harmony in this work, with obvious Baroque overtones in the first song. And the enharmonic treatment of that song's pre-cadential chord ('*Be*fore his look'), typical of many of the cycle's crucial harmonic movements, is far nearer to the textbook method (enter the chord with one key in mind; quit it with another) than to Stravinsky's conflated tonalities. Apart from his use of rigid elements, pedals or ostinatos (see, e.g., the bass reiterations in 'Now the leaves', and compare the funeral march in the Bridge Variations), it is mainly in freeing the timing of progression from abject metrical alignment that Britten has learnt from Stravinsky.

The transfer of the D major fanfare patterns in 'Let the florid music praise' to the voice (at *con bravura*) serves to underline the Baroque pastiche, but their return to the piano in the G minor section makes of them a ruminative commentary; in both sections the vocal line is organized by unobtrusive cross-reference. The strophic basis of 'Now the leaves' points up the moment at which deviations begin. Again the method is classical, tension being generated by repetitions of one fixed line against rising harmonies; and even the relationship of the peak G flat to the C of the tranquillo coda is essentially a conventional Neapolitan one. So it is not fortuitous that the fourth chord of this beautifully still coda (and of the introduction from which

74

it derives) lingers so potently in the memory, for its ambivalence (i.e., its dominant significance for either A minor or F minor) is far more complex than that of the various enharmonic chords in the song. To see how fundamental is Britten's reliance on traditional harmony one need only apply Brahms's acid test to the next song, 'Seascape'. Vocal line and bass reveal a simple framework, strong in linear organization and bold in the elaboration of pedals (notably the long dominant of the *da capo*). But the piano's accompaniment figuration adds the innumerable qualifying details that give the piece its quite new tang. Its waves, lapping in a 3+3+2 pattern, enclose subsidiary harmonic motions (their shape is admitted into the voice part only at the appropriate reference in the poem); a masterly touch is the incorporation of these wave figures into the whole harmonic span of the middle section while the interpolations retain a logical harmonic succession in themselves. The wealth of imagery in the vocal line is achieved without sacrificing motivic economy.

The 'Nocturne' takes such economy much further, depending throughout on juxtapositions, above block harmonies, of a rising arpeggio and a winding return figure, conjunct in essence. This throws a great responsibility on to the harmonic circuits: as in the second song, two identical strophes precede development. Here this involves the sequential pursuit of each figure in turn (with remarkable aptitude to the text), into a remote key area where the voice is becalmed on a monotone ('unpursued by hostile force') above a bass that uneasily abandons its otherwise conjunct movement. The vocal arpeggio which breaks this spell reaches out beyond the octave span and the standard phrase-length to effect the most transfiguring modulation in the whole work (see Ex. 8). The piano, becoming articulate at this point,

Ex.3.8

conducts the second shape towards the cadence in a rather prim diatonic texture, but the shape of the song as a whole is admirably executed. The last song, 'As it is, plenty', depicts in the monotonously clipped rhythms and the effete dissonance of pre-war sophisticated dance music (rather than of jazz) a complacent vacuity that has survived the war. It is viciously accurate, but offers little for the composer's future development: in a work that otherwise promises so much, above all in the reassessment of quite traditional procedures, this finale may appear a disappointment.

BALLAD OF HEROES, OP. 14, AND ADVANCE DEMOCRACY
Though the period flavour of *On this Island* remains pronounced, Auden's
avoidance of the most overt didacticism ensured that its immediate topicality should not become an obstacle to later audiences. The two choral works
of 1938 and 1939 in which Britten collaborated with Auden and with
Randall Swingler have not proved so well able to outlive the political events
that inspired them. *Ballad of Heroes*, for tenor soloist, chorus and orchestra,
a tribute to the British volunteers killed in the Spanish Civil War, takes so
many short cuts that it would appear to have been written in some haste. Nor
does Auden show his keenest edge in such jingles as 'The behaving of man is
a world of horror,/A sedentary Sodom and slick Gomorrah'. But the work
continues to interest the Britten student, if only for its confirmation of some
methods already sampled and its announcement of some new ones. The
ubiquitous fanfares are of several kinds—the still Mahlerian sound of the
opening (its chord of maximum dissonance being the augmented fourth
above a perfect fourth; cf. the Bridge Variations' funeral march), the quasi-
natural series up to the flat seventh (introduced at the rather clumsy transition to the second movement) and the meditative articulation of a recitative in a manner that strongly foreshadows the *War Requiem* (with good
reason at such lines as 'And the guns can be heard across the hills/Like waves
at night'). The vocal line of this recitative is mannered rather than characteristic, sometimes even platitudinous ('like rotting weeds'), but its measured
lento close achieves a true Britten ring. The Scherzo, subtitled 'Dance of
Death', arouses no memories of *Our Hunting Fathers*: a work composed, as
this was, for a 'Festival of Music for the People' must rely on far less tortuous
processes, and Britten makes of it his first ground-bass movement (on a
ten-bar pattern, abandoned only during a central interlude). The easily
memorized tune that is sung above the ground is of the kind that was to be
perfected in *The Little Sweep*. Finally in the dialogue between the chorus,
singing Swingler's hymn in square phrases but with some penetrating harmonic twists, and the soloist, declaiming Auden's lines in expanding melody,
there is achieved a fluidity of cross-phrasing that floats the work above the
earnestly pedestrian, and holds a promise the composer was to keep in
innumerable contexts from the churchyard scene of *Grimes* onwards.

The other political piece, an unaccompanied chorus, *Advance Democracy*, is almost crippled by its text. This tract by Swingler expresses high-
minded but imprecise sentiments in simplistic and hideously banal language.
Even so, Britten manages to make haunting the opening mood of apprehension and puzzlement, and just about justifies his later relapse into busy (and
wholly uncharacteristic) contrapuntal artifice by the reiterations of a constant G ('Time!'); but the Empire Day brand of truculent diatonicism is no
more acceptable when adapted to the promotion of democracy.

LES ILLUMINATIONS, OP. 18

After protest and exhortation the composer chose withdrawal, symbolized in his life by emigration to America. In his art the turning away is no less evident—from the brash topicality of the piano concerto to the elegant irony (and self-discovery) of the violin concerto, and from the blunt public address of the Auden-Swingler works to the esoteric language of Rimbaud's poetry. Before Britten's settings, *Les Illuminations*, for high voice and string orchestra, Op. 18 (1939), only cosmopolitan figures like Delius and Bernard van Dieren had looked beyond the confines of English verse in their songs. Whereas Delius in his mature work achieved a stylistic amalgam so uniform as to show little trace of alien influence, van Dieren identified himself so closely with the musical ambience of his texts as to produce a disconcerting diversity of idiom. Meanwhile the English tradition, built on the extensive foundations laid by Stanford and Parry, had tended to channel our musicians' response to a vast range of stimuli, spanning some five centuries, into surprisingly few moulds, both of manner and of mood. Even when the quasi-orchestral textures of his master were rejected, John Ireland, for example, introduced to his songs little more from exotic traditions than a pianistic iridescence that owes something to Debussy's example. Of course, the expressive nuances of *Ariettes oubliées* were unlikely to offer congruous comment on Housman's heavy nostalgia for a bucolic never-never-land. And if that poet's domination was far from absolute, composers could still indulge the predilection he represented, for the bitter-sweet fruit squeezed dry, in decorous but myopic readings of Elizabethan lyrics, or even of Keats and Shelley.

Largely by seeking fresh ideas in essentially instrumental methods, from Op. 3 onwards Britten's vocal writing had shunned this hermetic world—though conversely his instrumental lyricism had sometimes (for example, in the oboe quartet) betrayed his origin there. But with the Rimbaud settings he began to widen his vocal resources and expressivity in quite another way, seeking to penetrate into the unique worlds of feeling that other languages inhabit. It is by now a truism to point out that, while these settings, and those of Michelangelo which followed, inevitably took on nuances that recalled native treatment of the language, they also clarified his own tone of voice. Indeed, if we try to improve upon critical small-change like 'Gallic clarity', we are compelled to recognize that only at a few points are the key figures of modern French song, Fauré, Debussy and Poulenc, plainly identifiable in the background of Britten's emergent new manner.

The opening 'Fanfare', which sets out the recurrent verbal motto, 'J'ai seul la clef de cette parade sauvage', also establishes the fanfare-like arpeggio as the work's primary melodic cell and the opposition of B flat and E triads as a guide to much of the tonal scheme. Equally significant for the

77

rest of the work (and for Britten's subsequent development) is the euphony into which this tritone is resolved as E and B flat assume their places in the overtone series of C, introduced in glissando washes of natural harmonics. Even the final flat seventh never remotely suggests a dominant function; on the other hand, it affords a natural route to the Mixolydian mode, balancing the Lydian implications of the B flat–E relationship. In contrast to this one incisive epigram, 'Villes' demands the narration of a stream of fantastic images. Britten makes no attempt to seize on many other than the sonorous

Ex.3.9

ones (*mélodieusement*; *des groupes de beffrois*) and relies on a variety of reiterative accompaniments to sustain the hectic momentum; but the harmonic shifts by third relationships can become wearisome. 'Phrase' is short enough to be quoted in full (Ex. 9). Its simple design and subtle detail are telling even when deprived of a context. Everything here is shaped so as to throw into relief the ecstatic moment at the word *danse*. From monotone, motion begins by step, but falls back, gains momentum to swing higher in the next phrase, and then, through arpeggio, still higher; finally assertive crescendi are spurned, and the melody reaches out in a supreme calm for its summit. The immediate symbolism of these spannings of musical space is evident, but they also contain references to the work's musical motto, in the overall relationship E–B flat of the melodic peaks and in the harmonic series of C from which the B flat emerges. But the piece is also introductory, to the dance itself, 'Antique', and the surrounding of this transfigured B flat chord with its Lydian fourth and Mixolydian seventh prepares for the melodic characteristics of the dance.

Though its suavity of violin line and simple accompaniment figures prompted Donald Mitchell to a comparison with the Bridge Variations Romance,[5] in 'Antique' Britten has perceptibly moved away from the Gallic neo-classical cut of the earlier piece. No longer does he cultivate the studied insouciance which there ensured that melodic and harmonic implications should be contradictory. Instead, a succession of tonal centres rising by tones from B flat to E is represented by strummed common chords and vocal arpeggios, and elaborated more eloquently by a violin line that alternates between Mixolydian and Lydian inflexions; its pattern of upward arpeggio and downward, essentially conjunct, twist is comparable to that of the 'Nocturne' in *On this Island*. Tonal complexity, when it is admitted (from fig. 4) can rapidly create a crisis that justifies the relaxation of the final page.

From this ethereal B flat to its opposite pole, E major, we are swung by the pompous refrain of 'Royauté', a rondeau that uses neo-Baroque rhythms and Stravinskyan chord-superimposition deftly if not with any striking originality: typically the stylized vocal fanfares of the second episode (from fig. 3) sound the most individual note. 'Marine' is a near-strophic piece with final expansion, exploiting the dramatic tonal shifts of the earlier superimposed-fifth chords without relaxing the overriding harmonic logic that keeps Britten at this period so much nearer than Stravinsky to academic tradition, yet leaves his imagination unfettered. As in *Our Hunting Fathers*, there is an instrumental interlude, recalling the previous song in distortions, and to this extent Bergian. But the sinuous string lines look forward to Britten's own operatic orchestra, even if their variable modality produces uncertain harmonic tensions and eventually relapses crudely into the B flat Lydian that signals the return of the cycle's motto. Reflected against its simple

[5] D. Mitchell, 'The Musical Atmosphere', in Mitchell-Keller, p. 32.

harmonies, the string undulations become a merely decorative element, yet their serene commentary is one of the most prophetic sounds in this score.

'Being Beauteous' is a ternary song, classical enough even to echo the dominant cadence of its first section in its final tonic close. It is worth observing that the thirteenth chord of these cadences appears a solecism because of its stock resolution, whereas that of the opening vocal phrase (13–9–7–sharp 3 apparently on the V of E minor) proves to be an intensification of the melody's Lydian inflexion. This discovery of new contexts for old chords, particularly when it is prompted by modality, suggests the influence of Fauré, a composer who is brought to mind elsewhere by the economy of melodic movement (see, e.g., 'Phrase' Ex. 9 above). But here the voice's rising seventh, following a rising third, is far from Fauré's reserve: the flavour, though strongly evocative, has become distinctively Britten's rather than distinctively French, as we discover with the opening of Sonetto XXX in the Michelangelo set. 'Parade' unexpectedly reverts to a sound-world nearer Mahler at his most spectral. The vocal narration rises above a monotone norm in copying faintly the melodic inflexions of the orchestral march. After a tentative opening, establishing the two motivic shapes and the ubiquitous pedals, this is laid out as a miniature sonata, its wry Phrygian first subject giving way to heavy irony in the bitonal second; the motto ('J'ai seul la clef . . .') makes a final appearance before the latter is restated.

So two movements in C, major and minor respectively, have underlined the outcome of the initial E/B flat confrontation; yet 'Départ' closes the cycle in E flat. However, this very literal departure is not without one subtle link in a final structural dominant (sixth last bar) attended only by a flat supertonic: i.e., E flat is made another outcome of E/B flat. The song is of extreme simplicity, extending the opening vocal phrase (essentially C minor still) into two increasingly chromatic curves and in new harmonic perspectives; the plain, reiterative accompaniment makes each shift momentous. 'Villes' depended on similar methods but applied them too restlessly: by the end of this cycle one feels that Britten can trust his ability to keep still—an important gain in the acquisition of his mature style.

SEVEN SONNETS OF MICHELANGELO, OP. 22

That the Michelangelo sonnets, a cycle for tenor and piano written in 1940, demonstrate a greater sureness of stylistic aim than do the Rimbaud settings seems in the first instance to derive from hard, bright accompaniments which Britten the pianist-composer has known how to pare to their most incisive form; the string textures of the previous cycle were not always free from inventive overloading. However, it is not merely the quality but the nature of the instrumental contribution that has changed. In *Les Illuminations* it was commonly the musical essence, on which the voice could draw, or against which it could simply enunciate in an inflected monotone. Whether we trace the method to Debussy or to Wagner, it remains associated with the deployment of harmonic masses, to which melodic activity, even if highly organized in its cellular structure, is subservient. But in the tradition of Italian song, which triumphantly survived the nineteenth century's preoccupation with harmonic nuance, the shaping and balancing of melodic phrases is held to be the central act of musical creation. And it is in the design of great melodic arcs, spanning complete songs, that Britten has most obviously profited from the consideration of Italian models in the Michelangelo Sonnets. This implies the neglect neither of pithy accompaniment motives nor of illuminating harmonic commentaries and contradictions, but these attendant felicities will count for little if the composer's confidence in his melodic powers wavers or is misplaced. Scarcely an English composer of consequence in the decades before 1940 had so recklessly courted charges of banality or platitude as did Britten in the ample vocal lines of this cycle. This unbuttoning of a jacket of 'good taste' that had become inhibitingly tight was thus a significant moment in the history of English song (if we may class this work there); for Britten himself it established ideals which, modified in detail by a rediscovery of his native folk traditions, were to find their fulfilment in the melodic generosity of *Peter Grimes*.

The first sonnet (Michelangelo's sixteenth) provides a good example of the new breadth. Essentially through-composed, though with a brief return of the opening shape, the song is most obviously held together by the driving anacrustic motive that persists throughout the piano part. Already something of Britten's skill in drawing expressive profits from such small-change may be seen in a comparison of the two added-note chords that cap this figure at the opening and at the key-change: F sharp is common to both, but the ebullient clangour it represents in the A major context is exchanged for a wistful Lydian relation to C. A third stage is marked by a complete reconstruction of the chord at a lower level (at 'Chi semina') as a tortuous dominant of C sharp (see Ex. 10). This class of chord, in which perfect and

Ex.3.10 (a)   Tempo giusto

Ex.3.10 (b)

Ex.3.10 (c)

augmented fourths are superimposed, had already become a Britten symbol of *Angst* (see above, pp. 61 and 76), but the intrusion of its Bergian sound here is not quite congruous with the wholly unsentimental tone of the rest. Even so, if we now refer back to the text, we shall see how aptly these

variants of one motivic shape reflect the poet's successive states of mind.
What then is left for the singer beyond fastidious declamation? Not an
outburst of Baroque word-painting: even 'high, low and middle' is a temptation ignored, while the return of the opening fanfare at 'dubbie speranze'
would offend a diligent illustrator. Instead of shaping the line according to
the immediate suggestibility of this or that image, Britten has drawn bold
strokes that complete a musical design in their own right (see Ex. 11).

Ex.3.11

* = melodic pivots (usually V in function)
Ringed pitches = peaks/ troughs

Still more depends on the melodic line in Sonetto XXX, the most successful application in all Britten's early vocal writing of techniques so simple as
to make each avoidance of impending platitude an expressive triumph. As in
'Being Beauteous', the Lydian fourth degree is recognized to be the fifth of
the leading-note major chord, but now the whole song is based on similar
relationships between triads, usually a semitone apart. While one part of the
accompaniment presents a given tonal area in impassively repeated chords,

the other draws a quivering haze over it with arpeggios that fluctuate between the two areas; each change of the foundation chord is a momentous event. As in Sonetto XVI therefore, the accompaniment is well able to convey the crucial expressive backgrounds, but it is the subtle detail of the vocal line that makes this song so much more than inspired harmonic doodling. The placing of peaks and troughs, the semitonal inflexions that break arpeggio patterns, the striking intrusion of conjunct motion ('Col vostr'ingegno'), the progressive widening from monotone ('Nel voler vostro') and the following of a climax line that sums up the whole song with a plain statement of the widest interval (its E hovering ambivalently as dominant seventh to the leading-note arpeggio), all these devices are convincingly bound into a single span.

The songs surrounding this one, XXXI and LV, have accompaniment figures that, felicitous though they are, threaten to become humdrum in their rigid patterning. Again it is the spacious yet economical organization of the vocal line that saves the situation, aided in 'Tu sa' ' by the tension between two coexisting key schemes: the voice's G centre is only achieved in the bass of the piano (centred on a Lydian B flat) at the climax, 'Rompasi il mur'— when the voice itself has reached an E major that requires a conflicting G sharp. The tranquil coda is effective texturally, but its suave harmonies seem inconsequential here. All three songs, and XXXVIII which follows, show Britten's dexterity in introducing the return in a basically ternary structure at differing points in the melodic and the harmonic fields. 'Rendete a gli occhi miei' produces so piquant a harmonic twist (the classical gambit German sixth/dominant, conflated) at its first cadence that its wider-ranging progressions seem in fact less adventurous, but for the voice's final augmented line one telling intensification (implied Neapolitan plus tonic, conflated) is held in reserve. This wistful serenata, apparently a predictable response to the challenge of Italian texts, in fact attends a lament, a type which has commonly called forth heavily declamatory musical treatment. A pathos is here, notably in the monotone initiations of each vocal phrase, but in a form which can effectively be transformed to the lover's appeal implicit in the last line.

Still more determined by its last line is the setting of Sonnet XXXII: these anxious yet ecstatic conditional clauses all lead to a single question, one which has been prefigured so obsessively in the reiterated vocal motive (this is the most economical linear construction in the cycle) and in the clamorous unresolved seconds of the piano that it is eventually uttered in a pianissimo of nervous exhaustion. Finally, in the D major of so many of the most affirmative pages of early Britten, the cycle closes with a Baroque setting of 'Spirito ben nato' that alternates between (and in the middle section combines) ponderously scalic ritornello and boldly chiselled vocal declamation. Yet the boldness lies too much in the sequential repetitions of a tag (*a* in Ex. 12), while the culminating phrase of the first vocal paragraph (*b* in Ex. 12),

Ex.3.12

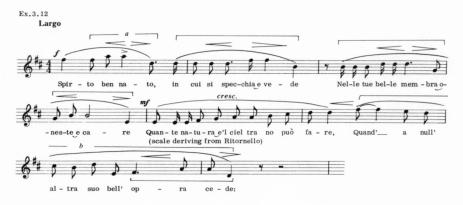

missing the mark of an Italianate bel canto, strikes instead the gestures beloved of English composers like Parry and the Stanford pupils (compare *b* in Ex. 12 with Parry's 'O that we soon again renew that song'). The tag *a* acquires new interest from the less rigidly sequential harmonization of its second statement, but these seventh and higher diatonic chords are still too recognizably the small-change (or perhaps rather the large-change) of early twentieth-century English song. As so often, the piece remains alive principally because neither key nor modality congeals into the predictable; the enharmonic twist by which a Lydian D is recovered from the extreme flatness of the middle section contrives an arresting climax. Even so, the most beautiful passage, which now follows, simply spells out that harmonic series by which Britten has so persistently illuminated his flat sevenths— compensated inevitably by the Lydian fourth of the final ritornello.

HYMN TO SAINT CECILIA, OP. 27

Britten's last work completed in England before he left for America, the *Ballad of Heroes*, was an uneasy political document, of frustrated idealism and growing embitterment. In America he avoided the choral medium altogether, but his decision to return home was given musical substance by the two works he wrote in 1942 on board ship, the *Hymn to Saint Cecilia* for five-part chorus, Op. 27 and *A Ceremony of Carols* for trebles and harp, Op. 28. The Hymn is another setting of Auden, but uses a group of poems in which the swingeing satire of the Ballad (and of the two early song cycles) is relaxed, though the sense of a lost innocence remains painfully keen in the third poem. Before that, however, Britten has been required to find musical imagery to match the strong serenity of the first poem and the mercurial lightness of the second. It is surely not reading too much into his response to find in it evidence of the load (of indecision, above all) lifted from his mind by making, and being able to act upon, the decision to return to England. Certainly no other work of his floats with quite the easy grace of this opening section or is able to distil more sweetness from simple triads. The impression of spaciousness is created both by a dual time-scale and by a dual harmonic scheme: the two strata (close position triads of the women's voices; tenor-bass canto fermo) can diverge and yet effortlessly achieve unanimity in cadence (see Ex. 13).

Ex.3.13

Given this noble command of time, Britten does not need to fuss over each of Auden's images in turn, though he accommodates some delightfully graphic touches within a fine sweep of phrase. The sustained richness of this setting is exchanged for the purity of very soft choral unisons in the invocation that is to end all three poems:

> Blessed Cecilia, appear in visions
> To all musicians, appear and inspire:
> Translated Daughter, come down and startle
> Composing mortals with immortal fire.

This unison statement of a musical idea that opened the work emphasizes its Phrygian melodic basis rather than its mixture of C major and E major elements. The scherzo setting of the second poem, however, turns to an E major unsullied by a single chromatic note except for one brief and telling deviation (back to a C major with flattened sixth and seventh). Sung very fast and lightly, its endlessly overlapping reiterations of a childlike five-bar burden suggest the tinkling of some magic glockenspiel; again a dual sense of time is created by a canto fermo-like strand (alto and bass octaves). The invocation following the scherzo is now harmonized, broadly and in preparation for the A minor in which the final setting begins. Here instrumental modes of writing are again adapted to Britten's purpose in the basses' repetitions of a ground, conveying the words impassively yet terribly clearly, while the upper voices' harmony provides the expressive nuances. Britten's cool Lydian tone perfectly marks the change at 'O dear white children, casual as birds', but the pedal above which this rapturous soprano line floats creates a cumulative tension that must be discharged: it gives way only when the Lydian blandness is shattered by the flattening at 'O weep, child, weep'—an excellently simple example of Britten's long-term musical preparation for an effect that the text demands. On the other hand, he makes no attempt to sew into the piece the instrumental references Auden incorporates into the following lines; nor does he commit the solecism of imitating the instrument at the reference to it, but instead uses the cadenza-like context in which each imitation is isolated to point up the poet's most poignant lines. The solo tenor's trumpet call, varying between fanfares of E major and of C major, provides an unforced route back to the tonal field of the refrain. By setting this to the texture (though not, of course, the text) which opened the work, Britten combines the feeling of 'refrain' with that of 'reprise', and a coda, with palpable logic, simply slows down the two strata at different rates. The twelve-minute duration of this work is modest by comparison with, say, *A Boy was Born*, but without recourse to the tight motivic disciplines of that work, there is created the impression of a highly unified emotional span.

A CEREMONY OF CAROLS, OP. 28

In the first of his carol cycles Britten had used an instrumental treatment of vocal textures, stiffened by intense motivic development, to break away from the rather woolly archaisms that had made such collections as the *Oxford Book of Carols* so appealing to his fellow countrymen. In the second, *A Ceremony of Carols* (1942) for boys' voices and harp, he seems intent on discovering how effectively he can contribute to this English tradition in terms recognizably his own. Thus he can reconcile the preoccupation with modality with his own concern for careful tonal planning across the whole cycle; *organum*-like blocks of choral tone are only one element in a textural range that inclines towards the single line and its canonic multiplication; and instrumental patterns contribute distinctive character and structural scaffolding, not merely adding additional harmonic wadding, to each piece.

Though the cycle opens and closes with a plainsong (the antiphon 'Hodie' for the Vespers of the Nativity), sung unaccompanied in procession, at this most prodigal stage of his career Britten does not draw his store of motives from this source, as was to be his later practice (see, for example, the *Hymn to Saint Peter* of 1955, but above all, of course, the parables of the 1960s). Yet the plainsong remains potently in the memory, and the central harp interlude is a 'pastoral symphony' in which the chant wafts towards the listener and recedes again out of earshot (cf. the quasi-programmatic scheme adumbrated in Op. 2); its ostinato undertow is neatly synthesized

Ex.3.14

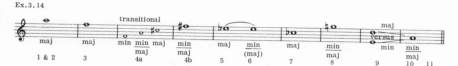

from the openings of nos. 2 and 3. The tonal path of the cycle may be summarized as above, though the internal fluctuations are no less carefully judged (see Ex. 14); the third relationships so important in this groundplan are prominent in the detail, especially of the early carols (2, 3 and 5). The later ones depend more on changes of modality with a fixed centre.

'Balulalow' stands between the two types, its essentially classical minor/ major oscillations giving way to a climactic swing of centre (illustrative of 'The knees of my heart shall I bow'; the amplified metrical scheme contributes equally to this moment). The belligerently canonic 'This little Babe' is rigidly Aeolian except for a Lydian interpolation that provides cadential momentum; only in its codà does the chain of thirds appear. 'In freezing winter night' puts canon to quite other ends, to repeat pitilessly the shiver motive created by the clash of its Phrygian intervals; the harp's tremolando and 6/4 position intensify the unrest. Yet a simple switch to the Lydian changes the entire character. Modulation again creates a climax before a return to the Phrygian motive, now background to more assertive lines, capable of achieving a tonic root. The 'Spring Carol' is as skilfully ambivalent as many a Stravinsky context, but the manner is Britten's own, foreshadowing, not surprisingly, the Spring Symphony boys' choir music. The harp's figuration is clearly D major despite the conspicuous absence of the leading note (a fairly constant trait of this cycle, together with the avoidance of the direct V–I). But the vocal line is heard rather as Dorian on E, so that the piece points both as IV and as V towards the returning A of 'Deo Gracias'. This has a pentatonic refrain, and turns to Dorian for 'Adam lay ibounden' and to Mixolydian at 'Blessed be the time'.

Because it is most grateful for the singers, brightly coloured and melodically memorable, *A Ceremony of Carols* enjoys a popularity that the first cycle has never achieved. If the composer in 1942 appears more circumspect than in 1933, he is none the less on his guard against vacuity, exploring a wide range of tonal and modal transformations to diversify a very simple melodic and harmonic language. In this sense the second carol sequence defines a territory to which Britten was often to return.

REJOICE IN THE LAMB, OP. 30

The festival cantata, *Rejoice in the Lamb*, for chorus, four soloists and organ, was written in 1943 in response to a commission from St Matthew's Church, Northampton for its fiftieth anniversary. It maintains the radiant tone and simple harmonic resources of the previous two choral works, but reveals an influence which, never so plainly evident before, was to assume still greater importance in the next few years—that of Purcell. The dotted-note Hallelujah section, on a firm crotchet bass (essentially its own augmentation) clearly derives from those of Purcell's verse anthems, though the mood here, of restrained mystical exaltation, is not to be found in Purcell's public exercises of piety. By bringing back the Hallelujah to end the cantata, Britten seeks to give it the force of a ritornello, as in much seventeenth-century music, but it may be thought that the extraordinarily diverse range of musics contained in this short work is not so easily made to appear coherent. Yet Hans Redlich, who points to what he feels to be a defect in this respect, acknowledges that the impression of heterogeneity is consistent with the nature of the text Britten chose to set.[6]

The eighteenth-century poet, Christopher Smart, wrote his *Jubilate Agno* in an asylum. It celebrates God's presence in all creatures and all things, and reveals how each in its characteristic way praises God. Fantastic diversity is of the essence, for in Smart's eccentric view of the created world the divine may be sensed in a cat or a mouse no less than in a man, in a single letter ('For H is a spirit and therefore he is God') no less than in a poem; even the praise which music can contribute is to be found in individual instrumental propensities, charmingly classified by Smart according to 'their rhimes'—'For the harp rhimes are sing, ring, sting and the like'. Redlich's division of Britten's setting, which lasts only sixteen minutes, into ten distinct sections, underlines how far the composer has gone towards retracing the poet's mercurial flights of imagination.

Yet if rapid changes of musical symbolism are our predominant memory of this cantata, we may still find the sum of its experience satisfying. No doubt it will appear pedantic to subject so fragile a piece to analysis, but the Britten critics who are disconcerted by the range of his imagery too rarely (I would suggest) seek out the underlying uniformity of his material. A few examples of connexions that tighten this work will need little commentary; the epigrammatic form in which the basic conjunction of step and perfect fourth is presented at the outset does not encourage the assumption that such connexions are fortuitous (though they would be no less active in any event).

The Lydian implications of Ex. 15a are fully realized in the section

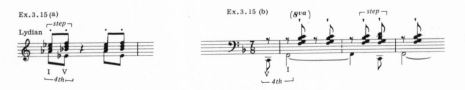

Ex.3.15 (a)

Ex.3.15 (b)

6   H. Redlich, 'The Choral Music', in Mitchell-Keller, p. 96.

Ex.3.15 (c i)

Ex.3.15 (c ii)

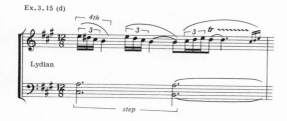

Ex.3.15 (d)

Ex.3.15 (e)

Ex.3.15 (f)

Ex.3.15 (g)

Ex.3.15 (h)

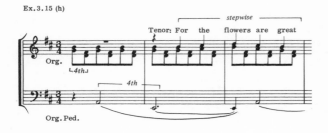

Ex.3.15 (j)

Ex.3.15 (k)

devoted to Smart's cat, Jeoffry, with that curiously equivocal innocence Britten's Lydian A was able to convey in the Saint Cecilia Hymn, though now a feline compound of grace and guile is added by the organ's obbligato line (Ex. 15d). Connoisseurs of Britten's symbol-forming process may detect a faint yet clear pre-echo in the 'flowers' section (Ex. 15h) of Lucretia's lamenting address to the orchids. Only the slow choral section that follows this has not been included in the relationships of Ex. 15; though its harmonic false relations appropriately strike the only note of pain in the work, its juxtaposition of triadic harmony and solo instrumental melisma represents a surprising approach to the world of Vaughan Williams's symphonic slow movements (even more than to his mystical choral works). Contrary to Redlich's implication,[7] the *vivace* that forms the finale of the cantata makes no serious attempt at imitation of instrumental effects (which is as well, given the number of instruments Smart mentions): how naturally Britten's fanfare arpeggios suit vocal contexts is emphasized in the beautiful

[7] Ibid., p. 95.

90

slowed-down version ('For at that time malignity ceases'; see Ex. 15k) that ends this section, in a mystic glow far more true to the composer than the slow section discussed above.

SERENADE FOR TENOR, HORN AND STRINGS, OP. 31

We have just seen how a most affecting moment in the festival cantata depended on the use of triadic arpeggios to symbolize rest. Living at a time when the triad's centuries-old hegemony has at last been called into question, Britten has tended, without any of the theoretical ramifications of a Schenker or a Hindemith, to see in the lower harmonics of the series (including, as we have often noted already, the seventh) the symbol of states of innocence, achieved or retained despite the shadows of experience. Fanfares have therefore less often been military signals in his music than evocations, nostalgic or even ironic, of a natural order, whether sublime or inexorable. (They may, of course, play both rôles, and this duality gives particular force to the musical symbolism of the *War Requiem*.) In his next work, the Serenade for tenor solo, horn and string orchestra, Op. 31 (1943), Britten gave full rein to a gift for simple Nature symbolism, reminiscent of the early German Romantics in the use of instrumental colourings.

The horn's prologue, played throughout on natural harmonics, is a handsomely-shaped three-part form in which melodic developments and fluctuations of tempo, metre and dynamics are all interdependent. Its initial motive is appropriated to fashion the strings' taut rhythmic figure in the first song, Cotton's 'Pastoral'. While this produces an effect of 6/16, the vocal stresses suggest a leisurely 3/4 (see Ex. 16), so that the piece moves on two

Ex.3.16

contrasted levels, an effect intensified by harmonic conflations that are usually open to two different interpretations. After the developmental third stanza, Britten brings the horn to the tonic for the final strophe, which is vocally a restatement, but neither voice nor strings recognize the horn pedal as home until the last line. We may hear a refinement and synthesis of procedures found in the Michelangelo settings and in the early sonata structures, but it is not far-fetched to see also in this closing section a picture of the dying light that follows the setting of the sun: structural method is made the means of musical illustration. The horn's last drooping call is transformed at a new level in the strings' characterizing phrase that opens the Tennyson 'Nocturne', but the voice postulates a diatonic chain of thirds rather than a true fanfare. If the single triad represents a state of rest, the third-chain represents an endless motion, for it constantly expounds the three fundamental units of the tonal system, IV–V–I. ('Our echoes . . . grow for ever and ever'.) Because Britten used this symbol of immanent motion in another context that did much to establish his popular reputation, the *Grimes* prelude, the device has been accorded exaggerated importance as a fingerprint of his style; it had appeared as one element as early as the finale of Op. 1. Most twentieth-century composers who have retained a 'higher diatonicism' (Stravinsky is the signal exception) have used elaborate third-aggregates, the *ne plus ultra* of traditional harmonic thinking, but Britten's typical chord building depends far more on the placing of the second (i.e., rather than seventh or ninth), while pure major diatonicism is less common in his work than are modal or chromatic variants. Here however it is so cultivated as to exclude all accidentals from the first stanza (the last has only a short-lived sharp 4 balanced by a final 'natural' flat 7). This simple sound-world can yield cleanly drawn medieval and elfin imagery, or a warmly reverberating haze for the horn-call's echoes. The chains of thirds traverse it but do not define its boundaries: neither voice nor horn cadences unequivocally.

In such a simplified reading of sound-relationships, chromaticism is once again inevitably cast as the canker. Britten has rarely demonstrated this more overtly or in more economical terms than in the next song, Blake's 'O rose, thou art sick'. Though the line of the horn solo that frames the song (and, as Pears has suggested, is its true essence[8]) only at one point fails to soften the movement of a semitonal step by a following perfect interval (fourth, fifth or octave), it ranges through all twelve notes (see Ex. 17). The

Ex.3.17

one protraction of semitonal movement, segment *c*, drives down to B flat, the chromatic antithesis of the tonic E, and the whole of the seven-bar cadential section *d* is needed to execute the swing back from B flat to E. As the middle-string harmony (two parts doubled) and the double-bass arpeggios make clear, this is potentially straightforward diatonic music, yet in both the melodic and tonal spheres it is disrupted. The tenor's recitative

[8] Pears, op. cit., p. 68.

offers Blake's metaphor of seductive corruption almost as a gloss on what has already been set forth in musical terms: the tritone transposition of 'thou art sick' at 'crimson joy' underlines the tonal point but otherwise the vocal line, despite its neat symmetries, lacks the extreme cogency of the horn's. Finally, the insinuating quality of the semitone is spelled out in the horn's portamenti.

And the singer picks up the same two notes to begin the burden of the 'Lyke Wake Dirge'. Now chromaticism adds painful detail within the closed statement of a descending G minor arpeggio; the long penultimate line in each stanza prompts the displacement of the last line by one crotchet, so that the ground's cadence does not coincide monotonously with the strong beat. A still more macabre fanfare is introduced by the bass strings as subject in a fugue that begins and ends in E flat minor but is tonally unpredictable in between. A further link with the preceding elegy is established when the horn, entering only at the seventh statement of the ground, delivers the subject in a stentorian E minor. Stretto reinforces the sense of obsession induced by this piece, a setting remarkably at variance with the decorously plaintive tone Stravinsky was to adopt in his response to this text in his Cantata.

After ground and fugue Britten uses other Baroque procedures in his *da capo* treatment of Ben Jonson's 'Hymn to Diana'. The recurrences of the horn ritornello are deftly overlapped with the vocal phrases in a true obbligato aria (*d'agilità*, we might add), faithful even to the Neapolitan mannerism and the singer's two tonic cadences. Apart from these flattenings, most key deviations are brightly sharp in direction, and, as dominants are preferred to tonics, the fleet impression is never endangered. Cross-references are now less harrowing: the tenor's opening fanfare is that of the first song, and the chains of thirds (bar 2, extended to form the cadences before fig. 26 and after fig. 28) are flippant melody, not the bludgeoning harmonic wedges of the bass before fig. 17 in the dirge.

The strange beauty of the final song, Keats's sonnet to sleep, lies in its

Ex.3.18

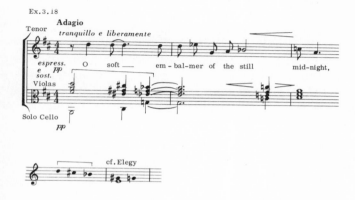

93

restless chromatic juxtaposition of triads in themselves luxuriously restful. Shadows of the earlier songs are faint but not to be ignored: the cello's opening fanfare (see Ex. 18), its G a 'natural' rather than a dominant seventh in effect, comes to the surface as an independent motive in the middle section, and the viola line can plausibly be heard to arrange in linear form (at the tritone) the nucleus of the Elegy. While the two quatrains are given essentially strophic treatment (the second transposed up a minor third), the vocal line thereafter is freer—but never casual—in its association of earlier shapes. Only two slightly too obvious examples of incidental word-painting (the whole-tone melisma on 'lulling' and the semitonal fluctuations at 'burrowing') momentarily disturb the unity. The drowsy last line, in a 15/8 that in two ways lengthens the basic unit, gives a foretaste of the power Britten was to find in monotone in the 'Great Bear' soliloquy of *Grimes*. And with the completion of the Serenade, the composer could feel himself equipped to deal with many of the problems of opera—the economical definition of widely differing characters, the setting of diversified verse and prose schemes (only the true parlando had been rarely essayed since *Our Hunting Fathers*) and the devising of formal schemes, each with its own climax yet all subscribing to the motion of the greater cycle. The problems that remained, of communicating dramatic motivation through an intra-musical sequence of events, could only be tackled in the operatic medium itself.

FESTIVAL TE DEUM, OP. 32

Among several small pieces produced while Britten was at work on the conception and realization of *Peter Grimes*, perhaps the most entertaining is *The Ballad of Little Musgrave and Lady Barnard* (1943), written for a group of British prisoners-of-war in Germany; it strikes an ingenious balance between strophic and cyclic treatment and creates graphic melodrama from slender resources (three male voices and piano). But the only piece to be graced by an opus number is the *Festival Te Deum*, written in 1944 for the centenary of St Mark's Church, Swindon. This is exceptional in Britten's output for its sustained use of two metrical strata. Unison voices declaim the text with a precision that requires constantly varying multiplications of the common quaver unit (5/8; 7/8; 4/4 and so on), but the organ works out its slowly-unfolding harmonic scheme in regular dotted minims; their grace-notes provide an almost motivic unity, while the vocal lines venture from pentatonic to Lydian and thence to fluid modulating shapes. The central outburst is more conventional, though still breezily unpredictable in metre, and the opening is effectively reworked on its final return.

4 Paul Bunyan

Though several works to which Britten assigned opus numbers were subsequently withdrawn, like the Occasional Overture in C written for the opening of the BBC Third Programme in 1946, only one piece, the operetta *Paul Bunyan*, of 1941, continued to attract much comment after its suppression. And comment was necessarily speculative for, whatever its significance as a trial essay in a medium the composer was later to cultivate with such success, and as his only operatic collaboration with Auden, it had been seen neither on stage nor in score by any of the writers who discussed Britten's work; not surprisingly therefore it acquired a mysterious aura during the thirty-five years between its first and second productions.

Both poet and composer had gone to the United States with the intention of settling there. Even so, it was perhaps foolhardy to offer among their artistic credentials for citizenship an opera on so quintessentially American a theme as the legend of the giant leader of the pioneer lumbermen, Paul Bunyan. Eric Walter White quotes[1] from the notices with which the New York press received the work at its performances in Brander Matthews Hall, Columbia University in May 1941, and they are almost uniformly dismissive: epithets like 'anaemic', 'flaccid' and 'undistinguished', together with the inevitable 'eclectic', must have been as discouraging to Britten as any he had suffered from the pens of the English critics. But clearly he too was far from satisfied with the operetta, for White says that many changes were made to text and music during the week's run. Thereafter it was consigned to oblivion, and Britten was persuaded to review its possibilities only in 1974, when, at the instigation of Donald Mitchell, he found in this activity a way of returning to composition[2] after his heart operation. His first initial verdict, that the opera 'badly needed cutting and revising'[3] seems to have been somewhat modified, in that only two numbers were eventually taken out, but the process of revision seems to have been widespread enough[4] to make

---

[1] White, p. 98.
[2] A. Blyth, 'Britten returns to composing', *The Times*, December 30, 1974.
[3] Ibid.
[4] Cf. C. Matthews, 'Britten's Indian Summer', *Soundings* vi, 1977, p. 44.

hazardous any resounding demonstration of compositional pre-echoes in the work. It was broadcast in a concert performance by the BBC in January 1976, and produced by the English Music Theatre Company at the Aldeburgh Festival later that year. This newly-formed company, successor to the English Opera Group but with a wider and more experimental brief, then toured the work extensively, giving many performances in a version for two pianos and percussion.

As a work for launching such an enterprise *Paul Bunyan* proved admirable, for it invited a stage treatment freed from preconceptions of 'operatic' propriety and offered many rewarding parts for a youthful cast rather than a few star rôles. The work's hybrid nature is already clear in that the hero, for obvious reasons unseen, is heard only as a speaking voice, and that some of the tallest incidents of the story are simply related by a ballad singer. Spoken dialogue and melodrama provide the cement in a structure built from separate, often basically strophic, numbers; *The Beggar's Opera*, Gilbert and Sullivan and Brecht and Weill are more likely to suggest themselves, severally or simultaneously, as influential memories (rather than as models) than anything in the mainstream of European opera and music-drama.

Auden's newspaper article on the work (quoted extensively by White)[5] can seem unduly portentous an introduction to the theatrical experience itself. We may subscribe intellectually to his view of the Bunyan legend as 'a reflection of the cultural problems that occur during the first stage of every civilization' and that eventually require, at the hero's own symbolic withdrawal from the scene, the exchange of a collective experience for the forging of unique human relationships:

> Gone the natural disciplines,
> And the life of choice begins.

Yet however sonorously Paul's closing couplets may point the morals of the piece, his own disembodied form (physically and musically) tends to leave this didactic element somewhat isolated from the series of incidents rounded out dramatically and vocally by the other characters. Auden, recognizing that Paul's could not be the chief dramatic rôle, gave this to Johnny Inkslinger, 'the man of speculative and critical intelligence, whose temptation is to despise those who do the manual work that makes the thought possible'. But that Inkslinger does in fact become the central figure of the work is chiefly due to the *musical* intensification of his introspective qualities at the climax of his extended song and still more potently in the minute, but contextually perfect, 'Inkslinger's Regret'. Similarly, though Tiny and Slim are far more nearly stereotypes, vehicles for Auden's most indulgent roman-

[5] White, p. 95. The article was also reproduced in the programme book of the English Music Theatre production.

tic parody, the individuality which marks their music's departure from the parodied type is so expressively appropriate to the situation that we are touched at least as much as we are amused. The total experience which the opera offers is episodic rather than cumulative (and in any event the general quality of invention declines in Act II), often charming and sometimes vivid but scarcely sounding the universal resonance Auden heard in the legend. Myth, of however homely a kind or recent a date, needs to enclose us within a consistent convention, but *Paul Bunyan* seems disconcertingly to require of us vacillating attitudes, without creating between them the ironic tensions that characterize Weill at his most powerful. Perhaps, as with some of Weill's work, the engaging qualities of the piece will acquire for it an audience that has little concern for deeper issues. Despite an over-refinement of accompanimental detail that would be unfamiliar, there seems little reason indeed why a work so full of appealing, apt and highly-memorable melodic invention should not enjoy the truly popular success that is accorded to the best in musical comedy. This would be less of an affront to Auden's memory than was the early success of Weill's music to Brecht's intentions, for if Auden's verse has a virtuoso quality foreign to Brecht, at the same time it is far less single-mindedly committed, far readier to succumb to the diverting irrelevance. In the light of the libretti Auden wrote later for Stravinsky and Henze, one easily regrets that Britten's early collaboration foundered, yet it may be that just that obsessive restriction of focus which made possible the composer's strongest dramatic achievements, in *Budd* or *The Screw* for instance, would have been less certainly maintained had he continued in partnership with so mercurially brilliant a talent.

Of all the musical structures in *Paul Bunyan*, the most rudimentary are in fact those sections which Auden dignified by a comparison to the Greek chorus. The narration of actions that exceed spatially or temporally the scope of theatrical presentation is carried on in three interludes, cast as ballads accompanied by guitar (possibly with the voice part doubled by a 'folk' fiddle). Given the recent popular enthusiasm for so many species of 'folk', 'country' and 'hill-billy' music, this reversion to so unsophisticated a musical manner may have lost some of its original piquancy. It is in the nature of these ballads to have innumerable stanzas and, when placed in the context of more highly-developed music, they could easily appear monotonous. Britten's inventions in this style are all economical in melodic shape, whether by use of internal repetition, sequence or variation, but tonally-displaced sections neatly substitute 'structure' for endless succession. The second interlude includes not only a shift to the subdominant level to form an ABA pattern, but a contrasted 6/8 episode characterized by its V (usually 9/7) of V position; this so deftly paints the softer world of Carrie's home county that it returns effectively when Paul introduces his daughter to the lumber camp.

Some of the music within the action is melodically scarcely less simple

Ex. 4.1

than the ballads, but harmonic detail and orchestration give more of an edge. The Farmers' Song (no. 19) for instance, acquires its stomping drive from the sharp second of its weak-beat accompanying chords (see Ex. 1), but goes on finding new uses for this B sharp. In the German-cum-French sixth of bar 5 this facilitates the B major move, while later it becomes a Mixolydian C natural at the transfer of the opening phrase to tonic level for the chorus refrain, and thence dominant to the F major of the climax phrase. A still more dynamic chorus, that of the lumberjacks (no. 4), develops the opening chromatic cliché in the resourceful modulations of the later stanzas, and the orchestral reiteration of the verse melody during the refrains makes a *moto perpetuo* as infectious as Offenbach. In another varied strophic piece, The Cats' Creed (no. 22), clipped, quasi-instrumental phrases recall the epigrammatic philosophizing of *The Beggar's Opera*; even the hemiolas are Baroque, though their protraction, as the harmony seeks out a tortuous route home from the Neapolitan degree, is evidently not. The flowery counterpoint added by the second cat in verse 2 is relegated to the orchestral bass for verse 3, in which the cats' proud D major turns at the penultimate phrase to a venomous D flat, not the sentimental E flat of man and dog. (In the earlier animal ensemble, the trio no. 8, also in D, Fido indulges in still more overtly Baroque trumpetings.) Of all the essentially strophic musical designs, the greatest dramatic weight is placed on the Blues, no. 9. This 'Quartet of Defeated', introduced by Paul as a warning glimpse of some American futures, occurs so early in the action as to suggest a merely self-indulgent rather than a motivated pathos. Auden has neatly fashioned the crucial third line of his first four stanzas to facilitate the poignant climax of Britten's harmonic circuit, yet it is with the musical breakaway from this burden that the piece rises above the mawkish, to evoke a tragic disillusionment. Again, modulation is the chief agent of the intensifying process, quickening as the voices begin to engage and eventually readmitting the tonic through a scale as fatalistic in its measured descent as any in Britten. The reprise distends the basic circuit slightly but momentously, the major ninth on the subdominant being made minor, and isolated as an orchestral reaction to the text 'America can break your heart', before the last phrase reverberates into the distance.

More elaborate tonal fluctuations within a basically strophic scheme can be found in no. 11, the Food Chorus, in text as well as music one of the closer approaches to Gilbert and Sullivan, and in no. 20, the Mocking of Hel Helson, a piece surprisingly astringent in the choral monotones that strike obliquely against the harmony. Its declamatory questions naturally approach an operatic style, while the more rounded set pieces of some other characters apply sophisticated structural methods to melody still redolent of popular music. Slim's Song (no. 12a), for example, is so open-handed in its diatonic refrain and its clopping accompaniment (reminiscent of Copland's prairie music) that the romantic *Angst* which invades its modulatory middle section seems almost uncomfortably intense. Tiny's Song on the death of her mother (no. 15b) which declares its sentiment in a hackneyed enough initial phrase can therefore appear *less* prone to sentimentality: tonal deflections that are rarely wholly predictable yet are securely balanced (Ex. 2a shows only the principal events), support spans of melody which absorb this opening pathetic cliché into a grander design. Britten's route to the last of the many cadential fifth cycles, shown at Ex. 2b, epitomizes the song's tonal behaviour.

If the music of Slim and Tiny (including their love duet) seems to prepare the way for Britten's refinement of a popular style in the warm music of Sid and Nancy, Johnny Inkslinger, whatever his superior intellect, may in his intimations of a richer experience eluding his grasp remind us of Albert Herring. In Inkslinger's account to Fido of his life (no. 14), the verse scheme

Ex.4.2 (a)

Ex.4.2 (b)

of three stanzas remains clear, most obviously through the literal appropriation by the voice in each last line of the forlorn orchestral cadence that colours the whole piece. But a steady growth of intensity is achieved as Johnny's imagination takes wing, from the desultory recitative style of the first stanza, through the regular accompanying texture of the second to the sustained melody of the third, initially in orchestral solos but finally, in broad octave phrases shared by the voice, encompassing his Utopian vision; only the static tonic chord underlying this aspiring peroration declares its impotence. The unfolding of character in this piece foreshadows Britten's mature operatic style, yet so in a contrasted way does the vignette which is Inkslinger's second aria. Coming immediately after the generous emotional outpouring of Tiny's song, 'Inkslinger's Regret' (no. 16) is a single tightly-controlled, but not tight-lipped, musical paragraph; the vocal line is beautifully shaped, the wandering orchestral lines are gently coloured (a 'chamber orchestra' scoring, of oboe, clarinet and bassoon) and unassertively illustrative, and a single dissonance betrays the pain behind the words:

> All the little brooks of love
> Run down towards each other.
> Somewhere every valley ends,
> And loneliness is over.
> Some meet early, some meet late,
> Some, like me, have long to wait.

It is when poet and composer match one another in such simple emotional precision, rather than in their headier conceits, that the severance of their partnership again appears saddening. The peculiarly English vein of wistful diatonic lyricism Britten tapped here was to be refined in many later operatic contexts.

So, of course, was his blatant parody of operatic styles. Indeed, the opening shape of the Cooks' Duet (no. 7) prefigures the sensuous cantilena Tytania sings over the sleeping Bottom, though grosser parody such as the final divergence of the parts at lugubrious distance is nearer the mechanicals' idea of elevated speech, for here the pretentious and tired clichés of the advertisement copy-writers are ridiculed in those of nineteenth-century Italian opera. As we have seen, pastiche extends back to Baroque idioms and forward to the Blues, and in the Western Union Boy's Song (no. 6) there is an example of that nonchalant syncopated style which the thirties found so smart; Britten had used it more ambitiously for the last song of *On this Island* but here, with no weight of irony to support, it is more delightfully apt.

Though Auden and Britten observe the operetta convention of 'numbers' separated by speech, both the use of connecting melodrama and the accumulation of a few extensive structures resist the excessive fragmentation their cultivated heterogeneity could easily cause. Melodrama does occur within the action (as, for example, at Tiny's introduction to the lumbermen when a pre-echo of the love duet is heard), and a secco-like punctuation is provided for some of Paul's words of command, but typically it is his reflections which are invested with the peculiarly momentous (though, as we have noted, dramatically distancing) quality that an aura of music around speech creates. At such points we recognize Paul's symbolic force, as 'the Eternal Guest' of his closing lines, and his association with the immanent sounds of nature reinforces this. The bird song and serene chordal background of his Greeting which opens Act I return in the second of his Good-nights, but the third of these, added by Britten in 1974 to Auden lines not used in the original production,[6] is more complex, its strained calls (high bassoon and bass clarinet) and dark harmonies painting the mystery of the night with a beauty that is no less individual for the evident debt to Bartók. Paul's last address to his men, Auden's summary of the 'harder task' the life of choice brings, is delivered against a horn melody, almost as elemental as that which frames the Serenade, and its progressive orchestral elaboration.

In revising the opera, Britten composed a new Introduction to it (in place of a lost overture)[7] based on this memorable theme. It leads into a choral Prologue still more haunting. The unison theme, unwinding one small shape, has strong Lydian inflexions and a final scalic descent that carry our memories forward to the framing choruses of *Peter Grimes*; the phrase-structure, the long pedal, and above all the expressive rather than structural weight given to dominant sevenths contribute no less to its utterly personal stamp (see Ex. 3). The broad calm of this Trees music gives way to dispute between the staid old and the restive young, generated from the *b* scales and the twisting figure of *a*. The wild geese's music, taunting the trees, also develops the scale, and as they announce that man is on his way (to a third-chain of slow arpeggios, which offers another fingerprint) *a* turns into an orchestral ostinato which engages against itself at various speeds, before making itself the swinging 6/8 theme of the final section. The choral refrain of this intensifies in lilting sequence the popular tone, though it then becomes involved in an elaborate working-out, pitted against the new form of *a* in double-choral textures before its radiantly simple peroration. Though

[6] Matthews, op. cit.
[7] A two-piano version of the overture was preserved; after Britten's death it appeared in an orchestration by Colin Matthews.

Ex. 4.3

the music of this prologue has moved a long way from Ex. 3, the pedals and the sensuous dominant sevenths as well as the ubiquitous *a* shape preserve strongly the feeling of a unified span. (Indeed, the *a* shape persists as an accompaniment element at least as far as the fifth number of the opera.) A scene no less sustained is that in which the fight between Helson and Paul and Tiny and Slim's love duet take place simultaneously. Since the fight is represented by a choral-orchestral commentary that animates an unbroken F pedal, inflected as Mixolydian and so potentially at least a dominant, no great ingenuity was needed to interpolate this in a duet in B flat minor/ major, but the co-existence of moods, frenetic and tender, is piquant. And the later modified return to the love duet, against the scalic orchestral ostinato of the Hymn (in itself a rather inflated piece) draws together a considerable stretch of music. The Mock Funeral March at its centre, as we should expect, yields some quintessential Britten ideas. By comparison, the remaining ambitious span of connected music, the Christmas Party which forms in effect the opera's finale, is rather anonymous in its jolly music, though the speeches, to a pattern set by Inkslinger, appropriately reinstate the folky note, and 'Carry her over the water' is an interlude of charming tonal fluidity. The scene continues musically through Bunyan's Farewell (noted above) to the concluding litany. This could be said to typify those uneasy relationships that mar the work from time to time, and that are partly implicit in Auden's text and partly set up or emphasized by the musical treatment. The refrain, always recurring at a new tonal level, is of an unaffected, even touching, melodic simplicity, whereas the conceit of setting a catalogue of abominations of modern life as a litany intoned by the three animals invites titters that are difficult to reconcile with the sombre mood of valediction. As the threnody of *Herring* and Tytania's music for Bottom were to demonsrate, beautiful music may be so inappropriate to the truth of a situation as to be absurd, and beyond that again prove to be deeply true; but it is confusing to offer sentiments at two levels in rapid alternation.

Paul Bunyan stakes no claim for inclusion in the canon of Britten's operas, yet enough has been discussed of its music to suggest the work's importance to the composer. While he cheerfully allowed it to disappear, he had been able to test in it the efficacy of many kinds of character and mood painting and many kinds of set-piece and ensemble structure. Though one does not know how much of the orchestral version broadcast to initiate the opera's revival was reworked in 1974, it would seem likely that its wide range of colourings, many of them idiosyncratically fusing hard-etched line and sonorous warmth, represent a further part of the preparation for the synthesis of Britten's talents to a well-focused dramatic end that was achieved in *Peter Grimes*.

5 Peter Grimes

By now it is even more obvious than it was in 1945 how fastidious Britten was in selecting poets and poems for the song-cycles that form one important branch of his work. A composer who seeks in both the sonority and the emotional and intellectual content of verse a powerful stimulus to his imagination must embark on an operatic enterprise with trepidation since, unless he decides directly to adapt an existing play (a solution Britten was not to attempt until his version of *A Midsummer-Night's Dream* in 1960), he runs the risk that his initial vision, even when embodied in the choice of a subject, may be dimmed by the actual verbal material to which his librettist commits him. Whether Auden and Britten could have founded one of those partnerships that have allowed some opera composers to perfect a method rather than constantly to essay new ones is a question that was touched on in discussing *Paul Bunyan*. But in any event, it seems probable that those sentiments which in 1942 impelled the composer to return home while the poet remained in America also required him to seek a collaborator more in sympathy with them, since the new opera was patently conceived as a token of Britten's Englishness.

As is well known, his nostalgia had been sharpened in America by E. M. Forster's article on the Suffolk poet, George Crabbe, and it was in Crabbe's poem *The Borough* that he discovered his operatic subject. Yet all the qualities of the verse that he must have found attractive, the hard grey light in which its characters are appraised and the unsentimental but closely-observed accounts of natural phenomena as well as the strong, measured use of simple language (albeit in the ponderous uniformity of heroic couplets), would have to be jettisoned in forging a rounded plot and a continuous dialogue from Crabbe's narrative. Almost inevitably, then, Montagu Slater's text depicts a borough that is not Crabbe's; but this libretto had the great virtue of offering challenges of a new kind to the composer in presenting dramatic situations that must test the truth of musical characterization, and in devising an elaborate pattern of verse forms and speeds of movement. We may be tempted to carp at a Peter Grimes whose dreams can be revealed in such articulate fantasy or at the women of the pub who can

104

rationalize so eloquently their rôle in men's lives, but these pretexts for lyricism are vital to the greater rhythm of an opera. A few formations lodge awkwardly in the memory ('Him who despises us we'll destroy' is a particularly laboured proposition to expound in an elaborate stretto) but Slater avoids both the heavily poetized language and the implausible *gaucherie* that have marred some later Britten libretti.

As the courtroom prologue demonstrates at once, he is ready to provide a transcript of that matter-of-fact speech in which people, preferring cliché to fresh thought, conduct their affairs. Though it has attracted much favourable comment (Swallow's magisterial locution, for example, is admirably rendered in a Baroque parody), Britten's recitativo secco here, with its laconic orchestral gestures, is not entirely characteristic. For at this stage we are simply spectators, while once the issues are clarified we are alive not only to statements but to implications: in later recitative, however dry vocally, the orchestra is likely to help us make the connexions. (In retrospect, of course, we can see how certain implications were already there in this opening secco: the quiet dominant seventh to which Peter takes the oath achieves its full meaning only in the last scene of the opera.) The pub conversations during the storm have no true accompaniment at all, yet the continuous percussion is enough to suggest the strained nerves behind this routine badinage; and the use of a sing-song pattern for much of the small talk (first heard in Auntie's 'That is the sort of weak politeness') helps to unify these recitatives as momentary refuges from a storm that, musically, embraces the Interlude and the entire second scene of Act I. Thus, although the dependence of the opera on set numbers is absolute, the rôle of recitative as their necessary link is rarely made too blatant; the stiffest joints in the work, surrounding Peter's 'Hi! give us a hand' (Act I, figs 20 and 21), probably show us Britten feeling his way.

Britten's own introductory comment on *Peter Grimes* emphasized his aim to 'restore to the musical setting of the English language a brilliance, freedom and vitality that have been curiously rare since the death of Purcell',[1] but he immediately pointed out how far this aim might lead the composer away from the servile criterion of speech-rhythm when the emotional content makes other demands. Purcell was old-fashioned by the standards of his time in his tendency to let all recitative aspire towards arioso, and in a century when *Sprechstimme* has provided a still lower rung on the ladder between pure speech and pure *cantabile*, Britten is no doubt equally old-fashioned, for he too passes from functional recitative into arioso at every flicker of the emotional thermometer. In Ex. 1, for instance, the Rector's non-committal question is taken up by Boles, in his customary nagging tones, but with a projection into more shaped melody as his fanaticism mounts. The Rector's bars revert to speech patterns, but Auntie's words

[1] B. Britten, 'Introduction', in E. Crozier (ed.) *Peter Grimes*, London 1945, p. 8.

105

Ex.5.1

to Ellen transform in a warm *cantabile* the crucial motive (*x* inverted) that has underlaid the earlier speech in the orchestra.

The regular crotchets of her line exemplify a method of word setting that, already employed in the songs (e.g., Michelangelo Sonnet XXX), acquires a special rôle in Britten's operatic style. He abandons the immediacy of verbal rhythms but also forgoes rhythmic developments that serve the ends of an intra-musical design. While the words are conveyed with utter clarity, their deliberately unnaturalistic delivery directs our attention beyond them to the expressive significance of each melodic interval. What in one sense can appear an understatement can therefore in another represent an emotional essence. Because the method easily leads to mannerism, Britten rarely uses it as the basis of a full aria. Ellen's arioso lines in Act II, Scene 1 provide memorable examples, at the climax of 'Child, you're not too young to know' and at the crux of the whole scene, perhaps of the opera, when she anxiously questions Peter (see particularly 'Were we mistaken?'). In the previous act, 'Let her among you' shows the method extended to furnish from a descending crotchet scale and a four-note figure that *is* subjected to rhythmic variation the complete material of a ternary arietta.

The emotional reverberations of this simple piece continue in an orchestral extension as background to pure *secco* dialogue. More commonly, Britten uses the arietta to provide a deft sketch of one of the minor characters. Just as his gift for the graphically 'characteristic' instrumental piece seemed at one time to deflect him from mastering large-scale structural thought (see pp. 26 and 44), so we may see in *Peter Grimes* an occasional acceptance, in Hobson's song, for example, or in the Rector's Good Night, of the picturesque when it contributes little of dramatic consequence. It is true that these vignettes help to create a tragic irony when such well-intentioned people surrender their identities to the venomous mob emotions of the march to Grimes's hut and the manhunt, but miniature closed forms that emerge and disappear so trimly may disrupt the flow without offering the catharsis of the true aria.

Britten's claim to have returned to 'the classical practice of separate numbers that crystallize and hold the emotion of a dramatic situation at chosen moments'[2] is indisputable, yet a symmetrically-balanced structure may be realized in terms that in fact remain progressive. The closest approach to a *da capo* aria begins with Peter's 'We strained into the wind' (Act I, fig. 41). Not only is this linked to the foregoing chorus by one of the orchestral motives that symbolize the impending storm (see Ex. 2a) but its chief vocal shape (b) is derived, by octave-transposition, from the fugue

Ex.5.2 (a)   Ex.5.2 (b)

Ex.5.2 (c)

[2] Ibid., p. 8.

107

Ex.5.2 (d)

Ex.5.2 (e)

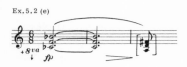

Ex.5.2 (f)

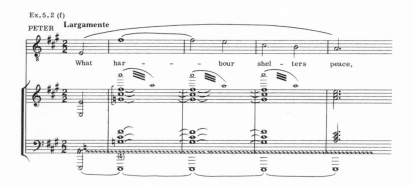

subject 'Now the floodtide' (c), while the end of the aria is swept into the
Storm Interlude (d), based on yet another transformation of the same shape,
crossed with the pithier motive shown at (a). So the aria is one stage in a
continuing process of thematic transformation. But within the aria too,
despite its clear ternary shape, we feel an onward movement. In its first span,
in A minor, Grimes looks back on a past traumatic experience; though
mounting terror pushes up the key in successive phrases, the paragraph
cadences securely before the storm breaks in again (fig. 43). The middle
section, from fig. 44, depicts Grimes's ambitions in an eager parlando (and a
stock Britten mode—D major with sharp 4 and flat 7); aspiring modulation,
round a circle of minor thirds, is already contradicted by an immovable bass
ostinato, but a chord (Ex. 2e) that has been acquiring fateful associations
since its first appearance at the word 'storm' in the opening chorus arrests
this flight of fancy when Balstrode offers more practical advice. Finally, the
return of the first section (Ex. 2f) brings the dream of a future shared with
Ellen, apparently beatific in its A *major*, but resting on a dominant pedal that
is ominously motivic (its E–F natural shake is part of the storm's Phrygian
figure, cf. a and d) and coloured ineradicably by the brass chord (e) that is at
its centre. This time there is no cadence, or rather cadence becomes a
mockery of the singer's vision, when his reiterated E–F sharp ('Where night

108

is turned to day') is seized on by the orchestra and turned to a G flat–F flat (by implication) preparation for the E flat Phrygian of the storm that now unleashes its full force. This conflation of closed-form principle and motivically developing textures is a characteristic feat of synthesis, and one that could be given new realizations in other dramatic contexts, as later operas were to show.

A distortion of Ex. 2 b/f marks Grimes's entry into The Boar in the following scene, and the E pedal of (f) carries on to initiate the scalic E major motive with which the strings illuminate his second aria, 'Now the Great Bear and Pleiades'. At the other end, continuity is again secured by the retention of E, now ethereal on the violins, but apart from the nieces' mocking parody of Grimes's own repeated E, there is no attempt to sew this piece by motivic means into the context. The scene is a social one and Grimes's hermetic vision cuts him off from any real contact with it. Simply to combine scale and monotone, as Britten has done here, might seem to court the threadbare rather than the economical, yet he achieves perhaps the most original piece of imagery in the opera, a sound-universe of serenely purposeful movements within a great stillness. The structural plan, three stanzas, executed musically as a-a-ba, is given point by the differing cadential outcome, C sharp and C natural, of the first two. Less satisfactory is the animato interlude: the tonal conflict here (involving the two previous cadence keys), the orchestral alarm signals and the startling vocal fioritura at 'a flashing turmoil of a shoal of herring' seem facile in their disruption of the calm; one feels more convinced by the timing of this demented outburst than by the terms in which it is realized. But the return to the earlier material brings its most intense form, and now a tonic cadence, of clear-eyed acceptance: 'Who can turn skies back and begin again?'

Grimes's last aria, embedded in the *scena* that begins Act II, Scene 2, reverts to the E of the 'Great Bear' soliloquy, but this is only for a moment glimpsed as a fully achieved major mode. The central strophic variations are A Lydian in the orchestra, yet the voice is so strongly centred on E that we more easily hear the accompaniment as a protracted IV, Ex. 3a; thus an instability persists that gives the lie to the self-induced confidence with which Peter rapturously embellishes his lines. Even so, this daydream quietens his tortured emotions; the arioso framing it (at figs 60 and 63), in which E major is more evidently undermined by the bass G natural, provides a transition between the earlier wild sequence of moods (making explicit those of the passacaglia interlude) and a nightmare in which the aria's phrases are distorted (see Ex. 3b), their harmony no longer A Lydian, but uneasily poised between A and its antipode E flat. (This association of Lydian scales and tritonally opposed key areas is one of the strongest unifying elements in the opera.)

That two of the three protracted lyrical moments which form our picture of Grimes as more than a dour brute are so convincingly related to their

Ex.5.3(a)

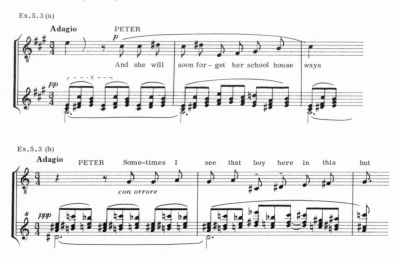

Ex.5.3 (b)

musical contexts does much to persuade us of their truth as character portrayal; the remaining aria ('The Great Bear') stands more isolated, as a pure set piece, just because it is a token of alienation. Ellen's one extended aria, 'Embroidery in childhood' (Act III, Scene 1), has at least as markedly the effect of a detached number, but in the context this is unfortunate. Indeed, the discovery of the boy's jersey, a cue as much for Ellen's reflections on her past as for her recognition of the present, seems faintly contrived. It attempts belatedly to give greater depth to a character who has existed for us mainly in her sympathetic reactions to Grimes and his work-house boy. The stylized vocal writing makes an apt enough illustrative device, yet its eloquence seems a strangely glib response to a chilling dramatic twist. However, by means of the repeated F sharps in the orchestra Britten does sustain some of the suspense which that note represented in the

Ex.5.4 (a)

Ex.5.4 (b)

previous recitative. Then, as an almost Bergian *idée fixe*, it throws a new light on the work's central motive x, in terms of which it acts as a VII pedal; on its own terms it is, of course, a V in B minor to which the motive is subservient, ending on VI (see Ex. 4). Now this equivocal harmonic situation is not new: in the scene between Peter and Ellen in Act II, Scene 1 (after fig. 16) the pedal F of the Creed carried on against the G flat Lydian of Ellen's 'Peter, tell me one thing—where the youngster got that ugly bruise' and 'Were we right in what we planned to do?'; the powerful relevance needs no underlining, but the allusion back is achieved by delicate means. Yet the aria's F sharp is already weaker (within a pure B minor context) than was the recitative's, and it is soon abandoned to permit the snapping of texture and tonality at 'Now my broidery affords the clue whose meaning we avoid'. In the second stanza of this strophic aria, this line is extended in sequential antiphony of singer and orchestra that only adds to the impression of redundant artifice. The following dialogue restores and, in a masterly passage, intensifies the original mood, reverting to the petrified F sharp and now using x and its inversion overtly in the voices, at 'We shall be there with him'; the B major chord here (cf. Ex. 15b), when black despair has overwhelmed those who must seek to offer a consolation they already know to be a mockery, may be thought of as a distant pre-echo of the great sequence of triads at just such a moment in *Billy Budd*.

As we see already in the Borough chorus that opens Act I, the minor characters, however much they may prize the individuality sketched so nimbly in their music, represent shades of opinion within a close-knit community, accustomed to acting as one man. So it is that the ensembles of the opera are almost always transmuted into choral texture before they reach their climax. The only exceptions are the first ensemble, 'I'll give a hand', from which most of the fishermen choose pointedly to abstain, the trio of the two nieces and Swallow, whose advances require privacy, and the women's ensemble that precedes the central interlude of the work. In this, the absence of the Borough chorus makes itself very potently felt: during the most extended build-up in the opera, just preceding it, the crowd's hatred of Grimes has been fanned into activity, the march to his hut. For the women who remain, only a dejected inactivity is possible. Their commentary on the comfort they may hope to bring to sordid lives has its moral for the whole work as well as an immediate one, yet it is the kind of sound that matters here far more than their words. This represents aspirations towards a very simple ideal of beauty, thwarted to produce some of the most complex tonal situations experienced so far. Even the flute ritornello's falling thirds, a symbol of the immanent established in the sea music of the first Interlude, are coloured plangently by simultaneous seconds (cf. the *Sinfonia da Requiem* finale), while the vocal textures produce constant blurs of adjacent notes by superimposing individually limpid constituents—arpeggios and scales—in different tonal areas. So the Straussian richness of vocal sound

111

never becomes self-indulgent: even the cadence of each refrain is immediately clouded by the flutes' aching dissonance.

Ex. 5 shows the third-chain in its original form in the opening chorus of
Act I as part of that tireless background of Nature against which human
endeavour must be measured. Here the plodding couplets that were
Crabbe's standby serve Slater well, though Britten makes his climax by

Ex.5.5

riding over the break (at 'as if in sleep') with the effect of an unexpectedly
great wave. He sets the drones in that Lydian A which is to be recurrent in
the opera, but the orchestral lapping of the sea, already established in the
preceding interlude, has far less warmth, its typical material being impassively 'white-note' without a defined modal centre (Phrygian, Aeolian, even
Lydian on F all suggest themselves at times). Just as this preludial chorus
includes interpolations by individual characters, so the reversion to it which
forms the opera's postlude contains dialogue, in which the sinking of
Grimes's boat far out to sea is judged to be 'one of these rumours'. The
phrase to which this is set is that motive *x* which has symbolized each
operation of the fate that pursued Grimes; in this 'white-note' context it is at
last assimilated with the eternal oblivion of the sea.

The later stages in the approach of the storm that is depicted in the central
interlude of Act I were discussed above. Before Grimes's aria, the Borough
folk have watched the warning signs with growing alarm. Their ensemble-
cum-chorus (from fig. 31) establishes the figures Ex. 2a and c and confirms
the early storm association of the chord Ex. 2e, thus making explicit in
advance the shapes of the Interlude (Ex. 2d). On Ex. 2c an elaborate fugue is
built, in which individual characters sing the subject while the chorus contributes exclamatory snatches of countersubject; the rôles are reversed from
time to time, and narrowing stretti betray rising panic. The subject is in
Phrygian D and several wide tonal circles return to that point; but at the
arresting moment when ensemble and chorus together deliver the subject, a
C sharp Phrygian statement is diverted so as to outline a great scale descending one and a half octaves from A to E flat (made Phrygian second of a
returning D centre); this relationship demonstrates the importance Britten
attaches to the antithesis represented by those two pitches (mentioned
above) even when they are regarded from the oblique viewpoint of another
tonal centre.

The first scene of Act I is framed by A tonality (interlude and Grimes's

'What harbour'), and the plunge to E flat for the storm is the basic structural move, since that key also closes the act with a few more gusts of the storm following the round 'Old Joe has gone fishing'. The whole protracted exposition of the round's material, i.e., up to the point where the chorus—following as usual the lead of the soloists—completes the last subject of this

Ex.5.6

quadruple counterpoint, has been supported on a tonic pedal (see Ex. 6) that allows no modulatory implications to the balancing sharp 4 and flat 7 shadings. Grimes's belated entry, however, seizes on the D flat as a tonic, further disrupting the comfortable flow by his augmented and diminished versions of the subjects. Only when Grimes drops out again is E flat restored by an enharmonic swing (at fig. 82); the final section presents a *tour de force* of contrapuntal resource.

The fateful motive *x* first becomes explicit at the moment in Act II, Scene 1, when Peter, tortured by Ellen's sorrowful reproach, 'We've failed', strikes at her blindly, recognizes in his own instinctive resort to violence his damnation, and cries out 'So be it, and God have mercy upon me' (see Ex. 7). The inexorable agencies of his fate are set in motion at once in the cumulative stretch of ensemble and chorus leading up to the march to the hut. The allegretto (fig. 18) conflates *x* as an accompaniment figure as well as fashioning it melodically into the taunt 'Grimes is at his exercise', and even the

113

Ex.5.7

So be it,— And — God have mer - cy u-pon me!

organ, pealing as the church doors open, takes up the motive. With the assembly of all the Borough folk, the orchestra converts it into an ostinato, that kind of obsessive reiteration on which rumour thrives; against this mechanistic malevolence, the few individual voices that appeal for some restraint make no impression. A graphic touch is the blatant crudity of the harmonic shift from C, to C sharp, to D (before fig. 27) as the crowd begins to scent the hunt. In the new key, x is underpinned by its mirror image for the agitator Boles's harangue; a momentary pathos is admitted at Ellen's entry (discussed above—see Ex. 1), and the crowd does manage to stifle its self-righteous indignation to hear her explanation of her motives in helping Grimes. Setting off in A minor (at the larghetto, fig. 31), this ensemble on a new theme seems at first too orderly in its balanced three-phrase pattern, but the listeners' interjections, by overlapping and superimposition, change the rôle of Ellen's burden to that of a canto fermo, a thread of compassion sustained through a maze of carping, malicious or sententious comments; the whole ensemble gains its affecting quality from the frame of simple triadic harmony on which this elaborate texture is woven. The chorus at last joins in, its totally uncomprehending reversion to the x motive ironically negating the warmer sound of the major mode at fig. 33, and Ellen's theme of compassion is soon bandied about (fig. 34) in derision. The wild excitement of this upsurge of popular hatred is checked by Hobson's drum but the processional music that follows is in fact more horrifying: this bare unison writing, with its ominous long notes at phrase ends, represents the sanctification of persecution in ritual.

By comparison with this scene, the ensemble and chorus that in Act III lead to the manhunt are slightly disappointing, in part because the situation is too close a parallel. The dance-hall galop against which Mrs Sedley raises the alarm is tenuously related to x (see Ex. 8), but the chromatic motive introduced by Auntie to 'My customers come here for peace' (at fig. 28) is

Ex.5.8

confusingly near Mrs Sedley's fantasies of crime, and its return at 'Our curse shall fall on his evil day' has no very convincingly ironic ring, despite the incisive added seconds. Indeed, all the material of this ensemble lacks distinction; though the close imitation of 'Him who despises us we'll destroy' provides some sense of the growing flood of venom, the cliché of its arpeggio seems misjudged. Ridiculous though any chorus can appear when required to sing 'ha, ha', the return of the dance-hall music at fig. 41 is far more powerful in the theatre than it looks in the score; the crowd's ecstasy of hatred exhausts the scope of their language, yet this exaltation is musically simply the apotheosis of their entertainment music—a revealing commentary. The analogy of the hunt is underlined at the climax of this scene (from fig. 42) by the distorted horn-calls to which the mob search out their victim; prominent among these is the storm chord (Ex. 9a), while it is not too

Ex.5.9 (a)

Pe - ter Grimes!   (= Ex.2 e)

Ex.5.9 (b)

Pe - ter Grimes!

Ex.5.9 (c)

Muted Horns

far-fetched to see (since one can undoubtedly hear) in the last great shouts (Ex. 9b) the crucial *x* motive. Between them, as the hunters listen, there is built up in the orchestra a chord of three muted horns (Ex. 9c), which becomes an eerie background to the Interlude that follows, a fantastic review of Grimes motives that charts the delirium we witness in the following scene. When, at the end of the Interlude, the sound emerges quietly out of the horn chord, we hear it not only through the fog that has fallen but through the haze of Grimes's disordered mind, in which the searchers' cries fluctuate between their actual imperious form and this lulling sirens' song. When Grimes gives vent to his fury, the voices, too, are vehement, but at his last vision of the peace that Ellen was to bring to his life, they have become his requiem, lapping with the gentle rhythm of the sea. Indeed, there is complete motivic continuity here, across the spoken dialogue, from the last phrases of Peter and the chorus, through the fog horn's last despairing moan to the opening of the postlude and dawn over the sea (see Ex. 10). The use of speech at the drama's catastrophe has sometimes been criticized, but in terms of Grimes himself it is entirely convincing: by now the musical

Ex.5.10

dream-world into which he has withdrawn has no connexion with reality, but Balstrode's spoken words penetrate into it with grim disenchantment. The whole scene, quite unremarkable in its musical means, is a highly original and perfectly integrated imaginative conception.

Of the six orchestral pieces, prelude and interlude to each act, four can be played separately under the title 'Sea Interludes'. Hans Keller has pointed out that one of these, the Storm, is interpreted in its dramatic context as a reflection of 'the turbulent and yearning aspect of Peter's mind'[3]. So there is a regular alternation between the static introductory pictures, of dawn, high noon and moonlit evening over the sea, and the three dynamic studies of Grimes placed at the centre of each phase of dramatic action. The nature of the dawn prelude has been discussed, but we may note how much of later significance is adumbrated in the chordal interpolations; in the Lydian I–II sharp–I progression is the seed of many later harmonic growths and also the essence of x, while at its contradiction by the natural IV of the bass, we hear a chord which is as close to the Storm's E flat minor as to A (see Ex. 11). Later developments point up this potential relationship (see the progression from

Ex.5.11

³ H. Keller, '*Peter Grimes*', in Mitchell-Keller, p. 115.

fig. 12). The origin of the Storm material (Interlude II) has been shown: not only the subject of this violent fugato (see Ex. 2d) but its scalic countersubject stems from the vocal fugue. Of the three episodes in this rondo structure, the first two may be related only to the physical storm (the trombone figure at 54 is a transformation of the fugue subject) but the third is an echo of Grimes's dream refuge (i.e., Ex. 2f) in its original A major. Its second motive ('away from tidal waves') is augmented on the brass while the woodwind make of it a pattering ostinato; when, at the end of the long tense dominant pedal on E, that note is recognized as the Phrygian second of E flat minor and the main Storm theme returns augmented, the ostinato can remain equally relevant for it is, of course, also the initial shape of the Storm theme. Innumerable thematic connexions of this kind are made possible by the extreme cogency of, and interrelationships within, the principal material.

The interlude that opens Act II ('Sunday Morning' in the concert version), standing outside the dramatic conflict, is less concerned with this material. It might appear sophistic to argue that Britten intends us to hear in the woodwind motive a foreshadowing of *x* inverted, but the connexion is there, just as the element that is lacking for complete identification, the sharp fourth, is the most prominent feature in the D Lydian stratum of the horns. Tempting though it is to regard this interlude as essentially in A, and thus part of that scheme of tritonal opposition so prominent elsewhere, details like the C natural (bar 14), Britten's characteristic flat 7 counteracting the over-sweet Lydian, confirm D as the centre. The new theme at fig. 2, however, is in A (again predominantly Lydian, as the great build-up of thirds—cf. Ex. 5—emphasizes). The reprise of the bell-like first subject is in D, though soon underlaid by B flat triads as the stage church bell joins in, and Ellen's sung version of the second subject retains D—thus completing a sonata form without development. But the B flat drone has a consequent in the E flat of the tenor bell, while the organ appropriates the horns' ground for its voluntary, so that the music carries smoothly on into the action, incorporating an imitative version of the second subject in E major, before the bell's E flat is accepted as tonic for both the hymn in church and Ellen's talk to the apprentice.

Ex.5.12

The ground on which the central interlude's passacaglia is erected (Ex. 12) is a version of the Grimes motive *x*, stated thirty-nine times, without transposition or rhythmic manipulation. Its eleven-beat shape ($\frac{3+3+3+2}{4}$)

prevents the inexorable degenerating into the merely monotonous and the material set against it never endorses unequivocally the 4/4 metre. This material consists of a continuous series of some ten variations (again of no consistent length) on the solo viola theme that begins at the third statement of the ground. Later events confirm that the theme is a vicarious expression of the mute apprentice's melancholy lot, but the boy can be mute just because he exists for the audience only as a symbol of one side of Grimes's nature, and this association of the two characters is confirmed by the shape of the viola theme: eloquent though this is, it is made up simply of innumerable juxtapositions of notes 2–4 of x, with the minor third occasionally diminished. Setting off in the F of the ground, it soon abandons that area, which is not regained until the final variation (fig. 54), so that tension is created by means directly comparable with those of the Dirge in the Serenade (see p. 93). Points of particular interest in the variations include the exchange of A for E flat (effected through their respective Lydian forms) in Variation I (fig. 45), the reappearance for the first time since Act I of the storm chord in Variation III (fig. 47), and the inversion of the three-note motive in Var. VIII (fig. 52). From Var. IX (fig. 53), the melodic elaboration is cumulative, preparing the way for the violent downward flurry and swing of key that prefigures Grimes's rage in the scene that immediately follows. And this scene, punctuated by brief reminiscences of all except the first of the variations, presents in dramatic form the fluctuating moods that have already been expounded in the orchestral character-study. The boy, whose misfortune it is to be the occasion of Grimes's fury as well as of his wistful reflection ('There's the jersey that she knitted'), is only brought to the centre of our picture after his death, when the viola again delivers its long, lonely theme in inversion. Even the *idée fixe* x is silent now until the last few bars, and the ghastly tinkle of the celesta that whispers on after all Grimes's hopes crash into emptiness at the boy's death, is the only accompaniment. Though we might trace this disturbing sound to Bartók's Music for Strings, Percussion and Celesta (see bar 78 of the first movement), we must recognize the remarkable sense of dramatic fitness that prompted its use here; Britten's use of this tone colour as a symbol of horror was to recur in *The Turn of the Screw*.

Interlude V, opening Act III, is the most truly independent orchestral piece in the opera, a picture of the mystery and the grandeur of the moonlit sea. Its textural formula is a typical route to Britten's simple yet not vacuous euphony—a primarily scalic theme is surrounded by two accompanimental elements, one a pedal, the other an arpeggio. This kind of construction gives a logic to the 'added-note' chords that they often lack in the apparently similar technique of, say, John Ireland (whose E flat harmony in the 'Threnody' of his *Concertino Pastorale* may profitably be compared with that of this Interlude). Furthermore, when the bass is so evidently merely the revolution of a single chordal object, not the clue to the upper harmonies,

Ex.5.13

the sound of the I 6/4 may be savoured for its own sake instead of a V preparation. 'Progression' now occurs across the phrases, rather than within them; Ex. 13 shows the II–V–I that leads to the second strain. This is punctuated by the triplet motive shown, which pursues another independent course that twice emphasizes the antipode A; the compromise area C is adopted to open the developmental middle section, and the recovery of E flat is celebrated in a climactic, enormously expanded I–V–I progression, each stage of which is represented in second inversion on a pedal.

The final interlude, while the most remarkable, requires least comment. Its fantasy around one chord shows an extension of a technique Britten had often enough applied to a single note or an ostinato figure (see Interlude IV, discussed above)—that of giving the unchanged object constantly new significance by its relationship to changing surroundings. The many angles from which we learn to hear this muted horn chord invest a commonplace harmonic unit with a mysterious quality that is made explicit, not dispersed, when the sound eddies in the fogs of the following scene, and the snatches of earlier motives that succeed one another so unpredictably foreshadow Grimes's demented train of thought in that scene. Their identification becomes unavoidable on a few hearings of the opera, but this kind of association remains potent even if the newcomer experiences it subconsciously. Indeed, there are shapes here which cannot be said to quote so much as to synthesize or distil. The bass line shown at Ex. 14 establishes an

Ex.5.14

identity between 'We strained into the wind' and 'Were we mistaken when we schemed?', and the crotchet figures from fig. 46 can be traced back to many sources and *on* to the searchers' cries and Grimes's retorts, after fig. 48. The great crescendo they initiate reaches its peak in statements of the *x* motive (inverted, straight and developed into a chain of thirds). The whole nature of this passage, noble and compassionate in tone, must remind us of

119

the final orchestral interlude in another opera, *Wozzeck*; the analogy between Berg's climactic quotation of 'Wir arme Leut' ' and Britten's quotation of 'God have mercy upon me' is particularly striking, and in both contexts we feel that the composer has exceeded his depicting rôle in order to comment on the lot of his hero/villain.

Enough reference has been made in the previous pages to the pervasive use of certain motives in *Peter Grimes* to make redundant any systematic survey of Britten's practice. But beyond the most obvious cross-references there are so many subtler derivations of material from common sources that a few music examples may usefully help to explain why a work apparently so prodigal of melody and so diverse in manner creates a unified impression. This is largely a matter of purely musical craftsmanship: it is, for example, of no importance to our grasp of dramatic issues that we do not immediately hear in x a simplification of the fishing round from the previous act (cf. Ex. 6). Of course, it might with justice be said that such examples as Ex. 11 simply demonstrate how much the melodic motive x has in common with the Lydian harmonic progressions of the whole work. Yet this is to underline how motivic in function all these Lydian references become. Though other modes are far less conspicuous, Britten tends to use them quite consistently within certain pieces to give a particular colour. Here too, some examples have been cited above, such as the Phrygian writing of the choral fugato preceding the storm and its transformation in the Storm Interlude. Further examples of that mode occur in the little song round the capstan (Act I, fig. 21) and in the Benedicite (Act II, fig. 12). Britten's view of Lydian and

Ex. 5.15 (a)

Ex. 5.15 (b)

Phrygian as tonally unified yet also antithetical is neatly demonstrated at an early stage (see Ex. 15a) and far more potently at almost the last stage (Ex. 15b), when Balstrode's Lydian x has a terrible finality that Ellen's Phrygian inversion, an anxious plea for reassurance, seeks to ward off. Britten also uses modal scales to effect smooth transfers of tonal centre. Thus the Gloria of the Responses, round an E flat reciting note, provides the figure which, interpreted enharmonically, can be retained in B Lydian as the accompaniment figure to Ellen's arioso. Mention has already been made of the ambivalence of the Creed's pedal F in the central dialogue between Ellen and Peter (Act II, fig. 16); Ellen's music makes it an added seventh pedal in G flat Lydian, while Peter's angry interjections treat it as a V in B flat minor, but his pathetic change to pleading 'My only hope' is conveyed by a soft Lydian with F now acting as I; the dramatic force of this passage is fully understood when the immovable F at last succeeds in fulfilling its rôle as a V (i.e., in following Grimes's will) by cadencing in B flat with the presentation of the x motive. Ambivalence of a simpler kind is to be heard in the minor/major fluctuations of Grimes's arioso 'By familiar fields' (Act I, fig. 38), while the D minor of Ellen's little aria in Act I is in fact compounded of pure F major against pure D major.

As was already evident in *A Ceremony of Carols*, Britten returned to England prepared to essay a style easily grasped by audiences to which much of twentieth-century music was still forbidding. He was willing to accept, with the example of Vaughan Williams and Holst still familiar, that modality, whether in very old or entirely new scale constructions, could provide some basis for a freshly-considered technique, though he had no concern for honouring the melodic or harmonic and textural ideals of his English predecessors. And in one form or another the flexibly constructed scale was likely to be the raw material of any composer in whose work tonality continued to play so fundamental a part. The score of *Peter Grimes* demonstrates in what was by far Britten's longest musical span to that date the same scrupulous balance of tonal forces that marked his earlier works, but now the dramaticism with which keys are juxtaposed (or superimposed) is explicit.

In a study of key centres in this opera, Anthony Payne demonstrates effectively the cardinal rôle of that opposition between A and E flat which has already been referred to in many contexts.[4] He sees in it a symbol of 'the impossibility of co-existence for Grimes and the Borough' though the musical facts do not enable him to allocate one key to each; in any event, even to define the significance of the key conflict thus far is to ignore the Sea Interludes, two of which are in E flat (storm and moonlit calm) and one in A (the eternal, impassive sea); these orchestral pieces block out the large scale tonal movements of the work. Further, Payne is given to bolstering a wholly tenable thesis with an unnecessary weight of evidence, some of which must

[4] A. Payne, 'Dramatic Use of Tonality in *Peter Grimes*', *Tempo* 66/67, 1963, p. 22.

121

be rejected: for example, to claim that 'the first important tonal incident is a juxtaposition of the two main keys' is to disregard the inconvenient (but to the listener no less palpable) material in G flat and C that precedes Mrs Sedley's interpolation in A (fig. 14). Payne's reading of the choral climax that sets off the man hunt (preceding the last interlude, fig. 42) is also difficult to accept. Despite some pauses that are formed around E flat (particularly forceful when this is made part of the 'storm' chord, see Ex. 9a), the orchestra's bitonal opposition here is, as Eric White says,[5] between F minor and E major; and White's reference back to the unaccompanied arioso shared by Peter and Ellen in the opera's prologue is telling. As Payne implies (and this context bears out), the fundamental opposition A–E flat is not always presented in direct terms, but its force continues to be felt in the deployment of keys closely related to those poles. The B flat minor of the central confrontation between Peter and Ellen (see above) and the E of Peter's dreams, for example, share much of the colour of the keys to which they stand in dominant relationship, while the D Phrygian of the impending Storm chorus in Act I is characterized by its flat II and V degrees, as the preliminary Storm chord (fig. 31) makes clear. That chord was first presented, after fig. 16, as an intensification of Lydian A's D sharp that swung the balance momentarily towards E flat (Ex. 16), and the way in which

Lydian propensities facilitate tritonal switches provides an interesting testimony to the integrated conception of the work (a precedent is to be found in some sections of *Les Illuminations*, see above, p. 78); an example of this modulatory technique in the passacaglia has been referred to.

Whereas Act I, both in the framework of its opening and central interludes and finale and in many more immediate juxtapositions, emphasizes its A to E flat function, Act II has only one important stretch of each key, the opening of the church service in E flat and the great ensemble in A minor/major. As we have seen above (see Ex. 3b), even fleeting appearances can be made momentous, or, more simply, motivic (see Ellen's reference to the storm which thrusts E flat minor into the Lydian B of her arioso after fig. 11),

[5] White, p. 119.

but the main structure of this act is not significantly committed to these keys—which may mean that it is rather committed to escaping from them. Act III reverses the pattern of Act I in moving from E flat back to A, though with much material (of the dance-hall in particular) quite outside the scheme. Its final interlude, underpinned by a simple chord (see Ex. 9c), has no single tonal moral; in relation to the chord its B flat opening acquires a dominant significance (as Payne notes) and the climactic *x* appears in A, so the dichotomy may still be glimpsed, but it is impossible to agree with Payne's view that Grimes's demented monologue sets out in E flat. The synthesis of choral chord and fog-horn tuba (at fig. 47) suggests a G minor which the vocal lines do not contradict; only in the later stages do the principal key centres emerge. But then it is to be noted how two of the crucial themes of the opera that originally appeared in 'dominant' areas achieve their destiny: 'Turn the skies back' (from the 'Great Bear' soliloquy) is now in A, not E, and the *x* motive 'God have mercy upon you' (directed now at those who have harrowed him) is in E flat, not B flat.

Hans Keller draws attention to several occurrences of what he calls 'Britten's own C major' in the opera[6] and it is tempting to seek a consistent rôle for this key, half-way between the poles, especially since the 'neutral' Act II gravitates to it. But it is not even possible to invest it with a single symbolic meaning: if Keller's references to turns to C in Ellen's Act I aria, in Peter's 'Great Bear' soliloquy and in his Act II dream of 'some kindlier home' do show a comparable use of the key for warm, deeply felt sentiments, the turns to C at the ostinato 'Grimes is at his exercise' (Act II, fig. 23) and for much of the dance music weaken such a reading. Yet Keller's point is valuable, above all when we look at some of the works in which Britten drew on the experience of *Peter Grimes*.

---

[6] Keller, op. cit., p. 117.

6 The Rape of Lucretia

The success of *Peter Grimes* gave real substance to hopes for British opera that had for centuries been sustained more on intentions than on fulfilments. But it could not improve a national situation in which only two houses, both metropolitan, were devoted principally to opera throughout the main season. And since one of these, Covent Garden, was to become again a showcase for productions depending on internationally distinguished casts, while Sadler's Wells had a demanding enough task in building its repertoire of classics-in-the-vernacular, practical prospects for native opera as anything more than an occasional indulgence were not bright. Outside London, however, there was Glyndebourne, a small house intended for short summer seasons which, immediately after the war, was not yet able to draw together casts to revive the repertoire with which it had achieved fame. Presumably it was because the size of the house suited his purpose so well, and because productions of his new works helped towards a resumption of activities there, that Britten's two chamber operas were presented at Glyndebourne in the summers of 1946 and 1947.

Certainly these presentations were only the most immediate part of the composer's purpose. As the formation of the English Opera Group made clear, Britten and his associates dared to believe that, by cultivating a scale of opera of which his two new works were at first the only examplars readily available, they would be able to offer rounded artistic experiences, not condescendingly watered-down arrangements, to audiences in many towns in Britain that lacked both the facilities and the tradition to support an operatic establishment. In fact, it must be said, this ambition proved too lofty: though the group undertook many provincial (as well as several continental and American) tours, these tended to become peripheral to its central activity, the presentation of chamber operas, by Britten and many other British composers, at the Aldeburgh Festival. Yet if national prejudices and financial problems conspired to qualify the contribution the English Opera Group could make to the establishment of provincial operatic activity, its success in realizing Britten's musico-dramatic vision proved so inspiring to him that in the years after *Grimes* only two out of a dozen operas demanded the resources of the largest houses.

The small orchestra he chose for the first chamber opera, *The Rape of Lucretia* (1946), was essentially that of the Op. 1 *Sinfonietta*—five wind (flute, oboe, clarinet, bassoon and horn) and one each of the standard five strings—to which were added a harp and percussion. To a composer preparing to explore further the ground opened up so fruitfully in *Grimes*, this drastic reduction of forces must not have been a self-denial lightly entered upon. Whatever the selective scoring that was to distinguish *Billy Budd* (i.e., after the chamber-opera experience was digested), in *Peter Grimes* full choral textures and elaborate ensembles had typically been supported by quite standard orchestral dispositions. The stage band, of course, was a tiny group of soloists, but its whole point lay in incisive representation of music within the action, against which the musical commentary on the action remained the province of the pit orchestra. Peter's 'Great Bear' monologue used only strings, but derived its effect from the multiplicity of layers in which their parts were heard and from that controlled warmth of sound which only massed strings can produce. Sectionalized scoring which could be re-created in the slighter medium is quite rare in *Grimes*: the string accompaniment to Peter's answers in the courtroom scene and the woodwind's spiky comments exemplify one obvious kind, and the thinly accompanied solo double bass and bassoon in Carter Hobson's little piece another. But even the women's ensemble that ends Act II, Scene 1, though it is the music in the first opera most prophetic of *Lucretia*, exceeds the bounds of later possibilities in requiring as well as the woodwind seconds and string arpeggios a third vital plane of sound—muted-brass harmony.

Solo strings not only bring a subjective nervous intensity to harmonic textures that makes the typical restful, contained tutti sound impossible to achieve, but their tone is singularly difficult to quell: even with mutes, they can scarcely retreat to that faint yet firm background which tutti strings invaluably provide. Yet to obtain a forceful attack the composer must have recourse to multiple stopping and the consequent extreme roughness of timbre. Similarly in the wind section, homogeneity of sound, sometimes difficult enough to achieve given the full orchestra's complement of two or three of each species, can only be simulated by special methods and must remain an exceptional effect. In this new kind of opera orchestra, every sound tends to become not only exposed but 'characteristic': because we hear it as an entity we attribute to it a unique significance in the scheme. The endless flow of warm sound in which subtle textural and instrumental variants can be smoothly made, inflecting rather than contrasting—the Wagnerian orchestral sound, to cite its extreme form—is wholly outside the realm of chamber orchestra style. (The student interested to test the point can ponder on the two current ways of playing the *Siegfried Idyll*.)

And this elevation of every instrumental detail to a 'characteristic' rôle reinforces the need to adopt that set-piece treatment which is the antithesis of Wagnerian musico-dramatic principle. When the addition or subtraction of a tone colour always makes a point, the composer, if he is to avoid a ludicrous and ultimately self-defeating proliferation of events, must plan an act structure as a succession of predominant colourings, not a kaleidoscopic confusion, must adopt, indeed, something quite closely comparable to the Baroque practice seen in the obbligato aria. Our recollection of the *Lucretia* score is likely to be of whole pieces in which a certain instrumental lay-out, often with a particular instrument given a true soloist's rôle, is maintained. When each timbre can be so individual in its characterizing (and thus, often enough, in truly dramatic) significance, the composer has to solve the problem of those sections in which he wishes to suppress the more involved kind of instrumental commentary, to allow words to make their impact with the minimum of simultaneous interpretation. Britten's solution is simple enough: robbed of that neutral accompanimental sound which the massed strings provided in much of the *Grimes* recitative, he reverts to the true secco convention, using the piano. As this is never combined with the orchestra, the functional distinction is absolute, though, with a subtlety that must have been learnt from Mozart, he often passes through a varied middle ground of accompanied recitative.

No commentator seems able to withhold a reference to the scoring of Lucretia's sleep music. Its most distinctive colours, bass flute and bass clarinet, were to become a favoured Britten means of conjuring up the mystery of night (e.g., Albert's return to the darkened shop, 'Out on the lawn' in the Spring Symphony, and Variation XI of the *Screw*). Both instruments have a curiously hollow timbre (partly because we tend to hear them against the brighter norm of the standard instruments), and the muted horn used here shares something of the same drained quality. The addition of harp harmonics with the entry of the voice is delicately luminous, even the placing of the initial B in this C major context creating a unique sound impression (Ex. 1). But a catalogue of orchestral felicities in this opera would be long. The use of the harp and of double-bass glissando to depict the sounds of nature, and to suggest the tension within the stillness of the

Ex.6.1

evening music in Act I; the strummed double-bass fourths with the gong that punctuate the spinning-wheel music of the second scene; the wind/string duets that eventually merge to form a quartet in the flower music of Act II, Scene 2; all these are examples of the pure chamber-orchestral style that makes this score so memorable a series of colours. Yet the tutti writing, too, is not a mere travesty of the full orchestra's sound, but exploits the peculiar edginess of the medium, nowhere more powerfully than in Tarquinius' ride.

In this first chamber-opera, Britten with the aid of his librettist extended the wind/string symmetry of the orchestra to the casting, of four women and four men. Though each group is made up of three characters and a 'Chorus' commentator, dramatic and musical demands ensure a sharp contrast in the treatment of their ensembles. Of all the women only Lucretia is truly involved in the action; though her attendants Bianca and Lucia are strong 'characters', they are, as Patricia Howard has written, 'the two facets of Lucretia—Bianca has the virtue without the passion, Lucia the passion without (we suspect) the virtue'.[1] Since the Female Chorus speaks for all women, she identifies closely with the other three, and so homogeneity of ensemble is the predominant impression of the spinning quartet, where each character in turn exemplifies a proposition of the Female Chorus, of the linen folding trio and the duets in the last act. (It will be noted that all this music is associated with the mundane household tasks, the passive filling of time.) Of course, the rôles remain distinct, Lucia's line in the trio being the most ecstatic, and so on, but the sentiment is essentially uniform. The rich lyricism of these ensembles, perhaps Britten's most unremittingly beautiful, affords at first a startling relief (following immediately upon the Interlude depicting Tarquinius' ride), but ultimately its almost cloying quality acquires a terrible irony in the aubade and flower-song. By contrast, the men appear to achieve one mind only in their snatches of a drinking-chorus, and in Tarquinius and Junius' duet in recognition of man's questing mission; indeed, they sing simultaneously far less than do the women. Each has a crucial dramatic rôle, and is given a characteristic music through which to fulfil it. It is true that Junius and even Collatinus soon pale as Tarquinius

[1] Howard, p. 36.

moves into the centre of the action, so that one might be tempted to extend Mrs Howard's interpretation and view the opera simply as being concerned with the female and the male forces (i.e., regarding Junius and Collatinus as aspects of Tarquinius' ambivalent nature); certainly the crucial musical function of motives representing Lucretia and Tarquinius (a point to be discussed later) supports this reading. Even so, the vocal lines suggest that the men act as individuals while the women await events together.

So long as the two worlds, of men and of women, remain rigidly apart—in Act I, Scene 1 and the first part of Scene 2—the Male and Female Chorus respectively describe and comment individually. This allows a graphic representation of the invasion of one world by the other as the Female Chorus's picture of a sleeping Rome alternates with, and is finally swept away by, the Male Chorus's account of the last stages of Tarquinius' ride (Ex. 2). With

Ex. 6.2

the exception of this one bar, the two singers are heard together only in the mysterious one-ness of the octaves in which, standing outside time, they offer a Christian commentary on the drama. Their urgent pleas to Tarquinius as he struggles with Lucretia are an extension of this rôle, and the culmination of this scene in an unaccompanied quartet by the two protagonists and the two Choruses ('See how the centaur mounts the sky'), and compounded of key material from both planes, is daring but successful. As irrevocable tragedy is set in motion, we look on, conscious both of the immediate issue and of its reverberations through time. On the other hand, this withdrawal of the orchestral clamour ensures that in its resumption for the Interlude's hymn we hear a representation of the abiding issue ('virtue assailed by sin') rather than an extension of the parable itself. Discussion of the Choruses' rôle in the Passacaglia must be postponed, since the ensemble techniques of that climactic movement can only be evaluated in relation to its place in a large-scale tonal design.

Extended solos of aria-like balance are far less common than are elaborate ensembles. The Male Chorus's depiction of an uneasily still evening in Act I is countered in Act II by the Female Chorus's sleep music, still quieter and even more tense; both depend on reiterations that fray our nerves. Tarquinius and all the minor characters are each given one short solo statement. Collatinus strikes at first a noble tone (note the prevalent perfect fourths) that borders on the sententious, but as the motives become more bound up with Lucretia (see below, Ex. 7) he appears in a more sympathetic light. Junius can imitate the righteous tone (and does, at 'The wound in my heart'), but it is this serenity which rankles, as the orchestral commentary makes clear after Collatinus has withdrawn. Junius' own character emerges most vividly in the arch insinuation of the crime into Tarquinius' imagination, to innocuous woodwind consonance (though we might hear in the odd scoring of these, with clarinet in the bass, bassoon and horn higher up, a hint of treachery); his outburst on Lucretia's name is a rather too facile piece of motive elaboration. How Junius' words work on Tarquinius is left to the Male Chorus to indicate, and so Tarquinius' only extended solo 'Within this frail crucible' is sung as he watches the sleeping Lucretia (Ex. 3). Though the

Ex. 6.3

muffled timpani pedal puts an ominous edge on the music, these spacious lines give substance to the Chorus's comment 'the pity is, that sin has so much grace', for the sensual never threatens to decline into the lecherous. The attendant women's solos have only marginal comments to offer, but Bianca's memories of Lucretia's youth acquire a keen edge of pathos against the shadowy scherzo of string quartet and tambourine, a happiness she recalls but can no longer comprehend. The complexity of Lucretia's character becomes manifest only in and after the outrage, but her tiny arioso 'How cruel men are to teach us love' has shown a depth of yearning in its rising sevenths (even though Bianca had introduced them less passionately) that remains in our minds. In touching contrast, the arietta in which she twines the orchids into a wreath, against the woodwind's transformation of the earlier flower-music, has a vocal line that only painfully rises from monotone. And monotone becomes still more significant in the lines she utters to the purple mourning of the obbligato cor anglais (Ex. 4a), a norm against which her three great curving phrases, the last (Ex. 4b) spanning a heroic compass, acquire inordinate power.

Ex. 6.4 (a)

Ex. 6.4 (b)

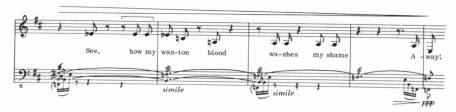

From the driest recitative (accompanied, as we have noted, by the piano) to the most lavish *cantabile*, Britten recognizes innumerable ratios in which verbal and musical qualities can be weighted, and he has acquired a much greater flexibility than *Grimes* showed in effecting transitions between them. This is why an opera so dependent on set-pieces, some of which may be counted indulgences to the ears rather than vital links in the dramatic chain, so rarely seems to hang fire: the instrumental figurations and colourings mark out the chief boundaries, but the vocal style is not abjectly subject to them. The opening pages of recitative, of the Chorus and of the men, are a virtuoso performance in pointed narrative—fundamentally syllabic so that any slurred syllable acquires innuendo, often enough monotone or conjunct for each bigger interval to give a specific weight of significance to the words, and often enough of matter-of-fact regularity in note-length for the pro- longations and accelerations to tell vividly. But still more music inhabits that middle ground where the singer maintains a very free relationship to the orchestra's coherent musical design, now concentrating on the etched rhythms of narrative, now reinforcing the instrumentalists' fabric; the Male Chorus's evening music provides the first example, his description of Tarquinius' ride one where narrative and quasi-instrumental functions are unified throughout. The consistency of tone that can be achieved across many changes of vocal style is nowhere more striking than in Lucretia's final scene: her first line (Ex. 5) sets up an attraction towards B that, as we shall

Ex. 6.5

see, remains powerful until (and meaningful after) her death, but it also sets up a habit of low monotone and disconsolately final scalic cadence (see, e.g., the superimposition of scalic cadences at Collatinus' 'I see only the image of eternity . . .') that draws together all the music of this scene.

No listener to this opera will fail to detect that another unifying force operating across its stylistic diversity is the use of motives. Indeed, there are moments at which the reiteration of the figure associated with Lucretia's name becomes an irritating labouring of the obvious; a shape so distinctive

Ex. 6.6

131

(Ex. 6*y*) tends to leap from the texture rather than to be sensed at work within it. Tarquinius' motive (Ex. 6*x*) is never used in this way to conjure up the syllables of his name; from the contexts in which it appears we may judge it to be rather a representation of that tyranny which his race exemplifies and that predisposition to sin from which his act springs. The two motives are, of course, of the identical stuff: Tarquinius' four-note figure, masculine in its scalically direct form and the generating force of the whole work, can be reconstructed in a more devious way so as to intertwine two feminine thirds. I take to be beyond dispute this general association of scale with male qualities and thirds with female; Eric Walter White's demonstration of the point is cogent,[2] and the Chorus's hymn 'Whilst we as two observers' (one male and one female) juxtaposes thirds and scales almost didactically. The scale that results from consistent extension of *x* is a regular alternation of tone and semitone steps (see Ex. 7c) and Britten uses this mode extensively,

Ex.6.7 (a)

Ex.6.7 (b)

Ex.6.7 (c)

Ex.6.7 (d)

Ex.6.7 (e)

[2] White, pp. 126 et seq.

Ex.6.7 (f)

fig. 30

Ex.6.7 (g)

TARQUINIUS

And I   am sub-ject to Lu - cre - tia

Ex.6.7 (h)

FEMALE CHORUS

Seek   -   ing   the   threads of   their   dreams

Ex.6.7 (i)

LUCRETIA

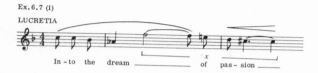

In - to   the   dream   of   pas - sion

Ex.6.7 (j)

after fig. 89

('The Prince bows over Lucretia's hand')

Ex.6.7 (k)

Act II
fig. 27

Ex.6.7 (l)

LUCRETIA

Yes,   I de - ny,   I de - ny.

Str.
+
Side
Drum

133

Ex.6.7 (m)

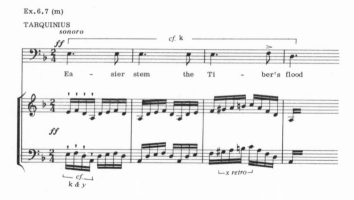

Ex.6.7 (n)

Ex.6.7 (o) i

Ex.6.7 (o) ii

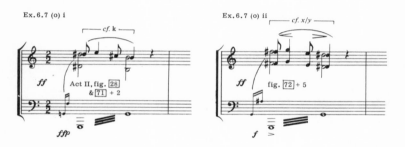

Ex.6.7 (p)

Ex.6.7 (q)

notably in the evening music; Ex. 7a and b show that piece's earlier derivatives from *x*. Similarly, the addition of two steps produces the minor third that dominates much more of the score than the direct *y* derivatives.

Sub-motives are formed by further rearrangement of the basic cell *x*, or of part of it. Thus Collatinus' reproach to Junius (Act I, fig. 26) is underlaid by a string texture developed from Ex. 7e, the first three notes of *y*, and this shape is later incorporated into a context which can be explained in terms of both *x* and *y* (see Ex. 7f). The same three notes, re-ordered, form a more crucial sub-motive in the rape scene (see Ex. 7k); as White has demonstrated, this thrusting of the horn's note within the oboe's minor third, an assertion of the male upon the female qualities, is a telling, yet extraordinarily economical, symbol of lust. A further re-ordering provides the head-motive of the Chorus's hymn following this scene (see Ex. 7n), close to *y*, but encompassing the total diminished-fourth in a way that is denied the participants in the action.

A complete list of *x* and *y* references would be long—and gratuitously insulting. Ex. 7 includes some of the less obvious and of the more debatable. No problem attaches to Ex. 7g or j, but they are fair examples of the ease with which Britten's motives, because of their identical constitution, can surely underline verbal points. In (h), sung by the Female Chorus, of women in general, and (i), sung by Lucretia, musical references to *x* (i.e., Tarquinius) drift into verbal references to passionate dreams, a circumstance which needs to be considered before the moral of the whole work is assessed. At Ex. 7(l) is a still more provocative reference, if it is one: *does* the orchestra conceal a recognition of Tarquinius at the very moment Lucretia denies him? It is true that later examples of these punctuating chords do not preserve this *x* content, but the last four (which are swept into a resumption of k) can again be heard in this light. Less debatable is Ex. 7m, where Tarquinius' line 'Easier stem the Tiber's flood', to sub-motive (k), is given an oddly Baroque illustration in the retrograde (i.e., turned-back) version of *x* that flits through the accompaniment figuration. The extension of (k) in Tarquinius' passionate demands is shown at Ex. 7o(i), but in Lucretia's feverish memories of the following scene it is soon distorted to o(ii), a pure *x/y* amalgam. Finally, two examples of the overwhelming presence of *x* and the burden of shame attached to it that haunt the closing section of the work: Ex. 7p is from Lucretia's own mourning music, and q marks the height of the Female Chorus's expression of despair at the human condition, just before a new hope is glimpsed (tonally, in the very next bar) and expounded by the Male Chorus. Nothing makes clearer the rôle of *x* as a symbol of man's universal weight of sin than this last reference and its subsequent expunction from the opera by the promise of redemption.

While the pronounced impression of unified material is clearly a result of these ubiquitous references to, and textural developments of, the basic motives, dramatic purposes are often served by a quite literal return of

135

material. Whether this serves a structural end, too, depends on the extent of the quotation and its assimilation into the musical context. Thus, as Lucretia, on her monotone low B, spells out to Collatinus the shame that has engulfed her, the orchestra punctuates with laconic memories of each stage of her traumatic experience; the dissociation of these from their context gives them a taunting quality. But when she summons up a *cantabile* line for 'O my love, our love was too rare', the connected paragraph has a structural force too: it brings back, with an aptitude that is moving, not a motive but a theme (Ex. 8) that has recurred across the opera, always with new relevance to its first text. Its other reappearances have been during Tarquinius' ride and in the unaccompanied ensemble that withdraws us from the enaction of the rape, to press home in metaphor its significance; increasingly, therefore, its occurrences acquire a strong cohesive effect.

Ex. 6.8

Peter Grimes could be seen to rely at certain cardinal points (and most obviously across the scheme of its Interludes) on the relationship between two opposed keys, A and E flat, but much of the material ranged widely and apparently discursively between these poles. It is no truer to say that *Lucretia* is an opera 'in C' than to describe *Grimes* as being 'in A', but it is certainly true to say that it is 'about C'. Far more than in *Grimes* we sense other tonal areas to represent significant departures from the one centre; the two chief deviations in Act II, C sharp and B, semitonal tugs in opposite directions, set up a tension that is only released by the Christian *deus ex machina* of the Male Chorus's return to C major. The details of this process are a good deal more complex, and we probably leave more loose ends in any tonal explanation of this opera's workings than in charting, say, the more schematic A–A flat conflict of *Turn of the Screw*. But we need only consider how many other subsequent Britten works oscillate between semitonally opposed areas (e.g., *Billy Budd, A Midsummer-Night's Dream*, Act I, and the Nocturne) to recognize how fundamental a rôle such a quasi-dramatic deployment of key plays in all his extended structures.

To say 'quasi-dramatic' is not to assume that the composer relied on some simplistic equation whereby key X represents one character or quality, key Y its opposite; tonal symbols must discharge satisfactory tonal *functions*, the tensions must make musical points that balance across the work. This, after all, is the basis of classical structural thought, and indeed, one need only pursue the extension of that thought practised by composers like Schubert and Bruckner to justify Britten's kind of process without reference to specific situations represented on the stage. He had employed it long before turning to opera (see the violin concerto's first movement for an unusual example), but, given an operatic context, it is not unreasonable to look for correspondences of some kind between this 'quasi-dramatic' musical action and the overtly dramatic sequence.

Excluding many short-lived centres (especially in the recitative sections) we might represent the tonal plan of the opera as follows. Capitals represent major mode, lower case the minor.

Act I, Sc. 1:	c–V of C(c)–g–b–b♭♮(B♭)b♭–e♭'(E♭)–c–e–(G)g
Interlude:	E♭–G–C–E♭
Act I, Sc. 2:	B♭–E–B♭–d–E–[E♭ GCE♭]–c
	└ wandering ┘
Act II, Sc. 1:	c♯–V of A(a)–C/E–c♯ ᵐᵒᵈᵘˡᵃᵗⁱⁿᵍ e♭
Interlude:	d imposed upon chaos
Act II, Sc. 2:	A [ᵗᵒᵘᶜʰⁱⁿᵍ ᵒⁿ b–c–c♯]–V of C–c–b–c♯–CB/C–C
	bass
	(modifications above)

Already it can be seen that the first act is far more simply balanced than the second. It begins and ends in C minor and its principal moves preserve basic relationships to that central key. Scene 1, apart from the major/minor ambivalence of the Chorus hymn ('Whilst we as two observers') has a bias towards minor modes that palpably symbolizes the men's heavy spirits; and only at two points, the toast to Lucretia and the duet 'What makes the Nubian', do these minor modes turn markedly away from flat key areas. In Tarquinius' ride, however, action after wearing inactivity, E flat major is set up as centre and the subsidiary themes use major modes too, G and C. Even so, these are still felt to be within the orbit of C minor, whereas the bright majors of the women's music in Scene 2 take us into an entirely contrasted world. The quartet sets off from and returns to B flat major (approximately) but is soon exploring keys as sharp as E major, and a pronounced Lydian penchant brightens the tone still further; the curious little arietta 'How cruel men are', in something near D minor, appropriately marks a glance towards the minor-mode area of Scene 1, but the linen-folding takes place to music of the most serene E major. Thereafter, however, reminders of every stage of Tarquinius' ride music, semitonally depressing the women's music and then sweeping it away, are ominous, so that the C minor which ends the act (to reiterations of the Tarquinius motive, accompanied by conspicuous 'feminine' thirds in the bass) is even heavier with portent than was the opening of the opera.

137

Act II at once establishes a new area, C sharp minor, with a theme that is later (after fig. 10) specifically associated with prophecies of violence. The Chorus hymn, still betokening observation rather than intervention, does not seriously challenge the new orbit with its dominant pedal of A (major/minor), but Lucretia's slumber (see Ex. 1) is in a white-note C major that, as elsewhere in Britten, can be taken to symbolize innocence. That being accepted, the opening of the rape scene in a restored C sharp minor seems to give that key the converse significance, as a symbol of sin. This leaves out of account the E major in which Tarquinius approaches the sleeping Lucretia (Ex. 3, above); but we have seen already that the Chorus's comment 'the pity is that sin has so much grace, It moves like virtue' has relevance to this aria, and so the E here is an *alter ego* of C sharp minor rather than a direct reference back to the key of the women's music of the previous act. The rape scene moves swiftly through many tonal fields, since a bass ascending semitonally is one of its chief sources of cumulative tension. Yet its opening is as clear in its C sharp minor tonality as in the symbolism of the motives (see above); the long stretch notated with two flats is full of wider tonal meanings—one particularly succinct opposition occurring to revealing words (Ex. 9)—and the outcome of the scene is the E flat minor into which

Ex.6.9

the unaccompanied quartet draws the music. Thus C/E has been followed by C sharp minor leading to E flat minor, and a logical outcome of this narrowing procedure is the D minor which the Chorus hymn (strongly marked by its C sharp–E flat inflexions) sustains against the tonal chaos of the orchestra's furious development. In a sense, therefore, this D minor finds a point of equipoise between the warring forces that have been let loose in the scene. Perhaps the procedure is here more structural than symbolic: certainly I should hesitate to assign to D minor any specific rôle in a wider account of the act's tonality. Indeed, the establishment of a D centre might seem to throw serious doubts on a reading of this act as concerned with C sharp (sin) and C (innocence). But one colour is still missing from the picture: it begins to emerge, after the ironically beautiful aubade and flower song, at Lucretia's first words 'Oh, if it were all a dream' on a low B. This is the voice of her shame, and perhaps of her remorse, for the loss of innocence

138

must induce a sense of guilt (as Collatinus tragically fails to understand); this is a point that must be considered more fully later. Her impassioned, even hysterical, soliloquy on the orchid (fig. 71) is a tortured recognition that Tarquinius' act (constantly recalled in the motives) puts for ever beyond her the world towards which the endless G natural pedal is striving. That pedal is released in C, in fact, minor not major, but Lucretia's little song as she makes a wreath never achieves a C-centred line: as she says 'Flowers alone are chaste. Let their pureness show my grief'. The B has already returned as a dark frame round Bianca's memories, whatever the accompanying scherzo's apparent gaiety, and after the longest stretch of piano-accompanied reci-tative in the work, Lucretia and the orchestra return to work out the full implications of B minor, in which the great adagio is set. The ironic twist of the Neapolitan C natural at the climax of the cor anglais solo is the most poignantly immediate touch of tonal symbolism in the work. Lucretia's confession to Collatinus was discussed above: only with the last of its three flights to escape from that obsessive B does the vocal line succeed, and this coincides with her suicide.

There follows the culminating ensemble of the work, a funeral march in passacaglia form. As discussion of this was postponed earlier, we may note here the nature of its ensemble techniques as well as its contribution to the tonal argument. With more singers heard together than at any other time, we are most conscious at this point of the missing two central characters. Ground-bass was recognized already in the seventeenth century as a pecu-liarly fitting vehicle for elegiac expression: it offers no release from an endless elaboration of sorrow. Though Britten was to use a comparable kind of structure in the Threnody of *Albert Herring* for a *tour de force* of characterization, he is not intent in this ensemble on illuminating nice distinctions: Lucia and Bianca share their grief in the warm thirds and sixths that have characterized their common language, and after Junius' oppor-tunistic burst of demagogism his declamatory phrases are not significantly differentiated from those of Collatinus. Despite a ground which, out of context, suggests E major (Ex. 10), only the variations dominated by the

Ex.6.10

women's Lydian inflexions (cf. their Act I music) escape harmonization in a C sharp minor sense. The Female Chorus's entry momentarily brings a new note (of rather highflown metaphor, incidentally) which coincides with a trans-fer of the ground (the burden of man's sin) to the upper part of the orchestra: equally striking is the move to a C natural (minor/major) orientation as the wreath is placed on Lucretia's head. But the burden invades all parts as the tonality swings back to C sharp. The singers' lines move towards ever closer and eventually complete identification in an octave passage ('How is it possible?') that seeks, more powerfully than before, to assert C major against the ground, but is swept back into limp reiterations of its final thirds, 'It is all'. This unanimity of hopelessness is the logical end of the drama: we have seen the last of its characters, locked inside that Hell which the Female Chorus describes in a declamatory passage of despair over human suffering and sin. The question 'Is it all?' flutters still in the background, often aspiring towards a C natural area, but held back by the fatalistic C sharp wind chords that underpin her narrative. Only after the climactic line (see Ex. 7q) do the thirds get support as a fragile dominant of C, and the Male Chorus momentously resolves this with his first words of hope (Ex. 11). This intensely beautiful recitative brings to bear on all that

Ex.6.11

has gone before the Christian message of redemption. Thus Lucretia's B minor of remorse can be purified into a serene B major ('For now He bears our sin and does not fall') that glorifies Christ's passion—human wickedness and death again, but that from which our salvation was wrought. Through this music there begin to sound intimations of C major, and in a few bars of intensely imaginative writing, where 'the accompaniment is powdered with major and minor thirds—the minor predominating—spread over the entire orchestral compass, like stars that come out in the firmament after sunset',[3] the last move is made to C for a final statement of the Chorus's opening hymn, now on an eternally sure tonic pedal. C major is not a restoration of

[3] Ibid. p. 132.

Lucretia's innocence but rather the achievement of a state of blessedness, throwing a glow back on the whole cycle of experience.

Of course, this protracted discussion of tonal operations can be dismissed as entirely subjective; I have no evidence at all that Britten made decisions for reasons I have suggested and at few points may one claim that the next move is 'inevitable'. But I believe that some terms such as those of this reading help to explain what we experience in the musical processes, and I consider that Britten has made unequivocally clear elsewhere how naturally attracted he is towards such a fusion of structural function and symbolic function in his tonal designs.

There remain two further questions which any writer on this opera has to face: is the Christian framework necessary, and does it in fact provide a logical commentary on the action? Other listeners may share my own discomfort, not so much at the framing contrivance which Ronald Duncan borrowed from his model, Obey's *Le Viol de Lucrèce*, as at his employing it to introduce Christian values which seem at odds with his declared intention to symbolize 'spirit defiled by Fate'. To construct such a metaphor, no frame at all would have been needed: the tragedy could have been played out entirely in its own terms and the universal resonances would have been sensed. And Mrs Howard has admirably demonstrated that, once we are introduced to the Christian doctrine of forgiveness, we are not concerned with Fate any longer but with sin.[4] However, given this transfer, I do not believe the work to be falsely argued. She claims that 'Lucretia has not sinned in a Christian sense, so no forgiveness is necessary', and if we accept this, then the epilogue must seem gratuitous. As may be clear from various references in the foregoing pages, my own reading is one that would justify the epilogue (on grounds other than the rightness of its musical function and its singularly rarefied music), for I find much incidental detail that builds up to a view of Lucretia as at once revolted by Tarquinius' assault and horrifyingly attracted towards the realization of a nightmare. Her struggles are real enough and, in this sense, she could be said physically to have defended her innocence, but her mental torture after the event suggests a recognition that revulsion and attraction can co-exist, that some part of her has shared the guilt. A brief review of the chief references on which this view is based must suffice.

A whole group of references can be held to imply that Tarquinius has exercised a powerful fascination in Lucretia's dreams; two examples have been cited at Ex. 7h and i. The second of these is the more convincing: even though the little piece in which it occurs—

    How cruel men are
    To teach us love
    They wake us from

4 Howard, p. 43.

> The sleep of youth
> Into the dream of passion
> Then ride away
> While we still yearn

—can at the moment be related only to Collatinus' absence and clearly has this surface meaning to Lucretia herself, the shadow of the Tarquinius motive is disturbing; in retrospect the whole passage can appear to foretell his intervention. It recurs when he confronts Lucretia at the end of the act (after 89): again, Collatinus is the foreground reference, Tarquinius a scarcely less plausible object of her agitation. And in her still greater agitation on being awakened by Tarquinius she lets fall the most revealing phrase of all:

> In the forest of my dreams
> You have always been the Tiger.

after which it is fitting that her first words of her final scene should be:

> Oh, if it were all a dream
> Then waking would be less a nightmare.

Other details are less consistently related. Tarquinius' taunt—

> Yet the linnet in your eyes
> Lifts with desire
> And the cherries of your lips
> Are wet with wanting

—is one of the memories that tortures her in her confession to Collatinus, and the orchestrally concealed x motive that accompanies her rejection of Tarquinius has been referred to above (see Ex. 7(l)). No doubt the hysteria of the scene with her women makes uncertain what weight can be attached to Lucretia's self-accusation, but one further pointer can be mentioned from the rape scene itself: the Chorus repeatedly urge Tarquinius to go, and they add

> Go! Before your nearness
>   Tempts Lucretia to yield
>   To your strong maleness!

It seems plausible therefore to assume that the Male Chorus's words in the epilogue—

> Though our nature's still as frail
> And we still fall

—do not refer to Tarquinius' frailty.

Alternative explanations for each of these moments is possible, and in basing some of these comments on Britten's treatment of Duncan's text and others on the text itself I have not been entirely consistent. But to accept the simpler alternatives is to be left with Mrs Howard's problem when the Christian epilogue is reached. Perhaps one is also left with Lucretia as a character who too patently symbolizes, rather than as one in whom the amalgam of human qualities is richly and curiously compounded. The drama that I find to exist within Britten's musical working-out of this theme seems to me proper to the second of these.

7 Albert Herring

Eric Crozier, who had produced *Lucretia*, provided the libretto for Britten's next chamber-opera, which followed within a year and was also first presented at Glyndebourne—though now by the English Opera Group. Crozier took his story from Maupassant's *Le Rosier de Madame Husson*, but transplanted it to a Sussex environment, where every person could become a familiar kind of English 'character' and local jokes could do duty for Maupassant's barbed ironies. Instead of the studied symmetries of the *Lucretia* casting, Britten was presented with a large number of individuals who find identity in the community. Such a cast gave opportunities for a wide range of ensembles, and the absence of a chorus meant that the density of tone of the most elaborate ensemble textures could take the place of the simple sonorities proper to massed voices. He retained the *Lucretia* orchestral forces for the new opera score, since so fundamentally contrasted an emotional world ensured his devising a new range of colours.

It was possible to see in *The Rape of Lucretia* a commentary on human conduct and its inherent predisposition to tragedy that made redundant the imposed reading in terms of Christian morality. When the flaws and the follies of human character influence events, all our experience makes us ready to believe in a progress towards catastrophe. This needs neither to be shrugged off as implacable fate nor to be transcended in the Christian doctrine of redemption for us to be harrowed: it is a deeper recognition of our own nature which most moves us in contemplating what has befallen others. In turning from tragedy on an antique story (and thus one already associated with a dense fabric of sonorous legend and ponderous meaning) to a domestic comedy of a period just distant enough to encourage the distorted view of ridicule, Britten might seem to have essayed an altogether lighter task, throwing off the burden of remorseless catharsis. But if comedy is to rise above the level of farce, the merest recording of foibles and mishaps, then it must depend on a chain of ambivalence, of subtly-afforded glimpses of a plane of experience on which the 'comic' incident has more sobering implications. That all comes out well in the end is likely to be virtually irrelevant on this other plane: here the end is to be found in terms of a 'moral', never in itself a mirth-provoking reflection on human behaviour.

It is clear that in those comic operas we most prize, above all, of course, those of Mozart, a fundamental awareness of this duality of experience, of the general implications behind the particular incidents, has influenced the quality of nominally 'entertaining' musical invention. Yet there has been no factitious introduction of portentous musical undercurrents; few musical phenomena more successfully resist really pointed analysis than does that poignancy we sense in many a radiant context of Mozart. That we do sense it so exactly tells us far more about the composer's assimilated understanding of human motivation than about any conscious exploitation by him of compositional techniques calculated to uncover an emotional sub-stratum. To write a comic opera that has no moral is to court frivolity, of however elegant an order, but to write one in order to expound a moral is to court inflation.

Britten's purpose in writing *Albert Herring* could have been no more than a wish to entertain by apt caricature of the familiar. Five years after making his decision to return to England, he might well have chosen simply to pay that tribute of affection which is shown in gentle mockery. Certainly the world he depicts is made up of characters who are more determinedly English than those of Grimes's borough; yet their failings, however ludicrous they may appear in distortion, are uniformly mild. Petty self-importance and pruriency were manifest in *Grimes* (in such characters as Swallow and Mrs Sedley, for example), but they were part of a climate in which brutality to a child and the hunting-down of a man could acquire a fearful inevitability. In *Herring* they are the foibles of a community in which no character takes on the solid flesh in which the canker of evil can flourish. As has often been remarked, there are times when, with disconcerting rapidity, the parody of their intense emotions takes on a musical intensity that is not at all humorous. But this is not central to the opera's aim: these characters exist principally as representative elements of an environment that is inhibiting Albert's self-discovery. And it is in accepting or rejecting Albert's initiation as a credible pattern of human experience that we determine whether the work involves us in more than a *divertissement*. Evidently enough, there is a moral to be drawn from this comedy: in Albert's words, 'It was all because you squashed me down and reined me in . . . my only way out was a wild explosion'. Whether or not it is a persuasive one depends on our ability consistently to identify with such a hero, to recognize the inevitability and the efficacy of the cycle of events through which he is emancipated.

Peter Grimes had shown how effectively Britten could adapt the 'characteristic' qualities of his early instrumental style to the depiction of minor figures in the drama. Indeed, there his vignettes could seem too nimbly sketched, too prettily coloured, so that they became momentarily isolated from the flow of incident. *Albert Herring* offered an opportunity to give much freer rein to this talent, for the trivia of these small-town characters' eccentricities are now more directly relevant in formulating the suffocating

145

ethos against which Albert rebels. But some critics have felt that, in attempting to make us both recognize each of these type-characters and laugh at their absurdities, Britten too easily gave play to a strain of schoolboy facetiousness which (as Newman thought[1]) reduced the work to the level of a charade; similar objections have to be weighed in judging the rustics' play in *A Midsummer-Night's Dream*. To pigeonhole stock characters Britten draws on stock musical idioms, of more or less appropriate period. Yet to import into his score the literal phraseology of, say, the Victorian anthem, would be to create an embarrassing stylistic incongruity and an implication that the imported style is self-evidently amusing. Though many superior persons may hold such a view, it is in fact peculiarly myopic. The harmonic clichés of the type will always remain unsubtle, but this provides no reason for our overlooking the essential seriousness of purpose that contributed to their assembly. If we are to be amused by characters who naturally draw on one fund of cliché or another (which in terms of everyday existence would mean the vast majority of our fellows—not forgetting ourselves), it must be because of the distortion that is the composer's own comment, the twist by which he suggests, not the falsity of a sentiment, but rather its disproportion to the situation.

The range of musical models is rather wider than the specified date of 1900 might appear to support; their appropriateness to a character's mode of speech and of feeling is the chief criterion. There is no period switch comparable in exuberance to that by which, thirteen years later, Britten cast the whole Pyramus play in terms of nineteenth-century Italian opera. But if we consider a single character, the Vicar, we shall hear in his little air in Act I strong echoes of the vintage Victorian drawing-room ballad ('Is Albert virtuous . . .'), supplanted in his speeches at the feast ('to introduce her Ladyship . . .') by the more 'tasteful' lines, with even an incipient folkyness, of the first decade of this century. Both help to convey an essential worthiness, tinged with aspirations he does not altogether trust (as his delightful hesitancy in reaching for *le mot juste* makes clear). The man is a prisoner to certain conventions, of his time and of his cloth, but he is not a humbug. He takes no part in the jeering which, under the thin disguise of good-humoured raillery, follows Albert's desperately short speech of thanks. And, if the consolation he offers Mrs Herring when she believes herself bereaved is so practised as to appear at first sanctimonious, as the quartet goes on, and we are involved in the tug between easy grief and noble restraint, the summing-up by the Vicar and Miss Wordsworth (curiously arousing a memory of Balstrode at the denouement of *Grimes*), 'In such an hour we scarcely dare pretend/We have the power to help our friend', rises musically far beyond the sphere of parody techniques, to one of Britten's most powerful chromatic epigrams (see Ex. 1).

[1] E. Newman, 'Mr Britten and *Albert Herring*', *Sunday Times*, June 29 and July 6 1947.

Ex.7.1

Miss Wordsworth, lost in hopeless admiration for the Vicar, often echoes his eager piety, but her own vocation is realized in parodies of that flaccid music thought appropriate to the English board schools and only recently finally banished from our educational system. Here the models are so wretched that even to parody them may lend a subtlety that destroys their quintessential vapidity; 'Glory to our new May King' is the most straight-faced piece in the opera, undermined only (though devastatingly) by a few jolts in its anguishedly rigid accompaniment. Yet the preparations for its performance show a livelier spirit in Miss Wordsworth than she is capable of injecting into her pupils, and this fluttering whimsicality makes plausible her speech at the feast: she may not be very certain of their direction, but she spins these lines with all the fervour of a thwarted poetess or *prima donna*. Some characters undergo no such intensification. Budd, the police super-intendent, is characterized throughout by brooding, stolidly repetitive, phrases, delivered after the manner of a brass band trombone solo. The Mayor, on the other hand, feels on all matters, not excluding his council's legendary water main, with the ready passions of an Italian tenor, whose highly-strung style he constantly emulates—even to a penchant for secco rapid-fire. Not unexpectedly, therefore, his most glorious moment comes with his Verdian contribution to the celebration of Albert's death. Florence Pike's character is more elusive, for she is allowed no convention distinc-tively her own. All too often she must simply reinforce—with a vindictive-ness that is the greater precisely because she is relegated to the rôle of a mouthpiece—the sentiments of her mistress. Her outburst provoked by Sid's late arrival in Act II neatly translates a Lady Billows-like indignation

147

into the more vulgar, jaunty rhythms of the music-hall, but only at one moment, at her 'But oh! sometimes I wish', early in Act I, is a revealing development promised, and the deputation's entrance cuts it short.

Lady Billows remains in the memory after most productions of this opera as the grossest caricature of all. But we should differentiate between the ridicule her words attract and that implicit in the music. It is true that at times she is personified by an inane flatulence in both speech and song. 'Rejoice, my friends', with its stale memories of Handelian bravura, its sycophantically homophonic choral responses and its 'loftiness' of language ('Her crown of simple and *refulgent* splendour') has many of the hallmarks of the Anglican festival anthem of the late nineteenth century. 'We bring great news to you' has the swagger of Empire-builders' music, and the bland preference it shows for rhythmic uniformity over verbal stress is in keeping. Like so much of the bad music in which this country took pride, this piece is distinguished by the dissolution of every phrase, however ambitious, in a weak cadential cliché. Even the splendidly momentous prelude's dominant pedal (over which the orchestra develops the Investigations theme) is reduced to fatuity by its cadential formula; that this should in fact land upon the 6/4, i.e., fail even to achieve its object, adds to the irony. But Lady Billows's two set pieces are less easily dismissed. Her aria of rage, 'Is this all you can bring', is a well developed piece, typical Britten in its unifying accompaniment figure and its varied strophic structure that, because of pitch shifts, is accommodated within one big linear span. The range of emotion, from eruptions of shrill fury to lachrymose self-pity and back again, is perhaps extravagant, but in another dramatic context it would not seem laughable and might be powerfully relevant. Once again, it is in the cadences that the deflation occurs, their banality being now underlined by Florence's obsequious repetitions; the intrusion of the striking clock upon the final cadence adds a gratuitous touch of farce. Lady Billows's speech at the feast is more fitful musically, including flagrantly disproportionate gestures like the vast fanfare arpeggio at 'the Loxford Urban District May Day Feast' side-by-side with the warm lyricism from 'Dear children', not significantly different in tone from entirely earnest moments in some of Britten's most direct works, like *The Little Sweep* or *Saint Nicolas*. If parody is intended in such a phrase as 'Think, oh think of Albert', then it can only be of Britten's own style. Crozier's text, with its uproarious succession of *non sequitur* quotations, spares an audience all subtlety of nuance, and Britten's later introduction of a phrase from *Rule, Britannia* transfers the music on to the same plane. But the habitual craft is still there, and is put to telling uses. The lyrical paragraph referred to acquires its urgent fervour from an insistent yet disoriented pedal (initially a leading-note), and this takes on a sudden triumphant tonic meaning with Lady Billows's arrival at that vice, Drink, which in her calendar outstrips all others. The *da capo* form too is piquantly handled: the music of her opening remarks returns to sentiments that are ludicrously different—yet apparently near enough to each other in her drastically simplified world-view, of good things and bad.

If all these characters represent the deadweight of small-town respectability which Albert eventually strives to throw off, his mother, herself not quite of the respectable set, provides frustrations of a more immediate and galling kind. To her, 'virtue' is sound economic sense, servility a self-evident requirement in human relationships. She demands both of her son with a command of automatically dismissive phrase calculated to make a moron of him. Even in the pseudo-gentility with which she addresses her betters the same tone can be heard (though tonal frictions betray some uncertainty), for Britten makes hers the only character picture in this opera that depends consistently on the deployment of a single motive. Occasional glimpses of her cultural bearings are afforded by overt parody of popular music, as in the second-hand sentimentality of 'Sleeping the sleep of the just' or the much-admired seaside music which comments poignantly on her grief. But the range of emotional situations to which Britten adapts the one scalic motive can be gauged from the following examples:

Ex.7.2 (a)

Ex.7.2 (b)

Ex.7.2 (c)

Ex.7.2 (d)

And the influence of this motive penetrates further: for example, in the quartet, where Mrs Herring acquires an apparently new *idée fixe*, of maudlin chromatic grief (its scalic nature in fact already establishes a link), the accompanying orchestral semiquavers are derived from her previous abject 'all, all'—itself the end of the motive. The result is that, despite her having fewer set pieces than many of the caricatured figures discussed above, Mrs Herring is able to emerge musically as one of the strongest personalities in the work.

For quite other reasons, Sid's musical character is a vital agency in the drama. He is consistently depicted in terms of a kind of popular song (post- rather than pre-World War I, in fact) that wonderfully captures the warmth, excitement and slightly illicit atmosphere which so disturbs Albert's peace of mind. In the everyday world of greengrocers and butchers, Sid is already an unnerving figure for his nonchalant acceptance of a freedom Albert has not dared to imagine, but in the nocturnal world of his relationship with Nancy, his example is still more alluring. However hackneyed the sentiments in which his songs reach their peak ('I love you', luxuriously protracted), these are full of suppressed energy and mystery; they are among Britten's finest achievements in *Albert Herring*. Critics who hold that his lovers too often lack conviction should not undervalue Sid and Nancy: the courting of the girl from the bakery by the butcher boy can have its illuminating flashes of truth if the composer does not patronize (a failing of which Tippett is sometimes guilty in the treatment of his mechanic and secretary, Jack and Bella). Though the couple sing limpidly diatonic lines, Britten refuses to oversim- plify, and his attendant details enrich these characters immeasurably.

The sequence in which Sid expounds his philosophy to Albert makes a heady introduction for the disciple. His recital of pleasures in a jaunty D major (Act I, fig. 68) throws into relief the swing to opulent harmonies of C sharp major as he settles down to elaborate on 'the King of all sports'. Sequential formulae are overdone in this little aria, for its crooning rep- etitions show Sid mocking himself as much as Albert. But with Nancy's arrival his romantic yearnings are focused in the seductive harp arpeggio at fig. 71: this 'peaches/kisses' motive is to recur as a symbol of all the excite- ments Albert has missed. The assignation is made to softly undulating woodwind harmony punctuated by the violins' wolf-whistle (a less inventive composer would certainly have reversed the rôles); the melody, unremark- able in itself, is given a teasing momentum by deft phrase extensions before each clipped cadence. After a few bars of unaccompanied ensemble, in which Albert's embarrassment is finely counterpointed, the couple sing their touchingly happy song in octaves while the orchestra adds undercurrents: 'arm in arm' calls for a canon 2 in 1 (compare Brahms's 'Wir wandelten'), and its dotted rhythms and syncopations suggest a nonchalance that the urgently pacing bass crotchets belie (Ex. 3). Albert's rueful survey of his mundane existence is only the first symptom of his infection by this fever.

After the indignities of the May Day feast (quite as much as the rum), the attraction of Sid's world becomes irresistible. Musing on it and, more

151

Ex.7.3

specifically, on Nancy, Albert begins unconsciously to ape that strain of popular sentimentality which is Sid's *forte*, in 'Why did she stare'. The articulateness he discovers through this romantic *Angst* is already startling, but still more remarkable is his ability to sense in advance the quickened pulse of the lovers' duet (i.e., his anticipation at fig. 78 of the fig. 80 music). The duet therefore only confirms a vision that has come to obsess his thoughts, of 'love and adventure'. It is the most elaborate of the couple's pieces in its rhythmic variety, its ambiguities of key and its structure—of two strophes (solo, then canonic), interlude (the kiss motive) and a third strophe (unison). The nervous excitement of its accompaniment and the latent sadness of so many drooping phrases, countered by the hopeful appeal of their inversions, are compounded in a complex mood. The orchestra's glissando-accelerando which symbolizes the protraction of the kiss gives a questionable edge of mockery to what is essentially a serious piece—as Sid's urgently monotoned 'Nancy', which quells the driving rhythms to create this interlude, has made clear. Certainly it is vital that this duet should have the ring of truth, for it immediately triggers off in Albert a cry of despair that is far from comic.

In Act III, Sid's rôle is essentially completed, but Nancy's character is given more definition, first in a lament for the folly of their act, 'What would Mrs Herring say'. Her artless short lines, of uniform metre, are given pathos by their incorporation, through the clarinets' expressive arabesques and the dominant pedal against which the harmonies tug, into a single musical paragraph: the Mahlerian quality of the cadence figure is highlighted by the banality of its deeply-felt words: 'We did it for fun:/Oh, we shouldn't have done'. The transfer of the pedal up a minor third in the third stanza produces an intensification bordering on panic, while the return to the original area for the refrain is the more powerful for now leading to the fatalistic full close avoided in the early stanzas. Nancy's edgy response to Sid, 'You're heartless', provokes a duet of frayed nerves, in pointed contrast to all their earlier music. But Nancy is at her best in the simple contribution she makes to the quartet, her reassurances steering a middle course between Mum's lugubrious burden of grief and the enveloping consolation of the Vicar and Miss Wordsworth.

It remains to consider what kind of character Albert's music makes of him. It is easier to catalogue what he resents and what he envies than to decide what he is and will be. For, although all the other characters exist to represent statically their conflicting qualities and his is the only one in which we see a fundamental development, we are still left uncertain of its true nature. From his first appearance we must discount Budd's description of him, 'a bit simple, of course': however spare and strained his speech throughout Sid's banter and flirting, Albert's musical delivery loses the automatic quality of his polite conversation as soon as he is left alone, and reveals well-developed powers of introspection. In tiny stanzas, each more elaborate in melodic detail as the details of the picture become more telling, he worries over the futility of his lot. (This kind of obsessive soliloquy is not new: we met it before in another character whose real existence had withdrawn into a private world—Peter Grimes, in the successive elaborations of his dream of domestic bliss in Act II, Scene 2.) The moral is drawn in measured terms (see Ex. 4), establishing a theme that is to play a crucial rôle

Ex.7.4

in later events. Its first two spans, with E and F sharp as sustained peaks, return conflated in the orchestra at fig. 79 as Albert recapitulates his train of thought after Emmie's interruption. But now his aspirations take wing in a third phrase, 'Oh, maybe soon I'll have the chance to get away', which, in achieving an A flat peak, symbolically bursts free from the mediant pedal that has held all this music in check. The theme is constantly remembered in Albert's first ineffectual attempts at revolt, after the deputation has left him

Ex. 7.5

with his mother (see Ex. 5), and eventually sings through the orchestra with an eloquence he dare not muster; as yet the competition of Mum's motive (Ex. 2a, above) is insuperable, as the last bars of the act demonstrate.

Throughout the feast we see Albert only as a virtually mute victim in the May Day rituals and as the hiccoughing victim of Sid's practical joke. But it is noteworthy that the May King motive of Act I, derided by Albert himself in his argument with Mum ('Why should they come and dress me up, like a blinking swan') is never used in Act II to its original text (the new anthem, 'Albert the Good', takes its place) but has become a much less crude motive, an expressive symbol of Albert's yearning to escape from the cloistered virtue thrust upon him. The horn solo that opens the act, with its flat seventh twist, establishes the new significance, and the fusion at the beginning of Scene 2 of this form (x in Ex. 6) with chromatic stirrings derived from the *Tristan* motive makes an important statement about Albert's development.

Ex. 7.6

(Beautiful though it is, the preludial nocturne from which this emerges is not peculiar to Albert: it accompanies his mother's return to the darkened shop at the end of the scene.) Albert's irreverent memories of the feast (the fugal version of the anthem and the vicar's unction) and his Tristanesque address to the matches as he lights the gas are entertaining enough, but drink appears, in rendering him garrulous, also to have turned him into a facetious idiot who is not easily squared with the earlier picture. The recall of Wagner's Love-potion motive (first heard as he drank the lemonade-and-rum at the feast) now acquires a keener relevance in that it prompts thoughts not only of the drink but of Nancy; the eloquence Albert discovers at this point has been discussed. As we have seen, he is learning Sid's tone even if, as so often, his memories must be tinged with some bitterness, as in his 'We never talked or walked', where the orchestra drily parodies the canonic theme of the Act I duet.

The first statement that is entirely his own is made at the crucial point of the opera, after he has heard with horror Sid and Nancy discuss his plight. Though the semiquaver motive from their duet spins through the orchestra ('like Catherine-wheels') in unpredictably juxtaposed diatonic scale segments that suggest Albert's dazed condition, his line is etched with the grimness of self-recognition and shame. But he soon takes characteristic refuge in distorting the music of his tormentors: the rhythms that punctuated 'Albert the Good' snigger as he devises his own embittered (and now defensively facetious) version of the anthem. Below this, the scalic shape of Ex. 4 is stirring in the orchestra, and its challenge quickly provokes the crisis. How typical it is of Britten that at this point he recalls one of the most trivial moments in the work: the cuckoo-clock music that interrupted the conference at Lady Billows's intrudes as Albert senses time flying from him (it is the eleventh hour that strikes):

> The tide will turn, the sun will set,
> While I stand here and hesitate . . .
> The clock begins its rusty whirr,
> Catches its breath to strike the hour,
> And offers me a final choice
> That must be answered No or Yes.

That we do not find this orchestral detail amusingly incongruous is due above all to the power of the vocal line it accompanies. Once again, sequence is the foundation of Albert's statement, but now organized with magnificent control of the shape across three phrases; for a moment at least this is the strongest character we have met in the work. Yet the other part of him promptly takes over in the juvenilia of tossing the coin and imitating Sid's distant whistle. And at the end of Act II we are as uncertain as Albert himself what he can hope to find on his journey of self-discovery.

Unfortunately, the cumulative tension that his disappearance creates throughout the first part of Act III is all too efficiently released by the witty

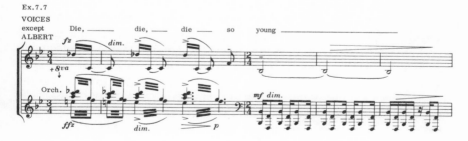

Ex.7.7

musical treatment of his return at the close of the Threnody (see Ex. 7). With the townspeople's loftiest sentiments so nimbly punctured, we are not ready to attend to Albert's testimony with much thought for his earlier aspirations; it merely gives added piquancy to the chagrin of his tormentors. Musically the inquisition goes by on a very prosaic level, and Albert's account of his night out, though it begins with a warm reminiscence of his yearning song, convinces us neither of pleasure nor of 'drunkenness, dirt and worse'. His outburst against Mum's repressive influence (see above, Ex. 2a) is more convincing, but only with the wry courtesy of his conclusion, 'And I'm more than grateful' (Ex. 8) do we sense a further emancipation in his musical

Ex.7.8

speech. His comment to Sid and Nancy, 'I didn't lay it on too thick, did I?' confirms that we may take the account of his libertine progress to be essentially symbolic, but the impression may remain that to have won the right to depravity is a hollow victory for the Albert we glimpsed in Act II. A symbol of another kind, which immediately follows, is more reassuring: Nancy kisses Albert and the bubbling pleasure he finds in this token is reflected in orchestral transformations of the kiss/peach motive. This incidentally triggers off his memory of the peaches, and he offers them to the children, whose old mocking song undergoes a mutation into a welcome to the new Albert. 'Jolly good riddance' throws out his May King image (i.e., the Ex. 6 *x* motive) just as he throws away the wreath. The prevailing euphoria is based on slender evidence, yet perhaps there is enough. The inexorable nature of his act and his persistence in justifying it have jolted him out of the old niche in people's minds: for the character he is to be we must rely on the glimpses afforded by the counterpoint of childlike geniality and amorous intimations of this final scene.

Britten's most common means of distorting his models are harmonic: melody and texture suggest a familiar musical type, but harmony either petrifies their flow or superimposes procedures that would conventionally be alternatives. Three examples must suffice to demonstrate a practice that has innumerable parallels in the rest of the composer's work. In Sid's first song (Ex. 9a), the automatic I–V swing of the bass belongs to the 'blow-suck' convention of the mouth organ, but the middle stratum, a sequential pattern

Ex.7.9 (a)

Ex.7.9 (b) i

Ex.7.9 (b) ii

Some of his lis - ten - ers are so - lemn-faced, ____ Some near to ___ laugh - ter.

Ex.7.9 (c)

MISS WORDSWORTH

Quick-ly, quick-ly,

Presto
Fl.

pp sempre
Str.pizz.

Harp + D.B.

come a-long! Come a-long!

of 6/3s (matching the vocal sequence) has no logical relation to it. A chord like that at the beginning of the fourth bar superimposes I, V and IV meanings, yet the effect is not Stravinskyan because the sequential pattern provides a propulsion even if the harmonic units in themselves do not. In Ex. 9bi, the hymn (a distant relation of 'Abide with me', the key and the inverted first phrase would suggest), the I–V oscillating bass again discourages true progression and the upper harmonies usually reveal two contradictory meanings in the organist's unselective clusters. (The touch of vocal fioritura for the choirboy was to return almost literally at the end of the choirman's burial in *Winter Words*.) A less hamfisted example of harmonic ambivalence is shown at Ex. 9bii, where a minor ninth on D is heard rather as a dominant seventh on D pulling against the E flat minor retained by the bass, i.e., solemnity is here a very precarious state. Miss Wordsworth's airy address to her charges at Ex. 9c is less heavily parodistic; its conflicting planes of simple diatonic harmony were from Britten's earliest period a means of substituting an attractive inconsequence for the swollen 'added-note' elaborations of conventional diatonic progression which the direct Stanford tradition had encouraged.

Harmony is not the only field in which superimposition affords the commentary that we find 'comic'. The fugal finale in which the committee sum up their plans for crowning Albert (Act I, fig. 42, 'May King!') crosses two textural genres that have rarely associated before, the 'learned' fugue (complete even to stretti and augmentations) and the 'oom-pah' march. Abrupt and undisciplined key swings reinforce the irony, as do the transfers of instrumental to vocal idioms (Miss Wordsworth after fig. 44, Budd before fig. 46). Key superimposition in Britten is more likely to be an extension of the harmonic practices discussed than a consistent polytonality, but certain passages rely for their effect on something approaching this. Mum's motive is commonly placed above a I–V accompaniment in another key (see Ex. 2a above) and the melodic clichés of the children's songs and games in the Act I interlude are strung on a taut net of conflicting key pulls. This is a strangely memorable piece, even a little sinister with its shrill whistles and furtive rhythmic refrain. The latter is already tonally uncommitted (two perfect fourths) and the harmonies added above it blur still more the tonal picture; the episodes in this rondo structure are emphatically centred melodically but accompanied tangentially (see Ex. 10); their conflation in the last episode

Ex.7.10

is a familiar Britten feat of legerdemain. The pity is that the children introduced by this music never assume its subtlety or its slightly eerie attractiveness.

A similar discrepancy between the orchestral music and what we know it to represent may be sensed in the central interlude of Act II. The *élan* of this virtuoso fugal piece scarcely accords with the Sunday School party tone of the feast it depicts, but we may take it to symbolize Albert's happy view of the proceedings under the liberating influence of the rum; even the subject's presentation of 'Albert the Good' suggests inebriation. In its textural variety the interlude is more akin to passacaglia than to fugue, and its position at the centre of the work also invites comparison with the *Grimes* passacaglia, of which it is the emotional reverse. The introduction at this point of music in which Britten need make no concessions in the cause of parody is very welcome, and the listener is unlikely to hear it as a mere device for covering the set change. The third act has no interlude, since the denouement must proceed so rapidly from the climax of Albert's presumed death. Instead, the orchestral introduction representing the frantic search for him is extended, and its material recurs as a ritornello in the act structure. Its last appearance, when the futile search is recalled, follows the Threnody, and it is this ensemble which stands as the central pillar of the act, even more imposingly than did the two interludes.

Just as the children's music was more complex than the children, the feast music more hilarious than the feast, so the Threnody plumbs a grief that we must know to be absurdly disproportionate to the situation. Yet even at so open an invitation as a fortissimo climax to the words 'Grief is silent', few listeners are disposed to laugh, for no trace of facetiousness is allowed to disturb the music's grand momentum. It is true that it begins almost as a parody of Anglican chant, a form of corporate solemnity with which the characters would be familiar. But even in the simple harmonic framework on which the passacaglia is to be built there are potent forces, as Ex. 11 demonstrates, and the chordal circuit is carefully organized. The unexpected dissonance, first provoked by and thereafter associated with the word 'death', is Britten's favoured perfect plus augmented fourth (cf. the discussion of this aggregate in the *Grimes* chapter, p. 108) though the bass B flat explains it as a dominant thirteenth, i.e., implies a move to the subdominant.

Ex.7.11

Instead the move is to the dominant (i.e., as though German sixth on a IV to a I), so that the position of rest too is unexpected. The next movement suggests an impending cadence on to the more relaxed relative major, and the drooping sixths also prepare for this, but the bass move to A natural (creating a false relation) thrusts back to B flat minor. Metrically the ground is striking both for its odd end-stresses and for the protracted final phrase: $\frac{3+1}{8}$; $\frac{3+1}{8}$; $\frac{3+1}{8}$; $\frac{(3 \times 2)+1}{8}$. If it begins in the sanctimony of chant, its literal repetitions soon lend it the hypnotic quality of incantation, and against this undifferentiated mourning of the mass the subjective cries of the individuals are heard in turn. Each solo line is true enough to a character created for us by parody techniques, but one opens the way for the next so naturally (in rhythmic and/or melodic contour) that their comic potential is no longer exploited. The duality of the scheme and the succinct nature of the ground make this a more powerful piece than the vocal passacaglia at the end of *Lucretia*. There the individual characters added their distinctive lines progressively, but here Britten holds back the superimposition so that suddenly the ritual of grief breaks down as all nine lines compete for our attention. Harmonically the ritual has been arrested by Sid's scepticism and then shattered under the weight of Mrs Herring's cries, and the superimposition is simply the elaboration of an entirely static F major chord. When this swings back to a tonic now major, the drum rhythm and the vocal unison bring a more conventionally funereal note, though the sforzando ninths (oddly reminiscent in rhythm of the reiterated 'Now' in the *Grimes* march to the hut) leave some edge, as well as preparing, as we have seen, for the deflation of Ex. 7. This final weakening of the emotional temper makes just tolerable our return to the provincial scandal that bursts about Albert's head. The earlier part of the Threnody, however, strikes a note of intensity that may even be regarded as misplaced. But a composer in re-creating an emotional situation may soon get caught up in that world of symbols which is his *métier*, and he cannot be asked constantly to withdraw to deliver shrewd comments and witty asides on the implausibility or the falsity of the situation. Susanna's *Deh vieni* is simply one of Mozart's most wonderfully passionate expressions, untroubled by knowing reminders that it is addressed to her wooer as a taunt to her lover, and *Soave sia il vento* is no less gravely tender because the women are to betray their departing lovers one act later. Musically, *Albert Herring* reaches its peak in the Threnody, and if Albert himself has become no more than a pretext at this point, we need not savour its richness the less. But, of course, the problem of the closing scene discussed above is made still more acute by its following so potently defined a mood; it is all too easy to disregard its few pointers to the new Albert, and to regard everything after the Threnody as a necessary but tiresome tying-up of loose ends after the crucial dramatic twist of Albert's return. Newman's talk of a 'charade' is based on such a reading, but Britten has created a character that seems worthy of a less contemptuous dismissal.

8 Billy Budd

Britten's opera, *Billy Budd*, to a libretto by E. M. Forster and Eric Crozier based on the novel by Herman Melville, was completed in Autumn 1951 and first performed at Covent Garden on 1 November of that year. Nine years later the composer conducted in a studio broadcast the first performance of a revised version in which the original four acts were drawn together into two; this operation was already foreshadowed in the original by the procedure (reminiscent of *Wozzeck*) of beginning Acts II and IV with the music that ended I and III. The one important change of musical substance, affecting the close of the old first act (now Act I, Scene 1), will be noted later.

One's first impression of *Billy Budd* is of a big, densely-written opera, but this may appear to be accentuated unduly by its place in the canon after the first two chamber operas. Yet to consider it in relation to *Peter Grimes* is to recognize that the sense of a towering, even menacing, work has not been created simply by the reversion to a full orchestral complement and a chorus. In *Grimes*, frequent changes of locale encouraged the deflection of some part of our attention from crucial dramatic issues to skilful paintings of the borough life—pub, church and dance-hall. Similarly, the lavish range of characters included some who, although also capable of sinking their identity into that of the crowd-as-protagonist, were chiefly savoured for their droll individuality of behaviour or speech. The crowd itself, though ultimately responsible for hounding Grimes to his suicide, emerged from and receded into a background of normal daily life that, if hardy, was none the less a resigned enough compromise with the elements: and the sea, which in storm could threaten life and livelihood, could also afford the luxuriant calm of the moonlight interlude. In *Budd*, any escape from a brooding concentration on man's potentialities for oppression and cruelty is far more difficult to achieve. As has often been pointed out, this stems in the first place from an acute sense of confinement to the physical bounds of the ship: every man here is a captive, the seamen's plight being the plainer only because systematic brutality compels them to accept it. The sea, as Eric Walter White demonstrates,[1] is the isolating medium, but one might say also that it is not

[1] White, p. 153.

truly present in the opera. In *Grimes* its potent influence derives from our being on land, but in *Budd* we are aware only of the ship and infinite space; and the hopeless nostalgia of the sailors' 'Into the harbour carry me home' declares the impossibility of bridging so vast a distance. No minor character is given a detail of illumination that does not reflect on the central predicament of this incarcerated community, on a daily life of which danger and deprivation are the constant background and strenuous labour and wanton cruelty the scarcely less constant foreground.

Even before we consider structural matters, a vital key to the single-minded forcefulness that distinguishes *Billy Budd*, we may observe how far removed its vocal lines are from the generous contours of *Grimes*. The use of exclusively male voices has already cramped the available pitch range, but the process is extended into the melodic detail, which is largely dependent on intricate differentiation within a restricted fund of predominantly small intervals: gestures and intervals as ample as Peter's 'We strained into the wind' or scales as protracted as Ellen's 'Let him among you without fault' could appear false or simplistic were they reproduced in this laconic context. (Indeed, it is the tendency of Billy's lines to burgeon which marks him out as the odd man whose spirit has been neither crushed nor warped.) Yet there is no threat of monotony, partly because of the endlessly resourceful variation of orchestral context in which Britten sets the voices, but chiefly because similarities of melodic shape are deliberately played on to create instead a sense of obsession. This brings us to the motivic usages in *Budd*, an aspect of its composition which other commentators, following Erwin Stein's lead,[2] have explored in some detail.

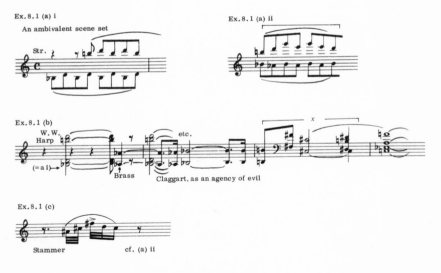

Ex.8.1 (a) i
An ambivalent scene set
Str.

Ex.8.1 (a) ii

Ex.8.1 (b)
W.W.
Harp
(=a i)
Brass
Claggart, as an agency of evil

Ex.8.1 (c)
Stammer   cf. (a) ii

[2] E. Stein, '*Billy Budd*', in Mitchell-Keller, p. 201.

Ex.8.1 (d) i

Worksong

Ex.8.1 (d) ii

(Potential) Mutiny

Ex.8.1 (e) i

Fls.

Obs.

etc.

Call to work (cf.(a) i)

Ex.8.1 (e) ii

8

Fls. + Vlns.   Bosun's Pipe

Ex.8.1 (f)

(and many related forms)   Billy

Ex.8.1 (g) i

Claggart's response to Billy

Ex.8.1 (g) ii

'O   beau - ty,   o   hand - some-ness, good - ness,   would — that I ...

Ex.8.1 (h)

Sax.

The novice; wanton cruelty

Ex.8.1 (j) i

'Star - ry — Vere'. '

Ex.8.1 (j) ii

Str.

The contemplative
Vere

Ex.8.1 (k) i

The French

Ex.8.1 (k) ii

' Don't like   the French'. '

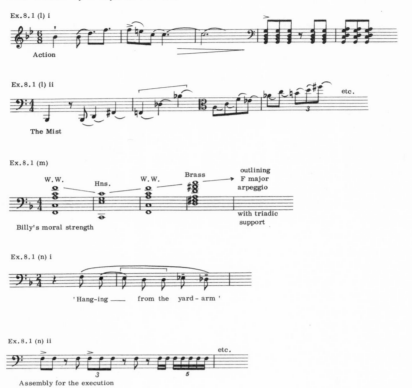

Ex.8.1 (l) i

Action

Ex.8.1 (l) ii

The Mist

Ex.8.1 (m)

W.W.   Hns.   W.W.   Brass   outlining F major arpeggio

Billy's moral strength   with triadic support

Ex.8.1 (n) i

'Hang–ing ____ from the yard – arm'

Ex.8.1 (n) ii

Assembly for the execution

Though a list of derivations would proliferate endlessly, the chief recurrent shapes are set out in Ex. 1; the labels attached to them should not be read too rigidly. Stein was able to demonstrate how many of these shapes could be referred back to an *Urmotiv* (of which, it appears, the composer was not fully conscious) consisting of the minor-within-major third of the opera's opening bars, Ex. 1ai, conflated harmonically in (b). More obviously the (b) theme, especially its *x* shape, a symbol of Claggart's malevolence, gives rise to many other fourth-dominated shapes, some (like Ex. 1gi and ii) patently relevant to Claggart himself, others reflecting in other contexts *either* his predisposition to evil *or* his bitter recognition of the beauty and goodness symbolized in Billy; this plasticity can create some confusion to the most literal-minded motive-hunter, though one is rarely at a loss in the theatre. A transfer of another kind operates between the two versions of (d): we first hear the men's working song 'O heave', then Billy's adaptation of it in his farewell to his old ship, the *Rights of Man*: this is misunderstood as a mutinous sentiment and is therefore used as a symbol of mutiny, usually suspected on faulty evidence, but when mutiny does stir, after Billy's execution, the crew's wordless figure is on Ex. di and we recognize how short a leap it is from the physical struggle that is their work to one that would overthrow their masters.

Intellectually, at least, we can also accept the fitness of Ex. 1h's being roughly an inversion of Ex. 1ji; (h), the theme of the ensemble in which the novice's friends try to comfort him, is used subsequently to symbolize a blind, arbitrary cruelty, while (ji) represents the wisely benevolent despotism the men see in Captain Vere; this makes notably powerful the orchestral application of the (h) form to Vere himself after he has accepted the verdict on Billy. But the circumscription of melodic idioms does produce occasional curiously inapposite echoes among so many telling ones; why, for example, should Claggart, in wrestling with his love-hatred for Billy, introduce Vere's formula (ji) at the words 'Having seen you, what choice remains to me?'?

At many points motivic references in the orchestra alone make pungent comment, and often these take us a step further in the action. The most economical example of the first kind must surely be the plaintive repeated D flat of the saxophone after Claggart, in the scene following Squeak's downfall, has lashed out at a boy who has stumbled; tone colour and pitch are enough to take our minds to the (h) theme and to re-create in a moment the hopeless compassion of the ensemble it initiated. Characteristically, Britten does not leave the note as a loose end: it is taken up by the trombone, Claggart's characterizing tone colour, and leads into his great aria, but it also touches off the men's 'Over the water', forlornly marooned in its C sharp minor over an F minor accompaniment remembered from Claggart's first arioso, 'Was I born yesterday'. The mood created by these interlocking references, none of them dependent on words, is complex but utterly precise. Of the second kind, several of the orchestral interludes provide clear examples, none more chillingly effective than that which follows Billy's farewell to the world and precedes the execution scene. This cross-cuts between his thoughts, dominated by the tortured phrase, Ex. 1ni, first heard to the death sentence, 'hanging from the yard arm', and sounds of the day's work beginning, preparations that, symbolized in Ex. 1ei and eii, point to the same end as Billy's thoughts. Many other contexts are as loaded as these two in their motivic juxtapositions and transformations; and many make their effect on the listener even before he has consciously traced the connexions. It is this labyrinthine quality of the motivic work which does much to enclose him in the isolated world of *Billy Budd*, and to make it not only the most individual in sound (The *Dream* provides a close second, perhaps) of all Britten's operas, but the most overpowering in cumulative effect before *Death in Venice*.

Outside the motivic scheme there are recurrences of another kind—of melodic entities such as Billy's farewell or of the great curtain of successive triads behind which Vere communicates the sentence; these two are assimilated in the epilogue. But the principal class of non-motivic pieces is that of the shanties, i.e., songs rather than sung speech. Except in 'We're off to

'Samoa', when the men try to outdo one another in facetious wit, Britten indulges in no whimsical distortions of the haunting airs, though he does play on the discrepancies of pitch range and timing proper to such an *ad hoc* body of singers. As we have already seen, the orchestra may throw their songs into a longer perspective, and the sweet sadness of the sailors' music, while it provides the chief lyrical relief in this oppressed work, does not dilute its essence. Parody techniques, which ran riot in *Herring* and were important even in *Grimes*, may perhaps be detected here only in a few touches like the 'forthright' English diatonic texture of the officers' chauvinistic 'Don't like the French' (see, for example, after fig. 5).

But the range of the harmonic language is so wide in this opera that one may scarcely claim that such writing departs from a 'norm'. At one extreme, Britten has elevated the triad to a symbolic rôle that is unprecedented: only in an age which has so strenuously sought to rid that unit of primacy in its musical thinking could his spelt-out major arpeggio with each note supported by a triad (see Ex. 1m but also the whole context) serve to represent the culminating moral drama and triumph of the whole work. And the distribution of the thirteen possible triads (see Ex. 2a) suggests that the

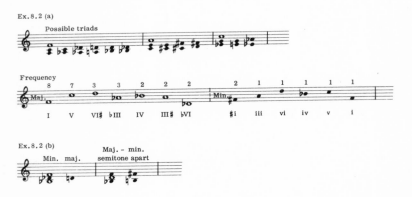

Ex.8.2 (a)

Possible triads

Frequency

Ex.8.2 (b)

Min. maj.

Maj. - min.
semitone apart

perfection of the major implies, as strongly as in older music, the imperfection of the minor. Much of the music of *Billy Budd* turns on a conflict between these two, while in still more this is extended into semitonal key opposition; how close the two are may be seen in the *reductio ad absurdum* of Ex. 2b. So at the other extreme are contents of which the harmony can only be explained in terms of two or more tonal strata; two simple examples and one more complex are shown at Ex. 3. The most elaborate dissonances are those built up by retaining successive chords in the depictions of the mist. Of more 'absolute' dissonance there is singularly little: even the kind of chord, made up from unequal fourths, that played so big a part in *Grimes* is far less common here. But another Britten fingerprint, the dominant seventh divorced from its old obligations, and savoured as an individual sonority,

168

Ex. 8.3 (a)

Ex. 8.3 (b)

Ex. 8.3 (c)

warm yet far from reassuring (cf. the last act of *Grimes*), is much in evidence; three examples show its range of application (see Ex. 4).

From what has been noted already it will be clear that few Britten scores depend more consistently on polytonal relationships and, we may now add,

Ex. 8.4 (a)

Act I, Sc. 1, before fig. 46

NOVICE'S FRIEND

Come a - long, kid,

Ex. 8.4 (b)

Act I, Sc. 3, before fig. 50

cf. x in Ex. 1 b

CLAGGART

So may it be! For what hope re - mains if love ...

x inverted

Ex. 8.4 (c)

Act II, Sc. 1, fig. 33

CHORUS

Wind, wind fill our sails MAINTOP: She's mak - ing, mak - ing! The Help our

Fren-chie's mak-ing fast! fight

ORCH.

on the listener's long-term memory for the colour of individual keys. Analysis of tonal schemes can easily disconcert the listener who is certain that he has no such faculty, but as we have already seen in the (admittedly, particularly simple) case of the saxophone's D flat, Britten takes care to aid our recognition by often reproducing characteristic sonorities too. But the temptation to set up a table of key references as cut-and-dried as that of motives shown in Ex. 1 must be resisted, for no composer to whom tonality remains a vital structural force could be governed by so unsubtle a principle. Nevertheless, as in *Lucretia* (and still more forcefully in *The Turn of the*

170

Screw), Britten has attached remarkably consistent dramatic connotations to certain tonal areas, and it can only heighten our admiration to discover how such extra-musically induced procedures are absorbed into convincing musical structures.

No listener can fail to understand from Vere's prologue that what we are to witness is a parable of good and evil: 'Much good has been shown me, and much evil, and the good has never been perfect./There is always . . . some fault in the angelic song, some stammer in the divine speech.' At this stage, however, we may take the ambivalence of key in the strings' gentle undulations (Ex. 1a) to be no more than the old man's confused gropings back towards this cardinal experience of his life. Indeed, this sense of time passing on inexorably into eternity is one important (and highly Mahlerian) meaning of these undulations, reinforced by their return in the epilogue. The opposition of B flat and B natural is poignant but scarcely absolute here: *pace* Stein, one is far more likely to hear a lower B flat (Mixolydian) stratum opposed by G Mixolydian (not B minor) above (cf. Ex. 1a). However, the prologue does prefigure, albeit faintly, the essential tonal drama, not only in introducing the more pointed opposition of Ex. 1b (together with Claggart's motive) but also in substituting for its original dominant outcome (of B flat—bar 15), a dominant position (at 'Much good . . .') that is of B minor, in due course opposing this F sharp with elements of F minor; and the vocal line does turn from B minor back into B flat at 'So much is confusion'. The listener will not understand at this point how much is to turn on the introduction of Billy's stammer (Ex. 1c) and the mutiny motive (Ex. 1dii), but the tonal outcome of the prologue in a clear B flat major after the words 'Who saved me?' marks that key a symbol of the state of blessedness towards which the whole work must ultimately aspire. How shapely a key structure Britten has devised while also making some important tonal predictions can easily be shown:

			Cadence	Cadence					Cadence
Cadence									
I → V⁷	↦ I		V of V → V		→ I	↦ I	→ I		
B♭ B♭	B♭		b	. . unstable . .	b	B♭	B♭		
unstable	(as					(as			
(B♮	before)					before)			
prominent)									
motives (a) (b)	(a)	(b) (a) (c)			(dii)	(a)	(b)		

The key of B minor combines both imperfections noted above, semitonal displacement from this ideal B flat, and minor rather than major modality. It is the dominating key of the *allegro energico* that opens Act I, but thereafter plays a far less prominent part in the opera. Its importance as 'not-B flat' is stressed in the opening of this scene where ambivalence at first persists (see, e.g., the harmony quoted at Ex. 3a above) and recurs from time to time, most obviously in the motives (ei) and (eii) (see Ex. 1). But the various appearances of the work-song 'Oh heave' (di) also strive to move from the B minor orbit (its dominant) into that of B flat (albeit minor) so that the immediate conflict of such bars as Ex. 3a is reflected in the long-term structure. As the two themes stand in the kind of contrast we associate with first and second group material, it is not an overstatement to call this scene, as critics have often done, 'symphonic'; the six appearances of 'O heave' trace the following path:

2nd party	—	a♯ (= b♭)	—	b♭	b♭	b♭	b
1st party	f♯	f♯	f♯	—	f♯	f♯	B
Orchestra	D	d♯	f♯	b	F as V	b♭	b	B
Figure	5	7	after 8	before 9	before 10	14		

The close of this design is particularly impressive as an apparently assured B flat outcome (fig. 14) gives way to a dominant of B, and the warm, low string harmony of the orchestral postlude that closes this first structural span expresses a powerful unrest. We need not look ahead to the recurrence of this sombre music at the end of the abortive mutiny (i.e., immediately before the epilogue) or to investigate all the other tonal conflicts in this 'first movement' to recognize that there is symbolized here a fundamental tension.

When we observe the contrast between the tetchy busyness of those who command (the (e) motives) and the slow strength of those who obey (di), we may try to oversimplify in reading this as a schematic conflict between the powers of evil and good (as Britten was to present in *The Screw*). But Vere's confusion persists here: in the crucial exchange between the Bosun and the Novice, for example, the former's B flat minor is answered by the latter's B major.

Elsewhere in the work we shall be conscious of this undermining of one key by its semitonal neighbour, though the conflict is transferred to other levels: for example, the scene in which the Novice tries to bribe Billy into service as a mutineer vacillates between F and F sharp minor; that in which Vere and his officers review the tragic history of the Nore places a C minor section within a B minor frame; and the attempted rising itself is quelled by the Officers' B flat commands just as its music achieves a climax in B, that is, the *status quo* is restored. But in several contexts quite free of this semitonal friction, the colour of B flat minor is introduced with the ruthlessness of a blow—whether of fate or some human agency, as in Claggart's intrusion upon the fight between Billy and Squeak. The return of the mist to a stupendous B flat minor chord, though it punctuates a scene based on G, puts paid to hopes of action that had begun the act in an optimistic B flat (Lydian) major—for in this one scene we see officers and men sharing the same hopes. The irony is intensified by the return of the opening, *quasi da lontano*, and its immediate collapse into Claggart's resumption (G minor/F sharp minor) of his lugubrious report to the Captain. With that many-sided fitness that distinguishes many Britten touches, a single G minor trombone chord at once closes the complete scene and reintroduces Claggart's baleful character to set in motion the next one. The mist and Claggart as instruments of an evil fate have clearly fused in Vere's mind in the B flat minor of his 'O this cursed mist' when the master-at-arms leaves, and the following interlude gloomily pursues this train of thought until Billy's arrival is anticipated with the swing to D Lydian. Yet it is the sound of F minor, in particular a fifthless wide-spaced wind chord with a cymbal stroke that repeatedly represents Claggart's malevolence, a quality that proves to be strongest after his own death at the hands of his intended victim. The chord first appears as he vents his sullen fury against his patronising superior officers ('Do they think I'm deaf?') and acquires a more sinister tone at his pitiless contempt for the flogged novice ('Let him crawl'): the whole ensemble then goes by in an F minor in which the sailors' compassion is overshadowed by that bestial response. Its place in a ghastly pattern is underlined later when Claggart strikes out at a boy to the same chord and, as we have noted, the saxophone D flat makes its appeal: so the climax of Claggart's aria extends this pattern, for his vow, against solemn repetitions of the chord (Ex. 5), to destroy Billy,

Ex. 8.5

is followed by the novice's appearance and saxophone theme, but now the boy is to become a pawn in an evil design of a quite new magnitude. The master-at-arms is too practised a dissembler for this token of naked evil to betray itself in his reports to Vere, but at the court-martial following his death the F minor symbol emerges again (now with brass and drums, fig. 80 and, complete with Claggart's own cadence—cf. *x* in Ex. 1b and Ex. 5—at 89), and as a dry third from the harp it hammers home the verdict. This means that we sense in the F minor of Vere's pitiful aria 'I accept their verdict' his recognition that it is he who has completed Claggart's design, and the orchestra's interpolation of Ex. 1h, noted above, reinforces this impression. Only through the mysterious cleansing process of the great succession of chords, as Vere makes his peace with Billy, is an F major achieved that finally expunges Claggart's evil power from the work. (It is recalled by Billy as he sums up his plight 'Captain Vere has had to strike me down . . . *fate*' at fig. 10 of the last scene.)

F major has in fact been used already in the scene for the trio in which the officers voice their sympathy for Billy's plight, but after this remarkable scene (or, literally, lack of a scene) the key is associated consistently with Billy's fortitude. The transfer to B flat major for his glowing farewell song links his fate with Vere's, but the turn to A major at the centre of this brings the clearest view of the special rôle that tonal area has been given at several points in the opera. Billy's song moves towards A (guided by intimations of the interlude triads) at the words

> But I've sighted a sail in the storm
> The far shining sail that's not fate
> And I'm contented, I've seen where she's bound for.

Now securely in A major, he continues: 'She has a land of her own where she'll anchor for ever', and the vision fades (though it is glimpsed for a moment at 'I'm strong', where the interlude triads are openly revealed). The only specifically Christian reference in the opera has come a little earlier when Billy tells how he has heard (apparently for the first time) the story of the crucifixion, a penetrating moment in which the execution motive sounds in the crystalline A major of the glockenspiel far above an earthbound double-bass pedal A. But Vere has twice prayed for 'the light of clear Heaven, to separate evil from good', and on both occasions in an A major context (both use a new figure, but lead into a reference to Ex. 1ji). So it is reasonable enough to find in this key-colour the symbol of an immanent good towards which we can only faintly aspire in an existence shot through with evil. But this in turn means that a very special significance may be attached to those few moments at which Billy's music has settled into A major—the fanfares signalling his victory over Squeak's evil acts and his descent from the foretop to be among the boarding-party (notice the men's response in the words of faith: 'He's with us! He'll come down to us'). In some sense, at least, we are encouraged to share Vere's awestricken view of the visitor to the world of the *Indomitable* when his F minor aria, 'I accept their verdict', swings to A (never quite achieving the major)—'The angel of God has struck, and the angel must hang'. This gives even greater force to Claggart's aria in which the A major beauty of sound (for this is a passionately beautiful piece) is eventually crushed by his own F minor; and he reverts to A for his denunciation of Billy ('A common seaman . . .').

Other key-colours are restricted in their use, if less momentous as dramatic agencies. C major obviously symbolizes the calm authority, founded on learning as well as experience, of Captain Vere—and C minor finds that authority faltering or irrelevant, in the Nore arioso and, most tellingly, in 'Scylla and Charybdis', where all his reading of the ancients serves only to reveal with the more harrowing precision his own dilemma. Despite the first scene's B minor, its relative major D has scarcely appeared in the entire opera until it brings a brightly affirmative note into the close of the misty orchestral interlude before Vere confronts Billy for the first time. Nor, except in the optimistic action-motive of Act II, Scene 1 (Ex. 1li), have Lydian inflexions played as big a part in the sound of this work as in most Britten. So a tone that is strongly reminiscent of his earlier music, D Lydian, complete with fanfares and figurations of superimposed thirds, is heard only during the scenes that concern the captain and Billy. Indeed, Vere's soliloquy before Billy is admitted sounds all too much like a parody of Britten's style (see Ex. 6), and it must be admitted that the scene which follows, in

Ex.8.6

which the sailor chats garrulously with his captain, strains credulity. Yet there is a young man's impulsive warmth of expression here, and a deep security in the long pedal Ds, that are to acquire a double irony: firstly because it is to a soft string chord of D major that Vere lays his hand on Billy's shoulder and, in effect, releases the pent-up strength which destroys Claggart, and secondly because Billy, when asked at his trial why he struck the blow, reverts to his D major music to protest his loyalty to country and King and again, more explicitly, to appeal to Vere: his D collapses tragically to F minor as the Captain remains silent. It is in this failure to acknowledge a mood he has shared with Billy, as much as in his refusal to expose the canker he has seen in Claggart, that Vere stands condemned and, of course, the second failure springs from the first.

The tonally-organized structures of the prologue and of the first musical span of Act I (up to the close in B and the fanfares that announce the guard-boat bringing Billy on to the scene) have been discussed. Such closed forms are less common as we move further into the action of the opera; though the set-pieces remain as clearly identifiable in *Budd* as elsewhere in Britten, the musical flow across their boundaries is unusually smooth. This is in part the result of a prose libretto: while it discourages the bland symmetries of musical metre and phrasing that verse can bring, it also discourages the isolation of a special prosaic-speech equivalent-recitative. Except at certain moments of apostrophe (Billy's farewell to his former ship or Claggart's 'O beauty'), we are not jolted when these characters exchange the language of communication for that of reflection, so imperceptibly are the transitions of level effected. The later part of Act I, Scene 1, provides a good example, for it passes swiftly through eight distinct sections, a straight-line structure that completes our understanding of the situation as it concerns the men and prepares for our moving on to the officers' problems in the following scene. The first piece, an arioso in A minor by the Sailing-Master, is the nearest approach in the opera to the *Grimes* vignettes, but its accompaniment arpeggios derive organically from the previous fanfares (Ex. 1f) and can therefore be assimilated again into the action at the end as Ratcliffe arrives with his pressed men. They can also emerge naturally to articulate the inquisition by Claggart: this is held together by its ominous pedal B, but also driven forward by the harmonic progression of the string figures (as well as an accelerating tempo). So a shapely structure emerges from what might have been the driest of secco exchanges, yet vividness of speech is in no way sacrificed. And this long pedal has another function, for its effect is essentially of a more and more imperious dominant, and so the swing to E for 'Billy Budd, king of the birds', is momentous, the completion of what now appears a single IV–V–I operation. At this point, however, there is a violent swerve, Billy's invocation of the *Rights of Man* stirring an echo among the men (Ex. 1d serving again its double purpose) that must be quelled by the B flat alarms and whistles of the earlier music (Ex. 1eii). The swerve is promptly converted to a structural end: while E is still prevailing in the orchestra, Claggart's 'I heard your honour' and subsequent arioso on his *x* motive set off from B flat, and plunge flatter still to the first appearance of F minor. The following scherzo (Claggart and Squeak) is built on diminutions of the paired-note figure underlying the arioso, played off in a rather Bartókian relationship against Billy's arpeggios. So it too is organic: though slightly macabre, it provides textural relief just where it becomes necessary. We have noted already how the ensemble led by the novice's friend, though thematically new, rounds out our understanding of Claggart's F minor. Perhaps more contrivedly, but poignantly none the less, the novice's last despairing seventh drops to a G flat (one more semitonal clash) which can then serve the practical purpose of effecting the transition to the quartet's F sharp minor. As Mrs Howard points out,[3] the scherzando figure on the clarinet that leads into this is a re-arrangement of the minor thirds of the novice's friend's kindly phrases, 'Come along, kid', while the bouncing seconds derive from the bosun's pipe (Ex. eii) of the first span. The whole scherzo reminds us that horrors and rigours that ought to be intolerable may somehow be lived through and that a wry humour may help. Finally, the changing of the watch is signalled by returning the seconds-motive to its original rôle, and the C major ensemble that ends the scene is punctuated by a new syncopated derivation from the motive. But this also approaches the shape of Vere's motive, which, as an overt demonstration of the affection he inspires among his men (Ex. 1ji) and as an orchestral ground, dominates every part of this excitable ensemble other than the denunciations of the

[3] Howard, p. 86.

French (Ex. 1ki). Britten's recasting of the opera in two acts required him to remove one or other of the two Vere scenes originally divided by an interval. In the 1951 'Starry Vere' scene, the captain himself prompted the men's ardour with a speech as notable for its dignity as for its incitement; though this created a splendid glow for the end of the act, its climactic note had to be subdued when it became merely the preparation for our first sight of Vere. Much of the original material is represented in a far briefer form by an ingenious process of cutting and patching, but an opportunity has been found to give a foretaste of the contemplative Vere we are soon to see, as the low strings throb (Ex. 1jii) below 'He cares for us like we are his sons'.

The sense of forward movement in this scene is irresistible, and affords a marked contrast with the following one, where the arched structure suggests a self-contained interlude: a diagram makes this clear. The scene serves more than one purpose.

Prelude and Vere's Soliloquy	The Officers discuss the French	'The Nore'			Distant Shanty of the men	Prelude Music returns
		Officers	Vere	Officers on their men		
C	E♭	b	c	b	E♭	C

It shows us Vere the classical scholar, whose officers must gape at obscure references, but also Vere who is at one with them in contempt for the French and fear that 'French notions', already mischievously active at the Nore, may burst out in mutiny. The centrepiece of the scene, a tiny C minor *da capo* piece, makes its mark by the quite extravagant agitation Vere shows—fast 5/8 rhythms and intervals wide with outrage. Yet within seconds he is reassuring his officers that the danger is not immediate: neither Billy nor a crew that can sing shanties so happily presents a threat to the *Indomitable*. This equivocal attitude to the possibility of mutiny establishes a pattern of behaviour that is to have tragic consequences in his response both to Claggart's 'foggy tale' and to Billy's fateful blow. But above all this evening scene is memorable for the intensely beautiful moments of introspection which frame it, where Vere's own motive has become a wisp of flute colour, and even the threat of the French (Ex. 1ki), intertwined on the woodwind does not seriously disturb the undertow of throbbing string harmonies, Ex. 1jii. Its later appearance, however (fig. 13), breaks more forcefully on to the officers' reflections, for it signals Lieutenant Ratcliffe's news that enemy land has been sighted; in this way the formal symmetry of the scene is heightened, yet a lead is provided into subsequent action. It is the sailor's apparent ability to share his reflective mood that reassures Vere as he listens to the distant strains of 'Blow her away': still underlaid by the harmonies of *his* music, they have a wistful beauty. But the following interlude converts them to a much harder sound, of naggingly insistent two-part counterpoint, and the singing men on whom the scene opens are far earthier creatures than their disembodied voices suggested.

This scene (Act I, Scene 3) in which Claggart's plot is unfolded, is more ramified, but it too is essentially arch-shaped, with the big aria in which Claggart commits himself to Billy's destruction as its centrepiece.

Shanties	Billy & Squeak	Claggart & violence (& Shanty commentary)	Claggart's aria	Claggart & Novice —violence (+ sax. theme commentary)	Billy & Dansker passacaglia
E♭ →G	A	b♭ → f (+ c♯)	AdE♭ A:f	F/f♯ F	E♭ → G

Once again we do not return to a literal *status quo*: Billy's high-spirited divisions in the finale show him even more buoyant than in the buffooning of the shanties, but below them the obstinate repetitions of Dansker's ground 'Jemmy Legs is down on you' (to bar 2 of the b motive) sum up the inescapable moral of the scene's developments. Though one's dominating impression is of a balance created by the three 'set' numbers—shanties, central aria, passacaglia—and of fluid connexions, even the chilling dialogue between Claggart and the novice is tightly organized, as Stein pointed out:[4] surrounded by the saxophone theme, it has an inner symmetry in the two appearances of the abject, broken music (of flutes, solo viola and harp) to which the novice pours out his willingness to sidestep evil by serving it, while Claggart's erupting violence marks its central point. The aria, 'O beauty! o handsomeness, goodness', is the most elaborate solo set piece in the opera

Fig. 45	Fig. 47	Fig. 49	Fig. 50	10 bars after 50	17 bars after 50
A	B	Devel. of A; framed by 'So may it be'	A fading out	B at slow tempo of A; fading out.	Coda
A maj.	D min.	From E♭ to B to	A maj.	No settled key	F min.

and among Britten's most probing character-studies. It is formed almost like a sonata movement, of ample dimensions though with a drastically abridged restatement so as to project quickly into the coda, with its terrible vow. What has appeared to be an unusually complete aria structure is therefore symbolically broken off short, for of course the sensuous *cantabile* of the main idea is a response to Billy's nature that Claggart at once owns to and seeks to stamp out:

---

[4] Stein, op. cit., p. 206.

The light shines in the darkness, and the darkness comprehends it and suffers.

The fourths that haunt Claggart's music throughout the opera are ubiquitous here, yet they never threaten to become stale, partly because Britten so subtly differentiates between the emotional significance of the rising and the falling intervals, but more importantly because the true progress of the piece is felt between the melodic peaks of successive lines, rather than within the lines themselves. The time-scale established by these opening phrases, for example, is magisterial (see Ex. 7), and the timbre of voice, bass strings'

Ex.8.7

arpeggios and trombone (in a smoother, heterophonic version of the vocal line) creates a night-music that is Stygian. It is also the music of suffering, whereas the allegro of the second section is that of rancour: here the fourths are left chiefly to the orchestra, and in his reiterated scales, a far more conventional image, Claggart has exchanged ecstasy for paroxysm. The middle section develops the first theme at the second tempo, against his motive (x in Ex. 1b) inverted in the bass, but it is noteworthy that this motive (i.e., the form with two successive fourths) is reserved in the vocal line for two cardinal points, immediately before the reprise at 'for what hope remains if love can escape' (see Ex. 4b above) and in the final vow of destruction. The passacaglia that ends the act is to spell it out *ad nauseam* without its message reaching Billy, his own variation which divides the bass (rather than descanting upon it) showing no understanding whatever of those powerfully bare fourths (see Ex. 8). So short a ground could easily lead to a bitty finale, but the repetitions are grouped into sections of uniform key and upper texture. The two inverted forms of the motive are merely illustrative of 'You'd better go back'. The appearance of a block of variations in F minor, when Billy burbles of his rumoured promotion, *may* foreshadow the

179

Ex. 8.8

fateful consequence of the interview with Vere which he believes to concern this matter, but the connexion here is tenuous. The closing block of variations, unified by Billy's most exuberant *fioritura*, gives stability to G major first by an extension of the ground into a three-bar unit (the motive × 2 and now passing from I to V) and then by a pedal, towards which it gradually sinks, in Dansker's last dismal warnings.

Act II appears on paper a more obviously symmetrical arrangement of scenes than Act I:

Scene 1   Main-deck and quarter-deck (Full company)
      2   The Captain's cabin (Vere & Billy; Claggart & officers)
      3   A bay of the gun-deck (Billy & Dansker)
      4   Main-deck and quarter-deck (Full company)

In fact, however, the effect is rather of a vast first scene in which the public drama of the encounter with the French ship is twice intruded on by the private drama that Claggart is engineering, and then of three scenes through which this latter is propelled with increasing momentum, so that the second assembly of the full company then seems an intrusion upon it. As many of the individual numbers have already been discussed in one context or another, comment on them need not be detailed. The first scene is unusual for this work in the importance attached to third relationships: its bright Lydian wind signal on B flat is countered by the more ominous rhythms of low strings and timpani in G minor (see Ex. 1 li), the two alternating in their pursuit of independent courses. Both are relevant to action when it comes (they are then counterpointed) but the thudding rhythms perhaps represent its dangers, the signal the crew's hopes. Certainly we have more than an inkling of what is in store when the rhythms solidify into the trombone triads that, so often a Claggart symbol, underlie his reports to the Captain; and the plunges to F sharp minor from G minor awaken the only strong memories in this scene of semitonal conflict. At the conflation of the Ex. 1 li figures, as the men move to action stations, the G becomes a major (Lydian) and the signal is now the refrain of a great choral ensemble, each body of men having a different theme (and often enough, key) just as each prepares to carry out a different task. Predictably, Britten then superimposes all these themes, but while the music is still in its modulatory flight, so that a still stronger climax is

180

left to him (after the call for boarding volunteers) with the eventual recovery of G and the unison statement by all voices of the complete refrain (the rhythms are now thunderous on stage as well as in the pit). Everything is now ready—except that the French ship is out of range of the *Indomitable*'s guns. And so this tremendous accumulation of energy must be held in check while the men call upon the wind to assist them: motion there is in the quietly rustling orchestral figures (see Ex. 4c) but the becalmed G below these seems a cruel test of their patience. The trial shot relieves nerves all too briefly for its reverberations give way to the returning mist: a mournful G minor and the shattering of all hopes in an explosive B flat minor lead to the dissolution of the scene in dismal transformation of the refrain, above a pedal D which leads to the ironic recall of the opening motives discussed earlier. Claggart's further depressing influence (we sink to F sharp minor again) is almost too much for Vere at this moment, as his irascible behaviour throughout the interview makes clear. Yet, if his refutation of Claggart's evidence against Billy reflects his exasperation as much as any very deep knowledge of Billy at this stage, it commits him to all that follows. After his over-bright B major (protesting too much—for Ex. 1dii in the bass suggests his fear of mutiny is real enough) the earlier motives are recalled in a B flat minor ensemble for the officers; but the mist they curse is no longer that which is troubling Vere:

> Disappointment, vexation everywhere, creeping over everything
> Confusing everyone. Confusion without and within.

The prayer for guidance with which he ends the scene threads its path as a brass chorale through the dense chordal mists of the interlude, with light bursting in, as we have seen, at the Lydian D that will characterize the following scene with Billy. Britten planned this originally as an entity, very roughly comparable to a sonata cycle of experience:

'EXPOSITION'	Billy & Vere (D Lydian)	Claggart's Accusation	Claggart's Death	
'DEVELOPMENT'	Vere's Aria and Quartet			
'RESTATEMENT'	Claggart's Accusation (orch.)	Billy's D Lydian	Officers' Ensemble (quasi further devel.) leading to	Death Sentence
'CODA'	Vere's Aria & the Chords			

But the conflation of the old acts III and IV ensures that we now hear across the orchestral chords to the last stage of a dramatic process in which Billy is isolated as the chosen victim:

	Vere	Vere	Vere		
Vere	Billy	Billy	Billy	Vere	Billy
		Claggart	&	Billy	
			Officers		

181

From Claggart's accusation onwards the music is strong, underpinned by motivic references that are potent, and without rigid symmetries so that the action mounts swiftly to the death-blow. Its catastrophic bass B sounds on as the Ex 1bx motives are drained of all energy in a pitiful decline: Vere, too, though he numbly acts and speaks in monotone, is paralysed while it lasts. His release through the mist motive (molto crescendo) is a masterly dramatic stroke: meanings towards which he could only grope are made terrifyingly clear in this moment. 'Scylla and Charybdis' represents the utter disintegration of order in Vere's world by its heterophonic accompaniment—a single strand but disaligned in time between upper and lower statements. His line above this appears more contained, though its Neapolitan (alias Phrygian) inflexions and obsessively repeated thirds betray his crushed condition, while the reprise 'my heart's broken' with a painful irony recalls, in words and falling sevenths, the forlorn novice of Act I. Only the orchestral whole-tone descent of major triads to Vere's repeated 'mine' (but, of course, to Claggart's fourth motive) suggests a momentary imaginative lapse in an otherwise tensely-sprung piece. Vere's recovery of C major formality at the entrance of his officers is not enough for him to attempt more than a monstrously bald statement of the case, 'William Budd here has killed the master-at-arms'. Their reactions are neatly contrasted in an ensemble of the kind Britten has always made a virtuoso feat: the first lieutenant displays a measured, dispassionate assessment of the situation in even quavers, Ratcliffe's warm sympathy flows out in *cantabile* triplets and the sailing-master's outraged clamour for revenge is in clipped semiquavers: to these three strata is then added a further stanza of Vere's aria.

The trial scene is framed by the muted trumpet rhythms (derived ultimately from Ex. 1ei) of a would-be dispassionate justice, though on both occasions Vere's distress sounds through in a chromatically mirrored phrase, prejudging the outcome. The two orchestral *grave* sections (evoking Claggart's accusation and his fascination by Billy's qualities) further shape the scene, one passing from I to V, the other rooted fatalistically on its F minor tonic. As in the Act I Scene 1 inquisition, the inquiry dialogue is unified by continuity of the bass and of the jagged snatches of Claggart motives, and Billy's D pedal serves a similar purpose while also acquiring forceful irony in Vere's failure to respond. The officers' deliberations have been singled out for admiring comment by other writers, and the effect of the apparently random overlaps in their speech (the heterophonic delivery of one line again) is indeed remarkably original and convincing. Mrs Howard points out,[5] of their conclusion, 'We've no choice', that 'these notes, like the dilemma, they try all ways round'; yet one wonders whether an alternative solution is not being whispered, if not to them, to their captain when the notes arrange themselves in the form of Ex. 1ji. (See Ex. 9.) Vere's accep-

[5] Howard, p. 96.

Ex.8.9

tance of the verdict is tortured both by the (now open) trumpet rhythms of this earthly justice and by the intimations of divine justice that have been vouchsafed him (the woodwind unisons here have that penetrating quality which Britten learnt from Mahler). The close of the scene has been discussed. Its recession into Billy's warm dreaming music (from his scene with the novice), interspersed with the cold-water of the low piccolo version of his fanfare motive, carries through successfully a difficult transition of mood. And the risk of falling into bathos which the use of Melville's lines in verse here induces is circumvented by creating an essentially independent musical structure. Though the bass turns sleepily between tonic and dominant almost throughout, there is a tonal scheme which embraces the whole piece, the reprise beginning smoothly as part of the penultimate stanza. An unexpected *frisson* is introduced by the transfer of Billy's line into F sharp minor above the strings' F minor at 'Heaven knows who will have the running of me up'.

Dansker's report on the disquiet among the men exchanges these lulling harmonies for a crabbed orchestral counterpoint of a figure and its inversion (Ex. 10). Bearing in mind also our previous example (Ex. 9), of which this is

Ex.8.10

the retrograde form, and his words 'The whole ship's trouble *and upside down*', we can take it that Vere's authority as represented in Ex. 1ji is questioned here. The scene is fitful, with significant motives interpolated appropriately as the conversation drifts (e.g., the death sentence sounds through Billy's 'thinking on what's no use' and its twists betray his thoughts at many other points), but the impulse of the opening carries us through to Billy's farewell to Dansker, an odd return of Ex. 1(l) motives. His more visionary soliloquy combines serenely even crotchets with a liberated metrical flow of two- and three-groups. Its later stages have been considered above, as has the orchestral interlude.

The final scene brings back the full company for the first time since the abortive action which began the act, and so far have we been drawn into the intimate drama, most of it never even made explicit, of Vere and Billy that this return to a wider scene is almost disconcerting. It is also, of course, heavily pointed in the contrasted moods we now hear in the identical succession of themes as the various sections of the crew take their places on

183

the main deck. But now, instead of the martial rhythm of Ex. 1li which underlaid the earlier assembly, there are the menacing drum patterns of Ex. 1nii, introduced in a fugal build-up that superimposes all the subdivisions in a terrible counterpoint. This reaches its climax as Billy ascends the mast, and the most blood-curdlingly slow version of Ex. 1ni symbolizes the execution; the height and serenity of its close around an E major triad cannot be ignored, however, and add one more nuance to Vere's reading of the situation (he, alone of the officers, stands with head bowed). The mutinous growls to which the crew now convert Ex. 1di were described by Melville, but to realize them in this rising fugal torrent was daring. In practice it usually emerges as a good deal more approximate than its notation, and its beast-like combination of the inarticulate and the goaded strikes home— particularly since it is so rapidly overtaken by all the sound-symbols of oppressive discipline. And because this 'mutiny' motive was always closely linked to the men's working song (see Ex. 1d), one always gives way to the rich sad sound of the other, to its string postlude, finally winning us to a position in which our involvement in the Billy story is matched by a pervading sense 'of compassion for all those who suffer'.

From its tonal ambivalence to that with which the opera began (Ex. 1ai) is now only a short step. Accompanied by the inexpungable Ex. 1nii rhythms (eventually augmented), Vere's epilogue draws us away from the scene into the old man's reflections on it. The conflation of Billy's vision and the absolving chords of the Vere-Billy interview creates a transfigured tonal spectrum before the last close into B flat (Ex. 1nii now a gloriously affirmative rhythm) and the withdrawal into silence. Comment on the detail of the epilogue is unnecessary, for all that was confusing (or, for us, simply uncommunicative) in the prologue has now unfolded layers of meaning.

Billy Budd induces a claustrophobic atmosphere, and it is easy to see why this should be so. Yet it does not become insufferable, chiefly because the concentration of motivic work is counterbalanced by an extremely wide range of orchestral invention, tirelessly exploring the colour and the possibilities of Britten's largest opera orchestra. Motives of the kind which must be succinctly telling, rather than germs in the growth of extensive paragraphs, are always highly characterized in timbre. An obvious example is the epigrammatic theme Ex. 1 b, instantly recognizable in the epilogue (though not heard literally since the prologue) less because of its clash between flute minor third and clarinet major third than because of the clash between its impassive wind tone and vibrant doubling by the harp. Billy's stammer and the tension it generates in bystanders are recalled by the muted trumpet's shake and a roll on the block with side-drum sticks even before the painfully compulsive woodwind snatches appear. Claggart's surrender to a malevolent will is, as we have seen, epitomized in a single chord of F minor without the fifth: Stravinskyan though such a spacing may look in piano reduction, it is again the orchestral treatment which makes of the chord so individual an

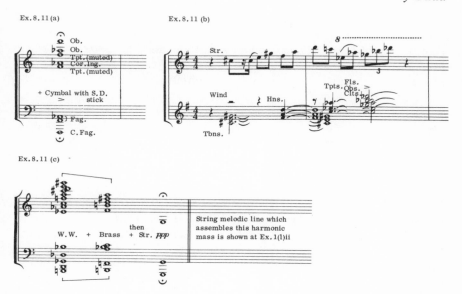

Ex.8.11(a) Ex.8.11(b)

Ex.8.11(c)

event. Its recurrent form is shown at Ex. 11a, and those contexts in which it is amplified (notably the adagio to which Claggart swears his terrible vow) preserve the spacing and reinforce the characteristics of this form. This motive is reserved for fateful moments in the action. More frequently Claggart is associated musically with trombone sonorities, usually in triadic contexts, whether in the solemn spacing (with tuba doubling the bass) against which his apparently benevolent remarks to Billy are made or the lugubrious movement in close position as he broaches to Vere the subject of Billy's treachery; here the darkness of sound is intensified by the melodic line of double basses, bassoon and double bassoon. In extreme contrast to this boorishly servile demeanour is the sound of Claggart's aria, 'O beauty': though no less dark, it is buoyed up by rolling double-bass arpeggios and a solo trombone doubles heterophonically the aspiring vocal line.

The immediacy of the saxophone's associations has been commented on, but a new significance is given to an identical musical situation (Claggart's F minor symbol followed by the novice's theme, at both figs. 42 (Scene 1) and 51 (Scene 3) of Act I) by the changed colouring of the other contrapuntal strand; bass clarinet and cello pizzicato becomes muted cellos' tremolando with harp and cymbal roll (cf. last bar of Ex. 5). Colours no less distinctive are those of the four flutes, which (doubled by violin shakes) create the screaming seconds of the bosun's whistle, and the two bass clarinets, in their rocking figure below the theme of Billy's sleep music (Act I, Scene 3, fig. 56) and their arpeggios that support his farewell to the world.

An association of hard wind (especially brass) sound with the rigidly disciplined and often violent life at sea, and strings with warmer human qualities, is not simplistically maintained, but is sometimes powerfully deployed, for instance in the first work scene on deck (Act I, Scene 1, contrast figs. 13 and 14) where the strings' postlude to the men's song is particularly poignant. Still more so are the muted string harmonies to which the novice's friend offers his futile consolations, chiefly because of the prevalent dominant sevenths (in non-classical contexts). A quite different string colouring is that which introduces Vere, reading in his cabin; the oblique, added-note character of the harmonies and the halting rhythms curiously qualify the gravely serene timbre of these lower-string chords. While the large wind-band frequently dominates the orchestral sonority, this is not always to violent ends. The elaborate texture at fig. 19 of Act I, Scene 1, and the 'mutiny' motive on oboes and cor anglais (Act I, Scene 3, fig. 57), later joined by muted trumpets, are contrasted examples of the strings' exclusion. The common use of the strings to delineate material progressively sustained by the wind is well exemplified in the firing of the trial shot: strings extend the 'action' motive through conflicting arpeggios which the wind hold as superimposed triads (see above, Ex. 11b). The method is taken to an extreme in depicting the mist; at the figurative mist through which Vere gropes to a sudden clarity of vision after Claggart's death (see Act II, fig. 72), 21 pitches are piled up by wood and brass, to which the strings add the one missing pitch-class, G (see above, Ex. 11c). At this climactic point, Vere's cry must momentarily dominate the total mass, before the rapid orchestral diminuendo. Elsewhere, Britten has been able to let his male voices be heard easily through the orchestral textures by a range of well-contrived spacings. Two random examples are Billy's first extended piece, 'Billy Budd, king of the birds' (Act I, Scene 1, fig. 31), which leaves a wide gap at the voice's register, and Billy's interview with Vere (Act II, fig. 59), where the solo horn elaborates on his ebullience in the same pitch area, but the rest of the accompaniment—two-part cellos with harp and double-bass pizzicato—is safely below; the later doubling of Vere's lines by octaved violins with flute and oboe still leaves the texture transparent.

Excluding scores for amateurs (most notably, *Children's Crusade*), only in the *War Requiem* does Britten call for as many percussionists—six—as in *Billy Budd*. Like the brass, they may be used with a weight that borders on the painful, yet even at such moments they are rarely superimposed automatically, but are given contrasted functions, in rhythmic shape and/or in illustrative significance. The sudden upsurge of the sailors' spirits at 'Beat to Quarters' and the prospect of some action is conveyed as much by the three-bar rhythmic ostinato as by their choral refrain (in two-bar phrases). But its underlining by the percussion is selective throughout the assembly until the four drummers on stage add their weight to the opera's most overpowering moment of optimism (Act II, figs 26 to 27). We have noted the acute irony that attends the recall of this assembly in that which precedes the execution scene. The percussion, now muffled, contribute still more crucially: three timpani players and the bass drum interlock statements of the new rhythmic ostinato, and are joined by side-drum, tenor drum and, at the execution itself, cymbals and tambourine; the xylophone's chatter at the appearance of the powder-monkeys is directly recalled.

The xylophone also adds inordinately to a memorable tutti sonority when Billy strikes out at the Master-at-Arms (Act II, fig. 70); together with trumpets, muted but *fff*, and strings *col legno*, and against that inexorable low B (underlined by the gong), this cleaving apart of Claggart's fourths-motive *x* has a ghastly, splintering sound. One final example of orchestral treatment that in itself is chiefly responsible for our emotional response is the interlude between Billy's farewell and the execution scene. Though the shape that haunts this interlude, that of the sentence, 'hanging from the yard arm' (Ex. 1ni), is already strained in its introverted chromaticism and its nervously accelerating counterpoint, and appears more so through its alternation with 'routine' sounds (Ex. 1ei and ii), it is the colouring of its lines that produces the excruciating quality in this context: oboe is doubled by cellos, or violas, both strings being taken to fearful heights, and finally double bass and double bassoon similarly strain to the upper reaches of their compass. The eventual carrying-out of the sentence (Act II, Scene 3, fig. 29) is symbolized in a tutti version of this motive, surely the most anguished two-part counterpoint in all Britten's work.

9 Gloriana

Two Covent Garden *premières* of full-scale operas only eighteen months apart must constitute a record in recent times—one that seems unlikely to be wrested from Britten. After the introverted action and music of *Billy Budd*, he had turned to an undertaking of an unprecedentedly 'public' nature in choosing to provide an opera in honour of Queen Elizabeth II's coronation and in basing it on incidents in the reign of her illustrious namesake. *Gloriana* was finished in March 1953 and was first performed on 8 June of that year. One suspects that the opera's first audiences felt cheated of another *Merrie England*, a sentimentalized picture of Elizabethan England adorned with vaguely archaic musical trimmings. But those who knew their Britten better may have been disappointed that he had relaxed so far the musical tensions that distinguished *Budd* as to devise a scheme in which set pieces are more patently isolated from their contexts than in any other of his operas, and in which the sonorous spectacle of tableaux is allowed to reduce the urgency of the action. For whatever reason, the coronation opera appeared not to have survived by long the occasion it celebrated, and memories of alluring moments could be refreshed only from the score. Indeed, in 1963, ten years after the first performance of *Gloriana*, Britten's fiftieth birthday was marked by a revival of the work in concert performance that seemed reminiscent of those consolation prizes awarded to neglected composers at various milestones in (or after) their lives. This renewed acquaintance with its delights swayed public opinion sufficiently for a staged revival to be planned, and the presentation of the opera by the Sadler's Wells Company in 1966 did much to suggest that its dramatic potentialities had been seriously underestimated. It now seems certain to come before a British public from time to time, though its dependence on some knowledge of the historical background will probably continue to keep it off foreign stages: this is the only Britten opera of which no singing translation has been made.

Yet the question may well be asked why this should be so when, for example, those selected scenes from Russian history and life that make up *Boris Godunov* have won a firm place in repertoires of opera-houses where the national background of the work brings no immediate evocations. Some part of the answer may lie in the sheer musical richness, the wide range of scenes and the quasi-symphonic depth in which they are executed and co-ordinated in *Boris*. But also, however fitfully Mussorgsky assembles his portrait of Boris himself, he sets it into relief against a picture scarcely less bold of the Russian people; as Calvocoressi wrote, 'the real tragedy of Mussorgsky's masterpiece [is] the fate of Russia'.[1] In *Gloriana* the chorus is used quite simply as supplementary evidence—of her subjects' love for Elizabeth and of her courtiers' fear of her barbed tongue. There are foils to the queen's dominating presence in the opera but, as we shall see, by far the most prominent of these, the Earl of Essex, too rarely appears to represent qualities more significant than the petulance of wounded pride, and our final reflexions on him are of an equivocal kind: in the epilogue, Elizabeth's thoughts are threaded on to an orchestral version of Essex's song, but in the snatches of melodrama which are interpolated it is the closing years of her reign that are reviewed, not just that part of them in which she entertained, wistfully and yet shrewdly, a love for him. So, unless we come to *Gloriana* above all for the rounding-out it offers of a character already in some degree familiar to us, we may complain that it lacks something of dramatic fulfilment.

It was in Lytton Strachey's *Elizabeth and Essex* that the librettist, William Plomer, found the seeds of the opera's central confrontations of character. Mrs Howard has roundly declared,[2] however, that the reference to Strachey 'is a red herring', for 'the opera is not an account of the relationship of Elizabeth and Essex. Essex is far too patchily drawn and the proportions are quite wrong for this to be so'. She also holds that 'the condemned Essex is deliberately excluded from the stage [in the final scenes] in case his tragedy either alienates our sympathy for or distracts our attention from Gloriana herself'. With the second of these assertions it is hard to disagree; though I doubt whether Essex, on the showing he has made earlier in the opera, would ever make a direct claim on our sympathy half as appealing as that made by his wife in the penultimate scene, his presence could seriously confuse our attempts to bring the last picture of Elizabeth to a focus. Yet Essex's influence does persist in the orchestral elaboration of his song: each musical line having been so wedded to its text, his words are powerfully recalled, and their relevance to the later contexts is always pointed and sometimes ironic. It is precisely because we listen in this divided way that the foreground voices are given no musical personality, but merely speak, while the few lines that the queen sings are direct echoes of, or pathetic reflections on, the original song. So Essex's rôle in the opera, while it may be 'patchily drawn', is to provide the one consistent relationship of characters from which we deduce most about Elizabeth. The opera could have no shape at all

[1] M. D. Calvocoressi, *Mussorgsky*, London 1946, p. 117.
[2] Howard, p. 105.

without its account of that relationship, and Strachey therefore remains an indispensable background to the work; none of which means that one could plausibly transfer his title to it.

In the opening scene of the opera, librettist and composer are at pains to establish some traits of Essex's character, even by the slightly contrived means of showing his quarrel with Mountjoy, thereafter to be apparently his closest ally in his restless resentment of the queen's authority (and of her susceptibility to counsels other than his own). It is Elizabeth who brings them together, in the splendid Ensemble of Reconciliation, yet one feels that Raleigh's sententiously waggish judgment of the case may have done more, in revealing a common enemy. For Essex, it is clear from almost his first words, is an enthusiastic hater. He cannot bring himself to watch the tournament in which Mountjoy is engaged, but every comment he makes on

Ex. 9.1 (a)

Ex. 9.1 (b)

Cuffe's report of its progress is bilious, colouring the prevailing G Lydian, and sharper, tonalities of this scene with flattening inflexions (see Ex. 1a). In the recitative that follows he is provocatively offensive, taunting Mountjoy with a phrase that is to acquire tragic meaning when it rebounds on his own head (Ex. 1b); and his explanation of the fight, after Elizabeth's entry has cut it short, is simply untrue. Raleigh's judgment provokes his *sotto voce* curse, whereas Elizabeth's magnanimous pronouncement is received in an ensemble that, for all its musical delights, does not differentiate character; the loyalty that the queen inspires seems as yet to be absolute.

The scene between Cecil and Elizabeth isolates the danger of so head-strong a character as Essex's: 'he might grow unruly, *and unruled*', but with his arrival and Cecil's departure we see a more complex personality. He strikes at once a romantic gesture (i.e., a stabbing Romantic dissonance and its blissful resolution) which even here sounds (see Ex. 2a) a little too

Ex. 9.2

practised an approach to the queen's favours; this is another motive which is to acquire greatest force when it goes awry. His two lute-songs, however, show for the first time some charm, and carry no more suggestion of dissembling than is to be found embedded in the amorous conventions of the Elizabethan lute-air. The first is a fragile little strophic piece, but it gains some dramatic point from an undertow in the bass which represents the persistence of those 'cares of state' the queen has asked him to subdue. The motive symbolizing these (Ex. 2*b* above) erupts at the end of each stanza, but never quite matches Essex's efforts to lighten her mood: while he moves up a semitone each time, as does the bass, they remain incompatible by the same amount, so that Elizabeth's refusal to succumb to gay music is palpable before she cuts it short. In asking for a song of another kind, she ordains quite specifically the mood he shall adopt, and it is illogical of her to tease him afterwards with its being out of character, a conceit. The dramatic interest lies in the kind of conceit through which she chooses to escape from her cares. To low brass cadences that prefigure the opening of his song, she asks that he

> Evoke some far-off place or time
> A dream, a mood, an air
> To spirit us both away.

No clearer evidence could be found that at this moment, as well as in the return of the song which ends the opera, she sees her relationship to Essex as part of an idealized state that can never be brought about. Indeed, the true warmth of feeling that exists between them is perhaps savoured by her more richly for the self-denial it demands. Essex, on the other hand, is unable for long to dissociate his titillatingly veiled protestations of love from the need to bolster his pride with the preferment he seeks, the Lord Deputyship of Ireland. The ambivalence of their beautiful duet, 'O heretofore', springs from the resigned flattening inflexions of the queen's measured *cantabile* (recalling the simple devotional strain of such a lutenist as Campian) and the snatched phrases of Essex with their anxiously sharpened degrees. The piece captures a mood of tension, but this is held in equipose—all the movement takes place essentially within a single static seventh chord. It is Elizabeth's declaration

> Then rejoice with me!
> I am a woman, though I be a Queen
> And still a woman, though I be a Prince

that destroys this balance and encourages Essex to launch into a more open protestation of love. Yet it is surely significant that the words she clings to, and the orchestra salutes, are 'Queen' and 'Prince'. And Essex's vow is, musically at any rate, almost too pat, an automatic construction of scalic 6/4s against a bass moving in thirds. This ardour is quickly exchanged for the fury that comes even more easily to him, as Raleigh's shadow is seen through the curtain. C minor, so rapturously sad in the lute-song, is now the vehicle of anger, the more sinister for its being controlled in this drily rhythmic monotone; both contexts create associations that are recalled when C minor returns as the verdict and sentence on Essex are pronounced. Also to appear again, with increasing significance, is the explosive horn dissonance on to which his lines fall, a motive that is consistently associated with Essex's ill-fated ambitions in the campaign against Tyrone (see Ex. 3).

Ex. 9.3

Act II shows still more directly that, whatever affection for Elizabeth may have warmed Essex's 'Happy he', it will count for nothing if those ambitions are thwarted. His ranting and repetitive ninths in the double duet already argue a lack of balance that neither the patient solicitude of his wife nor the admiration of his sister does much to correct; rather does the arrival of an audience encourage him to work his grievance into the more polished form of 'By Heav'n, my voice deserveth to be heard'. Yet it is the same three characters who fan the flames of treason in this ensemble who prove capable of the moving words of consolation offered to Lady Essex after she has been humiliated by the queen. Here again, Essex's pride is at the root of the matter, for it is he who has required his wife to wear the elaborate dress which, taken by the queen (as he must have foreseen) to be an assertion of rank, triggers off her splenetic outburst. And it is characteristic that sympathy soon turns with Essex to outraged concern for his own dignity, the venom which distinguishes him throughout the opera welling out in an ugly phrase: 'her conditions are as crooked as her carcass'. This gesture of defiance, of heresy indeed, jangles on in the orchestra as he is summoned before the queen to be appointed Lord Deputy in Ireland, a favour bestowed to the strains of Ex. 1b, though this figure is soon transformed into the salutation 'Victor of Cadiz' with which the company honours him. But at the end of the act, the pit orchestra sounds a heavy rather than triumphant portent as its A minor version of the 'Victor' theme engulfs the courtiers' D Lydian Coranto. The ominous comment is thus outside the action, where high spirits prevail and all slights are forgotten, following Essex's sonorous vow to quell the Irish rebels. This readiness to overlook an affront to his wife, provided his own cause is served, though it rests on a distortion of the historical record (which does not concern Lady Essex), goes far towards making the opera's Essex a character whose downfall and disappearance will create no sense of premature loss, of unfulfilled potentialities. And so the far more ramified character study of Elizabeth will assume an unchallenged primacy in our minds.

But first, in fact, there is another meeting between them, and it is noteworthy that we learn much more about the queen from it but merely confirm our impressions of Essex. Having burst impetuously into her dressing-room, he immediately appeals to her with a sorrowful version of Ex. 2a, and a protestation of duty that is immediately nullified by a plea to be forgiven. The queen's dignity in contrast is awesome, yet by no means lacking in tenderness. The whole scene is punctuated by dry pizzicato minor triads (eventually embracing all twelve) that convey a clear-eyed disenchantment, yet she is honest enough to recall what has been: the muted brass F minor triad brings a memory of that 'far-off place or time' she once sought, and earlier images are sadly re-worked:

> But the years pursue us
> And the rose must feel the frost
> And nothing can renew us
> When the flame in the rose is lost.

As Essex seeks to present his case, we hear a recurrence not only of the crucial chord of Ex. 3, but of its vocal line too. The chord has articulated the Act III prelude and the earlier part of the scene, in which we have heard from the Maids of Honour of Essex's failure. So the lion has already fallen in Elizabeth's esteem, yet she grants him leave to speak in a gentle arietta decorated by an almost skittish flute figure (derived from the subject of the fugal prelude). He promptly turns the same music into a self-justifying rant against unnamed slanderers. Though the queen's composure is ruffled by this dishonourable performance, it is left to the orchestra to press home clipped references to 'Victor of Cadiz, overcome Tyrone', a specific charge from her which he has dismally failed to carry out. Only when he seeks to reawaken her affection by striking once more the gesture of Ex. 2a does she passionately consign that part of their lives irrevocably to the past in a duet that unwinds over a gloomily reiterated C minor pedal. When this conjures up a poignant recall of the lute song ('Happy *were* we'), even Essex has recognized that their relationship is shattered. It is she who orders that he be kept under guard, and, his inevitable bid for freedom having become an open incitement to civil war, she who must weigh the horror of his death against the more pernicious dangers of national calamity.

The circumstances which influence her decision shed further light on the queen, but we ought to review now the exposition of her character earlier in the opera, sometimes in scenes that do not touch upon her relationship to Essex. Her first speeches, on interrupting the Essex-Mountjoy fight, show her acting as patently *ex officio* as the showy fanfares that punctuate them;

and like the trumpets she can easily sound too shrill. But her lines which open the reconciliation ensemble abandon fanfare shapes for a measured, conjunct melody of an attractive gravity; the Mixolydian B flat of the refrain, 'Fail not to come to court', underlined by a dominant seventh harmony, represents, as so often in Britten, an access of warmth but not of light. The ensemble ends with the theme that will symbolize her people's devotion throughout the opera (Ex. 4). Perhaps excessively mannered at first sight

Ex.9.4

and sound, it reveals the strength of its melodic construction (operating, rather as in the lutenists' *style brisé*, at various levels) through many repetitions. It is quoted by Elizabeth in her song to Cecil, bringing a lyrical note to an otherwise constrained piece, with its tight ostinato accompaniment that is to develop into the 'cares of state' motive (see above, Ex. 2*b*); here we see a monarch prepared to listen to others' counsels and to form sober judgments. The Essex scenes which follow (and were discussed above) reveal unsuspected qualities of fantasy and passion, yet her ability to cut short the meeting at the call of the 'state' motive is the more impressive, while the Soliloquy and Prayer which end Act I demonstrate, long before Essex understands it, how the divine charge of her office can never be neglected, even when it conflicts with the most ardent personal inclination. The Earl's vows are sorrowfully but firmly disowned, that is his theme is inverted at 'If life were love and love were true', and its underlying thirds have become fourths, for the 'Crowned Rose' theme (Ex. 4) repeatedly becomes uppermost in her thoughts. The plainsong-like melody of her prayer suggests the reservoir of spiritual strength that lies behind her other pronouncements in this conjunct manner.

Elizabeth on progress at Norwich admirably avoids regal condescension while attracting the most heartfelt homage simply by showing an apparently genuine concern for the old Recorder and an apparently genuine interest in the masque that Essex is finding so tedious. Her echoing of the valedictory choral dance in her speech, 'Norwich, we can never forget', is tactful, but the rise to high B flat in the following phrase argues a warmth of response that altogether exceeds formality.

By now we have a fairly consistent picture of the queen's musical character. How far out of that character her behaviour in the ballroom is may be heard at once therefore in the forced angularity—successive melodic leaps, often involving chromatic twists—of the Burlesque to which she parades in Lady Essex's dress. The gross tuba, trombone glissandi and *sul ponticello* violas that distort the *Lavolta* theme suggest a precariously balanced personality which emerges nowhere else in the opera; coming so soon after the Norwich scene, it shows how much more taxing than her meetings with the loyal but remote citizens are those with courtiers whose questioning of her absolute authority must always remain an unsettling possibility. She behaves abominably, and atones for it no more wisely in favouring Essex with the Lord Deputyship. Her official tone is invaded here by the fateful chord of Ex. 3: Essex is to know that the ambitions he has confided have helped to sway her decision.

This makes the more bitter, for her as well as Essex, the memories represented by that chordal motive as it reverberates through the scene in which his failure stands revealed. And, if she is firm in rejecting all his bids for renewed favour, she is even in danger of overcompensating for her earlier moment of weakness when she discusses Essex's actions with Cecil. His canny judgment, 'I see a certain danger', is swept aside by her self-induced indignation, 'Think of the waste . . .' (a rearrangement of 'overcome Tyrone'), and Cecil, merely by echoing her every sentiment, is able to elicit from her the command that Essex be kept under guard. She promptly drops the imperious tone as she recognizes 'I have failed to tame my thoroughbred', and her last phrase in this scene, conflating elements of examples 2 and 3, epitomizes the dilemma (see Ex. 5).

Ex. 9.5

The disastrous results of Elizabeth's action (whether or not it was precipitate) are seen obliquely, in the ballad-singer's news bulletins and Cuffe's haranguing of the populace in Essex's cause. But the effects on her of the verdict which the Council must pass are heard throughout the final scene of the opera, and in a very direct musical form: the B flat pedal that underlies the G major chord on which she enters to learn the verdict persistently looms up as she wrestles with the advice of Cecil, the pleas of Essex's wife and sister and, above all, her own divided feelings. Her reponse to Cecil, 'no prating to me of my duty', is a tetchy outburst (perhaps too near Lady Billows's style), but the following aria turns to the essential problem. This is the only passage in *Gloriana* in which Britten makes protracted use (the first lute-song was a mere illustrative touch) of the kind of semitonal tensions that are so vital to the dramatic argument of other operas. And with *Budd* in the immediate background of this work, it is particularly interesting to observe the reversion to a conflict between B minor and its leading-note's tendency to establish itself as centre of a major tonality (i.e., B flat major). A more literal musical representation of a dilemma is difficult to imagine, and its roots in Elizabeth's own ambivalence are painfully clear in the closing line (Ex. 6).

Ex. 9.6

The B flat retreats to its earlier rôle of a disturbing background in the trio of suppliants. Yet their music already has its own undercurrents—the constant seventh chords of the voices and clarinets imply one strain held in control, while their aspiration towards a C major outcome is prevented by the unyielding A minor arpeggios of the strings. So without sacrificing the intense beauty of sound that is vital to his dramatic purpose here, Britten lets us feel the manifold tensions that are operating in this situation. The queen's replies to the two pitifully monotone pleas of Lady Essex reinforce the character study created already. To the appeal for Essex's life, 'a Prince' responds with a proud derivation of the Crowned Rose theme, but soon collapses under the influence of that ominous B flat pedal into more introspective phrases:

>Alone, in sight of all the world
>Alone, and must not fail.

To the appeal for Essex's children, 'a woman' responds; the warm music of the trio, persisting now in the orchestra, softens the queen's speech into more flowing, conjunct lines. But even before Penelope's plea has been made, Elizabeth has received her with a chromatic edginess that does not bode well. And for Penelope to lead off with an encomium of her brother that also, via Ex. 1*b*, reminds the queen of favours she was once ready to bestow on him is monumentally tactless. Now as A sharp (in an F sharp major context) the *idée fixe* of this scene is at first the sole accompaniment of Elizabeth's replies, but the rhythmic figures of her soliloquy (see above, Ex. 6, bars 5–6) soon bring her back to the musical crux, and, goaded too far by Penelope's flaunting of what are more than half-truths ('he most deserves your pardon, Deserves your love'), she faces up to the B flat implications in decisively signing the death warrant. Yet the tumultuous orchestral scales which sweep us from this scene into the Epilogue's C minor are far from resolved in their conflation of B flat Mixolydian and B minor.

There is a nightmare quality about the return of 'Happy we', even without the interludes of melodrama, for what were delicate improvisatory details of line and accompaniment are now blown up in oppressive tutti textures, and phrases stalk out of their neatly cadenced frames, or engage with themselves in imitative contortions. The queen's exchanges with persons who, however weighty their business, are scarcely more than shadows never deflect her altogether from Essex's song; when the irony is particularly cruel, she brings the words to the surface by her own singing. So, for example, 'In some *unhaunted* desert' takes her directly to the B flat that is a spectre in itself. As it rumbles on, her own death is foreshadowed in the melodrama. And when the B flat returns to usher in 'Where when he dies' she at once interprets it as referring to herself—'*mortua sed non sepulta*'. Orchestral sequences protract the penultimate phrase of the song, wafting the music up from C minor till, in a magical twist of tonality and timbre, that fateful key is utterly lost, and in place of the song's final phrase, a more fitting last word on Elizabeth's whole reign is heard in the distant strains of 'O crowned rose'; now its overlapping entries help to blur the sonorous picture as the stage picture also sinks into darkness.

In an opera which relies more openly than any other by Britten on set (even titled and numbered) pieces, we are sometimes jolted by the crudity of the connecting matter and sometimes by the incongruity of certain of the pieces themselves. At times we may suspect that Britten conceived the units more or less independently, and relied only on a purposeful tonal scheme across the work (see Ex. 7) to provide a plausible relationship. A transition such as that of the recitative which leads from D into E flat for the final march of Act I, Scene 1, is journeyman stuff, even if the recurrences of 'O crowned

Ex.9.7

$$\begin{pmatrix} \circ = maj. \\ \bullet = min. \end{pmatrix}$$

rose' and the trumpet music which it connects complete an acceptably balanced structure. The extremely wide range of stylistic reference in *Gloriana*, incorporating various overt adaptations of historical idioms, is not, I believe, the chief cause of the opera's occasional jarring notes. Of two pieces which I find disappointing, one relies on pastiche and the other is far from it; both concern characters who are peripheral. Raleigh's song is packed with archaisms of rhythm, harmonic progression (including the inevitable 'false relation') and division technique, but a poorish melodic invention does not improve on repetition. Mountjoy's song as he awaits Penelope in the garden (later made into a duet with her) is surrounded by bewitching orchestral details of colour and figuration, but its melody is banal: Plomer gave the composer a start here with stilted lines like

> With enemies whose envy is more sombre
> Than cold unfathomed hollows of the seas.

In fact, it must be added that Britten later rescues this piece in two ways. The duet begins with a strangely beautiful passage in thirds, 'Let us walk in the paths of pleasure'—strange because of its modality that is poised uncertainly between F Lydian and the rare Locrian mode on B; and the sad sweetness of this music is sustained in a return to Mountjoy's theme that dispels its *gaucherie* with overlaid mirror images. A piece that is even more evidently a lyrical interlude than either of these, the Dressing-table Song in Act III, is also more successful, both because of its placing, after the tense last meeting between Essex and the queen, and because its workmanship is so refined: the quintuple metre allows a subtle flexibility of phrasing, and the accompaniment does not settle into predictable patterning until the choral refrain; but now interval is varied in the languorously arched phrases—fifths, sixths, thirds, fourths and sevenths lead to a close in octaves. Patricia Howard's reference to the 'harem' atmosphere of this scene is delightfully to the point.[3]

The opening of this same scene (the first in Act III), however, provides a reminder that there are structures in this opera which rely on a quasi-symphonic manipulation of material rather than on strophic symmetries. Its prelude operates on three levels: pedal (i.e., no motion), articulating succession of 'Essex' (Ex. 3) chords (i.e., slow motion) and rapid figuration (see Ex. 5, bars 3 and 5) of the fugal working-out. With the maids' conversation

---

[3] ibid., p. 117.

the subject becomes accompaniment pattern, but the bass now begins to move through ponderous progressions; the 'Essex' chords return as before but at longer intervals. At Essex's intrusion the original cycle of the prelude is repeated, but now each chord is protracted to support conversation; the pedal is eventually quitted for an augmentation of the fugue subject as he bursts in upon the queen. The scene between them has been discussed already in another light, yet structurally it serves as a development of the basic idea, persisting even in the 'larks' figure. Finally, after the emotional upheaval of 'Dear name I have loved', the reassurance of the dressing-table ceremony and the consultation with Cecil, the scene ends with a reversion to the opening material—now almost totally static, and with only one appearance of the 'Essex' chord, to fateful words (see Ex. 5). Rather more mechanical is the reproduction of the Act I prelude as the tournament of the opening scene, though this throws into greater relief Essex's sour deflections. The Ensemble of Reconciliation sets off as a simple song of balancing phrases, but by the superimposition of figurative detail and a steady unfolding of key it becomes a truly cumulative piece. The most ambitious structure in Act II is the quartet for Essex and his supporters, founded not only on the contrast between Essex's spikily canonic 'By Heav'n' and Penelope's suavely Lydian 'Call on the stars', but also on the progressive exposure of other significant component figures—Lady Essex's 'O be cautious' and 'Ourselves to rule the land'.

At the other extreme from such expansive forms stand the tableaux that begin and end Act II, in each of which a set of self-contained dances is threaded together by dialogue. One represents the masque offered to the queen by the citizens of Norwich, the other a court ball, and we should expect to find in them the strongest traces of Britten's debt to specific Elizabethan musical models. Yet the choral dances bring surprisingly few reminders. The Spirit of the Masque ushers in the Dance of Time with declamatory touches that are Purcellian, while the dance, despite its imitative technique, is an evocation of clanging bells that is remote from the madrigal. The serene Dance of Concord taps a strain of sensuous diatonicism that was beloved of a line of part-song composers stemming from Stanford; here it is appropriately restricted to pure triads throughout, preserved from bathos by new contexts and phrase variation. Nor are the following dances much nearer any recognizable madrigalian source —though they are no less engaging for that. Only in the final Dance of Homage does imitation of the opening phrase permeate the texture, but the density is uncharacteristic; the warmth of feeling these repetitions engender, as they emerge from and recede into the prevailingly rich sound, creates a splendid sense of climax by very simple means.

The palace dances are more stylized, adroitly re-creating the casually imitative five-part texture, keen rhythmic invention and improvisatory divisions of the type, but extending its modal freedom into a harmonic language

Ex. 9. 8

that existed in no century before ours. One example from the pavane will show how more or less idiomatic and, to the Elizabethan composer, quite inconceivable progressions jostle with one another (Ex. 8). The echo of *Lachrimae* is typically distorted by harping on a flat seventh which Dowland would have found barbarous, while neither the unresolved dissonance of the second beat nor the pungent dominant seventh of the second bar belong to a 'period' style. We are sufficiently persuaded by the prevalence of root triads and the fluid metre to accept this as a *token* of old music. Similarly, we can take pleasure in the harmonic adventures of the following phrase, propelled idiomatically enough by imitation, even while we recognize that only the first move is at all plausible (if not in relation to a G minor opening). Though rapid modulation was a source of great satisfaction to some consort writers, they would avoid this concentration of events in dance suites, and their criteria of part-writing were narrower than these. But a composer does no violence in looking at period characteristics from his own vantage-point. As with Stravinsky, the expressive essence is to be found in the deviations from the observed model, and Britten has shown elsewhere how creatively his imagination can be prompted by his affection for Elizabethan music. The two Dowland fantasies, for viola and guitar, take existing material as their starting-point (or finishing-point, see pp. 304 and 331), but in the opera there is very little direct quotation. The plangent opening phrase of 'Happy we' is taken from Wilbye's madrigal 'Happy, o happy he' (from the second set, 1609), but the affective declamation into which the song blossoms owes less to Dowland's late declamatory manner than to the English Baroque—and even then the echoes range from Henry Lawes to Purcell. The Ensemble of Reconciliation maintains semiquaver figurations typical of the virginalists' 'running' fancies, while the first act ends with the Queen's Prayer, a quasi-plainsong harmonized in the *faux bourdon* manner that was an English speciality some two centuries before her time. The ballad-singer, on the other hand, ushered in by orchestral textures that suggest Tippett, promptly converts the material to reminiscences of eighteenth-century ballad opera, despite his being accompanied by an instrument appropriate enough to the opera's period—the gittern.

The ultimate congruity of such diverse idioms is much assisted by the consistently modal nature of the score: already in the first scene we hear the Lydian music of the prelude countered by the Mixolydian of the trumpets' natural harmonic series (another happily misapplied archaism!) in the brilliant fanfares that herald the queen. A comparison of some interest (if severely limited application) may be drawn between the modality of *Gloriana* and the prevalent diatonicism of *Die Meistersinger*. Indeed, to find a precedent for so proudly national a review of musical styles we may consider Wagner's juxtaposition of fragments of Mastersingers melody and sumptuous Bachian chorale harmonization. And the Wagner is another opera that exploits set-pieces (including of course 'songs' crucial to, yet distinct from, the action) with unusual persistence, and achieves climactic points in great tableaux. However that may be, Britten has forged here some of the most attractive nationalist music of our time, while also drawing in Elizabeth one of his most detailed character portraits.

10 The Turn of the Screw

Britten's early impatience with the unduly self-conscious nationalism and the restricted emotional range of much English music in the thirties had encouraged him to seek out a music at once more full-blooded and more nervously tense: his discovery of Mahler was reflected in the phraseology of much of his early music, and it was Mahler's individual orchestral manner (rather than, say, the chamber orchestration of either Stravinsky or Schoenberg) that developed Britten's keen sensitivity in the use of the small orchestra of solo tone colours. So much was evident at many moments of the first two chamber operas, while in the Spring Symphony the method had been extended to a full orchestral palette. But in *The Turn of the Screw*, completed in 1954 and first performed at the Venice Biennale Festival in September, Britten seemed to reflect another aspect of Mahler, the strange personality racked by a conflict between youthful aspirations and self-consuming irony, the creator of a music capable of hinting at the emotional subtleties and undertones which, before and (if decreasingly) after Freud, make their effect chiefly at a subconscious level. Henry James, whose short novel was the basis of Myfanwy Piper's libretto for Britten's opera, was another pioneer in making an imperfectly glimpsed emotional world a subject of his art, though his delicately-shaded allusiveness reflects a *pudeur* that does not naturally prompt any direct comparison with Mahler's self-torturing assumption of a loudly public tone of voice. Yet James's careful depiction of the complacently disenchanted world of the English country house which is revealed none the less, to be undermined by indefinable (and therefore virtually unassailable) powers of evil, demanded for its musical treatment all the ambiguities, of innocence touched with worldly wisdom, of terror mounting below high spirits, that are of the essence of Mahler's art.

The choice of this source material proved to be highly imaginative, though a listener who approached the work straight from the hearty English humour (whatever the moments of disturbingly pointed truth) of the previous chamber opera, *Albert Herring*, might be forgiven for regarding it as unpromising. But in the intervening period Britten had written *Billy Budd*, a work combining within its overt drama a network of conflicting emotional forces that, despite soliloquies in which the three chief figures all glimpse something of their true plight, are never made explicit. If much remained here for the composer's process of extrapolation, at least the characters gave a clear direction in their words so that the void between those and their deepest meaning could be attempted. Much of James's point, however, is contained in the circumstance that his ghosts, Peter Quint and Miss Jessel, do not speak. Thus, we may find them palpably representatives of evil which, because it is indefinable, acquires a terrifying quality; it admits no possibility of a frontal attack and lays hold of the mind more cancerously because its presence may come to be suspected in all things (and particularly in oneself: thus the whole of James's story can be read in an inverted sense, the canker being in the mind of the Governess). But it is to deny the whole point of the operatic medium if two of the chief agents of the dramatic action are deprived of the music which will set them on the same idealized plane as the other characters. Indeed, music's ancient association with magic and the supernatural, its power to *enchant*, required that these two figures above all should acquire pronounced musical qualities. So if James's story was to justify operatic transcription, the ghosts must be made singing characters. And if they were not to become ludicrous bores, they must be given words to sing. How to provide them with a text that still left the nature of their evil influence on the children horrifying because imprecise was the librettist's chief problem. Her solution may affront the Jamesian who simply reads it, but it offers an excellent framework on which the composer can work and has imaginative qualities of its own. Her ghosts throw the children into an ecstasy of compliant terror because their words, of a heady 'poetic' quality on which a child's mind can feed, are intangible yet luring:

> I am the hidden life that stirs when the candle is out
> Upstairs and down, the footsteps barely heard
> The unknown gesture, the soft persistent word
> The long sighing flight of the night-winged bird.

At the central point of the drama, when the ghosts are heard alone voicing their will to control the children's minds, a phrase is borrowed from Yeats to sum up, once again without resort to definitions, the significance of a musical figure that has symbolized the corrupting power of evil on the innocent (as we shall see, the Governess is as exposed to the danger as are her charges):

> 'The ceremony of innocence is drowned'.

Wise though Britten and his librettist were not to depend on a wordless vocalise for their ghosts, they have found an opportunity in Quint's calls to the boy Miles for vocal melismata and attendant orchestral colouring, alluring yet disturbing sounds that are heavy with innuendo and create a fevered atmosphere more effectively than can any words in the original story.

In many other contexts, some of which will be noted later, music is able to awaken an ambivalent response in us that words could not touch off. But, of course, the decision to make articulate their ghosts means that Britten and Myfanwy Piper narrowed down the range of interpretations that could be placed on James's story. For example, the view that all its shadows of evil darken only the Governess's mind cannot be sustained in the opera. The Governess may be capable of receiving intimations denied to the stolid Mrs Grose, but it cannot be doubted that she shares that power with the children: quite apart from its scenes between the ghosts and the children in which she has no part, the opera attempts a sustained musical study, through the appearances of Miles's 'Malo' theme, of the boy's simultaneous attraction towards and yearning to resist evil. Yet if it necessarily makes more specific statements than did the story, the opera leaves enough unexplained to preserve the sense of poignant mystery with which one reaches the end of James's account. When so much must depend on inference, any attempt to construct one continuously unfolding dramatic action would have introduced a causality quite at odds with James's intentions. The opera was therefore planned to juxtapose a large number of incidents so that their composite pattern gradually became clear. The composer's first task was to conceive a sequence of self-contained musical episodes. But, of course, this immediately raised two problems, one of passing smoothly between them so as to prevent an impression of excessive heterogeneity, and the other of securing across this long span of small units the sense of relentless movement towards catastrophe which James's prose so powerfully conveys.

Britten's solution was to link up all the scenes of the opera by a chain of orchestral interludes. This device alone might simply have doubled the effect of prolixity and thus further diluted dramatic cogency, but Britten designed these interludes as constituents of a single musical argument, conducted *across* the intervening scenes. Indeed, because their progress is quasi-dramatic (i.e., it draws on principles of 'absolute' music commonly accepted as dramatic analogues), we feel the *musical* move through the interludes to a climactic situation as a far more direct one than that portrayed in the scenes; and in the work's finale the musical crisis coincides exactly with the dramatic. The interludes are all variations on one instrumental theme expounded in the prologue; their elaborate tonal scheme invites scrutiny first of all as an 'absolute' musical structure; see Ex. 1.

The theme already prefigures its tonal treatment in two ways, firstly by containing all twelve notes and secondly by disposing these in an orderly way so as to expose two simple scales. They are in fact whole-tone scales (i.e., odd-numbered notes/even-numbered notes) and they therefore imply an infinitely extended pattern; this screw can turn for ever. Though the theme is given very specific character by the selection of octave-register, by portentous double-dotted rhythms and by its sustaining of every note to form a single dense chord, the note succession is *too* regular to represent any single

205

Ex.10.1

Affekt: it provides ideal material on to which changing attendant circumstances can project changing characters, yet this will not conceal the immanent quality of those fundamental intervals. So the variations can at once refer to the emotional climate and even the visual or aural minutiae of the specific scenes they precede or follow and relate these to a process of fate that is relentlessly in train.

Britten's allocation of this cardinal rôle to a twelve-note theme gave rise to much comment, some of it ill-considered in encouraging a belief that the work marked a significant step towards his acceptance of Schoenbergian principle. While his use of such a theme as the basis of innumerable variants (and its influence extends into much of the opera's material beyond the interludes) is clearly indebted to Schoenberg's example, Britten neither here nor elsewhere has regarded the twelve notes as constituting a negation of tonal hierarchies, but rather as a ramification of them. What he sees in a note-row is not so much equality but *totality*: almost every one of his twelve-note ideas is in some sense the symbol of an *all*—a cosmos, one might more pompously say; many examples are cited elsewhere in this book. But within any given context, however rapidly fluctuating central notes may be, they are allowed to exercise their old powers of attraction. And since Britten rarely permits his harmony to stray further than the ear can retrace from a triadic norm, this twelve-note melodic material takes us nowhere towards Schoenberg's dissolution of the motive in the texture with its consequent abandonment of functionally directed harmony. (In the few special cases where Britten's *harmony* has a twelve-note origin, it is likely to stress its triadic origins with notable perversity. See *A Midsummer-Night's Dream*, Act II.)

Certainly in *The Turn of the Screw* we can see how in all but the last of the orchestral interludes (though the twelfth offers a somewhat tenuous relationship) the music is ordered consistently around the initial note of the theme, as 'tonic' in at least a broad and often in a quite traditional sense. Since the theme is progressively transposed, we therefore find in the interludes as clear a succession of keys as is suggested by the signatures Britten uses. It can be seen from the example above that the key centres are screwed up throughout the first act according to the succession of tone and semitone steps that form the Aeolian mode, but the final substitution of a semitone for the logical tone brings A flat in place of a return to A. Setting off from this A flat area, the second act unscrews its key succession in an exact inversion of the scalic steps of Act I, that is, descending Mixolydian on A flat. (This incidentally ensures that all twelve centres have been used, though of course some have occurred more than once.) But an uncertainty attends the final stages of the return: the twice-heard A flat that dominated the peak of this key structure appears by now to have a far stronger grip on events than the distant A from which they originated, yet exact inversion of the upward screw will require a final semitonal step to A. The ensuing crisis is given telling symbolic form. After the penultimate centre, B flat (Variation XIV), all centres are suspended in a variation which conflates all twelve notes of the theme in dense masses, then in the following *scene* the theme is presented in A for the first time since its announcement in the prologue. But this A is not to be unchallenged. The theme appears in passacaglia-like bass reiterations that at first do not attempt its further reaches, sticking to those notes 1–6 which can be securely accommodated within A major tonality; but as longer circuits are attempted and the seventh and eighth notes appear, strong currents in the upper texture swing the music towards A flat. At the climax, a final vast statement of the theme on A is achieved despite being pitted against a superstructure now entirely in A flat. Thereafter great pedals ensure the domination of A to the end, and the A flat threat progressively weakens.

This process draws on a kind of logic that, if in a less extreme form, has been well understood by all composers who since the classical period have sought to sustain an 'argument' in terms of opposing key forces: we do not need to relate such a musical chain of events to the specific characters and situations of opera to sense its dramaticism. But in this case, if we do turn to the events of the drama, we see at once how cogently the tonal progress of the theme provides a parallel to them. Thus, Act I represents a gradual move from the A territory of the Governess's resolute prologue (' "I will" she said') to the A flat domination of the final scene in which the ghosts' power over her charges is made manifest. Act II begins with more A flat, even expounding the ghosts' own reading of the situation rather than the Governess's, yet she proves ready to challenge them as best she can. So now the descending key moves operate until, when an outcome seems imminent—yet is entirely unpredictable—the fateful theme is conflated into no key; then the passacaglia scene wages the battle that may result in a victory for A, the moral courage represented by the Governess, or for A flat, the evil powers personified by the ghosts. The hollowness of her victory is therefore painfully evident in the shadows which A flat continues to cast (for example in the penultimate 'Malo' phrases, around fig. 138) even after A has achieved the power to dictate the final cadence moves.

We have touched in no more than the crudest outlines of what is a singularly detailed tonal design. Its execution across the orchestral variations is supported by some significant tonal cross-references within the scenes, so that the final scene's foreground (i.e., personified) waging of a tonal conflict that has been background (i.e., chiefly instrumental) simply illuminates what has long been implicit. Indeed such a detail as the recurrences of the variation theme in its original rhythmic and melodic form is nicely balanced between foreground and background significance.

Act I. 1. in A	Instrumental	Prologue
2. in A flat	Instrumental repeated instrumentally in a vocal texture	Act I, Var. VII sc. 8: fig. 87
Act II. 3. in A flat	Vocal	Act II. sc. 1: fig. 20
4. in A (but challenged by A flat)	Vocal and Instrumental	Act II. sc. 8: fig. 131

Apart from these literal appearances, the variation theme plays far less overt a rôle in the personified drama than do various motives which, while deriving ultimately from it, have quite distinct contours and implications.

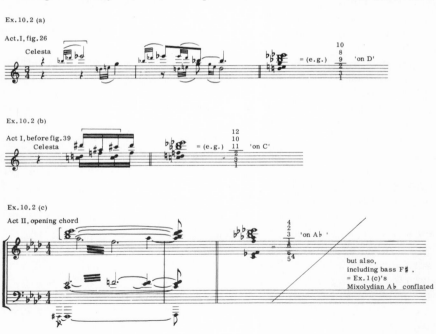

Ex. 10.2 (a)

Ex. 10.2 (b)

Ex. 10.2 (c)

Before examining either the variations or these other shapes, however, we should note how often the quality of a motive is attached to the key-colour of A flat, when it suddenly appears in some quite remote tonal context. In the most obvious examples, Quint's presence makes itself felt by the impending A flat of a three-note chord (notes 7–9 of the inverted variation-theme: 10 would be A flat); the distinctive instrumental colour of the celesta, quiet but impossible to ignore, sweet but hideously cloying, makes the point still more forceful. It can be seen in Ex. 2a and b how Britten sets this three-note segment of his twelve-note theme against similar but tonally opposed segments. (Innumerable other contexts in the opera are to this very limited extent 'serially' devised, and there results a considerable degree of harmonic homogeneity, perhaps even of deliberate monotony.)

As the ghosts' ascendancy becomes evident, this chordal motive is assimilated into pure A flat situations (like Ex. 2c). Another form of A flat intrusion is created by the clarinet arpeggios which constitute a further aspect of Quint's portrait: the most arresting example is their insinuation into the tritonally-distant, serene D major of the Summer Evening, Variation III, bringing a premonition not of Quint's appearance in the following scene (i.e., Ex. 2a) but, ironically, of the moment in it at which the Governess ignores the darkening sounds:

'My first foolish fears are all vanished now
are all banished now'.

Comparable assertions of A against established flat keys, which we might expect to find in the second act, are less common and altogether less schematic, yet they can be communicative: particularly strong examples are to be heard when the Governess braces up to face Miss Jessel, who has invaded her schoolroom (Act II, Scene 3: fig. 62), and when, recognizing the treachery of Miles's piano performance, she pits herself against the evil forces (see Ex. 3).

Ex. 10.3

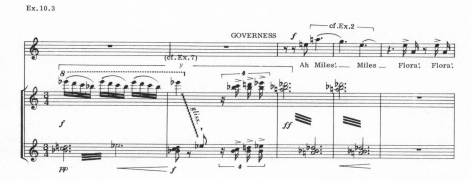

The variations are necessarily incomplete pieces, since they throw up ideas that continue to develop in the following scenes or (less often) they extend ideas from preceding scenes. However, they are scarcely less resourceful than many of Britten's independent variation sets. As we have noted, it is the changing attendant detail that most often gives specific character to these pieces, while the theme's schematic interval pattern is preserved with a passacaglia-like strictness. Even so, the detail, too, may be wholly relevant—as in the first variation where notes 1–6 of the theme are formed into an ostinato of two chords, establishing a pattern that underlies Scene 2; the ground is simply 1–12 plus reiterations of 9–12. Variation II uses a more sophisticated reading of the row (see Ex. 4) followed by a

```
Ex. 4   1  2  3  4  5
        1  2  3  4
        5  6  7  8  9
        5  6  7  8
        9 10 11 12  1
        9 10 11 12
```

literal inversion, and with a quasi-restatement based on 1–5 reiterations to stabilize the C major that will create moods of innocence in the following scene. The evenly-paced minims extend the Governess's serene mood ('For Bly is now my home') from one scene to the next (see the orchestral accompaniment to 'A good young lady'), but the busy rhythmic patterns above, an extension of the children's music from the previous scene, are phased out: their chord structure is again modelled on row segments. Variation III, the Summer Evening piece, seems like a complement to the nocturnal music that began the second scene of *Billy Budd*: both depend on low rich string chords and rhapsodically decorative melody. But here all is airier and more graceful, for this is as much a portrait of the Governess's rapt mood as the *Budd* music was a reflection of Vere's meditation. The theme is expounded in short leisurely oboe phrases, each transformed into flute arabesques; so the clarinet's intrusion (after notes 9–10) represents coloristically as well as tonally (see above) a deflection of the mood, while the final note of the theme is thrown into prominence as the Bartókian 'fluttering fears' of the bassoon figures. The following scene retraces the same experience in specific dramatic terms before Quint's appearance to Ex. 2a deflects it more radically, prompting the agitated figure, Ex. 5, an inversion of notes 1–3 (or, without transposition, 3–5) of the theme. The rest of the scene develops this, as do Variation IV and Scene 5. This is dramatically plausible enough, for the reverberations of her first shock have not died away before the Governess again sees Quint; and musically the extensive treatment of one motive is a valuable defence against an unduly sectional impression. The explanations from Mrs Grose and the Governess's vow to guard the children's innocence end the first span of the plot and so

Variation V marks a new departure. Its busy 'schoolroom' counterpoint is a wry Britten joke but a textural *tour de force* too; the initial notes of the subject and countersubject in each entry of this figure add two further notes from the twelve of the theme till the circle is completed in a coda that prepares for Miles's mnemonics in the schoolroom scene. But it is his second jingle, 'Malo', that throws disturbing shadows over Variation VI: it is threaded between woodwind arpeggios (I *versus* V), which herald the following scene by the lake, and pizzicato figures that gradually exhaust the twelve notes (as so often, the tonal circle is closed, here by adding 1.2 to 11.12 in the protracted final harmony). In Variation VII, the A flat statement of the theme restores its original form, as we have seen; its attendant texture is a complex of ghost symbols (see Exx. 2a and 3y, above and Ex. 12 below).

The repetition of this interlude as orchestral background to the culminating ensemble of the act (at fig. 87) helps to accumulate a big 'finale' structure, and its coda (from 88) gradually piles up on E flat (i.e., quasidominant of the act's structural cadence), segments of the row to the Ex. 5 rhythm till all twelve burst the music apart at the Governess's great cry 'Miles, what are you doing here?': for it is at this point that the boy's complicity in the ghosts' machinations can no longer be doubted. The arch phrases with which he strives to reduce a situation of blind panic to one of anti-climax gently parody the alarm of Ex. 5, and their 'sweet' harp accompaniment sets out from Quint's chord (Ex. 2). The act ends in a terrible quietness, leaving us tottering before a sickening vista.

Just as the final scene of Act I drew more heavily on the variation material than any other had done, so the variation that begins Act II (extending the A flat domain of the ghosts) draws heavily on the other music of that final scene, in a series of rhapsodic instrumental cadenzas. The references to each feature of the ghosts' temptation of the children are unmistakable. Their punctuation by dense chords is less obviously a structure built on the intervals of the Screw theme: thus as well as combining Quint's three-note chord (Ex. 2) and Miss Jessel's low F sharp (see Ex. 12), the first chord spells out all the notes of a Mixolydian A flat (see Ex. 2c). The progress is not schematic, however, and the unequivocal thematic statement is reserved for the centre of the following scene. Variation IX is the most elaborately

211

presented statement of the theme (and its retrograde) yet attempted, clearly a utilization of the principle of change-ringing appropriate in a piece dominated by the clangour of bells; the vigilant ear may note that Quint's chord creeps in even here (see, e.g., bar 9). This interlude is recapitulated in the course of the scene, underlying a vocal ensemble in which Mrs Grose recapitulates earlier lines; as the children's irreverent canticle is also brought back (at fig. 50), a structure of some subtlety and economy results. From the F sharp close, to which the Governess sings 'I am alone' after Miles has left her in this scene, into the F major of her despairing resolve to go away there is the most chillingly direct drop of key in the opera. It is this new material (its derivation will be discussed later) which is sustained through Variation X, above a peculiarly deadened version of the passacaglia theme. We are back in F, though far from the genial bustle of Variation V, and it is to the schoolroom that we return for Scene 3: Miss Jessel's presence there transforms the mode to the minor. Variation XI prepares us for a night scene with its bass flute and bass clarinet duet (cf. *Lucretia*, *Herring*, Spring Symphony), but it carries many more detailed suggestions: the ground's stealthy canonic movement progresses first only to the eighth note before being dissipated in fluttering figures, achieves ten on a second attempt, and finally all twelve—a graphic foreshadowing of the hesitant approaches the Governess and Miles will make towards each other's confidence in the following scene. The arabesques contain the obsessive minor-third reiterations of the preceding letter scene and they are soon heard surrounding 'Malo'. To complete a highly charged picture, Quint's influence flickers up from the background in glockenspiel touches of his chord.

Variation XII is one of the few that abandons a ground-like thread and the only one to include a vocal part; though the stage remains in darkness, we hear Quint, often in a furtive *Sprechstimme*, tempting Miles to steal the Governess's letter to his guardian. The variation develops dry pizzicato figures based on the 'Malo' shape (see Ex. 9 below), quickly exhausting twelve notes in their stretto formations, but only at the arrested chords to which Quint speaks solidifying into recognizable segments of the Screw theme. The scene itself is quickly over; and as Miles succumbs to the temptation, his 'Malo' theme emerges poignantly. It plays a big part in Variation XIII too. This piano study brings back the C major of Variation II but by now the 'innocence' of that key is patently a sardonic mask on the face of the young Miles. So every detail of his diligently-played Diabelli (or whatever) is turned slightly awry: neither in harmony nor scansion do the two hands quite correspond and soon little twists of key result in some poker-faced bitonality. Notes 1–10 of the theme are gradually pinpointed in the course of the piece, but 11 and 12 are given special prominence as opening notes of a bland subsidiary theme, setting off in E flat despite the left hand's indefatigable C major (see Ex. 6a). This is, of course, the 'Malo' shape, which gains ground until it achieves a still more direct reference (Ex.

Ex.10.6 (a)

Ex.10.6 (b)

Ex.10.6 (c)

6b). Miles returns smoothly to his opening, and even in their repetition during the following scene his references go unnoticed—both here and in his other piece (Ex. 6c)—until too late. Variation XIV celebrates his deception with the ground melodically elaborated in the orchestra while the piano's Romantic gestures of triumph (based on Quint's 'On the paths'), with crashing diminished sevenths to the fore, remind us that Miles, if precociously malignant, is still a child. Variation XV intensifies the blurred harmonic units of VIII, conflating now all twelve notes; its cadenzas refer back to Flora's 'I can't see anything' outburst of the previous scene (note how closely the piccolo scales resemble the scalic patterns of the acts: see above, Ex. 1b and c). The final variation is that incorporated within the last scene: its many revolutions of the earlier part of the ground on A before notes 7 and 8 are admitted have been noted, but the scene repays close study for it draws many strands of the work together. The complete plan is as follows

Notes 1–6 × 8	Notes 1–9
Notes 1–8 × 4	Notes 1–10
Notes 1–4 → 1	Notes 1–12 → 1

213

It will be seen (and it is certainly felt) how the earlier part of the conversation between the Governess and Miles remains defensively within that part of the ground that can be assigned to her A field of influence. But first clarinet arpeggios and then the celesta's intrusion with Quint's chord break in on this uneasy truce and Quint's call to Miles (cf. *y* in Ex. 3) admits the seventh and eighth notes in the bass. It is the Governess's action in pushing Miles round so that he cannot see Quint which secures the boy's confession that he stole the letter, and this moral triumph produces the celebration of A major at fig. 128 and a bass circuit that simply covers 1–4–1, that is, an affirmative tonal cadence. But Quint is not so easily repelled, and the next circuits extend to the ninth, tenth, eleventh and finally twelfth notes with an increasing urgency of bass movement: the fateful process is accelerated to its crisis. The diametrical opposition between the last statement of all, in the bass and sung by the Governess, and Quint's seductive 'On the paths' in A flat, epitomizes the conflict of the whole opera,[1] but its strains are too much for the boy: his denunciation of Quint above the recovered A is also his breaking-point. The Screw has turned for the last time, an inexorable fate has been discharged. Both Quint and the Governess are left to bemoan the situation they have brought about, but there is no further quotation of the variation theme.

Of the various themes and motives that derive from the twelve-note theme, most are confined to a specific character or situation, but one recurs in a wide range of contexts, if without the regularity of the turning Screw in the variations. This is first heard in the prologue: immediately after the Screw theme has amassed all twelve notes, its V returns to I for a jaunty rhythm in which unceasing timpani fourths mark the movement of the coach. Above these the new theme emerges in a middle part—the descending tetrachord of a major scale returning to its tonic again and then moving to a flat seventh from which the pattern is repeated; Ex. 7 shows a later, more common

Ex. 10.7

variant in which a return is made from the second loop to the original final. It also shows that the theme is no more than a filled-out version of the opening of the Screw theme, inverted. To deduce one single meaning from the more than twenty appearances of this *y* motive should not be attempted too

---

[1] To observe at how late a stage Britten arrived at this musical confrontation, cf. D. Mitchell, 'Britten's Revisionary Practice', *Tempo* 66/67, 1963, p. 15.

hastily, for it has two distinct, though related, fields of association. Through-out the opera it charts the Governess's progress, in Act I from uneasiness at the task she has set herself, to a recognition that 'things have been done here that are not good', and thence to a resolve to protect the children from evil influences, which is soon proved to be futile. In Act II, her awareness of evil bearing down on the house inspires a vow to escape, yet she cannot abandon the children to their supernatural mentors. But events once again drive her to admit failure, and to recognize how she has fallen a victim to that from which she sought to shield the children—'there is no more innocence in me'. Her last reference to the theme is transfigured into a simpler diatonic form (i.e., without the canker of the last seventh twist) at 'O Miles, I cannot bear to lose you . . . I shall save you', words that are soon to find a savagely ironic outcome. The other uses of this theme occur in Quint's music, in particular his seductive calls of 'Miles' or its instrumental echoes, and at the peak of the ghosts' scene, after they have laid bare their motives in seeking to control the children's thoughts, it carries their central line, the Yeats quotation 'The ceremony of innocence is drowned'; this appears three times in an elaborate structure, and is developed in taut imitations on its third appearance. The crucial significance of the y theme is, clearly enough then, the corruption of innocence, but at two levels—the directly exercised evil influence of the ghosts on the children and, through the terrifying spectacle of the increasing guile and malice that floods their still childish natures, its extension to the Governess: this is the meaning of her line 'O innocence you have corrupted me' in the 'labyrinth' aria. The dual application of the one theme, to the Governess and to Quint, reveals them as the central characters of the drama long before the final scene in which Miles patently becomes their pawn. As the Governess's last reference to the theme makes clear, a sub-stratum of her guilt concerns the love she has conceived for Miles, and Mrs Howard has convincingly related this to a thread that goes through the opera of her primary motivation by love for his guardian;[2] it is particularly clearly revealed in the prologue and the rich pathos of the letter scene.

We chart the Governess's progress no less in her changing vocal style. On her arrival at Bly, she sings in spacious lines of evenly-measured notes, savouring her new position as the controlling element in an ensemble to which Mrs Grose contributes simple-minded chatter and the children irre-pressible high spirits. (As so often, the structure of this scene depends on skilfully interlocked ternary patterns: the Governess completes a ternary span of melody, while the children's intervention at fig. 12 makes a ternary structure of the whole scene.) Her rapture in Scene 4 shows a more complex character; memories of the guardian lend a delicate tinge of regret to a consciously relished moment of serenity—her last in the opera, as the motive of alarm (see Ex. 5) breaks the spell. When its meaning has been clarified in

[2] Howard, pp. 131 et seq.

Mrs Grose's account of Quint and Miss Jessel, her vocal style verges on the histrionic as she vows to protect the children. Hysteria begins to threaten in the scene by the lake, when almost every statement is over-emphatic, and the reiterated sliding fourths of 'they are lost' (against Quint's chord) touch despair: by the end of the act she is wholly unnerved, as her frantic top B reveals at the twelve-note climax (see above). Her labyrinth aria in the first scene of Act II is in pitiful contrast to the music of her arrival at Bly: instead of gracious intervals, the line gropes in repetitive conjunct movements, twisting chromatically but returning impotently to the G sharp tonic. (How far Britten had developed this manner of writing in a decade may be seen by comparing the subtle twists of this piece—constructed entirely from two phrases—with such relatively crude contexts as Mrs Sedley's 'Murder most foul' or Mrs Herring's 'All that I did, all that I planned'.) The five-bar ground of the strings reflects the futile attempt to escape from G sharp (= A flat) territory on another level.

So her resolution physically to escape, following Miles's final taunt in the churchyard scene, represents in vocal terms a renewal of spirit—as the bold arpeggios bear witness (the pedal bass also demonstrates a stand against the wiles of the twisting *y* shape in the wind). The confrontation with Miss Jessel, whose phrases and arpeggio accompaniment patterns persist so implacably, reduces the Governess again to panic, exploding in the aria with which she drives the spectre away. The arpeggios still persist, however, as an agitated undercurrent to the one action in which she can hope to find some easing of her burden—the writing of a letter to the guardian. On its first instrumental presentation this is filled with a passionate yearning characterized by false relations between the parallel tenths, but as she then reads it aloud, sustained triads carry her into the warm, sweet textures of a daydream, in which the image of the guardian has for the moment taken precedence over her fears; the collapse of her climactic *cantabile* phrase into the limp close—'forgive me'—is particularly affecting. Scene 7, in which Flora is found by the lake, provides another insight into a character that is becoming dangerously unstable, bitterness ('And where, my pet, is Miss Jessel'—a straight quotation from James) quickly giving way to horror, anger, and something near self-pity as she is left alone. The *portamenti* of her previous confession of failure ('they are lost') are now widened to grotesque ninths. In the final scene she nerves herself for the crucial interview with Miles: her carefully prosaic E major scale 'All the same, go . . .' in the dominant preparation for the passacaglia is a revealing touch. In contrast to the stilted nonchalance of Miles's dotted rhythms, her lines well up impulsively in what is as much a confession as an inquisition (see Ex. 8). But Quint's intrusion brings back the agitation of the Ex. 5 motive, now twisted to a new use as the Governess substitutes a direct appeal to affection for moral pressures: 'Who is it? Who? Say for *my* sake!' Her words become repetitively importunate but her embarking, for the first and only time, on the Screw theme gives them a force

Ex. 10.8

she has never mustered before, and it is Miles who is crushed between this and Quint's relentless cajolery. The symbolic unison of the Governess and Quint, in which A flat is transformed to A as one celebrates the other's failure, has a mordant irony: her cries of 'you are saved' directly echo the terrible 'they are lost' of Act I, Scene 7, producing an antithesis that is the more painful in that both parts of it are evidently true. In the Governess's last surrender to terror, as she becomes aware of the boy's inert body, all her guards are swept away and her most impassioned phrase in the opera, 'don't leave me now', leads into her mourning song. As well as passing pathetically

217

through A flat territory in its second phrase, this great descending arc touches other memories: the 'sweet' harp chords (at fig. 138) recall Miles's childish delight in wickedness (cf., e.g., 'you see—I am bad' at the end of Act I), and the last line of 'Malo', with its sharp fourth and flat seventh, intertwines the minor thirds of the Screw theme as the timpani reverses its first two notes in a cadential fourth.

Perhaps the Governess's intensifying experience is the only truly developing aspect of the opera. It is difficult to judge whether the children grow in their knowledge of evil, or whether we, with the Governess, simply uncover more layers of their deceit; but the effect must be much the same, and Britten, while providing them with music that takes a demonstrative innocence as its starting point, has contrived that, armed with foreknowledge, we shall have a ready ear for false notes. The better we know the opera, the more likely are Britten's minute distortions of innocent children's song to suggest frightening vistas of self-knowledge. We may take as an example the moment at which the news comes that Miles is dismissed his school. The case for the defence, that he may be innocent of the charge of being a corrupting influence on his friends, is argued by James in a delicately oblique way—with a description of his sister, Flora, in which a wealth of unemphatic irony will convey to the reader a suspicion that he will do well not to accept the innocence of either child as finally established. In the operatic treatment of the scene, both children are in the background and their sudden piping of 'Lavender's blue' creates a curious strain on the listener. Like all surely designed musical effects, it is not curious at all: the Governess and Mrs Grose have been fretting, in chromatically introverted developments of Ex. 7 (= y), over Miles's reported 'badness' and the pure diatonicism of the nursery song remains awkwardly estranged even from their music of reassurance; great sweetness and uneasiness of sound coexist. So we may take the song to be an arch caricature of the innocence the children know they have left behind, or feel that this placidity is in some sense a true picture of one side of their nature, a side that makes more horrible the canker we shall increasingly detect in them. In Scene 5, another nursery song, 'Tom-Tom, the Piper's son', acquires a slightly sinister character from the tonal misalignment of tune and bass in the first two verses, the persistence of the 'Who is it' motive, and the nearness of that motive's percussive clusters to the Quint chord—which eventually emerges as the children dash into the distance. So far, only conjecturally can we detect malevolence or mockery in their singing, but their new words to the canticles before they go into church is a less equivocal declaration: what begins as mere schoolroom clowning, quoting phrases from earlier scenes ('O ye rivers and seas and lakes: Bless ye the Lord. O amnis, axis . . .') takes on a more sombre meaning at 'O ye paths and woods' (Quint's blandishments recalled), and their taunting of Mrs

Grose—'May she never be confounded'—is heavily underlined by the 'Malo' theme in the bass.

That theme (Ex. 9) is, as we have seen, still more prominent in both of Miles's piano solos, further refinements in the distortion of innocuous models, and the means by which he provides the cover for his sister's escape. Its rôle and its significance in a reading of the boy's character cannot be neatly pigeonholed. Whereas Quint's motives are direct spurs to evil

Ex. 10.9

= 1–5 of *x* set 'on A♭' or 6–9 of *x* inverted 'on A'

thought or deed, to which they lend allure, Miles's own theme (as he is proud to claim it to be, though its presentation in A flat and relationship to Quint's chord are telling) is a troubled song. It acknowledges the evil that is in him, and it puts a brave but wistful face on tragedy that he has not lost the power to wish averted; it is thus a movingly apt epitaph when sung by the Governess who has saved his soul at the expense of his life. Some of the incidental references to the theme are no more than gestures of defiance (as is also the recurrent 'I am bad' figure mentioned already), but one is particularly significant: in the ghosts' colloquy Quint seeks 'a friend/Obedient to follow where I lead/Slick as a juggler's mate to catch my thought' and the brittle accompaniment patterns reveal how suitable an accomplice he has already found in Miles, for the muted horn picks out the 'Malo' theme. It was originally characterized instrumentally by the cor anglais, and reappearances in that colour always seem to represent Miles's acceptance of a propensity to evil. Act II, Scene 4, is introduced by such a statement as the boy sits restlessly in the candlelight; it recurs when, the Screw theme having achieved its full course, Miles startles the Governess by blowing out the candle (to the 'I am bad' figure). Its note of pathos may appear disproportionate to such a childish prank, but the unseen figure of Quint prompted Miles's action, and the boy's (and our) reflections are intensified at the end of the scene. The variation that follows immediately presents the 'Malo' theme not as a reflection of Miles's true character but as material that Quint can manipulate; once again, after the tempter has won the day and Miles has stolen the letter, the ambivalence of his feelings emerges in the cor anglais quotation of 'Malo'. Some progress in evil may be detected in the quotation in his piano scene not only of 'Malo' (see Ex. 6a above), which is almost an *idée fixe* by now, but also of Quint's motives. In the final scene, however, Miles, trapped between conflicting powers, retreats into increasingly desperate snatches of speech and his own musical personality disappears

—to return with extreme power in the Governess's lament.

Flora is drawn in much less detail, but musically she is not without memorable characteristics. Her exaggeratedly childish behaviour in the schoolroom scene and her own geography lesson by the lake makes the more disconcerting her adoption of quite sophisticated melody and imagery in the lullaby to her doll. This develops a phrase sung by the Governess and seems to be balanced on a dividing line between intense sincerity and elaborate mockery; Ex. 10 shows the relation of its melody to the Screw prototype.

Ex. 10.10

That these bewitching strains should return as a spell (aided by Quint's and Miss Jessel's musical symbols) cast on the nodding Mrs Grose in the piano scene is entirely appropriate, for the whole piece is an incantation. After Flora has made her escape and is found by the lake, her reversion to the behaviour and sing-song repetitions of a little girl can only ring false, though the venom is genuine enough. The orchestral quotation of her lullaby in the ghosts' colloquy shows her as closely bound to Miss Jessel as Miles is to Quint; even though we see little more than tantrums in evidence of the pact, Mrs Grose's testimony in the final scene confirms her pitiful condition.

The colloquy is the only scene in which the ghosts are viewed out of relation to the children or the Governess, and even here they prey on the music of the children before reaching a climax in a juxtaposition of the corruption motive (Ex. 7 above) to the Yeats quotation and the Screw theme. It is in the previous scene, the last in Act I, and in Miss Jessel's invasion of the schoolroom that their most strongly characterized music is heard. Quint's motives, his key-colour, the three-note chord on the celesta and the enticing version of the corruption motive by which he calls Miles, have been noted, often in contexts where a few touches of one or both are enough to have wide repercussions. But it is in this scene that they fully take possession of the music. The ecstatic elaboration of the call is inevitably his most haunting moment, but the flow of imagery that follows, 'the riderless horse . . . King Midas with gold' and so on, is rapid and fantastic enough, verbally and musically, to suspend disbelief in so eloquent a spirit. Its effect on Miles is that of a drug, and the soft dragging motion of 'I am the hidden life that stirs' puts Britten's typical tonal ambiguity to a new use in its suave

Ex. 10.11

innuendo (Ex. 11). The duet Quint initiates, 'On the paths, in the woods', though exciting in its nimble stealth, is less immediately gripping; its impact is cumulative as the voices move into canon and the orchestral parts proliferate, but only on its return in the final scene of the opera do we gauge its significance for the work as a whole.

Ex. 10.12

Miss Jessel's motive takes various forms, the fullest, shown at Ex. 12, being heard when we first see her, by the lake. The low F sharp with gong is often sufficient elsewhere to indicate her presence, and the whole-tone complex (derived from the nature of the Screw theme) often flavours her music; this may account for the Lydian penchant that can be detected in much of Flora's music. Variation VII, a prehearing of the climactic ensemble of Act I, already incorporates her F sharp symbol, but we have seen and heard too little of her to find compelling the mannered vocal lines of her call to Flora in the night scene, and her solo 'All those we have wept for together', though sustained by the revolutions of her motive, is laboured. The simpler, initially almost banal, contours of her aria in the schoolroom strike home more certainly—perhaps Quint's absence helps almost as much as the obsessive rhythms and petrified accompaniment patterns. It will be noted, incidentally, that the first three notes of her motive have now formed a cluster in the bass comparable to Quint's chord; this creates an oblique kind of F minor, and the vocal Phrygian seconds emphasize the same mournful inflexion. On Miss Jessel's second lakeside visit to Flora (Act II, Scene 7) both the scooping intervals of her nocturnal calls to the girl and the

221

schoolroom aria (at 'we know all things') are recalled, though the Governess's agitation and Flora's shrill denials reduce her here to the merest symbol.

Ex.10.13 (b)

Ex.10.13 (a)

Even Mrs Grose has a pronounced musical personality. Her chief function is to recount the horrors that taint the immediate past of Bly, and her great sighing motive 'Dear God, is there no end to his dreadful ways' generates a whole scene, organized with unusual textural complexity; the derivation of this theme (Ex. 13a) from the Ex. 1 variation theme is shown and the link with the corruption theme (Ex. 7) is manifest. But Mrs Grose has another theme, Ex. 13b, an expression of her humility and consequent powerlessness in the face of evil, and this also recurs significantly.

The various motives that identify and often enough propel dramatic incidents have been discussed, and the relation of many of them to a common source in the Screw theme has been demonstrated. To reveal how powerfully they can act, even in making points that are nowhere stated explicitly, we may consider the single moment in the penultimate scene when the Governess is deserted by all and threatened by Miss Jessel's baleful influence: her sustained notes are literally trapped first between the Ex. 13b and Ex. 12 motives, then between a motive depicting Flora's spite and Ex. 12 (Act II, at figs. 110 and 111).

The Turn of the Screw is Britten's most intricately organized opera, and analysis could be extended with profit far beyond the scope of this chapter. In the opera house what matters is not the ingenuity of each detail but the magnificent interaction, so that a highly ramified yet overwhelmingly convincing experience is created. Much that analysis reveals may not have been consciously registered, yet all has been felt—which is one reason why so comparatively short a work can leave us so drained.

11 The Prince of the Pagodas

If we count the church parables among Britten's operatic scores, then there is no gap in the succession as great as that between *The Turn of the Screw* (1954) and *A Midsummer-Night's Dream* (1960). After *The Screw*, with some six full-length operas completed in less than ten years, the composer might justifiably have decided to cultivate quite other fields for a time, perhaps consolidating that brief return to purely instrumental problems he had made in *Lachrymae* and the *Metamorphoses*. In fact, a handful of tiny recorder pieces represent the only move in that direction, while the later part of this period is taken up by a virtuoso demonstration of word-setting in the contrasted manners of *Noyes Fludde*, the Nocturne, the Hölderlin songs and the *Cantata Academica*. But the first substantial work completed after *The Screw* (excluding the third canticle, finished later the same year) must have presented greater problems to Britten than could the challenge of a text or of logical instrumental forms. *The Prince of the Pagodas*, Op. 57, is a full-length ballet score, written for the Royal Ballet, which performed it for the first time at Covent Garden on 1 January, 1957; John Cranko was the choreographer and the composer conducted.

Its three acts play for longer than some of Britten's operas, yet he had denied himself not only the stimulus of precise verbal contexts but that of the complex dramatic situations which result from the interaction of characters whose motivation has been established to our intellectual satisfaction. 'Absolute' music can, of course, bring about complex situations when the behaviour of motives, themes, keys and so on is directed so as to acquire consistent 'meanings' (whether or not we seek analogues outside the purely musical terms in which these are presented). Indeed, it is a measure of the subtlety of such intra-musical argument that to deploy it in the service of the overt drama acted out by stage characters requires these to be created with considerable refinement of detail: Vere or the Governess can draw us into situations whose musical tensions are so intricately regulated only because we have plumbed so many depths of their characters in their earlier music and *words*. In the way that opera can support a highly ramified musical argument with exemplifying characters, ballet, deprived of the nuances of

223

language, cannot: it is therefore likely to encourage a music which, however elaborate, is essentially illustrative and episodic rather than dramatic and developmental. It may oversimplify to regard (as many critics have done) Tchaikovsky the symphonist as labouring under the hardship of his own brilliance as a ballet composer, but the essential point of such an argument is valid. Britten, it is true, has made no attempt to enlarge the orthodox symphonic repertory, but this study of his work has attempted to show that, after indulging in his first period a remarkable flair for the 'characteristic', he has placed great reliance, whether in instrumental or operatic contexts, on motivic development across big structures braced by elaborate tonal stresses.

Although we hear ballet music often enough in the concert-hall, now-adays· this usually consists of complete scores like the early Stravinsky works or Debussy's *Jeux*; suites drawn from full-length ballets such as Tchaikovsky's are no longer popular. In consequence, Britten's full-length score, dropped from the repertoire after its first run, cannot easily gain a hearing. The construction of the work certainly allows the detachment of many self-contained pieces that could be arranged to form a pleasantly-varied concert suite, and to this extent the parallel with Tchaikovsky remains relevant. However, such a suite would falsify the design of the work rather more seriously in Britten's case: at least those sections of the score which concern the central characters, Belle Rose and the Prince, are knit together by recurrences, variations and developments of a restricted body of thematic material, whatever the prodigality which distinguishes the work as a whole. So, although the ballet score does not remotely approach, either in the closeness of its motivic weave or in the dramatic force of its tonal relations, any of the Britten operas (even including *Gloriana*, the opera most like a series of tableaux), it does not jettison altogether those methods which can form it musically into an experience that is felt to span its playing-time of 125 minutes (longer than, for example, *Lucretia* or *The Screw*), rather than into a very long series of short pieces.

It may be that Britten decided to impose some of the unifying processes at a fairly late stage in the ballet's conception, for the orchestral prelude appears in the full score to have been added as an afterthought (even its cue letters are outside the numerical sequence of Act I): as the Prelude allows for a pre-hearing of important material relating to the Prince (see Ex. 1a and b), its place in the total design is eventually to be a significant one. The fanfare motive, Ex. 1a, always recurs as a magic signal; it marks the arrival both of the Kings' pages and of the Prince's emissaries, the frogs, in Act I, the appearance of the Prince himself as a salamander in Act II, the illuminated splendour of his palace as his subjects are freed from their enchantment in Act III, and (in the Prelude's form once more) the Apotheosis. The related Ex. 1b, one of the Prince's two themes, is also brought back in the Apotheosis, though its constrained movement has till then been associated

Ex.11.1 (a)

Ex.11.1 (b)

with the bewitched form of the Salamander (the quotation given is from the Salamander's first appearance). The Prince's true *persona* is embodied in a noble arpeggiated theme (see Ex. 2). Its trumpet colour and its initial emergence from the distance link it with Ex. 1a, while its Baroque double-dottings emphasize a debt to *Apollon Musagète* that is to be detected elsewhere in the score.

Ex.11.2

On its presentation in the Prelude, Ex. 1b is used to build up a protracted dominant pedal of F: above an ostinato of the string basses, wind statements of the repeated-note pattern *x* are superimposed at many pitch levels and shortening note-values to form an impressive crescendo. (There is a faint foreshadowing here of textural methods to which Britten was to turn much later, in the series of works initiated by *Curlew River*; both works were outcomes, the ballet an immediate one and the parable a delayed one, of the composer's visit to the Far East in 1955–6.) The I consequent upon this V averts the flaccidity of too early an affirmative outcome by punctuating, as V flat 9 on I of F, a climactic statement of Ex. 1b which refuses to recognize that key. This precipitates a breakdown of the texture, into imitative snatches of the arpeggiated figure *y* that fade out as the curtain goes up. We are not to hear this theme again until almost the end of the second act, but the manner of its reiteration ensures that it has lodged in our memory. Its reappearance, with the entry of the Salamander, is heralded not only by Ex. 1a but by the clangour (accelerating and fading after each initial impact) of the pagodas music, which sets the mode for its presentation. Taking the A major signature at face value, this is restricted to the pentatonic set 1 3 4 5 7, but both the melodic fixation and the static bass suggest C sharp as the centre. It is interesting to note that, in copying the effect of Balinese *gamelan* music here, Britten again approaches a kind of texture that he was to explore much further in assimilating the experience of Japanese Noh-play and its music: the complete five-note mode is constantly in circulation, and it is a matter of indifference which degrees sound against which as the various accompaniment patterns unfold. The sound is as hypnotic as its models, not least in its marvellous scoring. The melody, on glockenspiel, celeste, first piano and cello harmonics, is supported upon constant undulations of two low flutes with xylophone, vibraphone and second piano; lower still, pizzicato cellos reiterate the mode in oddly fluctuating rhythm, but the first beat of each bar is hieratically celebrated by gong and double-bass C sharp. No *gamelan* orchestra ever drew on such resources, but Britten's re-creative act is one more testimony to a singularly acute ear. Just as the Prince is imprisoned within the Salamander's skin, so this music is imprisoned within its rigid modal bounds. The symbolism is therefore very direct when that bass C sharp at last gives way, moving as the pulse quickens to non-modal pitches, until, with the emergence of C major, Ex. 2 appears: the Salamander's metamorphosis into the Prince has been completed. Yet Ex. 1b continues as a strident counter to the trumpet arpeggios; and, of course, before the end of the scene, the change is to be reversed when Belle Rose tears the bandage from her eyes. The irony of this reversal is pointed in the substitution of C natural for the original C sharp, a friction that persists until the curtain: now that we can hear what is locked within that strange music, its impassive revolutions create a strain as powerful as that bracing the end of some Britten operatic acts. The theme marks the Salamander's intervention in Act III, Scene 1, and in the grand illumination of the Pagoda Palace that follows it is combined in an orchestral fantasy with Ex. 1a, Ex. 2 and with 'pagodas' music. But only with its return in the Apotheosis is it at last given unequivocal tonal moorings, that F major which was circumvented in the Prelude being hammered home in a melodic statement thickened by added sixths, accompanied by the Ex. 1a fanfares (the origin of the many added-sixth usages in the work), and underpinned by an elemental bass ostinato, 1–4–flat 7–8.

The various appearances of the Prince's theme, Ex. 2, are as simply charted. Belle Rose's vision of the Prince in Act I consists of a statement (see

Ex.11.3

Ex. 2) and three variations, all on a huge G pedal that is a dominant to its C major (with balancing sharp fourth and flat seventh inflexions) though centrally placed within a scene unified by Belle Rose's own G-centred music (of minor modality—see below, Ex. 4). By the end of the act, however, at Belle Rose's departure escorted by the frogs, the Prince's theme is centred on G, ending in a blaze of G minor. And so it is not beyond the listener's powers to hear in the music which opens Act II, and accompanies each phase of Belle Rose's journey to Pagoda Land (see Ex. 3), an agitated quest for the object of her vision: the key is hers (indeed, its juxtaposition of G minor and A minor segments directly echoes her theme, Ex. 4 below), but its contours are of the Prince's theme. The latter returns in literal form (now on a C pedal) later in the act, as he emerges from the Salamander's skin, and it is the most driving force in the orchestral fantasy referred to above. This piece is constructed upon endless revolutions of B flat to C in the bass, but the Prince's theme appears at many pitch levels and in augmented forms before it achieves a brilliant C major form (the pedal now being of C upon G) that provides the climax of the scene and leads to the celebratory Pas de Six. It is no less predominant in the Finale. This begins with yet another momentous pedal G, above which entries are accumulated in quasi-fugal manner of a subject that, in dotted rhythms and arpeggios, inevitably recalls Ex. 2. But after a vast tutti texture has been assembled, its IV on V of C foreshadowing a crucial cadence, the last stage is withheld (compare the Prelude's procedure) and instead a gentle waltz sets off in F, using Ex. 2 in elegantly decorated form and joining it to a transformation of Ex. 4. After episodes which bring back earlier music in attendance on lesser characters, these two themes, still within the waltz tempo, begin a peroration that leads to the Apotheosis, discussed above.

Belle Rose's theme, which appears so jubilant in this waltz context, began as a far more wayward idea (Ex. 4). Its conjunct lines, of a nervously variable modality (prepared by the wandering introductory oboe solo), and its

Ex.11.4

Ex. 11.5

rhythmic habit of sinking wearily to rest in every bar, give it a character in pointed contrast to that of the Prince's theme. A middle section breaks from the tonic pedal, and achieves wider intervals (essentially conjunct still, but on two planes now); the return is a synthesis in that the scooping intervals form a countersubject to the original conjunct line. The note of wistful elegance which sounds in this more plainly recalls Tchaikovsky than does any other feature of a score that often declares his influence. Yet more open still, perhaps even to the verge of disconcerting parody, is the resemblance to Stravinsky in the theme of the other princess, Belle Epine (Ex. 5); here every detail of harmony, rhythm and string sonority (only strings are used) has been faithfully observed from the 'purest' neo-classical contexts; again *Apollon* comes irresistibly to mind, and we may recall how Pears identified the influence of that score in as early a Britten work as *On this Island* (see Chapter 3, p. 73). The themes of Belle Rose and of Belle Epine are subjected to variation or transformation, assembling a secondary source of recurrent material to add coherence to the total structure. Belle Rose's theme returns as a rhapsodic violin solo, with the sparsest of accompaniments and with its modal uncertainty intensified into expressive chromatic alternatives, as she tentatively explores Pagoda Land. In Act III it marks her return to the court now dominated by her sister, forming the first of three espressivo interludes in the atmosphere of heartless mockery flourishing there. And the Variation (in the balletic sense) for Belle Rose just before the Finale, though its bright E major and its sweet sonorities (of melody doubled at the sixth and octave above) show her achievement of a new serenity, effectively retains the rhythmic pattern ♪ ♩♩♩ ♪♩ of the Ex. 4 theme. Belle Epine's music has two features not shown in Ex. 5—an accelerating sequence of repeated chords based on the initial F sharp–E of the main theme, and a conjunct *cantabile* line that climbs three-and-a-half octaves above the baldest I–V oscillation. All three recur, but it is Ex. 5, symbolizing her haughty and intolerant nature, that punctuates her encounters with the four kings and that, swollen to an orchestral tutti, betokens her assumption of her father's authority at the opening of Act III. In this context, however, the two subsidiary ideas follow, the *cantabile* being counterpointed by a reeling ostinato for bassoon and tuba that represents her drunken accomplice, the Dwarf. A sizable orchestral movement is constructed from this

228

material before the old Emperor is brought on in a cage, to provide entertainment for the court. Brittle fragments of Ex. 5 create the heartless
atmosphere, and, by a neat stroke, Belle Epine's downfall comes when her
querulous authority is swept from her by the Salamander/Prince: at the
swing from her D major to his C major, her theme literally explodes, and the
reverberations of the undermining B flat in the bass echo on right through
the orchestral fantasy in which the Pagoda Palace is revealed.

The appearances of the old Emperor are not all linked by the use of a
single theme, but the colour of the saxophone signals his presence even more
consistently than trumpets herald the Prince, the oboe Belle Rose and
strings her sister. His failing powers are reflected in the small movements of
the theme to which he first dances, alone though surrounded by his court
(Ex. 6). Like Belle Rose's theme, this is wholly conjunct but employs

Ex. 11.6

alternative degrees to curiously wistful effect. Yet it can flare into an
authoritative gesture as he angrily places his crown on Belle Epine's head:
his motive is here fused subtly with that of his favoured daughter. By Act III
the fruits of that act of folly have ripened, and the Emperor, carried on in a
cage to the saxophone theme, is forced to dance to a new tune, like a maudlin
nineteenth-century street-organ ditty (Stravinsky's influence again?), but
given a painful undercurrent by the bassoon's accompaniment, shadowing
the saxophone line at a quaver's distance; and now it is the courtiers who
echo Ex. 6 in a sour harmonic form of mock homage. His dance is recalled in
the finale on tuba and double bass, when its lugubrious character serves to
throw into relief the rejoicing in a new dispensation which the Emperor can
share. Other material associated with the court may be mentioned briefly

here. The Emperor's Fool, Belle Rose's one friend at court, is represented in a mercurial music that juxtaposes scalic segments so as to suggest a ceaselessly shifting tonality; as with all the best fools, this crazy chatter (in orchestral terms) eventually yields the perfect last word, returning to celebrate the ballet's final F major cadence and the union of the Prince and Belle Rose. Belle Epine's accomplice, the Dwarf, is a more sinister figure, depicted in gloomy, sluggishly-moving trombone harmonies; we noted in passing the distortion of this motive to a jazzy form at the opening of Act III when the Dwarf, rather drunk, is enjoying the freedom to practise his malevolence on the whole court. The ceremonial music of the court, a lumpy wind-dominated march and a gavotte for strings that is one of the score's simplest inspirations (see Act I, figs. 5 and 7), allows for some effective later cross-references: for example, the dance theme recurs as the courtiers laugh to see the casket, which Belle Epine has failed to open, open of its own accord before her sister. But their fickle nature is still clearer when the same theme conveys their mockery of the old Emperor.

All the material described so far is recurrent, though not all of it serves essentially structural as well as immediate programmatic ends. But, as we might expect, some of the ballet's most vivid music occurs in set pieces that draw on quite independent, 'characteristic' material. In particular, the music of the four kings in Act I and that for the divertissement of the heavens, the sea and the fire in Act II required of Britten a fund of varied, and always colourful, invention that few opera scores embrace. Even in these two contexts, however, some unifying element is retained. We have seen that in Belle Rose's adventures it is the theme of her aspiration towards the object of her vision that acts as a ritornello. In Act I, the scene in which the four kings present their credentials in bidding for the Emperor's heiress is held together by reappearances of the music to which their pages announced their arrival, Ex. 7a. The close harmony of three flutes is momentarily reminiscent

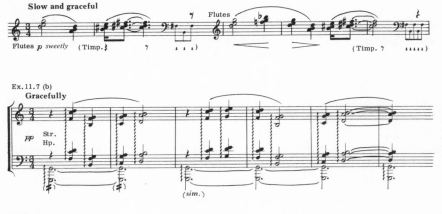

Ex. 11.7 (a)

Ex. 11.7 (b)

of the *Sinfonia da Requiem* finale, but there the varying diatonic clashes gave
an expressive fluctuation, whereas here each chord is an identical 4/2 colouring of the line, producing a bland, impassive effect; its amplification by a
dense chorus of muted strings intensifies the ritual impression. A strikingly
simple modification is therefore felt when, after several graceful but still
ceremonial statements of this theme during their reception at court, the
kings kneel before Belle Rose to a new version: merely by inverting the
intervals (i.e., 4/2 becomes 6/5) they appear to have invested their response
with a new warmth (see Ex. 7b). By more obvious means Ex. 7a is transformed to convey the kings' wrath after Belle Epine has spurned them all.
More surprisingly, it serves, in a melodically inverted form on gruff bassoons
and now with an *augmented* fourth as the containing interval (producing a
purely whole-tone situation except for the bass punctuations—now on
trombone), to usher in the four winged frogs who bear the casket. This is in
the best fairytale traditions, no doubt: it is the messengers of good fortune
whose appearance initially seems a gross caricature of all that is noble and
attractive.

The variations of the four kings have graphic qualities created by means
that could seem unduly simple in other contexts. But assorted exoticisms are
more to the point here than nice studies of character; scoring is therefore of
the essence in these pieces. The King of the North's *Gopak* is, as the
composer directs, both 'quick and heavy': its line is given a very incisive
quality from the doubling of the upper strings by clarinets on the flourishes
and oboes on the accents, while its nimble offbeat accompaniment is given to
trombones and tuba. Both melody and accompaniment form simple harmonic circuits but are usually contradictory (e.g., I–IV–V–I *versus* i–ii–III–
IV–V in the first phrase) and the phrase lengths are adroitly varied. To this
clear-cut sonority the scoring of the King of the East's variation offers a
perfect foil. A haze of string tremolando clusters is shot through by harp
accents with suspended cymbal and flutters of flute and clarinet, while from a
great distance sounds the melody of a stopped horn. As this widens in scope,
its oriental cantilations pass to oboes doubled by the violins, very high on the
G string, a strangely tense sound; the mode is established as G with sharp 4
and flat 7, but with a single A flat that is superbly climactic. Yet the tan-
gential relationship of melody to accompaniment (commonly sharp/natural
7/6/5/4 on D) gives this haunting piece a flavour quite unlike Britten's
stock Lydian-cum-Mixolydian. Less rewarding are the arid twelve-
note exertions that symbolize the King of the West. If this is parody, the
target is not clear enough for, whatever the internal retrograde movements
and so on, the rows used here, juxtaposing segments of various diatonic sets
and treated to create an overall G minor effect, are more characteristic of
Britten's usage than of any more 'orthodox' twelve-note composer's. The
twitching figure at the central V suggests Stravinsky as its butt (perhaps by
1957 the indisputable King of the West, following his appropriation of a

good deal of Schoenbergian territory), and the inanely mechanical canon of the reprise, aided by its modish xylophone, is a most effective monument to purposeless busyness. Despite its 'native drums', its superimposed rhythmic ostinatos and its 'blue' melody notes, the variation of the King of the South lacks abandon (though not orchestral artifice) and its ternary shape is too rigid: one does not question Belle Epine's failure to be wooed by this empty swagger. Her trial of each suitor is contrived musically by embedding his music into a waltz that she continues abstractedly until, impatiently reverting to Ex. 5 rhythms, she dismisses him. The fusions are as ingenious as we should expect of Britten, though they come too soon after the original variations not to strain our patience a little.

The greater part of Act II will test our patience still more if we look for any advancement of the dramatic situation. As in most full-length ballets, there is found at this point an opportunity to turn away from the principal dancers, and in the varied scenes of a spectacular *divertissement* to show off the skills and artistry of other solo dancers and the corps de ballet. Belle Rose's cosmological adventures are held together loosely by the theme representing her rapid transport by the winged frogs (see above, Ex. 3), but the individual tableaux are not musically interrelated. Though the ideas are felicitous and their scoring attractive, the long succession threatens to sprawl, and Britten tightens it up somewhat by rondo-like patterns and by his typical conflation of ideas. For example, the heavens are explored by the following route:

Brief glimpse of clouds and stars	Belle Rose arrives	Clouds extn. of	Stars extn. of	Clouds/ Stars
a　　　b	x	a	b	a v. b

The Moon appears	Clouds & Stars	Moon fades out	Clouds and Stars fade out
c	$a + b$	c	$a + b$

All this material is engaging, the most memorable colouring being that which signals the appearance of the moon: the trumpet's serene perfect fourth is supported on a low flute shake, and the answering idea is a clarinet major arpeggio (following the harp's *minor* chord) above a double-bass shake; the gong also contributes effectively. Later statements vary the scoring, culminating in the splendid tutti version at fig. 15, and the multiple subdivisions of the bar that characterize the arpeggio create a fluidity to counter the simplicity of the basic idea. Scoring again sustains interest in what is otherwise rather humdrum material in the aquatic scenes that follow: note, for example, the curious timbre of the dominant seventh arpeggio (at fig. 22) played on double-bass harmonics with doubling of piano and flute in alternation, the whole being a tonally oblique accompaniment to the melody of cor anglais and bassoon. The rippling of water and the crash of a great wave are depicted here in terms simple enough to be employed again in the texture of the 'Fish creatures' variation, after a brittle piece of Britten's assertively unadorned C major in the 'Sea Horses' variation. A galloping Coda rounds off this scene in terms that appear too conventional despite the ubiquitous glissando of the melodic line. Much stronger is the music of Fire that makes up the last of these scenes. The two motives that alternate in the *Pas de Deux* (Male and Female Flame) share a derivation from major seconds juxtaposed. The steadily advancing line drawn in the bass (by trombones, tuba and double basses) uses the seconds to produce an elaborately mixed modality, spanning F sharp to F sharp with eleven different pitches (the twelfth appears in the next octave span). The countering idea superimposes on brassy horn seconds glissandos of trumpet harmonics, the resultant effect being a series of explosively disorientated dominant sevenths. The Male Flame's variation simultaneously exploits metrical and tonal ambiguity, though its outcome in B is not seriously in doubt. The Female Flame's variation is more difficult to place, the darting line of violin and flute being held at a tangent to its apparent E major moorings both by the fixed A grace note and by an accompaniment that never advances nearer E than II–V; the middle strand continues to use the juxtaposed major seconds, sonorous on two cors anglais and violas. And the flattening moves (F sharp–B–E) continue when the Coda sets out in an E that might equally be an A Lydian. This splendidly driving piece recalls earlier features of the Fire sequence in its metrical oddity (now 3/8 groups against 4/4) and its underlining of accents by clusters of three superimposed notes, commonly two major seconds; the earlier motives recur literally in the middle section, and the *da capo* reaches a flashing climax in great scales, fortissimo and staccato, of the three-note clusters. Certainly this section of the ballet could well become popular in the concert-room.

The music of the pagodas later in Act II, though still more colourful, would be more difficult to detach from the context of the action. The first clangorous outburst (fig. 69) is magnificently unexpected: four pitched percussion (vibraphone, xylophone, glockenspiel and celeste) with piano duet and the clash of small cymbals combine to produce a glassy sound made more exotic by the uncertain modality (Phrygian from D, or even Locrian from A?). With the uniform texture established at fig. 72 (see Ex. 8), a clearer picture emerges, of a D scale 1–flat 2–natural 3–5–flat 6–sharp 7; it will be noted that its use avoids altogether the conventional (Middle rather than Far) Eastern colouring of the flat 6–sharp 7 melodic relationship. The layered texture has also been observed from *gamelan* practice: two piccolos (and the piano 'Primo') share the revolving demisemiquaver patterns, the xylophone has semiquaver figures, the fixed C sharp leading-note is reiterated in quavers on a very high timpano with harp *près de la table*, and an ostinato restricted to pitches 1 2 3 5 revolves in slow crotchets on vibraphone, celeste and piano 'Secondo', while below all a solo double-bass's lowest D and a

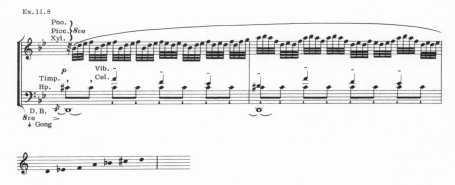

Ex. 11.8

gong mark the bass. In the dance (at fig. 73) the crotchet element becomes more prominent and melodic, but now each weak-beat note is delayed by a semiquaver. Like the Salamander music which follows (but was described above), this texture re-creates with convincing effect though quite different resources both the glittering colour and the soporific quality of Balinese music. Finally in Act II, the graceful *Pas de Deux* for the Prince and Belle Rose deserves mention, not only for the delicacy of its orchestral colouring but for the economy with which the first three-note cell of its melody (F sharp–B–A, one more derivative from the initial added-sixth chord of the score) generates almost all the subsequent melodic life.

In Act III the unwinding of the plot is easily followed through the recurrences and transformations of material that have been discussed. In the Pagoda Palace orchestral fantasia we can now note, in addition to Prince and Salamander motives, ostinato figurations taken from the pagodas music and a succession of tonal centres above that endless B flat–C alternation which covers all twelve pitches (in the symmetrical form C D flat B flat E flat A flat F G flat G natural A E D B) before triumphantly ushering in the incandescent C major which prepares the way for the celebratory *Pas de Six*. The sequence of music which this opens is again of a kind that can well be detached from its context and heard in a concert suite. The *Entrée* may have a link in its ♪ ♩♩♩ | ♪ repeated notes with the Salamander theme, but no weighty symbolism need be attached to so breezy a piece of orchestral bravura, of that uncomplicated diatonicism that Britten could still draw on at times without embarrassment in the late fifties. The ardent Variation I is tonally more elusive: though one may admire the skill with which these shifts are engineered, their cumulative effect is uncomfortable, and the melodic sequences are importunate. But the scherzo of Variation II shows Britten's habitual resource in rounding out a witty piece from a single insubstantial idea. Other delights in this sequence are the lilting 7/8 metre of the *Pas de Trois* (its melody beautifully coloured by clarinets in octaves and a haze of flute oscillations) and the *Pas de Deux* for Belle Rose and the Prince, in

234

which the melodic gestures of the strings unfold so slowly against the busy wind and piano ostinato harmonies, and the two kinds of momentum are then exchanged (e.g., at fig. 63). As natural as the *Pas de Trois* 7/8 is the 5/4 of the Prince's Variation, the melodic line of which is blazoned out by four horns against the syncopated dominant fixation of the woodwind. The remaining sections have been discussed in relation to the principal thematic material of the ballet, and the consolidation of this in the closing sections is particularly necessary after so much highly coloured but prodigally new music.

As in the *Young Person's Guide*, Britten's striving in this ballet score after consistently direct, 'characteristic' music, with none of the ramifications that in opera make the depiction of character an extremely subtle musical process, creates a predominant impression of brilliant (at times brash) display. The ballet audiences for whom, one presumes, he kept his music so unproblematic do not seem to have responded with much warmth, though it may be that the three-act structure discouraged them unduly. Yet, even with the cuts made in the admirable performance recorded under the composer's direction, so much orchestral brilliance with so sporadically integrated a musical argument is less likely to be heard out very often than are any of the operas. It would be pleasant to see this music restored to its original function from time to time, and thus to appreciate its composite artistic shape, but no less so to see one or more orchestral suites drawn from the score, for if its riches are of a kind that can cloy in too substantial a diet, they are riches none the less.

12 A Midsummer-Night's Dream

No great imaginative leap is required for us to see how each one of Britten's operas before *A Midsummer-Night's Dream* (not excluding the coronation pageant, *Gloriana*), can be interpreted as the composer's commentary on recurrent patterns of human behaviour, most commonly relations between individuals and the society to which they belong.

We may assume that, however circumspectly they avoided a crude formulation of the general predicament of which their work was to provide a parable, Britten and his librettists refashioned their received plots so as to tend consistently, if not didactically, towards some broader statement about man's nature. And when the whole fabric of language was woven afresh, it was natural for them to allow glimpses of this background to be revealed through specific foreground details. But in deciding to convert *A Midsummer-Night's Dream* to operatic ends, Britten was committed to a far less cavalier manipulation of his sources.

Whereas he had experienced no qualms in rejecting Crabbe's heavy grey verse, or the fastidiously-wrought but unsingable prose of James and Melville, and had evidently sought to re-create, not to translate, Obey and Maupassant, in turning to Shakespeare and some of the richest and most familiar of English verse he immediately awakened the literary conscience of the song-writer as well as the opportunism of the music-dramatist. Purcell, Britten's only peer in an English drama-through-music, may have been unperturbed by a book which aped Shakespeare's play without quoting a single line of his, but Britten and Peter Pears laboured to produce a text which, though necessarily much abridged, is of almost formidable authenticity.

Except for the invention of a single line (required by their exclusion of Hermia's father, with his tetchy insistence on dictating her choice of husband), their derivations from Shakespeare scarcely go beyond the reallocation of some lines to different characters in the interests of musically-balanced ensembles. Yet this is not to say that the opera is essentially a musical adornment of the play: whatever the magnificence of the verbal stuff on which a composer works, the worlds of feeling through which we move in an opera are those conjured up by the music, and Britten's *Dream* creates an atmosphere which, though markedly distinct from that of any other of his works, cannot be mistaken for Shakespeare's. As we should expect, the composer thrives on Shakespeare's piquant juxtapositions of mood and character: with the experience of song cycles such as *Winter Words* behind him, in which disparate scenes, without musically common material, achieve a composite meaning that is focused in the poet, he is ready to invent pointedly differentiated musical idioms to symbolize the three planes on which the fairies, the mechanicals (his term is 'rustics') and the lovers exist. Whereas Shakespeare left us to make what we might of this co-existence, propelling his story by the encounters between characters of different planes, but attempting no unifying cosmography, Britten has chosen to employ means of intra-musical unity that inevitably have the effect of subsuming the specific incidents, as though offering a view that embraces all. Doubtless the precedent for the method he adopts is to be found in the Nocturne he completed two years before this opera: in that cycle the common background of night and sleep imposed on diverse poems a unity of atmosphere that was absorbed into the musical fabric. The opening music of the opera, depicting the Wood as a primeval natural force rather than an inert backcloth to the action, recurs between the scenes of Act I as a ritornello; though the music of the fairies most easily merges into it, its vast mystery broods no less palpably over the other scenes, reducing almost to puppets the human characters, whether torn by desperate passions or by ludicrous aspirations. The unifying music of prelude, interlude and postlude in Act II again contrives an emphasis that is not explicit in Shakespeare, symbolizing sleep and dreams as the familiar gateway to a blessed realm of fantasy that is otherwise accessible only through enchantment. Thus humans and 'supernaturals' alike are shown to share an existence in which the absurdity may stand revealed as a clue to essential truth.

Throughout these two acts, as Britten and Pears have cast them, the characters never escape either from the wood or from the falling night. The hypnotic power which these natural forces exert is never challenged by the prosaic vanities of human institutions: but for some imprecise references to Athens and its harsh laws, the four lovers appear hermetically sealed from normal intercourse. Even the mechanicals are marooned in a world far from their native element: attempting in their play to plumb the depths of a heroic code that represents the purest fantasy to them, they are also vulnerable before the hidden forces of the forest.

The decision to postpone until Act III all sight and sound of Theseus' palace and of the painful commerce of courtly relationships was the biggest single factor in creating the opera's individual mood. Of course, many of the play's impacts have been sacrificed or much softened in the process. Not only do we lose the acid realism of Egeus' trading of his daughter, but many incidental touches that give extreme pungency to Shakespeare's kaleidoscopic

237

images have been suppressed. To create a sense of enchantment in music needs time, and the cynical or the facetious aside can break the spell: thus, for example, in the wonderfully languorous music in which Bottom enjoys the fairies' courtesies, long melodic paragraphs are spun out with few words but his more cloddish witticisms are omitted lest they disrupt the sublime musical poise between sensuousness and irony. (It will be noted that two scenes which are separated in Shakespeare have been run together here to aid the gradual intensification of one mood.)

At the beginning of Act III also, Britten protracts far beyond Shakespeare's representation the moment of the lovers' awakening. Again he has kept Theseus out of the picture, so that their sensation of transfigured reality seems directly linked to the music of the wood as it is now seen, in the cold clear light of early morning; in this same light, Tytania too has been freed from her nightmare fantasies, and even Bottom profits momentarily from its illumination. However, if the denouement is to be effected, the Duke becomes indispensable at this point, and the mechanicals set off for Athens as the orchestra begins the long orchestral interlude that translates us at last from the wood to his palace. I hope to show that Britten contrives this change of level with some subtlety, but the listener-spectator is bound to feel a sense of disenchantment, not least perhaps because, whatever his knowledge of Shakespeare, in terms of the operatic experience he has to discover a place for two entirely unknown and inevitably stiff characters, Theseus and Hippolyta. Outside the wood the lovers seem content to make cheap witticisms at the expense of the mechanicals, whose play is transformed into a monument of banality; in other words, everyday values are reinstated as though they had never been in question. Only with the strokes of midnight and the return of the fairies does the enchantment creep back, and now, though it casts a benevolent glow over the human characters, it excludes them. The dream fades more disconcertingly in Britten than in Shakespeare just because for more than the first two of his three acts we were drawn so persistently within it.

The rigid structural symmetry (ABCBA) of Act I assists the definition of contrasted musical idioms for supernaturals, lovers and mechanicals, though interaction has begun by the fourth scene.

i	$\begin{cases} x \\ A \end{cases}$		Fairies, Puck, Oberon and Tytania
ii		$\begin{matrix} x \\ B \end{matrix}$	The lovers—observed by Oberon and Puck
iii		$\begin{matrix} x \\ C \end{matrix}$	The mechanicals' casting of their play
iv		$\begin{matrix} x \\ B \end{matrix}$	The lovers; Lysander spellbound by Puck
v	$\begin{cases} x \\ A \\ x \end{cases}$		Tytania and fairies; Tytania spellbound by Oberon.

The dense string texture of the Wood symbol, the ritornello (x above), stirs and subsides in slow breaths; its illustrative function is more immediately obvious than its structure as a spaciously timed ostinato on a sequence of all twelve major triads. However, its initial G–F sharp ambiguity is made a fundamental *tonal* phenomenon, sustained throughout the Fairies' music in first and last scenes of the act (thus the Fairies' closer identity with the Wood's primal nature, mentioned above, is established). Their song 'Over Hill, over dale' is poised in an Aeolian F sharp over the Wood's tremulous G pedal (compare the C minor/D flat conflation in the Shakespeare sonnet which ends the Nocturne). Its scalic movement coloured by harp triads is to be recurrent as a Fairy symbol, while its cadencing fourths and their inversion provide an ostinato accompaniment to the middle section as well as a horn fanfare. But other kinds of symbol are being defined in this first scene. Boys' voices, a rare sound on opera stages, are the first of a series of 'supernatural' vocal colourings to be introduced: Tytania's coloratura soprano has the most obvious precedent and Oberon's counter tenor is an imaginative stroke if also a hazardous one. Puck delivers his lines in speech, usually with the freakishly rough timbre of a breaking voice. His part is rhythmically notated and his orchestral representation is by drum-taps on F sharp and fantastic trumpet calls, but his acrobatic tumblings are probably his most eloquent medium.

Oberon and Tytania first appear together in what has been shaped as a duet by the redistribution of Shakespeare's text. It is unfortunate that the contest of brilliant musical imagery (the 'progeny of evil') into which their quarrel develops is in the nature of things likely to be won hands down by Tytania's sheer superiority of vocal power. (Patricia Howard has suggested that Oberon's triumph over Tytania in the opera takes the form of breaking the magic of her vocal art.[1]) The imagery is unified by an orchestral undercurrent, a slow march dominated by a descending figure used as a free ostinato. Though this is moored to the dominant of A (essentially the key of this set piece), it is punctuated by triads on all twelve centres during the Fairies' introduction; then the pattern shown at Ex. 1, in which A is challenged by B flat minor (i.e. another semitonal relationship though here more conventionally Neapolitan), is reiterated. These twelve-note successions now appear in the instrumental elaborations, a middle section substitutes C versus C sharp minor, and there is a brief *da capo* at the original pitch. From this piece and the opening music of the act we can already deduce a technique that has an important rôle in much of the opera: with situations that explore the whole field of tonal resources (i.e. that demonstrate twelve potential centres or otherwise pointedly relate all twelve pitch classes), structural emphasis is given to one centre and a semitonally adjacent one; two recurrent patterns in Britten's earlier work are thus fused. Oberon

[1] Howard, p. 169.

summons Puck to find the herb for his magic charm, and we hear for the first time the music that will attend all his spells. It is shown at Ex. 2 both as a celesta figure and in the sinuous melodic form of the same notes. This confirms how important ostinato and inversion are to be as symbols of magical transformation and spellbinding, but there are other characteristics that give Oberon's music its curiously penetrating quality. The first is the eerily bright instrumental colour, the second is the confined range within which his lines are shaped, often with numbing monotone repetitions, and the third is the subtlety with which both semitonal conflict and the completion of twelve notes make their points: the celesta's ostinato can be resolved into totally symmetrical segments of E flat and of E minor—see Ex. 2b—(as can much of the vocal part) and the remaining four pitches are slowly added by the glockenspiel. This music moves, but within a charmed circle.

The predominance of percussion instruments, harp and harpsichord throughout this exposition of supernatural elements has been so great that the fuller, more conventional orchestral palette which introduces the first pair of lovers makes an inordinately effective point. And the new theme, tortuously chromatic, conveys a romantic *Angst* which aptly symbolizes a palpably human emotional plight. Indeed, it is because the four characters now presented are entangled in one complex situation that their music can spring from a single musical symbol, deployed with endless subtleties of inflexion. As may be seen in Ex. 3, where the basic shape is quoted to epitomizing words, three distinct motives can be isolated, and they remain aurally identifiable in inversion, changed succession and varied textural surroundings. Yet these *differences* are no less telling. They extend far beyond the basic contrast of accompaniment textures shown at (d) and (e). The exchanges of Lysander and Hermia intensify under the influence of the diminishing rhythm (d) on the brass, impatiently punctuating a static string texture; their rising affirmations (again the librettists have distributed anti-phonally lines originally given to one character) 'I swear to thee' in exhausting 'all the vows that men have ever took' also exhaust all twelve major triads, finally achieving a serene C major to round off a scene that opened in its minor (not without semitonal oppositions—Lysander's first phrase, for example, is essentially B minor). The rhythmic accompaniment shown at (e) at once abandons this ardour for a fretful tone; while the succession of Demetrius' brusque, angular phrases and Helena's painfully snatched semitonal fragments of the motive betrays nerves frayed almost to breaking point. There is no hint in the opera of Demetrius' former love, but the cruel vehemence of his rejections is not at variance with that. Helena's pathetically artless arioso 'I am your Spaniel' achieves its lachrymose tone by a harmonic conflation of the *a* segment above the A which, as a stabbing dominant pedal, has underlaid the dialogue (Ex. 3f). Transformations of this unobtrusive kind often account for music that *sounds*, but does not at once appear, wholly congruous. A good example follows in Oberon's 'I know a bank'. Setting out from his charm theme (Ex. 2a) this develops into rich neo-Purcellian declamation over a quasi-continuo accompaniment, an overt tribute to the artistry of Alfred Deller, who created this part. But its simple refrain 'There sleeps Tytania' (with muted string quartet), apparently quite new in its material, not only moves entirely within the fifth E flat to B flat of the charm, but incorporates a literal reference to the notes with which Oberon formerly apostrophized 'Proud Tytania' (compare Ex. 1 above). More obviously, 'weed wide enough . . .' restores the scalic triads of Fairy music, while at 'hateful fantasies' the charm motive is diminished and the refrain shape ('There sleeps') is twisted against itself in mounting wind imitations.

Whereas the lovers' music is obsessively tied to the one motivic source, that of the mechanicals ranges unpredictably. Their efforts to quit their customary earthy *parlando*, for heights of poetic rapture or of animal fury inspire them to a fine variety of ponderous clichés. But the orchestra unifies and propels their unruly scenes with a pair of jaunty figures for wind band; once more there is a strong element of semitonally-related bitonality in this material though with no consistent intention beyond that of striking a satirical note. Additional motives characterize the play's title (a I–V–I cliché to be much used later) and the crucial rôle of the lion. Curiously, despite the prodigality of nimble invention, more than any scene of the opera so far this has the effect chiefly of a pointed commentary on felicities already provided by Shakespeare; only with their later music do the mechanicals achieve a consistent (albeit consistently crazy) translation to an operatic mode of expression. However, it does establish Bottom musically as the obvious candidate for Puck's attentions, and it devises an engaging tone of timorous enthusiasm for Flute (here Britten's sometimes mannered word-repetitions are deliberately exploited) that goes well beyond Shakespeare's portrait in fitting him for his rôle in the mechanicals' play.

The rhythm of Ex. 3d is reversed to become a faltering woodwind support to the wearied phrases of Lysander and Hermia, who are lost in the wood, and sink down to rest. Hermia's riddling rebuff when he would lie too close is omitted. Even its delicate barb would dislocate the timing by which the beautiful music of their slumber is prepared: the impetus of the Ex. 3d rhythm finally subsides to a rocking pedal (muted brass and harp) and the sacred vows are intertwined in tightly chromatic weavings (beautifully doubled by two solo cellos) of Ex. 3a and its inversion. (The listener may hear as a model in the distant background of this passage another vow— Ellen and Balstrode's, 'We shall be there with him'.) How Britten profits from the simplicity of his motives may be judged from the moment when Puck discovers Lysander and, doing what he believes to be Oberon's bidding, squeezes the juice on his eyes: the delicate fusion of muted trumpet in D and drum on F sharp with an E flat celesta chord makes the point more swiftly than do his words. For the bewitched love scenes, which now begin

Ex. 12.4

Ex. 12.4 (c)

with Lysander's impassioned protestation to an incredulous Helena, new ideas appear; Lysander's vocal line takes on different contours, full of swaggering grace-notes (Ex. 4b) while the orchestra introduces a cross-rhythmed string figuration (see Ex. 4a) and a spare but tense wind disso-nance (one which had served Britten as a symbol of anguish since the Bridge Variations and the *Grimes* storm music).

An origin for this chord in the derangement of the superimposed fifths that underpinned their lullaby is suggested since, at Hermia's waking to find Lysander gone, she voices her fears (see Ex. 4c) against an echo of their entwined vows, and the dissonance is reiterated in a woodwind quintuplet which revives a memory of Ex. 3d. The connexions made here may read tenuously but again the simplicity of the basic motives makes the listener's associations precise. Yet these are not in themselves simple: the moment under discussion conveys Hermia's love assaulted by panic, together with overtones of irony which the musical as well as the dramatic chain of events has helped to create.

Just as the fourth scene advances a situation revealed in the second, so does the fifth develop both plot and musical shape of the first. The Wood music is expanded into a full restatement of its preludial form; above it Tytania addresses her Fairies 'Come now, a roundel', an arched arioso that rises to brilliant coloratura. The phrasing of the vocal line in relation to that of the ground is spaciously free, the phrasing across the ground's second start producing a particularly felicitous harmonic movement too. The whole span centres round F sharp, intensifying the original sway of key from the basic G, and as it sinks to rest on Tytania's command that she be sung to sleep, the Fairies begin their song in F sharp. This therefore corresponds exactly to 'Over hill, over dale' and the lullaby refrain reverts literally to that shape

243

Ex. 12.5 (a)

FAIRIES: So good - night with lul - la - by

Ex. 12.5 (b)

FAIRIES: in our sweet — lul - la, lul - la, lul - la - by ———

(with the scalic phrases reversed) before a narcotic close in which I–V rocking in G harmonizes the Fairies' pure F sharp cadence phrase (Ex. 5a). This happily resolves, without simply abandoning, a certain tartness— caused chiefly by false relations and other semitonal frictions (see, e.g:, Ex. 5b where every note is from the chromatic band of a major third)—that has characterized the song. In treating words as familiar as these, on which so much archness and whimsicality have elsewhere been lavished, with this slightly dry touch (*col legno* string rhythms, xylophone and wood blocks add to this quality), Britten has given them a memorable musical form. Oberon's casting of a spell on the sleeping Tytania intensifies earlier contexts in which his motive became merged into a blur of canonic ostinati, but the glittering, frozen sound recedes with him into the background of the Wood and this too fades from sight and sound.

This return to the fairy kingdom confirms our awareness of another way in which the three sets of characters evoke contrasted musical responses. In the outer frame of the act have occurred the most rounded set pieces—'Over hill', 'Ill met by moonlight', 'Come now, a roundel' and 'You spotted snakes'. Oberon's declamatory aria 'I know a bank', the most formalized piece inside the frame, is also sung by a supernatural. By contrast, even the most extended scene of the lovers, that at Lysander and Hermia's first appearance is much nearer 'endless melos', while the mechanicals whether uttering their normal *parlando* or affecting the monotonously-phrased rhythms they think poetic, are incapable of sustaining an ambitious musical structure.

At the head of this hierarchy of musical order stands, of course, the music of the Wood, immanent and all-embracing. Similarly in Act II it is the revolutions of the ground symbolizing Sleep that are structurally predomin- ant, articulating as prelude, interlude and postlude the whole act into two large composite scenes. Whereas the Wood music preserved the definitive nature of a ritornello, the Sleep music is an extended set of variations on a sequence of four chords; though we might call it a passacaglia, textural continuity is eschewed between variations and, indeed, within the theme

Ex.12.6

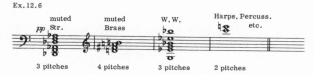

itself. This (Ex. 6) sets out all twelve notes without repetitions (other than octave doublings) in a subtly balanced curve of intensity and orchestral timbre. The tensest orchestral sound, muted brass, coincides with the densest chord (an added sixth), while the luminous sonority of harps and percussion surrounds the final limpid C major third, the mid-points of the curve being major triads on strings and woodwind, and in all the variations this rigid distribution of timbre is observed. The rising pitch area also helps to isolate these chords as discrete aural phenomena, so that the succession of chromatically adjacent notes is never directly demonstrated. The semitonally related centres do not operate simultaneously in that manner we have noted so frequently in the first act, yet their representation by triads in contexts which deploy all twelve notes suggests a distillation of earlier methods.

Ex.12.7 (a)

The first four variations establish the symbolism, being played before a stage empty except for Tytania who lies sleeping as at the end of the previous act. The fifth variation is interrupted by the arrival of the mechanicals, whose scene is again unified by orchestral material either restating that of Act I or corresponding quite directly to it; Ex. 7a shows the most important figure. Their discussions proceed exuberantly, throwing up images for the Wall and for Moonshine that will be more extensively drawn on in the final play scene. Both Bottom and Flute further develop characteristics already established, and Snug's slow-wittedness is graphically conveyed by his habit of expressing all the common sentiments in augmentation. Puck looks in just as the rehearsal begins and his fantastic trumpet explodes in a derisive snigger as Bottom presents himself to his colleagues, with his ass-head, symbolized by a braying trombone and timpani. Ex. 7a is transformed into a buzzing motive that is projected through the strings as the mechanicals fly in panic. Typically Britten brings back Flute (not Snout as in Shakespeare) to mourn tenderly Bottom's translation, which is then saluted in awe by the whole company, in their customary close harmony of mild dissonance. Deserted, Bottom keeps up his spirits with a stentorian ditty: its accompaniment is a further derivation from Ex. 7a but its line (7b) suggests a popular melody affected by the singer's fine disregard for niceties of interval (cf. Andres' hunting song in

245

Ex. 12.7 (b)
BOTTOM

The ___ woo-sell cock, so ___ black of hue, With ___ o - range taw-ny bill

Wozzeck). As his bellowing awakens Tytania, the scalic developments of Ex. 7a are magically converted into the bright sweet sound of the Fairies' harp scales, now in contrary motion. Under Oberon's spell (as his E flat key may remind us), Tytania greets in an ecstatic monotone the object that meets her eyes. A second verse from Bottom (in counterpoint to the original tune on the trombone) allows for a second transformation of his ungainly scales (at such moments the interaction of the opera's planes is made very palpable) and the absurdity is intensified when Tytania abandons monotone for arched lines that are rich and controlled, not extravagant and approximate. But the cumulative effect of the scene that follows is by no means farcical. Britten writes here the most sensuously beautiful music of the whole score, even while he never loses a delicate edge of irony in depicting Tytania's wooing. Whether Britten's cause has been well served by comparisons with Mozart that are not always specific enough is debatable, but I see no reason for suppressing a view I put forward when the *Dream* first appeared:[2] this superabundant musical richness that causes us to sense an ultimate truth behind a patent absurdity has only one operatic precedent—in *Cosi*. It is perhaps not surprising that that opera should have been influential in Britten's subconscious mind while he was setting a story of two pairs of lovers whose ideal matching is at issue, though in fact his music for them achieves a visionary level only at their final reconciliation.

Tytania's little *da capo* aria, 'Be kind and courteous', seems too mannered a piece of pseudo-Baroque stylization. The harps' mirrored ostinato and the ubiquitous scales of flute and clarinet brand it evidently enough Fairy music, but it remains an address from a queen to her subjects. Of the two colouring notes B flat and F sharp that disturb its placid C major, typically it is the second which, evoking memories of Act I's last scene, releases a passage of coloratura brilliance. Oversimplified though the piece is (especially in its cadence patterns), it provides an excellent example of the fundamentally opposite inflexions of mood Britten finds in flat 7 and sharp 4. So the orchestral refrain that follows and the Fairies' homage to Bottom, in juxtaposing both of these degrees in a familiar Lydian/Mixolydian compound create just enough tension to prevent a relapse into flaccid whimsicality. In particular, the melodic B flat–F sharp span of the Fairies' line brings back that sharp edge which has been heard in some of their earlier music. The monotony of the phrase alternations is of the essence of this piece, for it lulls

[2] P. Evans, 'Britten's new opera: a preview', *Tempo* 53/54, 1960, p. 39.

Bottom, and the audience, into a euphoric somnolence that is a highly receptive state for the daydream that follows. Tytania's arioso 'Come sit thee down' refines this mood in its lazy downward curve (juxtaposing both whole-tone scales—and so again systematically exhausting the twelve notes), and provides the characteristic motive for the following orchestral texture. This is a stream of warm yet crystalline sound, woodwind lines being woven together against a cushion of harp harmony. Even the ass's trombone brays with a peculiar sweetness as it enriches the string chord at each moment of rest; another of Britten's omissions in the service of protracting (which in music must also mean intensifying) a mood, is Bottom's witticism 'I must to the barber's . . .'. Conversely the fairy musical entertainment of recorders, blocks, and little cymbals, is an addition to Shakespeare, at least in its passage of time. It is so unaffectedly guileless as never to induce embarrassment, though Bottom's grotesque dance dangerously invites buffoonery. With the closing and most beautiful strain of the orchestral theme, Tytania adds her counterpoint to the wind lines, touching once more on that sweet-sad contrast of flat 7/sharp 4 before the magical rediscovery of the D flat chord which began the act. For the ground returns to throw into relief her three great sighs of love, and she and Bottom fall asleep as three further variations provide an orchestral interlude. The third of these introduces the Puckish rhythm ♫ which develops on Puck's entry into a new motive: his trumpet is now joined by xylophone in a fluttering texture that foreshadows his part in the confusions of the second part of the act.

After the protracted idyllic moment of the scene between Tytania and Bottom, this second section moves with far greater rapidity as Oberon's spells lead the four lovers into even more vexed misunderstandings and accusations. A complete account of the interrelations of the main motives here would merely provide one more instance of the sluggishness of words in the face of music's evocative precision, but there is much new material too, contributing to a juxtaposition of contrasted textures that accelerates by purely musical means the dramatic momentum. This impression is strengthened because the constituent sections now often suggest miniature symmetrical forms rather than the more freely expanding melos of the lovers' Act I music. So, for example, a new form of Oberon's music frames the first little scene, between Demetrius and Hermia, which in turn is framed by Demetrius' identical statements of an Ex. 3a/b derivative; its middle section includes a quite literal return of the music to which Hermia awoke in Act I (cf. Ex. 4c). Even the spell which Oberon, having discovered Puck's mistake, binds on Demetrius, is delivered in an impressively measured form of Ex. 2. Helena and Lysander, still at cross purposes, continue essentially as they were last heard, but now the enchanted Demetrius passionately enters a rival claim, also underlaid by the string cross-rhythms of Ex. 4a. This is rounded into another miniature piece, essentially of strophes punctuated by a cadence phrase on full wind. Britten's subtlety of melodic inflexion and

Ex. 12.8

phrase length here have been prompted by the verse (especially by the stop in each third line), but they facilitate a rapturous fleetness of delivery many an actor would envy. Yet the piece does not assert itself too uncomfortably as an 'aria': its accompaniment links it to the preceding music, and a third stanza, in which Helena joins canonically, collapses under her fury into recitative-like dialogue. Hermia's return completes the scene for a rising tide of recriminations, the more ugly for setting out from Helena's still subdued, and very beautiful, reminder of the women's ties of friendship. Looking back to a time of their lives in which the men had no part, this arioso momentarily escapes the convolutions of Ex. 3 for new material, an apt symbol of friendship in its mirror-image ostinato. Again its simple formal pattern is broken off under emotional strain, and soon the lovers are caught up in furious exchanges, with material patterned enough to constitute recognizably a 'quartet' set piece. The accompaniment is dominated by a hammering timpani figure that can be heard to derive from the Ex. 3b fourth: less obvious, but no less to the point, is the derivation from Ex. 3a of the abrupt little figure that projects across each bar; see Ex. 8.

When each paragraph has acquired sufficient momentum, there is an explosive tutti cadence figure, also modelled on the Ex. 3 shapes (e.g. the first occurrence consists of (a) thickened in triads against an inversion of (c)). And the vocal phrases that alternate and combine above this driving mechanism are all further derivatives, except for the descending scale (see Ex. 8)—though even that could be taken as the ultimate simplification of the whole Ex. 3 theme. Its stretti lead to the crisis moment when Helena yet again breaks up a musical process, one that aptly paralleled an argument which threatened to become endless, with her cries and a taunt at Hermia 'you puppet, you' which falls away into a charged silence.

Music demands of such a moment a protraction we should find intolerable in the spoken drama, yet it also induces a more powerful suspense than could any purely verbal treatment—the urge towards resumed momentum. So there is a significance quite incommensurate with the means in the deliberate

248

holding-back implied by the stately rhythms which accompany (on strings only) Hermia's considered reply to this insult. The imagery in which she contrasts her 'lowness' with the 'painted maypole' Helena shows her self-control disintegrating, and the oboe and bassoon ostinato of Helena's gentle plea, recalling their schooldays, now ironically points her retort 'she was a vixen when she went to school'. This little ternary piece leads into the final section of the scene where the men outdo one another in offering Helena their protection. So with the course of true love at its most tortuously deranged, Ex. 3 in its original key (on a V pedal of C minor) reaches a climactic augmentation in strained wind homophony followed by an inversion as the men swear in portentous unison to test their rival claims in combat. The achieved tonic chord, at which they rush off, gradually fades over string diminutions of Ex. 3 as the women exchange final accusations and also run out. Thus a scene that is not long by the clock has been built up from some six or seven distinct (and often formally well-developed) sections, so that the impression created is of an exhausting succession of nervous tensions, contributing to a steadily mounting hysteria.

The remainder of the act affords an easing of this state; as tailpiece to a big scene it balances the introduction (Bottom and his fellows) which preceded the scene between Tytania and Bottom. The motivic references are all uncomplicated. And the change of orchestral colour from strings and wind of the lovers to percussion and harps is very telling as Oberon turns on Puck in rage (Ex. 1a and the quasi-ostinato progression), ordering him to repair the confusion he has caused by bringing darkness and sleep to the lovers, then by unbinding the spell on Lysander. Ex. 2 is again transformed in a dragging lullaby (the 'leaden legs' of sleep) and Puck's activity prompts a renewed display of fantastic muted trumpetry heard through a mist of dense string harmony. Imitating Demetrius and Lysander in turn, he calls to the men till each despairs of finding his rival and sinks down to sleep. With less assistance from Puck, the women too fall asleep. This entire sequence is wonderfully organized as a single variant of the Sleep progression, Ex. 6, in relation to the lovers' theme, Ex. 3a. To the sustained D flat chord, Lysander sings a recitative and an arioso line based on Ex. 3a, then Puck's figures form a transition while he finds Demetrius, who repeats the process over the D added-sixth chord; with similar interludes Helena sings to the E flat chord and finally Hermia to the C major third. A remarkable fertility of new melodic shape continues to be found in the hard-worked Ex. 3a and a subtle distinction in mood marks each lover's lines. But they share in the unguarded moment of falling asleep a pathetic innocence that is perfectly answered by the entry of the Fairies (not Puck, as in Shakespeare) to sing a benison over them. The harp scale patterns of earlier Fairy music creep in over a turning-back of the Ex. 6 chords and the haunting Fairies' song retains mainly scalic shapes in thirds over slow revolutions of the Sleep ground. Britten shows his customary skill in writing vocal parts easily mastered by children yet not in any way vapid: the variety of thirds sets up networks of false relationships and the reduction to simply two keys (D flat/C, semitonal again) in the middle section brings a piquant reminder of some Act I contexts. Ex. 9 shows the closing lines as the Fairies withdraw, but there is a further variation in the orchestra, influenced by a delicate fusion of Puck and Oberon's music as Puck administers the charm, and dying away in the D flat chord from which the act began.

Ex. 12.9

Like the second act, the third is divided by an orchestral interlude, but this is not related to a wider symmetry, for its purpose is to mark a transition that is absolute. Before this imposing dividing line, three short scenes present the main characters in the order of Act I's exposition, but in an atmosphere of reconciliation: Tytania is freed from her infatuation and reunited with Oberon, the lovers are amicably paired (even if at the expense of Demetrius' remaining bewitched), and Bottom is restored to his natural shape—and to his fellow actors in time to conclude preparations for their play. The mood established by the orchestral prelude prepares us for these transformations. Though we are still in the Wood, we now see it in the clarity of early morning. Yet it is no ordinary dawn to which the sleeping figures of Act II will awaken: night, with its tortured fantasies, yields to a cold light of day that can reveal a greater wonder, a sense of transfigured reality. After the shifting yet solidly rooted tonalities of the Wood ritornelli and the Sleep ground, the music now floats in the thin air of a pure yet apparently rootless diatonicism. Setting out from the line Ex. 10a, three violin strands are intertwined in a sound of peculiar brightness but emotional neutrality; the viola pizzicato figure and the basses add two more planes to the texture, Ex. 10b. Seconds, sevenths and ninths are the characteristic encounters in this cool, imperturbable motion, and the first accidentals have inordinate power. They colour the word 'hateful' as Oberon, who has tenderly watched his sleeping queen, resolves to free her from his charm; as well as providing a Baroque illustrative touch, these flattened notes prepare for a delicate transformation of Ex. 2a, its E flat area kept within the frame of the prelude's F (central key of the act) by a continuing violin shake. So the Ex. 10 texture unfolds again, to acquire a specific meaning as Tytania wakes. But now it reaches a climax which tilts the key to A, recalling the progression that dominated their

Ex. 12.10 (a)

Ex. 12.10 (b)

Ex. 12.10 (c)

earlier scene, and a transformed Ex. 1a accompanies Tytania's reunion with Oberon, who has released her from a nightmare, recalled as potently by the trombone as by the ass-headed Bottom. Puck restores his sleeping figure to human shape, music is summoned and Tytania and Oberon dance a slow saraband. Though inversions have played so important a part in motivic workings, the presentation of the whole of this dance in mirror image ('take hands with me') strikes a new note, a solemn ecstasy heightened on the repeat by the piccolos' elaborate representation of the morning lark. Its mirrorings (resulting in a compromise B flat) are framed between Oberon's E flat and the F of the preludial music. The latter persists throughout and emerges literally again to prepare for the awakening of the lovers. At this point we hear for the first time the distant call of two horns off stage, as substitute for the viola figure shown at Ex. 10b. Britten has seized upon Shakespeare's direction at the end of the dance, 'Horns winded within', which was to introduce the scene in which Theseus and his hunting party arouse the sleeping lovers and witness their new and happier state. But a far more radical rôle has been devised for Britten's horn calls. However much they may on this first hearing evoke romantic associations with the mystery of the forest, they are in fact the agency by which we shall be transported to the prosaic (if also splendid) level of courtly life. However, as was explained earlier, it would be far too abrupt in an opera which has so far had no place for Theseus' world to plunge us into it yet. The horn calls mingle still with the violins' weavings of Ex. 10a, and the Ex. 3a shape drifts across these as Demetrius stirs and calls to Helena. In a scene that is Britten's rather than

251

Shakespeare's, its musical ordering as precise as that by which the lovers fell asleep—and its effect as poetic, Lysander and Hermia too are disturbed by the horns, wake to the Ex. 3a phrases, and call to each other. The horn signals draw nearer and are extended: by progressively adding Lydian fourths they gradually assemble the rising pattern shown at Ex. 10c; an Ex. 10b derivative throbs throughout the moments of new vision. The optional cut in the score here is regrettable, not only because it sacrifices some beautiful metaphors, but because the spacious timing of the original version was part of its captivating quality. Helena's 'And I have found Demetrius like a jewel, mine own and not mine own' is used as the text for an ensemble that seems suspended in time, a series of eleven different orchestral major triads being savoured, in alternation between strings and woodwind with harp, before the twelfth restores us to F and the momentum of Ex. 10b/c. As the lovers follow the horn calls, 'Let us recount our dreams' is woven as close imitations of Ex. 3a with a chromatic intensity that throws a shadow over the prevailing diatonicism.

Attention is turned to the last sleeping figure, Bottom, by the trombone that accompanied his translation, and he awakens to the line which was his cue in the rehearsal. He slowly discovers that he has missed it irrevocably and its distortions fade as he remembers what must be a dream yet is decked out with a wealth of detail he dare not voice. The music is less inhibited: Tytania's seductive strains crowd his thoughts until he gathers them for a pompous soliloquy, 'The eye of man', a travesty of her C major aria that miraculously preserves its delicacy. His musical recollections include the Fairies' salutations and Tytania's sighs of love (to the Sleep ground), coinciding with his words 'Bottom's Dream, because it hath no bottom'. His exit is followed by the entry of his fellows in search of him: now the orchestral figures that give continuity to their speech develop the Ex. 7a idea with an agitated semitonal dissonance reminiscent of Bartók. Despair at the loss of their most talented actor (including a lament by Flute at Bottom's missed opportunity of gaining recognition) is relieved by Bottom's voice and the fervent reunion turns to a spirited ensemble, checking all the necessary preparations when he tells them that 'our play is preferred' (to the 'Pyramus and Thisby' cadence). Though the impetus of this ensemble fades with their departure, its bass figures (i.e. the I–V–I of 'Pyramus and Thisby') are retained at a slower speed as melodic basis for a rhythmic ground for harps and pizzicato double basses in the orchestral interlude that now begins. Its organization is a re-tracing on a much larger scale of the process by which the horn call Ex. 10c was assembled: each horn phrase is followed by free elaboration on pairs of wind instruments. While the rhythmic ground's revolutions continue to pass between the F's, its middle note has been changing, each new pitch being sustained and marked by a gong-stroke until all twelve pitches have been completed by a C. This is ready to act as a powerful dominant preparation for the scene in F that follows despite F's having been a constant tonic pedal throughout the interlude; the whole piece is a remarkable example of the static and the dynamic harnessed together. But before the scene begins the bass patterning is suspended and the horn-call figure, having reached its climactic A once more, swings the music into A major for a noble new string theme, and the lights go up on Theseus' palace. The horn theme makes a splendid return, its meaning made clear as the duke and his court enter. The string theme, now restored to F (and on the interlude's pedal F) becomes a counterpoint to Theseus and Hippolyta's talk of their coming marriage—Shakespeare's opening dialogue. By the gradual thrusting into the foreground of the horn theme and its extension into a huge piece, Britten has created in advance the musical necessity for some corresponding stage representation; thus the sight of Theseus' palace and court appears as expectation fulfilled rather than the adventitious intrusion of some last-scene *deus ex machina*.

Even so, a considerable effort of adjustment is called for at this point, and the dignity of the new theme can appear particularly self-conscious when the lovers' entry to ask for pardon brings back memories both of their nightmare and of their clear-eyed awakening. Their explanations are cut short as Theseus releases Hermia from her father's choice of husband (Egeus has never been mentioned till now) and ordains a triple wedding ceremony. This is bound to appear a somewhat cursory way of sorting out the lovers' tangle: certainly no other point in the opera leaves us so uncomfortably aware of the wholesale excisions that have been necessary. So it is with a certain relief that we see Quince (not the Master of the Revels as in Shakespeare) enter, to convey us (via references to Ex. 7a in a double-bass solo) to the more familiar ground of the mechanicals' play. Their prologue, an exercise in fatuous homophony that recalls the *Herring* deputation, adds a few extra felicities to the original garbled punctuation, before Quince, at his most heavily decorous, introduces the actors in turn.

Throughout their play, Britten has marked all tempo indications in Italian, instead of the English used elsewhere in the opera. This is a mild witticism shared with the performer, but the audience cannot fail to take the broader point: just as the mechanicals' poetic delivery is ridiculously stilted and their acting is the richest ham, so their operatic language is for the most part a perversion of those clichés by which much nineteenth-century Italian opera steered its perilous way between the banal and the melodramatic. Complacently mechanistic accompaniment patterns bedevil the most touching moments, fluttering flute (appropriate enough to the character Britten has made of the bellows-mender/Thisby) or lachrymose trumpet (quasi cornet) share the melodic honours with the singers, and the dominant seventh has restored to it all that importunate quality of which Britten had deprived it long ago. But the delivery of Snout, as Wall, is a far cry from all this. As in Act II, the orchestra sets up a solid enough structure in the form of a sustained fifth on cello and double-bass but, by adding two octaves to the basic interval, they leave a vast chink. Snout's speech wanders forlornly in this, adopting the manner and notation of Schoenbergian *Sprechgesang*, and systematically exploiting the pentameters of his verse by touching on all ten notes (i.e., excluding the two of the drone accompaniment). When we notice also that his phrases reappear in retrograde and inverted motion, we can only hope that it was not with too malicious an intent that Britten gave this music to a character who elicits a barbed audience response:

> *Hippolyta:* This is the silliest stuff that ever I heard
> *Theseus:*   The best in this kind are but shadows
>   and the worst are no more, if imagination amend them.

Since the court audience in their recitative asides (accompanied by harp-sichord) treat the little opera as an object for merciless derision, Britten would have failed if he had not kept the theatre audience equally amused. And so we are, yet perhaps not without a nagging wish that parody could have made its effect without so total a surrender to the musical crudity of its models. Jests like Thisby's repeated attempts to find the right key for her aria are too unsubtle to wear well, particularly when the orchestral accompaniment offers nothing beyond tonic/dominant 7th alternations; and the inane word-repetitions are more piquant than the bitonality in the following duet. The Lion's motive is incorporated into a grotesquely decorous Polka, and Moon illuminates each of his phrases with the same gingerly-produced round-vowelled top note. Pyramus' address to the Moon seeks to recreate this refined touch, though falling short by a semitone: if the recitative of dismay on seeing Thisby's mantle finds him stunned, he and an obbligato trombone summon a heroic and neatly symmetrical challenge to the furies and the fates, before he kills himself—only to manage an incongruous *da capo*. In Thisby's death scene, the parody is so preposterous as to disarm criticism: 'dead' becomes a brilliant cadenza for voice and flute in thirds (or, by accident, the less conventional sevenths, finally classically resolved to effect a modulation) and her threnody to Pyramus' corpse is in succulently chromatic sixths rising to a veritable passion of despair on the dominant thirteenth. The Bergomask with which the entertainment is rounded off (its opening material had appeared in the prologue) recovers a more bracing kind of Britten simplicity in which varied metrical stresses and modality nimbly stave off too obvious consequences.

The first stroke of midnight brings the dance to an end. In one of the opera's most sonorous tuttis the 'Pyramus and Thisby' cadence is developed to become the accompaniment to Theseus' parting speech to his guests. His own theme is woven into his last words as the last stroke of midnight sounds. As they all withdraw a host of tinier clocks begin also to strike twelve, gradually moving from the G sharp centre of the first, and rhythmically counterpointed so as to produce a fascinatingly thin but active texture.

Ex. 12.11

Now, now the hun-gry li-on roars, And the wolf be-howls the

Moon: Whilst the hea-vy plough-man snores, All with wea-ry task for - done.

Against this twinkling background the Fairies sing 'Now the hungry lion roars'. This is the most unexpected of all the Fairy songs in the opera: though it is simple enough to sing, it is quite intricate melodically, incorporating several switches of tonal level (see Ex. 11). Its repetitions gain in effect from being heard against new pedals and a varied fourth stanza extends the final phrase of the pattern before ending with soporific repetitions of the first phrase. The piece is insubstantial yet it lodges in the memory with an intriguing potency. Its final twist from A flat to G flat reinstates the latter note (alias F sharp) as the key of Fairy music. This persists as a bell throughout Oberon and Tytania's duet 'Through the house', though the rest of the accompaniment is a reversion to that of their first duet (see Ex. 1 above); the order of the twelve triads is slightly altered to hold back F sharp till the end (as in their sarabande, 'hand in hand' is illustrated by stately mirrored movement). After this equivocal tonal situation the Fairies' blessing on the house is in the purest F sharp major. Its seductive lilt is created not so much by the Scotch snap in itself as by the sonorous and harmonic treatment of it, harpsichord playing one chord on the beat and harps immediately countering this a semiquaver later. The vocal melody that rides on this buoyant accompaniment is a two-bar strain so guileless as to court flaccidity, but on its foundation is spun a fine, bright web of counterpoints, drooping down in those steady crotchet scales that have characterized the Fairies' music. The homophonic middle section is also arresting in its modal deflections and its extensions into 5/4 units. One could perhaps use this song as a test-case of any listener's feelings about Britten's precarious stylistic poise. Such extreme simplicity can seem exasperatingly perverse, or it can appear an inspired response to verse that Shakespeare too has made disarmingly childlike. If one does surrender to the spell of this music, one would like the opera to fade away with its rhythms throbbing into infinity. Instead, the last words must be Puck's, and an unfortunately crude transition carries the music into D for a near-restatement of his original trumpet motives, now with woodwind harmony: the light, mocking note is well captured by Britten's multiplied Lydians in the orchestral quick crescendo that ends the opera. The last chord brings us down to earth so abruptly that we almost too readily believe 'that you have but slumbered here/while these visions did appear'. But the aural memories one carries away from a performance of *A*

Midsummer-Night's Dream are persistent, and the bright colour and melodic allure of the Fairies' music in particular represent an achievement of a kind without parallel in Britten's other music.

In this recounting of the opera's dramatic and musical incidents, enough has been said of colour to emphasize the vital rôle played by the orchestra. As well as a much bigger cast, the score calls for a bigger band than did the first three chamber operas; the wind is now two flutes (doubling piccolos), one oboe (doubling cor anglais), two clarinets, one bassoon; two horns, one trumpet, one trombone, and there are two percussion players, two harps, harpsichord and celeste. At the original Aldeburgh production a small string group left these more exotic colours predominant, but at Covent Garden and other big houses a large complement of strings has been used, to the detriment of the work's characteristically fragile but very bright timbres. The countertenor's rôle also becomes impossibly demanding in a big house, while the intimacy in which an aura of magic can envelop audience as well as actors is not easily achieved there. On every count except that of economic practicability, the *Dream* must be reckoned among the chamber operas.

13 Music for Children

By comparison with the other composite chapters of this book, unified by the medium of the works discussed, the assembly of pieces within this chapter must appear heterogeneous. And it could be considered not altogether logical a selection, since both the *Missa Brevis* and the *Gemini Variations* might with no less justice be regarded as music for children yet have been relegated to other chapters, whereas *Saint Nicolas*, though written for young people, is now at least as often performed by adult choirs. However, it seems to me worthwhile for once to look right across Britten's creative career, and to observe his response, always sympathetic but always changing both in its form and its tone, to the musical needs and ambitions of groups of children.

FRIDAY AFTERNOONS, OP. 7

Britten's reputation as a composer who has demonstrated almost unsuspected abilities in children to perform music of some subtlety and wit rests chiefly on works which, like *The Little Sweep*, *Noyes Fludde* and *Children's Crusade*, take them out of the classroom situation that so often appears to discourage the cultivation of either musical competence or musical enjoyment. But his first essay in writing for children was the set of twelve class songs, *Friday Afternoons*, Op. 7, composed at various times from 1933 to 1935 and dedicated, on their publication in 1936, to his brother, a schoolmaster, and the boys who would sing them. Forty years later, the collection remains delightfully fresh, perhaps for its melodic invention even more than for its resource in devising varied accompaniments.

The most memorable song of all, 'A New Year Carol', is also the simplest, only the final refrain departing from the model set in the earlier two stanzas. There are few melodic and fewer rhythmic shapes, while the alternation of I and II (III and IV for the third-shift of the refrain) is the sole harmonic activity until the final phrase; so the coincidence in that of the peak note and a spread seventh chord is inordinately strong in effect. The scalic descent through an octave offers a notable resolution of tension, but the final tonic coincides with the II chord of the switchback, which is therefore set under way again. The scale and the materials are slight indeed, but the song is no less an example of true artistry.

The varied-accompaniment songs range from the wittily economical 'Tragic Story' to the exuberant 'There was a monkey'; in between are pieces with a melodic character as strong as many a true folksong—'Ee-oh!' and 'I mun be married on Sunday'. The setting of Izaak Walton's 'Fishing Song' suggests a more genteel tradition, but its quintuple metre gives a charming lilt; only the smart reharmonization of the third stanza strikes a rare jarring note. 'Jazz-Man' is at the furthest remove from folkiness, and, just because it is so much of its thirties period, seems the most dated. Finally 'Old Abram Brown' is a piece of canonic artifice, simple yet cunning, and endlessly pleasurable to the generations of children who by now have demonstrated its permutations.

SAINT NICOLAS, OP. 42

More than a decade later, Britten wrote another work for a specific school. His first cantata, *Saint Nicolas*, written for the centenary celebrations of Lancing College on 24 July 1948, was tailor-made for the resources available on that occasion—a large four-part chorus of boys from three schools and the choir of a girls' school, together with amateur string players, percussionists and piano-duet team. The solo tenor who portrays Nicolas, the quintet of string-players who lead their sections and the first percussionist are the only fully professional requirements stipulated by the composer. The cantata therefore creates a very distinctive sonorous impression, founded on brusque contrasts: these are on the one hand between hard-edged piano and other percussion and the warm, inevitably slightly blurred sound that massed strings produce when the tolerance of intonation is considerable, and on the other hand between choral textures that, whether homophonic or polyphonic, are made up from individually very straightforward lines and an exacting solo rôle of far more sophisticated contours.

Eric Crozier's text was no doubt designed to place Nicolas in this exaggeratedly bold light, a character dominant not only in himself but by virtue of the centuries' accretion of legend through which we see him. Yet there is a danger, which Britten does not consistently overcome, of paying for the vivid *Affekte* which make up the composite portrait of the saint with a comparative insipidity in the music of the chorus, whether it participates in the action or interprets this for today. Britten's skill in devising choral textures that can be mastered by quite inexperienced singers is constantly in evidence, but is at times deployed in the service of a bland, rather faceless music. The dissonances and the dexterous modulation of Ex. 1 could have come from the pen of innumerable well-trained but pedestrian church musicians. Our interest in this piece (section VIII) is sustained only by the new harmonic contexts in which its ritornello figure is placed; the eventual transformation of this into an accompaniment figure for a long narrative

He led — us from — the val-leys to the plea-sant hills — of grace.

dolce

succession of semi-chorus entries exhausts its potentialities for surprise a little before the strongly-organized tonal scheme has run its course.

Significantly, the most impressive choral movements are sustained both by comprehensive orchestral designs and by the participation of the tenor soloist. The Introduction uses a formula for easy choral writing that relates every move to a central pedal, but over these pedals the strings build a long melodic paragraph. This makes three appearances, the first two, which open the work, retaining an E pedal and the identical harmonic progression. But whereas the orchestral prelude places the melody in a relationship to these elements that makes of E a dominant, the melody's transposition accompanying the first choral lines changes E into a centre. Already we can see how flexible is the modality of Britten's harmonic framework, but a still subtler change is made at the end of the movement (from fig. 6) when pedal and progression are both transposed up a fourth, but the melodic line is in yet another relationship, beginning on the flat seventh of the A tonality and thus affecting the paragraph with a flat bias that leaves the final A potentially a dominant. (The conclusion of the whole cantata in D is to give point to this.) Within the frame of these paragraphs there is an inner frame, in which the tenor develops the melodic fourths and E is assimilated into a context initially of C major (figs 3 and 5); between these a modulating section reaches a central point with A major and a new, march-like texture. The ground plan is shown at Ex. 2a, but a full description of this ingeniously-wrought movement would show how much the progression at Ex. 2b, the closing stage of the recurrent paragraph, influences the modulatory process of the middle section. The Ex. 2b phrase spans a minor sixth chromatically by mixing the mode, a Bartókian procedure we shall see used more schematically in later Britten. The successive perfect fourths of the strings' melody might suggest Hindemith, particularly in the coda extension, but a more prophetic touch here is their gradual assembly of all twelve notes, the last to emerge being an A that fuses with the underlying pedal.

This invocation to Nicolas turns about the moment at which his spirit replies 'across the tremendous bridge of sixteen hundred years' and a new vocal eloquence is achieved. The final movement of the cantata reverses this procedure: Nicolas's rapturous prayer as he aspires to a life beyond death receives an earthbound counterpoint in the chorus's *Nunc dimittis*, chanted

259

Ex.13.2 (a)

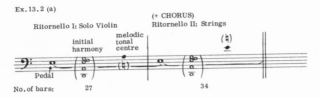

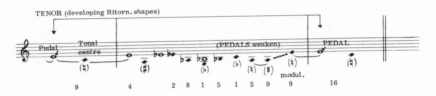

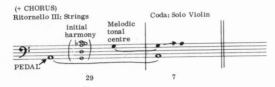

Ex.13.2 (b)

Ex.13.3

to a psalm-tone (fourth mode, fourth ending). The tone has already been heard in the orchestral introduction, a powerfully anguished sound of tremolando triads against semitonally clashing basses that is perhaps the most memorable instrumental colour in the work. But Nicolas's first apostrophe to death quells this clamour with its chains of thirds, aspiring in ascent or tenderly compliant in descent. With the choral *Nunc dimittis* a central paragraph is begun which is tonally stable on D, though the soloist's lines progressively enrich the modal range. Indeed, so far does his flattening of

260

degrees extend that the climax of this impassioned arioso is effectively in D flat, creating now a semitonal tension writ large, and, incidentally, a quite original route to that (allegedly) 'English' dissonance of simultaneous sharp and natural seventh; see Ex. 3. The inexorable chromatic fall from this peak which, coinciding with the choral *Gloria*, symbolizes Nicolas's death, is one of those superlatively simple gestures that allow us without presumption to recall Purcell while discussing Britten. Symmetry is ensured by the return of the orchestra's introductory clamour, and the way in which this gives way to the final affirmation of faith, rationalizing the D/C sharp conflict into a smooth hymn-book dissonance to admit *London New* ('God moves in a mysterious way') is adroit. But the comfortable tone of this setting, with its self-conscious harmonic crudities, makes a rather disappointing end to so strong a movement.

The setting of *Old Hundredth* ('All people that on earth do dwell') which rounds off the first half of the cantata is, if anything, rather more perverse in its distortions of an originally strong harmonic model while, in an effort to meet what is too often considered a necessary stimulus to hearty congregational singing, a brash 'descant' verse is included. The orchestral figures that punctuate the last verse derive from the countersubject of the choral fugue preceding this hymn; its subject is an inversion of the hymn's initial descending tetrachord. Though choirs may welcome this one opportunity to indulge in a polyphony of highly respectable antecedents, the protraction of such undistinguished material leads to some priggish writing—a practice of which Britten can rarely be accused.

Yet *simplicity* cannot in itself be a matter for disapproval (above all in a work based on legends of so childlike a nature), provided that the imaginative response is fresh. Thus, the dancing second movement, 'The Birth of Nicolas', is a catchy jingle, but a good deal more: the Lydian fourth leads through whole-tone extensions to piquantly ambiguous tonal situations in the alternate (E-based) verses, and the monotone refrain, 'God be glorified', is accompanied by harmonies that are consistently, not quirkily, modified. Nicolas's voyage to Palestine (section IV) is no less beguilingly simple in outline, but its compositional detail is fine. Consider, for example, how the initial flat second of the accompaniment and the singer's sharp fourth are reinterpreted in the major-mode restatement after fig. 23; both the phrase-lengths and the progressive modality of the vocal line here repay study. The dramatic interlude of the storm, though the *raison d'être* of the piece, is perhaps simplistic, and doggerel such as 'Thunder rends the sky asunder/ With its savage shouts of wonder' receives a treatment that is too well matched. But Nicolas's prayer, at which the turbulence is stilled, is a beautifully formed line in a strangely bright E; the fading of this visionary moment as elements of F are readmitted is masterly. Even in the episode of the pickled boys (section VII) the most mundane materials are set into a taut relationship. One melodic cell is common to the travellers' march and the mourning mothers' cry, but tonally they are irreconcilable, as the petrified harmonic situations make clear. Again it is Nicolas's intervention that brings mobility to the material: and after his seductive *dolce* invocation, unanimity can be achieved in the final Alleluias. The intensification of their A Lydian characteristics sweeps the music up to a B major close. Though this in fact preserves tonal unity across the piece, its effect is of a triumphant levitation.

The two solos for Nicolas develop contrasted moods in full recitative-and-aria moulds. The obsessive unease of the slow aria 'Heartsick' and the nervous tension of the fleet 'O man' strongly recall that world of fevered emotions Britten had created in the Donne sonnets three years earlier. The opening chords of section III not only set the tone of the recitative but provide a model, of semitonal conflicts from both sides of a central note, on which the succeeding arioso depends (see Ex. 4 below). Its phrases acknowledge the strophic text but are, like it, cumulative in their force. The later aria, section VI, is characterized by a ritornello of thin but tensely sprung rhythmic counterpoint. It deplores man's folly, and its one warm harmonic texture, appearing over a long tonic pedal at 'Yet Christ is yours', strikingly symbolizes what man has rejected; the singer's flat seventh here is one more example of Britten's ability to draw a wistful sweetness from the sound, without the old implications, of the dominant seventh. The explosion back to the original texture (to bar 1, in fact) at 'Crucified' throws into still greater relief the importance throughout this aria of the Phrygian second, E flat, confirmed in a *da capo* in which the singer takes over the strings' ritornello, to intensify further the quivering spiritual excitement of this piece.

Although there are few signs in this cantata of the detailed motivic organization that Britten was developing in his operas, we have seen already that these two arias share a tendency to reach crises through semitonal oppositions to a central note. How far this device (which may be no more than a reworking of the old augmented-sixth formula) goes towards produc-

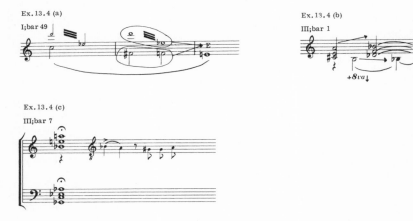

Ex. 13.4 (a)

I; bar 49

Ex. 13.4 (b)

III; bar 1

Ex. 13.4 (c)

III; bar 7

Ex. 13.4 (d)

Ex. 13.4 (e)

Ex. 13.4 (f)
SEMI-CHOR. S.A.

Ex. 13.4 (g)
CHOR. T.B.

Ex. 13.4 (h)

Presto agitato

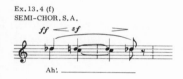

Ex. 13.4 (j)

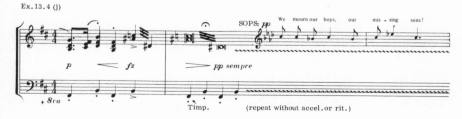

Ex. 13.4 (k)

ing a quasi-motivic unity across the whole work may be tested against the above list, by no means exhaustive, of examples (Ex. 4). And the unity of the cantata's tonal design can be still more simply demonstrated:

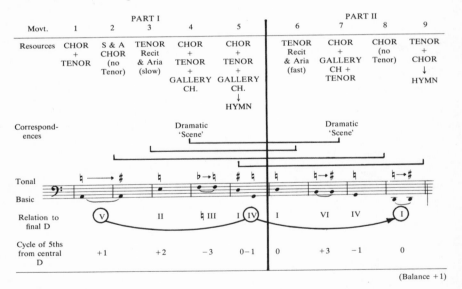

Movt.	PART I					PART II			
	1	2	3	4	5	6	7	8	9
Resources	CHOR + TENOR	S & A CHOR (no Tenor)	TENOR Recit & Aria (slow)	CHOR + TENOR + GALLERY CH.	CHOR + TENOR + GALLERY CH. ↓ HYMN	TENOR Recit & Aria (fast)	CHOR + GALLERY CH + TENOR	CHOR (no Tenor)	TENOR + CHOR ↓ HYMN
Correspondences				Dramatic 'Scene'			Dramatic 'Scene'		
Relation to final D	V	II	♮III	I ⟨IV⟩		I	VI	IV	⟨I⟩
Cycle of 5ths from central D	+1	+2	−3	0−1		0	+3	−1	0

(Balance +1)

THE LITTLE SWEEP, OP. 45

One aim of the English Opera Group was to introduce opera to areas with theatres far more modest than the metropolitan ones, but without resorting to patronizing adaptations or reductions of large-scale scores. Britten's crusade in the cause of opera took him in another direction two years after the group was founded, when in 1949 he and Eric Crozier devised an entertainment that should demonstrate to children both the mechanics of opera and its potential ability to tell a plausible story with an emotional intensity which, invested in words alone, might appear an embarrassment. The first part of *Let's make an opera!* is a play in which the writing and the rehearsal of an opera is depicted; the second part of the entertainment is the opera itself, *The Little Sweep*. Instructive though the preliminary exposition may be, one may doubt whether it is altogether necessary; certainly the effect of so rounded and lucid an emotional cycle as this little opera's quite effaces memories of the debates it nominally exemplifies. The music is some of Britten's most simple—most reducible to formula, it might even be said—but it takes hold in the memory (and in children's memories) with quite remarkable tenacity. Despite the connexion of its musical pieces by spoken dialogue (recitative being a constant stumbling block to the child logician), each situation can be recalled through a characterizing melody, rhythm or instrumental texture. This means that formulae of procedure are indeed vital, so that crucial ideas can be spun out to some length, and confusing subsidiary material can be kept to a minimum.

Similarly, the sophisticated musical transitions through which we move from one scene to a contrasted one in many of Britten's operas are not attempted here, for it would be impractical to expect an audience of children to regard such instrumental music before a closed curtain as more than a background to animated critical commentary (some of their elders have still to take the point). Rather than run the risk of disenchanting his audience at these necessary moments, Britten devises the excellent plan of taking them more vividly into the conventions of opera by allowing them to sing: and he does not restrict them to commentary on the action, but ranges from setting the scene (*vice* overture, in the first audience song) through representations of unseen action (the Bath Song) and of passing time (the Night Song), to a collaboration in the action (the Coaching Song finale). The audience songs thus offer the satisfying experience of rehearsing pieces out of context and then savouring their enrichment in context; but they also provide a safety valve for nervous excitement while still focusing attention on dramatic ends. Short of dispensing with the convention of a captive audience altogether, there can be few ways more effective of commanding its sympathetic involvement.

In that it does retain that convention and that it is pre-eminently a piece to which, as to a Christmas pantomime, children are escorted by adults, *Let's make an opera!* may not entirely escape an impression of patronizing its young audience. Some three eventful decades after its writing, we are hypersensitive to such nuances, and much current educational theory would reject this approach to the young in favour of one which encourages each member to participate in a joint improvisational experiment. Excellent though this can be in stimulating at least the few truly creative imaginations, it does not invalidate a demonstration of skilled artistry at the level of directly expressive communication which Britten achieves here. Similarly, some would prefer to form a child's new experience through models that relate to contemporary ways of living, and are disturbed on the one hand by the nursery surroundings of the favoured children at Iken Hall and on the other by the grotesque savagery of Black Bob and his son. Indeed, it is easy to sense a Dickensian mawkishness in such lines as Sammy's 'But it's time I began work, they say. I shall be nine next birthday'. Yet children's own fantasies thrive on blacks and whites rather than shades of grey, and they are not incapable of recognizing in this little parable a statement about cruelty and compassion: as clearly as in the *Cantata Misericordium*, yet without any hint of didacticism, the message emerges, 'Go, and do thou likewise'.

Certainly Britten does not attempt to soften the poignant contrast between the worlds of those who have and those who have not; nor does he in representing it renounce subtlety of a kind familiar in his other operas. Thus, the nursery romp in which Sammy has his bath is conducted to an infectious waltz that sweeps its participants—cast and audience—into a state of delighted self-congratulation. There follows the conversation from which Sammy's lines just quoted are taken, in which poverty and its inevitably evil consequences are exposed. When the music resumes, its reference back to the waltz theme is unmistakable, while the transformation to a desolate minor is as direct an assault on the sensibilities as any Schubertian change of mode. But there is a more complex mood created than that simple reversal, for the first vocal line is sung by Rowan and echoes her affecting arioso, 'Far along the frozen river'—the most tortured piece in the opera because it is that of a character caught between the two worlds. And the progress of the piece, though orderly, is never mechanical. The stylistic formula is a line each by two soloists, punctuated by orchestral refrain, three-part vocal refrain and Sam's own refrain 'How shall I laugh and play?'. The solo lines take a free course, the three-part refrain always sets off from the same pattern of 6/3 chords but arrives at a new harmonic destination each time, while Sam's line is always unchanged despite the new harmonic situations in which it is placed. Though the final false-relation cadence, admired by Eric Walter White,[1] is a device used in very many Britten contexts, its power here lies in the unpremeditated stab of harmony which Sam creates by once again repeating limply the self-evident question that surrounds his whole life, after the other children have been indulging in self-consciously (which is not to say artificially) 'pathetic' harmonic twists. This playing off of emotionally-charged variants against still more charged invariants has served musico-dramatic purposes well from Monteverdi, through Mozart, to Britten, and

[1] White, p. 148.

the child who has the measure of this ensemble's inflexions has learnt a great deal about the creation of expressive meaning in tonal contexts.

Movements founded on ground basses or other ostinato elements afford a particularly straightforward means of charting the free against the fixed, and they abound in *The Little Sweep*. The opening audience song preserves intact its six-bar tune throughout five statements (see Ex. 5) but the bass outlines one progression that spans the whole piece while the harmonization

Ex. 13.5

267

of the tune is a *tour de force* of exuberant variation, often taking its direction from ingenuities forced on Britten by the coincidence of the bass pattern with the harsh C/C sharp of the 'Sweep' refrain. So at once we experience the nightmarish *idée fixe* of Sam's employment (the false relation discussed above does not echo it fortuitously) and a purposeful progress as the sweeps ride to their work. The Quartet which follows depends on a different Britten formula, its first impression being of prodigality as in turn Miss Baggott, Rowan and the sweeps establish their musical characters in contrasted lines and accompaniment patterns: but the final conflation of all three lines and accompaniments is so transparent that a child can take the point—that operatic ensembles may emphasize conflicting personalities, not submerge them in an undifferentiated wealth of sound. The Duet of the sweeps plays on the ominous quality ostinato patterns can assume. Its stealthy dotted-note formula is articulated by sudden bumps that twist the key up one notch each time as Sam is prepared for his first climb. Then the ostinato and vocal lines are inverted and the key moves laboriously down, as the sweeps anticipate his return. The symbols are conventionally enough what children expect of creepy music but the purposeful working-out of this plan reinforces the menace. Britten again assumes some ability in his young listeners to make connexions when he echoes their sympathy for the sweep-boy in the instrumental return at the end of the postlude of Rowan's line from the preceding quartet.

The shanty's material is more slender still—one progression (I–V⁷–I–II⁷ major), its transposition to the dominant, and a modified circuit for the return. But added notes, suggesting contradictory functions, give just enough tang to flavour the artlessly swinging conjunct line and cadential intervals. One of the more sophisticated ostinati, a five-bar circuit that in fact undergoes considerable transformation, underlies Miss Baggott's inspection of the nursery; again it is used to build up terrified apprehension. The finale into which it is diverted by Juliet's resourceful fainting fit combines earlier devices in using a simple ground (the major scale rising through an octave in four bars) but also a variety of stylized counterpoints. Here not only are the characters' reactions differentiated, but those known by the audience to be feigned are neatly overdrawn: the children's baleful flattened sixth on 'ill' is the obvious example. Their three-bar phrase is just one of many devices for countering the rigid phrasing of the ground. It is quite an elaborate little piece, but the way has been so carefully prepared that its climax of method makes for an exhilarating dramatic climax too. The last tense moment of the opera, when it seems that Alfred and Tom may refuse to carry the trunk in which Sam is to make his escape, is the occasion for yet another ground. But

its lumbering fourths represent the hoped-for movement and it is the interludes of dialogue over arrested harmonies which create the tension.

Several other pieces are scarcely less dependent on uniform figuration,
and in few is the audience expected to sense the kind of expressive shape
created by a key scheme of any complexity or by truly developmental
procedures. The opera's two arias are a little more demanding, Rowan's
being perhaps the only piece that might have been appropriate to a context
in Britten's fully-grown operas. Its concentration is less of figuration than of
motive, so that the range of vocal styles and orchestral textures can be wider
than anywhere else. This helps to establish it clearly in the memory as the
most 'serious' piece—appropriately enough, for it is the most explicit statement of that compassion which is the opera's theme. It therefore follows
hard on the malevolent Trio in which the sweeps and Miss Baggott relish the
punishments in store for the missing Sam, and the crucial motive of tone and
semitone (itself relating back to the ensemble in which Sam pleaded forlornly 'Please don't send me up again') is introduced in Rowan's declamation over a chord which dislocates that on which the Trio was based. The
harmonic change that ushers in the accompaniment arpeggios of the aria
proper is one of Britten's most affecting: the E flat they introduce appears to
offer a way out of a highly equivocal tonal situation but the returning E
natural of the voice produces a new ambivalence (see Ex. 6). Instrumental

Ex. 13.6

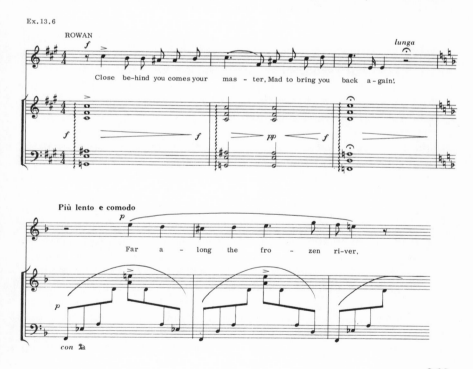

textures (including the faint cymbal) create the 'frosty' sound here but the harmony is not numbing in its effect: rather does it convey a burden of human pain. The agitated central section develops the motive and its inversion in both melody and accompanying harmony, and a despairing subdominant restatement rises to an impassioned yet still impotent 'tonic'. The children's echoes of Rowan's aria dissolve its strained mood, but the remedy they have to hand for the sweep-boy's plight does not still its wider reverberations.

Juliet's aria is less momentous. Whereas Rowan's compassion betrayed an experience far beyond the children's understanding, in Juliet's self-conscious assumption of her rôle as the eldest girl we see charity of a different kind. This is a serene piece, but dangerously bountiful, accurately reflecting Juliet's conviction that freedom has begun for Sammy with a gift of three half-crowns. The aria is unified by the obbligato violin melody, and a spaciously-planned bass movement; the voice roams freely, and flattening inflexions touch delicately on darker memories that can be consigned to the past.

Miss Baggott, a domestic ogre, is more easily made a parody figure than are the sweeps, bizarre but horrifying invaders from a world a long way outside the nursery. She does not achieve a formal aria but her finest hour is in the 'scena' that ends with her advance on the toy-cupboard to the ostinato discussed above. The Pantomime preceding her entry is a fine piece of Britten busyness, reminiscent of the edgier music of his first period and wittily breathless in its one endless phrase; the augmentation which represents the freezing of the children's furious activity into decorous immobility is facetious, but a young audience will forgive that—and at least they will take the point. Miss Baggott's tirade against the absentee sweeps is punctuated successively by the chromatic *Angst* of her physical ailments, the modal organum of her righteous indignation and some particularly fruity sequences from a putative Victorian anthem (the opera's date of 1810 is neither here nor there) at 'For they that mock . . .'. An audience that can respond to these musical captions is probably ready to move on to *Albert Herring*.

Though Britten in his other music for children has usually been able to assume some degree of aptitude and some consistent training in his performers, in the audience songs he has sought to provide pieces that can quickly be learnt by all comers (and of whatever age). It is interesting to observe that he has made them so memorable not by avoiding all deviations from those lowest common factors, the school song and hymn books, but rather by incorporating some features that at first sight may appear daunting but are quickly negotiated (due to unobtrusive aids elsewhere) and then become the spur to the memory. In the Sweep's Song it is, of course, the quintuple metre and the modulation from D minor into G flat which look dubious material for novices, but Crozier's lines make the former entirely natural while Britten guides the way through the latter with the dominant

seventh on B flat of the fifth bar of the song. The song of Sammy's Bath is
without tonal complication of any kind until the audience have dropped out
(when the stage children make amends rather ostentatiously), but they are
required to pit their hemiola patterns against the waltz accompaniment with
some resolution. While the six-bar pattern of the Sweep's Song closes into its
beginning, the Bath waltz avoids the let-down of traditional strophic forms
by closing always on the dominant (this gives splendid finality to Sam's
'Thank you all kindly' with its achievement of a tonic close). The Night Song
diversifies its strophic pattern in any event by the varieties of bird song with
which each verse ends, but there is also a feeling that the G minor closes are
not entirely final, so much of the verse having rested on C minor. In fact the
piece is one of Britten's happiest Phrygian inventions—the mode here
bringing nothing of archaism but adding something to the nocturnal mystery; orchestral detail in the varied interludes and the bird-song adds still
more. By comparison the Coaching Song finale gives the audience an unadventurous rôle, adding the same little refrain indifferently to the cast's tonic
and dominant verses but they are flattered to find themselves for the first
time true partners, if only at the moment of Good-byes.

The cynical would claim that to make 'opera' so enormously enjoyable to
the uninitiated, Britten has in fact deprived it of much that the connoisseur
would regard as fundamental to the medium. Yet it might be said in reply
that in doing so much to involve his young audience so closely in a potent
little drama, of which almost every stage is brought alive by musical means,
the composer has shown them more of the essence of true opera than by
subjecting them to displays of elegant vocal art, of tenuous relevance to a
plot discovered from the programme-book. It is in breaking down misunder-
standing as to the nature of the operatic experience that Britten has
triumphed in this unpretentious but satisfying work of art.

NOYES FLUDDE, OP. 59

Of all Britten's works written for children, the miracle play *Noyes Fludde*
remains the most perennially satisfying, both for the young performers and
for the listeners (though in any live presentation they should regard themselves as participants too). The score is carefully designed so as to give
opportunities to singers and players of attainments that range from the most
modestly amateur to the entirely professional, yet there are no bumps to be
felt in transitions between these levels, and the memorable invention is not
only shared evenly but remains of essentially the same order. This was not
true of *Saint Nicolas*, for example, in which Nicolas's own principal statements, above all the impassioned music in which he foresees death, were of a
more searching nature than the genial but at times parochially complacent
music of the choirs. In any event, choral music written for the resources
available to a number of public schools can scarcely escape some evidence of
its conventionally good breeding, and may not comfortably be transplanted

271

to less urbane contexts. The cantata was written moreover for adolescents, a notoriously difficult group for which to provide music and texts of uninhibited directness and unaffected simplicity. The children of *The Little Sweep* are, for the most part, a younger set and the music they and the audience share is enchanting. But, no less markedly than in *Saint Nicolas*, there appears a gulf between this powerful simplicity and the more sophisticated (which does not mean superficial) conventions in accordance with which their elders express themselves; thus Rowan, though her sympathy for Sammy's plight conveys itself to the children unmistakably, voices it in terms ('Far along the frozen river') that they might find embarrassingly mannered. Like many well-to-do children, of course, they are learning precociously to adopt adult turns of phrase, and the deliberate contrast with Sammy's restricted repertoire can be striking, as in the ensemble 'O Why do you weep'. But this serves only to focus attention on that world of nursery teas to which this little opera is most immediately relevant, and thus to give the work an estrangingly implausible quality to many children (and perhaps their parents, though earlier generations of the British lower classes were more familiar, albeit vicariously, with what they were expected to envy).

If *Noyes Fludde* never strikes an arch or a priggish note (and I believe this to be true), much of its success must surely be attributed to the text, which can never have embarrassed the composer as one suspects the less happy of Eric Crozier's formulations may have done at times. This is not to be offensive about Crozier's texts, but to stress how much more easily children can lose themselves (or perhaps without constraining thought *be* themselves) in the patent *enactment* of a legend when the language by its antiquity offers a ready-made *convention*. We may care to assume that the first participants in this Chester Miracle Play found it most natural to act out the story of the flood in their everyday language, but of course they were doing nothing of the kind: earthy though their speech may appear, its being cast in lumpily determined metrical and rhyme schemes must have represented a considerable feat of stylization, a making artificial in order to facilitate access to the illusory world of the drama. How far Britten was to take the superimposition of conventions in the church parables of the sixties could not be foreseen at the time of *Noyes Fludde* (completed in December 1957, and first performed at the 1958 Aldeburgh Festival), but the approach to the ancient story of Noah through an essentially medieval convention, realized in Elizabethan language of a fairly lowly order, was a splendid formula for arousing children's sense of the fitting.

On the other hand, Britten is well aware that this sense has little to do with questions of literal consistency. Whereas the church parables were to couch their most overtly spiritual sentiments in terms of, or cognate with, Gregorian plainchant, his children in *Noyes Fludde* most effortlessly recognize an act of praise as their own when couched in terms to which their conditioning has accustomed them—that is, those of the body of universally familiar

English hymnody. The three plainest statements of the work and the evenly-placed buttresses of its structure are settings, for actors and audience together, of hymns: 'Lord Jesus, think on me' is a plea from a sinful world for deliverance in the time of reckoning, 'Eternal Father' is a cry of faith from the centre of the storm, and 'The spacious firmament' a truly 'enlightened' vision of the blessed universe in which man has taken his place after the covenant of the rainbow. Similarly, the instrumental resources are not those proper to any one period, medium or environment: what they have in common is an established place in children's experience. And so representatives of the string class, the recorder group, the bugle band, the percussion band, and the handbell ringers can each be given music that is *sui generis*, while their combination, together with the contribution made by expert players (a string quintet, piano duo, organ, solo recorder and timpani), produces an extraordinarily individual tapestry of sound. It is not immoderate to regard Britten's response to the challenge of such heterogeneous forces as one of his major imaginative achievements; the many imitations that have followed his example do nothing to temper one's admiration for the original.

The strophic nature of hymns exemplifies for many children the most obviously satisfactory way of constructing an extended musical piece, and Britten has on the face of it made few attempts to introduce them to more sophisticated ways of extending and rounding out a structure. First impressions of *Noyes Fludde* are of a series of clearly strophic pieces connected by sung dialogue that also contrives the necessary modulations. Of Britten's typical operatic procedures of expansion, whether by development of accompanimental figures and manipulation of phrase lengths in homogeneous pieces or by the introduction of significantly contrasted material in others, there is scarcely a trace. And in consequence the work never feels like an opera: 'pageant', a term Britten's preface refers to, would probably be its most apt description. But its successive tableaux are not therefore wholly inert. Indeed, scenes like the entry into and exit from the ark naturally call for a process of varied repetition, while the strophic-variation form of the ground bass provides an evidently appropriate means of depicting the mounting and subsiding storm. Yet the most overwhelming manipulation of time in the work is achieved in the climactic setting of Tallis's canon where all the variational details coalesce into a wholly *static* texture, repeating one elaborate pattern as though into eternity, while against this the eight-part canon appears to offer a *dynamic* route to the same destination. The whole work affords an interesting study of these two qualities set into harness together.

For example, further acquaintance reveals how often ostentatiously closed forms contain shapes that can overspill into the freer connecting material, tightening it unobtrusively. The opening of the work is an instrumental 'play-over' of the first of the hymns, its first phrase being simultaneously

273

Ex. 13.7

expounded as a trenchant cadential assertion, and, because of the bass's first semitonal displacement (I–V–flat II), as a source of tension that demands explanation and/or resolution, i.e., implies a future (see Ex. 7). (To note in passing how graphically those F naturals, buffeted by the explosive splash of the tam-tam, plunge us into the flood where we expect firm ground, is to observe the recurrent facility with which Britten persuades illustrative and structural detail to coincide.) The issue is postponed in the first three verses of the hymn: though the retention of the characteristic limping bass movement blurs or renders ambiguous harmonic events, simple diatonic models are to be heard in verses 1 and 2, and the rising flood of the bass in verse 3 creates a logical route to an emphatic unison, from which the initial cycle sets out again, now as the last verse. But since this so clearly cannot be the end, its opening (Ex. 7) is reiterated: we can accept its upper parts as an epigrammatic reinforcement of the choral cadence but the enigma of the recalcitrant bass note is thrown into relief when the three-note pattern carries on alone. Its significance appears with startling clarity when from the thunderous F natural emerges the voice of a God of wrath. The reference of Ex. 7 is not limited to this single point, however: its rhythm, apparently devised in response to the three iambic feet of the hymn's first line, can also give weight to the short final lines of the Miracle Play's four-line verses (8 . 8 . 8 . 6 in hymn-tune terms). The device is transparent but, after a full statement of the hymn, hypnotically compelling; later, the pitch-shape of the words 'Lord Jesus think on me' is also to be used in these punch-lines, but God's supernatural otherness is defined by the use of stentorian speech. This is an excellent way, incidentally, of persuading children to accept without further debate the propriety of everyone else's singing their way through the drama: as soon as Noye has completed his repetition of the divine commands, he transfers to his natural medium—song. The disturbing F natural has disappeared from the accompaniment as God turns from man's sinful state to the means of saving Noye, and the repeated Es which now remain unchallenged as a tonic outcome gradually take on a new meaning, their function becoming that of a dominant as we pass with Noye's singing into his less awesome world (the string harmonies in this transition derive from the cadence of the hymn's second line). There are other examples in this work of passages connected by a common (though functionally contrasted) pedal, and the method is eventually amplified to give logic to the different tonal strata of the Tallis setting.

The A major tonality which is fully established at fig. 7 has, as well as the pedal E that gives it the buoyancy of a permanent 6/4 position, another characteristic that is retained in much of the work: its pentatonically-based melodic lines seem to gravitate towards a note other than the harmonic tonic, here the sixth degree, F sharp, so that there is a hint of modality in their cadences even while the harmony makes no concessions to the bogus-archaic. Much of the appeal (and certainly of the memorability) of the melodic jingles in which *Noyes Fludde* abounds stems from this oblique relation between melodic and harmonic bearings. Ex. 8a shows the punch-line in the melodic form it takes in Noye's first speech and in the ensemble that grows from it, but at Ex. 8b we can see the same notes set in an odder relationship, with A now competing with F sharp for the melodic 'final' rôle while E is central in the orchestra. A more sustained feat is to be found in a later E minor context dominated by Mrs Noye: while nothing more subtle is involved than her insistence (from fig. 55) on outlining the dominant seventh while the accompaniment is fixed on the tonic, the extension of this into a sizable strophic piece ('The flude comes fleetinge') by the gossips (Ex. 8c) invests it with an incantatory quality that seems to make an absolute of this odd scale (i.e., one no longer hears in the tune any implication of a tonic 'outcome'). Again, we can assume that Britten devised the method in direct response to the resources: children who might cope at best uncertainly with chromatic complexity or determined polytonality, have no difficulty in sustaining these diatonic lines.

Ex. 13.8 (c)

Ex. 13.8 (d)

The structure of the ensemble which prompted this digression is essentially strophic, from Sem's breezily syncopated 'Father, I am all ready bowne', but with the most unapologetic of modulations each verse is screwed into a new key. The anxiety of everyone to share that infectious cadence phrase (Ex. 8a) leads to increasing canonic protractions. Mrs Noye's verse swings to a lugubrious F sharp minor, but her gossips restore the original A major, the more effectively to mock it with their chattering, and complete a neatly patterned key sequence; it will be seen from Ex. 9 how

Ex. 13.9

the last two keys are reversed from their schematic order to close off the structure. The song's melodic shapes carry on into the recitative, the standard practice for securing a plausible continuity from the end of the set pieces in this work. The following ensemble, to which the ark is built, never quits F tonality throughout its five strophes, but avoids monotony by transferring its swinging bass fifths to a Mixolydian E flat–B flat position for the middle phrases of its monolithic melody, by the flattened third and its further consequences in the refrain (another quotation of 'Lord Jesus think on me') and by the accretion of instrumental figurations that surround it as the sawing, knocking, squeaking and scraping of the building progresses; the violins' open strings can rarely have been put to more effective use than in these textures. After a verse that expands the tune in echo phrases, the final verse swings unexpectedly up, reaching its climax transposed a fourth higher, from which point the refrain takes three statements, of a moving gravity, to recover its original close. The curiously oblique angle at which the following duet between Mr and Mrs Noye is set has been shown at Ex. 8b.

Here monotony is deliberately courted as the couple repeat the same phrases maddeningly, testing each other's patience with a skill that betokens long experience. The mode to be deduced from this is very shadowy indeed—assuming E to be final there is a flat seventh and sharp sixth, but virtually no third, the two which appear briefly in Mrs Noye's 'frynish fare' leaving Dorian and Mixolydian as alternatives: but all that is required is a stubbornly-held position, for no true harmonic movement is attempted. Their argument might go on for ever did God not seize on the E pedal to launch his symbolic warning (Ex. 7—timpani figure) and issue further instructions. As his words fade out, it is the F, the sign of his anger, that carries on in the timpani as he prepares to loose the flood. Noye for his part prepares to embark his crew, to a new contraction of the hymn in the strings. Still in the D minor context of this, the bugles' B flat fanfare is heard for the first time, setting off the animals' march into the ark. Britten's resourcefulness in accommodating the one limited harmonic series into a variety of tonal contexts is ingenious, though not wilful: the processions into and from the ark are both centred on B flat.

This march is a charming invention, its melting violin parts recalling the suavity (but not the underlying irony) of Britten as early as the Bridge Variations. Against their support the children can use crisp rhythms in the verses which announce the inventory of the animals, and a change of key each verse gives some nice inflexions of character. The verses are preceded by bugle calls and followed by the animals' single-minded refrain, *Kyrie eleison*, to an urgent pattering in the orchestral bass. Not only modulations but acceleration of harmonic rhythm diversify the verses, but the *da capo* settles down to a I-V switchback on which canons *ad infinitum* can ride; the sudden freedom of the bass to stomp scalically gives the instrumental postlude an inexorable power confirmed in the choral *Kyrie* and even surpassed by the wild blare of the tutti bugles' natural flat sevenths. After all this brilliance, a series of minor triads has a sobering influence on the *Kyrie* repetitions, though their upward succession is halted in G major where a distant plainchant *Kyrie* momentarily transfers the prayer to a universal level. The dialogue that follows is compounded from the basic *Kyrie* figure and elements of the hymn, but Mrs Noye's contemptuous dismissal of her husband's appeals (bass drum with double-bass tremolando D sharp) is gradually transformed (from just after fig. 54) via the hymn cadence, into the theme of the gossips' ensemble (Ex. 8c). Indeed, it would not be impossibly far-fetched to regard their strophe as a variation on the hymn model. As with Mrs Noye's earlier stubbornness, this piece remains rigidly fixed harmonically, though it explores different segments of its total chord (Ex. 8d = E minor I + V^7 + natural VII) in each line. Verses 2 and 3 add offbeat timpani, and an imitative part for Mrs Noye, followed by a descant above her tune, but their most memorable feature is the cool solo recorder doubling the acrid stabs of the tune. In the last verse, the counterpoint is provided by

Noye's children, who hoist up their mother (at which point the fixed harmonic position must be abandoned at last), and the ensuing turmoil comes to its head in a version of the song's peak line that pulls out of a dive just in time to cadence sonorously as the Ex. 8a melody; to this apt phrase Noye welcomes his wife into the ark, and she adds a percussive commentary by boxing his ears.

At this point comes the most patent modulation of the work (Ex. 10). It

Ex. 13.10

may even appear unduly crude, though the enharmonic conversion of that abrasive D sharp, paraded so malevolently by Mrs Noye and her cronies, into the E flat of a distant C minor organ chord aptly enough makes Noye's point. More importantly, a fundamental structural modulation is operating here: the E minor–B flat major–E minor circle of part I of the work gives way to the new area of C in which the whole of the storm scene will be carried through. With this change, and Mrs Noye safely in the fold of those whose salvation has been assured, the E minor of sinful humanity is to lose its centrality. But there is one last and very beautiful recall as, in humbled tones, Noye's family pray to the literal strains of the penitential hymn (see fig. 70). Already this is tonally disorientated for the steady onset of the storm has begun in the revolutions of a ground bass (Ex. 10 above, from fig. 67). Eric Walter White has commented on the use of all twelve notes in this ground,[2] though in a total of nineteen this is perhaps not notably clinching in effect; certainly its moorings round C are made very secure initially by the anchoring Gs and the cadence which links its repetitions. The effect is of mildly chromaticized diatonic music, and Britten's purpose in using such a shape, not obviously congruous with the earlier melodic material, is, partly no doubt, to suggest the serpentine creeping onward of the waters but, more practically, to prepare an ambience in which Dykes's hymn, 'Eternal

[2] White, p. 190.

278

Father', will not appear ludicrously incongruous: both lines 5 and 3 have helped to shape this ground. Its development is markedly sectional so that the repetitions (twenty-one statements, a ground-less hymn verse, and then another six statements for the dying away) suggest, if not forty days and nights, a vast passage of time during which the storm mounts. The instrumental details of each variation bear a designation ('rain', 'flapping rigging' and so on) to give precise focus to the pleasure young performers will take in executing them: the slung mugs against staccato piano arpeggios are a particularly happy *trouvaille*. A variety of alternative tonal explanations of the ground are sampled without supplanting C, and at the 'panic of animals' chromatically rising triads offset a change to descending sequences and a tonic pedal for three statements of the ground. The original form returns when, stemming the panic, though not quelling the instrumental roar, the whole cast pits against the storm its new hymn. As purely intervallic counterpoint to the ground this works at some points less smoothly than did the first hymn, but the angularities create tensions appropriate to this testing moment. By the second verse, the hymn has already tamed the elements to a more orthodox harmony, and with the third we escape momentarily from the storm's musical grip into Dykes's own harmony and a treble descant; in other words we move into church, to reflect for a moment on still broader issues than Noah's flood. How well Britten's ground has served one of its purposes can be heard in the impression Dykes's harmonies give of being a reduction to simplest terms of ideas that had been jostling in less orderly form—peace out of chaos, as Whiting's words have it.

The resumption of the ground is accompanied by ruminations on 'Eternal Father' in the solo strings, much as they kept alive the memory of 'Lord Jesus' (in fact a quotation from this is incorporated into their first phrase); above them, the illustrative counterpoints reappear briefly, more or less in reverse order. Before these have run their course, the ground has been eased out of the music and the hymnic phrases have cadenced memorably. An augmented recall of the ground (bar after fig. 94) attends Noye as he watches from his window the last slow drops die away. Seizing as usual on a familiar pattern, he soon leads in his recitative into quite new territory, and the tonal uncertainty of these scenes in which first the raven, then the dove, is sent out to prospect for dry land is not only appropriate to their exploratory mission but a welcome respite after being confined to the ark's C-centred conditions for so long. Introverted chromaticism, familiar in much other Britten but wholly avoided in the vocal writing of this work, gives a new tone to the cello solo representing the raven's flutterings, but its music is derived from Dykes's third line (as the accented crotchets make clear). The dove's waltz is designed to provide the kind of palindromic music which can be heard effortlessly as such; now it is the accompaniment (piano, sometimes with muted strings) which provides the shifting tonal basis while the treble recorder pipes and coos in pure

279

white-note terms. As the dove's return flight ends, even the references to the ground which still underline Noye's speech take on a retrograde form, bringing them near line 3 of the hymn before its final line forms a richly affirmative coda to the whole section.

But the strings' harmonic progressions carry on beyond C now: *via* bar 1 of the ground, they gently assert B flat, leaving C sounding on only in the timpani as God commands Noye to disembark. Not until the twenty-fourth bar of the processional music does that memory of the storm disappear from the music; we note here another of those overlaps created by the use of pedals. Bugle calls and B flat create an obvious symmetry with the entry music, and the animals' Alleluias correspond to their earlier *Kyries*, rhythm as well as 'Landini sixth' cadence giving an archaic note to the new refrain; the persistent C below naturally encourages a Lydian harmonization. When the animals are followed by Noye and his family, the C stops but Lydian progressions characterize the little hymn of thanksgiving they sing in coun- terpoint to the Alleluias. Its peak is marked by a countering swing to the Mixolydian seventh (fig. 110) while the bass gets lodged on the sub- dominant: though the voices cadence roundly in B flat this new harmonic situation (Ex. 11) has been created to overlap with the next section, for the

Ex. 13. 11

handbells make their magical first appearance as a soft afterglow from the final chord. God's promise, betokened by the rainbow that spreads across the stage during his speech, is delivered against the handbells' reverberating cluster and punctuated by delicate peals, in a haze that might be a potential E flat, a Mixolydian B flat or even a Lydian A flat. From their final clashes, B flat appears to be emerging, but it is deftly sidestepped by the G major of Tallis's tune, a moment that remains touching even when it is no longer unpredictable.

Not only does the clashing chord carry on to form another overlap between sections, but B flat is to be accommodated in other ways into this last big tableau, for the bugles, *faute de mieux*, must reiterate their calls in that key. After two verses of Addison's hymn in which the clashes of the bells are set against a string counterpoint of purely diatonic dissonance (the inner parts of verse 1 recur, one note up, in verse 2, and the V pedal has become a III), the bugles' entrance swings the key to F for the third verse. This depicts

280

the moon with cool recorder harmonies but its nocturnal character owes still more to the oddly-timed oscillations between II and III in the bass, and the chasm that yawns between these two elements of the texture. With the canonic development of this in the next verse an impressive picture is painted, by the most economical means, of the rolling planets in a divinely ordered universe. The organ's interlude which follows this visionary moment provides, for this listener at least, the only jarring note in *Noyes Fludde*. Reminiscent of all those meretricious devices by which officious organists have found it necessary to demonstrate changes of key to pre-sumedly witless congregations, its eruption at this point breaks the spell surely more drastically than the composer intended—even if it does achieve its purpose of reminding listeners that they are in church, and are now required to behave appropriately by joining in the next verse, Tallis back in G with almost the original harmonies and the canon 2 in 1. The 'solemn silence' of Addison's verse is represented by the withdrawal of all instrumental counterpoints, but the spheres ring again to dramatic effect as the last chord releases all the instrumentalists, who superimpose their most joyful signals (Ex. 12a). This splendid maze of sound is designed to act, in literal

Ex.13.12 (a)

Ex.13.12 (b)

repetition for bar after bar, as a support to Tallis's canon, now 8 in 1, in other words to fit with the harmonic cliché of Ex. 12b, but the constituent instrumental patterns range from G major (strings) through Mixolydian (recorders and bugles) to B flat (handbell) and the last of these is extended beyond the frame, its augmentation colouring God's blessing on Noye, and then being multiplied in a stretto which leads to a final great celebration of Tallis's progression V(7/5/4-3)-I; the handbells' fading glow of benediction colours the tonic faintly but affectingly with B flat.

So lengthy an exposition of so transparently simple a work may appear to treat it with a disproportionate *gravitas*. But to write childlike music that communicates powerfully (and not only to children) on repeated hearings is less likely to be a knack than the imaginative practice of compositional skills. This account has concentrated on only some of these, the refreshing use of quasi-modal melodic orbits, the variety of strophic usages and the means of linking across evidently 'set' pieces. The last has involved a good deal of reference to tonal procedures, and it might be helpful to close the discussion with a *résumé* of the chief tonal events of the work (Ex. 13); the ties to

Ex. 13.13

bracketed notes show the retention of pitches as influential pedals in succeeding stages. E minor has remained the only minor mode used at a structural level of significance, and the transfer to its relative major to end the cycle is effectively symbolic of the change in man's state through which the story has led us.

PSALM 150, OP. 67

Surely the shortest of Britten's works to bear an opus number in its own right, the setting of *Psalm 150*, Op. 67, is also among his most unassuming pieces. The *ad lib.* principle, usually implying a preparedness to make do with less than the ideal instrument (or number of instruments) has been all too familiar to British composers: major scores of distinguished figures like Vaughan Williams and Holst show that even in an entirely professional performing context some cheeseparing was likely to be required. In writing for amateurs, however, the principle can be interpreted in the opposite sense, as inviting the presence of more and more participants rather than permitting the absence of some: Vaughan Williams, in works like his *Household Music* and *Concerto Grosso* demonstrated a variety of approaches, and Britten's *Psalm 150* offers still more choice. It was written in May 1962 for the centenary celebrations of his old preparatory school; instead of tailoring

282

it to the exact resources available there at a given moment (cf. *Saint Nicolas*, above), he paid the school the greater compliment of associating it with a piece that could be performed in innumerable other environments—wherever, indeed, some children's voices, one or two treble instruments, a drum and a keyboard instrument could be assembled. These are the essentials, but some refinements are indicated, like the reservation to a brass instrument, if available (*or* harmonica, *or* oboe, if not), of the fanfare that always attends 'Praise Him in the sound of the trumpet'. And the musical textures are designed to ensure that, even with minimal forces, nothing of the essence is lost, yet the basic nature of every part allows its multiple doubling to enrich a quasi-orchestral (rather than to disturb the delicacy of a chamber) ensemble.

The structural plan can be summarized as abca, tonally C–F–A–C. The march which frames the design has two contrasted ideas, both on pedals, and their sequence in the instrumental prelude is repeated when the voices enter, but with two effective modifications:

1ab	2	1c	//	1a	2	1c	1b
I	V	V		I	V	I	I

One could point to innumerable touches no more subtle than this, in the progressive chromaticization of the chordal stratum lying between melody and pedal, or in the lengths of phrases, that guard such childishly simple music against insipidity, but analytical sledge-hammers seem particularly unwieldy before so tiny a nut. The F major section in which the instruments of praise are detailed uses a 7/8 metre with an infectious delight in its fluctuating inner stress (3 . 2 . 2; 2 . 2 . 3) that recalls the finale of *Rejoice in the Lamb*. By twice transposing a vocal phrase, through a transition that gains remarkable weight from its very modest context, we gain the level of A major for 'Let everything that hath breath', though the bass revolves 4–flat 7 while the vocal span is between Es; we could regard the conflation as no more than an alternation of the sharp 4-2s on D and G, yet the ambiguities are sufficient to keep the phrase braced through the innumerable repetitions it undergoes when the singers try it as a canon 4 in 1. In the modulation back to C, the blunt swing, on traditional fifths in the bass but not quite traditional superstructure (note how tersely the central chord recalls the F major section) is made an impressively climactic moment before a literal (though abridged) 'as it was in the beginning' for the Gloria.

One suspects that the success of a work like *Noyes Fludde*, the finest of all Britten's children's pieces, hangs so much on the long-term disposition of related musical events of which operatic experience made him a master that it is unreasonable to expect its example to bear very succulent fruit in the parched soil of 'educational music'. But there are many lessons in the deployment of simple ideas that could be learnt from this psalm setting by school musicians of musicality but modest creative endowments.

THE GOLDEN VANITY, OP. 78

As *Psalm 150* effectively demonstrates, Britten's wish to speak to children with immediacy is pursued so far as to call for participation in the musical performance by people of very modest skills. And when children have uninhibitedly pointed the way, it seems quite natural in *Saint Nicolas*, *The Little Sweep* and *Noyes Fludde*, for members of the audience, whether children or adults, to take part too. This release from inhibition, indeed from the requirements of formalized 'training', is an important factor in creating the communal effect of those works; and we shall find the same spirit in, for example, the free percussion writing of *Children's Crusade*, so that the work, although the audience plays no part, remains very much a children's work in this special sense. In contrast, neither the *Ceremony of Carols* nor the *Missa Brevis* (nor of course the boys' choir in the *Requiem*) is infused with this spirit, for the realization of these works is evidently a task to be undertaken only by boys who have acquired many of the disciplines of professionalism. It is into a similar class that we must place *The Golden Vanity*, Op. 78, described by the composer as a '*vaudeville*' for boys and piano, and written for performance by the Vienna Boys' Choir at the 1967 Aldeburgh Festival.

I am not convinced that children as an audience for this work would find themselves strongly drawn into it, while adults might find disconcerting the precosity with which its charade needs to be presented. No doubt I am seeking to rationalize my own lack of sympathy for the piece, yet it can be difficult to succumb to enchantment in a work of this kind when it is accompanied only by a piano, its part as neatly polished as the vocal parts. No doubt the Viennese singers are heirs to a very different tradition from that English amateurish enthusiasm (in some respects an appalling obstacle to the development of really high technical standards among the young) on which some more engaging Britten scores depend, but it therefore seems perverse to have presented them with this expansion (by Colin Graham) of a well-known English ballad. The work is certainly not lacking in the composer's habitual craftsmanship, and it thus marked a notable addition to an uneven repertory, but only at a few moments does it reflect his habitual expressive warmth.

The resource with which the basic structure of the song is kept audible without monotonously literal repetition makes of the work one more of Britten's *tours de force* in variation technique. An easily memorable verbal-rhythmic shape allows wide divergences in melodic detail, and the 'Lowland sea' refrain, widening the unison into harmony, can take many variant forms, the final one preparing a satisfyingly oblique last chord. The merging of song derivatives with free writing is smoothly contrived. Thus when action is first called for, after three plain stanzas, two lines, melodically distraught but rhythmically intact ('The Captain turned pale . . .'), give way at the Captain's panic to the nervous development of a single figure in alternation with the pirates' gloating jingle. But when more rational counsel prevails with the bosun's words, the song outlines reappear once more, to fade (*via* a blatant borrowing from *Billy Budd*) into a depiction of the firing of a broadside. Each time we relapse into narrative the ballad is discernible, but the chief characters take on substance in music that has a life of its own. Most memorable are the cabin-boy's open-handed 'What will you give me?', the Captain's more canny reply and the duet to which it gives rise. For the boy's underwater expedition a smooth variant of the song floats over two simple images, one of the sea, the other of his steady strokes, and narrative and direct action are nicely counterpointed at the moment of his spectacular success.

In desperate reiterations of a mirror form, the swimming motive betokens the boy's plight as his Captain and his shipmates refuse to help him aboard, and his steadily falling minor thirds provide a graphic picture of his sinking. Rescue comes too late, and to a funereal version of the piano's original ritornello material, its flippant bitonality now rendered elegiac, the cabin-boy's death, his last rites and (in solemn canon) his lingering spirit are saluted. The postlude confirms that we are not required to surrender too abjectly to the pathos of the occasion.

CHILDREN'S CRUSADE, OP. 82

Britten's anxiety to put his art at the service of institutions and causes whose aims commanded his sympathy was not always sufficient of itself to summon his most spontaneous invention. *Saint Nicolas*, for a boys' school centenary, is a piece which, whatever its occasional *gaucheries*, is full of unforgettable musical images; the *Cantata Academica*, for a university's quincentenary, is far more ingeniously wrought, but the wit we enjoy in its performance does not inspire the affection that would hold for it as secure a place in the memory. Similarly, we might contrast the composer's response, structurally disciplined but emotionally profoundly committed, revealed by the superb *Cantata Misericordium* (for the International Red Cross's centenary) with that we find in *Voices for Today* (for the United Nations' twentieth anniversary), a worthy but wordy salutation that makes too many points ever to convince us utterly of any one. The ballad *Children's Crusade* is yet another birthday work, written to be performed in St Paul's Cathedral on the fiftieth anniversary of the Save the Children Fund, 19 May 1969. But Britten ensured in two ways that his tribute—to an ideal that is persistently reflected in his own work—should not fall a lifeless victim to stiffly charitable sentiments: he chose a text from Brecht, and he conceived the work for the heterogeneous resources of a school music group—the very skilled Wandsworth School Boys' Choir and a large band of percussion players, together with two pianists and an organist. The work that resulted is not directly related to the rest of Britten's output either in genre or in the manner of the musical discourse.

Not that the composition of a 'ballad' for voices and orchestra was without

285

precedent: the *Ballad of Heroes* in 1939 (see Chapter 3, page 76) had been a vehicle for Britten's moral outrage in a more burningly topical cause—the Spanish Civil War. Whatever the bitter, ironic and even macabre qualities of its musical ideas, they were contained within movement structures that would have been unexceptionable in a festival cantata. Brecht's text, however, is more truly a ballad, a continuous narrative, told in a calculatedly flat, matter-of-fact way, its rhyming verse scheme like a child's sing-song and its sentence structure primitive—'There was . . . and there was . . .'. The total rejection of polished language, of descriptions of subtle (or any other) emotional states, and of the first person, discourages the formation of 'set' musical pieces of a conventional kind. This matches well the practicalities of the situation in that boy soloists need not be exposed to the artificially protracted attention required by an 'aria'. Britten goes still further towards Brecht's ideals in devising the most consistently syllabic word-setting of all his works: in many sections even a single slurred two-note group registers as exceptional, and the one passage in the whole score which exploits the espressivo quality of such groups ('So there was faith') is clearly set apart in various ways from the main narrative, being a reflective interlude that moralizes and also allows for the passing of time on the children's wanderings.

So heavy a reliance on a laconic recitative style must be balanced by more patterned music in the instruments. Britten forms the principal structural units of the piece by working out the possibilities of instrumental ideas, these providing a uniform frame within which the voices can freely pass between the swiftly changing topics of the narrative. The introduction, declaimed by the two-part chorus, is articulated by a series of explosive sonorities that give at once a peculiar stamp to this work. Some percussionists execute rhythmic figures at different tempos, while others make patterns quite independently of any fixed pulse. The xylophone's prominent pattern also provides cue notes for the voices, as does the electronic organ, which adds harmonic underpinning. The two pianists mark the detonation of these sonorous bombshells with conflicting rhythms (initially ♪♪♪ against ♬♬ at extremes of compass (see Ex. 14). Once again, as in the parable textures, Britten has not hesitated to find suggestions for his own music in that of a younger generation. The sound is not remotely that of any other composer, as a moment's scrutiny of Ex. 14 will confirm: the sustained organ chord is that symbol of tension (conflating as it does both semitonal and tritonal conflicts) which has been remarked on so repeatedly in this study, while Piano 1 sounds the crucial melodic note D with tone and semitone neighbours, twice marking out major seventh drops, and Piano 2 covers a V–I gap chromatically to drive in an A flat bass as the opposite tonal pole. Bar 2 shows the same ambivalence of tonal centre extended into the vocal writing, and gives a first example of the individually very simple voice parts that are constantly made to yield less simple products. Each explosion singles out a new reciting

Ex.13.14

pitch from which the next line of narrative will set out before forging melodic shapes, and gradually the dynamic level subsides until the seventh and eighth blocks are retained in alternation, to form a plane of quiet sound as we hear of the children gathering together. But a great crash as the pattern is resumed (fig. 4) now is heard to be a direct symbol of the violence of war from which they seek a refuge; again the dynamics subside and the last two blocks form a clear cadential movement (melodically semitonal, B flat–A; harmonically V–I; i.e., the opening principle has been retained) on to A. The achievement that *could* mean is revealed in the text: 'And one fine day they'd come/Upon a land where there was peace'. This last phrase of the text and its setting as a duet that closes on to a major second (see Ex. 15) is to provide a recurrent motive for the whole work. Meanwhile the introduction has provided a symbolic prefiguring of the children's search for that land in

287

Ex.13.15

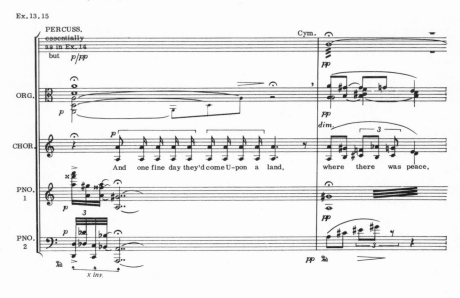

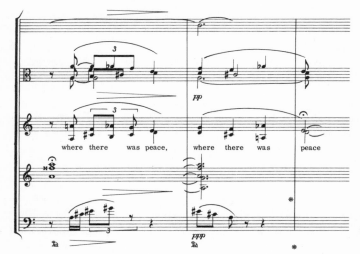

trying for the reciting-note of each block (e.g., the D in Ex. 14) a different
pitch, always at variance with the bass until the cadence upon A, the last
possible pitch.

   The long narrative section which follows (figs 5 to 18) has no such unifying
design. It is a deliberate reproduction in musical terms of Brecht's artless
'There was . . . and there was . . .', Britten's equivalent introductory phrase
being a rhythm first heard on the side drum. The child's delight in banging a

drum provides the simplest and the central symbol of this work, its quasi-military form of play obviously enough epitomizing the whole crusade. Presumably Britten developed the idea from Brecht's introduction in this section of a boy who finds a drum in an abandoned village. He is allowed to play it only when the company have wandered into country so remote as to ensure that its noise will not betray them. But the commentary of side drum, and successively other instruments of the solo percussion group (tambourine, wood block, tenor drum, bass drum, triangle), helps to preserve rhythmic tension and differentiation of colour, if not character, throughout the series of tiny sketches that make up this section. Although the alignment of strata is just as free in this work as in the church parables (to which in temporal matters it owes much), the effect is totally unlike, partly because of the hard piano sounds which replace the more flexible chamber group, but principally because of these regimented percussive figures that wear on the nerves by constantly asserting themselves against the more freely unfolding elements of the texture.

In turn we see the leader of the crusade, a little Jew, two brothers (twins, their canon might suggest) who specialize in strategy, a boy from the Nazi legation, and the drummer-boy. A different soloist presents each character and the pianos add a distinctive accompaniment pattern, most of these maintaining in their roughly bitonal cast a link with the introduction's sound-world; between each sketch, the chorus voices the longing for peace (modelled on Ex. 15, though always refashioned). A new sound, the scraper (the Latin-American *reso-reso*) introduces a dog which joins the company, and then the whole chorus joins in antiphonal strains as a concert is staged, to which the percussionists make a spirited contribution—a sudden upsurge of more elaborate musical sound that is remarkably vivid in comparatively barren surroundings, though it is soon disrupted by the drummer-boy's over-enthusiasm. Equally vivid is a love-scene some eight bars long, its material touchingly derived from the preceding 'where there was peace'. This makes doubly ironic the eruption, just as those words are repeated at the end of this scene, of a war against another company of wandering children. Now the military rhythms can be recognized for what they are, and pianos and voices (in mirror formation) clatter with precision; Britten's extension here of his Lydian penchant through whole-tone to bitonally conflicting situations is particularly telling. The war blows itself out as inexplicably as it began, and by now the relevance of these children's behaviour patterns to those of their elders is too uncomfortable to be ignored. True to type, they must now stage a trial, with pompous solemnity of monotoned rhythm, though by a nice twist it is the judge who is condemned. Another ceremony follows, the funeral of the little Jew (to reminders of his earlier piano figurations and a disembodied *vocalise*), and in an impressive ensemble the whole company, 'Protestants and Catholics and Nazis' alike, joins to observe the last rites; the heavy irony does not tempt

289

Britten to parody the musical representation, and only by allocating the words to a form of 'where there was peace' does he make a wry comment on the concluding moment of the funeral—'At the end they heard a little socialist/Talk with confidence of mankind's rebirth'. (Hans Keller, who translated Brecht's text, has paraphrased here, but to good effect, 'von der Zukunft der Lebendigen'.) And this transfer of socialist doctrines to Christian connotations is extended into the opening of the reflective interlude referred to above: 'So there was Faith and Hope too,/But no meat or bread.'

Britten's use of the twelve pitches one by one to articulate a structure with symbolic intent in the Introduction of *Children's Crusade* was typical of a practice common in his work. The interlude of the ballad provides an example of the opposite extreme in twelve-note usage—a piece that constantly builds up and dismantles the same harmonic complex of all twelve pitches. Again the textural continuity is provided by the instruments, chiefly the pianos. To a rhythmic ostinato, they pile up successive pairs of notes (most of them minor thirds) to form the peak bar shown at Ex. 16a, and then reverse the process. It is against these regular waves of sound (varied only in the detail of the solo percussion parts) that the *cantabile* reflections on the children's plight already mentioned are set. The tonal wanderings of each vocal line take place between fixed octave-positions of each pitch-class, and

Ex. 13.16 (a)

PNO. 1

PNO. 2

Ex. 13.16 (b)

Ex. 13.16 (c)

CHOR. Tr.

CHOR. A.   They wan - dered— stea - di - ly —— south - ward ——

the identity of the material becomes clear when the voices reach a climax with the row itself (see Ex. 16c) and its retrograde. It will be noted that the first three notes of the row (Ex. 16b) form a shape (*x* hereafter) of a tone and a minor third that has already played an important part in the work, initiating many vocal phrases (most obviously in the 'concert'); it was prominent in the bass figures in the introduction (see Ex. 15) and also formed the first three reciting pitches of the introduction's row. Its use becomes obsessive in the section that follows (from fig. 21) as the children follow the dying soldier's clue and search for Bilgoray. But all this section can be explained too as further revolutions, with some permutation, of the Ex. 16b row. When the stasis of the choral harmony (notes 1–6 + 12–11 + 10 . . 9) betokens the fruitless outcome of their search, it is with reiterations of *x* in retrograde (completing with pitches 7 and 8 the unfinished set) that their leader pathetically reassures them, 'it must be there'. But the version of the pianos' ostinato structure that follows is a distortion of the row (Ex. 17) that

Ex. 13.17

(cf. Ex. 13.16 b)

excludes *x*, and a disconsolate tone is created by vocal lines that merely creep a short distance to and from the initial E, on which note we finally lose sight of the children. Yet the new row had an affirmative feature: it closed with the major third on A, a tonic outcome to that E. The meaning of this becomes clear in the following section, a quiet recapitulation *in* A (even to the key signature of its major mode) of the introduction's instrumental music (cf. Ex. 14) in which the narrator (represented corporately by an ensemble of soloists) visualizes the children, joined by countless others 'high above them in the clouds'. This apotheosis draws Britten into his warmest Lydian-cum-Mixolydian vein, troubled by other accidentals only at a reference to the place the children are now leaving for ever. With a splendid choral recital of the achieved A at three octaves ('mighty crowds too great to number'), supported by a clangorous affirmative version of the opening piano figures (cf. Ex. 14), the work seems to be pointing towards a closing visionary glow.

But to beatify the children in this way would be to sentimentalize their tribulations, and Brecht's return to a prosaic narration of events is startlingly brusque. Britten's is, if anything, more so. Suddenly the dog barks—its piano motive and the scraper make the point before the narration—and the last chapter in the tale is told, of the dog's success in reaching a human habitation with an appeal for help from the children, of the blank response to it, and of the dog's death from hunger. The children's message is a distant echo of the apotheosis, and at the words 'We're the fifty-five' an echo of 'where there was peace' makes an unforced but forceful connexion. Even now, however, we are not to end with this elevated music, for the dog must die to his own rough motive. The briefest of epilogues, a twelve-note set in the pianos, is his requiem, and a terser comment than was the apotheosis on the fate he shared with the children; the tonal ambiguity of the dog's music persists to the final G sharp above A, so that in this way too the great affirmation is set into question again.

Britten's score is underlaid with both the German text and Hans Keller's English version. Keller turns some phrases that pungently reproduce Brecht's dry, loaded understatements:

> But none should rebuke the needy man
> Who would not part with a slice:
> For fifty-odd children you need flour—
> Flour, not sacrifice.

He is somewhat given to heavy-handed inversions like 'Homes and aims they haven't any' for the powerfully direct 'Heimatlose, Richtungslose'; and there is nothing he can do to invest 'leader' with the associations aroused by *Führer*. How faithful Britten is to Brecht is probably a matter to be left to the Brechtians, but it will be clear from the account given above that he has reproduced musically many twists of the original, and has not hesitated to forgo the kind of elegiac statement that one would have expected to find as his most personal contribution to the climax of such a work. Perhaps already in setting the whole text for boys' voices he has introduced a note some would find too open to sentimental associations, yet throughout he writes for his vocal forces lines that are sufficiently braced, both by tonal strains and by unyielding attendant percussion detail, to stave off any threat of the wistful or the coy. Of all Britten's works for children, this one most bluntly reminds us how much their world is a microcosm of our own.

WELCOME ODE, OP. 95

Britten's last completed score, dated 19 August 1976, less than four months before his death, was the *Welcome Ode*, Op. 95, for young people's choir and orchestra. It is a much slighter piece than *Saint Nicolas*, *Noyes Fludde* or *Children's Crusade*, but does not duplicate in resources and intention any earlier work. Thirty years earlier, it was reasonable to assume that the elaborate choral groupings of *Saint Nicolas* could be mustered from a few schools in collaboration, but that the instrumental parts to be played by young people would be restricted to strings and be less demanding than those of their professional section leaders. The remarkable development of instrumental teaching throughout the British educational system and the consequent flowering of youth orchestras in the intervening decades made it possible for Britten to write in this ode for really competent, though not virtuoso, full orchestral forces, while it is for the chorus that concessions have been made. The choral texture is of three lines only, sopranos, altos and basses, though there is an *ad lib*. tenor strand in one section; all the parts can easily be mastered by singers whose experience is limited, and there are no soloists to expose the limitations.

The ode is a continuous cycle of five short movements—March, Jig, Roundel, Modulation and Canon—of which the second and fourth are for orchestra alone. The text of the first piece, by Thomas Dekker and John Ford, beginning

> Haymakers, rakers, reapers and mowers
> Wait on your summer queen

is a picture of a holiday pageant that inevitably recalls the May Day festival which ended the Spring Symphony. On its more modest scale this march recaptures some of the ebullience of that superb tableau. Its energy springs both from the 7/8 interpolations (recalling Bartók in 'Bulgarian' mood with an unusual directness) and from the sensation that virtually the entire piece rests on a dominant pedal. In fact this B flat is equivocal: while the key signature and many melodic/harmonic contexts give it a dominant meaning, it is scarcely less valid as the tonic of a flexible mode, and eventually the cycle is rounded off by a B flat movement which ends with pronounced Mixolydian inflexions. The orchestral jig is fast and texturally transparent; its lack of rhythmic quirks is compensated for by dexterous phrase manipulation, its innocuous G major refrain by an explosive middle section in which F sharp seeks to oust it. The robust open fifths on G which end the Jig subside in the Roundel to become the chord between whose appearances a ground bass is stretched. But the upper parts of voices and orchestra are clearly enough in D, so that there results an equivocal situation (Lydian G/D with a subdominant undertow?) equal and opposite to that of the March. As in that movement, metrical variety (3/4 and 2/2) keeps the altos' simple melody buoyant, and the subsequent varied statements are characterized by Britten's gentlest dissonance (S and A) and neatly interweaving imitative counterpoints (S and A above the basses' extended form of the melody). 'Modulation' is the unapologetic description of the functional interlude that prepares both key and material of the final 'Canon'. This jaunty piece begins with a choral unison delivery of the infectious tune which later proves to work in a knockabout canon. A homophonic refrain offers a brief escape from the bouncing V–I of B flat reiterated in the orchestral bass; on its second appearance this is extended to introduce, as climactic underlining of 'merry', the A flats from which the cadence progression is formed (see above). The clipped witticism of its last statement must represent one of the strangest endings to a distinguished composing career in the history of music. Yet it is a singularly happy comment on Britten's view of his mission that he was ready to devote some of his last working hours to this wholly unpretentious piece, and that its high spirits effortlessly carry conviction.

14 Later Instrumental Works

STRING QUARTET NO. 2 IN C MAJOR, OP. 36

The Second String Quartet, Op. 36, was first performed on 21 November 1945, the 250th anniversary of Henry Purcell's death. On the following evening, also in the Wigmore Hall, Britten and Pears gave the first performance of Op. 35, the cycle of Donne Sonnets. Not surprisingly, both works are heavily influenced by the composer's admiration for his great predecessor, but it is in setting texts that Britten has learnt the more profoundly. The quartet's tribute lies chiefly in its final Chacony, its first two movements inviting comparison rather with the classical quartet literature.

Thus, as in so many of the instrumental works of Britten's early career, we instinctively measure the events of this first movement against a background of the sonata principle. Just because the music is so demonstrably (indeed, demonstratively) tonal, the listener is likely to become aware very quickly how far from orthodox an interpretation of the sonata thesis this is going to be. He is probably far less conscious in the first instance that the three opening paragraphs, each announced by gesturing tenths, constitute significantly different *themes* (since their textural colour, of three instruments in octaves against a drone tenth, and prevalent note-values are so similar) than that they appear to define three different key areas. That epic swing to the dominant area from which an entire movement sought to recover momentum in an eighteenth-century scheme is not only achieved in the first twelve bars, but it is followed after another ten by a further swing in the same direction round the circle of fifths, i.e., to D. It is true that, by using a minor tenth at the next position (on A) and then reproducing this as the cycle is reversed, Britten cancels the sharp move and powerfully reaffirms C as *status quo*. But he has deliberately weakened the force of modulations that once determined structure by making them appear almost casually achieved (and the Lydian penchant of his themes tends to suggest that the next move is due). Similarly, by demonstrating the unity of the three paragraphs in this immediate juxtaposition, he appears to have prejudiced other dramatic potentialities—of pointed thematic contrast and ultimate reconciliation.

294

Ex. 14.1

However, both of these are to be exploited in due course, though our response to them is much affected by their being found within the complex of ideas we first accepted (tonal perambulations notwithstanding) as essentially a single 'first subject' statement (shown at Ex. 1). Transition duly begins, strenuously extending in jagged quaver figures (first introduced to activate the static eleventh built up in the Ex. 1 process) a series of entries of the basic tenth. Again sharp and flat ventures cancel out, however. But in the following misty texture of drones and imitative entries of Ex. 1a, the superimposed fifths (now still more obviously inspired by 'natural' open-string resources), C–G–D, suggest a centre of G, and the air clears into this orthodox second-group key for a first violin statement of Ex. 1b in a new rôle, accompanied by *a* in floating parallel chords. Released from the original drone, the theme quickly moves sharpwards and the cello's inversion of it carries on the process across the enharmonic divide, to perorate logically (mirror movement of the two soloists) in A flat. Ex. 1b has thus acquired the extended *cantabile* function of a 'second subject' and now Ex. 1c, cadential even on its first appearance, is transformed into a swaggering closing theme. Yet its A flat loses confidence, the authority of its vast dominant seventh being undermined by reiterations of the cadence that might have been—of G (four bars before letter G). The texture disintegrates and when the middle section opens (at letter H) the dominant seventh is the faintest background to the cello's ghostly reminder of the original tenth C–E (via a glissando to a harmonic). There follows a highly imaginative passage of harmonics that slowly changes under the influence of a succession of these sliding tenths; like so many features of this work, one may savour the moment but suspect that it is too divorced from the life of the movement. But the motion that begins to develop at letter I is a good deal more relevant than most commentators have allowed: while the staccato of the middle strings soon becomes a clear Ex. 1c derivative, the winding first violin five-note ostinato is ingeniously derived from the rather Waltonian twist of Ex. 1b; the bi-tonal conflation here is typical of most of the middle section; when 'exposition' can range so far tonally, development can only hope to intensify the situation by superimposed keys. Yet the whole section also draws heavily on ostentatious fifth relationships, the C major V–I see-saw from letter K being a particularly felicitous irony; b/c compounds are to be found in all this passage. Alternations of this leisurely tranquillo with a brusque agitato (inversion of the Ex. 1b shape and of the basic 10th) do not signally affect the impression of dispersal rather than cumulation that makes of this section another Britten 'development' to defy most classically-founded expectations. Ex. 1c in its closing-theme form eventually suggests a determination to clinch matters, though in the event the viola's F sharp–A tenths have to be reinterpreted most unexpectedly in order to admit C major and recapitulation.

This *locus classicus* among Britten's abridged restatements provides a cogent enough solution to the problems posed by so idiosyncratic an exposition. Nothing could redeem the tedium of rehearsing the division of one into three which characterized that: with a sleight of hand that is unashamedly virtuoso, Britten now demonstrates that the one can represent three-in-parallel as well as in series. Over cello arpeggios the upper strings conflate a, b and c into contrapuntal relationship. This does duty for first and second groups, and tonal 'reconciliation' could not be more schematic (though only the cello's reiterated open Cs ensure that we relate all this diverse activity to that tonic). But the closing group's function must still be exercised and, 122 bars having been represented by 16, the original pattern of events is resumed with Ex. 1*cii* (at letter N); *ci* has the last word in the coda, when in the purest C major it is strummed gently by the cello against a wall of limpid tenths, and is reinstated in its original rhythmic shape to make a final neat point.

On any hearing or reading of this movement, the superimposition of the three thematic ideas must appear the climactic moment. Yet repeated hearings may make one wonder whether too much weight has not been thrown on this contrivance: a development so episodic in character and a restatement so drastically abridged can invest the return with a rhetoric that sounds spurious. And that one does measure the movement against 'sonata' norms may create an acute feeling of imbalance; though statistics are not to be trusted too far in such matters, they are indicative of the very odd proportions here:

Exposition	*Development*	*Restatement*	*Coda*
148 bars	91 bars	37 bars	31 bars

A somewhat comparable inverted pyramid was to be found in the *Sinfonia da Requiem* but its effect was quite different: there the superimposition of ideas represented a dramatic, even tragic, collision and, because of the programmatic undercurrent and the continuity of the total structure, that movement could be left quite simply without a resolved outcome. There it was the restatement which represented the knot of complexity often made the business of development; in the quartet a grandiose 'resolution' is offered for which all too little dramatic conflict has called. Indeed, the movement is perhaps more accurately regarded as a balanced alternation, fundamentally as much decorative as dramatic, between statements and developments:

44	36	31 + 37	91	37	31
Statement	*Development*	*Statement*	*Development*	*(Re-) Statement*	*(Coda) Development*
abc	of a	b c	of b/c	a	of c
		(a)		b + c	
				c	

This would throw further light on Britten's careful disarming of tonal forces in the opening paragraphs but would conflict with the broadly 'sonata' scheme of tonal organization. Thus, imaginative though this structural *tour de force* may be, I find a more permanently satisfying relationship between form and content in the equivalent movement of the first quartet, and a better realization of that Britten ideal of a 'straight line' sonata derivative in either the Violin Concerto or the *Sinfonia da Requiem*.

The latter work provides a precedent for the quartet's retention of a single central tonality across a three-movement cycle. I have just suggested that the first movement of the quartet was not a highly dramatic structure, however, and despite the careful balancing of flat and sharp proclivities, there is little sign in it of the symbolic powers commonly attached to tonal relations in Britten's dramatic works. Of course, the *recognition* of a home tonic continues to play an important part in Britten's argument: the 'irony' attributed above to the tonic and dominant arpeggios underlying part of the development is made clear even to the listener without a developed key sense by the open-string pointers. Still more in the other two movements, we shall savour the composer's powers of oblique allusion only if we retain some feeling for that C around which the music skirmishes so dexterously.

Ex. 14.2

In the Scherzo this offers no problem, for the flying staccato arpeggios constantly incorporate prominent open strings, while reiterated chords of C

297

minor (and eventually major) aggressively punctuate the design. The actual harmonic units are more problematic (as the opening I–V at Ex. 2 makes clear) and the theme's use of protracted Neapolitan relationships adds piquancy. Against the *pp* arpeggios, its *ff* unison acquires an ejaculatory force that is not easily paralleled in the quartet literature; though its construction from scales and fourths is simple and schematic, inversion and phrase extension prevent a lapse into the utterly predictable, and so the oddly frantic tone persists. Nor does the Trio banish it, when an augmentation of the same theme is imposed on a new *sotto voce* accompaniment pattern, essentially based on a six-bar ground, though much varied by extension and contraction. Tonally the Trio provides yet another example of a rudimentary pattern (I–V–I in F) executed with a wealth of conflicting detail. On its reprise the Scherzo material is transformed into a high-pitched whispering of imitative voices, still within the Trio's tonal area. Only after protracted searches by the subsidiary idea (i.e., the scales superimposed to form alternating seconds and thirds) are C minor and the original texture rediscovered: the theme is reduced to its explosive first two notes, around which a symmetrical formation of arpeggios presents an epitome of the earlier harmonic movement without ever seeming likely to dislodge again that fixed tonic.

The ground of the Chacony is characterized by heavily cadential fourths and fifths, yet their very frequency makes tonal implications flexible (the *Screw* theme eight years later was to use them to move through the whole chromatic field), and only the repetitions of bar 7 and the step to a leading-note in bar 8 make C an inevitable outcome (see Ex. 3). A long series of variations on a mono-tonal ground might court our boredom, but a series on a ground that repeated the same modulatory process *ad infinitum* would undoubtedly win it. Britten has therefore placed C firmly in our ears as the destination of these explorations in order to allow innumerable points— dramatic, witty or poignant—to depend on the constant deferment of its complete achievement; similarly the tonal flexibility of the earlier part of the ground can be reinterpreted in innumerable different ways while the free string parts can (and frequently do) exist on their own quite separate tonal planes. As the Cello Sonata was to confirm, years later, the innocuous description 'in C' seems to inspire Britten to feats of tonal dexterity that do not belie the term but vastly enlarge its meaning.

The tribute to Purcell's age extends further than the structural method and the spelling of its title. The stylized rhythms of the Sarabande appear here in a well-drilled, French, treble-dotted form, and the nine-bar sentence is made up of units that contract, through two hemiola groupings, so as to accelerate events.

Basic rhythm

Less easy to reconcile with Purcellian habits of mind are the cadenzas that articulate the structure as follows:

6 harmonic variations	cello cadenza	6 rhythmic variations	viola cadenza	6 variations of a new melodic counterpoint	1st violin cadenza	3 variations reaffirming the ground's properties and (ultimately) C major

The growth within each block of variations is so steady as to cause one to question whether this sporadic exchange of corporate order for individual fantasy was necessary: in anything less than an eloquent performance these cadenzas can sound the most contrived of links. Paul Hamburger's comment on their 'dynamic' purpose 'of preparing, as every good recitative does, the ensuing ensemble, by musical meanderings that more and more approach their sequel as they progress'[1] gives an accurate description, but may not reconcile us to the loss of that cumulative tension on which so many of the greatest ground-bass treatments, Purcell's most notably, have depended. Of course, the interpolation of recitative into a ground bass aria was common enough before Purcell (it can be found effectively used, for example, in Cavalli) but the dramatic contingencies which govern such a procedure are difficult to simulate in a non-verbal context.

Ex. 14.3

To enumerate the details of each of twenty-one variations would labour much that emerges with great clarity in performance: Erwin Stein's analytical note issued with the score provides a check-list for the newcomer to the work. As in so many Britten harmonic contexts, the variations of the first group make their point by movements logical in their own terms engaging against static or delayed elements. Thus in variation 2 (fig. 3) it is the cello's pedal C against which the ground and its two harmonic attendants pull, whereas in much of variation 3 the pedal C has become a static F minor, leaving only the ground out of line; in variation 4 the pedal has changed to B flat (i.e., the other end of the span) but the revolving major/minor arpeggios of the middle strands invariably come to rest on B flat and C, so that we hear links carried across from one variation into the next. And in the final harmonic variation (fig. 7) the idea of C and B flat is amplified into the colour of the dominant seventh that dominates this reversion to homophonic movement. Though the rhythmic variations begin by multiplying the jolting

---

[1] P. Hamburger, 'The Chamber Music', in Mitchell-Keller, p. 232.

semiquavers of the ground into regular dotted-quaver groups, these are restricted by the third variation (fig. 10) to the violin's chordal ground and so interest transfers to the fundamental rhythm (see above) of the cello and the arabesques of the middle strings; by the next variation, the dotted-notes have been abandoned in favour of a free interplay around Ex. 3 as canto fermo. This is followed by using the arabesques of variation 3 as anacrustic preparation to the cello canto fermo, allowing a new accompaniment rhythm to permeate imitatively the upper strings (fig. 12). From these insistent quavers to the triplets of the last rhythmic variation is a logical step, and the fierce unison is a bold means of divorcing rhythm from all harmonic considerations.

If the viola cadenza too ostentatiously winds down the excitement of these triplets, the sustained second violin C throughout it makes a beautiful point when it proves to be the opening of the melodic counterpoint from which the next group stems—yet also to be no tonic, but the leading note of a suavely conjunct line in D flat. This set of variations is one of the most consistent and unforced passages of polytonality Britten ever produced. The accompaniment (i.e., ground) rhythms have sunk back to the more lethargic ♩ ♩. ♩ shape, and textures never rival the primacy of the melodic thread (assigned to each player in one variation or another) until the last variation of the group (fig. 19), where melody bifurcates into a rich counterpoint. After the first violin cadenza, we hear for the first time a statement of the ground framed by pure C major triads. This simplicity extends to the intervening harmonies and their timing, and the next variation (fig. 21) inverts the textural disposition—simple three-part harmonization of the cello's C major descending scale being opposed by three-part harmonization of the ground in the first violin. Finally the ground returns to its original unison condition, but C major has now so insinuated itself as to appear in an explosive chord after every long note of the ground: the chords outlast the ground and C major remains, unchallenged for the first time in the finale and, for this very reason, strongly reminding us of similar moments of tonal achievement in the first two movements.

THE YOUNG PERSON'S GUIDE TO THE ORCHESTRA, OP. 34
Whereas the Donne Sonnets and the second quartet's finale make clear that an attraction which was no mere response to the anniversary celebrations drew Britten towards Purcell's music in 1945 and 1946, the variations written in the latter year do not significantly extend their debt to Purcell beyond the theme, a hornpipe from *Abdelazer*. The work was intended to illustrate, with the aid of a film, the instruments of the orchestra, and on its transfer to the concert room a didactic purpose was still declared in the heavily jocular title, 'The Young Person's Guide to the Orchestra'. Nowadays it just as often appears on programmes as *Variations and Fugue on a theme of Purcell*, and there seems no good reason for considering it together

with Britten's music for children, since it was not designed for them to play. In any event, the didactic function could scarcely outlast a first hearing, and so we may assume that the work has kept its place on the strength of an inherently musical appeal.

It may therefore appear churlish to suggest that the popularity of a piece so far from Britten's best does him a disservice. Yet there are, I believe, few of his works which play so readily into the hands of those who have recognized in him no more than an ingenious manipulator of facile ideas. Similarly, those who find uncomfortable the stylistic dichotomy of Britten's piano-accompanied Purcell song realizations will be no less discomfited by the portly orchestral guise in which Purcell's theme is presented—for all the world as though successors to the firm of Handel-Harty had come into business.

To complete an expository section which presents not only this tutti, but the four chief orchestral families in turn, Britten extends the theme to round out an exemplary tonal circuit, I–III–flat II–IV–V–I, though this is weakened by the connexions originally made necessary by the spoken commentary; even in their abbreviated form these do not altogether escape the puerility of the 'till ready'. Some neat phrase contractions loosen up the eight-bar model (2; 4 × 1; 2) and help to identify the chief motives that will be used in later developments.

As the variations are all very short, there is no opportunity to show much more than one aspect of each instrument's character. So we find Britten, a master of imaginative instrumental colouring in almost all his major scores, dealing in stock responses—twittering flutes, soulful oboes, arpeggiating clarinets, and so on. The bassoons fare better in a little ternary piece that allows their popping staccato to be exchanged for a mellifluous *cantabile* (modelled on the earlier oboe version of the theme); the reprise is inverted, and the tonal scheme of the whole variation is more adventurous than the breezy Lydian B flat of the clarinets' variation, less mannered than the modulations of the oboes'. Accompanying string textures are incisive without encroaching on our interest too far. The brass take over this function in the violins' variation, a brilliantly vacuous *polacca* that for the first time in this work reminds us of the gentle ironies of the Bridge Variations, though by now Britten also has a manner of his own to parody—as the chains of thirds make clear. Violas demonstrate their varied tone-colour in a blank espressivo, but the cellos are given less perfunctory treatment: Crozier's patronizing commentary prepares listeners for 'splendid richness and warmth', yet most of the piece is restrained, almost hesitant in its syncopation against a delicately scored accompaniment, while its scalic variants are a sign that Britten is not deserting all his most personal expressive devices. Inevitably, the double basses bring lugubrious humour, but, like the bassoons, they are allowed to develop two ideas from the theme in a ternary piece (again with inverted reprise), their ardent *cantabile* platitude being accompanied by a woodwind stretto of their earlier arpeggio figure. Instruments featured in one variation often continue to play an important secondary rôle in the next, since the whole nature of the design prevents any recourse to the kind of continuity Britten uses in his passacaglia variation sets. So the basses now provide a spacious pizzicato bass to a variation displaying the harp as a heavily diatonic instrument, innocent of all the subtleties Britten had discovered in it long before this score.

It redeems itself with the delightful detail it adds to the following variation, for the horns; by this means the obvious device of their reiterating the arpeggios of the sequential bars 3–6 of the theme is sidestepped, throwing into more effective relief their opening and closing (inverted) fanfare derived from bar 1. Trumpets chatter in familiar Lydian/Mixolydian patterns, their rapid alternations owing something (though no trace of terror) to the scherzo of the *Sinfonia da Requiem*, and trombones and tuba find some unexpected ways of distributing ponderous augmentations of the theme. The array of percussion instruments is introduced by the timpani, playing a truer fanfare than any of the brass were given; the length of this section encourages a more ambitious treatment, with much bizarre attendant detail from the strings.

The fugue in which the instruments are all brought back in the same order derives its subject essentially from the sequentially arpeggiated bars 3 to 6 of Purcell's theme, though in fact it ingeniously conflates many other features. A witty kind of monotony seemed a deliberate part of the original, and Britten reproduces something comparable in the exasperating yet infectious proliferation through innumerable entries of his subject: it is therefore vital, however, that the subject itself should *not* share the squareness of its model. How systematically he ensures this can be seen in the $9 + 7 + 5 + 3 + 2 + 2$ construction of his subject (Ex. 4). Against this

Ex.14.4

a variety of countersubjects play, some rigidly accommodated to the 2/4 metre, others no less at odds with it. In the interests of clarity rather than to simplify the contrapuntal problem (for Britten's dexterity in this knockabout polyphony is great), the woodwind move into homophonic rhythms when the strings enter the maze. The texture is drastically thinned for the harp, but is quickly reassembled in an episode before the brass entries begin. Throughout this activity, the countersubject most directly based on the opening of the theme has made itself increasingly prominent, and its intimations achieve their full meaning with a chorale-like brass statement of the whole theme in D major (after a kaleidoscopic variety of key implications), against which the fugue subject maintains its garrulous course; indeed, it is still there after the theme has blown itself to a standstill, imposing its asymmetric rhythms on the drums against the reiterated orchestral cadence. Though the harmonic language is humdrum and the figurations parody Baroque formulae, the sheer verve with which so much activity is sustained in this fugue commands the kind of breathless admiration with which we reward a juggler. The effortless solution of technical problems makes one wish that Britten had set himself more of them in the unduly relaxed variations that make up the rest of this work.

PRELUDE AND FUGUE ON A THEME OF VITTORIA (1946)

Britten's only work for the organ, this prelude and fugue was written, like *Rejoice in the Lamb*, for St Matthew's Church, Northampton, a church with a distinguished record of artistic patronage. One suspects that the composer was never tempted to return to the medium, for he lacked that special affection for the organ which its best composers, players almost to a man, have had. At least his lack of the player's experience meant that he was immune against the stultifying clichés to which generations of English organists succumbed; no fingers wander idly around this music. But it must be owned that his imagination was not set alight by the instrument's resources. The prelude is chiefly a pedal recitative, though the dispersal of its quintuplets across the whole texture produces a momentary felicity of metrical asymmetry. The fugue, in its *p-ff-ppp* dynamic plan, calls for all those mechanized gradations, whether of stop changes or swell pedal manipulation, that make nonsense of extensive fugal textures. As in the fugue of the Purcell variations, there is no lack of contrapuntal resource, sometimes giving point to neat harmonic deviations, but the lay-out is often ineffective, principally because of a congestion of left-hand and pedal strands. The transparent diatonicism of the final canonic pair of entries is the most memorable sound in an uncharacteristic piece.

LACHRYMAE FOR VIOLA AND PIANO, OP. 48

The second quartet was to be for fifteen years Britten's last instrumental work related to classical sonata principles. Though the period immediately preceding *Grimes* had seen the centre of his activity move markedly towards the vocal sphere, after the opera the quartet and the Purcell variations gave no hint of the remarkable withdrawal from instrumental structures that was to follow. The only two instrumental works to be produced before the cello sonata of 1961 were *Lachrymae*, Op. 48 (1950) for viola and piano and the *Six Metamorphoses after Ovid*, Op. 49 (1951) for oboe solo. Both quite short, they were written while *Billy Budd* was the composer's preoccupation, as tributes to particular artists and for performance by them at Aldeburgh.

Paul Hamburger's analysis of the viola piece,[2] a series of 'Reflections' on John Dowland's song, 'If my complaints could passions move', demonstrates the originality with which Britten has solved the problem of accommodating developmental procedures while observing the framework of individual 'variations' proper to a theme of quite square and cadentially finite phrases. Dowland's song, of three eight-bar strains (each repeated in the original) would be unwieldy material for either division or canto fermo techniques, and any method that compelled us always to reconstruct the full cadential scheme (in which there is already an element of variation by amplification: Strain 1(a)'s cadence is reproduced in Strain 2, Strain 1(b)'s at Strain 3) would soon reduce to parody a monotony that in Dowland had a fatalistic intent. The point of his scheme (as in so many of his songs) is that each momentary glimpse of the light of hope is bound to be followed by a plunge into the darkness of despair: the turns to the relative major in the second and third strains are beautifully scaled, the first subsiding on to a half-close of the minor and the second rising to the peak of the melody's aspiration only to fall back finally into a full minor cadence. In reserving the whole of this paragraph of the song for the close of his work and basing his variation procedures entirely on its first eight-bar strain, Britten finally secures an expressive power that would have been utterly drained by repetitions of the same harmonic structure.

On the other hand, he makes sure that we have already taken the point of these inexorable returns to C minor from other evidence. In a work rich in bitonal implications, C minor (often with its ironic Picardy third) is repeatedly found to be the only point at which unanimity can be achieved. The sixth variation in a foreshadowing of the denouement attempts an equivocal relative major in introducing a quotation from Dowland's great *Lachrymae* song, 'Flow my tears', but the constant relapses (contracting the original melodic span) on to an accented B natural reinforce the supremacy of C minor. The whole of the final variation (fig. 10) is bound by a pedal C: above it a kaleidoscopic series of harmonic events proves incapable of dislodging it, and the viola's heroic efforts to implant the theme in a new territory (from the 16th bar) are tragically deflated in falling sequences. So, though Dowland's relative major affords a brief intense sweetness, it is accepted in the certainty that it must revert to his minor: thus his is the simplest and most perfect statement of a proposition relevant to the whole work.

But these strains can also be held back because, for that process of development Britten has called 'reflection', the first eight bars already provide a sufficient store of shapes—x and y in Ex. 5. It will be seen that y

---

[2] P. Hamburger, op. cit., p. 233.

appears inverted in the second strain, and to this extent Hamburger is not quite accurate in suggesting that no hint of the later strains is heard before their transfiguration (if we may so describe what is in fact a literal appearance): in bars 18–20 of the opening Lento, for example, the inverted *y* shape emerges prophetically. However, the essence of the Lento lies in the conflation of *x* and *y* (Ex. 5a) and in the piano bass statement of the first strain, fading out in the course of its repetition into a reverie from which we return only with the complementary strains that end the work. With no leaden thematic pro-forma, the intervening 'variations' work out highly

Ex. 14.5 (a)

Ex. 14.5 (b)

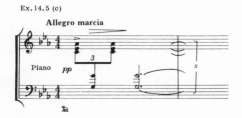

Ex. 14.5 (c)

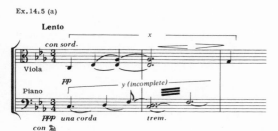

individual character studies at varying lengths, *x* and *y* (and less often their sequels in strain 1) giving rise, without ostentation, to innumerable new and fantastic ideas; Ex. 5(b) and (c) are quoted only to show how pervasive the initial principle of vertical conflation becomes. To analyse the procedures of each section in detail would help less than in much Britten towards an appreciation of the total achievement. Much of this music is deliberately spectral in its relationship to the model: the succession of images should seem even a little blurred, for our ears must strain ahead to find the focus of the magical closing bars—pure Dowland set in an imaginative frame that is quintessentially Britten's.

SIX METAMORPHOSES AFTER OVID, FOR OBOE SOLO, OP. 49
Even though Britten was subsequently to write the far more ambitious suites for solo cello, the little solo oboe pieces he wrote in 1951 for Joy Boughton to play on the water at Thorpeness still appear a remarkable achievement, less for the virtuoso effects they demand (which are not inconsiderable) than for the poetic qualities discovered in purely monophonic resources. On the face of it many instruments would seem more suited to 'metamorphosis' than the oboe, with its highly distinctive yet uniform timbre and its comparatively limited range. How simply Britten's transformations are effected may be heard in the first piece, 'Pan, who played upon the reed pipe which was Syrinx, his beloved'. The opening shape (see Ex. 6a) is developed in widen-

Ex. 14.6 (a)   Ex. 14.6 (b)

ing arabesque phrases but all within pure A major, and all entirely conjunct. The contrast at the appearance of the (b) motive springs partly from the intrusion of a tonally disturbing chromatic note and a leap; the implications of both of these are then worked out to form the middle section of a miniature ternary piece. On the return of (a), tension is built up by the restriction of range to a mere fifth (throughout the accelerando passage) so that the A major now becomes an intolerable frustration, whereas the sudden outburst with which the (b) shape makes a final appearance spans the movement's highest and lowest notes. It is in the delicate balancing of such slender materials that Britten creates a memorable chain of purely melodic experience.

This is not to imply that he avoids familiar arpeggiated harmonies: yet in this music, intended to be played in the open air (and its generous articulation by pauses, vital to the player's survival, is only really convincing under such conditions), one tends to accept even a dominant seventh (and 'Phaeton' is full of them) as a natural harmonic series rather than as part of a

306

functional progression. It is possible, of course, to hear in the opening phrase of 'Niobe' the implication of a rather glutinous piece of nineteenth-century appoggiatura harmony; the complete movement discourages such an interpretation, however, for the misalignment of the A natural is developed into a persistently contrasted tonal plane so that the final quiet statement of a great D flat major arpeggio (the 'natural' phenomenon *par excellence*) freed from this disturbance is a touchingly fitting image for the metamorphosis of Niobe 'who, lamenting the death of her fourteen children, was turned into a mountain'.

Perhaps 'Bacchus' does depend on our imagining an underlying harmonic framework: certainly its phraseology suggests a depleted village band, struggling to triumph through the hiccups and histrionics of the final bars. The mirror images of the second statement in 'Narcissus' are an obvious response, but the fantasy of their arrangement is not; still less foreseeable is the tranquillo third statement in which the mode is purified to C major and the theme, twice before thwarted by a B natural/C sharp impasse, finds its natural tonal outcome. The oboe is not a notably liquid instrument, and an attempt to engage it in *jeux d'eau* could appear ludicrous: Britten's fountain in 'Arethusa' falls almost languorously, but this means that we sense all the more each variation of the basic pattern. Throughout much of the first section the lowest note of these figures, F sharp, is our point of reference, tonality changing around it smoothly. The final section (from 'animando') builds up the cascade again through a process of expanding tessitura that typifies the extensive melodic thinking of this finely wrought work.

SONATA IN C, FOR CELLO AND PIANO, OP. 65

Admirable though each is in discovering new expressive resources in an instrumental tone-colour, the viola and oboe works appear as brief digressions in a long period during which almost all Britten's energies were devoted to equating texts, whether dramatic or lyrical. They were programmatic (*Metamorphoses*) or at least dependent on quasi-programmatic events (*Lachrymae*), while the one major work of the fifties to dispense with a text, *The Prince of the Pagodas*, was more closely bound than most of the operas to the presentation of a series of tableaux that depended on a scenario rather than on an intra-musical logic for its coherence.

During these years it became possible to believe that Britten had fallen victim to those critics who were ready to assure him that his purely instrumental designs had little beyond ingenuity of craft to compensate for the loss of the imaginative precision with which he responded to verbal and dramatic stimuli. In retrospect, we can see that what he required was stimulus of another kind, that provided by a performing artist of compelling and individual musicianship. So the artistry of the Soviet cellist, Mstislav Rostropovich, which eventually spurred Britten to a resumption of instrumental writing, was subordinate only to that of Peter Pears in the degree of influence

307

it exercised on the composer's choice of medium. Beginning with the Cello Sonata of 1961, Britten wrote five works for Rostropovich, and in the Cello Symphony he produced his biggest 'absolute' instrumental score.

The sonata is on a much smaller scale, its five short movements exploring a mode of concise but not constrained speech that had been forged in some of the more laconic vocal works (the Chinese and the Hölderlin songs, for example) written since the expansive days of *Grimes* and the second quartet. As each movement bears a title, it might appear that, like Britten's one violin-and-piano work, this is in fact a suite. But its first movement is undoubtedly to be heard against the background of sonata tradition, and scherzo and slow movement are also orthodox; as the extra movement is a march, we might think of the work as a divertimento, bearing in mind the honourable association of that term with mature classical forms. Certainly the embracing key scheme demands the thought across movements which we consider a sonata unity: Britten's framework is C–A minor–D minor–A flat–x to C. The disarming innocence of the inscription 'Sonata in C' should warn us that, no less than in the second quartet, such a tonal scheme may be executed with some licence, and the finale's scuffle to reach a home so long deserted would be a private joke for those with absolute pitch but for the cello's open-string clues. But this elation is the resolution of a complex sequence of moods: much of the sonata is subdued, its scherzo is phantasmal, its march bizarre rather than jocular, and its centre is an elegy of poignant understatement.

This sequence is well considered, and we have noted the key scheme which contributes to its logical realization. Even so, there remains a deeper source of unity in the melodic life of the sonata. To say that this springs from scalic motion may seem a truism in view of Britten's constant dependence on a flexible diatonicism; we have seen in many earlier works how he has drawn inordinate effect from entirely conjunct movement, but in the cello sonata he narrows the focus to the quality of the individual moves, to the expressive difference between tone and semitone steps. In the scherzo this produces a Bartókian introversion, and leads to scales that regularly alternate tone and semitone (Messiaen's second mode of limited transposition, though again Bartók is the true parallel). The other movements reveal the same preoccupation in different lights, so that we may consider a subtle motivic principle to be at work, even though it cannot be exemplified by any single thematic shape.

The second quartet had deployed a great wealth of material, whatever the unity imposed on the three subjects of its first movement by a common head-motive. In the cello sonata's gentle 'Dialogo', one idea is enough, with a derivative as cadence theme or belated 'second subject', and the climax is placed centrally in the development. The opening statement, Ex. 7, sets out from an uncommitted E–G that is to make E an important pole in the whole movement; the tendencies to E minor in Stravinsky's Symphony in C offer a

Ex. 14.7

parallel, though Britten had already explored such relationships in the D major/F sharp minor of the *Missa Brevis* and was to return to that pair of keys (reversed in weighting) in his *Cantata Misericordium*. The scale pattern of the piano's thirds is as vital a part of the theme as the cello's gradual coaxing into eloquence of its broken tone and semitone phrases; the two elements are offset in a rhythmic relationship of nervous sensitivity. The same material is later converted into a transitional forward thrust: now seconds collide vertically while horizontally they are concealed in octave transpositions that may recall another Stravinsky work in C—the piano sonata. Though the passage is repeated from the dominant, a modal A is the key in which the piano offers an apparently new theme. Except for octave transpositions, this is merely a variant of Ex. 7, complete with the left-hand scales, yet the bright colour (immediately suggestive of fairy symbols in the *Dream*) gives it a second-group contrast, so that Ex. 8 appears as cadential

Ex. 14.8

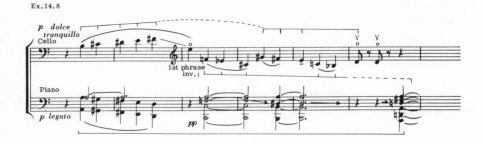

appendage. The scalic structure is on more than one level and eventually leads to a close on E, from which the exposition is repeated.

The middle section sets out as if to use Ex. 7 again, but complications of key involve the instruments in increasingly warm exchanges that flare up in heavy scales in opposite directions, reaching unexpected unanimity on the E that is the central point of the movement. In the other half of the development, Ex. 7 in the piano mounts through semitonal dissonance, gradually fading into the transfigured E with which it begins the restatement. Below its crystalline sounds, delivering Ex. 7 in a new metrical guise of 4/4 crotchets (compare the lengthened bars of the Violin Concerto's restatement; see p. 49), the cello oscillates between the scalic patterns which were the piano's earlier province and a pedal C. This already sounds a valedictory note, and Ex. 8 becomes sole second-group theme, dropping eventually through a whole-tone scale to the pedal again; over it the cello recalls the original rhythmic shape of Ex. 7. Finally, the piano scales climb into a distant brightness and the cello follows through its C string harmonics, capturing the innocence we instinctively associate with this key.

The 'Scherzo-pizzicato' is a furtive movement, which escapes from the main idea only into quasi-episodic developments of it. The cello's new manner of exploring tonal and semitonal adjacencies produces so uncertain a tonality that the piano cadences brusquely on to A four times in the first section. In rushing to its last cadence, it follows through the implications of the cello's alternating whole and half tones in a scale of that construction; this idea is worked out more fully in the next section while the cello plays an open-string ostinato (wittily suggested by the piano). The passage is repeated in melodic inversion, symmetry extending even to the cello's beginning the ostinato on its lowest string. After some tentative returns to the opening snatches, the piano leads off with an apparent platitude around A flat (a key relevant to the cello's opening bars). Now the pattern of steps (t–t–s) is strictly inverted within the phrase, producing a Phrygian flattening on the return. But the phrase itself is repeated in inversion, and the cello, interpreting the final chord enharmonically, sets off in A and in diminution to develop the figure against the piano's inversions. This strangely rigid manoeuvre induces a claustrophobia which, together with the casting of the whole movement in pizzicato, betrays the influence of Bartók's spectral fantasy more clearly than any other context in Britten's work. But the percussive reiterations by the piano at the climax of this section have none of Bartók's brutality of dissonance, and they re-establish A as the key held firmly by the piano throughout the cello's brief *da capo*.

At the opening of the first movement's transition, the piano seconds provided a striking deviation from the thirds it had played till then. They were produced by moving the upper note of the preceding minor third down a tone and the lower note only half a tone. Britten seizes on this pithy summary of the idea which has preoccupied him in this work, and adopts it as

Ex.14.9 (a)

Ex.14.9 (b)

a constant principle in the piano accompaniment of the 'Elegia'; see Ex. 9a. This means that he is combining two tone-plus-semitone modes as used in the previous movement (see Ex. 9b). Above the entirely stepwise movement of this motivic formula, the cello's restrained song is able to make a profound effect with simple intervals and repeated notes. The basic melodic idea dominating the whole elegy is given a tone step in bar 4 and a semitone in bar 6 (5 and 7 are decorated repeats of this conjunct motion). As the accompaniment's symmetrical modes offer no single key centre, the passage is only felt as D minor because of the cello theme, which eventually cadences on to the dominant. The piano takes over the theme in high octaves with a time-lag that later grows into elaborate heterophonic right-hand ornamentation (cf. the piccolos' decoration of the saraband in the *Dream*). The cello's accompaniment begins far below but rises into rich chordal texture as the climax is approached: even in these chords the tone and semitone motivic pattern may be traced. At the *largamente* climax, the one theme of this arched design reaches an incandescence that is difficult to parallel in Britten's chamber music. After it has faded, the earlier piano textures are recalled in brief alternations before the cello draws a last noble curve from the theme and closes again on the dominant. The parallel that comes to mind here, with the Adagio of Elgar's cello concerto, is perhaps not too far-fetched if we are willing to recognize an association of certain instruments with subtly individual moods—the pathos of this last word unspoken seems peculiarly appropriate to the cello.

We may wonder whether the freakish 'Marcia' was conceived as a tribute to the musical satire of Rostropovich's compatriots, Prokofiev and Shostakovich. The distortion of its main theme is produced by the crudest bitonal twist (tune in G, accompaniment in A flat), but it is the aggressive banality of this tag which is chilling. Apart from the semitonal key relationship, the scalic movement of this pattern and of the cello roulades is the only obvious link with the unifying principle we have traced elsewhere. Nor is this very apparent in the Trio, essentially in D with semitonal pulls exerted from both

311

sides. When the march reappears, its former martinet precision is blurred by
the sustaining pedal in high piano sonorities and the cello's roulades are
converted into glissandi of harmonics.

Because Britten uses for long stretches of the 'Moto perpetuo' finale the
symmetrical scale formation discussed above, it is impossible to assign a key
to it that has much relation to the listener's impression. Of course, within its
segments the theme *i* in Ex. 10 touches on a succession of minor keys, while
the piano accompaniment idea *ii* seems major, Lydian or Ionian. This
enigmatic conjunction provides the entire material for a movement of some
140 bars, though, as in the scherzo, it acts as its own episodic relief so
successfully that a comprehensive formal pattern emerges:

A; B1 & 2; A; B1 & 2; momentous transition to A.

This rondo scheme requires little annotation if the ostensibly similar but
functionally (and texturally) distinct elements are observed. The first exposition of A (beginning as at Ex. 10) is the longest, for the instruments
exchange rôles, and then drop *ii* in favour of canon on *i*. As the canon is at
seven quavers' distance, it reinforces those accents on every seventh quaver
which are the natural articulation of the theme; the effect of this simple
device is to prevent the monotony of the compound metre to which the
quavers unambiguously belong on a lower level, and to propel the music by
the palpable impulses of a higher time scale. In the second of the subsidiary
ideas, the seventh-quaver impulses occur *between* quavers, giving a still
more powerful thrust to each revolution. In the central A, *i* is on the cello C
string (*ruvido*) and there is a suggestion of development in the piano's
treatment in octaves of the falling semitones of *ii*. With an absurd elegance,
pointed by the cello's pizzicato accompaniment formulas, the piano brings
back B1, and so B2's line goes to the cello. The approach to the final refrain
is prepared through the build-up of harmonic blocks on D sharp, C sharp
and finally C natural. Inevitably this therefore sounds like a dominant, and
A*i* duly sets out from F in five gargantuan octaves (i.e., the cello in the
middle) and rolls on in intoxicating waves of sound that are truer to the title
than some much faster but fundamentally motionless displays of brilliance.
Here the full significance of Britten's use of the symmetrical mode becomes
clear, for there seems no reason why the chain should ever break; indeed,
the competing minor-key implications it includes (cf. Ex. 10) are only
silenced by a tumbling descent from which, miraculously, C major emerges.
In thus escaping from a vicious circle, the sonata closes its own key circle,
with a brave flourish.

Britten's concern for instrumental balance often results in very original
dispositions. The piano writing has all the finesse of his song accompaniments but this is exploited in a still greater variety of textures. It never
becomes virtuoso in style, and the cello part makes a similar impression;

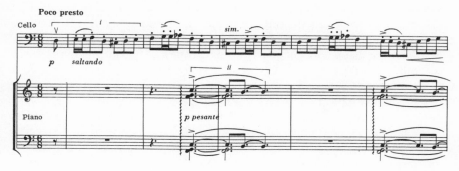

only on closer scrutiny do we notice that its demands have in fact been pitched quite high. Britten paid Rostropovich a musician's compliment in assuming that the technical mastery demanded here would not be allowed to overshadow the deeper beauties of this sonata; how justified he found his confidence is to be seen in the later cello works.

SYMPHONY FOR CELLO AND ORCHESTRA, OP. 68

Among these, the Symphony for Cello and Orchestra, Op. 68, stands out as a work conceived on the grandest scale of any Britten instrumental work since his earliest period of composition. It was completed in May 1963, but because of the soloist's illness was not given its first performance until March 1964, when the composer conducted it in Moscow.

The traditional label for such a work, 'concerto', has come to imply an ascendancy of the individual instrumentalist over the mass, achieved as much by demonstrable superiority of technical resources as by innately superior eloquence. Concerto structures have been strong or weak according to the degree of musical plausibility with which composers have been able to invest those sections in which the soloist's activities are essentially a display to defend his position against all comers. To accommodate such moments within the framework of a traditional *sonata* structure is almost inevitably to dilute its concentration on intra-thematic issues. It is often pointed out that the sonata-concerto tends to substitute an overt conflict of instrumental forces for that subtler argument which is provoked by the musical ideas themselves. Dramatic juxtaposition becomes more important than organic extension: in the greatest examples of this form, Mozart's piano concertos, this is recognized both in the large number of themes and in the reservation of some of them as orchestral interpolations. But the sonata-concerto in which the soloist proposes all the good tunes and is promptly seconded by a faithful band implies no conflict of any kind, so that the obligatory outbursts of soloistic demagogism may easily strike a hollow, if not meretricious, note.

313

This not uncommon failing of concertos in the nineteenth century has sometimes been avoided in our own by reversion to a pre-classical distinction between orchestral definition and episodic solo display. But Britten has shown no enthusiasm for this solution, the automatic propulsion of the neo-Baroque being conspicuously absent from his stylistic amalgam. Even so, with his idiosyncratic early sonata essays in mind, we may think it surprising that he chose to execute his frankest sonata scheme in a medium, of soloist and orchestra, to which it is not necessarily most appropriate. And here we discern the significance of Britten's title. Having conceived a first movement in which sonata principles are cardinal, he decided that concerto virtuosity would be a tiresome irrelevance. There is no conflict, genuine or spurious, between soloist and orchestra, and no place for the importunate rhetoric of passage-work. On the other hand, this is not a symphony for orchestra 'with cello' after the model of *Harold in Italy* or d'Indy's *Symphonie cévenole*; rather is it a sonata in which a cello is partnered by an orchestra. Britten therefore merely respected the curious habit of reserving a special label for the sonata when it is played by an orchestra in calling the work a 'cello symphony'. Of course, we might much more simply conclude that its claim to the title rests on its having four movements. Yet, if we look beyond the opening movement for signs of that kind of musical thought we call 'symphonic', we shall find it most convincingly in a relationship between the last two movements so embracing that we may be inclined to view the work as being in three movements after all. Thus, despite a final passacaglia considerably shorter than that of the violin concerto, the composer accumulates a structure weighty enough to counterbalance his fully worked out sonata opening.

The symphony has more than a solo instrument in common with the cello sonata. Though the slow movement draws all Britten's old power from melodic thirds, it is the manner in which he uses fundamentally (and sometimes obsessively) scalic material that continues the sonata's train of thought. In that work he subjected the idea of scale to an analytical scrutiny, notably by systematically contrasting the expressive effects of the half- and full-tone steps, as individual gestures or in a regularly alternating scale, but to secure an impression of more open-handed melody, in the first movement he diversified scalic movements by changes of octave register. Such scales are taken to far greater lengths than ever before in the Symphony's first movement, and they continue to play some part in the scherzo.

Even the opening (Ex. 11) can be related without sophistry to that of the cello sonata (cf. Ex. 7, above) in its scalic, quasi-ostinato accompaniment and its cello line that reiterates notes before emphasizing a crucial interval, here the semitone, *c*. But now it is the scales which are monodic, while the cello provides its own harmony. Though the I–V assertion of a D tonality is less equivocal than the sonata's delicate Phrygian/Ionian balance, the independent routes followed by soloist and bass suggest a far richer modality, of

Ex. 14.11

alternative notes (rather than the merely chromatic descent which could be considered the composite meaning here); the counterpoint of phrasings is also subtler in the later work. The rigidity of the falling tetrachords *a* is offset by the rubato effect of the link bars *d*. These lead to transposed repetitions of *a*, yet the essential continuity of the cello's discourse ensures that the whole of this paragraph, extending for twelve bars beyond Ex. 11, is heard as a nobly expanded progression in the tonic. As the soloist's fervour mounts, we note an early sign of the co-operative policy which unites the forces in the wind band's discreet sustaining of chords he can only sketch. The most poignant of these appoggiaturas (first heard in bar 11 of Ex. 11), stirring Britten memories from *Grimes* to the *Requiem*, gives way to a new extension from the rhythmic figure *b.*. A first impression of orthodox dissolution of authoritative statement into transitional small-talk proves illusory. The cello's minor-third figurations elaborate a descending scale, and *a* has another, still more devious, offshoot in angular brass octave-transposed figures, so that 'scalic' succession is maintained with near-serial strictness at this stage (hereafter B1; from fig. 2 of the score). The Mahlerian echoes of that *Urmotiv*, the rocking minor third triplet, are intensified by the horn's

315

rocking sevenths, to which the crucial *c* is appended. Later the same elements re-form in a more connected, but beautifully transparent, texture (hereafter B2; six bars after fig. 4).

Since the initial D minor was abandoned, it has not been clear which of its two traditional opposed centres will be set up, for tendencies towards both have been held in equilibrium. The undulating thirds and sevenths fade out, but the cello still ruminates upon the semitonal appoggiatura figure *c*, transforming it and its inversion into broken, sighing phrases (again compare the sonata); and these, at a wide variety of pitches and registers, form the entire melodic material of the tranquillo 'second subject' (hereafter C; fig. 6; it is in fact, of course, the third melodic stage). Its sustained accompaniment appears to settle the key question in favour of an A major in which the mediant is the most important note, the tonic rarely present (again, comparison with the sonata's opening is interesting). But this peculiar brightness of a major suggested most often by a minor third is clouded by more than the soloist's semitonal tensions: an equally persistent, though furtive, delineation of the other classically related key, F major, often in Mixolydian form, is simultaneously proffered by the pizzicato violins and double basses, their erratic contours extending the dislocated scalic patterns established in B1. Though the duality of progression heard at the opening of the work has thus been magnified into one of tonal centre, the ear accepts the weightier, harmonic, evidence, and the theme closes serenely in the dominant. So an exposition is completed in which three distinct thematic spans have been derived from two simple principles, the scalic succession and the scalic (semitonal) step.

The cello abruptly leads the way into the development with the B1 thirds pattern, and this alternates with an orchestral exploration of A around F, the centre which has just been eliminated; the bass pattern *a* + *d* is now inverted, and *a* becomes involved in close stretti that force the pace, reducing the theme (woodwind and trumpet) to fragmentary interpolations. On its re-entry, the cello reiterates the *d* figure as elaboration of a stabilizing pedal C that heralds a new section. This, despite obvious derivations, forms a reflective interlude rather than an intensive working-out. After repeating the section in triplet figurations, with brass instead of wood, the cello passes easily into the undulating triplet thirds of B2, against which woodwind soloists develop its lines. The brass continue to interpolate the A rhythms and their harmony suddenly clarifies to a patent dominant that signals the restatement.

But the key they have prepared is the F in which the development began. So the woodwind can now achieve around that centre the full restatement of the first subject from which they were distracted earlier; the cello again shows its freedom from virtuoso fixations by assuming the menial task of the underlying *a* + *d*. Since it presented all the main ideas in the exposition, it now consistently leaves the dominating rôle to its partner, and the orchestra enthusiastically accepts the exchange: the B1 material returns on *ff* wind, swinging the centre away from F back to D (major, essentially). The original extension of this section, B2, does not return, for the cello re-enters, to take over the octave-transposed scales (in an approximate B flat) in a restatement of theme C in D major; the original solo line is now shared by the strings, and the chordal accompaniment is in the wind. A long dominant pedal suggests that the movement is completing its cycle without a return to soloistic eloquence, but the cello, recovering an even keel after its tortuous patterns, gently insinuates itself as soloist into an extension of theme C. The valedictory tone of this is underlined by a return to predominantly minor tonality and by the steady descent in the accompaniment's bass to D. The home tonic is achieved, but by a measured scalic movement that brings to mind *a* and thus the first subject, untried by the cello since the opening of the movement. Britten's skill in adapting entirely classical procedures is well demonstrated in the I–V–I revolutions of *a + d* (revealing still more plainly its ostinato nature) which support the coda. Above them, the soloist brings to the pizzicato return of his first statement a great arc of intensity that calls on the support of cellos and then violas to double his chordal progressions as the peak is reached. And the wind are given a no less vital rôle, for they bring back B2, omitted in the restatement. Thus a true counterpoint of melodic interest in the coda supplements the development's antiphonal treatment of the same themes. As at the opening of the movement, alternative modal spellings and independent phrasing schemes characterize this richly imaginative coda: the woodwind melody (essentially major), the bass scales (essentially minor) and the cello's chords (free-ranging, but finally major) reach one after another their quiet cadences.

	EXPOSITION				DEVELOPMENT	RESTATEMENT			CODA
Themes	A	B1	B2	C	of A and B2 with central interlude	A	B1	C	B2 ⎫ A ⎬
Key centres & modes	D minor	transitional (towards A or F)	A 'major' versus	A 'major' versus F mixo.	F . . unstable	F minor	D major	D 'major' versus B flat mixo.	D minor + major
Chief melodic thread	SOLO	SOLO	SOLO + ORCH.	SOLO	SOLO & ORCH. in antiphony	ORCH.	ORCH.	ORCH. finally SOLO	SOLO + ORCH. in counterpoint
No. of bars	26	26	20	23	32+22+41	24	24	28	37
			95		95		76		

This movement marked a quite new development in Britten's attitude to the sonata structure. In particular, so complete and literal a recapitulation was unexpected, though easy to explain by the egalitarian principle he applied to soloist and orchestra. The movement's fine balance, in thematic and instrumental distribution, may be summarized as shown on page 317.

The scherzo, *presto inquieto*, presents the antithesis of such symmetry, only the most shadowy *da capo* rounding off its chain of continuously evolving patterns. Their source is again scalic, a cell of three notes (*e* in Ex. 12), moving by a tone step, then a semitone; the composite interval of a

Ex.14.12

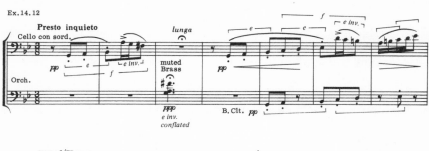

minor third also plays a prominent part in the stringently economical, yet prodigiously fertile melodic life of the piece. Its opening six-note motive (*f* in Ex. 12) establishes rhythms for future development but is melodically already a development of the basic shape (*e* plus its inversion). The seventh leap preserves the feeling of octave displacement familiar from the previous movement, as does the muted brass conflation of the *e* inversion. These chordal statements of the cell punctuate the whole scherzo, and are almost its only truly harmonic element. Between their appearances, a spectral counterpoint between soloist and woodwind is drawn from endless scalic derivatives of *e*. The shape *f* is so definitive, of mode as well as centre, that it is true to say that an initial G minor is displaced by C sharp minor, though the strings momentarily restore the tonic when they enter with a wedge of superimposed quaver scales. The motive's ability to act as its own episodic relief emerges in the following cello statement (fig. 32), an augmentation of *f* that is repeated in inversion and otherwise developed, between scurrying mixed scales from the strings. The later episodic section, from fig. 35, is more concerned with the minor third, though the cello's ostinato accompaniment has *e* at its core. After a brief return of the augmented *f*, a new section begins, in which the soloist works out the semiquaver scale figure in innumerable mixed-modal juxtapositions, over a drumming (*col legno*) string background. This texture provokes the first general *forte* of the movement as the brass discover a route back to G minor (and, inevitably, to *e*). Restatement of a kind is left to them, while the cello's busyness and the strings' drumming dominant pedal work up a crescendo the more dynamic for following so prolonged an undertone. Abandoned suddenly by soloist and strings, the brass restatement collapses dramatically, and in a final section the strings' superimposed scales (shadowier than ever—*sul ponticello*) are answered by the soloist's memories of his opening figures in harmonics. The brass chord of bar 3 also returns, but at sepulchral pitch. It ends a scherzo that calls to mind no convincing parallel in Britten's music—and none in anyone else's, for now the furtive, claustrophobic atmosphere he creates from these flickering shapes, always new yet always eerily familiar, has thrown off the debt to Bartók of the cello sonata's scherzo.

The simple profundity of the Adagio, on the other hand, is achieved through devices that have long been recognized as Britten's most personal. A plain ternary structure throws all the weight of the movement on to the recurring thematic span, a paragraph of some fifty bars that is superbly fashioned. Yet the subtleties analysis reveals are compatible with an aural impression of complete spontaneity. After the timpani have established a ceremonially slow but taut pulse with the G natural of the scherzo's key, the cello and string harmony begin to expound the theme (see Ex. 13) from an E major that does not attempt to absorb the foreign bass note (contrast the apparently identical, but resolvable, clash at Grimes's 'In dreams I've built myself some kindlier home'). The friction set up is maintained throughout each phrase, for pizzicato double basses and staccato tuba outline a variety of bass movements that connect two G naturals and assert a G tonality, of variable (usually 'flat') modality. Meanwhile the string harmonization of the soloist's phrases describes wider, and

Ex. 14.13

Ex. 14. 13 (ii)

always contradictory, tonal arcs. Restricted entirely to common chords, each line moves from and to its own tonal centre, and, since the last line is centred on the first line's E, the whole scheme thus forms a tonal succession at a higher level (E–A flat–F minor–B flat–E).

The soloist's melody is for the most part entirely consonant with the accompanying harmony, but its magnificent linear construction suggests that in fact it was conceived first. Its basic units are the third (minor or major) and the two rhythms ♩.. ♪ and ♩. ♪ ; in later phrases these are extended to include a few compounds of thirds (i.e., fifths and sevenths) and the contractions ♫ and ♫ . From this stock of commonplaces, Britten forges an adagio that justifies the classical associations of the term. Its phrase-structure alone gives us some idea of the structural logic at work: a five-bar statement, of compliant falling thirds; seven bars in which, with notably more effort, the thirds rise to repeat the opening at a higher octave; three bars only, relaxing to hover slightly below the peak just achieved; a five-bar development of this line, lower still yet more exploratory; finally, a twelve-bar phrase that rises from a greater depth than before to a higher peak, in urgently contracting rhythms and with the only fourth of the entire theme thrown into high relief after the cadence in a return to the basic rhythmic formula (Ex. 13ii). These five phrases of one monumental proposition are separated by rhapsodically fluctuating woodwind interludes, all patterned on the modal sixths, *g* in Ex. 13i, and all underlaid by the drum's assertion of G that began the movement.

320

Both of these features are carried over into the horn counterpoint and violin decoration that attend the subsidiary theme. This, ultimately derived from Ex. 13ii, is to become the melodic basis of the passacaglia, and the form in which it appears there may be seen at Ex. 14. The soloist's fourth phrase (cf. Ex. 14, bars 17–21) is here extended over a huge compass, losing all the theme's originally clear-cut A tonality. A more violent timpani interruption stirs up an agitated development in which the soloist applies his own impetuous rhapsody to the interlude figure *g*, while the strings dissect the subsidiary theme. This subsides into A major underlaid by C natural, from which point a subdominant restatement of the main theme is a natural consequence. It is played by the brass soloists over wind harmony, and the cello plays the interludes. Only one modification is made, a bar being interpolated to move the climactic statement, Ex. 13ii, back to its original E orientation. At the same moment, the timpani abandon their C for the original G. The tutti breaks off but the movement's opening drum rhythm carries on, fading to become a background to the first part of the cello cadenza.

Britten's violin concerto provides the obvious precedent for a cadenza which leads into a passacaglia finale. It was a *tour de force* that summed up the first two movements before adumbrating the ground of the third. Although it secured continuity, it was necessarily dissociated from the scheme of the movements themselves. In the cello symphony, the cadenza is concerned rather to establish the link that makes an entity of the last two movements: it may be viewed as a second development in a design which places the restatement of the slow movement's subsidiary theme at the head of the finale.

	MOVEMENT III				CADENZA	MOVEMENT IV		
Themes	A	B	Devel. of A & (mainly) B	A	Devel. of (mainly) A & B	B	extended as variations (new passacaglia bass)	Coda on A
Key Centres	E → A		fluctuating	A (with 4-bar close in E)	fluctuating→	D	(with fluctuating interlude)	D
Melodic Interest	SOLO	SOLO with Horn Cpt.	ORCH. with SOLO	ORCH.	SOLO	Tpt. with Cello accompt.	Interest shared consistently throughout variations	SOLO

All the cadenza's derivations are clear, its climax coming with an impassioned statement of the main adagio theme, punctuated by its own pizzicato representation of the drum figure. The less stressed feature of the subsidiary theme, the rhythms of its counterpoint (originally in the horn), is then recalled, so that the eventual restatement of the theme itself (see Ex. 14), on the trumpet with a cello counterpoint establishing the new passacaglia element, is quite unforced. The solemn close of the adagio's first theme (Ex. 13ii) forms a tailpiece to the statement, underlining again the interrelation of the two movements. Some faint reminders of the first movement in this material are noted in the example.

321

Ex. 14.14

Despite the ambiguity of key produced by the strict patterning (minor third; tone) of the fourth phrase, this is the most frankly diatonic tune in the symphony, and Britten extends it into a bright D major final section by simple variation procedures. The ground, first presented by the cello, persists, but interest centres on modifications to its tuneful descant rather than on new counterpoints. Little in the process calls for analytical investigation, and the variations may be summarized as follows.

I. The ground on wind, the tune in 6/4 on first and second violins in canon at the fourth. Some phrases are extended by the insertion of segments transposed, a practice maintained in later variations.

II. The tune a third higher on cello, double-stopping another part in contrary motion; a typical Britten near-Lydian. Ground (still at original pitch) on strings. The tutti tailpiece expands to represent also the third-higher pitch level.

III. Each phrase of the tune is delivered in 12/8 and in fivefold imitation by the woodwind; the ground retains its tonal hold (now on brass with the soloist's pizzicato) in the face of these conflicting assertions.

IV. The ground on lower strings' pizzicato, while the cellist tries a jaunty version of the tune at the fifth. After the third phrase, the ground, the strict

melodic model and the basic tonality are quitted in favour of free development of the texture, making a scherzando piece far more genial than anything in the second movement. This leads into

V. An expansively rhapsodic interlude (i.e., without ground) in which the
cello muses, *senza misura*, on each line of the tune between wind elaborations of the tailpiece, *h*. Key is flexible. After dwelling affectionately on the
drooping final phrase, the cello sketches in arpeggio form the last statement
of the ground—

VI. This is supported by the lower strings, while wind take up the tune at
all three of the levels tried earlier (i.e., unison, third and fifth). Doubled at
various octaves, this produces a dense texture, reminiscent of a 'folky'
composer like Martinů. The tone is lofty and the fourth phrase reaches a
splendidly sonorous climax.

As it ends, the cello emerges from its accompanying rôle for the last time,
and climbs to deliver an intense coda, discovering still deeper expressive
potentialities in the fourths of the tailpiece, *h*. This drawn-out, rich solemnity, stemming from the adagio's main theme (Ex. 13ii), emphasizes once
more how indissolubly mingled are the last two movements. Yet in the
steady scalic descent of the parts that make up the accompanying polyphony
we may perhaps hear another distant echo of the work's earlier preoccupation. In so many ways this coda helps to bring to the composite finale an
emotional weight which counterbalances the first movement that one may
regret the impression given in performance that it is just too short to perform
the task ideally: we appear to end while still drawing a great breath, not in
exhausting one.

In the symphony's later movements, Britten has been just as scrupulous as
in his sonata opening in giving the orchestra and soloist equal shares in the
statement, or restatement, of thematic material. And yet the cello has never
been granted those faintly contemptuous rests in which soloists appear to
watch the underlings strive, but has contributed subsidiary interest or quite
menial accompaniment. When the orchestra is thus encouraged so frequently to match soloistic eloquence, its scoring demands particular finesse,
and when the soloist to be supported is a cello, the composer's task is no less
demanding. Britten solves problems so unostentatiously that we may overlook their existence. Already in his choice of orchestral specification he has
prepared for a quite new range of effects. Apart from the usual strings
(unusual, however, in the relatively minor rôle of the violins), he calls for
two flutes (one doubling piccolo), two oboes, two clarinets (one doubling
bass clarinet in the scherzo); but one bassoon and a double bassoon are used
throughout, the latter often being the more prominent. The brass section has
two horns, two trumpets, one tenor trombone and a bass tuba; the percussion section includes a metallophone. This is scarcely a chamber orchestra,
but it can provide a great variety of transparent textures. The inclusion of
tuba and double bassoon makes possible, together with the string basses, a

range of positive colours at a very low pitch, so that the cello can be accommodated in its lowest register without having of necessity to be the functional bass too. The upper woodwind tend to be used as a composite group in a fairly high register, so that their tubby middle harmony shall not blanket the soloist. It is clear that the unusual specification stimulated Britten's imagination, and he was to return to its essential form for *Owen Wingrave* and *Death in Venice*. Among the many new sonorities in the symphony are the development's dialogue between double bassoon and high clarinet (later oboe) supported only by the soloist's oscillating thirds, the scherzo's loud, nagging cello figuration surrounded by a high oboe octave, *pp*, and a Stygian chord on horn pedal, tuba and double bassoon, *ppp*, and the rhapsodic fifth variation's background shimmer of empty fourths on vibraphone and flutes, later translated to much lower register by horns and tam-tam. Delightfully new though the work often is in its colouring, it is for the nobility and economy of its ideas, and the masterly structures in which their potentialities are realized, that we may regard the Cello Symphony as Britten's most considerable achievement in the field of purely instrumental music.

SUITE FOR CELLO, OP. 72, SECOND SUITE FOR CELLO, OP. 80 AND THIRD SUITE FOR CELLO, OP. 87

Britten's subsequent works for Rostropovich were cast in the far more modest mould of the solo cello suite, yet, since he completed a set of three of these, they represent a significant addition to the literature.

Since Bach's magnificent example, the unaccompanied string sonata and suite have been cultivated chiefly by composers of pronouncedly neo-Bachian tendencies, such as Reger and Hindemith. But Bartók's solo violin sonata, for example, showed that the influence of Bach, though in these media almost impossible to shake off, could be assimilated into much wider terms of stylistic reference. Obviously enough, Britten's cello suites declare a debt to Bach's textural methods, and in more than their fugal movements. Since a string player cannot sustain more than two notes at once, the convention, supremely exemplified in Bach, has been to change pitch register so as to sketch in now this part, now that, of a 'texture' that can exist as connected threads only in the mind's ear; the process is closely comparable to the *style brisé* of the French lutenists. To what purpose Britten had studied the convention may be seen in almost all the movements of these suites (as also in the guitar *Nocturnal*, written shortly before the first cello suite, but discussed below), yet only in a few movements is it relevant to consider Baroque models. For the rest, a succession of contrasted character pieces, nimbly exploiting different technical possibilities of the cello, suggests comparison rather with Britten's own early instrumental writing. Not surprisingly, the dedicatee, a great Bach player and an executant with a variety of special techniques effortlessly at his command, has been a dominating influence. But Rostropovich has also been a great ambassador for Soviet music, and, as in the march of the cello sonata, it is possible to hear links in these suites with the world of Prokofiev and Shostakovich.

The first suite, Op. 72, in G, was written in November and December, 1964, and was first performed by Rostropovich at the 1965 Aldeburgh Festival. It is framed and punctuated by a Canto, Ex. 15. Memorable though

Ex. 14. 15

the effect of this 'song' is, one scarcely recalls it simply as a tune: certain basic melodic shapes emerge from the peak notes on the opening presentation, but they are just as likely to reappear in the middle or at the bottom of the texture in later statements. As the parts alternate swiftly between melodic and harmonic functions, a very rich sonority is implied, even though no more than two notes are heard at once. The sound of these diatonic sevenths and ninths recalls the transfigured world on to which Act III of *A Midsummer-Night's Dream* opens, and the Canto's ritornello function is made as evocative as are the recurrent images which articulate that opera.

In the Fuga a long subject with three distinct features makes possible a variety of pointed episodes. Though the most witty exchanges depend on the figure of two staccato notes, the flowing semiquaver passages (punctuated by common chords that reveal the wide tonal range of this piece) are no less relevant, containing the subject within their figurations. The Lamento is a pure solo-line piece organized with great resource and expressive power by expanding the first drooping phrase and its inversion. With no harmony other than that implicit in the line, Britten here creates again those tensions that depend on semitonally conflicting tonal centres (E challenged by E flat). The brief second Canto leads into a Serenata that recalls the Pierrot-like fantasy of Debussy's sonata. It is played pizzicato throughout, the unequal intervals of the strummed opening chords influencing the modality of the whole piece, which is rarely stable and often, like the rhythm, bizarre.

The Marcia exploits the 'natural' sounds of the cello—open strings and their upper partials. Its two ostinato elements are a delicate bugle-call of natural harmonics and a drum rhythm played on open-string fifths with the bouncing wood of the bow—elements of such simplicity as to court vapidity. As so often, it is the witty arrangement of these materials that sustains our interest, the unpredictability with which the fairy trumpet and drum interrupt the trudging forward movement of the third idea, a clipped rhythmic pattern with a rising melody that is also heard against open strings. Stealthy though all this is, a steady crescendo is at work, and the peak of the movement's single dynamic curve arrives with a new, 'trio', tune. This begins in stentorian tones and a more confident key area than the march ever achieved, but chromatic complexities arise that drain away the swagger. With the *da capo* of the march, the mysterious quality is intensified, so that an almost programmatic significance seems attached to each gesture.

The Canto's third statement is the most tense, chromatic relations tending to predominate and tonal orientation to be at best ambiguous. So a single open-string D provides an immutable drone in the Bordone that follows. After a flurry of minor-third figurations and a more menacing left-hand pizzicato figure have confronted each other from both sides of the drone, this becomes background, but rarely harmonic accomplice, to a more pastoral dialogue. The last of these virtuoso studies, the Moto perpetuo, remains clear in outline even at breathtaking speed, for every pair of semiquavers is a semitone step, and so the motion is heard as, in effect, that of decorated quavers. The turbulent course is made more precipitous by frequent metrical contractions, but it evens out, to admit phrases of the 'Canto' in its original form and key; and gradually the ebullient figurations are harnessed to provide embellishment for the final statement of the suite's dominating theme.

Three years later, in August 1967, another suite was finished and it was presented at Aldeburgh in the following June. This second suite, Op. 80, in D, opens with a Declamato, an eloquent line that suggests improvisatory abandon but is subtly organized both in its incorporation of apparent asides into the main argument and in the unification of its melodic spans by very systematic widening and contraction of the constituent intervals. Such a movement shows very clearly one of the ways in which in his later style Britten can achieve a strong sense of logic without depending on progressive harmony. The Fuga is even more ingenious than that in the first suite.

Ex. 14. 16 (a)

Ex. 14. 16 (b)

Because of the placing of rests in its subject (Ex. 16a), the player is able to set against this a countersubject and then to execute stretti of two and eventually three 'voices' (Ex. 16b), all without ever sounding more than one note at a time. As early as the Bridge Variations Britten had demonstrated the paradox of a monophonic fugue exposition (cf. Chapter 2, p. 43), but this working-out of a complete fugue (including a canonic episode and a statement of subject-plus-countersubject in mirror form) is perhaps the most elaborately consistent use of the *style brisé* ever attempted. Yet there is no impression of an arid or earnest exercise: the subject's necessarily odd rhythmic shape has the virtue of stamping the whole piece with its attractive blend of hesitancy and haste.

The Scherzo has two main ideas, the first characterized by scurrying cross-rhythms and an abrupt end-accent, and the second a little chordal refrain which avoids monotony by always carrying a new harmonic meaning; after the two have been heard in alternation, they are finally telescoped together in rhythmically unpredictable situations. The fourth movement bears no title but carries the speed indication, Andante lento. Though composers have commonly regarded those terms as contrasted alternatives, Britten justifies their juxtaposition, for the pizzicato figures are in typical 6/8 andante quavers, while the bowed melodic lines use slower dotted-quaver units (i.e., are in quasi-2/4 for much of the time). The melody's addiction to thirds, constantly alternating here between major and minor, emphasizes a resemblance to the Cello Symphony that can be heard in structural matters too: in later developments the pizzicato, originally on open strings only, blossoms out into an independent chromatic idea, in antiphony with the *arco* melody recast as a duet. The inverted melody completes the scheme, and through a few transitional bars a way is found into the tonal area and the briskly dotted rhythms of the final allegro. This Ciaccona is on a five-bar ground bass, adapted from the most common of all the Baroque prototypes, the descending tetrachord from tonic to dominant, but a Baroque uniformity of triple measure can never be taken for granted. After the first build-up of twelve variations there is a quiet interlude, using the inverted ground as a basis for freer figure development in a wider tonal field. With the return of D major and the dotted rhythms, ascending and descending variants of the ground alternate. While pedal Ds and As within the figuration spell out a simple tonal assertion, the chromaticism of the ground creates a play of intervals that provides at least a memory of the opening declamatory movement of the suite.

It was not until seven years after the second suite's appearance that the third was heard. In fact the work had been composed, in nine days, in early 1971, and taken to Rostropovich when Britten visited Russia in April, but it was held back from publication until the Soviet cellist was able to visit England again to give the first performance, at a Maltings concert in December 1974. At first glance the third suite appears to draw again on many of the figurative, textural and colouristic possibilities Britten had already found in the solo cello. Over the whole suite the technical problems may be slightly less consistently daunting than before, but the continuous unfolding of its nine movements, lasting some twenty-two minutes, clearly calls for reserves of concentration as well as of virtuosity.

As we get to know them better, even movements of a type evidently recalled from the other suites reveal themselves as highly individual, while in one obvious respect the work is sustained by means quite unlike those used hitherto. For this suite is based throughout on four Russian themes, three folksongs from Tchaikovsky's arrangements and the *Kontakion* of the Orthodox Church. However, as in *Lachrymae* and the *Nocturnal*, the material that has been varied emerges only to end the work, the four themes being played in simple succession at the close of the ninth movement, a passacaglia. By this time their melodic shapes are familiar, for each theme has had at least one movement quite closely derived from it, yet there have also been contexts in which they have been interwoven or blurred into one another; so the final process of unravelling is an obvious but satisfying outcome.

Last of all the themes is the *Kontakion*, a Hymn for the Departed, presented with impressive solemnity in a version that expands from monody to a chordal climax. In it we recognize the source not only of the passacaglia's ground but of the suite's introduction. This opening Lento evokes its lines in a veiled parlando, suggesting the rhythms of chant but freely deflecting through six or seven tonal fields. These are measured against the fixed point of the plucked open C string, a pitch which is to recur as a true tonal anchor in the final full statement of the hymn and the suite's faint last note. With no such reference, the following march inhabits a tonal limbo; its bizarre opening can be traced to 'The grey eagle' and its spectral second idea, a revolving figure followed by mounting or falling thirds, to 'Autumn'. Instead of conventional recapitulation, songlike phrases are interpolated, soon emerging as the tonally vagrant Canto of the third movement, based on the folksong 'Under the little apple tree'. The following Lento is a barcarolle which incorporates in its arpeggio figurations the complete melody of 'Autumn', transposed up two degrees within the major system. This is repeated with the original G-string pedal made drone fifth to a C-string pedal, but a third verse, in trying new figuration that cuts free from the pedals, soon also abandons tonal moorings. These are reinstated in the fifth movement by the open strings, incorporated in turn as pedals in the elaborate pizzicato harmonies which are one element in the opening dialogue; melodically they outline phrases from the *Kontakion*, whereas the brusque bowed figures derive from 'The little apple tree' and later the rising thirds of 'Autumn'.

Britten's third fugue for solo cello is in particularly marked contrast to his second: instead of its witty *trompe l'oreille*, this fugue builds a weighty arch from initial subject (very literally quoting 'Under the little apple tree') to the sonorous chordal texture in which subject is opposed by inversion, to a tranquil final inversion in the original pitch area. From a mercurial reassessment of its last three notes, the next movement (VII, marked *fantastico*) is born, a recitative full of dramatically contrasted gestures, making clear references to 'Autumn' and 'The grey eagle' and shadowier ones to other shapes. Again there is a link across to the *moto perpetuo* in the cell, minor third-plus-semitone (descending), but this shape now begins to suggest the *Kontakion*'s opening, albeit faintly in the haze of so much chromatic movement. Only with the re-ordering of the same pitches in the slow, drooping phrase of the passacaglia's ground is the relationship made obvious—yet uncertainty persists, not only in the unpredictable timing of its appearances, but in that its last note, leading-note of the chant, just as often acts as a tonic in relation to the texture's upper strands. These offer a final review of the cello's eloquence, and fleeting references to the three folksongs are clarified until, after a gradual winding-down of its opening phrase, we are led into 'Under the little apple tree', followed by its three companion themes.

Though we heard in both the earlier suites unmistakable echoes of Rostropovich the Bach player and the envoy for Soviet music, this last of Britten's five tributes to him is the most personal, and affectionate, of them all.

NIGHT PIECE (NOTTURNO) FOR PIANO SOLO (1963)

Britten the conductor, of his own and other music, has been comprehensively preserved for future generations on gramophone records, but Britten the pianist will be known only as a superlative accompanist. The lack of interest he showed, from the time when he gave the first performance of his own concerto, in solo performance was paralleled in his composition. After the early *Holiday Diary* he was only once persuaded to write solo piano music, and that a modest test-piece for the Leeds Piano Competition of 1963, entitled *Night Piece* and allotted no opus number. Like some other examples of the composer's night-music (including the last movement of *Holiday Diary*; see Chapter 1, p. 27) it owes a debt to Bartók, chiefly in the murmuring sextuplet figure, Ex. 17c (compare the quintuplet that punctuates the slow movement of the Sonata for Two Pianos and Percussion) and in the mysteriously fluttering and chirping cadenzas that protract the recapitulation of Britten's ternary design. But the characteristic sonorities are not at all Bartókian. The formula of tune unwinding against long-held pedals with uniform accompanying patterns in between is Romantic in origin, yet the oscillating stepwise, rather than arpeggiated, movement of the central component gives it a separate, motivic, existence (it is, of course, the origin of the sextuplet figure) and prevents a warm harmonic blend. (This innocuous-looking texture was worthy of the contestants' efforts—it is not at all easy to realize perfectly.) The harmonic plan of the theme shows a straightforward move from B flat to B and back (see Ex. 17a), the second tonic area being a sequential copy of the first and of exactly the same length. And the progressive introduction of all twelve pitch-classes (Ex. 17b), though it could be

329

Ex. 14.17 (a)

Ex. 14.17 (b)

Ex. 14.17 (c)

ppp (murmurando)

regarded as an arbitrary by-product of the modulation, seems no less carefully planned. The extension of the final B flat chord in Ex. 17a adds a new element, of luminous chords winding down; the bass now takes over the accompanying pattern, but soon the sextuplet form adds a new middle element, one that generates the central climax, and passes to the top of the texture for the restatement. The melody is now two octaves lower than at first, and it is arrested (at the three asterisks in the harmonic plan, Ex. 17a) as the high sextuplet line blossoms into fantastic cadenzas. In much of this detail B continues to suggest a counterpole to B flat, and the return of the chordal element intensifies the tension until the closing bar's resultant resolution into a distant B flat of sympathetic vibrations. Unimportant though the piece is in Britten's output, in every aspect of its making it reveals his hand.

NOCTURNAL AFTER JOHN DOWLAND, OP. 70

Later in 1963 a far more spacious 'night-music' was completed. Britten's love for the music of Dowland had been creatively exercised in his *Lachrymae* of 1950 (see above, p. 303), a poetic work of which the crowning beauty lies in the emergence, complete with Dowland's own harmonies, of the second half of one of his airs, after ten variations have elaborated the shape of only the first strain. In writing a piece to exploit the imaginative artistry of Julian Bream, it was natural for Britten to turn again to Dowland, whose music Bream the lutenist has done so much to bring alive, even though the work was in fact conceived for Bream the guitarist. In the *Nocturnal*, Op. 70, for solo guitar, it is a complete air, 'Come, heavy Sleep' (1597) which, with its original accompaniment, emerges at the close. There

has been no opening thematic definition, but each movement has incorporated a distorted version of Dowland's line and/or features of its
accompaniment. So when at last we achieve the simple statement, the song
seems to represent the repose of sleep, and the preceding eight variations the
changing, often tormented, moods through which the poet has groped
towards it. The air has two strains, of which the second should be repeated,
but each variation leaves incomplete this repeat, falling away as though in
despair, and passing to the new approach of the following variation. When
the repeat of Dowland's own second strain fades out, however, to end the
whole work, it is the achievement of oblivion.

No feature of the work more convincingly supports such a programmatic
reading than does its harmony. Much of this remains shadowy, implicit
within the guitar's characteristic *style brisé*, but Britten also makes powerful
use of the fourth-dominated chords that stem from the instrument's tuning.
In all the tortuous weavings of the first seven movements the repose of a
rooted major triad without tonally conflicting elements is never achieved.
Only out of the turbulent climax of the following passacaglia does the rich
sonority of pure E major appear, and its reiterations provide the calming
influence that directs the music into Dowland's air.

The opening variation has an improvisatory waywardness of rhythm (see
Ex. 18a) and its lines twist and develop Dowland's shapes so that they are

Ex. 14. 18 (a)

Ex. 14. 18 (b)

uniform in neither tonality nor modality. But the opening of the second strain preserves the drumming homophony that is so marked a feature of the song (see Ex. 18b). Variation 2 abandons this introspection for compulsively repetitive *moto perpetuo* figurations, interrupted by clangorous open-string chords; the second strain continues to be marked by the E–F conflict of Ex. 18b, now realized in arpeggios. The steady accompanying triple pulse of Variation 3 is belied by the antiphony of melodic lines above and below it, which subdivide the bar into quarters; the use of inverted phrases, particularly effective in the reiterated fourths of the second strain opening (much prolonged in the coda), leads to the beautifully logical mirror movement of the air's final phrase. Variation 4 is restless and tense, with flurries of notes that juxtapose alternative degrees, and with decelerating tremolandi—both features that give a Bartókian flavour rarely wholly absent from Britten's nocturnal fancies. By contrast, Variation 5, marked 'March-like', appears a relaxation, because its characteristics are so definable, though there is nothing swaggering about these obsessively thrummed open-string rhythms (the ♪♫ of Ex. 18b) or the melody, essentially an inversion of the air's contours, enclosing them within its two-octave doubling.

Open strings again prompt the composer's imagination in the sixth variation, strings 2 to 5 affording a central chordal unit to which the successive yearning harmonic movements all return. But alternate phrases of the air are represented by flickering patterns of harmonics, creating a fantastic interplay proper to a piece with the Schumannesque heading, 'Dreaming'. In Variation 7 the open strings create slow bell-like points of colour against the high tremolando in another tonal plane. It leads into the final variation, a passacaglia on Dowland's first accompaniment phrase; this is shown in Ex. 18a, but now it falls from C to E through the 'white' notes, creating by simple means a conflict between 'tonic' and 'final' that prepares for a greater tonal conflict, of a kind familiar from many dramatic Britten contexts, and thus invests the achievement of the closing E major with that decisive quality we have noted. Whereas most ground-bass treatments are studies in simultaneity—counterpoints against the ground, new harmonizations of it, developing rhythmic activity above it, and so on—the nature of guitar technique makes of this passacaglia something nearer a dialogue. Since the ground is so persistently at variance with the unfolding argument it interrupts, the piece acquires a dramaticism that may well be unique in the repertoire of this instrument. There is no longer a line-by-line paraphrase of Dowland's melody, but a developmental process in five stages (like variations within the one span), the fourth leap of the second strain playing an important initiating rôle in most of them. E major first emerges from the maze of tonal implications at the climax of the chordal fourth stage, but it is conflated with the C of the ground. The ground's scalic pattern is then pursued, straight and inverted (which equals retrograde) throughout the instrument's compass and the tonal universe, until the E major triads that articulate it have their subduing effect. It is a moment of deep poignancy when we hear the ground return to its original C–E descent for the last time and usher in its own transposition in Dowland's opening texture (see Ex. 18a).

This work deserves a far higher place in the common view of Britten's achievement than it has yet gained. Its demands upon the player are not lightly overcome, and perhaps its moods are not those to which many guitarists' recitals have acclimatized their audiences. But the prevailing melancholy is as natural to the guitar's sonorities as it is appropriate in a tribute to John Dowland; the strange flights of fancy that constantly flicker in the gloom are no less a tribute to the artistry of Julian Bream.

GEMINI VARIATIONS, OP. 73

The most interesting aspect of these variations and fugue seems likely to remain the circumstance which brought them into being—the composer's meeting with the gifted Hungarian twelve-year-old twin brothers, Zoltán and Gábor Jeney, and his being persuaded by them to provide a piece that would exploit their abilities as pianists, and respectively as flautist and violinist; they gave the first performance of the work at the 1965 Aldeburgh Festival. In homage to the father figure of musical education in Hungary, Britten based his variation set on an Epigram by Kodály. If one looks back on some earlier Britten themes for variation, whether his own or borrowed, this rather pompous statement appears scarcely epigrammatic enough, and its complete structure is not reproduced until a *da capo* which, as in the Purcell Variations, crowns the final fugue. For the rest he relies on developing and contrasting the two kinds of shape, disjunct and conjunct, that alternate throughout the theme.

His old facility in turning out nimble or affecting character pieces had not deserted Britten, though the irony he brought to such tasks in his early period is nowhere to be sensed here. Probably the dedicatees enjoyed the opportunities for maintaining individual metric schemes and the jaunty counterpoint of canon and fugue, but the listener glimpses Britten as more than a *Gebrauchsmusik* purveyor in reflective moments like the romanticized fanfare of Variation 9 and the gravely beautiful mirror movements, 6 and 11; the first of these, with its subtle adjustment (in itself symmetrical across the piece) of interval relations, is a particularly concentrated form of a Britten *idée fixe*. It is difficult to foresee much of a future for this work, since the dedicatees will have outgrown it, and the version for four players has little to compensate for the loss of the *tour de force* quality that justified the original; but the piece stands as a pleasantly eccentric testimony to a quixotic impulse.

THE BUILDING OF THE HOUSE, OP. 79

Britten had written an Occasional Overture in C, his Opus 38, to mark the opening of the BBC Third Programme in 1946, but he withdrew it subsequently. So the overture he wrote for an occasion certainly no less important for his own plans, the opening of a new concert hall, The Maltings, Snape, at the beginning of the 1967 Aldeburgh Festival, remains his only extant contribution to that once popular *genre*. It is, furthermore, an odd one in including a chorus, which sings a metrical version of Psalm 127 ('Except the Lord the house doth make') to the tune known best as *Vater Unser*. Though additional brass or an organ can substitute for the chorus, the disappearance of the text reduces the *raison d'être* of the hymnic thread in the work.

Writing for a standard orchestral specification for the first time since developing the methods of the church parables, Britten did not extend the freedom of alignment enjoyed by their small groups of players. But his interest in distinct temporal strata finds an outlet in a consistent superimposition of the units shown at Ex. 19; the instrumentation given is that of the opening and final sections.

Ex. 14.19

Trumpets and Horns

Violins and Violas

Woodwind

Cellos, Basses and Tuba

The overture is played at great speed ($\textstyle$ = 172), so the texture could be thought symbolic of the various craftsmen going about their different tasks with admirable zeal. A tonal dichotomy—wind's F sharp major and string' D major (Mixolydian in the bass)—further differentiates the activity, though it also provides the clashes which make of each outburst, released by a bell-stroke and gradually fading, a joyful peal. The detail of the strata is inventive in an open-handed way, but their lack of dominating contours is explained when they become attendant on the first line of the chorus's psalm. This leads off, in unison in F minor, but the string basses who prompted that convert it down to D during the orchestral fade-out, and in that key the verse is sung in full, broadly and idiosyncratically harmonized in triads. Even here metre is far from unanimous, woodwind duets in a jaunty 3/8 accompanying each line; another wind pair (later doubled at the octave) decorates each cadence chord. The collapse that the ending of a paragraph so evidently finite can bring is staved off by a typical Britten close on to a major second, and this becomes compositionally important in the following section. This is a quiet string fugato on a sinuous line derived from the hymn's opening shape; the initial note of each entry is offset by a xylophone rhythm one tone lower: . It will be seen that the rhythmic units originally separated are

334

now used in linear succession, to produce a highly fluid dolce texture. Energy is restored by unsubtle means, and the wind develop snatches from the hymn in canons of varied temporal units (here a device common in the parables is quite directly recalled) against free string tremolandos. The return of the original fleet movement is this time sustained throughout the psalm's second verse—in stentorian unison, but at unpredictable tonal levels: F sharp minor, achieving two successive lines, seems in the ascendant, but with the last line D is triumphantly recovered. In the huge flourish of the Amen, the orchestra is given *carte blanche* to render their parts *ad lib.* within given rhythmic (i.e., as in Ex. 19) and pitch restraints. Very much an occasional release of high spirits, the overture is structurally unambitious, but texturally marks a new stage in Britten's orchestral style.

SUITE FOR HARP, OP. 83

It would be an unwarrantable assumption that Britten's enthusiasm for writing instrumental pieces for his close colleagues and friends deprived us of more works in the standard media—violin sonata, piano trio and so on—since this survey of his late instrumental music suggests that the stimulus of a particular soloist's performing style was needed to release a flow of ideas in instrumental terms. If the standard media were little enriched by Britten in his later years until the magnificent third quartet, some subsidiary repertoires made significant gains; to those of the guitar and the cello he added in 1969 that of the harp, with a Suite, Op. 83. It was written for Osian Ellis, a player who had made a distinguished contribution to the Aldeburgh Festival performances of the three parables, and who introduced the work in a recital at the 1969 festival.

The harp is of all modern instruments that most tightly harnessed to a diatonic conception of pitch resources: though chromatic amplifications are available by pedal changes, at any one moment the harp is set to produce across its entire compass only seven of the twelve pitch classes. But, as we have repeatedly noticed, even when borrowing some part of Schoenberg's regulating principle, Britten never wrote music which abandoned the use either of irregular (i.e., in their mixing of tone and semitone steps), *scalic* contours or of triadically referable harmonies and the polarizing effects which are their consequence. His most typical situations, juxtaposing or opposing tonally distinct scalic segments or chordal units, remain accessible to the harp even without pedal changes. For example, if the instrument is set as shown in Ex. 20a, a C major (or minor) triad might be treated as central,

Ex. 14. 20 (a)

Ex. 14. 20 (b)

but strong implications of B major or E major/minor could also be played on, as could the suggestion of D flat brought by its dominant seventh (i.e., C's 'German sixth'). Ex. 20b shows a situation more liquid and yet more committed: the whole-tone scale affords a tonally indifferent pitch material, but the interpolated F natural inevitably casts itself as the centre of a predominantly 'minor' mode (with flat second and third degrees, sharp sixth and seventh). In fact, this Ex. 20b scale is used without deviation throughout the Nocturne of Britten's suite. Though the writing is elsewhere less rigidly circumscribed, few of the work's most telling effects are dependent on frequent pedal changes, and it is clear that the composer has taken pleasure in confining his music for long stretches within the modal limitations natural to the instrument.

He has also restricted himself to the instrument's traditional resources—arpeggios of all kinds, glissandos, dry chords in close position, and so on; only one passage is in harmonics, and of such modern extensions of the medium as knocking on the soundboard or using the tuning-key as a beater there is no sign. To a layman it appears as though harpists would find much satisfaction in a work that is both taxing and idiomatic, yet there is little of the didactic aura of the Conservatoire test-piece about it: the listener will take it to be a piece by Britten that happens to be written for the harp, not *vice versa*. Nowhere is this more obvious than in the Overture, the first of the suite's five short movements. The ceremonial opening defines C major, counteracting its platitudinous quality by lithe rhythms and inflexions of other tonal areas (comparable passages can be found in *A Midsummer-Night's Dream* and in the first movement of the cello sonata); Ex. 20a, taken from this context, has already served to demonstrate the kind of relationship that can be set up. From its pitches 7.1.2.3, a bass ostinato is formed, but 5 and 6 are now sharpened to produce the E major with flattened sixth in which the drily syncopated new idea is harmonized. Its texture is expanded through some twenty bars to a vehement climax, during which C natural has not been dislodged from its place on every beat of the bass. With the restatement of the first idea, the same mode continues to break from this in affirming G sharp major triads, but this evaporates quickly into a return of the Ex. 20a mode and its inflected C major, which persists through a distant reminder of the central idea, its ostinato (in the treble) now confirming C by an identical interval succession 5.6.7.1 (=7.1.2.3).

The last flourish of the Overture is immediately converted to form a ubiquitous triplet head-motive in the Toccata. Whether in its crossing patterns, its whimsical changes of texture or its long stretches dominated by whole-tone relationships, this is markedly reminiscent of French pianism, though its tight little formal scheme is not at all Debussyan. The opening chatter of bars 1–4 appears three times, with only slight modifications, while the idea that follows it each time is more fundamentally altered for its central appearance (thus A B A B₁ A B), though it never escapes from its mooring to a pedal. The Nocturne is, as we have seen, still more confined (see Ex. 20b, its inflexible modal limits). The notated 6/8 metre, though it accounts for the melodic line in isolation, cannot consistently be heard in this way against the regular crotchets of the bass patterns, but their organization as a *four*-crotchet ostinato does aid the impression of two schemes operating independently—one carrying impassively the tread of time through the nocturnal hours, the other responding to the nocturnal spirit with a wistful human song and the scurrying sounds of natural life. As the description is intended to convey, this is yet another of Britten's night-pieces that owes its basic poetic conception to Bartók. By recasting the position of his ostinato (but not its mode), Britten contrives to imply many tonal areas other than the initial F minor, but this is finally restored in a rich version of the song-like strain that winds down two-and-a-half octaves to its cadence, logically formed of a whole-tone penultimate chord and a resolution into pure F minor, the two conflicting principles of the piece. Britten's experience in the cello suites serves him well in the Fugue. Even though the harp needs less recourse to subterfuge than the cello in presenting a polyphonic texture, the same featherweight touch is preserved in this scherzo. Its deft subject, in 5/8 metre and compounded of fairylike fanfares in B flat Lydian, is the kind of Britten idea that seems a parody of his own style. The scalic second half (bars 4–6) establishes a countersubject rhythm (usually restricted to a monotone) and the simplest of melodic shapes for sonorous quasi-episodes ('quasi' because they can all be regarded as consequents of middle entries), in which the fanfare converts itself into accompanying arpeggios. It would seem unforgivably heavy-handed to detail every inversion, elision and tonal deviation in this tiny piece, but the final entry, uncertain as to its timing, its direct or inverted form, and its register, is a particularly neat witticism.

With the final Hymn, variations on the Welsh tune, *Saint Denio*, Britten pays tribute to the dedicatee and to his native land, so proud of its long history of harp playing. Truth to tell, this is not the happiest theme for variations: its first two and last lines reiterate essentially the same cycle of melodic thirds attended by primary triads, and cadence unequivocally in the tonic, while the third line is simply an extended tonic arpeggio and a dominant. Britten decides on three alterations which all make for greater flexibility. He casts the repeated lines 1 and 2 up a third, where their contour is reminiscent enough but cadential possibilities are less restricted, he reduces line 3 to repetitions of a chord but always swerves to an unexpected destination at the I–V point, and he takes the identity of line 4 with 1 and 2 as an invitation to carry straight on into the next variation. Characteristic results are often obtained (as in the first two statements) by playing off conjunct lines, sometimes themselves thirded, against the theme's thirds; elsewhere these melodic thirds are filled in so that long scalic passages reach out to new tonal areas. But the peroration is stated in the purest 'white-note' terms, with a hammering ostinato rhythm between each chord; the mere

337

rearrangement of lines 1, 2 and 4 so as to begin respectively on tonic, mediant and dominant prevents the torpor the full tune might have induced here. A reflective coda further dispels any effect of brashness, and allows the suite to fade out in romantically shadowy sounds more appropriate to the nature of the instrument.

SUITE ON ENGLISH FOLK TUNES, OP. 90
Though Britten's arrangements of folksongs for voice and piano are not discussed in this book, the orchestral suite, which works traditional material into much more elaborate structures, demands notice. One movement, 'Hankin Booby', was written for the opening of the Queen Elizabeth Hall in 1967, but the other four were not added until seven years later; the whole suite was first performed at the 1975 Aldeburgh Festival. The orchestra required is quite modest, and the technical demands are not excessive, though every texture calls for great precision of execution and balance.

Britten's was a generation of composers that tended to find uncongenial the consciously cultivated folk influences so evident in the work of many of their English forerunners. Yet it is significant that an interest in treating folk material blossomed in about 1942 together with Britten's recognition that, whatever travels both he and his musical language might have undertaken, their true place was within a peculiarly English environment. From the early song arrangements onwards, his practice appears consistent. He accepts that to 'set' a folk tune is artificial, ensures that the nature of the artifice adopted is in some sense prompted by the tune, but then makes no attempt to suppress his own inclinations in developing it. This orchestral suite stands therefore at a considerable distance from the modally 'appropriate' harmonizations of, say, the well-known Vaughan Williams suite. In any event, the material used here includes only three melodies from that body of rural song rescued at the beginning of this century as against seven dance tunes from Playford's *The Dancing Master*.

The opening movement, 'Cakes and Ale', is a scherzo characteristic of Britten in its incisive clarity of sound and in the contrast of both time scale and tonal allegiance maintained between the two dance tunes on which it is based. 'The Bitter Withy' has a more affecting duality between the edgy brightness of the harp and pizzicato double bass and the veiled sonority of the other strings. Both melodic lines are stated in octaves that contain their harmony, but the harp's homophony, a sound that could come from early Britten, answers string textures that are loosely aligned rhythmically after the manner of Aschenbach's E major scalic superimpositions in *Death in Venice*. At the central statement of 'The Bitter Withy' the string octaves are left unadorned and a sombre new colour, of low horns and bell, is added. The return to the opening string texture suggests an unremarkable ternary pattern, but increasingly dissonant encounters between the strands provoke a belated crisis, stilled but not forgotten in the melancholy coda.

338

'Hankin Booby' is for the other half of the orchestra, double woodwind, trumpets and a drum, the latter dominating the piece with the military vigour of its rhythmic patterns. The contrast between the two tunes used is again sharp, though neither is allowed an opulent treatment: the spiky dotted rhythms of the one engage in a rather acid two-part counterpoint and the other's smooth flow does not conceal the strain imposed by the middle of its three octaves being a degree too high. So the swinging rhythms and clangorous open strings of the four-part violin band in 'Hunt the Squirrel' take on a special brilliance; the piece recalls that carefree virtuosity with which Britten presented his credentials in the Bridge Variations.

Only in the last movement, 'Lord Melbourne', is a song quoted *in extenso*, as an eloquent solo statement. Even this, its rhythmically flexible cor anglais line reproduced from Percy Grainger's notation, is not so much harmonized as freely suspended above a string texture of interweaving ostinati. The melody is framed by snatches of a dance tune, 'Epping Forest', but its climax recurs and is extended by a process of fantasy in which the impassive pedal at last gives way to a harmonic circuit; the poignancy of this moment seems to illuminate the Hardy quotation which provides the suite's subtitle, 'A time there was . . .'.

STRING QUARTET NO. 3, OP 94

Just as admirers of Sibelius reassured themselves through the long years of his silence that an eighth symphony must exist, so many musicians nurtured on rumour and wishful thinking for some thirty years the belief that Britten's two string quartets would have a successor. The BBC proposed to commission a third quartet, and the composer's return to instrumental composition with the Rostropovich works of the sixties added more substance to a widespread hope. Yet throughout those years, as we have seen, Britten wrote scarcely a work that was not prompted by the desire to pay tribute to the highly specific performing style of some great artist; although many quartet ensembles have what might be called a corporate individuality, the musical ideals of the medium are essentially foreign to the enhancement of a personal performing 'character'.

It seems that Britten himself shared the hope that, when time should allow, he would turn again to the quartet medium; in the event, it was only when he must have known time to be running out that he set about the task. The Third Quartet, his last instrumental score, was written down during October and November of 1975, and given its first performance by the Amadeus Quartet at The Maltings on 19 December 1976, shortly after the composer's death. The profound impression it made then might appear an inevitable consequence of the occasion, but greater familiarity with the work confirms that the simplicity of its language and the serenity to which it aspires represent a distillation, not a dilution, of Britten's expressivity during this most poignant period of his life. 'La Serenissima' is the subtitle which is attached to the final Recitative and Passacaglia, and the epithet has several applications. It links the quartet with Britten's beloved Venice, where some of the work was written, but also very potently to Britten's last opera, from which quotation is made; even so, finally it seems most appropriate to the radiant atmosphere, resigned yet not renouncing, which pervades the quartet, in particular the outside pair of its five short movements.

After the three-movement plan of his apprentice quartet of 1931, Britten had adopted a classically orthodox succession of four movements in the D major Quartet (1941). With the second quartet (1945) he reverted to three, but now, through the enlarged structural proposition and intensified restatement of the opening Allegro and the ramified variation design of the Chacony, he attempted a more symmetrical balance of forces across an arched design. In using an arch of five members in the third quartet, he would seem to have invited comparison with Bartók's fourth and fifth quartets. Certainly a correspondence of mood between the outside movements, as noted above, encourages us to view the two scherzos (2 and 4) as complementary and so to isolate the violin cantilena of movement 3 as centrepiece. But there is little to remind us of Bartók's models in the music: the structures here are much more slender, and corresponding movements do not so evidently re-work common material (though see below). The title of the second scherzo, 'Burlesque', does suggest a debt to Bartók's sixth quartet, but Britten's irony makes a less barbed, more elusive impression; persistent echoes of popular entertainment music, especially in the eerie waltz of the trio, suggest another link with *Death in Venice*, notably the wry distortions of the travelling players' music.

Britten at once disowns the grand sonata designs of classical tradition in modestly entitling his opening movement 'Duets'. Rather as in the cello suites, a fluid succession of textural variants is to be more important for this work than an embracing argument, tensed by motivic concentration and schematic tonal opposition. It may be that the short spans of activity to which the composer was restricted during the years of his illness necessitated this reduction of scale, but in any event the lyrical impulse of the material implies no striving towards epic climax: the movement's central eruption, though evidently built on the same motivic ideas as the rest, feels more like a dramatic interlude than an organic 'development'. Of course, the whole piece is developmental in that so much springs from the swaying seconds of the opening bars (Ex. 21a). That 'sonority of the second' first discussed in this book in relation to Britten's first instrumental work (see p. 19) achieves in this last score its most sustained and luminous use. The other shapes bracketed in Ex. 21 remain influential but the movement gains its highly individual stamp from the gentle friction of these seconds, flowing across, then relaxing into the broader momentum of the compound metre. Inevitably the quiet lapping of water is suggested. Though the closest parallel to this rhythmic propulsion in *Death in Venice* is far from placid—the fretful

Ex. 14.21 (a)

Ex. 14.21 (b)

Ex. 14.21 (c)

theme to which Aschenbach pursues his search through Venice (see Chapter 21, Ex. 5a), already some relationship of the quartet to the opera seems implied. And so it is probably not fortuitous (while in the final Recitative it is most pointed) that many of the pitch-collections form intervallic cells of the x^1 or x^2 class that was so fundamental to the opera's growth (see Chapter 21, Ex. 6b). Here we sense no crucial symbols at work, yet the play of alternative degrees causes the music to inhabit a tonal limbo not unlike that which characterized Aschenbach's quest. A disembodied second, whether major or minor, is in itself tonally enigmatic, and the whole movement amplifies that phenomenon (cf. Ex. 21b) so that, while local tonal attractions can be isolated, they are rarely unequivocal or protracted, and the fascinatingly

341

elusive quality of sound that results can draw the listener on without recourse to patently intensive 'working-out'. Only in the coda, from bar 76, does an outcome in G minor (a key towards which, without Britten's key signature, one might earlier not have felt impelled to look for pointers) become a clear goal: even here the second pair of instruments (second violin and viola in Ex. 21b) are scarcely less intent on implying a dominant of A flat.

The progress of the movement does not call for elaborate analytical comment. One of its principles, that each of the six possible 'duet' pairings shall be used, is made to reinforce the simple logic of the coda's return to the opening. The dialogue shown at Ex. 21a reaches a peak and drops back to an undertone, when it is joined by a delicate commentary of single pitches alternately above and below from the other pair, first violin and cello. As well as vastly expanding the musical space, this commentary sounds all twelve pitches without repetition, a complement to the central duet's more leisurely unwinding of a twelve-note succession through its multiplication of a semitonal figure derived from the shape marked *2* in Ex. 21a. At bar 19, as

	1	2	3	4	5	6
Possible Duets	(V1	V1	V1	V2	V2	Va
	(V2	Va	Vc	Va	Vc	Vc

Bar Nos.	1–10	11–18	19–27	28–39	40–57	58–63	64–75	76–end
Duet Type	4	4 + 3		3 + 4		1 + 6	5 + 2	3 + 4
Structure	A		B		C	A	B(?)	Coda
					–based on			chiefly on
					elements			A (but
					of			quoting
					A and B			B and C)

the diagram above shows, the neat pairing and the extension of the opening *cantabile* dialogue break off. A duet principle persists in which one element is a knotted chromatic pattern, essentially scalic and plainly related to the opening bar but much edgier in its heterophonic presentation by pizzicato and bowed-trill lines. The distribution of these varies, but the answering element is always the first violin with fragile snatches of melody characterized by the alternation of sixth leaps (the fourths of bars 4 and 5 in Ex. 21a had already been expanded to fifths in the sequel) and returning steps. This curiously wistful passage gives way to a resumption of the earlier duetting (as from bar 11) but with the rôles of the pairs reversed, and then a more radical deviation occurs—the central section of the movement (bars 40–57), described already as a dramatic interlude. The change from placidly alternating quavers of the compound metre to alternating semiquavers (at $\downarrow . =$ $\downarrow$) is not drastic, but their expansion of conflicting pitches into conflicting chords quickly generates the movement's crisis. So do the rapid consequents, either scalic or derived from the first violin's earlier wistful phrase, and the principle of dialogue between two elements preserves congruity even though the duet disposition is abandoned. It is more appropriate to look back to, say, Britten's early piano piece 'Sailing' (from *Holiday Diary*, see p. 27), where a squall momentarily disturbs the smooth motion, than to look at his sonata development-into-restatement contexts for a parallel to this central section. And this squall as easily blows itself out in a smooth transition back to the earlier swaying rhythms.

These central 18 bars were preceded by 39 and are followed by 37 bars, so that an obvious ternary balance is achieved. But in fact the final section only faintly reproduces the deflection that articulated the first: the violins' sixth phrases may be recalled by the chordal sixths of violin 2 and cello from 64, but they are more potently octave-transposed to thirds in the first violin's ethereal dolce phrase from bar 71. The shape is retained in the coda from 76 (Ex. 21b, second and third bars) and both the central eruption and the original first violin phrase are more literally recalled at the one tense moment (bars 84 and 85) of this intensely beautiful closing paragraph. The bright chord through which the movement subsides into silence (Ex. 21c) conflates as its top three pitches the violin's rising-sixth, falling-step shape, but it also contains many other delicate tensions of seconds converted to sevenths or ninths—not surprisingly, since it is made up of six adjacent pitches, Mixolydian G minus its E. The penultimate gesture (bars 92 and 93) in which each of these pitches falls away through space complements the G set with hints of an A flat opposing pole, so that yet again the opening seconds have thrown a long shadow.

The application of octave transposition to a scale segment could be said to be retained in the first scherzo, 'Ostinato', for its ground is a series of sevenths; the first two bars of Ex. 22 show the version which acts like a

Ex. 14. 22

refrain in the structure. The opening unison E is more persistently a tonal reference than was G in the previous movement, though the proposition that fans out from it superimposes cadences on to E minor, A minor and C major; the resulting chord also appears as a consequent to that which ended the first movement. On to the lunging crotchets of the ostinato sevenths (rising or falling) in one part contrapuntal lines are threaded in others. Their syncopated rhythms (shown in bars 5 and 6) and very fast scalic successions rarely fall into exactly predictable formations so that an excitement is generated quite unlike that produced by the more motoric virtuosity of the earlier quartets' scherzos. The refrain returns to introduce a more *cantabile* theme, enclosed by its harmonic accompaniment and, but for the ostinato, initially much nearer a stable tonal area (B major, i.e., the putative dominant) than the earlier material. The simplicity does not continue, though Britten's highly characteristic placing of 'expressive' harmonies (see the dominant sevenths at 43, 52 and 54) does. After a codetta in which the new idea, augmented and spaciously harmonized, briefly escapes from the ostinato, the treadmill is set in motion again. Now the ostinato operates at more than one level, rhythmically out of phase, to produce textural situations of some complexity (see from 86, for example). At yet another brusque signal from the motto refrain, a final section reviews epigrammatically earlier stages, to end with the *cantabile* theme's expressive dominant seventh cadencing unexpectedly, not in E minor, but its relative, G major.

The central slow movement, 'Solo', appears to set aside all the previous tonal uncertainties in that its spacious cantilena, for first violin in the upper register, is supported on a series of triadic arpeggios. Reading these baldly, one arrives at the following tonal structure (see Ex. 23a).

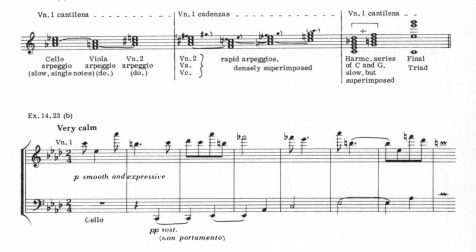

Ex.14.23 (a)

Ex.14.23 (b)

Thus, apart from the V–I implied in the last section by sounding the G harmonic series of the second violin's lowest string against the C series of viola and cello (and the superimposition blurs any suggestion of cadential *motion*), all the relationships of the movement are simple third shifts, turning about the tied pitches marked in the example. Section 2 reverses the process of Section 1 before moving to the C major which is then sustained to the close. However, the effect is far less rigid than the explanation. Not only does the opening set out from C in both solo part and cello arpeggio, but it at first suggests C minor at least as strongly as A flat; and at each tonal level, the first violin's accidentals similarly create momentary alternative readings. The organization of the solo line (its opening is shown at Ex. 23b) is unobtrusive but subtle: sentence and phrase lengths are supply manipulated, a few basic rhythmic and melodic shapes are constantly reworked (compare bars 1 and 2 with 5 and 6 in Ex. 23b for a simple example) and not only across the melodic peaks but at some three pitch levels within the line can firm, primarily conjunct, connexions be drawn. In the central sequence of cadenzas the superimposition of the accompanying arpeggios is freely timed, after the manner of the church parables, while in their new 'lively' form the cruelly high first violin shapes take on a hard glitter. The sense of relaxation as their original calm flow is resumed is intensified by the cool sound of the series of harmonics played by the accompanying trio. Again Britten finds a far greater range of tonal suggestion than the procedure implies, but the final C major (its last triad spaced as shown at the end of Ex. 23a) achieves in its tonal clarity a visionary gleam.

The 'Burlesque' so constantly reiterates its opening (and closing) scalic upbeat pattern that it appears more obsessive than the previous scherzo, while the speed borders on the frenetic. Textures are therefore rarely intricate, the main theme being expounded by the first violin against arpeggio octaves of the other three which always at their peak coincide with a melody note. This reinforcement of what are in fact (though not unambiguously) last beats is ungainly, but a still more bizarre effect is created by the accompanying strings' completing their pattern just before the cadence point of each violin phrase, leaving it to complete the line and breathlessly to begin the next with no more than a single beat's extension of the basic triple measure. At the *da capo* return the textural formula is reversed, all three upper parts having the theme against the cello's arpeggios. This section bears the label 'maggiore', and its anacrusis figure duly sharpens what were formerly natural sixth and seventh degrees: but this would have been no less valid (indeed, more orthodox) in the A minor to which the piece roughly belongs, and, of course, the irony is made clear by all the other scalic readings thrown up in the movement—an essay in alternative degrees, and in this sense at least a slightly Bartókian piece. The development of the scherzo, including a self-important fugato, reaches pungent climax which evaporates in a transition made tense both by the suspension of the driving rhythms and by strange scoring (high viola scale with first violin at the third below, on a sustained second in cello harmonics). The trio establishes E flat, though A remains prominent as a grace-note in the cello's wooden pizzicato bass, to which the second violin adds *col legno* off-beat chords in a quick waltz; now the scherzo theme has exchanged its bizarre qualities for the complacent banality of the first violin's I and V⁷ circuits. The final chilling touch is given to this interlude by the viola, which interpolates between, then during, phrases a mad flourish of arpeggios executed on the wrong side of the bridge. In Britten's quartets this trio holds a place, uncomfortable but not to be ignored, comparable to that of 'O du lieber Augustin' in Schoenberg's second and the barrel-organ tune of Bartók's fifth.

Because the final Passacaglia is explicitly related to *Death in Venice* through its subtitle, one can accept with conviction the point made by Desmond Shawe-Taylor in his review of the quartet's première, that its E major is Aschenbach's key.³ The scalic ground (Ex. 24) reinforces the point

Ex.14.24

(consider the Aschenbach theme quoted as Ex. 4 in Chapter 21) but also underlines that congruity of material which is strongly sensed throughout this quartet. If we turn back, with this shape in our ears, to the work's opening (see Ex. 21a above), we recognize at once that both halves of the ground were adumbrated, winding up in bars 1 to 2 and down in bars 3 to 4. A still clearer pre-echo is to be heard in the contrary motion of the pizzicato figure and the whole-tone clusters that articulate the finale's Recitative. The gentle rhythmic undertow already revives earlier impressions of a limpid

³ D. Shawe-Taylor, 'A note of serenity: Benjamin Britten's farewell', *Sunday Times*, 2 January 1977.

water music, and in the first solo recitative, the cello smoothly converts the undulations into a direct recall of the barcarolle that accompanied Aschenbach's gondola journeys (see Chapter 21, Ex. 6e). Given so familiar a quotation, we are readier to detect those which follow—the theme of Aschenbach's longing (Ex. 5b in Chapter 21) on second violin, 'Phaedrus learned' (not quoted but see Act I, figure 158) on first violin pizzicato, and 'While this sirocco blows' (Act I, figure 107 and elsewhere) on viola. The last of these, one of the 'canker' forms in the opera, grows rapidly in intensity, and cells of the crucial intervals (see the discussion above and in Chapter 21) dominate the accompanying clusters till a biting melodic unison at bar 23 throws the minor-major third shape into stark relief. As in the opera, the figure is founded on C, but at this moment of crisis it is the E natural which displaces the E flat (contrast the fatalistic contraction from major to minor third of 'Marvels unfold') and which gradually washes from the piece, as the flow of the passacaglia's revolutions swells, the memory of that searing figure. It is as though we have been vouchsafed a new light on Aschenbach's fate that the opera withheld. In the serene unfolding of Britten's last ground-bass movement we shall surely hear, as in the passacaglias of *Lucretia* and *Herring*, a threnody, but now it is as much for the composer himself as for his hero.

As may be seen in Ex. 24, the ground (undulating always in *tone* steps) is overlaid by a first violin descant that is an expanded form of its own rise and fall. The further counterpoints added as this tune is taken up by second violin and viola are also essentially scalic, so that a steadily widening musical space is filled with calmly winding but rhythmically interacting lines. The recurrent Mixolydian D natural induces many gentle declensions to the flat side, in which the C natural so fateful earlier appears transfigured. When this first

Ex. 14.25

great arc of the movement has been spanned (at bar 71) the viola briefly takes over the ground and the cello tries the descant line at dominant level en route for its return to the ground two octaves above its original level; the ground itself is never transposed, and its revolutions seem less 'events' than a symbol of eternity. Now the upper strings become eloquent in closely overlapping chains of semiquaver thirds, and as this brightness dims the ground is restored to its bass register and a tender new counterpoint is introduced (bar 89), again taking the D natural as cue for some poignant flat excursions. The last semiquaver wanderings of the first violin wind gradually down to lead, with beautiful inevitability, into the original descant, and the harmonies that link it to the ground are now of extreme diatonic simplicity. The coda in which the motion is gradually halted, and reflections from the ground throw up a luminous haze, is still simpler, and the quartet seems about to end with as delicate and widely-spaced a sonority as did its first movement. The sudden upsurge of energy in which a passionate sigh is made the last word (see Ex. 25) cannot be paralleled in Britten's instrumental music, and the tension created between its long dying bass D and the melody's G sharp (i.e., the extremes of the ground) is enigmatic yet profoundly satisfying. Though not his last work, this passacaglia is surely his last artistic testament.

15 Later Vocal Works

THE HOLY SONNETS OF JOHN DONNE, OP. 35

The completion and popular success of an undertaking as ambitious as *Peter Grimes* gave Britten the dangerous right to assume that an interested public would eagerly await anything he now chose to produce. These years after *Grimes* show him a superbly confident and astonishingly prolific composer: whereas the first opera had occupied him for well over a year, with few and small distractions, the next two appeared at yearly intervals despite his also completing substantial scores in other media. Yet the chamber-operas, a tragedy and a comedy, jettisoned most of the resources he had deployed so fluently in *Grimes*, and demanded solutions to quite new problems, as we have seen. In his other works of the period, too, Britten showed no tendency to restrict himself to proven recipes. In two of these scores, the String Quartet in C, Op. 36 and the orchestral variations, *The Young Person's Guide to the Orchestra*, Op. 34 (written in fact later than the quartet) he appeared ready to pursue further the career of an instrumental composer from which he had been deflected by his return to England, while *The Holy Sonnets of John Donne*, Op. 35, reverted to the cycle of songs with piano. But in each case some fresh approach to the medium is to be found, and the three works suggest an attempt to colour in several contrasted ways the basic stylistic amalgam Britten had achieved in *Grimes*. *The Young Person's Guide* simplifies still further the language of the opera to produce the least problematic diatonic relationships in Britten's work since the Simple Symphony; the Quartet applies the opera's motivic underpinning to a sonata argument; while the song cycle intensifies the motivic practice, the modal variation and the norm of dissonance.

One link between the three works is a debt to the music of Purcell. While this is declared in the Chacony finale of the quartet, written for the 250th anniversary of the composer's death, and in the orchestral variations on a theme from his *Abdelazer* music, it is scarcely less certainly to be identified in the declamatory word-setting of the Donne songs. Though Purcell set none of Donne's poetry, a setting of 'A Hymn to God the Father' by Pelham Humfrey appeared in Book I of *Harmonia Sacra* (1688), and it is in Purcell's own contribution to the Divine Hymns of that collection that the most striking precedents for the fevered spirituality of Britten's cycle are to be found, as well as some quite direct influences on the shape of his vocal declamation. (In the next few years Britten was to publish his own realizations of some Purcell vocal music, including settings from *Harmonia Sacra*.) The opening apostrophe of 'Oh my blacke Soule' intensifies the procedure of dissonance following an arpeggio that Purcell had used in 'Lord, what is man' (*Harmonia Sacra*, Book II); see Ex. 1a. The second pair of quotations, from Britten's fifth Sonnet and Purcell's 'Awake, Awake' (*Harmonia Sacra*, Book I) at Ex. 1b, again show arpeggio-plus dissonance but they are com-

Ex. 15.1 (a) i

Ex. 15.1 (a) ii

Ex. 15.1 (b) 1

Ex. 15.1 (b) ii

parable too in the use of repeated notes for reproducing verbal rhythms, the placing of stressed syllables (*hell, slaughter*) on nominally weaker beats, and the slurred fall of a fourth (diminished in Purcell, perfect but approached from the tritone in Britten) for violent emphasis.

Both composers construct vocal lines in which the words dictate rhythmic shapes of such individuality as to form highly asymmetrical melodic phrases. The figured-bass accompaniments in Purcell's sacred songs regiment this free declamatory treatment only in their cadential moves; elsewhere neither harmonic rhythm nor bass figuration is predictably patterned. In Britten, however, the same kind of rhythmic freedom in the melody is balanced by orderly harmonic phrase structures and persistent figurative designs in the piano; and it is often achieved within a line that is tautened by unobtrusive (because not rhythmically uniform) motivic correspondences. Thus both piano and (less single-mindedly) voice endorse one generalized *Affekt* appropriate to the whole song, while to the voice fall the additional roles of conveying every significant verbal inflexion and of colouring with melisma the most evocative words. To say that a Purcellian line is grafted on to instrumental parts influenced by later Baroque principle is therefore true enough, but our anxiety to recognize a synthesis quite new in English song should not blind us to the parallels here (in method, not style) with some of Wolf's work.

The first of Britten's Donne settings has a granite quality of which neither the Rimbaud nor the Michelangelo cycle gave any hint. One rhythm hammers relentlessly throughout the accompaniment, tenser for proving at the voice's entry to be a reaction, not an anacrusis, to the main beat. The entire vocal line is built up from two shapes, that quoted at Ex. 1, often inverted, and a chromatically introverted one (Ex. 2). Like several of the sonnets, this

Ex. 15.2

sets out from the dominant, achieving an unequivocal tonic B minor only at the thematic reprise ('Oh make thyselfe'), where the piano's octaves are changed to triads, each given a sharp edge by the addition of some semitonal friction (analogous to the '*b*' twists in the melody). Thus, despite patent restatement, the song is felt to pursue an unbroken forward movement just as Britten's sonata movements have been seen to do. Similarly in 'Batter my heart' the root tonic (of C minor) only appears in the last section, though it then provides a pedal for the rest of the song. Endless reiteration in the piano (and, less blatantly, by the voice) serves a different purpose here, creating musically the pent-up state Donne conveyed with his successions of monosyllables:

351

for you As yet but knocke, breathe, shine and seeke to mend
. . . bend your force to breake, blowe, burn and make me new.

Yet as with other fast even-numbered songs (i.e., excluding the lyrical no. 6), one may feel that the execution of an appropriate enough scheme is flawed by a routine treatment of detail; here the melismata, excluding the inevitable 'ravish', seem redundant, the powerful climax on the remote V of B is spoilt by the glib pianissimo phrase that follows, and the postlude uses a regrettably obvious device.

After these two assertive songs in B minor and C minor the wavering indecision between B and C that opens 'O might those sighs' makes a dramatic yet not unmotivated contrast. This serves fittingly also as the coda to the song, introduced beautifully by Donne's enjambement 'to poor me is allow'd/No ease'. In between there are three quatrains which Britten sets strophically. The melodic line, essentially contained within the fifth above and semitone below the singer's initial B, develops from a Phrygian opening, through a more orthodox minor that achieves a peak on the high F sharp, only for the true emotional climax to appear with the swing to E flat in a poignantly sequential last phrase, B flat acting as a leading (-back) note, and so balancing the original flat second. But this recurrent curve is realized afresh in note- and phrase-lengths (and in new accompaniment textures), producing an effect analogous to that of Donne's uniform background of the ten-syllable line, and foreground of constantly varied sentence structure.

The fourth sonnet is declaimed over a *moto perpetuo* accompaniment that makes resourceful use of the motto figure presented by the voice at 'contraries meet in one', but the final melisma (*'shake* with fear') seems disproportionate, however clinching. Far better integrated is the single chromatic melisma on 'crucified' in 'What if this present', a piece tortuously 'Baroque' in almost any sense we care to give to that abused term. The vigilant ear will have detected that some melodic gestures struck first in the Serenade have been given new significance in this cycle: even the melisma on 'shake' just mentioned is comparable in function to 'excellently bright', the close of the first sonnet looks back to that of the Blake setting ('life destroy') and the *alter ego* of that semitonal move, the opening of the Lyke-Wake Dirge, has become the melodic crux of 'O might those sighs'. In the fifth sonnet it is the heavy ornament of the dirge's accompanying fugue subject that is brought to mind, though the detailed chromaticism of the fourth bar (perhaps the nearest to Hindemith that Britten ever ventured) gives a frantic tinge to this vision of the last day that is in sharp contrast to the relentless balance sheet of good and evil in the dirge. The opening yet again is from a dominant position, but the tonic G at bar 6 (bass) is challenged by the persistence of G flat in the voice; after a middle section in which no centre is even momentarily absolute, this is balanced in the reprise (bar 22) by a no less prominent A flat challenge. But even the fantastic detail of the piano right-hand part intensifies tonal strife, rather than bursting into atonal freedom: the music is so vehement just because it is pitted against the orderly progressions of the heavy bass chords. This means that the bass reassertion of G at the reprise ends the fundamental tonal circuit (though there is a supplementary cadence seven bars from the end) and this admirably contributes to the lightening of character that sets in here, with mellifluous sixths and a new chromatic shape at 'all my profane mistresses'. This is transformed to a still more relaxed form in the coda ('This beauteous forme') and is at once taken up in the opening motive of the sixth sonnet.

So we are to some extent prepared for the limpid flow of melody and consonant harmony of this setting, 'Since she whom I loved'. At first it suggests comparison with the luscious textures of 'Being Beauteous' and 'Départ' in the Rimbaud cycle but its chordal moves are less savoured as isolated sensations, more integrated into a single unfolding experience. Their timing, at first entirely according to a four-bar phrase structure, gradually loosens under the influence of vocal lines that treat the three-beat measure as a most elastic guide to stress; the song was Britten's most successful achievement so far in a music that floats freely above a still uniform measure rather than modifying bar-lengths in order to retain first-beat domination. The mood here is not all serenity, and the intensity of this wide span of melody springs from its extreme motivic economy. A complete analysis would involve the whole song but a few examples will show typical transformations; see Ex. 3.

'At the round earth's imagined corners' is more openly unified by its vocal quintuplet and piano texture of fanfares and tremolandi—all in a splendidly Baroque D major last used with such overtones at the beginning of *On this Island*. The Lydian G sharp of the fanfare strives towards an A while the

Ex. 15.3 (a)

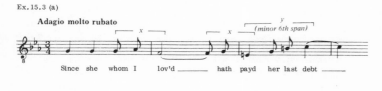

Ex. 15.3 (b)

Ex. 15.3 (c)

353

voice's G natural signals a move back to D in a brilliant pendulum. This bimodality is repeated at the dominant level for the second quatrain, but the recital of catastrophe here forces up the centre semitonally till a tonic return celebrates the poem's peroration. A single minor third, advance notice of the qualifying conjunction 'but', is enough to set the more passive mood of the rest of the sonnet. The fanfare rotates at an abased level while the bass descends forlornly through an octave made up of flattened degrees: the voice's lower tessitura similarly marks the faltering spirit. Its flat seventh completes the synthetic mode ♭7 ♭6 5 ♯4 ♯/♮ 3 2 1 (one that the reader may care to trace in an earlier English work—Vaughan Williams's fourth symphony). So in both the quiet resurrection of the fanfare, and the voice's recovery of its original pitch area and brighter modality, the close of the song wonderfully reconciles the conflicting experiences:

> for that's as good As if thou hadst sealed
> my pardon with thy blood.

'Thou hast made me' is another *moto perpetuo* for the piano, highly organized from a cadential motive (see Ex. 4) and descending scales of

Ex.15.4

flexible modality. The dominant opening here provides the potential of a tightly wound spring and the voice unfolds a single urgent line between two portentous cadential phrases; there is irony to match Donne's own in the E flat major arpeggios at the peak, harmonically insecure and soon swept away by 'our old subtle foe' in the form of the flat second; thus the postlude contraction of the motive (Ex. 4*b* above) represents an assimilation of the unstable element into an affirmative state—aptly enough.

The open declaration of Purcell's influence in the five-bar ground bass of the final song, 'Death, be not proud', appears to be contradicted by an opening melodic contour that savours more of a nineteenth-century rhetoric. But the internal metrical fluctuations of this bass and the unpredictable timing of the accompanying chords prevent a ponderous squareness of phrase: the effect most often created is (1):4.3.3.3.3.4. Furthermore (and this *is* a Purcellian trait) the bass is so devised as constantly to run across into the following statement; only by means of prolongation is the path of the twelfth (and last) statement diverted into the song's one true cadence. From a near-drone (F sharp persisting for the first 21 bars), the accompaniment steadily gains importance, reinterpreting the key, first merely as G sharp minor, with which the ground co-exists well enough, later as D major, with which it clashes violently. At this point, the syncopations also become more tense and a new military *Affekt*, characterized by dotted-notes, invades the piano texture. The voice has declaimed freely, in unison with, imitation of, or felicitous counterpoint to the ground, but it is in drawing the music back to the tonic area, after the alarums and excursions, with a bold statement of the opening motive (leaping from A into D sharp major and thence to B), that it first assumes command. Its magisterially augmented lines in the restored tonic—of the cycle as well as the song[1]—open up a new time-scale ('One short sleep past, we wake eternally, And death shall be no more'), making possible a final taunt ('Death, thou shalt die') that is powerful without being histrionic.

This was Britten's biggest song cycle since *Our Hunting Fathers*. If its demands on the singer are less obviously for virtuosity, they are unremitting, while the emotional intensity is not even relaxed in the lyricism of the sixth song. It has therefore become one of the most rarely performed of all his cycles, while *Grimes*, also dating from 1945, remains the most popular of all the operas. Yet its more intricate processes, in particular the fanatical persistence of its motivic work, are a fitting response to language and thought infinitely more ramified than were those of the opera. In this highly-strung music there are intimations of a Britten tone of voice that was perhaps too rarely heard in his later work.

A CHARM OF LULLABIES, OP. 41

A Charm of Lullabies (1947) was written for Nancy Evans, who had shared with Kathleen Ferrier the part of Lucretia in the original production of the opera in the previous year. The gentle diatonic dissonance of the first and last songs may faintly recall the music of the sleeping Lucretia ('She sleeps as a rose'), but here there is no dramatic context to give tension, and the contrast provided by the whimsical and bizarre middle songs of the cycle seems rather factitious. While there is none of that unity which the verse of a single poet can bring to the most diverse subjects (even *On this Island* feels like a cycle because it reveals a consistent response to Auden, and *Winter Words* was to demonstrate still better the same focus through the poet), there is not much scope for the imaginative flights opened up by the previous anthology, the Serenade. Night and Sleep are subjects that draw the listener into a rich visionary world, whereas a lullaby merely bids another enter it. The tone may vary from the coaxing to the querulous but, as Pears comments, 'a lullaby is—a lullaby, *sonst nichts* or almost *nichts*'.[2]

The Blake 'Cradle Song' creates a pleasingly soporific atmosphere from the gently undulating bass and the largely conjunct murmuring upper line of

---

[1] On the tonal designs of this and other cycles see A. Whittall, 'Tonality in Britten's Song Cycles with Piano' *Tempo* 96, 1971, p. 2.
[2] P. Pears, 'The Vocal Music', in Mitchell-Keller, p. 72.

the piano, which clashes at the second with the voice. The drowsy sensuality of this effect is in danger of being reduced to cliché, but the white note/black note bitonality of 'the cunning wiles' transfers the tension to a more fundamental plane, and the clashing seconds return with a new significance for 'the dreadful lightnings'. Though the key scheme of this song, mapped out by the few essential pitch moves of the bass, is convincingly shaped, some cadential corners are turned with a crudity that does not suggest Britten's most fastidious craftsmanship.

The Scotch snap of 'The Highland Balou' seems to have taken a circuitous route, by way of Stravinsky's *Apollon Musagète*. Graceful though the piano motive is, the artlessness of the vocal line sounds studied and the structural return to the tonic is by means of an ineffective ellipsis. 'Sephestia's Lullaby', a neatly-turned miniature, is harmonically more sure-footed, with a witty treatment of chromatic relations that has not appeared before. But the fourth song, 'A Charm', is characteristic rather than merely apt. The opening clash between D and C sharp centres sets a pattern for much of the harmony, and the rapid 7/4 phrases are made cumulative with typical artifice. The first bar is literally repeated, bar 3 is repeated sequentially, while bar 5 is retimed so as to carry across into a sequential extension and thence into a third bar for the last note; below this, the piano bass escapes at last from its tonic reiteration to walk up a symmetrical scale (t.t.t.s.t.t.t.) and the voice then inverts this to clinch the stanza with great force. The tonal circuit, essentially I to V by step, despite many parenthetical implications, is completed by guitar-like fourth chords above the dominant that seem unduly bland for this oddly venomous little song. It having closed in D, we naturally hear the unaccompanied refrain of 'The Nurse's Song' as still centred there; the recurrence of the refrain at the end of a piece which the piano's first entry shows to be in B flat is therefore both identical and entirely differently apprehended; the intermediate appearance is absorbed into the fluid key movement of the main song. In this Britten touches that certain mastery of the simple device that eluded him in the early numbers of the cycle: the melody bewitchingly varies two formulae (see Ex. 5) and each modulation has that delightful inevitability which is free from predictability.

WINTER WORDS, OP. 52

The Hardy cycle *Winter Words*, Op. 52, completed in September 1953, was the only work written between *Gloriana* and *The Turn of the Screw*. The unassuming description 'Lyrics and Ballads' prepares us for a far homelier music than that of the lavish court tableaux on which Britten had been working, but there is no sign of the prescription for economy in diversity he was to adopt in the quasi-serial variation structures of the chamber opera. Already in the earlier tenor cycles, and especially in the Donne Sonnets, Britten had been achieving securely unified songs by motivic work; if we feel that the Hardy songs are notably sparer, this is not because of an incipient

356

Ex. 15.5

concern for the serialist's integrating methods. More significant in this cycle is a tendency to prune musical ideas back almost to their stocks, discouraging the proliferation of florid textural detail. This accords well with Hardy's sober, if at times simplistic, verse and helps to ward off the sentimentality that can lurk behind it, but above all it makes congruous, however remarkable, the bald terms of the final song in which Britten turns from Hardy's acceptance of the minutiae of a rural existence to the nihilistic philosophy which lay behind it.

The first song relies on tonal complexity of a kind that is not common in Britten: there are not simply two poles but shifting modulatory processes, in which each chord contains a new contradiction. As Ex. 6 shows, tonic *versus* dominant, major *versus* minor, and semitonal oppositions follow upon one another in these unadorned textures with a hard and grey, yet invigorating, sound; despite some hesitation at the tritone, no clear objective emerges, and the music falls back to the D from which it began. Though the song is headed 'quick and impetuous' these repeated drooping descants of the vocal phrases suggest a homing instinct that, after a very restricted tonal circuit (i.e., as delineated by the cadence, not the internal chords: a-I; a-I; b-V; a-I)

357

Ex.15.6

is satisfied in a long final section which hovers constantly between I (+V) and V(I) in beautiful yet never self-indulgent sonorities. Motivically, the figure *x* in Ex. 6 is all-important, but to do justice to the melodic construction of this song one should do much more than identify that tag. Above all it is the gradual widening and contracting of musical space in successive peaks and troughs that gives such grace to the line: on the last page there is added to the piano's ruminative drone an inverted pedal as recurrent peak of the vocal phrases, so that all developments point downward, the final D being reached with palpable logic.

It is not the purpose of this book to attempt more than to demonstrate how consistent processes of musical thought make satisfactorily rounded pieces, but, even in a song which has so little that we may flatly label 'word-painting', the listener is unlikely to miss connexions that exist between what happens in this music and Hardy's subject-matter. The danger that attends directly imitative sound symbols, such as those of the train's whistle and its clanking motion in the next song, 'Midnight on the Great Western' is that, having made so obvious a connexion (whether with pleasure or contempt), the listener will have too little concern for that intra-musical process in which the symbol serves not inertly to 'represent', but to construct across time a pattern analogous to an 'experience'.

A very simple example is provided by the blurred triads which act as ritornelli in this song. These provide an apt enough reminder of the sound made by a train-whistle, falling off in pitch and then reverberating across the countryside. But they are also symbolic in less mechanistic terms: the initial C minor triad is at once confused, first by being reduced to a grace note to B major, this chord is itself turned minor, and finally the whole complex gives way, as the pedal is released, to a distant echo of the original triad, the more mysterious for being without initial impact. Obvious though all this may be, it already constitutes a musical organism, a miniature cycle of experience, but one which can give rise to a cycle much expanded. And this duly takes place when, in the central section, the tonal development of the song is carried through entirely in terms of these shifting minor triads: their utility in the tonal architecture is patent, their relevance to the text scarcely less so:

> What past can be yours O journeying boy
> Towards a world unknown,
> Who calmly, as if incurious quite
> On all at stake, can undertake
> This plunge alone?

But their relation to the sound of a train-whistle is by now almost entirely incidental. And if the final bars seem to epitomize the tonal experience of the whole song, they also add a further symbolic interpretation, for now that disembodied last chord is inevitably heard in terms of the last stanza (of which it is the representative in the epitomizing progression):

> Knows your soul a sphere . . .
> Our rude realms far above?

'Wagtail and Baby' prepares the ground for a final dart of gentle satire with nonchalantly co-existing (rather than significantly bitonal) piano strands, the wagtail fluttering in 6/16 against the baby's 6/8 musings. As in so much Britten, a far slower motion still is described by the logical bass movement. Though keys seem so casual, the opening impression of an oblique approach to A is eventually confirmed. The unobtrusive reprise at 'A perfect gentleman' is thrown off course by the E flat to which the wagtail bolts; in the grotesque piano comment (*molto rall.*) an E flat cadence sounds forlornly above an A minor one, but in the coda a return route from E flat to A is painstakingly worked out. This song and the next, 'The little old table', are sketches thrown off in a few practised gestures, yet this is not to say to a formula: they absorb their illustrative touches into a chain of musical causality. 'The Choirmaster's Burial', a ballad, is more heavily dependent on a chain of incident, yet the total impression is of a straightforward ternary pattern in which the recurring element is the piano's hymn-tune 'Mount Ephraim' (by B. Milgrove, 1731–1810). Both of these B flat statements are

Ex.15.7 (a)

Ex.15.7 (b)

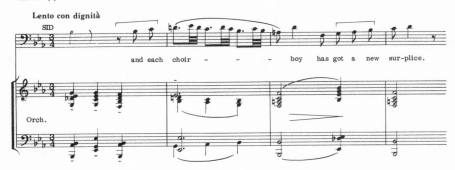

introduced by the narrator's own A flat, and a frame is completed with the final phrase in that key. Though Britten's free recitative above the hymn is affectionately, not maliciously, artless, it is curious to note how he has echoed another commentary around a hymn—Sid's description of the festive service in *Albert Herring*: see Ex. 7. The vicar's comments, on the other hand, strike a ponderously prosaic note, cadencing frequently as befits a man who knows his is the last word. The A tonality here is countered by B for the hurried funeral service, before a B flat reprise; in this the hymn is transformed into the misty glory of the 'band all in white like the saints in church glass'. Another miniature follows, 'Proud Songsters', an ebulliently happy piece constructed entirely from one kind of chord (in which the clangorous second predominates) and the two melodic shapes of the singer's first phrase. Analysis would be otiose, but one more characteristic adaptation of necessary musical device to verbal contingency is worth citing: after the rising sequence at 'no finches were nor nightingales nor thrushes' has swept the key to its brightest area, a magical (i.e., enharmonic) return to the tonic coincides pointedly with the final line 'But only particles of grain, And earth, and air, and rain'.

Spareness of texture is taken furthest in 'At the Railway Station, Upway', where the piano plays a part conceived entirely within the limits of a single

360

violin. This dry sound and the singer's cool recitative present the anecdote without labouring its pathos, and the apparently improvisatory sequence is unified by a regular alternation of two ideas, the first being developed to accompany the central song of the convict. Though the tonal cycle implies upward transposition here and an eventual *da capo* reversion, key centres remain indefinable, creating the wistful mood that makes so transparent a piece memorable.

The simplicity of the last song, 'Before Life and After', is still more evident and, indeed, a wilful crudity can be heard in the endless close-position root-triads at the bottom of the texture. Out of context, piano writing like that of the last two bars of this song is remarkably near the vampings of the most misguided player 'by ear'. But Britten, having chosen these impassively reiterated triads as symbol of a primeval state, incorporates them into a musical scheme that is sophisticated enough. Ex. 8 shows

Ex.15.8

the bass movement of the entire song; this aspires by measured upward steps to serene perfect cadences, the third time with far greater difficulty (i.e., the steps are chromaticized and the cadence itself is now clouded by a strong false relation), then the stepwise movement changes to accelerating descent, the last span leading right down to the final tonic. Needless to say, descent supplants ascent at the crux of Hardy's poem, when 'the disease of feeling germed'. So the musical ground plan accords with that of the poem, yet the progressive widening and quickening of tonal events (including those not shown in Ex. 8, created by the relationship of the upper parts to the triadic bass) can be timed according to purely musical criteria. The long-spun imitative dialogue between the piano's right-hand octaves and the singer wanders freely at first, but its chief shapes, an auxiliary-note figure and a succession of perfect fourths, are abandoned at the crisis in favour of anxious upward scales (i.e., in direct opposition to the bass movement), returning only with the regained tonic and the cry for a regained nescience. This is not an elegant song, but it avoids the pitfalls of neo-primitivism and, in a well-controlled performance, powerfully recreates Hardy's own progress to a momentous conclusion from unaffectedly simple phraseology.

361

SONGS FROM THE CHINESE, OP. 58

In one of the most illuminating analytical commentaries a Britten work has elicited, Jeremy Noble described the six *Songs from the Chinese*, Op. 58, for high voice and guitar, as a 'work that can stand with any of his song cycles'; 'as a whole', he wrote, 'they make a statement about life (and particularly about the transience of youth and beauty) as poignant and personal as Mahler's own settings from the Chinese'.[3] The cycle was written in the autumn of 1957, one year after Britten's extended essay in *chinoiserie*, *The Prince of the Pagodas*. But in the precise, laconic language of Arthur Waley's translations, these poems do not invite a treatment that would give more weight to their exotic origins than to their oblique but universally relevant illumination of the human condition. Whether the poems prompted the choice of instrument or *vice versa*, it is clear that the composer arrived at his musical material from a consideration of the guitar's unique qualities and limitations, never from an intention to evoke an archaic Chinese music.

In the first song, 'The Big Chariot', the guitar provides harmonic support (in pure triads apart from the odd passing note) to the voice, but also adds a commentary at the opposite end of its compass in trickling conjunct semiquavers. Just as each of the three verses looks away from 'the big chariot' to 'the sorrows of the world', from public pomp to private despair, so a clangorous accompaniment with chords above and running commentary below fades away into short furtive chords below and the edgy sound of the semiquavers high above. Each verse is pitched higher but, while the chariot music rises by tones, the sorrow mounts by thirds. Noble points out how the final verse is made climactic by the repetition of verbal phrases and by the peak of tension reached here between the two strata of the guitar's 'sorrow' music. His explanation of the enigmatic postlude, where the guitar's semiquavers run on beyond an F close to a remote G minor cadence, that it is too early in the emotional cycle for true resolution, is acceptable, but it is worth noting how much of G minor was adumbrated in the nominal F major of the song's opening bars.

Whereas this song was restless in its tonal moves, 'The Old Lute' remains fixed until its last lines in the most rigid Lydian Britten ever used. Noble likens the effect of its strange quasi-polyphonic lute texture, in which each of the four strands moves within a highly circumscribed range of three or four notes, to 'rhythmic variants of a single chord-progression'. Alternatively we may trace the 'remoteness' specifically called for by the composer to the total absence of any true progression. Provided that the restrictions imposed on each part are observed, any notes of the mode may appear together; the timing of the moves is therefore directed mainly towards a balance of rhythmic interest, as in the lutenists' *style brisé*, but without the progressive implications of that convention. The effect is comparable to that of a

---

[3] J. Noble, 'Britten's *Songs from the Chinese*', *Tempo* 52, 1959, p. 25.

suspended object gently swaying so that the light catches different features in turn. This is an embalmed music, of 'ancient melodies, weak and savourless', but in creating it Britten has ventured remarkably near a modern textural ideal, of a single harmonic complex given a free interior mobility, one that he was to exploit in the church parables, inspired by Japanese Noh-plays. The singer's line moves within a single octave of the mode, but the degrees on which it pauses show a comparable freedom; the use of a 'dominant' arpeggio that exceeds the compass, on '*cold* and clear', is therefore extraordinarily arresting, an emotional surge from which the singer immediately relapses into his disillusionment. Britten's final switch to a 'modern' mode (G major despite the prominent VI that relates it to the Lydian E), seductive arpeggio guitar textures, and neat little harmonic circuits, provides a graphic symbol of a popular music without destroying the dreamlike quality of the whole song.

In 'The Autumn Wind' Britten's ability to incorporate the most fragile texture into a cogent structural scheme makes possible contrasts of feeling that belie the uniform appearance of the pages. As in the first song, the two elements of the guitar part frequently exchange rôles; though they are here conflated into a single line (in accordance with a lutenist tradition equally familiar to us in, say, Bach's solo string works), we mentally reconstruct a duet in which the upper voice's melody, typically coloured by doubling at the second, is held up at times so that the lower voice may abandon its sustained bass for more eloquent line. The singer doubles whichever strand is melodic but his phrases remain terse, even aphoristic, and Jeremy Noble shows how the guitar's two registers have prepared in advance the antithesis of the protracted last line: 'Youth's years how few, age how sure!' Before that, the setting has fallen into a two-verse structure, the parallels being imaginatively free. After a pair of lines which depict their subtle harmonic movements the unrest that Autumn brings to everything, the third line appears more poised, dwelling on life's sweetness but, as the insistent dominant pedal makes clear, with a tension which must make it intolerable and which can find release only in a surrender to inner thoughts (see Ex. 9). In this poem's few poignant juxtapositions there is as powerful a recreation of that complex interfusion of moods Autumn represents as in many a more sonorous treatment in western literature; Britten's achievement is to have translated this into musical terms no less restrained.

A simple frame, comparable to that of 'The Choirmaster's Burial', surrounds the narrative of 'The Herd-Boy'. The main song contrasts an engaging instrumental reproduction of the ox's ponderous gait with a strong graceful vocal line representing the nonchalant boy. Noble's consideration of the placing of its sustained peaks can be extended to the troughs too, while the economy of these apparently generous phrases is well shown in the conflation in the fifth phrase ('On the long dyke') of elements from all the earlier ones. As in much of this cycle, we observe how Britten can imply an

363

Ex. 15.9

elaborate series of harmonic progressions, including even the kind of bi-
planar motion we saw in the first Hardy song, in a guitar part that is in single
notes throughout.

'Depression' finds its musical starting-point in the peculiar melancholy of
the guitar's glissando. The struck chord must be rapidly followed by the
position shift if we are to savour the evanescent sound of the new one, and so
the characteristic rhythm of this sound is preordained. So too is the use of
strictly parallel movement with all the piquant false relations and conflicting
tonal implications that can bring. The singer sets the melodic pattern,
restricted almost throughout to steps and perfect fourths; yet the weary
snatches of the opening are warmed to moving eloquence in Britten's great
expansion of the last line of this most desolate song: 'Though my limbs are
old, my heart is older yet'. And the guitar echoes this cry in its own way,
progressively thickening its figures from single notes to glissandi of that
strangely thrilling six-part chord to which it is tuned.

After the distant glow of the last of these chords, with its full octave slide,
has faded, it is disconcerting to leap into the savage gaiety of the concluding
'Dance Song', with its pounding 7/8 rhythms. Noble's reading of the poem as
combining triumph and lament, like the ceremonial dismemberments of
every religion, is borne out by Britten's ritualistic treatment of its three
verses. The singer's lamenting glissandi ('Alas for the unicorn') abandon the
tonal area, held so tenaciously in the preceding shouts of the hunt, more
effectively than do the rather stereotyped 'horror' chords (augmented
triads) of the guitar. In the last verse each line is given a sinister new
emphasis by a twist that repeats it at a higher pitch. After the last great wail,

364

the ritual is ended: there is a furtive, disenchanted 'alas', and the guitar's arpeggio, dominant after the earlier verses, now spells out a tonic that reaches almost beyond earshot. So bright a sound leaves a curious impression, less perhaps of irony than of a passive acceptance that embraces the experience of the whole cycle.

SECHS HÖLDERLIN-FRAGMENTE, OP. 61

Waley's translations take most English readers as far as they can hope to travel towards the just appreciation of an exotic tradition of poetry. Simply by abandoning his usual accompanying instrument Britten found himself in the Chinese Songs obliged to devise a range of new expressive symbols, and their very aptness to the poetic moods gives the cycle a special stamp among his songs, without our needing to look for specifically oriental musical stimuli. But in his next venture outside English traditions he turned to the late eighteenth-century German poet, Friedrich Hölderlin, setting the texts in the original language. In this way he continued the process, begun in the Michelangelo and Rimbaud cycles, of diversifying his own fantasy in facing the problems of prosody and of expressive nuance that a foreign literature imposes; such a process can scarcely fail to include some consideration of solutions achieved by native composers, though, as we have seen in the earlier cycles, the result is likely to constitute a particular inflexion of Britten's tone rather than a direct imitation of theirs.

However, these German poems offered less tractable material than Britten had found in Michelangelo or even in Rimbaud. A fusion of Lutheran theology and fervent Hellenism formed Hölderlin's attitude to the poet's task; the exposition of a philosophy is more his concern than is the recounting of a subjective experience, while the mastery he achieved of verse forms (often with direct classical roots) and syntax contributes as vitally to our apprehension of his poetry as do the verbal images. In selecting short poems and fragments, Britten avoided the virtuosically varied metres and formidably involuted language that characterize much of Hölderlin's work, but his selection spans from the years of the poet's maturity into those of his madness. If he seems to circumvent the metrical problems of 'Die Jugend' by adopting an ironic rhythmic cast of his own, he distributes the variable feet of 'Hälfte des Lebens' across an inflexible accompaniment with a freedom that not only points up the words but is curiously appropriate to the complex mood they create.

Although Hölderlin lived through that great flowering of German lyric verse which had a consequence in the German *Lied*, few of the most popular Romantic musical types could be adapted to make appropriate vehicles for his verse. Indeed, the *Lieder* composers never found inspiration in Hölderlin, the most celebrated nineteenth-century setting of his work being Brahms's choral *Schicksalslied*. Even if Britten's aversion to that composer had been less publicized, we might infer that so ponderously aspiring a piece

365

would not contribute much to the many-faceted picture of the poet's ethos which the song cycle attempts. Of nineteenth-century textural ideals only the second and fifth songs show clear influence (oddly, it is to Brahms, in a song like 'Wir wandelten', that we must look for precedent for the canonic second song) but the remaining songs, in texture and structure, are highly individual even in Britten's own work.

The first song, 'Menschenbeifall', establishes at once that the composer's response to Hölderlin is to be a sterner asceticism than he practised either in the plain textures and imagery of the Hardy cycle or in the spare but aurally fascinating figurations of the Chinese Songs. The bare opening octaves renounce all sonorous charm in an assertion that makes a highly constructive musical point—each link in a chain of perfect fourths is spanned more securely—but does not invite interpretation in terms of any verbally definable symbolism. The first five bars of Ex. 10 show the figure co-existing

Ex. 15.10

366

with, but in no conventional sense 'expressing', a word that within the lyricists' tradition would have justified a significantly enriched music; Britten merely allows it unusual length. It will be seen that he treats the piano figure with a freedom that leaves to the singer the clarification of the basic metre, and so the writing avoids the squareness that characterized much nineteenth-century German song. But the habit of juxtaposing strongly diatonic segments so as rapidly to explore the entire chromatic repertoire is here reminiscent of Hindemith (a composer for whose ideals Britten had rarely shown sympathy elsewhere), particularly because of the addiction to the perfect fourth. The succeeding passage (Ex. 10, bar 6 to end) extends the likeness to the harmonic sphere, though the embracing of all twelve notes in a few chords also reflects Britten's interest during the late fifties in Schoenbergian practice. There follows a section in which the despicably unaspiring reactions of common men are deplored, and in the constant use of the more 'expressive' minor third here we may detect Britten's irony adding to Hölderlin's scorn; even the accompaniment figure has lost its strong fourths and suggests a nightmarish insistence in terms first discovered in *The Turn of the Screw*. For Hölderlin's final line, apparently of superb arrogance,

> An das Göttliche glauben
> Die allein, die es selber sind

Britten restates the piano's opening but now its questioning rests are filled in by the singer's commanding line (inverting his original vocal shape). Yet in a quiet postlude the piano figures of Ex. 10, bars 1 to 5 are broken down so as to move to the cadence in an oddly abstracted way. The motive remains a musical device: we cannot 'interpret' this treatment of it as parallel to anything specific in the verse. On the other hand, it compels us to reflect that, whatever Hölderlin meant by that last line was not, in Britten's view, a monumental boast.

With the drooping melodic sixths and lapping accompaniment of 'Die Heimat', Britten moves nearer to the lyricism of Romantic song, but ultimately the impression of rigorous design counts for more than does the sensuous charm of the melodic line. The organization of later phrases from fragments of the opening lines ('Stillt ihr der Liebe leiden', for example, conflates the first three vocal phrases) draws off any suspicions of undue opulence, though not without leaving a significant emotional upheaval implicit in the inversion of the initial sixth at 'ach gebt ihr mir'. But the line is further objectified in being echoed throughout by the piano in canon, 2 in 1 at a bar's distance, except at the emotional turning-point just mentioned where it is intensified as 3 in 1 at two beats' distance. The reversion to the simple canon at the crucial word *die Ruhe* coincides with the thematic reprise, the return of the original tonality and tonic pedal and the accompanimental seconds' achievement of their restatement at the octave higher,

367

after a climb that has spread over the whole song. Until this point all its elements have been unfolded as independently timed structures, but now they are assimilated on to a single plane—of rest that yet is not rest, as the questioning sixths and the endlessly unresolved 5/4 makes clear. This organization on several levels (none of them precisely coincident with the poem's strophic structure) is no doubt a more consciously intellectual process than supported the generous invention of the *Grimes* period, but the same imagination is at work, reacting subconsciously to a comparable situation in comparable music (see Ex. 11). Peter's dream of a return from the sea to the quiet haven of home is almost precisely paralleled by Hölderlin's metaphor here.

The third song, 'Sokrates und Alcibiades', is structurally one of Britten's most transparent. A long melody is first heard on the piano, entirely unharmonized though rich in implications, as background to the singer's free declamation; it is then sung, against the piano's succession of root triads on all twelve notes. So the same musical object is present both in the question and in the answer, but while in the first it is obscured by the speaker's niggling rhythms, in the second its graceful phrase structure and rich tonal meaning stand revealed; as a musical parable the scheme perfectly complements the poem while it also recognizes in an unusual way its strophic design. The rôle Britten has allotted to the triad, as a symbol of beauty, makes of the second stanza a statement of the composer's own artistic beliefs, while the manner of juxtaposing the triads in unexpected ways, recalling the empty-stage scene in *Budd*, symbolizes, as it did there, the recognition that beauty must awaken love.

'Die Jugend' is through-composed, of materials that sound contrived and, at times, self-consciously bizarre. Against a dry little drum-tap (cf. the violin concerto's opening) the singer delivers brittle cross-accented phrases of closing-fan shape with some flippant word-repetitions. When the piano's scalic fragments cohere into a flowing ostinato the voice relaxes into conjunct *cantabile* ('und wie du das Herz der Pflanzen erfreust'), the whole complex hovering on a single seventh chord with both perfect and diminished fifth that twice resolves luxuriantly into the submediant at 'Vater Helios' and 'Heilige Luna'—the most characteristic procedure in the song. Modulation back to the tonic is achieved in a cadence to words ('wie euch meine Seele geliebt') so crucial that they echo on in the piano left-hand for the rest of the piece, a reworking of the earlier seventh chord below the laboriously achieved vocal spanning of an octave. Harmonically all hangs together admirably but the diversity of textural types, however apt to the catalogue of the youth's education at the hands of the gods, makes for an uncomfortably quirky song.

Apparently more typical is the retention in 'Hälfte des Lebens' of a single piano figuration throughout; yet its two forms, one wearily slow and bound to a low tonic pedal, and the other fluttering up in agitation, provide the antithesis as well as the unity in this song. The fitful alternations between them in the second stanza, the voice's obsessive semitonal slurs and its inconsequential end at the peak of a rising phrase after its first disconsolate descents, all subtly suggest that borderline between fantasy and dementia at which this painfully beautiful poem seems placed.

The final song 'Die Linien des Lebens' emerges almost automatically from its text, the most moving of all the poems written in Hölderlin's madness:

Die Linien des Lebens sind verschieden,
Wie Wege sind, und wie der Berge Grenzen.
Was hier wir sind, kann dort ein Gott ergänzen,
Mit Harmonien und ew'gem Lohn und Frieden.

Each slow vocal line appears only after its exposition has already begun on the piano in a texture of contrapuntal entries that cross in trance-like motions. Though the completed vocal shape (canto fermo in that most German of structures, a chorale fantasy) shows a simple cadential symmetry in its two contrasted (minor/major) workings of a two-line scheme (see Ex. 12a), the piano lines move without regard for harmonic meaning. Only with the affirmation of the poem's last line does tonal order emerge from this maze; both the 'completion' of the opening musical line (by its inversion) and its harmonization are achieved in the piano's postlude (Ex. 12b), a passage of symmetrical scalic movement around tritone poles that was already characteristic in its clangorous second aggregates, but is perhaps still

Ex. 15.12 (a)

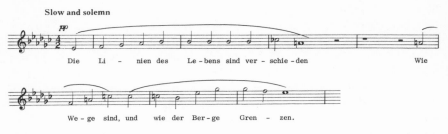

Ex. 15.12 (b)

more prophetic of the *War Requiem*'s procedures. To those critics who regard Britten's susceptibility to poetic stimulus as a snare this song must offer a model example, for its musical scheme is virtually dictated by the text. It remains one of the composer's most impressive songs, not only because everything is explicable in terms of the poem but because the music is entirely logical in its own terms. Although in several of the earlier cycles (the Michelangelo, Donne and Hardy sets provide the best examples) Britten had striven to make the final song a statement by particularly simple musical gestures of some fundamental philosophical tenet of his poet, one that could in retrospect embrace all that had gone before, in none had he succeeded as certainly as in this spare yet magnificently cumulative song.

NOCTURNE, OP. 60

The Hölderlin songs were not published until 1963, which may account in part for their acquiring a reputation as one of the composer's rare esoteric works. Since publication they have been performed by singers other than Pears, including Elisabeth Schwarzkopf, yet they seem unlikely to become ready material for the large public recital. Earlier in 1958 Britten had written another cycle that plainly does require the concert platform, the Nocturne, Op. 60, first performed at the Leeds Centenary Festival in October of that year. In setting an English poetic anthology linked by a common theme of Night, Sleep and Dreams, for tenor with string orchestra and obbligato instruments, he appeared intent on applying to expressive and technical problems comparable to those posed in the Serenade fifteen years earlier the musical ways of thought he had developed and refined in the meantime.

His choice of verse already shows, however, that a duplicate of the Serenade was not planned. In place of the short self-contained poems of that work, Britten now includes several excerpts from far more ramified contexts. The lines of the Fourth Spirit of the Mind from Shelley's 'lyrical drama' 'Prometheus Unbound' (1819) are broken off here before the final couplet that linked them to the dramatic context. Coleridge's verses from 'The Wanderings of Cain' (1798), all that was written down in poetic form of an abortive project planned in collaboration with Wordsworth, acquire an added mystery when dissociated even from the prose scenario Coleridge drafted. The Keats lines formed only the first stanza of the long poem 'Sleep and Poetry' (1817), and the Wordsworth excerpt from 'The Prelude' (1805) introduces us in mid-narrative.

Though there are convincing musical reasons too, one reason for the unquestionable finality of the Shakespeare Sonnet at the close of the work is that it traces a full cycle of experience while most of the other verses appear to leave the circle incomplete. This facilitates the musical process by which one setting is made to merge into another, usually with the opening orchestral material acting as a link. This ritornello acquires therefore an extra musical significance, seeming to symbolize the interludes of peaceful, deep-breathed slumber in a succession of dreams; aptly enough the Wordsworth setting—an insomniac fantasy—is the only one neither prefaced nor concluded by the ritornello.

The earlier cycle depicted Night, its beauty, mystery, cruelty, only being absorbed into it at last with the sleep of the Keats Sonnet. The Nocturne inhabits a dream world (references to dreams frame the cycle) that is less regulatedly picturesque. So the simple strophic forms of the Serenade have given way to a free arioso style, the vocal lines rarely forming symmetrical periods and being less prone to rely on literally scalic or arpeggio shapes. Similarly the instrumental imagery is more fantastic in the later work, even the horn abandoning those nature symbols of the Serenade in order to outdo Middleton's onomatopeic representation of the animal world at midnight. Despite Britten's retention of key signatures (as usual, quite accurate guides to the fundamental tonal premise of each movement) the tonal situation has become far more fluid in the Nocturne, and the characteristic harmonic aggregates are ambiguous. In many contexts, melodic and harmonic, a given set of pitches is quickly complemented by the rest of the twelve-note repertory, yet a place remains (see the opening of the Coleridge setting, for example) for conflations of the diatonic resources. At the end of the cycle, the apparently conclusive C major in which the opening bars return is supplanted by a major third on D flat. In retrospect it becomes clear not only

371

that the final Shakespeare setting fused these two tonal assertions but that the D flat outcome was already prepared by its V in the third bar of the work. And this challenge to simple tonal orientation by a closely neighbouring note is to be heard elsewhere too—in the obstinate open A string sounds in the B flat minor of 'The Kraken' and in the E sharp against F sharp of the timpani's *idée fixe* in the Wordsworth setting.

The opening pages of the Nocturne show a manner of blurring tonality by superimpositions more dense than Britten had used before, yet the first movement is felt subconsciously as a secure enough I-v-I experience. Typically, the bass only achieves a 'tonic' C at the point (three bars before fig. 1) where the upper harmony is most elusive, but the middle section (from fig. 1) stands for a kind of G minor, and the G duly converts to a V function to make a simple return at fig. 2. The melodic activity of the first section is derived strictly from three 'shapes that haunt' (see Ex. 13) while the mid-section

Ex. 15.13

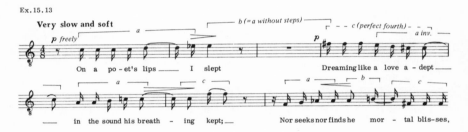

employs harmonic intervals rather than motives. After an abridged reprise, the vocal line suddenly takes wing, symbolizing the poetic vision in a magnificently shaped descent. This alights on that D flat which we have already seen to be the outcome of the whole cycle; on its way, against pure white-note string harmonies it passes through various tonal fields, touching on every pitch of the chromatic set except A natural, a note promptly thrown into relief as the open-string irritant against the B flat minor of 'The Kraken' (see Ex. 14).

This is a setting in which almost extravagant detail, of the singer's word-painting and the obbligato bassoon's virtuoso figure development, is balanced by a structural plan simple to the point of crudity—a ground bass. The gargantuan three-bar tonic arpeggio is sustained against the new tonal areas explored by the soloists for the varied images of the central section. Only after restatement has begun (at fig. 6) does the ground break from its

Ex. 15.14

moorings to achieve an expiring final statement in the strained high register of the bassoon. So obvious a means of depicting the Kraken's rise at 'the latter fire' need not exasperate, for it is carried out with admirable precision of attendant detail, and the association of the note A with the last word 'die' illuminates its rôle throughout the structure.

Though the ground provides a link with the Dirge of the Serenade, neither in the tonal complexities of the string ritornello nor the curious fusion of fantastic arabesque with driest of accompaniment textures are there direct reminders of those sounds which seemed Britten's most characteristic in that earlier period. But the Coleridge setting which follows takes up again the exploration (through harp figurations) of the 'total diatonic' sound of A major which the *Grimes* sea-music and the *Lucretia* aubade had made a celebrated Britten resource.

The figurations are no longer so dependent on long chains of superimposed thirds: at first they derive from the vocal phrases, then for much of the song (e.g., from fig. 10) they form palindromic decorations of a simple I-IV-V (- I etc) harmonic treadmill. As in 'The Kraken', the string parts add little but points of emphasis to the voice/obbligato duet, but this achieves a beautiful suppleness from the playing-off of a flowing Lydian vocal ostinato eight minim beats long against a harmonic circuit of three bars (i.e., nine minims). Because this idyllic sound could apparently flow on for ever, its interruptions by the staccato wonderings of the narrator convey an unease which heightens powerfully ambiguities already manifest in the poem.

The centrepiece of the anthology is formed by following a setting in which the Sleep ritornello is omnipresent with one from which it is entirely banished. The musically diffuse stream of onomatopeia with which Britten surrounds the Middleton text is effectively unified by the ritornello, and the exchange of miaows between soloist and obbligato horn brings back the Ex. 14 ('Nurslings') theme; see Ex. 15. C major is thus restored at the centre of the cycle, though its presentation as iv + I + v facilitates a semitonal transition to the tritonal pole of F sharp on which the Wordsworth setting begins. The brooding menace of this piece is created evidently enough by the dynamic and pitch curve of the timpani obbligato, but scarcely less by

Ex. 15.15

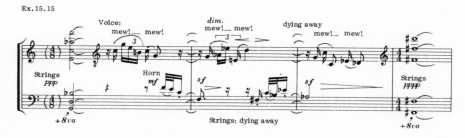

progressive tonal instability. The initially serene F sharp string octaves are already made problematic by the timpani ostinato, which inclines them towards a V function; the voice also suggests B minor but its wanderings pull the attendant string harmony into obscurer regions. When the security of the bass F sharp also is lost (at 17) the poet abandons disturbing fact for nighmarish fantasy. The calculated banality of the new theme ('the horse is taught his manage') is offset by the distorted accompanying harmonies, not the only Mahlerian process in a cycle dedicated to Alma Mahler. Restatement (fig. 19) transfers the pedal to B but the singer now inclines towards F sharp; the explosive outburst 'sleep no more' realizes the portents of the second theme, while the F sharps that began the piece are shattered into the G-E sharp (F natural) from which they emerged.

If the measured march that lies behind this Wordsworth setting seems an inexorable preamble to catastrophe, the far slower detonations which fade into an impassive background to Owen's 'The Kind Ghosts' contribute to an elegy following catastrophe. It is possible to find this more chilling than anything in Britten's later treatment of Owen in the *War Requiem*. The cor anglais makes its most sustained appearance since Lucretia's mourning of her impending death, but its melody has none of the tonal inevitability of that context: its few figures twist upon themselves chromatically and even the calmer arpeggio motion (at 22) is full of inner contradictions. Meanwhile the dry pizzicato tread too contains no hope of harmonic resolution, though every chord is a pure triad except for a conflicting bass. And, above all, as though in a trance, the singer delivers phrase upon phrase coloured by warmly consonant intervals, only at the most terrible line of all ('Nor what red mouths . . .') threatening to disrupt a calm that is as charged musically as is Owen's fusion of beauty and horror.

The reappearance of the ritornello, though it begins hesitantly (and marked 'cold'), allows an escape from the obsessive atmosphere of this setting, and into a Keats setting that is one of Britten's airiest pieces. The tenor line smoothly explains and unifies the exuberant imagery of flute and clarinet, alternating then duetting, but the moment to which all this has been tending is created by the return of the strings with a soft rich chord of C major. Its key colour reminds us of the ritornello, its lay-out as a 6/4 chord may remind us of the Keats sonnet in the Serenade: in any event, we scarcely need the singer's help to identify this as the symbol of that sleep which surpasses all the joys that have been enumerated. Gradually it achieves the breathing rhythm of the ritornello, and to the pure white-note undulations that accompanied its first appearance, the Ex. 14 theme ends the poem. It ends on D flat, therefore, and the obbligato instruments, joining forces for the first time to provide a body of sound that can challenge that of the strings, gradually bring warmth, and indeed passion, to the major third of D flat. Shakespeare's sonnet 43 thus becomes in the cycle's slow finale an impassioned tonal duologue. This is not, as in 'The Kraken', a matter of an irritant note but of two entities that can merge into a higher unity: one can choose to hear either key, a Lydian D flat or a Neapolitan C minor, as predominant in the crucial opening phrase, and the ambivalence is sustained to give impressive profundity of meaning to the simple textures, beautifully scored to give a highly Mahlerian sound; see Ex. 16. (Even the reprise—bar after 38—is prepared by dominants of C and of D flat respectively.) The meaning of this rapturous coexistence is only made clear when the great climactic tug has slackened and, to an inversion of Ex. 14, the singer surrenders to sleep and dreams. Lulled by snatches of the ritornello, this familiar yet strangely new shape works out its course around D flat only to swing ultimately to C (i.e., just as its progenitor turned from C to D flat): the final words 'thee' and 'me' are thus in different tonal planes and we understand the ecstatic fusion of Ex. 16. The last faint sound is in fact of D flat, a resolution of the previous two bars, but therefore also of the sounds which opened the whole cycle. This long-term effect is only the most conspicuous of the many features of its organization that indicate how Britten had profited, since the days of the Serenade, from the association of tonal structure with dramatic argument which he had refined in the operas.

Ex. 15.16

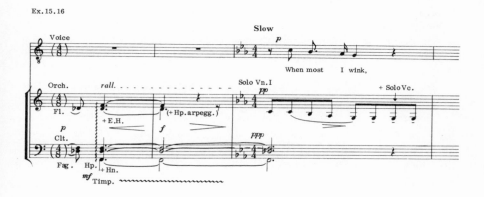

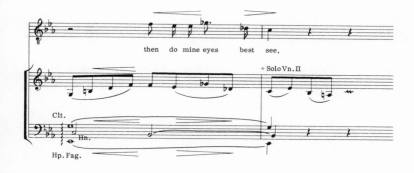

SONGS AND PROVERBS OF WILLIAM BLAKE, OP. 74

Britten had set verses by William Blake in three of his anthologies, the Serenade, the Spring Symphony and *A Charm of Lullabies*. His decision to fashion a complete Blake cycle may therefore have been arrived at slowly, after pondering how best to offer a sustained musical reading of that elusively direct poet's vision. But it seems no less likely that he was led towards Blake for this work (written in 1965 and first performed at the Aldeburgh Festival that year) by the very nature of the voice for which he had chosen to write, that of Dietrich Fischer-Dieskau, which had already influenced the *War Requiem* four years earlier. The distinguished German baritone was recognized in the mid-sixties, when the cycle was written, both as an operatic singer of remarkable versatility and as one of the foremost *Lieder* singers of the day. Like Pears, Fischer-Dieskau has contrived to put a highly individual vocal quality at the service of a commanding musical intellect in such a way as to encompass a far wider range of characterization than many singers with a less idiosyncratic timbre. But it is probably true to say that his unique sound, dark yet unforced even in a high baritone tessitura, is most perfectly adapted to expressions of world-weariness or even of utter fatalism, tempered by a philosophic resignation that never degenerates into emotional detachment. Certainly Britten's use of this voice in his setting of Owen's 'Strange Meeting' had endorsed such a view, and if we may read so much into a specific vocal tone-colour then we may say that few texts more fitting could have been found for Britten's cycle for Fischer-Dieskau than the Blake Songs and Proverbs selected by Peter Pears.

Unlike the earlier cycles with piano, this is performed without a break: six excerpts from the Proverbs of Hell alternate with six Songs of Experience, and a last aphorism, from the Auguries of Innocence, leads into the last song, the closing verses of the same set. Blake's recurrent images and ideas have enabled Pears to fashion cross-references between proverbs and songs that link the subject-matter compellingly. For example, the first song, 'London' ends with those searing lines:

> But most thro' midnight streets I hear
> How the youthful Harlot's curse
> Blasts the newborn Infant's tear
> And blights with plagues the marriage hearse

and the proverb that follows, 'Prisons are built with stones of law/Brothels with bricks of religion', at once offers a moral relevant to the foregoing song and makes a point about the hypocrisy of institutional religion that is to be developed in 'The Chimney Sweeper', which follows. Two songs of bitter social protest give way, in 'A Poison Tree', to one in which the canker is owned to be in each of us, but the central song, 'The Tyger', appears to promise a respite from such dark reflections. Yet its apocalyptic tone (and the muted frenzy of its setting) prevents its forming too relaxed an interlude.

The three remaining songs, as arranged by Pears, treat with steadily increasing power of one cosmic theme, life and death, time and eternity. So in this quite modest span a considerable range of Blake themes is covered, but at the same time a sense is conveyed more strongly than in any other Britten cycle of inexorable movement towards a final concentration of the whole experience; the nihilism of the last Hardy song can appear almost shocking after the delicate miniatures earlier in the cycle, and the stark tracery of the last Hölderlin song, though it provides a superb ending, represents a further fateful twist, whereas those hopeless revolutions into eternity which we hear in the last Blake song are more overwhelming because the whole cycle has allowed no other kind of outcome. We need only compare Ex. 17b's *x* shape with Ex. 15.2 to be reminded how this links up with a preoccupation of the Donne cycle; and indeed, the Blake songs invite comparison for their singular intensity of utterance with the *Holy Sonnets*, but in place of that work's feverish Baroque ecstasies, a grimmer, steelier tone is to be heard, a vision to be glimpsed that is painfully stripped of illusion about the human plight.

The continuity of theme is assisted by the unbroken musical fabric, but its articulation is clearly marked, the proverbs serving as ritornelli. The idea from which they all derive is itself a musical aphorism, all twelve notes arranged as three four-note segments; though the systematic construction is best seen from the following example (Ex. 17a), the note orders within

Ex. 15.17 (a)

Ex. 15.17 (b)

segments are in fact variable and the most pregnant shape for the whole work is the twisted arrangement of the chromatically adjacent notes shown as *x* at (b). At first these sets of pitches appear only in the piano, reiterated across many octaves in clangorous conflations or as a measured pacing against which the baritone declaims in a free tempo. As in the church operas, non-alignment offers no problems when all the accompanying notes can fuse into a single harmonic unit. The vocal line begins as portentous monotone with terminal inflexions, but in successive ritornelli it aspires towards the shapes of the note-row. Proverb IV juxtaposes three statements and an inversion of *x*, comprising ten pitch-classes, Proverb V extends the *x* principle into sinuous scale patterns and uses all but one pitch, Proverb VI, though of only nine pitches, begins to shape phrases related to the piano's row segments, while in the final proverb, the whole twelve-note statement (Ex. 17*c*/*b*/*a*/*c*) is achieved by the voice, to particularly apt words:

> To see a World in a Grain of Sand
> And a Heaven in a Wild Flower
> Hold Infinity in the palm of your hand
> And Eternity in an hour.

The singer thus relieves the piano of the need to delineate the row melodically, single tremolando chordal statements of the segments extending a textural idea from the previous song. And the achievement of unanimity in the musical material of Proverb VII extends into the last song, which retains the harmonies of the segments and an ostinato movement drawn from 'To see a world in a grain of sand', reinforcing that sense of inevitability noted already as the dominating characteristic of this song.

The earlier songs are less overt in their relationship to a common source and our immediate experience is of their individuality of character, but repeated hearings confirm some links that can be demonstrated analytically. The ostinato-like accompaniment of the first song, 'London', is a wholly predictable Britten response to a wanderer's poem, yet a new note is struck in the agitated revolutions of its five-against-three rhythms. The same synthetic scales, including prominent whole-tone components, operate in the vocal lines, though a cadential shape resolves the scalic ambiguities as it always leads to a pure triad in the piano. But the illusoriness of such repose becomes clear when one possible centre after another is tried, eventually embracing all twelve notes as roots of triads. If the piano's wanderings are restless, the voice's are forlorn, each new horror being spelt out with the painful clarity of its simpler divisions of the beat and the only melismata being like cries of despair. From its first line all the remaining phrases are developed in a typical Britten scheme, concealing a three-part structure by a control of the melodic extremes that welds together a single arch; this plummets to its lowest point in the last line 'And blights with plagues the marriage hearse' where the scalic impetus is momentarily lost. Its recovery in the coda promises nothing more than a still gloomier review of the whole experience, and instead the proverb summarizes before we move on to view more closely a single victim of 'the mind-forg'd manacles' in 'The Chimney Sweeper'. The spare, crystalline piano sonorities of this still winter scene come first as a relief after the turbulent motion of 'London', but the simple intervals in either hand of this part rarely fuse into a single harmonic entity, so that a sense of strain begins to develop. Ironically, tonally definitive harmony (albeit with a major/minor ambiguity) is achieved only with the piano's reiterations (from bar 21) of a tag that echoes the voice's words 'to pray'. This hops along gamely enough both times the sweep boy sings of his happiness, but the desolation behind the acceptance of his lot is revealed by the placing of the rests within the phrase. The tag can be regarded as an expansion of Ex. 17*a*, and the shape *x* gives a wry twist to two phrases. Despite the recurrence of the 'happy' section, this is a far less tightly organized piece than the first song, almost wayward in delivery so that its outrage is all in the implication, never the statement: even so, the descent of the last phrase 'Who make up a heaven of our misery' to a still lower note than in the previous song is telling.

'A Poison Tree' is the biggest song of the cycle and the only one that presents a developing dramatic situation. The piano's introductory rumbling conceals a twelve-note arrangement, interlocking cadences of E flat minor and E minor. The opening vocal shape shows another way of interpolating an E minor suggestion within an E flat minor span, and it initiates a twelve-note melody palpably related to the Proverbs' row and including a direct form of *x*, but harmonized in spacious minor-mode sixth chords; see Ex. 18.

The line 'I told my wrath, my wrath did end' naturally prompts a cadential return to a thirteenth note identical with the first. But in the contrasted sequel 'I was angry with my foe/I told it not' the inverted row is never completed, for from the sequential repetition of 'I told it not', vast consequences begin to develop ('my wrath did grow') as a dense polyphonic web is spun from crucial motives. The shapes *b* and *c* of Ex. 18 (the second bringing repetitions of 'My wrath did grow' that are musically compelling though not in Blake) together with a sinuous new line that incorporates *x*, first introduced at 'I water'd it in fears', engage with each other in straight and inverted forms, in a texture that dispenses with all less potent material and moves steadily to a climax of a kind that cannot be paralleled in Britten's songs. That much of this build-up of intensity goes by very stealthily adds to its grimly fascinating quality. After an almost seductively light piano texture for 'my foe beheld it shine', vast octaves in the bass of the piano begin slowly to turn again the inverted row of 'I was angry . . .'. But now its course is

379

completed, arriving at its E flat destination as the singer savours the bitter triumph of 'glad I see/My foe outstretched'. Here a near retrograde-inversion of the row (including the sequential repeat of *b* but never reaching *a*) brings back the opening piano texture, but now the sixth chords are major; the fading to the rumbling introduction's return suffices to measure the emptiness of this victory. Every thematic usage in this song can thus be assigned the most obvious symbolic relationship to Blake's lines, but it is the piece as a whole that so remarkably echoes the terrible force of the poem.

Of Blake's *Songs of Experience* none is more dangerously over-familiar than 'The Tyger', and a composer's response to it might easily be jaded. Britten's opening sounds disconcertingly platitudinous, but as this pattern takes its place in a larger one, spanning the whole song in minor-third shifts, its repetitions throw into relief the many taut rhythmic variants. Similarly, the piano's scalic figurations, though unduly simple at first sight, contribute to a sensation of furious, quivering energy held in restraint. As a separate piece, this setting would perhaps be too uniform, but as the centrepiece of this cycle it appears scarcely weighty enough, its neat Lydian-cum-Mixolydian shapes sometimes offering a routine handiwork rather than a fearful symmetry. At least its *scherzando* mood never suggests a flippant one, and if one genuinely quick song was needed, this transitional point was the place for it. Not only its speed but its unequivocally major colouring is new. The gentle song on 'The Fly' is more difficult to categorize: though F is roundly prepared by the final note of Proverb V, it is never established as a tonic (major) except by implication, the whole song hovering around the diatonic seventh on the supertonic G. The peculiar weightless quality that results is intensified by the absence of a functional bass (the melody, doubled at two octaves' distance, encloses the harmony) and by the limply fluttering figure which unifies the piano part. The motive *x* appears in the voice as a symbol of death, viewed here without passion; yet the mood is not one of indifference, but wistfully questioning in its Schumannesque obliquity of harmony. The next song, 'Ah, Sun-flower', expresses passionate longings, but the ecstasy towards which it aspires is hard won; the vocal phrases, characterized by successive thirds often in yearning ♫. rhythms must try to unfold against the dragging undertow of the marching bass line. The song moves between a conflation of Ex. 17b and one of Ex. 17c, that is it passes from B (major or minor) to F (major and minor), the key areas that are the most important in the whole cycle (songs 2 and 4 in approximately B minor and B major; songs 5 and 7 in approximately F) though they nowhere else generate dramatic conflict. The weighty bass line develops a type which originated in the *War Requiem* and reappeared in the first movement of the Cello Symphony. Its elaborate quintuplet groups do not conceal that its essential motion is relentlessly pushing down by semitones, while the right hand chords are pulling in the opposite direction; the progress of these extremes of the texture is summarized in Ex. 19.

380

Ex.15.19

1) ⟶
2) ⟶   4) mid-section   5) cf.3
3) ⟶

Three times the first span is essayed, only with the last of these (from 'traveller's journey') achieving the tritonal pole, an F minor which remains static (even with a final touch of major) as the singer recounts what is to be found in the 'sweet golden clime' we are momentarily savouring. But the bass begins to traverse the complementary tritone as the longings reassert themselves for what is still only a vision, 'where my Sunflower wishes to go'. As the singer repeats these words to his original drooping thirds, B natural is in fact omitted by the bass and we pass to the B flat point of the first span, which has its outcome in the postlude in an F that is now both minor and major (as we have seen, segment *c* of the proverbs' row); the tonal area of B is not forgotten however, as the ambivalence of the final bass quintuplet groups makes clear. To explain the mechanics of this intensely beautiful song can no doubt seem crassly insensitive, but it is a particularly clear example of Britten's making a tonal objective and the stages of the journey impressively direct symbols of the poetic essence.

And with that last chord identified as the escape from time into eternity, we move through the proverb to the hymnic phrases of 'Every Night and Every Morn', distilling the whole experience, and the Experience too, in Blake's sense synonymous with man's fall into hell. For Eternity now rolls on through the piano bass, yet no golden clime is painted by these harmonies of mild but irresoluble dissonance, which convey again the burden of human misery shared by the dwellers in Night; not even the climax's apocalyptic vision of the true Day banishes the profound yet totally resigned sadness of this song, and the final slow turn to a consolatory major chord in fact intensifies this mood. The derivations from segments *c* and *a* (from 'delight', bar 23) are pointed, that from *b* less direct (from 'light', bar 52), but with the word 'Night' in bar 33 we hear a form that is not strictly of the row but is very familiar; as it is played off against itself in mirror movement ('We are led to believe a lie/When we see not through the Eye') its reference back becomes clearer – it is the opening shape of 'I was angry'.

The Blake cycle may never become one of Britten's more popular sets of songs, for its despondency is not of the easy kind in which audiences like to envelop themselves. But these reflections on the human condition, darker than any he had betrayed before, are among his most disturbing achievements.

381

THE POET'S ECHO, OP. 76

Whatever the sources of new stimuli to Britten's invention, he was always prepared to put to use in quite different contexts every addition they brought to his technical armoury. The techniques of the parables, which accepted within a European musical convention some elements of Japanese practice—heterophonic elaboration of line, non-harmonic textures and instrumental predilections—were not obviously reconcilable with Britten's established practice in other media. Yet he soon found ways, in *Voices for Today* and the proverbs of the Blake cycle, of admitting at least some influence of the church operas' flexible temporal alignment. Clearly then, the composer saw nothing exotic and limiting in the device. So a further modification of it in the Pushkin song cycle has nothing to do with Japan, or indeed with Russia, but it is made very evidently appropriate to the theme of the work—*The Poet's Echo*.

That Britten would some day turn to a Russian text seemed inferable both from his earlier range of language and from his high regard for the Soviet artists with whom he had been working for several years. The Pushkin cycle, a tribute to Galina Vishnevskaya and her husband, Mstislav Rostropovich, was written in the House of Composers, Dilizhan, Armenia, in August 1965, and was first performed by the dedicatees in December at the Moscow Conservatoire. The composer's setting of the poems was facilitated by his hearing them read in Russian, even though his understanding of them was bound to be formed by translations. Since Peter Pears fashioned an admirable singing translation to Britten's lines, English listeners are able to hear a version which seems to lack nothing in immediacy.

As in Britten's other sets of songs, the six poems he has used from Pushkin do not constitute a cycle in any narrative sense, but there is a strong link between the first poem, 'Echo', and the fourth, 'The Nightingale and the Rose'; both show it to be the poet's lot, after he has given of his utmost, to receive no answer. And in the final poem, even the sounds that torment him at night bring no certain message. Musical connexions between these three songs are therefore particularly clear, but elsewhere too the influence of the work's opening complex is pervasive. Without so patently unifying a device as the proverb-interludes in the Blake cycle, this set is securely bound into a musical entity; that the ties are of faint evocation as often as of direct recall makes of the work a series of stronger and fainter echoes. Thus, despite the wide range of song types, the listener is left with one dominating sound-shape reverberating in the memory, that of the opening bars—Ex. 20, bars 1–4.

It will be seen at once how this multiple echo, with its varied timings of a single phrase and its harmony compounded entirely of melody notes, derives from Britten's practice in *Curlew River*. But the harmony is far removed from the plainsong conflations that characterize the parables. Though the phrase cadences, the augmented fifth and the opposition of both tritone and

Ex.15.20

major seventh create a situation in which we cannot take F to be a tonic, the immediate sequel suggests that it may rather be a leading-note. Some later phrases establish centres, and F seems assured at the climax, only to evaporate into the initial uncertainty again. Each line is treated in echo canons, but in the central bars an important subsidiary melodic shape is accompanied by a new kind of heterophony; its displacements create a chain of seventh and ninth relationships. This subsidiary idea is thrown into relief on its return, for now, after every sound of nature and of man has drawn an answering call, to the echo itself, as to the poet, there comes no response, and a few sparse chords replace the earlier resonance.

The unusually simple scheme of this first song, avoiding all detailed word-painting, is underlined by its directly sequential treatment of the figure *c* in Ex. 20, and later of its inversion. The extent to which nineteenth-century Russian operatic style (that of the Pushkin opera *Eugene Onegin*, for example) lies behind this sequential rhetoric is made clearer in the second song, where it has pointed relevance to a poem in which old, passionate yearnings have kindled to a flame once more. The opening melodic shape stems from *b* in Ex. 20, but in this new form, with an initial rising sixth and neat phrase development within a straightforward diatonic framework, it leads us into a very different emotional world; only the subtle fluctuations of phrase length and the constant sevenths (cf. *a* in Ex. 20) that brace the delicately figured accompaniment remind us that this is an echo, not a recreation, of a past music. In the third song, however, the strongest echoes are from Britten's own work—lithe octaves like those that open the Hölderlin cycle are

383

followed by a triad that is blurred like those of 'Midnight on the Great Western'. The two ideas have in common their reinterpretation of the F-E tension in Ex. 20, but they are symbols respectively of Satan and the Angel; their confrontation is succeeded by their fusion when Satan is moved by the sight of his shining adversary. Most of the triadic relationships turn on semitonally adjacent roots with a common third (e.g., the opening F minor-E major), but the addition of the major seventh often adroitly transfers the process to another level, so that Britten contrives with yet another triad usage to avoid platitude. The vocal line is suitably free for a narrative poem, but in more than its climactic sevenths the influence of the *b* curve in Ex. 20 can be detected.

And the notes that ring through the trembling seconds of the introduction to 'The Nightingale and the Rose' build up Ex. 20*a*. This song is of a fragile beauty that Britten has rarely surpassed. The accompaniment never uses the lower part of the piano and its 'sonorous seconds' are a constant background to a rhapsodic vocal line, nervously conjunct at first, and with inflexions that oddly recall the Madwoman's speech in *Curlew River*, but flower into a spacious derivative of *b*. At the central point, a simple enharmonic swing takes us on to another tonal plane, with the rhapsodic song now in the piano, as the moral of the scene for the poet is drawn. The closing bars' juxtaposition of the harmonic series' flat seventh and a Lydian fourth offers an epitome of a lyrical vein that had served Britten well for a quarter of a century. After this the 'Epigram' inevitably sounds somewhat graceless. Its clipped cadences point up the major seventh and the complete chord *a* is also outlined, but this caricature stands aggressively apart from the rest of the cycle.

So the drawing together of threads in the closing song, 'Lines written during a sleepless night', is all the more welcome; it is also extremely subtle. A comparison of its opening with that of the first song shows relationships of varying degrees: the major seventh is now a nightmarish ostinato that ticks away time (an idea to be developed further at the close of *Owen Wingrave*; cf. p. 517), the intervals of *a* are modified, while the *b* curve can be heard behind the piano left-hand figures and in the vocal span; and a figure related to the subsidiary theme (unquoted in Ex. 20) of 'Echo' plays a big part in this song. Gradually these and other relations are made more evident as the vocal line takes in a reminder of the fourth song while outlining *b* ever more exactly, and the *a* substitute is joined by its original form; both then melt into the superimposed triads of the third song. This troubled fantasy reaches its peak at 'Answer me, I long to hear' with an ironic return of the echo's music (i.e., Ex. 20) before the ticking ostinato emerges from it. The final dry repeated B's are technically consonant (against a G and D drone) but the seventh remains so powerfully in the memory that it is impossible not to hear in this state of rest an irresoluble unease. The work's cycle thus fittingly closes with an echo which is in fact inaudible, a poet's echo.

WHO ARE THESE CHILDREN?, OP. 84

The song-cycle *Who are these children?*, Op. 84, was written to mark the 700th National Gallery of Scotland Concert, and was inscribed to Tertia Liebenthal; as her death preceded the first performance of the cycle, at Edinburgh on 4th May 1971, it was given in memory of her. In fact the cycle had been completed almost two years earlier, and part of it was given at University College, Cardiff in March 1971, an odd circumstance for a work in which eight out of twelve songs are settings of Scots dialect poems. It may appear odd already that Britten should have chosen to set some of the lesser-known pieces of a not particularly well-known Scottish poet, William Soutar (1898–1943). But the occasion for which he was writing clearly required him at least to avoid quintessentially English verse, and in the event, he was able to undertake the work as no token act of homage, for in the Soutar of the four big poems here, written in English, Britten found a writer with whose themes and manner of realizing them he felt a strong sympathy.

Soutar died at just about the time of Britten's return to this country, and the preoccupations these English poems reflect had been voiced by the composer during his first period of activity. Man as the murderer of living things in nature or of his own kind, including children, or the two aspects in confrontation—these are themes that easily take us back to the Britten of *Our Hunting Fathers* and *Ballad of Heroes*. It is true that our route would be through parts of the *War Requiem*, yet the elaborately layered nature of that work prevents its ever recalling the rounded statements of protest of the late-thirties Britten. Furthermore, the tone of an Owen, who finds himself part of the machinery of murder, is inevitably different from that of an Auden, who is a troubled but determinedly rational observer from afar. We are told that Soutar was an admirer of Owen, but by the time these poems were written, the passion of his protest had to feed on what he read in the newspaper or heard on the wireless. How cuttingly he could put to his service such material is seen in the poem that Britten chooses for his cycle's title, written after seeing a photograph published in 1941 of a hunt picking its way through a bomb-damaged village; not until two stanzas have appeared to dwell on the elegance of the hunting party does the implied comment crash into the open:

> Is there a dale more calm, more green,
> Under this morning hour;
> A scene more alien than this scene
> Within a world at war?

Neither 'Slaughter' nor 'The Children' adopts this oblique approach; the latter has a terrible finality in its long third lines that amplify the second lines:

> A wound which everywhere
> Corrupts the hearts of men:
> The blood of children corrupts the hearts of men,

385

while the shadow of another poet to whom Britten had been attracted, Blake, seems to lie behind 'Slaughter' (see the quotations given in the discussion below).

Soutar lived the withdrawn life of an invalid in his last years, noting the minutiae of uneventful days in his diary. Yet he was as concerned to turn his experience of a Scottish home and the characteristic domestic scene to poetic account as to comment on the world scene, and his verses written in Scots, for children, are pithy miniatures; the social commentary in 'The Larky Lad' is as revealing as many a survey. Of course Britten's juxtaposition of these jingles in dialect and the English poems gives the cycle no definable subject area; as in *Winter Words*, the very range serves however to round out the composer's view of its poet.

The Scots songs match Soutar's simplicity of language in being each worked out from one or two simple musical formulae. For example, 'A Riddle (The Earth)' has piano refrains in which two chords alternate, suggesting G or the dominant of C, but the jigging pedal that sets off from F natural samples every conflicting flat pitch (i.e. behaves as though it were in D flat) before finally gravitating to G. The two vocal stanzas are doubled by the piano octaves; each consists of the same four-bar phrase and its slightly elaborated repeat, C Lydian now tending to outweigh G in the balance of probabilities. Relationships between these two ideas, which remain discrete, are in fact very close, for all the vocal melody except its peak notes is drawn from the piano's harmony. 'Analysis' of pieces so transparent always appears risibly superfluous, but the song makes its point wittily only because it is well composed. 'A Laddie's Sang', which follows, is redolent of much earlier Britten in its lapping waves of pure D major added-note chords, troubled only by a single flattened sixth. Again formulae control the two piano strata, ensuring among other things the characteristic melting second on the weak part of each pulse, but it is the melody that makes this a striking song for those who admired the Britten of almost three decades earlier, so certain of the strength of his invention as to embrace platitude in order wonderfully to refine it. This could be taken for a bogus folk-song but it is nothing of the kind, as all the modifications of its second stanza insist: it is an essay in melodic construction in which scale and arpeggio are at once norms and extremes, and it is absurdly old-fashioned from any point of view except that which recognizes a tiny but potent expressive achievement in the result. 'Black Day' (no. 4) is a wry little piece, flailing tritones against dour minor triads graphically underlining the petty hazards of a Scottish childhood. 'Bed-time' (no. 5) reverts to major seconds, their colour painting three sequential lines of each stanza before the texture widens into cadence. The sequences, though essentially no more than dominant sevenths, leave tonal bearings elusive, but the cadential scales meet at the plainest G, so a new independent bass is needed to generate momentum in the otherwise unchanged second stanza. Another riddle, 'The Child You Were' (7), is closer to other late Britten in the range of contrasted scalic forms through which its parodies are pointed up; an impassive drone completes the enigma. In 'The Larky Lad' (8) also, mixed scales (compounded of F major and F sharp minor) make for a sinuous line, played off against a mirror; nonchalant whistles in the piano add pedals that hold the piece firmly within a simple F-D-F circuit. A stranger pedal is that which underlies 'Supper' (10) for it rocks on the tritone 4-7 of B major to which the right hand adds the dominant (but *not* the supertonic that would complete the plump platitude V7d); for two stanzas the vocal melody also traces its repeated patterns between notes 7 and 4. The last stanza widens the rocking bass interval progressively from tritone up to octave, the upper harmony moving in parallel to touch on a range of distant key areas, before an enharmonic return on the peak note guides the line back to its original moorings, though with a new and surer cadential form; this is yet another economical structure that realizes its expressive aim with certainty. The last Scots song, held back to serve also as the last song of the cycle, 'The Auld Aik', is related to the graver themes of the English poems, though its intense pathos is all implicit:

> The auld aik's doun:
> The auld aik's doun:
> v.1 Twa hunna year it stūde or mair,
> (v.2 We were sae shair it wud aye be there,)
> But noo it's doun, doun

It thus provides a fitting closing epigram to the whole cycle. Musically too it represents simplification taken to an extreme—a series of grave triads in alternating piano registers and a recurrent drooping shape for the burden; even a functional dominant seventh is made touchingly symbolic when its resolution falls so far below; see Ex. 21. By transferring the burden up at the

Ex. 15.21

end of the first stanza and continuing still higher to begin the second, Britten welds the song into a single melodic arc, one of his baldest statements but one that is weighty enough to demand silence as its sequel.

The first of the English songs, 'Nightmare' (no. 3), is also of a tree and the axeman, but the fantasy of Soutar's treatment here is far removed from the flat statement of 'The Auld Aik'. Britten seeks to create this dream world by recourse to free alignment, an F major piano ostinato first defining the shape to be declaimed freely against it by the singer and then being transmuted through a few lines of unified metre into the next ostinato shape. The unified passages are weighed down by a low two-part accompaniment to the voice, with which the flowing right-hand figures conflict tonally, initially and finally in the relationship F/F sharp minor; the contrast between leaps in the ostinati and derived vocal lines and conjunct movement in the metrical sections further confirms the imagery as of light, freedom and nature opposed by darkness, bonds and murderous men. The disappearance of the ostinato as the dream fades allows the second image to prevail in a homophonic texture chilled by semitonal clashes, but the first line of all is recapitulated to form the last, now underlaid by an F sharp minor bass that is like a death sentence. The sixth song of the cycle, 'Slaughter', shows one of the most relentless workings-out of a single accompaniment figure since the Donne Sonnets, with which work it shares an impetuosity and a largeness of vocal gesture that had rarely been evident in the intervening cycles. Yet if the general effect of this apocalyptic statement is remarkably akin to much earlier Britten, the detail reflects its later date. The piano motive, endlessly pursued in straight or inverted form at a quaver's distance between the two hands, interpolates the semitone missing from its initial tone move before plunging down a fourth (*x* in Ex. 22). And the vocal line, though it outlines a

Ex. 15.22

scheme based on C minor and related areas (i VI vi flat I flat IV V of V i——I) is within each phrase consistently introverted chromatically. The big scalic movements of its later phrases generate a heat that is only quenched after the explosion of a climax, in which the piano motive *x*, harmonically conflated, throws up great tonic pedals against which the singer can hurl his crowning denunciation:

> All are the conquered; and in vain
> The laurel binds the brow.

The move to final cadence through the contrary motion of whole-tone scales (another device which is found so literally more in later than early Britten) is subtly interwoven with augmentation of the *x* motive, so that would-be impassivity fails to conceal the experience of the song:

> The phantoms of the dead remain
> And from our faces show.

'Who Are These Children?' (No. 9) is a song which requires some awareness of the poet's stimulus (explained above) if the immediate target of its outrage is to be identified; the published score usefully reproduces as its cover the photograph which so incensed Soutar. But ultimately both poem and song reach beyond that circumstance to reiterate the central theme of the cycle in showing how man (and it may be highly cultivated man) has guarded himself with insensitivity against recognizing the part he plays as a killer. Both the hunt and the war serve to exemplify, but it is the hunt which provides the musical symbols—two horn calls that alternate and combine in the piano, Ex. 23. For once a roughly tritonal polarity seems to have no

Ex.15.23

symbolic force, and the whole complex can be regarded as an enlarged D. The vocal line, almost languorous in its depiction of the hunt party's effort-less command, tilts from D minor into whole-tone movement on F and sequentially E flat as dominant pedals, but at the word 'whips' the music cracks back into the original orbit with motive *a* jostling brashly against itself. Enharmonically revalued, it is transformed to begin the gentle oscilla-tions around the dominant of E minor above which floats the line 'Is there a day more calm . . .', another flashback to early Britten. But merely by twisting the revolving bass from B-F sharp to B flat-F natural, the scene is set askew, its 'alien' quality disturbingly suggested rather than bitterly denounced; and the horn calls, fading, are further transformed to a soft reverberating question. Just as we notice in the photograph the boy with the bicycle, observing his betters with studied blankness, only after we have taken in the hunt and the bomb damage, so the last stanza emerges from Britten's setting only when the hunt seems to have passed by. The literal horn calls return but now sound on automatically as in the memory while the free alignment between piano and voice once again suggests a state of reverie. By the contrast between this musical 'dissolve' and the sharply edged word-setting, Britten drives home Soutar's crucial lines:

> Who are these children gathered here
> Out of the fire and smoke
> That with remembering faces stare
> Upon the foxing folk?

What Soutar called 'Bairn-Rhymes', a 'Bairn's Song' ('The Auld Aik') and riddles make up the eight Scots poems. The poet's pleasure in writing verse that would appeal to children must have been another bond with him Britten discovered. But Soutar's awareness of children's vulnerability and his passionate concern for their well-being in a world ordered by their guilty elders are qualities that had already stirred Britten to a range of expression embracing *The Little Sweep*, *The Turn of the Screw* and, most recently, *Children's Crusade*. After a significant single line in 'Nightmare' ('The branches flowered with children's eyes'), the theme comes to the forefront in the last stanza we have just considered of the title-song, and its brooding treatment in 'The Children' (no. 11) is matched by Britten in a song that faces unremitting tragedy with intense yet never indulgent melancholy. The monumentally calm sadness of 'The Auld Aik' seems to be won out of this bitterest experience of the whole cycle. The opening figure, of two minor thirds connected by a passing figure of another minor third (Ex. 24a) is the

Ex.15.24 (a)

Ex.15.24 (b)

idée fixe but its lack of a single harmonic meaning leaves it inert, acquiring specific emotional force only according to the context in which it is placed. In the first stanza the bass E pulls it into a dominant (minor ninth) situation, but this too is immobilized, the bass E flats failing to acquire more than auxiliary function, and the elaborate fanwise upper harmony of the 6/8 section arriving back at the same harmonic situation – as it must, for Britten consistently makes these third lines elaborate the contours of the second, quickening the pace to 6/8 for Soutar's expansion of the metre (and of the sense). The second stanza repeats the pattern of the first but treats the *idée fixe* as a minor ninth on a dominant G; high tenor G is also established as a peak of the vocal line (bright afternoon) to acquire a luminous quality in repetition especially in the fifth stanza, but to be exceeded only in one climactic phrase. In the third stanza, the motive is conflated in a tremolando and the earlier dominants have been replaced by tonics in a modulating bass A/C, yet still there is little sense of movement, except in the restlessly straining intervals of the voice. It is in the fourth stanza that, with dramatic urgency, movement is released in every dimension of the texture: the motive is multiplied to involve all three diminished sevenths (and thus all twelve pitches) in close relationships (see Ex. 24b) and these are progressively arpeggiated, the bass traces an eleven-note curve (excluding the A which appears to be its original destination, and instead preparing C by its dominant), and the dynamic level, till now almost entirely pianissimo, rises steeply to fortissimo. The words treated in this way emerge powerfully:

> A wound which everywhere
> Corrupts the hearts of men:

but the third line, fading as quickly and dropping in tessitura by an octave to end on a low B, is still more indelibly impressed on the listener:

> The blood of children corrupts the hearts of men.

Now the motive is restored to its original slow form but at a new pitch (up an eleventh) and, with a secure underpinning of bass C's, this serene texture accompanies a melodic form of the motive, setting out always from that luminous tenor G as the silent, ordered movement of the stars is imagined. From the end of this stanza the minor thirds proliferate in a new and greater fanwise movement of harmony, supporting the voice on its slow rise to an A flat that initiates the one melisma in the whole cycle:

> But from earth the children stare
> With blind and fearful *faces*.

Again a powerful climax (now principally the singer's) is emotionally assimilated by a quiet repetition at the octave below, 'And our charity is in the

The Music of Benjamin Britten

children's faces'; the motive has returned to its original blank form and the bass that starts on a dominant G wanders down to the alternative E, where it began.

I do not claim to know what symbolic significance the composer attached to these two tonal readings of his motive but this does not prevent an aural recognition that the song operates between these poles, and is thus one more example of the most common form of Britten's tonal thinking. If only for this song the Soutar cycle could not be written off as a peripheral work, but I hope to have shown that all the four English settings reflect a highly imaginative response, while the little Scots songs include some delightfully wrought miniatures.

A BIRTHDAY HANSEL, OP. 92

Britten's last song-cycle, *A Birthday Hansel*, Op. 92, sets verses by another Scottish poet, Robert Burns. Not surprisingly it reflects far more evidently than do even the most idiomatic of the Soutar settings an openness to suggestion from native song, though with scarcely a hint of the genial satire that was turned on such material in the *Scottish Ballad*. The cycle is for tenor with harp, partly no doubt because, as with the fifth canticle, the composer wished to provide a repertoire for Pears's new partnership with Osian Ellis, but still more obviously because the world of Scottish minstrelsy, whether ancient or recreated, appears to be dominated by that instrument. It was composed as an offering to the Queen Mother (for her 75th birthday), and completed in March 1975.

Just as Britten showed elsewhere, for example in the songs of *A Midsummer-Night's Dream*, a complete lack of inhibition in giving music to words already associated with other settings, he does not hesitate to include Burns poems like 'Afton Water' and 'The winter it is past' which many listeners will have thought inseparable from their familiar music; nor does he fail to bring to them a fresh response. No one of his settings consistently suggests any particular model, melodic or rhythmic, in Scots song, yet each owes much of its flavour to echoes, clear or faint. Pentatonicism and drones co-exist with bitonality, square-cut initial phrases are progressively modified, and so on, creating effects which avoid the crude extremes of pastiche and wilful distortion. The result is a cycle that treats its poetic material with affection, but, as befits a birthday gift, does not attempt to point morals or encourage profound reflection. Thus, although its verse is that of a single poet, there is little sense of that cumulative illumination of his creative character which distinguished Britten's cycles on Donne, Hardy, Blake or Hölderlin. Perhaps the *Charm of Lullabies* (which included a Scots setting) comes nearest to a precedent for this delightful but undemanding set of songs. In one literal respect, however, it is more obviously a cycle than were most of its predecessors: the songs are performed without a break, the harper (surely a more appropriate term here than our modern 'harpist')

392

making transitions between them which, in an improvisatory manner, exchange one mood for the next.

The opening is in itself a 'Birthday Song', to a highland chief. A proud march punctuates the singer's tribute without curbing its declamatory fervour. His opening lines show one of the ways in which Britten inflects shapes that declare pentatonic origins. The inflected pitches have a further significance in that they belong to the second tonal level, of C, maintained in parallel with B throughout the song. This typical tonal device might appear as no more than a recurrent Neapolitan sixth deviation, but for some typical refinements. The harp never sounds the D sharp that would enrich into a B major triad its rhetorical strummings, but its march strains are initiated by complete C major sixth chords and develop at the end of both halves of the song into quotations from the reel, 'Mrs McLeod' which substantiate C major; the voice, on the other hand, emphasizes the missing D sharp but in its C ventures always avoids the major third, E. Since this D sharp often provides a contradictory minor third to the harp's C major triads a delicately equivocal situation is produced; it is sustained in the reflective penultimate section (after the De'il's expulsion) by a new scalic collection that can be related equally obliquely to either field, and in a climactic harp descent in sixth chords outlining a succession of pentatonic groups from C to cadence in B. Obviously enough 'Mrs McLeod' was the stimulus to this song, but it has been assimilated into a subtler organism.

The second song, 'My early walk', includes the directions 'casual' and 'meandering', which admirably fit its apparently unpremeditated tonal excursions. Here the poise achieved is between two kinds of material, as in the contrast between the first three lines and the last line of the first stanza: the one, reminiscent in its uniform repeated notes of Britten's own early style (cf. e.g., the opening of Canticle I), acquires a Scots accent from the rhythmic variants introduced during its progressive development, the other, lavishly graced, suggests the elegant Scottish songs familiar to the late eighteenth-century salon; the accompaniments are scarcely less disparate. The second element, having been played down in the third and fourth stanzas, takes over the whole of the last, establishing the D major at best only implicit elsewhere—a simple symbol of the rose's full bloom. 'Wee Willie Grey' is aptly a miniature, both halves of its musical strophe, nicely contrasted in registers as well as figurations, turning nimbly on the same G major–E minor point. In 'My Hoggie' progressive variation of a model strophe reaches its peak in the fourth stanza: opening with the relaxed sound of the major with sharp fourth and flat seventh and an expanded phrase, it suddenly reverts to the model, but at a strained higher pitch for the catastrophe, from which doleful repetitions of the last line fall to the close. Of the two reminders here of the variable opening mode, the major third intensifies the poignancy (as in Schubert) even more than the flat second. The harp postlude recalls the owl's eerie cry of the third stanza, but the anxious dominant pedal is now balanced by a hopelessly final tonic one.

As such contexts confirm, the harp has been used so far with as much textural fluidity as a piano in response to poetic promptings, but its most stereotyped accompanying device has scarcely been called on. In 'Afton Water' Britten suddenly releases a torrent of those warm, liquid arpeggios we associate with the harp writing of *Grimes* or, still more, of *Lucretia*. The song's squareness of phrase is offset by continual invention in the reworking of the basic melodic shape, unforcedly accommodating a host of transitory images; the modified *da capo* of the last verse achieves its gentle finality merely by enlarging the phrase to escape from compound grouping at two points.

'The Winter' is perhaps the most memorable song in the cycle, for its melodic patterns are few but distinctive, and their deployment of simple harmonies is elusive. What begins as a swift and orderly tonal movement, from Lydian A flat to B flat at the stanza mid-point, is then becalmed in this area (major then minor), before it is finally pulled down by the bass to A natural (see the outline at Ex. 25). The evident analogy to the text here is

Ex.15.25

intensified in the second stanza, where the gain of a tone from the new key, A, to B is immediately lost (the second A major thus has a peculiarly pathetic impotence), and the pull of the last line is down to G sharp (i.e., A flat). The last song, 'Leezie Lindsay' is a reel, and it applies the principle, so fundamental to Scottish folk dance, of phrase transposition up one degree and back, to drone bass and melody, but then, influenced by the harp's inflexions of the major to the minor third, a sudden tonal shift rounds off the D major verse with a cadence phrase in F; the same process is applied to the two subdominant episodes. Returning to D, harp and voice embroider the basic eight-bar idea frenetically before the energy winds down for a final epigrammatic juxtaposition of D, E and F natural. Neatly organized as it is (and often almost stealthily soft), this song gives more than a hint of the untamed abandon which has kept true Scottish music so alien to the mainstream of the cultivated European tradition. In his last songs, Britten directed nearer home that susceptibility to foreign influences which had distinguished a long line of his settings beginning with the Rimbaud cycle.

394

PHAEDRA, OP. 93

All Britten's earlier works for solo voice and orchestra belong, like those of Mahler, to the genre of song cycle, however pervasively a unified theme (as in the Serenade and Nocturne), or the character of a single poet's language (*Les Illuminations*), or both (*Our Hunting Fathers*), may draw from diverse texts a single complex experience. In *Phaedra*, composed in the summer of 1975 for Dame Janet Baker and first performed by her at the following year's Aldeburgh Festival, Britten wrote his only solo cantata. His declared debt to the Baroque type extends to the use of harpsichord and cello for the recitative interpolations; the orchestra for the arioso-cum-aria sections is of strings, timpani and percussion. In its alternations between these two types the Baroque solo cantata was comparable to an operatic *scena*, the stage (so to speak) being dominated by a single character but the dramatic action and its emotional consequences continuing to be developed. Writing in the years after *Death in Venice*, when it was clear that an operatic scale of creative activity was denied him, Britten compressed into the modest span of this cantata almost a sequence of event proper to an opera. Yet because the plot begins as retrospective narrative, once it moves into the present the inevitable catastrophe cannot be far away, and so the time-scale never appears congested. Nor in such an interior conflict between passion and remorse does the absence of other characters (in vocal terms: orchestrally they are graphically present) strain verisimilitude.

Janet Baker had created the part of Kate in *Owen Wingrave*, a troubled character whose proud, edgy behaviour masks until too late the depth of her affections. The strain of immature petulance did not seem entirely appropriate to the warmth and authority of the voice; a tragic figure far better matched to that was Lucretia, and Janet Baker had interpreted this rôle with great distinction. So in conceiving a work in tribute to her artistry, Britten's thoughts turned not unnaturally towards another classical heroine, Phaedra. Her dying words, in the verse translation of Racine's *Phèdre* by Robert Lowell, from which Britten drew his text, would not seem misplaced were they given to the dying Lucretia: 'My eyes at last give up their light, and see the day they've soiled resume its purity'. But whereas Obey's and Duncan's Lucretia is obsessed by a stain to whose blackness she may or may not have contributed (the point was discussed at some length in Chapter 6), Racine's Phaedra is in no such romantic predicament: though she sees herself a victim of Aphrodite, in the drama of her sin she was the conscious and only protagonist. Whereas Lucretia celebrated her death in the purple sonorities of her aria with obbligato cor anglais, and was mourned in the long reverberations of the passacaglia ensemble, Phaedra's death is accomplished in a single mounting paragraph, and only a series of spectral fragments in the orchestra review her story. This exchange of a rich, sombre eloquence for a dry-eyed laconism matches very exactly the change Britten's musical personality underwent in the thirty years between *The Rape of Lucretia*, an

395

opera memorable for some of his most generously beautiful music, and *Phaedra*. The cantata does not lack musical symbols as apt and arresting as those of the opera, but they are never expanded into lyrical effusion for its own sake. The restriction to a single singer and the lack of seductive tone colours (wind and harp sounds dominate one's memories of *Lucretia*) already determine much of the work's character, but its musical working-out greatly intensifies the ascetic note. This study of 'passion and the abyss' is indeed perceptibly terser than *Death in Venice*, for its focal point has been moved, to dwell with an awareness totally untouched by self-pity on the inevitable sequel, death.

As in *Lucretia*, key associations and motives complement each other, playing a cardinal role which is structural and dramatic. But while the opera provided one of the simplest examples in Britten of melodic shapes used more or less as character labels, the cantata demonstrates the practice, typical of his last period, of drawing from a cell of intervals, or a regulating intervallic principle, diverse melodic and harmonic characteristics in the whole work. Thus, while we can establish easily enough from the other contexts in which it appears that the graciously inclining string theme of the opening (Ex. 26) relates to Theseus, it soon becomes clear that two of its

Ex.15.26

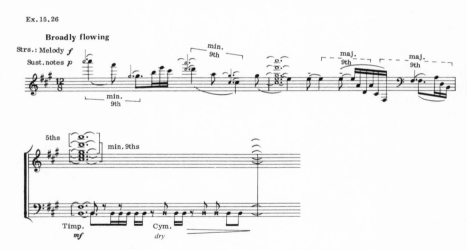

prominent intervallic classes, the perfect fifth and the minor ninth, are no less active in quite contrasted thematic material. The key colour of A (the entire major mode is heard in the sustained chord, luminous yet given by its 'supertonic' placing a hint of tension that the percussion's rhythms intensify), on the other hand, is specific to Theseus. The key is capable of implying a reference to him athematically, as at the turn to A major-minor from E major-minor three bars before fig. 19, which palpably underlines 'I go to meet my husband' even before the Ex. 26 theme appears in inversion (the relevance of a co-existing V-I of C in the cello becomes clearer only later). The later succession of references to Ex. 26 is dramatically self-explanatory, from its transformation to a flurry of semiquavers, agitated yet still in command, at fig. 23, when Theseus arrives to hear the confession of his dying wife—one of two string textures in this work oddly reminiscent in sound, not shape, of Tippett's *King Priam*. Theseus' reactions punctuate Phaedra's speech, but at the climax before fig. 26 the grand modification of his theme in which C and G of the Ex. 26 chord are naturalized, is rather her tribute to a nobility of spirit she must acknowledge even though she has betrayed it. Reduced to a solo string line, the Theseus theme fittingly leads off the recall of themes that ends the work in a numbed undertone.

Less immediately comprehensible may be the ostinato form of the theme which appears in the right hand of the harpsichord when Phaedra tells of her attempt to appease Aphrodite (last bar of Ex. 27). The significance becomes clearer if one hears this A major in relief against the D sharp (alias E flat) territory of the left hand and cello. The crucial bars in which E flat emerges as potentially important are just before this (see Ex. 27), and the suggestion that this opposite pole to A symbolizes the fatal powers of Aphrodite can be substantiated throughout the rest of the cantata; here we witness Phaedra's determination to cherish a legitimate love. But the goddess's agent in the

Ex. 15.27

destruction of Phaedra is Hippolytus, her husband's son, and the D minor concealing E flat meanings which represents the mad infatuation he inspires in her is already implicit in the superimposed cadences attending 'executioner'. The perfect cadence in C that follows foreshadows several contexts (two have been noted already) in which that progression and tonal field symbolize Phaedra's tragic fate; even the arpeggiated thirteenth chord is to reappear just before her last words, while the momentous G pedal to which she sings that line which will haunt the rest of the work, 'Death to the unhappy's no catastrophe' (see Ex. 28 below), is answered by the still more momentous low C on which the entire coda is supported.

If these readings of key significance are accepted (and that such a scheme should have come to Britten's mind after reflecting on his own *Lucretia* would not be surprising), then the rest of the work is seen tonally to fall quite logically into place. The music of Phaedra's infatuation, 'fast and impulsive', is orchestrally so angular and scrawny as to appear tonally elusive, but its rapid juxtapositions and superimpositions of D minor and E flat major/ minor are confirmed by the voice part's fretful arched phrases, traversing the two fields. The oblique D major music to which this gives way (fig. 8) is richly compounded in its references: it portrays a Hippolytus not just the cause of Phaedra's frenzy, but his father's son, as witness the airy string harmonic chords of interleaved fifths with A at their peak, the minor ninths against the bass, even the rhythm, all related to Ex. 26. This image of a graceful prince is tarnished only by Phaedra herself, in her dragging the minor ninth to the melodic surface and in her obsessively wrenching the melody on to an E flat plane. Two points concerning key may be added that take us beyond the context of this work. Phaedra's lines on death, already quoted, are set to a slow rising scale ending with a whole-tone phrase (see Ex. 28), and the B sharp peak of this certainly throws into prominence the pitch round which turn her dying speech and its impressive orchestral accompaniment of layered scales (a dark, thick sound which is the other texture reminiscent of Tippett). Yet the scale itself is unambiguously of E major, and one is tempted to question whether, as so movingly in the third quartet, Britten consciously made an association here with the last of his tormented operatic

Ex. 15.28

heroes, Aschenbach. And the C major itself towards which Phaedra's own music aspires was not only the key of Lucretia's chastity but also of the state of blessedness of the opera's epilogue, in which the sin is not erased but transcended. Britten's choice of the same key may suggest that Phaedra, however 'responsible' her defection, was a helpless victim of Aphrodite's will; if her death throws no such beatific afterglow as did Lucretia's, the adagio of her last speech seems to carry at least a promise of apotheosis.

It would be tedious to trace every appearance of the intervals noted already as fundamental to the aural unity of this cantata. The minor ninth in particular is used with great subtlety so that the degree of dissonance experienced varies constantly. A simple example is the contrast between the sustained chord of Ex. 26 and the second chord in bar 2 of Ex. 27; the major/minor chords of Phaedra's second recitative give another kind of significance to the same interval. While the string adagios amass dense blocks of low sound from mainly scalic movements, the phrase thrown into relief at the triadic end of each block (i.e., derivations from bar 4 of Ex. 28) always includes at least one minor ninth tension against the triad; by doubling the phrase in major sixths the effect is softened to that of bitter-sweet false relations in the first adagio, but in the second Phaedra's solo phrases strike far more acutely. The contraction of the music to this second adagio after her salute to Theseus, when she tells him of the means by which she has resolved to die, is one of the most chilling moments in the cantata (from fig. 26), and its material proves to be entirely congruous. Setting out from the modified Theseus chord (i.e., Ex. 26 with C and G naturalized), its perfect fifths continue the slow scalic movement of Phaedra's music in contrary motion, to arrive at a chord in which the ninth tensions are emphasized rather than balanced out.

The cantata is composed with all the control of interrelated detail that had distinguished Britten's work before his illness. Its effect in performance is curiously disconsolate, partly because of the shadows into which the music seems finally to retreat. Both the Theseus music and Phaedra's dying music remain strongly in the memory, and if the distraught music of her passion ('My mind whirls') is perhaps less sharp in profile, its rôle in the dramatic scheme is apt, while musically it provides the only fast propulsion in the work. The sections which strike home least certainly are, I find, the recitatives even though, as has been noted, they contain dramatically telling phrases and accompaniment details. But the sound of harpsichord and cello, while entirely adequate for carrying the simple harmonic implications to complement a Baroque line, is altogether too tenuous to discharge adequately all that Britten entrusts to it here. Not only do melodic movements tend to sound miserably disembodied, but astringent harmonies that, marked perhaps *ff* in the score (see Ex. 27), look to have clinching force, emerge as puny side by side with the powerful sonority of massed strings, the weight of timpani and percussion. Britten's reasons for reinstating the 'continuo' resources are evident enough, but it could be argued that his expressive purposes would be better served if, as in some of his operas (including, of course, *Lucretia*), the piano were to assume the rôle.

16 The Five Canticles

Apart from the few early songs without opus number that have been published, most of Britten's activity as a song writer was channelled into the
composition of the cycles discussed above. Though these are never of the
linked narrative type familiar in Schubert and Schumann, we have seen that
they may approach a single subject from a variety of angles suggested by an
anthology of different poets' works (the Serenade, *A Charm of Lullabies*
and the Nocturne could even be regarded as pursuing aspects of one subject
through three works) or they may consider many subjects through the words
of a single poet. The second may remind us of the concentrated attention
Wolf habitually gave to a particular poet, but Britten never sustained this on
a remotely Wolfian scale, and he preferred to arrange his songs in a fixed
order, yielding a cumulative experience. Within these groups individual
songs rarely provide a developing (as opposed to intensifying) experience:
the kind of structure that supports fundamentally strophic vocal patterns on
an accompaniment of ostinato-like consistency, recurring from the
Michelangelo to the Soutar cycles, has been justified by innumerable
memorable songs, none of which, however, can yield its full effect when
performed out of context. That this is so evidently the case ought to have
silenced years ago those critics who see in Britten's work only a flair for the
'characteristic' touch. If they were right, then a song like (shall we say)
'Midnight on the Great Western' might be expected to retain its highly
distinctive character with no loss of power, divorced from the other Hardy
settings; the multiple reverberations created by its context are a product of
an act of long-term musical judgment, albeit not of long-term deployment of
material.

From time to time, however, Britten chose to set poems that, because of
their length and the scope and spaciously developing presentation of their
subject, demanded to be treated as entities: now the cycle of experience is
within, not across, a span. The description he applied to all five of his
extended settings, 'canticle', might be thought simply to recognize that all
treat of religious subjects (though among their diverse texts, ranging from
miracle play to Sitwell and Eliot, is nothing that resembles the liturgical

canticles Britten incorporated so convincingly into two of the church operas, and only the first owes its inspiration to the Song of Solomon). But many of the composer's other religious songs are evidently not canticles in the sense he gave to the term; a mood of spiritual elevation intense enough to demand realization in an ambitious musical structure seems to be the essential prerequisite.

The five canticles date from 1947, 1952, 1954, 1971 and 1974. In a perceptive analytical study of the first three,[1] written in 1960, David Brown used them to chart aspects of the composer's development; his claim, that they reveal 'mounting achievement' has been substantiated by listening experience now spread over some two decades. For although the eventful creative period covered by the three canticles was no more than seven years, no addition to the group appeared for seventeen years. The gap is therefore far too great for us to be able to use the five works as a comprehensive index in matters of style or method; in particular, the whole area of Britten's activity in which the liberation of textural strata from rigid temporal alignment is essayed would be quite unrepresented. Even so, in reviving the term 'canticle' the composer openly invited comparison across the gap. Perhaps he also acknowledged a backward glance at his earlier achievements, one that seems to have told on other works of the same period—some of the Soutar songs and parts of *Owen Wingrave*, for example.

Canticle I, Op. 40, was written for the Dick Shepherd Memorial Concert on 1 November 1947. It derives ultimately from the Book of Canticles, Solomon's Song, in that Francis Quarles's rapturous poem is a meditation around his paraphrase of the biblical line: 'My beloved is mine, and I am his'. Strophic musical structure would have appeared to be the obvious treatment for a poem of which the regular stanzas are further unified by the recurrent use of a final line based on this quotation. On the other hand, Quarles's long series of images and antitheses could easily have staled in uniform musical surroundings, while the oblique approaches to the subject of the third and fourth stanzas would have lost much of their impact. Britten therefore decided to cast it as a miniature cantata:

STANZA	1 + 2	3	4	5 + 6
	in binary relationship Barcarolle (flowing andante)	Recitative (fast verbal rhythms slow harmonic movement)	Canonic Scherzo (presto)	in modified binary relationship (lento)
	g–D; G♭–E♭–g	modulating	d(–b♭)D	B♭–G

D. Brown, 'Britten's three Canticles', *Music Review* xxi, 1960, p. 55.

The drawing together of two stanzas to begin and again to end the work provides two substantial pillars, the major modes of the second palpably stemming from the G minor of the first. If the structural ordering is essentially symmetrical, the textural is essentially alternating. The first movement is contrapuntal with an interpolation of harmonic blocks shortly before the end, the last movement chordal with a contrapuntal interpolation at the parallel point; in between the recitative is accompanied by decorated harmony while the scherzo is almost entirely in three-part counterpoint.

Considered without reference to the text, this is a neatly executed design. There is some justice in David Brown's suggestion[2] that its diversity of musical character has been imposed upon the poem, yet it is difficult to imagine a more rewarding approach to the task. For if Britten avoids monotony by this sectional treatment, he also avoids the opposite pitfall of too immediate, and therefore heterogeneous, a technique of illustration. The opening stanza shows how a musical image may be valid far beyond the words that provoked it: the nonchalant two-part writing of the piano, each strand pursuing its own course in modal-cum-tonal independence, is an obvious symbol of 'two little bank-divided brooks' but it is maintained throughout this stanza and into the next. Following the words 'after long pursuit', the upper strand literally pursues the lower in a triplet-against-duplet descent, and inevitably catches up at 'we joined', from which point a single flowing line is carried along by the voice, supported now by a spacious harmonic piano texture. But this graphic imagery is not allowed to disrupt the balance of the movement, for Britten turns to his purposes a later line 'Our firm united souls did more than twine' and, anticipating this with a twining of vocal and right-hand piano strands, is able very naturally to restore the original textural disposition to round off the structure. In its postlude the triplets are recalled, to provide an accompanying pattern for the following recitative; again they conflict with duplets and set up bitonal relationships, so that strong links with the first movement help to strengthen what is a rather conventional piece of early Britten declamation.

The scherzo material is more subtly linked to earlier ideas. In the refrain of both the *alla barcarola* stanzas the central text 'So I my best beloved's am, so he is mine!' was illuminated by a phrase in which a falling sixth was complemented by a rising one (see Ex. 1a; there is of course, another sixth, in mid-phrase, but this merely reinforces the first whereas the last sixth obviously symbolizes the verbal antithesis); and minor interval was complemented by major in both the original and inverted forms. Now the scherzo sets off with a subject and its canonic inversion, in which the sixths are similarly complementary; see Ex. 1b. The whole scherzo, in developing this subject with nervous excitement, celebrates the central text, which finally has its words restored at the jubilant climax, marked by the major

---

[2] Ibid.

Ex.16.1 (a) i

So   I   my   best   be - lov - ed's   am,   So   he   is   mine!

Ex.16.1 (a) ii

So   I   my   best be - lov - ed's   am,   So   he   is   mine!

Ex.16.1 (b)

mode and emphatic augmentations. Yet there remain two stanzas before this D major's dominant function can be realized in a G major close. The sense of an outcome deferred is therefore strong at the opening of the lento where a turn is made to the other closely related area, B flat major (so far not used structurally at all); the halting Lombard rhythms, the divergence of piano and vocal harmonic designs and the voice's succession of phrases that begin identically reinforce this sense. But at the thinner texture that opens the final stanza a more fluid line is drawn, and as the pedal F is relinquished, the move begins that leads to G major, and the wonderfully liberated vocal shape, straight and inverted, of the last refrain. With the tonal outcome achieved, the piano's rhythms are no longer tense but send out slow ripples from tonic to dominant and back.

The second canticle, *Abraham and Isaac*, Op. 51, was written and first performed in January 1952; to the tenor and piano which are the constant elements in the first four canticles is added here an alto. This makes possible the vocal characterization of the father (tenor) and son (alto), but also a representation of the voice of God, which acquires a supernatural aura from the use of both voices indissolubly linked in the delivery of speech rhythm at close intervals. Britten's text is from the Chester Miracle Play, and he sets it as a dramatic scene, alternating between recitative, arioso and set piece in response to the implied action. The structure that results is therefore more evidently apt than was the 'cantata' treatment of the Quarles poem, but its many short sections could have prompted a heterogeneity that reduced music's rôle to that of a glib attendant upon, rather than the principal agent

404

of, the drama. It was no doubt to avoid this snare that Britten drew so much of his material from a restricted store of melodic shapes; this ensures a musical unity palpable even before we observe how consistently certain shapes are given symbolic meaning. David Brown's labelling of three such basic motives, as representative of 'summons', 'sacrifice' and 'will' may suggest a Wagnerian fixity of meaning that is nowhere paralleled in Britten's operas (perhaps *Lucretia* and *Death in Venice* most nearly approach it), but their recurrences are fluidly modified and, over this small span, never become importunate. Indeed, what Brown calls the 'summons' motive, the opening words of God (Ex. 2a) is no more than the cell of notes from which are formed the derivatives he lists.

Almost as awe-inspiring as the voice of God is the piano figure that punctuates his words. Such a fifthless arpeggio had played a strikingly similar

Ex.16.2 (a)

Ex.16.2 (b)

Ex.16.2 (c)

Ex.16.2 (d)

405

part at the opening of the first quartet; the comparison can be extended to the close diatonic dissonances of the upper strings, their recitative-like yet synchronized rhythms, and the expansion and contraction into *da capo* of the whole *Tempo primo* paragraph. It would be surprising if broad parallels of this kind did not appear in a composer's work, but the origin of this sonorous idea in an instrumental piece offers an instructive reminder that Britten's most characteristic *trouvailles* have not always depended on textual stimulus. More blatantly even than in Canticle I, Britten draws on the dominant seventh, in his first statement of the 'sacrifice' motive, three ascending thirds and a step down (see Ex. 2b). After this central V on the piano's I pedal, the 'will' motive (Ex. 2c) cadences by arranging thirds and steps in a new pattern, and closes off as an E flat prologue God's command. Action begins with the rapid growth of the Ex. 2b shape in the piano, sharp fourth and flat seventh providing the stock Britten enrichment of, and then escape from, the mode. In a few bars of recitative, Abraham's resolve to obey passes to A major, the opposite pole, so that *his* cadential Ex. 2c ('Thy bidding done shall be') is tensely contrasted to the immanent certainty of the prototype. The following scene between Abraham and Isaac is all conducted at the new tonal level, and is further shadowed by a piano part that ruminates on Ex. 2a in the right hand and connects Ex. 2b to a dry *idée fixe* in the left hand. Yet its vocal exchanges, father and son always in complementary areas of the octave, are blandly lilting as they set out to 'do a little thing'; the folky tone even extends to sequences reminiscent of 'Greensleeves' ('to do your bidding most meekily . . .'). The same artless melody intrudes touchingly upon the next section, the recitative in which Abraham reveals God's command to his son, but its dominating shape is Ex. 2d, heavy fourths departing markedly from the God-given motives' thirds in token of a human response nowhere foreshadowed in the prologue: a rapidly plunging succession of minor triads underlines the breakdown of Abraham's simulated composure.

The 'sacrifice' motive in the piano finally prompts him to say what he must, and it is converted into an urgent accompaniment figure for the set piece, a duet that, no matter what tonal deviations are attempted, plummets back to an inevitable D minor. The impression of strophic structure is strong when Abraham repeats Isaac's opening to initiate the duet texture, but Britten's symmetries are not based upon the simple 4. 4. 4. 3 feet of the text; yet he profits from the urgency of that foreshortened line in depicting the boy's agitation. In contrast, Abraham's long notes spell out a resolve on which his son's pleading must founder. The music passes back to recitative as Isaac seeks his father's blessing, and key changes freely again, between warm major chords of the added-sixth. The elevated tone of this scene may call to mind a still simpler chord succession, that of the scene in which Vere and Billy strengthened each other before the sacrifice; with this canticle so close in time to *Billy Budd* we cannot suppose the links between the two subjects to have escaped the composer. Even the compliant V-I movements of the bass in Isaac's 'Father, do with me as you will' could be compared with those of Billy's lyricism at 'Ay, all is up, and I must up too'. But of course, this little piece must carry a still greater emotional weight in the scheme of the canticle than did Billy's musings (to be succeeded by the apotheosis of 'And farewell to ye, old *Rights of Man*'). Its transparently simple plan of two strophes and a coda scarcely promises the strength of the impression left by its superb variation of phrase-length and by the transfer of the V-I pendulum to new levels in the second stanza, the climactic modulation (to A major at 'I come no more') thus realizing in full an expressive deflection hinted at in the first stanza.

This farewell unforcedly echoes the cadencing shape of Ex. 2c, but unsophisticated melody now gives way to vocal monotone, reiterating tremulously the pedal C sharp which, in the extreme bass of the piano, counts away the moments of Abraham's final preparations for the sacrifice. Having been the tonic of the farewell, this C sharp now sounds obliquely (often as a leading note) against the piano's vast build-up of the sacrifice theme. Yet at its peak the cadence theme (Ex. 2c) interposes a deflection to E flat, and the pedal C sharp explodes in conflict with that note. From this dramatic arresting of the sacrifice, E flat alone emerges serenely, to throw up its shaft of gentle light (Ex. 2a arpeggio) as God speaks once more (cf. Ex. 2a—but the (b) theme is beautifully modified). In an extraordinarily rapid return to earthly practicalities, the magical Ex. 2a is converted into a crisp accompaniment motive, as Abraham rushes to complete the amended prog-ramme. This necessitates a brief trip through various tonal areas but an amalgam of Ex. 2b and c in the piano, announcing the sacrifice of the lamb, carries the music to a pregnant dominant seventh of E flat, in which key the moralizing final section (*Envoi*) sets out. It is a modification of the earlier section in A major (Abraham and Isaac's journey), but without the ominous attendant piano details; instead there is a gentle peal of bells that inevitably casts the mind forward to the moment of deliverance in Britten's other Miracle Play setting, *Noyes Fludde*. The two voices, no longer of characters within the drama, move in loose canon, the repetitions of their coda broadening to a hymnic last strain (a curious further reminder of *Noyes Fludde* in its echo of Tallis's Canon) and a distant radiance from the divine image of the Ex. 2a arpeggio. Thus, with sonata-like precision, the themes of God and man, originally divided by the greatest void (E flat–A), have been reconciled after the central dramatic action.

Undoubtedly the second canticle remained strongly in the composer's mind when he forged a comparable duality as a representation of the divine voice that signals the 'Dawn' at the end of the third canticle. And the drawing together in that final page of two elements which have been struc-turally disparate throughout the work may be viewed as an intensification of the second canticle's process of 'reconciliation'. But in most other respects

Still falls the rain, Op. 55, stands in the sharpest contrast to its predecessor. It was written towards the end of 1954 for performance at a concert in memory of the pianist, Noel Mewton-Wood. Britten departed from his usual practice in choosing to set verses by a living poet. Although the poem from Edith Sitwell's 'The Canticle of the Rose' bears the sub-heading 'The Raids 1940. Night and Dawn', its imagery belongs to the Passion scene, and its searing tone rises to an ecstatic climax with a quotation from Marlowe. Britten, as familiar with the religious exaltation of Donne and Quarles as with the convoluted imagery of Purcell's sacred songs, was well equipped to set this richly suggestive text. Yet his musical design can be described in 'absolute' terms almost throughout, and only at one point (the reference to Dives and Lazarus) does the treatment have recourse to patent archaism. A series of declamatory recitatives is unified by a refrain ('Still falls the rain'), while the piano's accompanying commentaries always echo the preceding interlude. These interludes are developing variations for horn and piano on the theme presented at the outset. Its arched paragraph is made up of statements and inversions of a single figure that rises by whole-tone steps before falling a perfect fourth (see Ex. 3). The way in which line 3 expands from development into denouement is masterly.

Ex.16.3

THEME

Not only the lowest note, which frames the horn theme, but the highest note too marks out B flat as its chief tonal reference. E natural, however, is almost as prominent, while the piano chords, of clangorous seconds and perfect fourths, set out from a G flat centre and cadence there too, albeit as an interruption. But a short recapitulatory postlude deflects to B flat, and this is reproduced fairly literally at the end of almost every variation, so that each verse is prepared for (and most of them are dominated) by the final B flat open-fifth chord of this passage. With *The Turn of the Screw* completed just before this canticle was written, it is not surprising that commentators have looked for a further appropriation of twelve-note serial principle in its theme. Though schematic, as Ex. 3 shows, it is by no means as evidently so as the *Screw* theme, while its cadential implications are less numerous and less direct. The horn's melody eventually draws on all twelve pitches but the more obvious twelve-note usages are in the harmony's juxtapositions of a complete diatonic major field with those pitches of its tritonal opposite needed to exhaust the chromatic total: the sequence is D flat all 7 pitches + G 5; G 7 + D flat 4 (no B flat); E 7 + B flat 5; G4 (no B natural) + D flat 7.

In the starkest contrast to these densely interwoven sonorities are the crystalline B flat open fifth chords that support the first verse; the regularity of their repetition with only one inflexion up a semitone, seems to offer no hope of a sequel, and it creates a powerful symbol—of the rain, the hammerblows, the blood. Against this unchanging background the voice's Lombard rhythms and tentative melismata sound stricken. The pattern the verse forms is of the refrain phrase, spanning only the fourth C–F around the initial E flat, then a new arrangement initiated by the fourth and widening a semitone by its final disconsolate descent to B natural, this being twice repeated in modified form, and finally returning to the initial E flat. Though Brown assigns this whole paragraph to the piano's B flat, or possibly to C minor, the effect of this return phrase is powerfully cadential, and so E flat must now be viewed as another important tonal level of this work.

The process of variation applied to the horn theme is also schematic, the whole tones (and to a lesser extent the perfect fourths) of the model being alternately expanded and contracted as shown:

Var. I	Tones	→ 3rds	4ths	→ 5ths ±
Var. II	"	→ semitones	"	→ 3rds or 4ths
Var. III	"	→↓4ths	"	→ 9ths
Var. IV	"	→ unisons	"	eliminated
Var. V	"	→ 5ths	"	→ (aug.) 11ths
Var. VI	"	diatonically conjunct	"	→ 4ths/5ths diatonic

In the final variation conjunct movement and cadential perfect intervals achieve their simplest, traditional rôles within purely diatonic shapes, while horn and voice achieve complete unity of melodic style in mirrored movement. Earlier, the vocal derivatives from each preceding horn variation, though unambiguous, have been generally less pervasive than the piano's retention of its figurations. In verse II, the thirds that were quite relaxed in the smooth horn line of variation I appear only as aching diminished fourths, but the piano's six-quaver groups which, in unpredictable overlaps, provided the sole accompaniment of the variation, three times rhythmicize the open-fifth background of the verse to point up poetic references. Similarly the oscillating accompaniment of variation II articulates verse III, but here it is the horn's chromatic movement transferred to the voice that provides forlorn images, the last 'that worm with the brow of Cain', presumably the original inspiration for the musical figure. Variation III, a rapid three-part invention, is dominated by superimposed perfect fourths so that its palpable unrest remains unfocused; and in the following verse the variation figures are far less telling than is the central invocation. The B flat open fifth is dramatically abandoned for its opposite on E, and the first true harmonic movement begins, which has at its peak the first two pure major triads of the work, a climax matched by the voice's great melisma on 'mercy', sung to the G natural that is the highest sung pitch. Between variation IV and verse V relations are closer again in the retention, of both the piano tremolando and the horn's wild monotone quintuplets. A significant change of level, up a minor third for the repetition of the initial refrain, underlines the modification 'Still falls the *Blood*', but from this disconsolate verse it is the new *depth* of vocal pitch (low D) that remains in the memory. The perfect fifths of variation V, like the fourths of III, seem too objective to invite close identification with the poem, though perhaps the piano's triads suggest a series of futile leaps that extend the image of the hunt. (The use of fifths in double-dotted rhythms inevitably brings the strongest memory of the *Screw* theme, yet I cannot see that the connexion is more than fortuitous.) This is the horn's last outburst, and its final plunge of two and a half octaves, from E natural to B flat, forms an important structural cadence in the piece: thereafter the B flat open-fifth chord (here a logical product of the variation's principal feature) is to mark out the concluding paragraph of the canticle. Underpinned by reiterations of the bass G flat to B flat (deriving directly from the theme's coda) which ended variation V, the chord moves slowly up to E flat—the singer's key—during verse VI, so that by the end of that verse the B flat element appears to have been drained from the work. Indeed, the vocal line, distinguished now by wearily falling diminished octaves, has clearly prepared for the E flat minor into which the piano's figures finally coalesce; not even the *Sprechgesang* which is Britten's oddly inverted response to Edith Sitwell's interpolation of an anachronistic element (a quotation from the close of Marlowe's *Dr Faustus*) seriously contradicts this reading. Yet this is no more than the IV of a plagal cadence, made explicit with the return of the open fifth on B flat that ends the coda of variation VI and the whole work. And before that coda, the variation itself has demonstrated the two key areas held in serene equipoise—the horn's theme in a diatonic B flat (with one Mixolydian seventh) being shadowed by the voice's inversion in E flat (with two Lydian fourths); the level of the inversion ensures that B flat and E flat always complement one another, until the horn moves ahead to establish cadentially a B flat that the voice too accepts. The music under such ponderous discussion is in fact of a lucidity bordering on the transparent, yet the sense of inevitable resolution created by this music of dawning light can only be explained in terms of a key dichotomy that has persisted through the whole canticle, a work which remains among Britten's supreme imaginative feats in its adaptation of abstract compositional procedures to specifically expressive ends.

Seventeen years later Britten again employed the term 'canticle' to describe an extended setting of twentieth-century verses, this time one of the best-known of Eliot's poems, *Journey of the Magi*. Canticle IV, Op. 86, was composed during January 1971 and first performed at the Aldeburgh Festival of that year. The decision to use three singers, counter-tenor, tenor and baritone, followed obviously enough from the choice of poem, but in fact it leads at times to some prolixity when three voices have to be given an opportunity to deliver what are evidently the reminiscences of one of the Magi. In seeking to convert this necessity to more positive virtue, Britten indulges even more than is his custom in word-repetitions of an incantatory kind, often pointing them up by oscillating the notes of a stationary triad (see Ex. 4 below, bar 6). This may appear a highly questionable practice, however, when he is setting a poet who relies on a few tight-lipped repetitions for special effects. That the peculiar jugglery (to which Eliot is prone) of the following lines as they appear on paper –

And I would do it again, but set down
This set down
This:

is lost in a musical treatment, is perhaps not too important; the essential repetition is preserved easily enough. But if innumerable other words and phrases are repeated by the composer, then the force of the poet's sparing use of the device is much reduced; and in the instance of Eliot's tersest statement (one not free from a certain self-conscious laconism)—'It was (you may say) satisfactory'—it can be argued that his point is altogether abandoned when the final word of the phrase is echoed by the singers some eight times. No doubt the composer could reply that he had done no more than compose out the resonances which the word sets up in the mind. And in thus discarding one of the poetic subtleties he has fashioned a musical one, for it is this word 'satisfactory' that introduces a shape which, stated in full by the piano, is revealed as the plainsong melody, *Magi videntes stellam*, the only explicit acknowledgment of the Christian frame of reference within which words and music make their effect.

The melody and its subsequent development or distortion by the voices form the climactic episode in a rondo-like structure, of which the refrain seems to betoken the jogging, stumbling progress of the journey by camel (see Ex. 4). The piano's bass ostinato, though rhythmically variable, remains fixed in pitch, indicating obliquely the G area to which (in accordance with the key signature of G minor) the work finally aspires. But the ambiguity of this ground pattern can plainly be heard: its G flat to A flat drop can serve to support flat-key implications, as in the opening bars of Ex. 4. The alternation shown here, between minor third plus major third (the minor triad 'coming') and a chord made up of a tone plus a major third ('cold', and the piano right hand) epitomizes more than the work's equivocal tonality: its entire

Ex. 16.4

harmonic life springs from these two intervallic cells, the second in particular, whether used straight, inverted or multiplied upon itself, colouring the sound of almost every bar.

After the introductory section, all after the ritual manner of Ex. 4, a new piano figure compounded from the two chords quickens the movement, for narrative which the singers share, prompting and echoing one another freely. The most diverse pianistic imagery, of the 'silken girls bringing sherbet' and the 'camel men cursing', for example, is audibly derived from one or both of the cells, so that the literal return of Ex. 4 material appears a summary of the 'hard time' related. The next episode ('at the end we preferred to travel by night') is still closer in its relation to the refrain, for the original bass ostinato is augmented and extended, while the clusters above it conflate the two cells: though the voices' conjunct movements within the clusters prevent an unduly monotonous impression, the constriction of resources is clearly intended to be burdensome. A new tremolando accompaniment aptly symbolizes the descent to a lusher countryside, and the vocal lines relax somewhat too, yet without straying far from the field of intervallic relations already defined. At the abortive visit to the tavern, the same accompaniment takes on a lumpier form, the voices are edgier with perfect fourths prevalent and their words are distributed in a *pointilliste* manner that is rare in Britten. Only after an unusually long return of the refrain material, during which the singers' chords subside gently in pitch and volume, do we arrive at the place appointed and that measured verdict upon it.

Though the reflective episode to which this gives rise is held on the thread of the plainsong, even here the piano's percussive drone contains both a minor triad and a tone + major third + tone formation. As for the reiterated word 'satisfactory' itself, that is, of course, the simplest scalic statement of the basic intervallic resources. So there is a peculiar sense of human constraint even at the moment when the heavenly hymn (if so we may regard the rhapsodically-delivered plainsong) is pealing out. Subsequent events confirm this impression, for the scalic pattern returns to project at 'Set down This' a crisis, the piano now vehemently conflating chords of the two classes. After a pause the singers try to bring logic to bear on the disturbing experience: their understanding of the plainsong's message from 'There was a Birth, certainly' is imperfect but as ardent as their unison delivery can make it; and the chromatic distortions they introduce bring the melody down to an earth where 'bitter agony' is a familiar condition. Their closing unison line 'like Death, our death' refers back to their own experience still more directly in quoting the augmentation of the bass ostinato heard in the section 'At the end we preferred to travel by night'. Inevitably, the whole section is underlaid by the piano's reiterations of the drone that accompanied the plainsong, but now the chords, all motivic in their derivation from the two cells, wander turbulently. The return to the refrain material is facilitated by the singers' augmentation, and the entirely literal nature of this return (Ex. 4 opening, but with right-hand part now an octave lower) makes clear that the central revelation has receded. Yet it is not quite a *status quo* to which the Magi's music reverts. The homophony heard at 'So we continued', before their arrival, marks a long, darkly uneasy withdrawal from the scene (note the *descent* of the piano right hand now, countering earlier ascents). Minor triads predominate, but not until the final line 'I should be glad of another death' is the G minor that is the central implication of their coda brought back in the context and form heard in bar 6 (see Ex. 4). Though the piano postlude continues to dwell on an arpeggiated G minor triad, above its drone there floats once again the plainsong melody at its original pitch level (see Ex. 5), creating a clarifying Lydian sonority at the close. This affecting coexistence of human resignation and divine intimations is achieved by a

Ex. 16.5

typically simple piece of Britten's symbolism, but its force stems less from the mere juxtaposition than from the recognition that this outcome was implicit in all that went before; for here are added together yet again, and with a new clarity in the contrast between them, the two intervallic cells that have dominated the whole canticle.

Few listeners will find this piece as overwhelming in its immediate impact as was its predecessor of seventeen years earlier. Its revelation is far less certain, ecstasy lies beyond its grasp and its misgivings are not to be brushed aside. Britten's attempt to match Eliot's tone by intensifying the detail of his habitual craftsmanship commands our concentrated attention, even if the slight dryness of sound that results deprives the work of our affection. But the Eliot set by Britten in his last canticle is a far cry from the familiar *Journey of the Magi*; after its chilled passion, the tone of his early poem *The Death of Saint Narcissus* appears lacerating. Britten's response offers scarcely less marked a contrast, and his Canticle V, Op. 89, composed in memory of William Plomer in 1974, is among the most affecting of that handful of works written during the years of his illness.

After the more elaborate resources of the middle three canticles, the fifth reverts to one voice and one instrument. But the piano, so memorable a participant in all the other canticles in the composer's own performances, is here replaced by harp, as it was also in the *Birthday Hansel* of the following year. The harp suite of 1969 (and indeed the harp parts of the church parables before that) had shown how Britten had come to admire the artistry of Osian Ellis, and it is characteristic that, recognizing his own activity as a pianist to be at an end, he set about providing a repertoire for a new partnership, that of Pears and Ellis, who first performed the fifth Canticle in January 1975.

Britten's choice of subject both in his last opera and in most of his settings of words thereafter openly confirms a preoccupation with death that haunts the listener in so much of his late music. Of course, a facile argument could be constructed to show this as a continuing thread of his entire work, from the funeral marches and dances of death of the thirties, to the *Sinfonia da Requiem* and on to the pre-ordained victims of his operas (Grimes, Lucretia, Budd, Miles, Wingrave, Aschenbach), and the indiscriminately doomed— the soldiers of the *War Requiem* and the children of *Children's Crusade* and the penultimate Soutar song. It may be conceded that the earliest of these examples, up to the 'Dies irae' of the *Sinfonia*, express in common a sense of outrage at the macabre inanity of death. But in the main body of his work Britten's passionate concern is with all those human impulses which darken life. In the dramatic form he gives to his parables (using the term in the wider sense that is applicable from *Grimes* onwards), the logical denouement comes when the destructive will achieves its end, yet death is not a central theme of these works. Consider again, for example, the threnodies, shaped as passacaglias, which form the climax of *Lucretia* and *Herring*: in the first, death opens a way from human frailty and sin to the promise of redemption, whereas in the second poignant reflections on the immutable fact of death can be indulged precisely because they are to prove extravagantly beside the point. Billy, Miles and Owen die, but their defiance of the dark powers that have beset them throughout the opera is dramatically more crucial than the price they pay for it; and in each case at least one character (Vere, the Governess, Kate), but by implication we all, will have understood the moral victory. The early sense of impotent outrage before the futility of death returns, of course, as one searing strand of the *War Requiem*, yet this work, more urgently than any other by Britten, is addressed to the living: the grandiose wickedness of war is compounded from innumerable pettier debasing impulses which none of us can disown.

Death in Venice marks a new development in that, in every sense but that most literal one represented by the plague, the canker is now wholly within the central character; indeed no other character is allowed to take on fully plausible human substance. The death, spiritual as much as physical, which its ravages bring about offers no redemptive gleam within or outside the dramatic context; the abyss is man's destiny, whether he treads the Apollonian or the Dionysiac way. It perhaps remains for future commentators justly to assess the fortitude of spirit that enabled Britten to complete this merciless work under the shadow of his own serious illness. After its completion, recognition that surgical treatment had afforded no more than a respite meant that the shadow lengthened as the composer's remaining work was done. In pieces like the suite on folk-tunes and the *Birthday Hansel*, it is triumphantly disregarded; in others it is still more couragously regarded unwaveringly and put to artistic purposes. So these late Britten works, the opera, the Medieval Lyrics, the quartet, *Phaedra* and the last canticle, while sombrely coloured by reflections on death, remain wonderfully free from the hysteria of over-emphasis.

In the *Death of Saint Narcissus*, simply by amplifying correspondences already present in the poem, Britten shapes a beautifully controlled structure:

Shadows	Expository	A(1	*bars* 1–20
The gray shadow on his lips	with coda	(2	21–27
He walked . . .	Expansive	B(1	28–64
He . . . became a dancer before God		(2	65–76
He had been a tree	Episodic	C(1	77–88
a fish		(2	89–108
a young girl		(3	109–123
So he became a dancer . . .	Tersely	B2(+1)	124–138
. . . the shadow in his mouth	recapitulatory	A1 + 2	139–145

This chart gives a complete enough account of the thematic correspondences of the piece, but conceals one aspect of its shape that relates at once to the composer's consistent structural predilections and to Eliot's narrative scheme. Recapitulation involves not only abridgment, but a climactic intensification of material: Eliot's references back are interleaved with his account of Narcissus's fate.

> So he became a dancer to God.
> Because his flesh was in love with the burning arrows
> He danced on the hot sand
> Until the arrows came.
> As he embraced them his white skin surrendered itself
>   to the redness of blood, and satisfied him.
> Now he is green, dry and stained
> With the shadow in his mouth.

Ex. 16.6 (a)

Ex. 16.6 (b)

The feeling of climax which Britten brings to this final section is created by melodic and textural means, but the no less strong feeling of resolution is, as we might expect, dependent on a tonal ordering that spans the whole canticle. The opening section (A1 of the chart) is founded on lapping harp arpeggios in which triads of C major and C sharp minor are intermingled, the vocal line being similarly ambivalent tonally (see Ex. 6a). The first 'accidental' to disturb the system, A sharp, qualifies both fields (i.e., is simultaneously flat 7 and sharp 6) and 'modulation' is through A major/B flat minor to the orthodox dominant, G major/G sharp minor. By different means the B section of the structure reinforces this tonal duality (see Ex. 6b), whereas the three episodes that make up the C section move as elusively as the strange imaginative flights they depict. Even here however, at any point the material suggests two conflicting areas: for example, the harp scales, of semitone/minor third alternations at 110 and 122 ('young' and 'old') are still compounds of two triads, but now third-related (the possible readings are E major/ C minor; A flat major/ E minor; C major/A flat minor). And these third relations accurately foreshadow the transforming process of the final section: the closing Bs of this episodic section serve as introductory dominant to an E field which unobtrusively draws towards it the returning C major and C sharp minor, until the closing vocal line and the piano in turn lead to an outcome, at the one pitch common to the originally conflicting triads. Looking back, we see how implicit this outcome was, notably in the voice part, within the opening sections; yet there the semitonal relationships were the characterizing ones, here the third relationships. Both types of tonal duality were constantly employed throughout Britten's work, but this exchange of one for the other is particularly striking.

It can be seen from Ex. 6 that the triadic arpeggio (shown as z) is also one of the melodic shapes of the canticle, active in the vocal line of A and in the accompanying patterns of A and B sections. The curve x is a head-motive common to these sections, while y, used literally or inverted for all the repetitions of 'shadow', also remains influential rhythmically in the 'walking' harp octaves of the B section. Again the C section stands apart: though the opening shapes of both voice and piano at 'First he was sure . . .' derive palpably from the closing bars of the previous section, the mercurial movement of these episodes cuts the music loose from the earlier motivic weave. This section can admit, as well as the most bewitching harp sonorities of the piece, such specifically illustrative touches as the chromatic vocal descent at 'slippery white belly held tight'.

By comparison with much of Britten's piano writing in the earlier canticles, the harp textures are tenuous; whatever the special rôle reserved for the triad, in much of the piece the progression of harmonic blocks is renounced entirely (see Ex. 6b). The composer's invention of figured accompaniments, always so resistant to mere formula, seems revitalized by the challenge of new instrumental capacities, yet idiomatic limits are never threatened.

417

Ex.16.7

Perhaps the single most arresting effect is the simplest—the terrifying eruption of loud high C major arpeggios that three times depicts the arrows in the
restatement section (see the stanza quoted above). The whole canticle is
quite brief, its range of musical gesture considerable. Ultimately its great
power springs from a voice part which, capturing the expressive nuances of
contrasted sections, is also spun across them to bind the piece in a single,
magnificently subtle line. Reference has already been made to some of the
connecting devices (the common pitches between Sections B and C, the V–I
relationship between C and B's return) and the others are no less clear. In
addition there is a network of correspondences of small groups of pitches
within the sections, and meticulous control of the voice's pitch extremes
that, even reduced to the skeletal form of a diagram, can be seen to have
crucial relevance to the way in which we hold the entire cycle of experience
in our memory (Ex. 7). The white note-heads represent peaks and troughs,
the black note-heads a few of the most important connexions. Studied
together with the score, this diagram can be expanded to show innumerable
refinements of compositional detail, but even at a glance it reveals some
significant relationships (e.g., that of the troughs in Sections A and B) and
distinctions (e.g., between the approaches to the three top G sharps), and
explains very simply why section C is felt to expand in a manner so different
from the rest of the work. The last canticle is as moving as any of the set, and
many words could be expended on our emotional reactions to it. As ever, it
succeeds not only because Britten was able to share the poet's vision, but
because he encompassed it in a musical organism of perfect aptitude.

17 Later Choral Works

SPRING SYMPHONY, OP. 44

In his cantata, *Saint Nicolas*, Britten had been able to create a sense of unity across a succession of heterogeneous movements both by the unfolding narrative and by carefully ordered key relationships (see Chapter 13). The choral and orchestral work which he completed a year later, in June 1949, might seem to have contained in its title of 'Spring Symphony' the promise of a still more rigorously unified musical structure, though the narrative thread had been abandoned in favour of a poetic anthology. The composer's explanation of the title is worth quoting once again, for it does not encourage misunderstandings:

> For two years I had been planning such a work, a symphony not only dealing with the spring itself but with the progress of Winter to Spring and the reawakening of the earth and life which that means. . . .
> The work . . . is in the traditional four movement shape of a symphony, but with the movements divided into shorter sections bound together by a similar mood or point of view.[1]

This makes clear that, even on the verbal plane, a feeling of logical sequence is no less important than is the arresting articulation of each new poem, and that the grouping of poems is intended to amass 'movements' that will reproduce the 'shape' of symphony. Britten does not claim that they will reproduce the thematic rhetoric of the classical symphonic style. Only because the label 'symphony' attracted so exaggerated and inhibiting an esteem during the nineteenth century did it become possible for certain critics to denounce Britten's use of it here and for others, retaining the same criteria, no less fervently to defend this. Yet the criteria are not necessarily relevant: Beethoven's choral finale, in introducing a text, already demonstrated that a structure may remain appropriately massy even when pointedly unlike sections are juxtaposed, and although a fundamental tonal/thematic dualism and the proliferation of texture by vigorous figure-development are

---

[1] B. Britten, 'A Note on the Spring Symphony', *Music Survey* ii, 1950, p. 237.

jettisoned. With three operas behind him, Britten had mastered means of building musically convincing act-structures from discrete set-pieces as surely as in his first period of composition he had found congenial ways of turning the sonata principle to his own ends. In choosing an arrangement of four composite but continuous structures in which the slow meditative one comes second and the scherzo mood third before a weighty finale rises to peroration, he worked out an expressive scheme familiar in the orchestral symphony while preserving the control of imagery proper to vocal writing.

Part I of Britten's scheme is not so evidently referable to precedent. Though we hear a slow introduction, 'a prayer in Winter, for Spring to come'[2], give way to a succession of animated aspiring gestures culminating in the affirmation of the Milton setting, the proportions do not support comparisons. The long first piece, on an anonymous sixteenth-century poem, instead of opening like a classical introduction into the elaborately structured allegro, presents in itself one of the most detailed formal schemes in the work. Indeed, we might think that it provides a direct parallel to the structural syllogisms of Britten's sonata movements with conflated restatements. Yet the 'argument' concerns only the instrumental episodes (see Ex. 1a, b, c and e), each being for a different section of the orchestra, which later contributes its distinctive material to the culminating tutti texture at fig 7. There is no direct 'progress' between these episodes, for they are separated by choral passages of necessarily diverse imagery, and each is prefaced by a ritornello, the percussion figures heard at the beginning of the work (which also underlie the final tutti). That the resultant structure does not sound decoratively additive (in the conventional sense and in an extra one) but expanding can be attributed to several aspects of its composition. One is the fugal growth of the three orchestral episodes, a second the derivation of many figures and harmonies from a common fund of intervals: Ex. 1 shows some relations of instrumental and vocal contexts to the opening timpani shape. The use of pedals underpinning episodes 2 and 3, on G and E respectively, is essentially a static element, contributing to the feeling of inertia which is so marked in the choral lines (and so relevant to the picture of winter). But the E which returns at the end of the superimposed orchestral textures, that is, when *interaction* is beginning to operate, is a dynamic element projecting the structural V–I of the orchestral movement (i.e., to fig. 8), reiterated in the fading orchestral interpolations. From this point the chorus lines make one connected progression towards their cadence, in essence a I–V opening harmonically into the next piece (melodically A–F sharp provides the connexion). Though almost every choral chord in this introduction has the gnawing unease of contradictory elements (occasional open fifths being the nearest to the affirmative outcome of a triad), there has been a clear move from tonal wanderings to a close around A minor—a

[2] Ibid.

Ex.17.1 (a)

Ex.17.1 (b)

Ex.17.1 (c)

Ex.17.1 (d)

Ex.17.1 (e)

Semitone relations, in canon at tritone.

Ex.17.1 (f)

point from which we chart all future excursions and to which the finale reverts to begin its tonal design.

The introduction has also established a principle of orchestral usage in allocating a distinct body of material to each of the four instrumental groups.

421

As Erwin Stein pointed out in his commentary on the symphony, 'Britten is continuing what he began when he chose the instruments for his operatic chamber orchestra'.[3] But now, of course, the number of homogeneous ensembles available is far greater, while the number of selective mixed groups is infinite. With a quite Baroque strictness, he allocates characterizing colours to each piece, and retains them throughout it or, as in 'The Driving Boy', realizes two poems in terms of two instrumentally underlined *Affekte*.

'The Merry Cuckoo' (Spenser) employs three trumpets as both cuckoo and the rest of 'the quire of birds'. It is deft but a little too dependent on cues for immediate imagery. After its A major has been displaced by the tritone E flat, a return is made to the dominant: thus the flat deviation again, as well as the suddenly more sober texture, gives a typical Britten reading of the qualifying—'*But . . .*'mongst them all'. No unequivocal A major returns after this: a string dominant seventh pull towards G is conflated with the final A triad. By simply reversing the viewpoint, 'Spring, the sweet spring' begins in G with a strong attraction towards its supertonic. Britten's two-chord switchback can bear its tantalizing repetitions because it can never complete the tonal circuit that is contained within it; see Ex. 2. There are three such

Ex. 17.2

progressions (though the word is a misnomer) and a *da capo*, forming one symmetrical tonal progression: G–E–B flat (approx.)–G. Everything else depends on swinging ostinato figures and the snatches of counterpoint the soloists spin above them. Transitions come through the interpolations of bird song, which appropriately have an accompaniment modelled on the last bar of the previous setting: this is played by flutes, clarinets and trumpets, the only absentees from the accompaniment of the verses.

Another simple connexion, the incorporation of the D–G falling fifth into a new accompanying figure, carries us across into the contrasted tonal area of 'The Driving Boy', for woodwind band, jingling tambourine, and a tuba indefatigable in treading a II–V–I circuit of E flat that is now wholly unambiguous. The wind harmony is less committed (see Ex. 3), so that the outcome of the movement in F is not wholly capricious. The boys' choir setting of Peele's verse, nimbly side-stepping the obvious in its metrical variety, provides a fund of melodic shapes on which the soprano ruminates in the Clare, high violins transforming the harmonies to a new mood. The

[3] E. Stein, 'The Symphonies', in Mitchell-Keller, p. 256.

Ex. 17.3

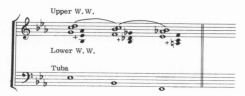

boys' climactic whistle is another cuckoo-call, and in the Milton aubade that ends Part I falling thirds dominate both brass accompaniment and choral refrain. Tonally this piece is the least adventurous so far, its few detours retaining a clear relation, and making a quick return, to F. The feeling of stability is strengthened by a bass line that scarcely ever moves by more than a step and by the chorus's confident octaves. The recognition of a triadic norm confirms how much has been achieved since the uneasy harmonies of the Introduction, though one may wonder why Britten allowed himself the Stravinskyan final dissonance—splendid though its vibrant choral sonority may be, it appears to be justified only in terms of the bells which, having alternated between A and B flat throughout, now sound them together.

Part II paints, the composer wrote, 'the darker side of spring—the fading violets, rain and night'.[4] Except for a moment in the eruption towards the end of the Auden setting, this darkness is a matter of shadows, not of a black despair. There is a less emphatic swing to flattened key areas than in the traditional symphonic slow movement, but modality is so elusive in the first

Ex. 17.4

[4] B. Britten, op. cit.

two pieces as to confound simple tonal reference and the third piece wanders restlessly despite the choral refrain's insistence on B flat (as at least a recurrent point of departure). The use of the contralto in both the outer settings is supported by orchestral textures thick in lower harmonies; a simple ternary impression is produced therefore by the tenor's floating line, accompanied only by the violins in 'Waters above'. Its quality of light (to extend the image) is created by their *ponticello* triplets, for the higher harmonics vividly suggest points of pale sunlight reflected from wet surfaces. The withholding of the violins from the Herrick setting makes their return a simple but effective symbol of the welcome rain. The Herrick piece, 'Welcome, Maids of Honour', is worth examining to observe once again how Britten could compose to a formula and yet keep the result alive. Here the process can be summarized: given three elements, an arpeggio figure a (of harps coloured by woodwind soloists) a string texture b (of violas moving in major seconds, cellos and basses in major triads) and a vocal stanza c (followed heterophonically by the violas), then the pattern is

$$
a1 \rightarrow b \rightarrow a1 \begin{vmatrix} c1 \\ \text{accomp. b} \\ \text{articul. a1} \end{vmatrix} \qquad a1 \rightarrow b \rightarrow a2 \begin{vmatrix} c2 \\ b \\ a2 \end{vmatrix} \qquad a2 \rightarrow b \rightarrow a3 \begin{vmatrix} c3 \\ b \\ a3 \end{vmatrix} \quad \text{etc.}
$$

The symmetry is emphasized by the phrases of the vocal stanza being a direct reflection of the rhyme scheme, i.e. x y y x. Tedium and coyness alike are held off solely by the variation of the model in tonal bearings, intervallic structure and, on the last two statements, length. Ex. 4 shows the entire voice part. The double extension downwards of the last stanza not only affords an appropriate touch of illustrative detail, but also leads to an A which closes on a recognizable dominant the tonal scheme—D–E flat–C (V?)–G sharp (V?)–A. References here are to central melodic points, for the few chordal movements within the two string strata prevent any consistent tonal structure in the harmony. One need not be derogatory in suggesting that so transparent a scheme, in conjunction with total consistency of orchestral layout, may have been realized by the composer very quickly. Indeed, its uniformity (though not without nuance) allows the piece the more easily to fulfil the rôle of one element in the wider scheme of this tripartite 'movement'.

'Waters above' (Vaughan) appears to be an altogether less constrained structure, though in fact its recurrences—of the first (and basic) four-note shape, the high/low climax of the motives first heard at bar 11, and the arpeggio texture and vocal shape of fig. 4—are admirably balanced. The essentially ternary pattern is subservient to a comprehensive melodic curve, i.e., the G peak which the first section never achieved emerges magically (three bars after 5) at the close of the second, and so can be incorporated easily into the short reprise. Britten's key-signatures, as we have often noted, commonly provide an accurate enough background to his tonal plans,

424

but here B minor is, at best, by inference. The A sharp from which this beautifully arched melody springs sounds like a leading-note only in the mid-section; elsewhere it is in fact a 'final', but it would be futile to define its mode, beyond noting its predominantly diminished fifth. The curiously wistful effect created by such treatment of a nominally 'leading' note may be heard in other Britten contexts (see, for example, p. 126 *Lucretia*, and p. 199 *Gloriana*).

'Out on the Lawn' is the most substantial piece in the centre of the work and the only one in the symphony that ever questions a vernal optimism. The verses Britten took from Auden range widely in images and feeling, and his first concern has been to provide a common factor. At first sign, the wordless chorus's 'Ah' as a ritornello smacks of desperate contrivance, and its underlining of a mystery and finally horror that are implicit in the orchestral textures can appear gratuitously to prompt the listener's reactions. But the piece works rather the other way round: the five-note motive from which all the choral refrains are made has infiltrated the verse-settings (a few instances are shown at Ex. 5a). The music provides a patent allegory in that our attention is given to seductive foreground detail of the score (without strings) throughout the first three stanzas—the alto flute and bass clarinet of Britten's nocturnal pictures, the trio of double-reeds, and the fluttering flute demisemiquavers. In this last the brass harmony that has provided a dark but distant background takes on a certain menace in its sporadic triplet appearances, yet even so, the outburst that overtakes the fourth stanza, of trumpet and trombones now in tonally conflicting fanfares, is shockingly unforeseen. The progression of which it forms a suddenly exposed climax, is shown at Ex. 5b. The review of the first three stanzas' material in a telescoped restatement is the more forlorn in that the brass support has now disappeared entirely. This is not one of Britten's overt statements about war, but its message is clear.

The scherzos of Part III are of progressive density. The first, Barnefield's 'When will my May come', is a study in mirrored arpeggios alternating between strings and harps, strictness of interval inevitably producing bitonal situations; the tenor's line is resourcefully developed from his declamatory first statement. A final extension prepares the A of the next setting while the last arpeggios, of A and F, suggest its bitonal slant. The woodwind solos that float above or below the voice parts move constantly between opposed tonal fields. Oboe, then flute with soprano, complete the first half of a binary pattern, which is then repeated by the tenor with the counterpoint inverted, on bassoon, then clarinet. The complementary section follows a similar pattern, but the tenor repeat is limited to the motto ending 'They that do change old love for new . . .'. Then the whole pattern is repeated but with voices and their instrumental counterpoints in canon at two quavers' distance. Now the segments of flat tonal area in one wind part coincide with those of a sharper in the other, producing a delightfully vertiginous sensation

as they bowl along in endless quavers. But the vocal parts, already ingenious in rhythm because of the irregular placing of ♩♩ groups in the 6/8 bars, pursue one another in the most pointedly cross-accented context in all Britten. The texture is stiffened by drumming string pizzicato semiquavers, their 6/4 version of the tonic keeping it in mid-air. The last scherzo uses the full orchestra except for percussion, pairing instrumental and vocal groups.

Male Voices + Brass a1	Female Voices + Woodwind a2	Boys + Strings b	→ Refrain on a + Female V & W.W. + Male V. & Brass	Orch. Tutti on b

426

The devices of the preceding scherzos are recalled in the closely knit dialogue of *a* (which also incorporates an inversion) and the mirror movement of *b*. Reiterations of 𝅘𝅥𝅮𝅘𝅥𝅮 in the orchestra and dynamics which constantly sweep between extremes give a sensation of a corporate joy that is still an entirely childlike one—a fitting treatment of Blake's poem.

Britten described the finale as 'a May-day Festival, a kind of bank holiday',[5] and he shaped its continuous music like a big operatic tableau. The last scene of *Die Meistersinger* comes to mind more than the *Gloriana* pageant, for that scene preserves a decorum proper to a royal entertainment while this, like the Wagner, seems to exploit the gathering momentum of a great crowd's high spirits. Its large-scale ternary structure provides the weight to draw the whole work together, yet the variety of available vocal and instrumental resources is sampled more prodigally than in any earlier movement in response to the many images thrown up by this exuberant speech from Beaumont and Fletcher's *Knight of the Burning Pestle*. In the tonal field too, the finale stabilizes the symphony, reverting, after the simultaneous or rapidly shifting areas of the scherzos, to less equivocal situations and eventually to the broadest of C majors, underpinned by the crudest of V–I reiterations in the bass. However, this key is one of two possible outcomes from the A minor in which the symphony began. As the orchestral waltz theme that opens the finale has no bass, one hears it as (Aeolian) A minor rather than C major, while the Maylord and the blast on his horn with which he punctuates his speech tug towards the latter key; their 2/4 against the waltz helps further to separate the planes. The restricted set of chime-like notes from which the tenor fashions his lines also suffices for the choral texture into which this first section grows; and it recurs in the Maylord's declamation at the end of the work. Its iambic cadencing fourth provides a link with the central Allegro, an extensive movement that seems to have settled on the *tonic* major as the destination of the symphony. The chorus's drumming quaver patterns with their 𝅘𝅥𝅮 | 𝅗𝅥. braying extensions (and expansions) of the fourth at the ends of lines, provide one recurrent element, the orchestra's 𝅘𝅥𝅮𝅘𝅥𝅮 | 𝅘𝅥𝅮 or 𝅘𝅥𝅮𝅘𝅥𝅮 | 𝅘𝅥𝅮𝅘𝅥𝅮𝅘𝅥𝅮 rhythms another in a rondo-like structure, of which the chief stages are as shown:

Cue figure	5 to 9	10	11	12	14	15+	18
	Chor. + Orch. Refrain	Soloists' Episode	Chor. Orch. Refr.	Boys Ch.	Soloists + Choir Episode	Choir Episode (Orch. refr.)	Tutti Orch. refrain . . .
	A(often Lydian)→ c♯	b♭(& B♭)	b♭	Transit. via V⁷ of C	C (as V?)	c/a	V of A

5 Ibid.

427

Ex.17.6

At the point where our diagram breaks off, a long section begins that substitutes for square episode truly expanding paragraphs on a pedal. And the introduction here of a theme built on thirds in a triplet rhythm (see Ex. 6) suggests that this embraces both parts of the movement so that, despite a lengthy preparation for A major, the eventual swing towards a return of the waltz does not appear factitious. The soloists again assert C major but now the thirds theme is given to the chorus who treat it as a great V below the soloists' I, an exciting preparation for the moment at which the original form of the waltz recurs in stentorian two-part imitation. Here an orchestral opposition movement strives to deviate into less obvious key areas, and the chorus try a few of them, but C major's hold by now is supreme, and the playing-off of the waltz's choral two-part counterpoint against the boys' 'Soomer is icoomen in' is as aggressive an assertion of that key as Britten has ever contrived. At the end the final bass revolutions of the waltz remind us of its original position on A, now assimilated as the added sixth.

No mention has been made of this movement's many textural felicities. As ever, they consist in choosing a disposition of voices and instruments proper to the verbal imagery in weight and colour, and maintaining this until the next verbal cue: there are no momentary splashes of sound but no blurring of instrumental colourings into a uniform brown varnish. Two examples will suffice to remind the reader who has ever heard this work of its individual sonorous precision. In the first episode, 'The lords and ladies', the soloists' smoothly flowing three-part harmony, is given a glittering edge by the staccato quavers with which the harps double it; already there is substance without stodginess, and the strings add another subdivision of the unit with semiquaver scales that traverse some five octaves, giving inevitably the impression of a very rarefied texture indeed. The 'little fish' episode similarly has three elements, but here a dense yet very quiet sound is required without loss of detail. In the first place, Britten introduces canon because it immediately makes the detail intelligible, provided the entry-points are clear: the soloists' 3 in 1 is taken up *inverso* and 4 in 1 by the chorus, building up to an undulating sound (at fig. 15) that evidently represents the creeping snails, yet has been achieved from a logical growth of material relevant to the movement as a whole. Similarly the woodwind elaboration of each vocal part maintains the paired semiquavers with which the Allegro began. And finally, that all these conjunct movements virtually cancel out to a static harmony is recognized in the thick string background.

The range of this work is impressive, even if its subject almost entirely excludes any representation of some of Britten's most intense sentiments. To look back to his previous big cycle with full orchestra, *Our Hunting Fathers*, shows how far he simplified the construction of distinctive sonorities here, while to consider his early works for chorus from Op. 3 onwards is to see how carefully he had prepared himself for this transformation of the traditional English choir into an apparently virtuoso body, an achievement the more remarkable in that their material is not insuperably difficult to master.

A WEDDING ANTHEM (AMO ERGO SUM), OP. 46

A work written shortly after the Spring Symphony which has never achieved any general currency is the Wedding Anthem, *Amo Ergo Sum*, Op. 46, for soprano and tenor soloists, choir and organ. This was composed for the wedding in 1949 of the Earl of Harewood and Marion Stein, and the occasional nature of the piece, consistently underlined in Ronald Duncan's text, has discouraged performances out of context. This is a pity for, without stretching the bounds of feasibility in writing for church choir and organ, Britten provided them with a work in which his freshest tone of lyricism sounds through. Perhaps we should not be surprised that in setting Duncan again he naturally responded with some memories of the sunniest moments in *Lucretia*; these are particularly clear in the writing for the soloists, in which he makes no kind of concession towards the traditional range of anthem moods. The soprano, after a Lucia-like recitative, sings a little air that avoids preciosity by progressive extension of its Mixolydian flattening to degrees other than the seventh, and by the displacements of its accompaniment. The tenor's simile aria, with its brook accompaniment, is less newly-felt, but the rapt canon-by-inversion in which the two celebrate a mystical union is a *trouvaille* that was to be recalled in some later contexts. While the nature of the symbolism here is entirely Baroque, the levitating effect of the Lydian mode, based on a final that may not be a tonic (i.e., we are conditioned to hearing such a passage in a dominant seventh sense, as well as able to savour its Lydian flavour), is a Britten peculiarity—as is the subsequent balancing by the flat seventh for the climactic mirror movement at

'Amo ergo sum!' Later in the duet, Lydian movement and the stepwise bass provide links with the material of the opening choral passage, which acts as a ritornello across the structure. The final section, in which the B flat of the duet is transformed to the B which opened the anthem, affords a neat example of Britten's use of leading-note pedals.

$$\text{I} \qquad \text{VII} \quad \text{of} \quad \boxed{\text{B}} \; = \; \text{C}\flat \qquad \text{I}$$
$$\boxed{\text{B}\flat} \; = \; \text{A}\sharp \qquad \text{I} \qquad \text{II} \quad \text{of} \quad \boxed{\text{B}\flat}$$

FIVE FLOWER SONGS, OP. 47

During the following year, Britten composed more choral music for a married couple, the *Five Flower Songs*, Op. 47 for unaccompanied four-part choir, written to mark the twenty-fifth wedding anniversary of the Elmhirsts, of Dartington Hall. His previous purely choral cycle, *A Boy was Born*, of 1933 (see Chapter 3, p. 64) had made a determined assault on the limited horizons of the English part-song and carol traditions, bringing to bear on them a host of instrumentally-derived textural innovations and of organizing methods owing much to continental models. Nine years later, the *Hymn to Saint Cecilia* and, more markedly, the *Ceremony of Carols* showed a guarded return to a patently English tradition after the American years and the Rimbaud and Michelangelo song cycles. But in the Flower Songs we find accepted as a still profitable starting-point most of the conventions of the part-song as it was practised by, say, Stanford and the later generation of Finzi and Moeran; thus, from a norm of diatonic homophony with fastidiously placed verbal accents and with dissonant sevenths or ninths, the music will tend to achieve truly contrapuntal textures (i.e., of significant rhythmic independence) only at an extreme territory across a wide middle ground of pseudo-imitative techniques. The result seems less consistently bland than some earlier part-songs principally because Britten makes the parts, even in nominal homophony, pursue courses regulated by more stringent linear considerations (often including detailed yet unostentatious motivic work) and recognizes a wider range of diatonic dissonance—used to keep the strands apart, not just to mark with a particularly scented blend each emotional high point. Even so, there remain whole lines in these songs which, but for perhaps a couple of chord spacings, could be mistaken for other men's work, and it is worth observing how much the absence of accompanying textures may weaken the individual flavour of Britten's vocal music. The solution had been, of course, in the Op. 3 cycle and the Saint Cecilia hymn, to provide quasi-instrumental accompaniments from the vocal resources, but only in the 'Ballad of Green Broom' does he do this. The indiscriminately alternating tonics and dominants of a ballad-singer's guitar strum in the accompanying voices of the first two verses; thereafter their texture is disintegrated progressively so that each voice acquires more independence until the imitative writing of verse 5; the last verse restores the accompaniment in an appropriately grander guise, pure homophony underscores the concluding lines, and the accompaniment achieves its final clangorous form. So many words on so slight a piece may appear disproportionate, but this use of textural variety to create a structural shape more comprehensive than would mere strophic variants is typical of Britten's approach to the medium.

Hans Redlich, writing in the 1953 symposium,[6] considered the first song, Herrick's 'To Daffodils', to be overshadowed by the following two. To me it appears a good deal stronger than the following Herrick setting, 'The Succession of the Four Sweet Months'. Its four-part opening texture is lit by few rests, yet this is not hymnic homophony. At least three sources of tension are operating simultaneously: the derivation of every line from a single four-note shape, the drag of the middle two parts behind the outer two, and the ostinato-like bass's resistance to the downward, then upward, movement of the rhythmically identical soprano part. The second section offsets short snatches of homophony in the upper voices with a bass line that now is responsible for the true (and slow) movement of the piece. The restoration of the tonic after this detour is nicely managed, providing the structural cadence, after which the parts recall the opening movement, but all are now confined, as was the bass, to a static reiteration. The 'Four Sweet Months' are introduced fugally, and in decorous terms that many a well-schooled English composer would find an echo of his own response. The mood intensifies a little with the completion of the texture and the flowering of stretto, but the ending is too tenuously related to what has gone before.

In 'Marsh Flowers', Britten sets an unpromisingly bleak inventory by George Crabbe of the 'contracted' (and, on the face of it, distasteful) 'Flora of our town'. He accommodates plenty of illustrative detail, but not until he has established a distinctive tone that can unify the whole piece on its return. Taut rhythms and unharmonized octaves serve his purpose, and thereafter octaved two-part counterpoint (i.e., S–T v. A–B) keeps the music wiry. Even four-part homophony (at the 'fiery nettle') is kept chill, by melodic poverty, and so the fern, sprouting from every chink of an ingratiating little canon 4 in 2, suggests a comparative warmth, sustained through the following line. The seaweeds roll in two-part mirror movement (octave-doubled) and thence we move back to the bare octaves of the opening, and a disconsolate drop to an unexpected final. John Clare's 'The Evening Primrose' is set in what might be a parody of the well-mannered part-song, so smoothly and regularly does its homophony give way to snatches of imitation. But its rhythmic life is a good deal more varied than the 4/4 signature admits, incorporating innumerable groupings based on the dotted crotchet unit (the closing phrase is particularly happy); harmonically too, not all is predictable.

Yet one returns to the opinion that, with their many felicities, these songs do not convey much of the quintessential Britten. One has only to consider

[6] H. Redlich, 'The Choral Music', in Mitchell-Keller, p. 90.

The Music of Benjamin Britten

such Tippett part-songs as 'The Windhover' or even (in a sphere more akin to the central English tradition) 'The Weeping Babe', to discern how much more of that composer's strength and individuality of manner can be conveyed through the medium of unaccompanied voices. But singers will undoubtedly find that Britten's settings can be more securely mastered, and that they always 'sound' well.

HYMN TO SAINT PETER, OP. 56a; ANTIPHON, OP. 56b

Though written a year apart, these two of Britten's occasional pieces of church music share the opus number 56. The earlier is the *Hymn to Saint Peter*, written for the quincentenary of the Church of St Peter Mancroft, Norwich in 1955. Its words are from the gradual of the Feast of St Peter and St Paul, while musically it derives from the plainsong 'Tu es Petrus' (essentially the Alleluia and Verse for the Common of Holy Popes). After the organ has stated in B flat the first two lines of this melody, the second of them is conflated into an ostinato eleven quavers long which, played off against the common time of the choral hymn, yields the maximum diversity of relationships. The hymn itself, 'Thou shalt make them Princes', is based on the ascending pentatonic shape of the plainsong's Alleluia; its lines fan out from unison without ever relapsing into the plumpness of orthodox four-part texture. A miniature scherzo ('Instead of thy fathers, sons are born to thee') begins in neat closed forms—G Aeolian section repeated, then the same up to B flat, repeated—but then undergoes modulatory expansion; the quasi-instrumental use of dabs of vocal colour here reminds us of earlier Britten choral contexts. Around the new tonal centre of D, the organ now states the remaining two lines of the plainsong ('aedificamus Ecclesiam meam'), conflates them into a new eleven-quaver ostinato and runs this off against a second verse of the hymn. But this reaches no close in D, fading out with a flattening inflexion. A treble soloist now sings the generating plainsong to its Latin text, each line being followed by its translation in the quietly repeated triads of the choir. Their final added-sixth does not seem an indulgence, for it so evidently stems from the pentatonic source of the piece; the organ meanwhile climbs up through the Alleluia shape while its bass brings back the original quaver ostinato. The work is as modest in its demands as in its use of material, but its cogency is preferable to the extravagant panache of much 'festival' music.

The *Antiphon* for choir and organ was written in 1956 for the centenary celebrations of St Michael's College, Tenbury; it is a setting of George Herbert's 'Praised be the God of Love/Here below/And here above'. Those three lines furnish the composer with a textural formula—full choir's unison against a swinging organ accompaniment, lower voices' solemn, quiet homophony, and treble soloist (or semi-chorus) continuing the flowing lines of the tutti against the quiet harmony, now in the organ. The slowly unfolding harmonic plan and an appropriate diversion to jagged imitative work at

432

'He our foes in pieces brake' serve to prevent too mechanistic an impression. As coda there is a sinewy fugue on two subjects, though its highly unorthodox doublings in the cause of choral sonority discourage the use of so pompous a description; once again, the text has directly prompted the device: 'Praised be the God alone/Who hath made of two folds one'. After a hymnic climax, the piece dies away in antiphony between the fixed tonic-triad 'one' of the treble soloists and the determinedly divergent triads which the rest of the choir choose for their 'two'. But finally they also arrive at the tonic, and the work can end literally at 'one'. Superior minds of our age no doubt find such naïve symbolism offensive, though a seventeenth-century composer would have regarded it as a necessary response to such a text. Church music, and church acoustics, are not often served best by extremes of complexity, and this piece puts its simplicity to an expressive effect worthy of the poet.

CANTATA ACADEMICA, OP. 62

Not until ten years after the Spring Symphony did Britten return to the medium of chorus and orchestra. It is not simply that he was that much older which makes the *Cantata Academica* appear to spring from a less spontaneous upsurge of his creative spirit. Everything about the work, from the tombstone Latin of the title-page onwards, suggests a slightly uneasy attempt to combine academic dignity and academic jocularity; to be pompous with a light touch is a formidable undertaking. One wonders whether the composer had seen the text before he accepted the commission to write a work for the quincentenary of Basel University (where it was first performed by the Basel Chamber Choir and Chamber Orchestra under Paul Sacher on 1 July 1960). The unremittingly worthy tone of such 'founders and benefactors' orations can be disconcerting to anyone bound by no direct ties of affection, and it must have presented a quite new problem to a composer whose genius had thrived in matching the abundant imagery of English verse. However, the Latin text, while still prompting some musical symbolism (most obviously in the many-entried fugue at 'venerint ex omnibus orbis ternarum regionibus'), is likely to conceal from all but the most alert ears the incongruity of setting such ponderous stuff as

> Then, indeed, Aeneas Sylvius,
> the Romulus of our Rome,
> who adorned the city to which he was indebted
> with a university, provided
> with the rights of every faculty

to a duet as seductively lilting as (if less rhythmically ingenious than) 'Fair as fair' from the Spring Symphony. Clearly enough, Britten decided he must write his own kind of music, however he might pervert the tone of the text. His concept of 'academic' has therefore become a very generous one. At face value, he provides this Latin oration with a no less 'learned' music,

433

including an *Alla Rovescio* (mirror movement) piece, a pair of *Soli* that, complete with accompaniments, conflate into a *Duetto*, a *Canone ed ostinato* and at the centre of the work a *Tema Seriale con Fuga* which epitomizes the tonal structure of the whole work—not to mention innumerable contrapuntal felicities elsewhere that are not dignified with labels. But, like Brahms in his *Academic Festival Overture*, he recognizes that academic celebrations concern students as well as their studies, and so the music almost throughout is relaxed, by Britten's own standards (let alone those of the 1960 European scene he was entering), aurally undemanding in its succession of simply-structured miniatures, and with a strong undercurrent of sociable song. Indeed, this becomes overt in the soprano's little *Arioso* which is repeated above a male-voice *Canto popolare*, hummed as from the distance. Elsewhere sturdy unison singing is given a prominent place, and even the soloists' canon would not be out of place at a *Liedertafel*.

Before the first performance, English readers were able to examine the structure of the cantata in an analytical article by Susan Bradshaw.[7] She demonstrated that the thirteen-note succession (all twelve, plus a return to the first) of the *Tema Seriale*, though never subjected to serial manipulation more stringent than the flippant retrograde of its woodwind diminution (after fig. 30), *does* ordain the series of notes around which the 13 movements are built. In fact the correspondence is not absolute since the *Tema Seriale* and its fugue stand outside the scheme, and so movement VII uses two centres (see Ex. 7); it will be noted that the *Tema* articulates the series of

Ex. 17.7

the work at the same point (after note 8 has appeared) as it is itself articulated into complementary phrases. The choral fugue is on a new, ironically diatonic subject, but the successive notes of each entry, sustained instrumentally throughout its length, spell out the series. Stretto quickens the succession and the woodwind interjections diminish it still further, so that we have heard the theme delivered in the following basic units

and, by the end of the work, also in a vast canto fermo that embraces its entire length.

Engaging though all this serial 'super-ordering' may be, it represents one of Britten's less serious encounters with the principles of twelve-note music. Thus in *The Turn of the Screw*, for example, although his succession of tonal

[7] S. Bradshaw, 'Britten's *Cantata Academica*', *Tempo* 53/54, 1960, p. 22.

434

centres in the interludes was chosen in accordance with criteria quite uncon-
nected with the twelve-note theme (but very closely connected with the
unfolding drama), the theme remained the basis of each variation, and so the
twelve notes were in a state of revolution (melodically, at least) more
constant than in most of his work. Here, however, nothing is pre-ordained in
each movement except the one pitch, sustained as a more or less obvious
pedal, around which it moves. These pedals are 'centres' but not necessarily
tonics. Indeed, Britten exercises much ingenuity in arranging his music at
different oblique angles to these fixed objects. In movement II, the object is
a complete F major triad, though the choral melodic lines and inversions still
contrive to traverse other areas. In the short recitative that follows (III)
segments of some ten other tonalities (major or minor) are sounded against
the pedal E flat. The *Duettino* (V) is poised on an F sharp that is, more than
anything else, leading-note of a flexible G mode, while the D of the scherzo
(VII) emerges at the same point in every choral entry but from an entirely
different tonal context; even more versatile is the G sharp in the canon.
Reversing the procedure, Britten takes the bell-like melodic figure (see fig.
5) which ended I (itself a G as V movement) with a swing to F Lydian, and
uses it at the end of the *da capo* finale XIII to reinforce G as tonic.

The same figure makes a fugitive appearance in the tenor recitative no.
VI, a piece which strikes a few florid gestures of a kind which in many
another context Britten has brought to life; here they do not convince. And
in several other movements he has been satisfied to work out a tidy little
scheme by recourse to formulas: consider, for example, the harp scale of
inverted sevenths from which the soprano arioso (X) has been constructed,
or the threadbare stuff of the solos in IX: their only merit appears to lie in the
ingenuity of their eventual contrapuntal ço-existence. I must confess to
finding the *Tema Seriale* itself an uncomfortable experience: that sonorously
strummed E flat harmony and pious vocal descant (*Abide with me* seems
quite as relevant to this as to the hymn parody in *Albert Herring*) suggest a
sanctimony which the subsequent melodic twists and complementary harmonic shifts (to D and to E) may outrage but do not eradicate.

But there are things far worthier of Britten in this work, if nothing of his
most penetrating invention. Even the *Corale* which frames it is distinctively
his, and for more than the interlinked third chains of the brass: the choral
and string 'white-note' harmony occupies a middle ground between
Stravinsky's empirically selected added-notes and orthodox movement on a
pedal. The delicately pointed *Duettino* has been singled out already, but the
following scherzo is full of witty inflexions, quite apart from the fundamental
hilarity of such word-settings as Ex. 8. Its 'trio' section, around B flat as V,
returns in the coda where it provides tonal parentheses of E flat in D that
prepare for the *Tema*'s early parenthesis in the opposite sense (of D within E
flat). The big ternary structure of this scherzo and that of the theme-fugue-
theme give a necessary solidity to the centre of the Cantata. The *Canone ed*

Ex. 17.8

flo - reat stu - dium ge - ne - ra - lis, stu - dium ge - ne - ra - lis,

flo - reat stu - di - um, _____

Ostinato, leading in to the *Corale*'s return, provide a balance at the end. The canonic subject is converted into a five-bar ostinato, while the rhythms that the soloists have reiterated at fig. 38 (maintaining the canon's fifths relationships) carry on in the side drum. The choral tune in which the praise of Basel reaches its peroration works equally well above the ostinato in E, D and finally A. As in the Spring Symphony finale the ostinato's superimposed thirds prepare the return to a first idea (the fanfares) dominated by that shape.

One hopes that Basel received the kind of work it was looking for, but clearly this *pièce d'occasion* could not be consigned to a university chest after the occasion. An alternative form of the text deletes all specific references; perhaps the lofty language becomes still more curious when deprived of any certain object, but a choral and orchestral piece so congenial to the performers can survive on the assumption that their audiences will probably be oblivious to the text.

MISSA BREVIS IN D, OP. 63

The *Missa Brevis*, a setting of the Ordinary excluding the Creed, shares some of the character of Britten's music for children, yet this in no way detracts from its liturgical propriety. It was written in 1959 for the boys of Westminster Cathedral choir and their director, George Malcolm, who was about to retire from his post. Though he has become better known in other fields—as a harpsichordist, but also as a conductor entrusted with Britten opera performances—Malcolm as a choir-trainer was notable for his cultivation of a boys' tone that was hard-edged to the point of stridency, a sound fundamentally at variance with the blandness of recent 'cathedral' tradition. Since the Spring Symphony at least, Britten had treated the boy's voice as an incisive wind instrument, shunning the sophisticated espressivo nuances of the trained adult singer, and so he responded to the Westminster tone with a piece that is subtle enough, but becomes so from the way in which individually uncomplicated parts are related. Observe, for example, how confident tuning of the crucial dissonance in this cadential phrase is facilitated by the easily mastered shapes of the constituent strands (Ex. 9a) or how a twelve-note row is assembled from short overlapping phrases (Ex. 9b). Similarly the 7/8 metre of the Gloria becomes easy to realize with the organ's ostinato shape (see Ex. 11 below) to serve as mnemonic. The varied subdivisions of

Ex. 17.9 (a)

Ex. 17.9 (b)

the bar give this setting an exhilaratingly jaunty flavour that makes it truly children's music. Such a joyful noise deserves a place in the liturgy, and one might hope that it would help to reveal as the abomination it is that matey vulgarity which the specious 'folk' movement has foisted on to modern church music.

The mass is described as being 'in D', almost an assurance that a fairly wide interpretation is to be placed on the term. Britten's cello sonata 'in C' affords an obvious comparison, Stravinsky's 'Symphony in C' a still better one in its elegantly sustained poise between C major and E minor, for when this work begins, D major is apparently no more than an adjunct to F sharp minor. In the Gloria the same two fields change their relationship (i.e., D now predominates over F sharp major), in the Sanctus D is encircled by F sharp but also by B flat (i.e., is central in a major-third chain) and in the Agnus Dei D has become of minor modality and B flat the most consistent counter-attraction: thus the final relationship is a transposition of the first (see Ex. 10). Details like the episodic move into B flat at 'Qui tollis peccata mundi' in the Gloria and the extension of the Agnus Dei ostinato through an F sharp major triad one bar before the close give depth to this scheme, one of Britten's most satisfying explorations of third-relationships, despite the minute scale on which it is conducted. Only the G–C(–F) orientation of the Benedictus, for material that is just as addicted to a chain of fourths, takes us outside the scheme. As markedly as in the Benedictus of the *War Requiem*, this gives a special feeling, here almost of levitation, to this music of beatitude; the less obvious *links* with other material will be noted shortly.

The close tonal relationship between Kyrie and Gloria (see Ex. 10)

Ex.17.10

extends to their thematic material. Though the Gloria's shapes evidently derive from the opening intonation, retained as an organ ostinato (see Ex. 11a), they have already been in circulation in the Kyrie (Ex. 11b). In that the

Ex.17.11 (a)

Ex.17.11 (b)

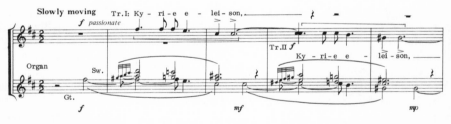

Kyrie motive spans a fourth and thus appears successively in the three voices at fourth transpositions, the Benedictus is not wholly unprepared. The voices merge for a refrain of oscillating harmonies that ends each of the Kyrie's three clauses, Christe being an inversion of the first, and the second Kyrie a *da capo*. The Gloria has scarcely less clear a return after its subsidiary idea has worked round through B minor back to D. (We have seen how the initial B flat of this idea anticipates the colour of the Agnus Dei, at appropriate words, but its scalic motion introduces another characteristic of the Benedictus.) The legato form of the ostinato first heard at 'Gratias' winds down further now and a contraction to 5/8 beautifully varies the momentum before the close.

The tonal fluctuations of the Sanctus (see Ex. 9 above), symbolically threefold, form the most eventful stage of the work's cycle, and in other ways too its climactic nature is established. The melodic material revolved so constantly in it is a twelve-note proposition (see Ex 9b), the exploration of all pitch resources providing an apt symbol for 'Pleni sunt caeli et terra gloria tua'. At this point the row moves into the organ pedal, while at 'Hosanna' the organ bursts out in a decorated form of its original paired intervals (cf. Ex 9a and b), supporting the wedge-shaped harmonic block of the voices' peak phrases. This brilliance fades as dramatically as it emerged (through the organ's drastically graded dynamics) and the Benedictus offers in its place a quiet ecstasy. The origins of this material in earlier movements have been noted, but a link with the Sanctus is preserved in the rhythmic pattern (essentially ♪♪♪♩ ♩ despite the halved note-values). The treatment is transparent—a solo centred on G is repeated on C and then delivered in canon at these two levels—but it is difficult to say why counterpoint apparently so casual should create so poignant an impression, at its most heart-rending at the final synchronization of the two voices, inevitably in a descending scale of perfect fourths. A succinct reprise of *all* the forms of the Sanctus ground gives the second Hosanna epigrammatic force.

The burden of the Agnus Dei, a five-beat chain of thirds, lacks altogether the exploratory quality of the twelve-note ground. It appears moored to the one spot in that the E flat to which it rises can only plunge again to the initial D—yet is it *rooted* to that spot or is this the upper part of a B flat major thirds-chain? The edgy rhythm of the organ right-hand figure clarifies nothing, for its semitonal clash between B flat and A only heightens the ambiguity. And the vocal line, conjunct like the Benedictus but now far more cramped and semitonal, sets off from B flat. Its sequential patterns (quasi flat 3 2 1 sharp 7 1) descend forlornly with no clear tonal destination until unison gives way to harmony ('miserere nobis') that retrieves D minor from a potential B flat minor. This disconsolate succession is repeated at a still more oblique angle to the ostinato bass, and the organ figure thickens to more tense dissonance, leading to a third and highest invocation in which the voices' C minor is fused by the organ with a B major triad—a harsh cry in a piece that has by now grown from *pp* to *f*. But at this point, 'miserere nobis' gives way to 'dona nobis pacem', and the voices abandon their anguished figure for the limpid plea of repeated notes. These are overlapped up and down the B flat major scale, and now even the organ's clashing seconds have become explicable within the one diatonic field—a touching symbol of dawning hope. At the peak of the curve, however, the prayer for peace provokes a recall of the earlier tonal conflict, and the organ's figure creates frictions that only fade out (*via* that illuminated moment where F sharp echoes distantly) in the final whispered plea—on a D minor triad but hovering in the 6/4 position.

439

CANTATA MISERICORDIUM, OP. 69

Britten's first choral work after the *War Requiem* is difficult to view in a context altogether divorced from that of the *Requiem*. In the *Cantata Misericordium* there is even so direct a reminder as a dialogue of tenor and baritone soloists that culminates in a soft, bright music (to which harp colour contributes distinctively) to the words 'Dormi nunc, amice'. Violence is no longer thrust before us as a central issue—the assault on the traveller is quickly related—but rather man's need to counter it with the practice, not merely the sentiments, of compassion. No more apt theme could have been chosen for a work written for, and first performed on, the Commemoration Day of the Centenary of the Red Cross, held in Geneva on 1 September 1963. As it was conceived to celebrate an international occasion, Britten chose not to prefer any one modern language but to use Latin, a common heritage of the whole western world. Certainly he was not seeking to profit from the hieratic solemnity associated with Latin, for the parable of the Good Samaritan is a simple tale. And he set Patrick Wilkinson's text in so direct a form that listeners can rely on their familiarity with the sequence of events to carry them through obscurities of language. The instrumental resources are modest, yet they create a highly individual sound world—string quartet and string orchestra, piano, harp and timpani.

The character of this sound is no less a product of certain harmonic-cum-tonal relationships that permeate the whole work. Whereas the tensions of the *Requiem* were symbolized in a tritonal polarity, the cantata makes much of third relationships, above all that between F sharp, its principal tonal field, and D; we have seen precisely this duality (though with roles reversed) at work in the *Missa Brevis*. Though the semitonal frictions (especially of simultaneous 'false relations') which are implicit in the method can be played upon to create moments of acute harmonic stress, ambivalence rather than flat opposition is the typical tonal situation of this work. The motivic importance attached to an F sharp major triad plus D in the bass is established in the opening salutation of the merciful, by the convergence of the successive 'Beati' cries on to that chord; see Ex. 12. It is then deployed in many ways, some very simple as in the 'Dormi nunc' music, others extending its ambiguity: in Ex. 13, a to c, can be seen three contexts in which the

Ex.17.12

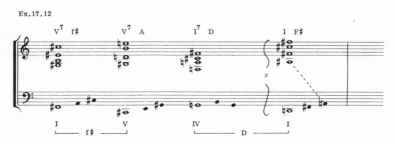

Ex.17.13 (a)

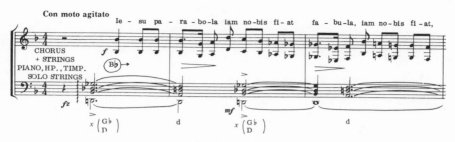

Ex.17.13 (b)

Ex.17.13 (c)

Ex.17.13 (d)

Ex. 17.13 (e)

attraction of one or more additional tonal centres can be felt. These more complex situations are created by the use of sinuously varied scale patterns, and the whole cantata affords an excellent study of this important element in Britten's technique of this period. Not surprisingly, given the major thirds in the augmented triad of the Ex. 12 x chord, the whole-tone scale often helps to establish the multivalence of centre, but much use is also made of that regular alternation of tone and semitone Britten had relied on so heavily in his Cello Sonata, two years earlier (see Ex. 13d). A simple example of its operation has already been shown at Ex. 13b above, and others can be found at three bars before fig. 6, from fig. 12 and, most schematically, in the unaccompanied choral mirror-writing just before fig. 13. At their most tortuous, Britten's scalic lines draw on all twelve notes by the Bartókian procedure of returning movements that fill in the pitches omitted in whole-tone steps: the agitated section beginning at 'Dure, sacerdos' (after fig. 16) is the most sustained example.

The score of the cantata gives the impression of many short sections, yet they are far more closely linked in their pitch material than a perfunctory glance would suggest, and, for once in Britten, some of the key signatures are misleading in implying more nearly absolute contrasts than the listener will sense. Even so, contrasts of many other kinds—of texture, speed and rhythmic patterning—succeed one another very swiftly, and the effect of a blur of images might have resulted. It suited Britten's structural purpose very well, therefore, to treat many of these passages as episodes in a design bound together by the appearances of a ritornello. The intertwining figures with which the string quartet opens the work assume this function and, as the chorus (doubled by the quartet) take up the same rhythms and imitative texture at the first appearance of the word 'misericordes', the idea is made a text for the whole cantata. The accompaniment is the common Britten pattern of scalic movement of a chord (initially a 6–4–2 against a tonally-grounded arpeggio bass: we have seen the fundamental harmonic movement in Ex. 12).

A wedge-shaped motive (at fig. 4) supported on the x-chord, provides a subsidiary unifying element; it is used to create expectancy, here ushering in the words of Roman and Jew, later bringing on to the scene in turn Priest, Levite and Samaritan. After the soloists' question 'But who is my neighbour?' has fashioned x into a memorable epigram (shown at Ex. 13e), the same chord is reinterpreted in the new tonal sense shown at Ex. 13a, as the choir announce the parable and lead into its action. Their rôle embraces narrative and commentary: while the baritone enacts the traveller and the tenor the Samaritan, the other participants are silent, their actions being followed through the reactions of the chorus. The pace of events is rapid: the lonely traveller's fears, voiced against an edgy accompanying line and sudden unnerving triads, are realized with the chorus's warning shouts; the ambush is depicted orchestrally in terms of percussive dissonance, and the anguished cry of the traveller is a powerfully harmonized derivative of Ex. 13a. (If *Peter Grimes* comes to mind here it is by way of the apprentice's theme in the passacaglia interlude and the 'storm' chord that affects its later treatment—see fig. 48 for example.) Tonal ambiguity makes uneasy the quiet music in which the chorus ponder on his fate—'Who will help this man in such a wilderness?'

The string quartet ritornello represents the passage of time, but its implicit appeal for mercy sounds forlorn. So the choral wedge-theme that stirs into life above the static x chord brings the first hope, prompted by the appearance of the Priest. Urged by the chorus, the traveller cries for help (making reference to the 'misericordia' motive again), but his appeal falls away into the uneasy stillness of the x chord. We follow the Priest into the distance only through the hasty step of the orchestral texture and the reproaches cast at him, 'Dure Sacerdos', by the chorus in their tortuous unison lines. A similar sequence of events begun by the quartet ritornello marks the Levite's appearance, though most of them are presented at lower pitch and the choral reproaches strike a new note of outrage in their seventh and ninth drops (see above, Ex. 13c). The effect of these two encounters is far greater for there being no attempt to represent Priest and Levite in singing parts: their actions take on a peculiarly despicable quality that could not easily be captured in music, apt though that can be in symbolizing more ample forms of evil. Doing nothing is, very palpably, the sin against which this work speaks.

For a third time the quartet ritornello begins the cycle of events, with an appeal for mercy that is so halting (most of its rhythms are by now reduced to half-speed) as to betoken the abandonment of hope. And the choirs' wedge-theme, at lower pitch than ever before and without its usual quickening of pulse, greets the Samaritan's appearance without confidence. Yet the despair of the traveller's cry, falling to his lowest pitch level, is answered by a mysterious stirring in the strings that restores x to the octave position which it has not occupied since 'Beati' (fig. 3), and by the voice of the tenor, also absent since the introduction. This beautiful turning-moment in the piece is given an inevitable quality by the Samaritan's direct appropriation of the choral version of the mercy theme (cf. third bar of fig. 3). His line grows generously as he tends the traveller's wounds and a peculiarly sweet tone is created by the A major (faintly Lydian) in which the chorus applaud this change of fortune. By contrast the business that must be transacted between the Samaritan and the keeper of the inn to which he conducts the traveller is done in a crisp, prosaic C major, perhaps less creatively derived from Stravinsky than Eric Roseberry, the work's first commentator, would have us believe.[8] The following section (from fig. 26) neatly enough counterpoints the Samaritan's fussing care and the traveller's slowly rising spirits, but its material is too mechanically worked out. However, its D major gives release to a tonal area that has customarily been an element of tension. At the close of the section, after the traveller has asked his rescuer to reveal his identity, we hear as the Samaritan gently refuses a concealed form of the 'Who is my neighbour?' epigram, now founded on D—a delicate allusion. Again dwelling on the 'misericordia' theme, but now accompanied by string quartet harmony, the tenor steers the music back to the ambiguous x chord. But now F sharp is to be represented by the serene major of his lullaby, 'Dormi nunc' (its line a further derivation from the epigram, cf. Ex. 13e above), and D by the Lydian of the plainsong-like melody the chorus male voices now introduce. This resolution of a conflict not by banishing differences but by accepting them in a new and rarefied state of tonal equipoise is quintessential Britten, and the moment of illumination towards which the whole work has been directed.

The chorus revive more acute tensions when, in their homily on the story, they speak of a world in which disease and war still prevail, but their peroration richly affirms faith in the unifying power of charity. The epigram (Ex. 13e) is literally recalled as its earlier question is answered ('Who your neighbour is, now you know') and the falling close of the work bridges the whole experience by recalling its opening section (from the crucial x chord of fig. 3—with parts inverted) for the deceptively simple moral 'Go and do thou likewise'. The D major arpeggio that rotates throughout fades out on a final F sharp. Stravinskyan though we may find the scene at the inn in its rhythmic chatter, in manipulating this Stravinskyan scheme of third relationships Britten never suggests that it arose from anything other than a contemplation of the parable, its dramatic situations and its underlying theme.

VOICES FOR TODAY, OP. 75

As an extended piece for unaccompanied chorus, *Voices for Today* takes its place in the line begun by *A Boy was Born* and continued by the *Hymn to Saint Cecilia*, but it does not attempt to reproduce the virtuoso feats of those scores. Whereas they deployed voices with a quasi-instrumental brilliance and in time-spans suggestive of 'movements', this anthem uses them above all as a vehicle for the clear delivery of words, in textures that restlessly change with each clause of the text but are typically very thin. Only in the final section, a setting of excerpts from Virgil's fourth Eclogue (in Latin) is one textural disposition, of a hymnic line for boys' voices floating over choral homophony, allowed to develop into a rounded section. Virgil's vision

[8] E. Roseberry, 'Britten's *Cantata Misericordium*' (review), *Tempo* 66/67, 1963, p. 40.

emerges naturally enough from the final lines of the preceding anthology of pithy texts (to be sung in the vernacular, whatever that may be, of the country of performance)—Shelley's 'The world's great age begins anew/The golden years return'—and from this point, the choral refrain with which the work began, 'If you have ears to hear, then hear!', effectively frames the closing span. But the earlier rapid succession of texts is musically all too insubstantial, whether or not its primarily monodic events are supported on the cushion of harmonies offered at times by the optional organ part. A truly cumulative texture, to which the boys' choir adds the peak, distinguishes the line 'The young are people', and prepares the shape for the final section's descant. But only with the reiterated bass rhythms of 'Ring out . . .' does the piece acquire real momentum.

Even Britten's setting of the Eclogue is restrained; setting out from the VII triad on I pedal of the refrain ('If you have ears') it dwells on a succession of such simply dissonant harmonies activated only by verbal rhythms. It is the boys' descant that charts the growth of this section. But with the onset of a hesitant polyphony (from 'At tibi prima, puer'), the interest is more evenly balanced, and C major is abandoned for a more graphic middle section. A little word-painting is admitted for the goats, the lion, the serpent and the poisonous weed, but the choral texture soon reverts to an essentially mono-dic delivery of the text. This makes more weighty the effect of the return to C and the textural build-up at the vision of the world ('Aspice convexo'), and the climactic moment at which the main choir takes over in octaves the boys' chant to words that have already acquired meaning, 'Incipe, parve puer'. The choir completes the entire hymnic shape, while the boys add 'If you have ears' as a closely canonic counterpoint. The ending, with its tonally deviating versions of the chant's opening line, brings a significant but unforced remin-der of Yevtushenko's 'The young are people'.

Nothing makes clearer than this reference the central concern Britten had in addressing this anthem to the United Nations—his heartfelt hope that the endeavour of one generation might yet secure a peaceful future for younger generations. His work was written for the U.N.'s twentieth anniversary, on 24 October 1965, and was given on that day in New York, Paris and London. To read the aphorisms Britten selected is to recognize how coherent a statement he was making, yet one may regret that he chose to deliver so many sentiments in so short a space; for until the Virgil setting the impres-sion is of a music not so much lean as undernourished.

SACRED AND PROFANE, OP. 91

In view of the preponderance of vocal music in his work as a whole, Britten's entire output for unaccompanied voices was surprisingly small. *Voices for Today* was his most ambitious attempt to make of the medium a vehicle for a deeply-considered personal statement, *The Flower Songs* were neat 'charac-ter' pieces yet for once the character was not consistently unmistakable as

445

Britten's alone; deference to the English part-song tradition sometimes has dulled his response to the texts. *The Hymn to St Cecilia*, on the other hand, was radiantly personal, using the voices to create newly-imagined textures without the rather self-conscious virtuosity of *A Boy was Born* (1933). The Auden setting was assisted by an underlying unity of thought in the poems and by the refrain, so that it could naturally grow into a single musical cycle; the much longer span and diverse texts of *A Boy was Born* had to be controlled by more contrived means, every piece being made an evident variation on the work's opening shape. Even so, this rigorous treatment allowed Britten to handle medieval texts without dipping far into the ragbag of sentimental archaisms from which the English 'carol' manner of the early twentieth century had drawn too heavily. A response markedly nearer the conventional one in his second carol cycle, *A Ceremony of Carols* (1942), preserved a highly individual flavour partly by the neatness of device but principally by the typically inventive yet economical accompaniments for harp.

More than thirty years elapsed before Britten wrote another cycle for voices on old English texts. The Eight Medieval Lyrics, *Sacred and Profane*, Op. 91, set for five solo voices (SSATB), were completed on 9 January 1975, and received their first performance at the Maltings in September. As the title implies, this anthology has no central literary theme, and its texts range from the mid-twelfth to the mid-fourteenth century. Yet our very remoteness from such poetry, its imagery as well as its language, helps us to sense (though perhaps also too fancifully to imagine) very strongly the unified ways of thinking and feeling that allowed unselfconscious passage between the sacred and secular. Perhaps Britten, working under the handicap of his illness, turned to these poems, most of them short, because they could be treated individually, without the need for the elaborate unifying schemes of his first carol cycle. There are clear cross-references, usually from one setting into the next, and the emotional sequence is well considered, but, unusually for Britten, there are settings here that could make their effect out of the context of the cycle. And if this were tried, it would not always be easy to date the Britten to which we were listening for there is a clear retrospective quality in some settings from which others, invested with a new acuity of vocal dissonance, stand out the more starkly.

The earliest text, 'St Godric's Hymn', is given a clear rhythmic profile by simple homophonic treatment. Britten's typical flat seventh on the tonic C triad is used primarily as a pivot to E minor/G major (i.e., quasi German sixth; as so often, comparison with Stravinsky's Symphony in C is interesting) but its influence is also heard in the deviations to flat areas of both strophes. Though the second is essentially a variant on the first's harmonic events, the strong impression of rise countered by fall conceals this; the invocations of the coda, aided by long pauses, discover a mystical quality in the piece's basic progression. Britten's title for his second setting 'I mon

waxe wod' is not the opening (of the familiar lyric, 'Fowles in the frith') but
the central line and, as a reiterated alto declamatory interjection, it is the
musical core too. The obsessions that foreshadow madness are represented
in the framing lines, delivered simultaneously, 1 and 2 in the two sopranos, 4
and 5 in tenor and bass. These are repeated mechanistically and are also
mechanistic in interval structure: the sopranos' nervously fluttering material
is a cell of two minor thirds joined by a semitone (e.g., A flat, F; E, C sharp)
reproduced canonically at the lower fifth while the men's dour burden
juxtaposes two major-third chains. The composite effect is of B flat centrality so that the alto's line, texturally dissociated yet sharing the same intervallic fixations, drops away to a final A that is forlorn. This is immediately
transformed into the melodic starting-point of the brightest piece in the
cycle, 'Lenten is come'. Its lilting metre (3 + 3 + 2) and easy development of
the complementary strands are so engaging as to make the piece seem at
once familiar, though models that come to mind (like the 'Spring Carol' from
A Ceremony of Carols) do not threaten its individuality. As in the first
setting, an early Mixolydian seventh facilitates later flattening inflexions,
and the strophe mounts sequentially from a central trough to a sonorous
peak. Only after its music has been repeated for the second stanza is the
wistful sweetness of the Lydian G sharp introduced (at 'the moon'), to be
given ironically reversed meaning as A flat when the piece loses its buoyancy
in a much-flattened minor mode.

This gives piquant effect to a quotation of the theme restored to the bright
major which, like a last glimpse of summer, opens 'The Long Night'. It is
displaced by winter's 'strong weather', of fugato that is angular but rather
anonymous (cf. the similar resort to fugal texture in the third quartet's
'Burlesque'). More characteristic sonorities give force to the central ex-
clamation, yet the treatment seems too diffuse for so short a piece. There
follows a magnificently terse setting, 'Yif ic of luve can', a contemplation of
the Passion. Britten has set the first seven short lines as a single musical
strophe in four-part homophony, punctuated by long reflective pauses; the
crucial last line, 'for the luve of man', is a broadened conflation of the first
two. Tonally B major/minor is never seriously disputed, yet the repeated
deflections to chords that suggest C minor (see Ex. 14, bar 3) create an
ambivalence such as underlines some of Britten's weightiest structures. On
this minute scale it is reinforced by an unusual concentration of dissonant
harmony to suggest a controlled anguish. This is allowed more eloquent
expression in a repetition of the complete strophe to which the first soprano
adds, in a wide-ranging descant (see Ex. 14), the moral of the poem's
remaining three lines:

> Well ou ic to wepen
> And sinnes for to leten
> Yif ic of luve can.

Ex.17.14

As in 'St Godric's Hymn' there is a mystical fervour here that cannot be exactly paralleled in Britten's work. Even 'Jesu, as thou art our Saviour' (third variation of *A Boy was Born*) creates a far less feverish mood; if one thought of Vaughan Williams there, albeit to chart then the crucial differences, here one thinks rather of Messiaen, even though Britten remains essentially uninfluenced by that master's harmonic methods.

The sixth lyric is simply entitled 'Carol'. When we observe that Britten has added the curious direction 'Flowing, with parody!', we may be tempted to believe that what is parodied is just that harnessing of folky lines to sophisticated harmony which had distinguished the tasteful pseudo-medieval carollings of many of his English predecessors; Warlock's *Adam lay ibounden* offers an obvious (if superior) example of the type. But of course the text itself, with its repeated hesitations and questionings over an incompleted line in each stanza, invites whimsical treatment. Britten intensifies the exasperated persistence of the dialogue by extensions and transpositions, but each stanza ends with the musical refrain literally recalled. This is a phrase so insidiously platitudinous that it has a fascinating memorability. So it very naturally persists in the next piece, 'Ye that pasen by', but now as a series of declamatory solos; these round off lines in which the chaste homophony of the Carol has given way to the sound, 'slow and dragging', of third chains overlapping scales, giving a blurred and peculiarly desolate effect. This second Passion scene is less elevated, more pitiable than the first, but in his final setting Britten remorselessly checks the inventory of 'A Death' that is now all too grossly human. Even when the grotesque declamation of single voices becomes dogged by a second, and later a third, voice, in close linear parallel but spitting out the crucial verbs with malevolence (a new use for heterophonic techniques deriving from the parables), no detail is allowed to escape us. The vast phrase in octaves, 'Al to late! Wanne the bere is at gate', no doubt fortuitously throws the memory back to the central motive of *Grimes*, yet the reminder does not seem wholly pointless: this headlong despair could be that of the mad and tormented Peter. The fluttering from bed to grave is made graphic by a further heterophonic technique of flowing parallel seconds versus a rapid phrase of the same pitches at another octave. From the opening, implications of E tonality have been recurrent but elusive, and the sudden relapse into a typical Britten major, with balancing Lydian and Mixolydian inflexions, mirrored melodic strands and buoyant rhythms, answers horrifyingly well the macabre nonchalance of the poem's last line. The irony is powerful, but one is grateful that Britten lived to fashion in Aschenbach's E major the sublime valedictory music of the third quartet's finale.

18 War Requiem

It has not been the purpose of this book to record the fluctuations of Britten's critical stock, for such an account would not bear much demonstrable relation to the quality of the music he was producing at any given period. However, it may be that in taking the *War Requiem* to be a landmark in the composer's creative career one is too much swayed by the reception it was originally accorded and the subsequent anxiety on the part of writers who had joined in the paean to qualify their praise. In a period when the concept of a masterpiece is widely considered to be suspect, ludicrous or just irrelevant, the profound effect this work made on its first audiences was unsettling, and spontaneous reactions were soon examined to detect flaws that reason suggested must be there. A comparative glut of performances in the *Requiem*'s early existence probably did the composer's critical reputation a disservice even while it gave to this one of his works a popular esteem none had enjoyed since *Peter Grimes* changed the fortunes of English opera. The *War Requiem* was intended to communicate very directly a specific message, highly appropriate to the occasion for which it was written, the celebrations at the consecration of the new Coventry Cathedral, where it was first performed on 30 May 1962. It represented not only an effort to mark worthily a triumphant recovery from the ashes of war, but also a conscious resolve on the composer's part to put the experience of his entire creative activity to that date at the service of a passionate denunciation of the bestial wickedness by which man is made to take up arms against his fellow. One could prefer that a work so overtly didactic might be kept free from the importunate note that too frequent hearings will tend to bring to it, yet it was precisely because Britten had found means of communicating in broad effects to audiences with little experience of the music of our time that the demand for performances rose so remarkably, and for the same reason that critical sensibilities proved delicate in the face of repeated exposure to the work's assault.

Viewed in a more dispassionate light, however, the *War Requiem* will continue to be noted by students of Britten's music as a watershed. Having set up within one frame the resources of works as contrasted as the *Sinfonia*

450

da Requiem and *Cantata Academica*, the Nocturne and the *Missa Brevis*, and stylistic traits recalled from a host of earlier works, culminating in the direct appropriation of material from Canticle II, Britten was evidently bent on consummating them, and the corollary which became evident soon afterwards was that he had in that very act exhausted, at least for the time being, their power to stimulate his invention further. Both the instrumental works that followed the *Requiem* and, still more strikingly, the church parables, seem to mark a deliberate withdrawal from the territory it mapped out with a mastery bred of long familiarity.

This encyclopaedic quality distinguishes the *Requiem* from any one of the operas (though *Owen Wingrave* may be thought to approach its width of stylistic reference), yet in its vast scope it can only be compared with the operas, as also in its development from dramatically conflicting elements. In choosing so audaciously to juxtapose the Mass for the Dead with war poems of Wilfred Owen, Britten could not rely merely on the anthologist's good taste which had served him well elsewhere. Unless the two sources could be shown to engage with one another, or at least to confront one another relevantly, perhaps violently, the result could only be a painful disaster. The pattern of correspondences and analogies he was able to uncover has become well-known, yet the appropriateness of such an association as he forges between the Abraham of the liturgical text, of Owen's poem and of his own earlier canticle setting remains uncanny. For the greater part of the work, however, dramatic conclusions that the listener may draw are not the product of overt musical interaction between the performing groups; the three spatially distinct ensembles move most often on quite separate planes, presenting the impassive calm of a liturgy that points beyond death (boys and organ), the mingled mourning, supplication and guilty apprehension of humanity in the mass (choir and main orchestra, sometimes sublimated, rather than personalized, by the soprano soloist) and the passionate outcry of the doomed victims of war (male soloists and chamber orchestra). It follows therefore that, however dramatic the impact of the brusque confrontations when the music moves from one world to another, Britten's scheme does not call for the symphonic drama of musical involution: when no texture is required to propel the entire emotional cycle of a movement, there is no need for the working out of material through a crisis of complexity to a regained equilibrium. So it is that a truly large-scale work is able to rely on simple musical ideas almost throughout.

The impression is therefore of some of Britten's most open-handed invention: while thematic cross-reference is used to obvious effect, there is far less dense a network of motivic growths than in the preceding operas (*Budd*, *Screw* and the *Dream* in particular). The principal unifying shape, the tritone, is a melodic, harmonic and sometimes tonal determinant, but the frequent appearance of so primary an element should discourage us from attaching too limitedly programmatic or 'dramatic' a significance to it;

451

beyond noting that it always appears in relation to the idea of 'requiem' we need not characterize it. As so often in Britten's music, the tritone is used to set up tensions (thus 'rest' is always associated with musical unrest) but in no other of his works is their resolution of so equivocal a nature. The first escape from the mutual incomprehension of the bells' blank F sharp and C is into an F major resolution, but this cannot be regarded as the 'outcome' in a long-term (or even notably logical) sense of each of the three movements which cadence in this way. Of the other two movements which employ the interval (it plays no important rôle in the Offertorium), the Sanctus yields no resolution at all, and only the Agnus Dei achieves a final statement of an equipoise in which the strains of the whole movement are balanced out. It is noteworthy that this setting, of the liturgical text and Owen's 'At a Calvary near the Ancre' in parallel, demonstrates the closest alliance, of feeling and of musical material, to be found in the work, and in the final tonal resolution a meeting-point is recognized between Owen's salutation of the 'greater love' and the liturgy's prayer for 'requiem sempiternam': Britten's substitution of the non-liturgical 'Dona nobis pacem' in the tenor's cadential phrase underlines this very clearly (Ex. 1c). The Agnus Dei is the only movement consistently controlled by a tritonal tonal relationship. Its melodic material springs from scale segments that span fifths from the poles F sharp and C, in opposite directions but by the identical succession of tones and semitone; Ex. 1 shows the two interlocking patterns which this may produce, (a) being used as an ostinato almost throughout except for one transfer to the 'domin-

Ex. 18.1 (a)

Ex. 18.1 (b)

Ex. 18.1 (c)

ant position' of (b) and climactic extensions at the end of each choral refrain, (c). The impression of this ceaseless burden, sung or played, is predominantly of B minor alternating with its Neapolitan sixth, but the tenor's descanting lines for Owen's poem often reverse the apparent stress in this scheme (i.e., sometimes one bar, sometimes the other seems to bear the weight), an effect aided by the extremely supple 5/16 pulse. The sombre colouring of the woodwind harmonies also prevents the scalic operations from acquiring too mechanistic (as opposed to inexorable) a sound, while the *da capo* structure throws into relief the central solo lines (the second coinciding with the transmuted ground, Ex. 1b) in which Owen reflects bitterly on the priests and all those who give their blessing to wars they do not have to fight. The singular economy of gesture in this movement is not simplistic: the tone of noble sorrow it engenders is the most subtly interfused mood of the *War Requiem*, and one of Britten's supreme achievements.

At the other extreme to this homogeneous (yet bi-planar) piece is the first movement, 'Requiem aeternam', where the tritone is the obvious unifying element common to three wholly distinct kinds of music, each of which puts it to a different purpose. Its relationship is most tenuous in the sections for chorus and orchestra. Here its two pitches provide the sole material not only for the passing bells but for the chorus's many repetitions of the liturgical 'Requiem aeternam dona eis Domine, et lux perpetua luceat eis'; their muttered phrases (with an obvious debt to Verdi at the outset)[1] do not

[1] Cf. M. Boyd, 'Britten, Verdi and the Requiem', *Tempo* 86, 1968, p. 2.

formulate the prayer for peace with any glib persuasiveness, and they are set at an uneasy tangent to the D minor in which the orchestra begins its slowly unfolding threnody. In basic tonality and contours this is reminiscent of the 'Lacrymosa' from the *Sinfonia da Requiem*, but it has a new inner tension, derived from the burdening of these nervously lithe quintuplet upbeats with the full weight of the lethargic harmony (see Ex. 2). These crawling chords,

Ex. 18.2

confined between melodic octaves, are almost invariably minor thirds, and the orchestral texture acquires all the ceremonial gloom of the minor mode while ranging very widely in tonal implications and scale pattern. D minor continues to be the central implication, active chiefly through its dominant; the last bar of Ex. 2 shows the extent to which the tritone of bells and choir can conflict with this field. This is a tortured music: though the words are of the liturgy, they are a commemoration of the dead weighed down with the self-searching of the living. The liturgical tone is sounded by the hymn of the boys' choir and organ (Ex. 3a): cool, chiselled and immanently certain, it hovers at a great distance from this human abasement. Yet it is not irrelevant to the foreground scene, for the crucial tritone is still there, but no longer tonally at odds with its context: instead it appears sublimated as the poles between which the melodic phrases and their inversions pass smoothly. The underlying series of triads is founded on all twelve roots, producing a weightless movement; we may accept Britten's F major key signature as basic, but the whole section turns on the doubly tritonal proposition F–F sharp/B natural–C (see Ex. 3b).

The vocal curves are progressively simplified until only C and F sharp (as dominants of F and B) maintain a gentle oscillation, when the return of the bells and the main choir restores to the identical tritone all its former unrest. The orchestral theme (Ex. 2) works its way up more quickly than before but, as in Ex. 2 bar 2, its cadential impulse is nullified by the tritone. Suddenly the

454

Ex.18.3 (a)

Ex.18.3 (b)

interval is given its third meaning, sounding from yet another source in a tremolando of the harp in the chamber orchestra. The change is more radical than before, to a new urgent pulse, the immediacy of solo voice and instruments, and the directness of the vernacular in Owen's 'Anthem for Doomed Youth'. Tonally the change is to a background of B flat minor's dominant (as the key signature indicates), but however familiar an orientation G flat–C might be thought to provide in this context, the simpler definition is calculated to give pungency to an ironic exploitation of simultaneously contradictory harmonies, while the athletic bass line (see Ex. 4) constantly wrenches against tonal bonds. This bass theme is related to that of Ex. 2 (and like it,

Ex.18.4

distantly to Britten's earlier *Requiem* opening), and its wild gait and wiry textures seem like a reproach to the heavy propulsion of Ex. 2 even though they depict the rifle's rattle and the wailing of shells. The effect is dramatic but not melodramatic: poet and composer offer a challenge to the luxury of opulent mourning, 'mocking from prayers or bells', that naturally implies a conflict between the two sections. Cross-references such as the tenor's tritone oscillation for 'prayers' are self-evident, but some are more subtle in their interfusion of sources and resources. In choosing to use a boys' choir to provide the third, ethereal dimension in his spatial plan, Britten must surely have been prompted by Owen's next lines:

> What candles may be held to speed them all?
> Not in the hands of boys, but in their eyes
> Shall shine the holy glimmers of good-byes.

This inevitably, and movingly, brings back the musical shape of those boy-servants of the liturgy first heard at Ex. 3a. But the impassive organ tone is replaced by solo colours more warmly human yet more spectral in their *ponticello* shading. The final augmentation by the tenor of Ex. 3a 'And each slow dusk' has that peculiarly penetrating quality that Britten can distil from slow equal notes. The tonic pedal drumming the rhythm of war below this seems to be confirming F as the outcome of this composite movement, but it gives way at the melody's cadence on F sharp to admit a scurrying echo of Ex. 4; the tritone thus reinstated is then returned to its original colouring in the bells and chorus to produce a faintly recapitulatory impression. The choral Kyrie twice fails to escape the impasse of that sound, only in its final clause sinking on to F major once more. This coda must be the shortest setting of the Kyrie in any large-scale work: it rivets our attention on to its meaning rather than dispersing this in ritual ornament. After the dead have spurned our mourning, we are fittingly reminded that there is much to mourn in ourselves.

So we are prepared in some measure for a Dies irae which eschews grandiose horror; though the words remain those in which the living commemorate the dead, we await those moments at which the dead reinterpret them to the living. Thus the climaxes of this movement are those of the battlefield, even while the analogy of the day of doom is pursued; the last trumpets are also forlorn bugle calls. To say that Owen's is the essential world in such contexts is not to question the propriety of Britten's drawing on the liturgy: if he refuses to portray a God of wrath, his man-made *dies irae* must appear the more terrible a denial of the God of pity so sublimely invoked elsewhere. An elaborate structure is assembled from the interpolation into the complete liturgical sequence of four extracts from Owen. Britten had exploited fanfare motives in so many earlier works, embracing implications ranging from the acutely ironic to the elementally affirmative, that the parade of ideas shown at Ex. 5 can both unify the movement and

Ex. 18.5

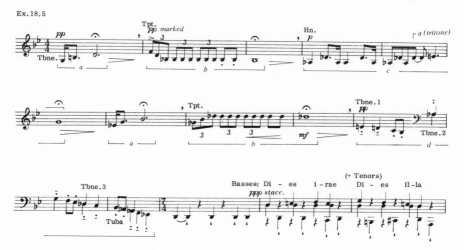

accommodate significant changes of emotional emphasis. Thus, although he accepts the almost inescapable convention (even Mozart's *letzte Posaune* utters one 'natural' brass call before its disconcerting access of eloquence), Britten can avoid *gaucherie* with a resourcefulness developed elsewhere in his work. The various tonal quarters from which calls sound and their rhythmic distinctiveness make them appear programmatically introductory, yet the succession is tightly secured, and is to be developed *in toto*. The brass material alternates with even simpler choral lines (the limping 7/4 metre giving point to almost wholly scalic contours) for the first four choruses, but it becomes steadily more dense so that 'Tuba mirum' (in which the implied tonic, G minor, is at last achieved) is presented by a blaze of sound as overpowering as Verdi's. But after the choral climax the fanfares lose their definition in hazy superimpositions (of tonalities as well as motives) preparing for the feeble groping of 'Mors stupebit'.

This shattering of an illusory splendour sets the tone for Owen's poem 'Bugles sang, saddening the evening air', in which all the motives of Ex. 5 reappear as pathetic commentaries by the chamber orchestra (its only brass instrument, the horn, acquires a prominent role as partner to the baritone). Despite the fleet woodwind writing (appropriately reminiscent of the Nocturne) to which Ex. 5*b* gives rise, the music is underlaid by long-held string triads, giving a foretaste of the timeless quality that is to be so wonderfully sustained in 'Strange meeting'. Britten's key signatures confirm the background of this setting as a move from G minor to A major/minor (the tonal centre of the whole middle section of the movement) but throughout it expressive use is made of merging or conflicting tonal fields. The opening conflation—horn B flat/strings G—at once creates a typical Britten situation in its semitonal clash and resolution in an 'absolute' flat seventh chord: the second statement has more semitonal frictions and the two major triads are now on C and G flat, the tritonal proposition of the previous movement. The baritone's line is fashioned from fanfare arpeggios poignantly at variance with the sustained harmonies, its climax being achieved when these lilting shapes are abandoned, at 'Voices of old despondency, resigned, Bowed by the shadow of the morrow', for the conjunct Ex. 5*d*, the shadow, that is, of the *dies irae*.

Returning to the liturgical text after poetic moments like this we may feel reluctant to surrender fantasy for formal symmetries. But the spatial separation of the groups helps us to accept the gulf between the ritual quality of the Latin text and the specific, urgent quality of the English poems, and Britten makes the distinction absolute in his material. The soprano's proud flourishes at 'Liber scriptus' are worked out in patterned extensions and inversions. Yet formal rigidity does not exclude dramatic effect: the juxtaposition and eventual superimposition of this recording angel's voice and the no less schematic but utterly abased choral 'Quid sum miser' unify these central choruses in a single span of dramatic tension. The crawling motion, chromatically introverted, of the choral texture, in that Bartókian vein Britten often tapped, is kept within a clear tonal field, and a I–V–I succession of pedals underpins the whole span. This supremacy of A nominally continues in the duet, 'Out there we've walk'd quite friendly up to Death', a buoyant setting which immediately reflects on the timorous apprehensions of the preceding chorus. Again an ironic multitonality is at work, however, with particular ferocity at the cadences which *begin* each line. Thematic cross-reference is now more tenuous, but at 'We chorussed when he sang aloft' the vocal line derives from 'Liber scriptus' while piccolo and clarinet deride the pitiful twists of 'Quid sum miser'. There is a terrible ebullience, a will to survive, in this music, to which the return of the 'Bugles' fanfare adds a sense of outrage. The unusual cadential structure throws into relief the final crucial words shared between the soloists:

> When each proud fighter brags
> He wars on Death for Life; not men for flags.

'Recordare' for four-part women's chorus is followed by 'Confutatis' for four-part men's chorus, and both accumulate by schematic procedures without relapsing into academicism. Above a pulsating figure (reminiscent in its seconds of much earlier Britten), a single theme is wound round itself into a close texture, the rhythmic shape of its main motive allowing statements at one beat's interval to sound through; a similar texture given to the four trumpets creates a strangely glowing effect. In this section the tritone becomes prominent again, notably in the mixed scales of opposing whole-tone segments at 'Mihi quoque'. The basses' 'Confutatis', punctuated by the brass, is succeeded by, then added to, the tenors' 'Oro supplex' and its querulous oboe accompaniment; the extreme marcato–legato contrast

makes for a high degree of permeability while the false relations in both
groups stress their relation of mood. By conflating textures in such ways,
Britten prevents the diffuseness which can easily infect the middle areas of
lengthy liturgical settings.

With the entry of the baritone and the chamber orchestra for Owen's 'Be
slowly lifted up' there begins what can be viewed as a reversed restatement.
The section corresponds to 'Bugles sang' in that the vocal lines are separated
by the main motives (Ex. 5) of the movement. But now it is no twilight scene,
and Owen's passionate anger before the great gun and the human arrogance
it represents demands the trumpets from the main orchestra at these points.
Two other important details which define the vehemence of this section, the
timpani quintuplets and the baritone's tritonal phrase endings, take our
minds back even to the previous movement, but an orthodox restatement
pattern is continued when the chorus introduces a climactic 'Dies irae' in the
original setting and key. The G minor is, of course, Verdi's key, and it cannot
be coincidental that Britten continues the parallel so far as to turn now to B
flat minor for 'Lacrymosa'. The lurching 7/4 rhythms are pulled back
throughout 'Quantus tremor' and the same pattern then forms the choral
background to the soprano solo (Ex. 6a). When so much is patterned, an
intense expressive burden is put on the changing contours. Britten's pointing
up of the salient notes (often implying dissonances—tritones and false
relations—against silence) by woodwind unisons adds to their pathos. The
dissonant notes serve another purpose when soprano and chorus begin, in
broken phrases, to repeat 'Lacrymosa', for from them the solo tenor lines
escape to the contrasted tonal region (nominally A major, though its

Ex.18.6 (a)

Ex.18.6 (b)

dominant position suggests a tritonal rather than a semitonal opposition) in which he sings, in recitative, Owen's 'Futility' (Ex. 6b). But each verse of this in turn gravitates back towards the 'Lacrymosa' shape, beckoning in another soprano phrase. The interaction of the two groups at the desperate moment when we see the futility of life in witnessing a death is the more powerfully affecting for coming at the end of a movement in which they have tended merely to coexist. The background to the poem is of simple tremolando chords, the vocal inflexions Britten's most sensitive, with one curve of intensity linking the interpolated phrases. The last phrase cadences on to the fundamental 'requiem' tritone, C–F sharp, echoed by the bells, for 'Pie Jesu' is a renewal of the prayer for rest. As in the first movement, the unaccompanied chorus leads that interval to resolution, yet F major represents a turning away from rather than a resolution of the issues raised in the Dies irae.

The Offertorium, by setting up a tonal relationship between C sharp minor and G major, appears to be transferring to a broader level the familiar tritonal opposition. C sharp minor is established by an introductory passage in which the boys sing 'Domine Jesu Christe' with an archaic economy of interval (inverting around a central C sharp/D sharp) and to organ roulades that directly recall the *Missa Brevis*. The tritonal F double sharp is prominent in the formation of these, and the orchestra's projection into the choral entry juxtaposes potential dominants of G major with C sharp segments. But with the fugal 'Quam olim Abrahae', G takes over unambiguously. The derivation of this theme from *Abraham and Isaac* is striking, but Britten's immediate concern is for its possibilities as a 'subject', which he provides with a regular countersubject and works out in inverted entries and stretti— the nearest approach to traditional choral craftsmanship in the work— culminating in contrary motion, doubled by parallel fifths. The main orchestra passes the subject to the chamber orchestra, its accompaniment changes to the 2/4 of the canticle, and the soloists begin Owen's paraphrase of the biblical story. Transferences from the canticle's material are never exact, and the old man's preparations for his son's ritual murder are underlined by motives from the battlefield music of the earlier movements, notably the Ex. 5 group, of which *d* (the shadow of the *dies irae*) tellingly accompanies the moment before the knife must fall. In the miracle play version it was the voice of God which stayed Abraham's hand, and Britten retains the luminous two-part texture (and the enveloping fifth-less arpeggios) for the angel's words here; Owen's longer lines sometimes make for a more arresting working of the canticle's shapes. Though the battle motives intrude again, musical understatement intensifies the horror of Owen's sequel:

> But the old man would not so but slew his son
> And half the seed of Europe one by one.

This is simply set to the 'Quam olim' subject, a shape from which expressive potentiality has largely been drained by its contrapuntal working-out; and before the impact of the words is fully assimilated the organ and boys' voices have divided our attention. Again there is a notably medieval flavour in the boys' 'Hostias', and the organ drone is compounded, as was the passage at fig. 63, from C sharp/D sharp and C natural/D natural, but its hypnotic sound is new, a dazed marking of time (its measure the human pulse) as the soloists insistently jab home their last line till all motion has ceased. Then with a symmetry no less chilling for appearing inevitable, the chorus repeats its 'Quam olim'; the counterpoint is strictly inverted in both senses, and the scherzo rhythms now scurry past in a chastened undertone.

The Sanctus reinstates F sharp and C natural as the poles of the tritone, intensifying the kind of juxtaposition which began the previous movement. But the tone at this middle point of the whole work is suddenly changed. We find a release from preoccupations with war, death and human folly in the words of a liturgy that has hitherto brought no more than momentary consolation. Sanctus and Benedictus are messages of serene joy, even in a mass for the dead, and Britten accepts them as such, however ambiguous the attitude in which he then looks back on them through the Owen poem he appends. Even the passing bells' tritone is less oppressive when it mingles with a Sanctus bell that glitters like the fairy music in the *Dream*; and it might almost be Tytania who sings these flashing soprano lines. Britten had offered a hint of the cosmic vision at 'Pleni sunt coeli' in his earlier mass by systematically revolving the musical globe of all twelve notes in the organ part. With the far greater forces of the *War Requiem* he is able to conjure up a pulsating universe of sound by the simple expedient of allowing the choir to repeat the text freely (i.e., with a constant flutter of consonants) across a wide range of pitches (usually introduced in a s-l-d′ succession) and with a steady crescendo. Like other Britten innovations, its nature seems obvious yet no other composer had hit upon this interpretation of this context. It prepares a ceremonial D major from which vocal Hosannas and brass flourishes range jubilantly while the basses hold to the opening 'Sanctus' shape and the tonic. Equally rooted to a pedal is the Benedictus, but this is of a subtler kind: its recurrent bass pattern is a V–I cadence in A, but as its melodic lines are constantly paralleled at the lower fifth there is a steady pull towards IV, and these opposed tendencies give great resilience to so still and unemphatic a piece. The crude parallel fifths are converted into sixth chords by the bass whenever it can escape from its cadential rôle, and the upper lines, controlled by the soprano, gradually widen their range. The mechanisms are simply explained, the result (notwithstanding an obvious debt to the buoyancy of the Benedictus in the *Missa Brevis*) remains fascinating in performance.

The Hosanna is reworked, ending with a blaze of brightly affirmative sound in which all the work's earlier obsessions appear to be exorcized. From the apparent silence that follows its cut-off, a soft pedal D emerges,

461

and the baritone enters, meditatively but pointedly, with Owen's lines beginning 'After the blast of lightning from the East'. A single F natural suffices to throw a long shadow over the brilliance that still rings in our ears; despite the pattering instrumental figures (reminiscent of the dying of the *Grimes* storm) which punctuate and accompany this recitative-arioso, the setting is as disconsolate as the poem. Britten appears here at his most enigmatic, for this questioning of the general resurrection in the context of a Christian mourning rite intensifies the poet's doubts. The accompanying figures become increasingly bitonal or bi-chordal, often opposing tritonally-related areas, until in the last section the texture is reduced to distant, irreconcilable arpeggios; the D major that appears to be clearing in the last vocal line is quickly lost again in the postlude's tonal mist, the basic C–F sharp interval emerging at the cadence. Original and beautiful though the total effect of this passage is, some debt to Stravinsky may be traced in its chord distribution—and perhaps even to Webern in the suspension of crystalline intervals within a vast musical space. Yet the literal-minded will correctly note also that the close of this movement can be construed (in retrospect at least) as a quite traditional approach to the dominant preparation for the B minor of the Agnus Dei.

In its marvellous embodiment of an emotional crux in a tonal structure the Agnus Dei marks the musical high point of the *Requiem*; as we have seen, the tritone here operates at the most comprehensive level and for a moment we can rise to a serene acceptance of what elsewhere had seemed the very token of dissension. But having engraved the text 'Dona nobis pacem' so memorably at the close of this movement, Britten cannot allow us complacently to echo the lip-service which generations of warmongers have paid to it. If the lacerating experiences of the Dies irae and the Abraham episode of the Offertorium have faded a little as the bright Sanctus has given way to the gentle Benedictus and the resigned Agnus Dei, then in the Libera me we must live again through the horror of war. The review of earlier musical material by which Britten recapitulates his subject is compressed into a nightmarish sequence, and a blind panic excludes the nobler emotions of awe that the Dies irae could still admit (e.g., at fig. 20). The opening immediately conflates the quintuplet rhythms of Ex. 2 (with which the drums of war return), the jagged bass lines of Ex. 4 and the Dies irae key (see Ex. 7). The *idée fixe* of the choral entries recreates the abject, forlorn tone of 'Quid sum miser', but is drawn to a still tighter chromatic knot. As the choral texture swells, the orchestral line grows more insistent, and it suddenly doubles speed, so that the Ex. 4 figures regain their original agitation, i.e., we pass from quasi-restatement of the first section of the first movement to that of the second section, a process clearly reflected in the new vocal shape, 'Dum veneris', modelled directly on the tritone span of 'What passing bells' (cf. Ex. 4). Though by now the constant accelerando has led to a considerably faster tempo, the chorus deliver their statements of this idea in the same ponderous

Ex. 18.7

metre which began the movement, so that there is set up a conflict that intensifies each time the orchestra adopts a shorter metrical unit. At one of these points the solo soprano introduces 'Tremens factus' to a transformation of her 'Liber scriptus' (with its accompanying harmony) in which majesty has been exchanged for quivering terror. At the next point it is the complex of fanfares (Ex. 5) that reappears, hurled by the orchestra at a furious speed into the gaps of the still heavy choral 'Libera me'. The inevitable sequel to this must be a return of the Dies irae; its 7/4 rhythm is hammered out in the orchestra, but choral scales now spill over in a panic outburst as the catastrophe is reached. The rôles are thus reversed, and it is the orchestra which turns here to a monumental, and overwhelmingly loud, restatement of the bass theme, while the chorus desperately interjects its 'Libera me' figures. The orchestral sound ebbs away, and the voices fade till only broken cries reach us from the pit that has swallowed them. No other interpretation can be sustained for this vision, apocalyptic even though its Doomsday is the battlefield.

And it is into the terrible calm of Hades that we pass when the chamber orchestra picks up the last G minor chord for the tenor to begin Owen's 'Strange Meeting':

> It seemed that out of battle I escaped
> Down some profound dull tunnel long since scooped.

The vocal line literally escapes from its opening twists of the 'Libera me' figure (i.e., the petition seems to be granted) and from all dynamic thrust, to move through melodic spans that have a new, timeless quality. Though the G minor sixth chord underlying this remains immobile, its calm is threatened by the tritone chords which swell up against it, and as the first words are exchanged the crucial tritone is exposed melodically. As the baritone looks back on 'the undone years', expressive instrumental details colour his lines, and Ex. 5a, first heard in the evening stillness, symbolizes 'the pity war distilled'. Other familiar shapes appear, but the most careful analysis does not account fully for the spell cast by this slowly unfolding recitative—on

463

paper indeed it appears too fragile to bear the emotional weight. Below it, the accompanying chords are turning on a pivotal D through a vast progression, until with their recovery of the G minor sixth they at last break off: it is here that the singer too cadences in the tonic, with a phrase so artless for 'I am the enemy you killed, my friend' that it would be futile to quote it out of the context which illuminates it.

Equally simply, G minor and its heavy associations are put aside after this moment of reconciliation. With the same tone colour (harp and clarinet) as Britten used for the accompaniment pattern in the *Sinfonia da Requiem*'s finale, he sets in motion the last section of this work. At last the cool tone of the boys' choir is at one with the foreground mood, and its hymn, 'In Paradisum' (a simplified 'quam olim Abrahae' pattern) rides serenely over the soloists' pentatonicism; an odd reminder in the baritone's opening 'Let us sleep' shape of an important figure in *Noyes Fludde* (see p. 275, Ex. 13.8) is to be followed by a stronger reminder of that work. The hymn is taken up by the main choir in a polyphony of eight parts (most often in canonic pairs) and the modality becomes richer, though elusive—thus the G naturals sound like Mixolydian A rather than plain D, while the G sharps sound like Lydian D rather than plain A. The peak is added to this splendid structure with the solo soprano's high descant. As the arc curves down again the passing bells' tritone rings through, associated as ever with the central pleas for 'Requiem aeternam', which the boys now intone. But, surrounded by their serene yet exultant waves of sound, this is not a mourner's petition so much as the token of a promise: it fittingly brings to mind the benediction of the handbells at the covenant of the rainbow in *Noyes Fludde*. For a third and last time the unaccompanied choir resolves the tritone, its extra-liturgical words 'Requiescant in pace' (compare Britten's addition of 'Dona nobis pacem' to the Agnus Dei) giving a final significant emphasis to this impassioned musical indictment of the wickedness of war. Yet the musical means here can appear modest to the point of anticlimax. That the ending of the *Requiem* in fact impresses itself deeply on the listener is explained partly, of course, by the apt symmetry of this recall of two earlier closes, but no less by the recognition that no grand last word is called for, or could be found. The liturgy's glimpse of paradise must fade, and Owen's poem is incomplete; the mood they leave behind as we withdraw to that curiously disengaged chord of F is not easily analysed, and not easily thrown off. The *War Requiem* does not answer all the questions it poses, but for that very reason a well-realized performance reverberates disturbingly in the memory. We should be grateful that, after its early success at the box-office, the work has been recognized as pre-eminently an occasional piece; in this way its searing message need never be reduced by over-familiarity to lukewarm truism.

Fortunately, its elaborate resources will tend to discourage its overexposure. The *Requiem*'s orchestral specification equals Britten's previous largest, even before the chamber orchestra of twelve is added, but the apparent complexity of means is rarely put to complex textural ends. In demanding three spatially distinct groups Britten has neither revived Baroque *concertato* methods nor aped the *avant-garde*'s concern for the revolution of sound in space. Only at certain moments (of which we have seen Agnus Dei to be the most memorable) is there any overt musical interaction between the groups, though poignant connexions may often be formed in the listener's mind that bridge the three isolated planes. And within the groups the textures are not often notably daring or new. Indeed, the composer's steadfast refusal to diversify with subsidiary ornaments and counterpoints in the large orchestral body may give a first visual impression of disappointingly conventional doublings (comparison with, say, the Spring Symphony score would bring this forcefully home), but such faith in the strength of his musical ideas is amply justified in performance. In fact, the broad scheme of orchestral sonorities does not wholly exclude the penetrating subtleties that can attend Britten's utmost simplicity: the trumpets introducing 'Recordare' and the woodwind emphases of the soprano's dissonant notes in 'Lacrymosa' are examples of musical ideas inseparable from their colouring. Yet the main orchestra remains a corporate body of sound, intimidating in its power at times (the brass writing is Britten's most violent) but deliberately deprived of individual nuance. So the graphic immediacy of the chamber orchestra's subjective instrumental commentaries strikes home the more tellingly: though Britten had been perfecting such techniques from *Lucretia* to the Nocturne, they take on a new meaning, of urgent personal involvement, in this larger frame. In the obvious precedent for this bi-planar technique, *Wozzeck*, it is a foregone conclusion that the emotional summing-up of the opera will come, not in the Schoenbergian chamber orchestra, but when the full warm flood of the main orchestra is released. Britten's remarkable achievement is to move to his emotional climax in following the cataclysmic events of Libera me, the one big dynamically evolving structure of the work, with Owen's 'Strange Meeting' and its almost static chamber orchestral accompaniment. It is a measure of the intensity we have come to find in these individual colours that we are able to accept their interjections of broken phrases as a disturbingly articulate commentary on the crucial moments of the whole work. The release that follows, into benediction or oblivion, is scarcely less remarkable, for the textures to which at last all three groups contribute, each still maintaining its distinctive character, are of extreme luminosity even when they achieve a peak of apparently unwieldy density.

It was stressed earlier in this discussion how conscious an effort Britten must have made to draw together various facets of his work in the formulation of a statement that, while being deeply felt, should be of an unambiguously public character. Few composers of our time have recognized as he has an obligation to simplify their utterance so as to re-establish communication with those audiences who have too readily withdrawn from the musical

465

explorations undertaken by their contemporaries. In works like *Saint Nicolas* or *Noyes Fludde*, with relatively unambitious narrative aims and clear moral summaries, he could move certainly towards easily-defined goals, but in the *War Requiem*, an initial complication of emotional response, sorrow for the victims of war and anger or despair at the human folly and wickedness which make for war, was further complicated (as it was also symbolized) by the choice of parallel texts so unlike. All we know of Britten might have led us to expect the result to be one of his most introverted works, valued by the connoisseur of his music but estranging in some degree the less committed listener. In sustaining a manner of address so direct through transitions of mood so problematic, he achieved a feat of a kind that is not paralleled elsewhere in his work, and which remains undimmed by the critical strictures that have been levelled at the *Requiem*. The effort must have cost him much, and it is significant that both in the appendix to this work, the *Cantata Misericordium*, and (still more so) in the parables which mark a new departure in his methods, he speaks in a far more muted voice, and to an audience that is ready to hear the subtle inflexions that may be conveyed in undertones.

19 The Church Parables

CURLEW RIVER, OP. 71

It was stressed at the outset that this study of Britten's work would not be threaded on to a connecting narrative of his life. And for the most part, this is practicable enough. It is true, of course, that we need to know something of the company he kept in the immediately pre-war years to understand such works of protest as the *Ballad of Heroes*, and that the homesickness he experienced in North America directly prompted the determinedly English tone of the music that marked and followed his return. The biographical facts which are summed up in the Aldeburgh Festival can be seen as the spur to a great succession of works, while meetings with superlatively gifted interpreters have often directly inspired his explorations of new musical territory. But there is little in Britten's mature work that one can account for only by a picturesque or dramatic biographical incident. The notable exception is the church parable, *Curlew River*, a work first performed at the 1964 Aldeburgh Festival.

Yet his reaction to the incident was far from immediate. Eight years earlier, in 1956, Britten had visited Tokyo and had been deeply impressed by the performances he saw there of Noh plays, in particular the *Sumidagawa* of Juro Motomasa (1395–1431). The experience, related by Prince Ludwig of Hesse in the Britten birthday book,[1] remained vividly in the composer's memory, and a means of transmuting it to his own artistic ends must have clarified gradually in his mind. At first sight, the stylization proper to Noh ritual is so remote from modern Western conventions as to discourage any substantial borrowing. It is the more remarkable, therefore, that the book William Plomer (the librettist of *Gloriana*) devised should have proved to be one of the most aptly executed that Britten had worked on. It confirmed Yeats's discovery that the Noh technique in which dramatic and narrative presentation are fused has a strong appeal to the modern mind; and Plomer's use of simple (but mercifully, not *faux-naïf*) phrases, often repeated in short-lined structures, achieved a dreamlike quality, the

[1] Prince Ludwig of Hesse, 'Ausflug Ost 1956' in *Tribute to Benjamin Britten on his Fiftieth Birthday*, London 1963, p. 56.

sense of another plane of experience, that is for us the most compelling aspect of ritual. Decisions which naturally followed from such a Noh-inspired text concerned the manner of staging and the style of acting; all action was to take place within a severely restricted area, on a small circular ramped stage that forbade all 'realistic' deployment of the characters; wearing masks, they would mime with movements 'as spare and economical as possible' requiring 'an almost Yoga-like muscular, as well as physical, control'.[2] Clearly enough, decisions about the nature of the music had to be of no less radical a kind: a dramatic world so far from that explored in Britten's operas could not be peopled by the opulent characterizations in which his music for the stage had been so rich. But the road to a new kind of musical restraint had been opened when it was decided to bridge the gap between the pure Noh conventions and the Western artistic legacy by abandoning all specifically Japanese reference, and transplanting the drama to medieval Christendom, for in converting the ritual into that of a medieval liturgical drama, Britten naturally found his attention directed towards a great body of musical source material, the plainchant of the Western church. Even so, formidable hazards faced both writer and composer in seeking to unify inspiration drawn from two ancient arts and to embody it in language more vital than the bogus archaic.

It was not difficult to extrapolate from the Noh-play story, of the Madwoman who crosses the river seeking her lost son, and is restored to sanity by a revelation at his grave of the boy's consoling spirit, so as to fashion a specifically Christian parable, which could then be placed within the framework of a medieval monastic community who act it out in their church and point its moral to their flock. Indeed, the idea of a frame was taken further: the monks enter in procession chanting the plainsong hymn *Te lucis ante terminum*, the Abbot outlines the story to be enacted, and an instrumental fantasy on the plainsong leads into the parable as the actors don their masks; the triple frame in reverse rounds off the work. This leisurely conduct of an audience into and out of the action helps to set this at a distance, to emphasize its being a *convention* of representation and thus naturally subject to a high degree of stylization. Musically too a transition could be effected quite gradually from the pure plainchant to techniques of sound manipulation sophisticated enough to bear the weight of an elaborate structure of symbolism yet still highly economical in resources, and gestures. The instrumental ensemble Britten chose—flute, viola, horn, double bass, harp, percussion and organ—was much smaller than that of his chamber-operas, and was not in their sense a miniature orchestra but a range of discrete tone-colours. A conductor was dispensed with, the performers being allowed a good deal of licence in the timing of their parts, and a system of arrows and other marks, including a new fermata (the 'curlew' sign indicating

---

[2] C. Graham, 'Production Notes . . . on . . . *Curlew River*' (issued with the score, London 1965), p. 3.

the retention of a note until another performer reaches a certain point in his part), being devised to co-ordinate the different strata of the texture. The important roles allotted to the flute and the percussion (especially in the use of bells) obviously stemmed quite directly from the Noh plays. But so unexpectedly stark were the sounds Britten drew from this group, and in particular so little dependent on his familiar harmonic propulsion, that listeners were ready to trace direct exotic influences in many features of the score. *Curlew River* was the least predictable work the composer had written for many years, and it retains, even when very familiar, its power to enclose the listener in a unique world of feeling. Yet it is possible to claim that every technical innovation in the work has precedents of a kind in Britten's earlier music. The Japanese experience was, of course, a vital catalyst, as was also the quickened interest in the melodic ideals of plainsong, but neither could have facilitated a new stylistic fusion without using basic elements from the composer's established practice.

Most of the talk about exoticism was prompted by the heterophony of the instrumental interludes of the inner frame. Now it is true that the techniques of anticipation by which a single melodic line is rendered as several asynchronous lines may be found in the traditional music for voice and koto; and the fascinating mist of ornamental quaverings and slides that blur the plainchant here is certainly remembered from Japanese models. However, Britten's interest in heterophonic presentation of a line can be traced back to examples as diverse as the witty one-part fugal exposition of the Frank Bridge Variations, the third Chinese Song, and the piccolos' ornamentation of the Saraband in *A Midsummer-Night's Dream*. And in the first two of these we can also find precedents (to which innumerable others could be added) for that renunciation of harmony as a primary phenomenon which is so arresting a feature of *Curlew River*. Much closer in time, the Scherzo of the Cello Symphony showed a remarkably concentrated exploration of a melodic motive which also provided the only harmonic unit in the piece. In the parable's interludes, of course, there is virtually no harmony at all (see Ex. 1a), but the type of texture that characterizes the work is supported by chords which are simply aggregates of all the melody notes in a given phrase: the clashes of asynchronous heterophony are thus rationalized into a simultaneous presentation of the entire line (see Ex. 1b and c). It might be said that some uses of the *Screw* theme showed such a technique developing from Britten's serial investigations: but he does not join Schoenberg's search for a diversified yet consistent harmonic *vocabulary*. Indeed, to use the melodic total in this way is rather to reject (as Schoenberg fundamentally did not) that idea of a harmonic argument on which so much Western music, including most of Britten's, has depended. It is rather like beginning again from monody, and creating a new role for harmony: that plainsong should have suggested this rôle will not surprise anyone who has heard it sung in a large resonant church, for there the line is supported upon a mass of reverberations from earlier notes. Thus we hear monody transformed into a species of polyphony—one that Western music chose not to pursue very far, though it is worth noting that the mensuration canon is not unlike Britten's more systematized forms of proliferation. But 'counterpoint' as an art which requires a considered resolution of the harmonic problem at each point in

Ex. 19.1 (a)

Ex. 19.1 (b)

Ex. 19.1 (c)

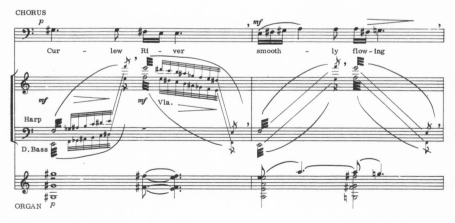

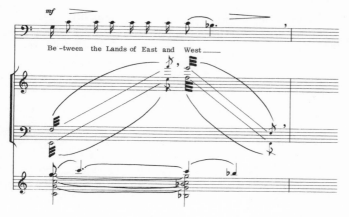

time is abandoned in the church parables: the exact timing of intervallic encounters becomes irrelevant when the individual melodic lines, complementary or heterophonic, merely contribute to the fluctuating motion within one static harmonic aggregate (often sustained by the organ in tone-clusters); see Ex. 2. Japanese music and Schoenberg's conflation of the horizontal in the vertical have already been cited as models. We may also consider Stockhausen's intense activity within fixed note-groups (e.g., in *Gruppen*), for there is no reason to assume that Britten's ears were closed to the music of a younger generation: the colours of his little band are perhaps not fortuitously suggestive of Boulez's palette, itself evidently subject to oriental influences. Far more prosaically, but not at all irrelevantly, we should note Britten's well-established practice in his operas of freely superimposing conversational exchanges so that the note-content, but not the note-coincidence, is settled. He was, it may be seen, well versed in simple

Ex. 19.2

'non-alignment' techniques long before they had become an obligatory part of every composer's equipment. It is the scale of their use that is new in this work, and which allows us to consider that his most remarkable achievement in it is the deployment of time: in the dreamlike world of *Curlew River*, it seems altogether natural that each character's speech should pursue an independent rhythmical course, and the resultant musical discourse is wonderfully released from that sense of time which is imposed by its unanimously metronomical division.

Yet it will be obvious that these liberations, from metrical co-ordination, from 'counterpoint' and from harmony as cause rather than effect, thrust a new weight of responsibility on to what must now be the chief, almost the sole, propelling agency of the music, *melody*. Perhaps only in contexts where he had invoked the aid of plainsong, the greatest repository of pure linear artistry in Western music, could Britten have dared to stake so much on his powers of melodic invention. *Te lucis ante terminum* is preserved intact as a three-verse hymn sung during the procession, and the Abbot's introduction to the parable makes obvious references to its contours, the last leading into a further literal quotation of the whole melody to begin the instrumental interlude. Thereafter it is not heard in a pure form until the complete hymn is repeated for the recession. But its influence can be detected in almost every section of the work and is always strongest when Christian overtones are touched on, e.g., at the Traveller's prayer 'May God preserve wayfaring men' (fig. 16), the boy's *Kyrie* as recalled by the Ferryman (fig. 65—a complete statement of the melody but in a changed mode) and at the Ferryman's counsel to the Madwoman that she should pray for her child's soul (after fig. 86). The no less obvious quotation at 'God have mercy upon us', fig. 54, prepares the way for an instrumental piece (fig. 55; see Ex. 1b) for the hoisting of the sail, which develops from a version of the first line; and this piece at fig. 56 becomes the important vocal refrain 'Curlew River' (see Ex. 1c). As an instrumental undercurrent it can be heard throughout the Ferryman's narrative as he plies across the water; the *Kyrie* therefore only brings into the open what has never been absent. More subtle assimilation, of the plainsong shapes into new motivic patterns can easily be found. For example, the Ferryman's horn figures (from fig. 8 to fig. 9—see Ex. 3a) remain within the fifth span of the hymn, cadencing frequently on the second degree (the 'final' of the plainsong), while the River refrain which is drawn from his music, Ex. 3b, makes the connexion clear.

It is in these horn motives of the Ferryman that we hear intensified a process of chromatic introversion that twists essentially scalic music into tauter relationships. The move from modality towards chromatic diversification had begun in the later lines of the instrumental 'frame' (i.e., the music that led us into the action) and the sinuous twists of Ex. 3a establish a manner that persists throughout much of the action, playing the rôle that would be accorded to dissonance in textures more dependent on

Ex. 19.3 (a)

Ex. 19.3 (b)

harmonic sensations; in later more complex contexts it is of course often supported by aggregates far more dissonant than the diatonic clusters produced by the plainchant. The melodic method has often been referred to in these pages; it may be seen in the mechanicals' music of the *Dream*, and in simplified form in the alternative scales of the *Requiem*'s Agnus Dei: the pivotal cell on which it turns, of a tone step in one direction followed by a semitone in the other (or *vice versa*) was powerfully used in Britten (e.g., in the Donne Sonnets) long before he began to make consistent use of Bartókian mixed scales. It is prominent in the tremulous agitation of the music to which the Madwoman and her *alter ego*, the flute, make their appearance

473

(Ex. 4a). Her opening cry, which is to become also the cry of the curlew, lodges in the memory as the most racked shape of the work. Though no more than that addition of unequal fourths which Britten had so often used, against so cautiously regulated a melodic norm these intervals acquire a demented, almost violent, quality; their later repetition by the full ensemble creates a nightmarish moment (from fig. 43). Calmer themes, of the bystanders and the Madwoman herself, that juxtapose only perfect fourths point a contrast very immediately (see Ex. 4b and c) for they are heard against the harmonic aggregate of the Curlew motive. And at one of the most tender

474

moments in the work, when the Ferryman guides the Madwoman to her son's grave (see fig. 80), the perfect fourths form themselves into a solemn thirteen-beat ostinato that presents the motive in a form restored to sanity (Ex. 4d).

At the opposite extreme from the disjunct line of this symbol of yearning anguish is the music in which the Madwoman tells the story of her son's disappearance. For here the melodic norm becomes a hopelessly reiterated monotone, with an emotional twist given to each line by the rise or fall of a tone that ends it. The intensification created by narrowing these moves to a semitone is inordinate: the climax is underlined by the coalescing of the instrumental parts into a unison tutti (fig. 35). Until then their reiterations of the one melodic germ have been at conflicting levels, again amassing harmony as though fortuitously. This piece (from fig. 33) and its later development, the duet of Madwoman and flute, 'Hoping, I wandered on' (fig. 81), are the most daringly simple passages of the whole work: on paper they look ludicrously impoverished, but in performance their effect seems surely calculated. While the basic shape remains limply uniform, in the first piece quintuplet and septuplet rhythms prevent too blatant a symmetry and the intervallic encounters are always unpredictable. In the later piece, the Madwoman's plaint has a central cry 'Did I give birth' in which the alternative-note scales suddenly return to build a vast arc: though the scope of this statement is much greater, it prompts comparison with another mother's grief over her lost son—Mrs Herring's 'All that I did'. The Madwoman's less harrowing music, the gentle song to the curlews which she recalls, 'Birds of the Fenland', is again extremely simple—a major scale segment made poignant by a minor sixth at its peak. Yet from this one melodic shape is built a dense harmonic choral ensemble (a fragment was shown at Ex. 2) with the flute soaring above, achieving simply by multiplication an ecstasy of yearning that strikes a new note in Britten's music (here where the variety of pitches in circulation is very great, the supporting harmony is not strictly an aggregate but a V over I of F in endless suspense).

Many other melodic cells are fundamentally scalic. An important one is the figure to which the Ferryman ushers his passengers ashore: it descends an E flat scale to land on E natural (Ex. 5) and this seven-note figure, spanned by two notes of the demented curlew cry (cf. Ex. 4a), becomes an (oddly

Ex.19.5

Holstian) ostinato below a new statement of the 'Curlew River' refrain (see above, Ex. 1c) as the whole company approaches the tomb of the boy. It reappears as a harmonic conflation during the following dialogue between the Madwoman and the Ferryman, and supports an ensemble of consternation as the truth about her son is uncovered. But its crucial significance is revealed fully only when the boy's spirit speaks to the mother with a promise of peace and reunion. The ostinato figure is spelt out in the organ while his words are set to the same note-repertory; and this persists until a final statement of the ostinato by the instruments leads into their framing interlude and *Te lucis*. An exhaustive study of the melodic developments and interrelationships in *Curlew River* would leave very little of its material isolated: to an extent rare in Britten's music, the whole work seems to have grown from the obsessive cultivation of a few disparate ideas until a host of associations has grown up between them, so dense as to make them appear to merge in a single field of musical experience.

Yet this does not prevent his giving a distinctive stamp to each of the chief characters in the parable. We have noted already some of the motive forms that are peculiar to the Abbot, the Madwoman and the Curlew, the Ferryman and the River. The Traveller's music is less evidently dependent on the central store of motives, except when he directly quotes *Te lucis* as a prayer. Like the other characters he is surely identified by instrumental colouring, but these wide-ranging harp arpeggios, successive triads a semitone apart, can seem alien among the less spacious gestures of the rest of the work. Of course, their undercurrent of trudging double-bass chords makes a graphic point, and it is probably not too misguidedly probing to detect in the shape of these a derivation from the crucial d-r-f-m figure of the plainsong's second phrase, and its inversion (see Ex. 6). Whereas the Ferryman's motive, because of its rôle in the music also of the river, remains a powerful element in the later stages of the work (note its reappearance in the bells and the horn at the climactic moment, fig. 90), the Traveller's music plays no part in the many restatements that give the parable so satisfactorily rounded a structure.

There is nothing classicistic about these returns of material—all are naturally prompted by the dramatic situation—yet they do reinforce one's impression of this work as a single musical span, articulated neither by acts and scenes nor by set-pieces as self-contained as those of all Britten's operas. It has been left to others to coin the description 'church opera' for this work

Ex. 19.6

= Te lucis, line 2

and its inversion

and its successors: the composer regarded them as of quite another *genre*. If one charts the appearances of the various thematic elements in *Curlew River* (and, ignoring the common motivic origin of many, there are some fourteen), one's first impression is of a mosaic not unlike the design of some works Tippett, to whom this work is dedicated, had been writing shortly before this time—his *King Priam*, second piano sonata, and Concerto for Orchestra (a work dedicated to Britten). But whereas Tippett tends to treat his pieces of disjunct material as essentially inert objects, finding the momentum of the work in ever new encounters, in juxtaposition and superimposition, between these pieces, Britten used both this method and that of developmental extension: not infrequently the working-out of one idea is carried on against more-or-less literal returns of several others. And although at some stages of the work, there is a rapid succession of ideas drawn from diverse earlier contexts, Britten has grouped much of his material so as to form sections broadly unified by the prevalence of one or more themes. A full diagrammatic representation would be very complex, but the interested reader can easily fill out many details lacking from this simplified account:

Section	Thematic Material	Bar nos.
FRAME	1a *Te lucis* 1b Abbot's address (based on 1a shapes) 1c *Te lucis* fantasy	bar 1 fig. 1 + 3 fig. 5
I The RIVER	2a Ferryman (horn; chromatic introversion) 2b River (choral adaptation of 2a) 2a – Traveller (incorporates 1a element, but does not return) 2b	fig. 8 fig. 9 fig. 10 fig. 13 fig. 18
II The MADWOMAN'S STORY and the CURLEW SONG	3a Madwoman and Curlew (unequal 4ths; flute) 3b Bystanders comment on 3a 3c 'Clear as a sky' (derived from and accompanied by 3a) – 'Dew on the grass' (does not return literally, but cf. 5) 4 Motive of Madwoman's song 3a Tutti 3b Instrumental 5 'Birds of the Fenland' (cf. other scalic themes, including 'Dew on the grass') (3a/2a interpolated) 5 as Tutti (canonic ensemble) 3a superimposed Transition recalling 2a 1a 2a to section III	fig. 20 fig. 26 fig. 27 fig. 30 fig. 33 fig. 43 + 1 fig. 45 + 1 fig. 46 after 49 fig. 50 fig. 52

477

Section	Thematic Material	Bar Nos.
III The CROSSING and the FERRYMAN'S STORY	6a 'Curlew River' (from 1a) instrumental 6b 'Curlew River' vocal 6 as accompt. to Ferryman's story (touches of 2a; 1a at 'Kyrie') 6a 2a 7 scalic figure spanning Eb–E♯ (cf. 3a) 6b with 7 as ostinato	fig. 55 fig. 56 fig. 58 fig. 68 fig. 68 + 3 fig. 68 + 4 fig. 69
IV The TRUTH REVEALED	2a/4 as at figs. 39–40 etc. 4/7 conflated 3a themes amplified climactically 3b 2b/4 3a	fig. 71 fig. 73 fig. 75 fig. 78 fig. 79 2 before 80
V DESPAIR and CONSOLATION	8 New use of *perfect* 4ths (cf. 3a) 9 Madwoman's duet with flute (derived from 4) 10 Peak of chromatic-alternative scales (cf. 2 themes) 10 developed with snatches of 9 11a *Diatonic* scales; perfect major triads; bells; preparing way for— 11b CUSTODES HOMINUM (joined later by 3a, curlew (flute) and Madwoman and 5, curlew (flute) and Madwoman)	fig. 80 fig. 81 fig. 83 3 before 85 fig. 87 fig. 88
VI VISION	3c ⎫ 4 ⎬ Instrumental fantasy 3a ⎭ 7 conflated in organ as accompt. to the Boy's spirit. Melodic contraction ('We shall meet in heaven') developed as Amen. (Interpolations of 4) 7 as first line of—	fig. 94 fig. 96 fig. 97
FRAME	1c *Te lucis* fantasy 1b Abbot's homily 1a *Te lucis*	after 97 fig. 98 fig. 100

From this it can be seen that, excluding the monastic framework, there is a short setting of the scene (riverside and the ferry) and then two main expository sections (II and III above), the stories of the Madwoman and the Ferryman, which are made into coherent structural entities by the arrangement of themes into what we might loosely call rondo patterns. Between them a transition briefly recalls earlier themes, but it is a far more elaborate process of recall and development that gives to section IV the quality of both a restatement and of a summarizing coda; in particular the peroration on the Curlew theme 3a, when the Madwoman's grief bursts out in the full knowledge at last of what she is mourning, evidently marks the principal caesura in the work's structure. Though almost every theme in section V can be related to earlier shapes, the effect is pronounced of a new tone. This is immediately felt in the superimpositions of *perfect* fourths in the ensemble during which the Madwoman is guided to her son's grave. The crazed quality of the Curlew motive's unequal fourths is banished, and although the Madwoman's despair is yet to reach its crisis, she is now surrounded by warm human sympathy that can help her to escape from the isolated hell of her madness. A further stage in this therapy is marked when, after her terrible soliloquy, the little bells of ritual mourning sound (a direct derivation from the Noh convention) and the chorus sings a plain diatonic scalic shape 'The moon has risen', resting on a major triad. Gradually these scales rise in pitch, till they move on the new plane of a consolation that exists outside time, symbolized in the hymn *Custodes hominum*. It is the context from which this simple setting has sprung, as well as the richness of its harmonic aggregates, that make it so moving an evocation of an 'abode of eternal happiness'. Though the bells' ostinato has touched on C (by analogy with River motives), all this music is securely founded on a white-note mode, and so the effect of the flute's intrusion with D sharp is inordinate: the Curlew motive returns to arouse in the Madwoman a last cathartic frenzy. And at the symbol of the Trinity (canon 3 in 1; the tune has now moved up a fifth) the voice of her son's spirit pierces through the tomb, eventually halting the magisterial progress of the hymn with highly dramatic effect. The onlookers are reduced to an awestricken silence as the spirit takes on visible form, to an oddly disembodied instrumental fantasy on Curlew themes. The moment is not prolonged and the boy's blessing on his mother is in the simplest terms, supported on the ostinato scale of Ex. 5. Almost before the experience is assimilated that theme has led us out of the parable and into *Te lucis* and the outer frame of the work. Again we can note how thematic restatements following new material have ensured a musically rounded form, but our sensations as listeners are likely to be far more concerned with the dramatic fitness of every move in these closing pages.

The intensity of experience that this parable offers, an obsession recorded in a musical language that seems obsessive in its restrictions, its renunciations of so many well-tried methods, is unique among Britten's work.

Though he was to find many new applications of techniques he first practised in *Curlew River*, none was to recreate the dreamlike suspension of time and the hermetic world of feeling which characterize that work.

THE BURNING FIERY FURNACE, OP 77

After the production of *Curlew River* in 1964, Britten professed himself 'too naïve' to say what the style of his parable might portend. But he was already planning with William Plomer a second work for church performance 'for the same instruments . . . probably using the same kinds of technique—but something much less sombre, an altogether gayer affair'.[3] In the event their choice of subject, the story of Nebuchadnezzar and the young men in the fiery furnace, prompted the addition of one instrument: for the biblical sack-but Britten revived the splendidly virile alto trombone. As Plomer adapted it, the story, if not unremittingly gay, provided scenes of feasting, comic entertainment, idolatrous ceremony and spectacular miracle, a range of mood so much ampler than that of *Curlew River*'s shadowy world that the composer must have faced many problems in drawing again on techniques devised specifically in response to the dreamlike ritual of *Sumidagawa*, as he had seen it performed in Japan. *The Burning Fiery Furnace*, completed in April 1966 and given at the Aldeburgh Festival two months later, took over quite exactly the format of the earlier parable: its monastic frame, its use of plainsong as a source for melodic material and its realization of the climactic miracle in an extended setting—the canticle, *Benedicite*, taking the place of the hymn, *Custodes hominum*— in which supernatural intervention swells the human invocation. But whereas the muted tone of *Curlew River* could be maintained throughout scenes in which all action was reported (the stories of the Madwoman and the Ferryman), in the new parable the entire action had to be brought to life on the restricted stage area devised for its predecessor. While this called for a still more stringently regulated stylization in production if ludicrous incongruity was to be avoided, it intensified the need to widen the range of musical gestures.

Fluctuations between textures in which there is considerable freedom of timing and those in which all strands are exactly aligned are more frequent than in *Curlew River*, for in this parable we pass more often between individual thought and corporate faith or concerted, even regimented, action. Indeed, the parable turns not so much on the particular question of racial toleration which is somewhat ostentatiously drawn to our notice by such lines as 'Young Jews, a bunch of foreigners!' as on the still broader one of the private conscience in conflict with the dictates of authority. Thus 'the sound of the cornet, flute, harp, sackbut, psaltery, dulcimer, and all kinds of music', symbol of a demand for unreasoning obedience, is represented in the most rigorously co-ordinated strands in the work. The sycophantic courtiers'

[3] Cf. 'Britten, Russia and Opera', *Faber Music News*, Summer 1965, pp. 13 and 14.

jollity-to-order is also cast in uniform metres. A distinction of another kind is made between the prayers offered by the Israelites and that of the Babylonians: the three young men address their unseen God in fluid but serenely unanimous rhythms whereas the futile address to Merodak, the image of gold, soon develops into chaotic frenzy.

Though the preservation of a triple frame as used in *Curlew River* ensures that the markedly oriental quaverings of the instrumental plainsong fantasy reappear, there are fewer contexts in which heterophonic presentation of a line directly recalls Japanese sonorities. For example, the instrumental flourishes (later vocal as well, to the words 'Greet and Salute') which punctuate Nebuchadnezzar's ceremonial entry, though of this kind, are mere arabesques above a grim undertow of harmonic blocks in the strings and organ. Rhythmic freedom and heterophony are both handled at times, however, with a subtlety surpassing that of the earlier parable, notably in the music of the Israelites after they have given offence at the feast and are left alone to reflect on their dangerous situation. Their chain of thought is built up across the three vocal strands, creating the effect of a soliloquy while yet preserving three distinct characters through the contrasted speeds of their delivery, till, at their recognition of the rôle that must inevitably be theirs, their parts coalesce, but in a heterophony (based on line 2 of *Salus aeterna*), that remains true to their defined characters (see Ex. 7); only in the homophonic refrain of their prayer is all individuality finally submerged.

From the above example it can be seen that, co-existing with rather than denying the heterophonic principle, there is a careful regulation, if not of harmonies, then of intervals. In particular the deviations of the three voices repeatedly create the vertical interval of a perfect fourth, this tendency eventually giving rise to a network of vertical and horizontal fourths at the name of Jehovah. No doubt it is chiefly because of the *organum*-like fourths to which the Israelites sing their *Benedicite* at the end of the drama (see Ex. 13 below), that the tone of Western medieval Christendom sounds even more strongly from this parable than from its predecessor, but in fact that passage is simply the climactic example of a sonority which has dominated the entire work in one form or another. We could derive it from *Salus aeterna*, the plainsong hymn (see Ex. 7b) which frames this parable, for many of its lines operate within a fourth-span and its opening line gives prominence to a direct fourth leap. But Britten makes much use of the plainsong by evocative reference, especially to the whole of that beautifully arched first line, always with specific local significance, whereas his use of the fourth as a fundamental unit throughout the work is more obviously constructive than symbolic. Even so, it is tempting to attach a certain consistency of meaning to this interval. In that the final *organum* of the canticle celebrates the supreme justification of the Israelites' faith, we can plausibly relate its fourths back to the theme of faith expounded early in the work, a theme that recurs as frequently and as palpably as the plainsong, and in which melodic perfect fourths and their doubled form of minor sevenths are predominant (Ex. 8). Once embarked on this line of enquiry, we shall have little difficulty in uncovering the important rôle played by the fourth in most of the music of the three young men. But a moment's further consideration

Ex.19.8 (a)

ABBOT

They ne - ver must in ___ a - ny way Be - tray ___ their faith.

Ex.19.8 (b)

MONKS

Tenors & Basses — God give us all The ___ strength to stand A - gainst the burning, bur - ning, Mur-d'rous world! ___

Baritones — God give us all The strength A - gainst ___ the Mur - d'rous world! ___

Ex.19.9

ASTROLOGER & COURTIERS

Slow, with movement

Horn (+ Hp.8va↓) — Me - ro - dak! (Hn.) Lord ___ of cre-a-tion, (Hn.) We bow ___ down be - fore you (Hn.)

___ A-dore you (Hn.) im-plore you, (Hn.) To glo-ri-fy our nation, our nation, To glo-ri-fy ___ our nation! (Hn.)

reveals the interval to be no less ubiquitous in that of Nebuchadnezzar and his Astrologer. And the faith of the Babylonians as they bow before Merodak is expressed in abject howls that span a fourth (see Ex. 9).

Despite this strong unifying factor, we are aware of a clear distinction between the music of the two races, created chiefly by contrasted modality and tonal implications. It would oversimplify to associate diatonic modes with the Israelites and chromatic ones with the Babylonians, yet to hear the work on the most general level is to be struck by the progress from the serene mono-modal line of *Salus aeterna* to the tangled strands in semitonally conflicting tonalities of the Babylonian orgies, and back: whatever the niceties of detail with which Britten executes such a plan, the fundamental (and essentially traditional) dichotomy it recognizes between two species of pitch relationship will not surprise any student of his methods. The very first chromatic relationship, in the Abbot's opening address to the congregation, comes at his reference to Babylon, the name being thrown into relief by a rhythm that will always characterize it (see Ex. 10; (b) shows the form used later in the herald's pronouncements) and by a triad that, consonant in itself, conflicts with the prevailing tonality. A more pungent example occurs shortly afterwards when the theme of the Israelites' faith (see Ex. 8a) is

Ex.19.10 (a)

ABBOT

To that im - pe - rial ci ty,   Ba - - by - lon,

Ex.19.10 (b)

Alto Trombone

repeated to words that test it against the wickedness that is to be represented by Babylon (see Ex. 8b) i.e., against an incursion of chromatic movement. As we move into the drama the continuum between the true faith and heathen idolatry is neatly demonstrated in the instrumental counterpoint to the herald's words (after 'acclaim you', bar after fig. 8): we hear the faith theme in the horn (bar 1), distorted (from bar 2) in the context of 'Babylon' (bar 3), and finally cadencing with the phrase to which Merodak will be worshipped (bar 5). It will be clear from the examples given already how much turns on setting up segments of semitonally adjacent triads or key areas. In particular, D major (the basic key of the work as established by its framing plainsong) and E flat minor often co-exist in the Babylonian music; the last four bars cited show a simple context, while the central procession is to provide an elaborate one. The bibulous chorus 'Good cheer' grows from a shape that spans from E flat up to D, setting up the two unequal fourths (perfect plus augmented) that contrast with the two equal ones of Ex. 8a (faith). But endless perfect fourths too can be pursued into chromatic territory, and the flickering symbol of the astrologer's magic (Ex. 11, it was foreshadowed by the king at fig. 14) plays on this device. Similarly the worship of Merodak, 'a grovelling, barbaric and superbly pagan utterance',[4] drives on from its initial D–A fourth and clashing E flat into territory that introduces every note but one in a great circle of perfect fourths (from fig. 67). There is an impressive consistency of method here yet no trace of monotony in the results.

Ex.19.11

Very fast

Flute

pp   mf   dim.   p   etc.

D.Bass

[4] Howard, p. 213.

The procession is more diverse in its material, Britten having chosen to provide each of the six biblical instruments (or their nearest equivalents) with highly distinctive ideas. Each player tries over his phrase during the Herald's pronouncement, and when the processing round the church begins, ten different superimpositions of the six ideas (each a five-bar sentence) are played; at the elevation of the image of gold, they merge into an intoxicating whole. The method is familiar (it was used, for example, in the children's games in *Herring*), but in conceiving a music that circles through space, revealing new facets of an essentially unchanged object, Britten was again adapting to his own ends a principle much exploited by a younger generation. The example shows how far his material remains from any direct debt to such models (Ex. 12).

Ex. 19.12

It will be seen that the D major/E flat minor conflation of earlier contexts has now been amplified into a more complex situation. The viola's patterned figures offer the clearest tonal regulation of the passage (half-bar alternations of D and E flat finally accelerating for an upward chromatic movement to G and a plagal return), but no other part taken at face value confirms exactly this scheme: the glockenspiel part appears to be in D Lydian throughout, whereas the little harp suggests E flat Dorian, punctuated with a *ficta*'d leading-note, and the flute's wailing line seems to centre around F

485

sharp; the two brass parts are less securely moored, the horn calls (derived from Ex. 10—'Babylon') deviating towards the E flat minor area between the dominants of D which enclose it, and the trombone describing a most introvertedly chromatic line that, because of its initial flat seventh, could as easily be taken to chart C territory as D. It is because of these varied implications that the earlier encounters of a few strands all produce markedly different results; the whole concept, simple as it is, could only have been realized by a composer as experienced as Britten in handling tonal ambivalence. What may not be clear from a reading of Ex. 12 is the barbarous ecstasy of sound to which these simple ideas can attain, given surroundings of such restraint. On a greatly reduced scale Britten caught no less surely than Schoenberg the abandonment with which man can worship the tangible god: perhaps it is not fortuitous that he wrote this parable shortly after *Moses und Aron* was produced at Covent Garden.

The reader must be left to trace the further consequences in the Babylonian music of the D/E flat juxtaposition. What should be mentioned, however, for it provides an essentially musical 'parable', is the conversion of those two notes, which have by now given rise to so much tortuously chromatic music, to a usage in which they open the way to a serene major triad as the young men's voices are heard, out of the furnace's uproar and the spectators' gloating cries, with the opening of the *Benedicite* (Ex. 13). Thus

Ex.19.13

is the impious act of the Babylonians transformed into the glorification of the Israelites' god: note how it is the *angel's* resolution of E flat to D that, after creating momentarily a chord of two perfect fourths, finally resolves into the triad. This miracle scene may rely on the most austere musical resources but they are supremely apt, and I do not find altogether convincing Mrs Howard's claim that 'both Parables [i.e., this one and its predecessor] court the opportunity of portraying miracles in music and both deal with the visions in a style so self-effacing at this point as to throw all the emphasis onto the verbal or visual account of the supernatural'.[5] While its sparseness is not in

[5] Ibid., p. 216.

question, this music is not 'self-effacing': not only is it a powerful resolution of tensions that have been experienced throughout the work, but it is of a most individual sonority, brought to a glowing climax in the working-out that follows Ex. 13, and lingering in the memory long after a performance. Though other Britten closes can be recalled that have a somewhat comparable effect, perhaps the most striking parallel, since it turns on semitonal inflexions within triads, is that of the violin concerto, written a quarter of a century earlier: the adventurous techniques of the composer's parable style in no way invalidated those of his youth.

Not all the extended sections of the work turn upon this central tonal point. As we should expect, the Israelites' earlier music is often on quite another plane, as in their prayer, 'Blessed art thou, O Lord God of our Fathers'; though this is sung against the instrumentalists' preparations for the procession, it takes no account of them but works out an eloquently arched line, coloured with *organum*-like fixity by a major seventh and major third, a chord which first appeared in their plea 'Lord help us in our loneliness', and which in its curiously resigned sound (rooted and with no obvious resolution implicit, yet dissonant) is the nearest we are to come to a state of rest before the later, *Benedicite*, chant.

Less evident is the consistency of pitch relation that unifies the scene in which the young men attempt to explain to Nebuchadnezzar their failure to accept his hospitality at the feast. The preceding music had fluctuated between the D-centred idea to which they were given new names (from fig. 17) and the E flat-centred chorus of the feast to which the innocuous entertainment of the boys provides as interlude a further touch of local colour, with their pipe-dance that sounds like a psalm-tone in the Locrian mode. But a new and more ominous situation is foreshadowed as the Astrologer begins his malicious reproaches (at fig. 33). The horn sustains notes that rise to an F natural, which then becomes fixed in disturbing contradiction to the king's gentle chiding; those who notice the strong echo of *Saint Nicolas* at his repeated 'Come!' will feel the uneasiness of this contrasted context to be intensified. From fig. 35 the horn outlines a series of notes each of which is sustained by the organ, to form the chord shown at Ex. 14a, two aggregates of minor thirds radiating from a central tone's interval, what the Bartók commentator, Ernö Lendvai, has labelled the *alpha* chord.[6] This chord is in fact an alternative form of that scale (see Ex. 14b) formed of alternating semitones and tones, which Britten, like Bartók, has frequently

Ex.19.14 (a)   Ex.19.14 (b)

[6] E. Lendvai, *Béla Bartók: an analysis of his music*, London 1971.

used (e.g., in the cello sonata; see p. 310). After the chord has been assembled, it is dismantled as a falling arpeggio, to the words 'we are very small eaters', and then a long section begins in which as an upward arpeggio it forms an instrumental ostinato background to the foreground dialogue. The strictly measured revolutions of this seven-note ground (cf. the identical device in *Curlew River*, from fig. 69) become a threatening, inexorable element even while the king remains at his most urbane: his melodic lines draw suavely on the diatonic scale segments latent in Ex. 14b, and indeed the whole discourse is founded on that mode. So the trombone's aggressive statement of the Ex. 14a arpeggio leading up to D sharp instead of E dramatically twists us to a new level of action. From fig. 38 the ground sets off again a semitone higher than before till it in turn is wrenched out of mode by a vehement arpeggio sung by the three men, 'By the sacred laws of Israel', which overshoots to a high G. The third rotation (fig. 39) is a tone higher still (i.e., a cross-section of the original mode), and it accompanies the hubbub of the crowd who have witnessed the Israelites' apparently insulting response to the king. When the trombone again spells out angrily the arpeggio in diminution, the extra note that displaces the mode is an F sharp, mysteriously added by muted horn. This provides the link with the following section, for this one pitch is to underlie the whole scene between Nebuchadnezzar and his astrologer. It is heard as a constant yet distant sound (often potentially a dominant pedal) behind each recitative-like passage, these occurring between arioso phrases accompanied by the flickering flute theme (shown above at Ex. 11); the alternation of the two textures gives a nervous stealth to this scene that graphically captures the power of the magician and the superstition of those on whom he exercises it. The scene ends with the withdrawal of all but the three Israelites, and only at this point does the horn move on from F sharp to state (at fig. 45) the opening line of *Salus aeterna* (Ex. 7b).

The new scene was discussed above for the flexible heterophony it demonstrates. Structurally it is less straightforward than the two scenes it follows. The ground reiterated at rising levels symbolized rising indignation, the fixed-pitch a numbing fear of the supernatural. But the young men's ruminations on their situation are a fantasy founded on chords built by the instruments chiefly from phrases of the plainsong (though a clear reference to Ex. 14a identifies the conspiracy against them); their own lines only once directly quote *Salus aeterna*, at 'what we are we remain', though the motive of their faith (Ex. 8) is frequently to the fore. An example of the more veiled references can be seen in Ex. 7a, line two of the plainsong. In short, this scene is far more fluid, even improvisatory, in feeling after the rigidly simple schemes we have just examined: once again Britten makes a distinction between his characters at a quite fundamental compositional level.

In concentrating chiefly on textural, tonal and structural aspects of this parable, I have not intended to imply that its motivic usages and interrelationships, referred to only incidentally, play a minor rôle in the dramatic unfolding. Very often they make points with precision and economy. We have just noted the epitomizing words to which the Israelites quote *Salus aeterna*, and the plainsong is introduced at least as tellingly when Nebuchadnezzar, marvelling at his victims' preservation in the fire, is filled with awe at the sight of their companion, 'And the form of the fourth is like the Son of God'. Quotations and distortions of the 'faith' theme (Ex. 8) are so frequent and so unmistakable that they need not be listed; similarly the dotted-note group of 'Babylon' (see Ex. 10) is self-evident. A motive that appears literally only at a late stage is that symbolizing the 'Burning fiery furnace', first introduced by the king (see Ex. 15) when he is interrogating the

Ex.19.15

Israelites on their refusal to bow down before Merodak. In fact its closing shape, a perfect fourth filled out as a mixed mode, is a retrograde form of the harping innuendoes of the astrologer much earlier ('this rash innovation, invasion of immigrants'—before fig. 41). As the furnace is heated and the Israelites are consigned to it, the motive, with its inversion, is developed as a vocal obsession and an instrumental ostinato divided between horn and trombone, and is recalled later in a comically furtive form as the king approaches circumspectly the intended victims. The motive also serves the Abbot well when he comes to draw the moral of the parable:

> Friends, remember,
> Gold is tried in the fire,
> And the mettle of man
> In the furnace of humiliation.

The supremely fitting quality of every musical and dramatic contrivance in *Curlew River* could not be reproduced in this more opulent drama. It is not difficult to imagine ways in which Britten could have painted an uninhibitedly bold canvas for many scenes of this work had he not chosen to conceive it as a companion to his first parable. Yet their realization in this restricted medium is never implausible and is sometimes impressive, chiefly because of the wide range of musical gestures across which he operates. Above all, the creation of two musical worlds as unlike as those which symbolize the exulting paganism of the Babylonians and the introspective faith of the Israelites, and the creation of dramatically convincing bridges between them, these are achievements that justify the composer's decision to put his new-found 'convention' to so contrasted a use.

489

THE PRODIGAL SON, OP. 81

Almost twenty years earlier than the church parables, Britten had devised the new kind of operatic resources that proved appropriate to a classicist tragedy, *Lucretia*, and had turned very promptly to a consideration of their effectiveness in the provincial comedy of *Herring*. But only after an interval of seven years did he return to the chamber opera medium, and then he not only chose another strikingly contrasted subject in *The Turn of the Screw* but also demonstrated a significantly modified musical treatment. The trilogy of parables written at two-yearly intervals from 1964 does not show a comparable development in the composer's view of the potentialities of his new medium. Certainly the contrast between *Curlew River* and *The Burning Fiery Furnace* is as marked as their subject-matter demands, but when we approach the third work, *The Prodigal Son* (1968: Aldeburgh Festival), our first impression may be that the drastic limitation of resources and the retention of the same textural formulae and stylized presentation are in danger of reaching beyond uniformity to monotony. However, we are left in no doubt that much of the uniformity is deliberately cultivated, so as to emphasize the ritual aspect of these dramas; for example, the three stages through which we pass from medieval Christendom to the Noh-influenced actions of the inner play have by now acquired the inevitability of ceremony. And it is just because Britten remains in most respects so faithful to the rigid practices he established in *Curlew River* that each deviation from them in the later parables is made telling to the initiates. The mere addition in *The Burning Fiery Furnace* of the domineering alto trombone to the instrumental ensemble could epitomize a transfer from an introverted personal drama to a social drama of personal belief in conflict with the dictates of authority, while in *The Prodigal Son* the insinuating D trumpet's meretricious brilliance, whether or not we associate it with the snares of the devil, clearly enough symbolizes that self-indulgence from which springs the evil that in this moral drama is ultimately to be confounded by love.

And to the devotees, familiar with the rite, another most obvious innovation to be noted from the outset of the third parable is that the preamble is delivered by the Tempter, a character of the inner action. Yet by analogy (and indeed by his voice) they will be ready to identify the Abbot, who duly sheds his disguise and declares himself in the moral tailpiece. This preview of the one character serves to suggest his existence outside finite time, a concept that is clarified when the Tempter stands revealed as man's other self, a constant and insidious guide along the road to evil. The revelation is effected by transparent but startlingly effective means when the Tempter and the Younger Son echo one another in close canon at the unison. Like so much of the symbolism in these parables (e.g., the framing and the characterizing instrumental colours) this kind of image has notable Baroque precedent, but Britten's intensely practical imagination was evidently no less touched off by the uncanny similarity in timbre between the voices of Peter Pears and Robert Tear, the first interpreters of these two rôles.

Britten's obsession with problems that spring from man's propensity to evil is well-known. But, if the line of victims whose plight he has illuminated is long, he has rarely attempted to round out musical studies of the agents of evil. The character of Claggart is no doubt the nearest approach, though even that is more a portrait of inner torment than of a simple abandonment to malice. Elsewhere, as in *The Turn of the Screw*, Britten has relied on music's emotional ambivalence, evil being sensed in innuendoes of what may be behind an alluring façade or, as in *Grimes* and the *War Requiem*, the quality of compassion has flooded over even that which must first have prompted the composer's anger. In this parable, therefore, a morality in which any bid for 'realism' could only undermine our acceptance of an elaborate superstructure of convention, it ought not to astonish us that Britten has made no attempt to depict in luridly graphic terms the rake's progress which forms the centre of the action. The Siren's song of boys' voices is more forlorn than enticing, and the Younger Son's companions at his initiation in vice seem a jolly enough crew. Though the instrumental contribution to these scenes is more barbed, it does not approach the abandon of the processional music in *The Burning Fiery Furnace*. Yet if neither the sottish nor the lascivious appears as more than a token gesture, there is in this music a perceptible growth of 'corruption', which Britten is as prone as was Bach to symbolize by chromatic distortion. The contrast between the most tortuously chromatic moments of the rake's city experience and the B flat tonality and sonorous triad which betoken his Father's simple country life is of a very familiar kind, and directly comparable to that which has been examined in the previous parable.

Britten's use in that work of symmetrical mode (the alternation of tone and semitone steps) was noted. In *The Prodigal Son*, far more consistent use can be found of material drawn from another of these 'modes of limited transposition', now the third in Messiaen's codification of such resources,

Ex. 19.16 (a)

Ex. 19.16 (b/c)

The Music of Benjamin Britten

the filling out of the whole-tone scale by the insertion of a semitone step between alternate tones (see Ex. 16a). While it can be restricted so as to yield the intangible contours of whole-tone music, this mode also contains potentialities for triadic definitions (on six roots, each major or minor), for playing off a 'black-note' cross-section against a 'white-note' one, for juggling with no less than nine major thirds, and so on. Curiously, Britten chooses to make most play with the *minor* thirds it contains (only six, as opposed to eight in Mode 2, used in the earlier parable). The Tempter's music is riddled with that interval from his first intrusive ululation, Ex. 17a, a jazzy motive that is to become associated with his characterizing instrument, the trumpet. The veiled sneer that we often detect in his lines owes much to the prevalent minor thirds, whether within the mode, as at his first approach to the Younger Son (Ex. 17b), or smartening up chromatically the B flat world of the Father's peaceful, orderly home (Ex. 17c). More essentially related to

the mode are the organ flourishes punctuating this first speech, and their vocalized form (Ex. 16b and c).

The ramifications of this body of material take several forms. Most obviously, the Younger Son soon learns to ape the intervallic characteristics of Ex. 17b, justifying his appeal to his father, for freedom and his portion, with both music and arguments well learnt from the Tempter. The space of a major seventh or diminished octave that is prominent in Ex. 16b and c can be heard in several contexts in addition to literal quotations of these motives. The trumpet develops 16b, usually in retrograde, as the parasites surround the Younger Son on his entrance into the city, and when they offer him wine a new development of that motive, arpeggiated in a Brittenish third chain, dominates, straight and inverted, both trumpet and chorus parts. Perhaps the most significant use of this motive comes when, his fortunes at their nadir, the Younger Son's resolve to return home is stated to a phrase (Ex. 18) that is still deeply involved with Ex. 16b, but is repeated more

Ex.19.18

confidently in a near-Lydian, and is then worked out instrumentally, the first statement (by the viola) being purified under the influence of *Jam lucis*, the plainsong quoted by the voice at 'Father, I have sinned', to the simplest major mode. At such moments what can appear simplistic in Britten's symbolic code proves capable of making an impressive yet quite unforced contribution to our understanding of the drama. The son's return journey is made to an instrumental fantasy in which the development of Ex. 18 continues against the flute's elaborated form of the plainsong, the whole texture being one of the most luminous and imaginative uses in Britten's loosely-timed manner of contrapuntal rather than heterophonic relationships. It leads to the Father's appearance and a great upsurge of the motives and the B flat tonality associated with him. But it will be noted that one of these motives, a scale from the Lydian E natural to the orthodox E flat of B flat major, spans a diminished octave in a gesture not so very unlike Ex. 16b. The scale was there from our first meeting with the Father, stemming each flow of the alto flute undercurrent to his speech. It is difficult to believe that the relation is fortuitous in the work of so careful a motivic craftsman; perhaps we are to draw the relevant moral that things which appear similar may be very different at the heart—as the semitonal conflict of F sharp minor/F major in Ex. 16b and the secure B flat diatonic core of Ex. 18 declare.

Another pervasive aspect of the Tempter's material, related to these diminished octaves, is the inflection between alternative forms of a scale degree; the prototype is the minor/major third of Ex. 17a. Used consistently, as in the modified repeats of his speech 'When quite alone, have you never thought' (after fig. 17; see also fig. 37) this creates an oddly insidious tone; a single twist can give a mournful tinge to a phrase, as in the servants' farewell to the son as he departs to risk the snares of evil, 'Go, if you must go' (note especially its final shape, twisting out of the security of B flat). But the whole scene of the son's initiation into the city's ritual of vice is unified by the recurrences of a motive (Ex. 19a) that derives from the principle. In particular the howling voices off of Ex. 19b provide a refrain between episodes which present the stages through which the prodigal son's debauchery is completed—drink, the flesh and gambling. We have seen that the first of these (from fig. 43) is based on Ex. 16b; the second is a grotesque parody of salon music, 'Nights are days, days are nights', that unwinds through alternations of semitone and tone steps (Ex. 19c). Its gruesome sentimentality reaches a peak in unusually straightforward harmonic textures so that the writhing semitonal shifts are more crudely displayed than elsewhere; but its abandon is belied by the dark ostinato pattern of hard and double bass. As a

Ex. 19.19 (a)

Ex. 19.19 (b)

Ex. 19.19 (c)

Ex. 19.19 (d)

terrible memory of the whole experience and a depiction of the son's utter wretchedness, his characterizing instrument, the viola, introduces (just before fig. 61) a theme whose scalic degrees are constantly twisted into new contortions of despair: Ex. 19d shows the opening of the paragraph in which viola and voice treat this idea in dialogue. It is from this abasement that the purging process begins which gradually filters out chromatic complexities as the son resolves to return home (see above). Only once more is the use of chromatically alternative degrees to make a point—at the words 'and prodigal come home' in the Abbot's closing homily. The reference is slight, but sufficient to recall dimly the city nightmare; more strong is an echo of 'Go, if you must go', that saddened recognition of human folly.

Finally in this study of the Tempter's musical ubiquity, we may note the various contexts in which the whole mode from which much of his material springs (Ex. 16a) is employed with some consistency. A brief example occurs when the servants praise the virtues of hard work, in particular its ability to keep 'From idle hands all sly Tempters away' (just before fig. 27); here the top two parts of the three-part choral writing are in the pure mode and only the bass insistence on G and E flat, foreign notes, helps to steer a course to the B flat major that ends the phrase in 'home' territory. The third episode in the rake's progress (fig. 53), his disastrous *début* as a gambler, is cast in a transposition of the mode (Ex. 16a up a minor third), holding Britten's favourite 'canker' chord of augmented above perfect fourth as an *idée fixe*, but with harp close-position chords that pass down the mode in a manner far nearer Messiaen's than is Britten's customary modal practice. When the prodigal son has been stripped of the last of his portion and famine has struck the land, there comes, in a ensemble above a ground bass (Ex. 20), a distillation of the misery he must share with all the poor and outcast.

Ex. 19.20

cf. Ex. 16a

This shape is drawn from another transposition of Ex. 16a (up a tone), and the vocal parts above it, apart from a few appoggiaturas, are similarly derived; they are a mixture of rigidly and loosely timed entries, creating a vivid counterpoint of the common burden and the individual cry of despair. That the ground so unambiguously cadences with each revolution only intensifies its fatalistic ring, but no less obsessively does it remind us of all those minor thirds through which we first learnt to recognize the Tempter, whose victory this piece celebrates.

Whether or not the devil has all the best tunes, he certainly has most of the colourful ones in this parable, not only in pitch relations but in instrumental figurations. Only the organ accompanies his speech in the prologue, but the

Tempter's first appearance in the action, when he approaches the Younger Son, is to an attractively bitonal harp figure (see Ex. 17b) that fades out suggestively on a semitonally oscillating pedalled portamento. The muted trumpet's reiterations of the Ex. 17a theme add a heady note, making the horn of the servants' chorus appear stolid by comparison, just as the Younger Son's viola seems earnest after the seductive harp. Even when the Tempter joins the son on his journey, the viola merely plods on while the harp adds a wealth of breezy arabesque, until the trumpet announces arrival at the city with its meretricious virtuosity. The rake's progress is painted with a fine range of new colourings, the refrain shown at Ex. 19b being supported on organ clusters and surrounded by a haze of the viola's harmonic series while the alto flute adds the semitonally oscillating motive introduced earlier by the harp; viola is exchanged for double bass and flute for horn in the passages in which the Tempter interprets the message of the distant voices in a histrionic *Sprechgesang*. The trumpet provides a racy obbligato to the first taste of vice (drink), and its contribution to the sensuality of the second episode reaches a peak in the lachrymose vibrato of its postlude. In the third, the harp chords referred to above are elaborated by flute tremolando and trumpet's serpentine triplet figures while the tritone of the sustained organ chord is hammered out in a little palindromic rhythm of the wood blocks. The stripping away of all such instrumental conceits in the stark unisons of the famine ground makes another forcefully direct comment, as does the lonely viola which carries on through the Younger Son's soliloquy.

Neither in instrumental sonorities nor in wealth and intricacy of motivic shapes can the music of the Father and his mode of life compete with the blandishments the Tempter offers. In one of the simplest symbols Britten has ever devised (Claggart's idiosyncratically spaced F minor chord is an obvious precedent), a single chord of B flat major (Ex. 21a) is made to convey the warmth, frugality and uneventfulness of life at home. No less symbolic is the fact that, having stated the text that orders this life (Ex. 21b) in his opening homily to his sons and his servants, the Father draws upon its stock of four notes repeatedly, permuting this into many new shapes that all reflect reassuringly their origin. Eric Walter White lists eight of these permutations,[7] and if we include instrumental citations, then fourteen of the possible twenty-four note-orders are to be found. And the pair of perfect fourths in this interval-set figure prominently in the alto flute solos which articulate the Father's discourse, together with a more decorative figure (Ex. 21c); as was noted above, this ends with a flourish spanning from Lydian E natural to E flat. Other vocal phrases are accompanied only by double bass, with derivatives of Ex. 21b. All remains uncomplicated, and the deflections from the purest B flat major are rarely more than Lydian and Mixolydian touches. It is by pursuing such inflexions simultaneously that the servants'

---

[7] White, p. 222.

Ex. 19.21 (a)

Ex. 19.21 (b/c)

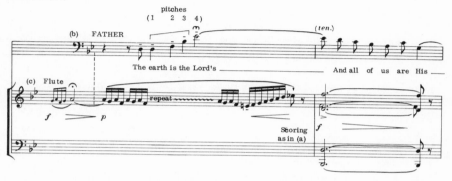

music arrives at its dissonance A flat–E natural–D, a pattern of intervals (major third plus tone) which is then made characteristic in a series of resourceful approaches to such chords. Horn calls provide the starting-points for these fanwise movements and a new degree of freedom in the textural alignment permits the individual singers of each group to enter one after the other. With these various images established, little happens to them as such, though they may become telling in brusque juxtaposition with images from the glossier world for which the Younger Son pines. The musical course of events as he explains his longings to his father turns almost entirely on such juxtapositions, though sometimes on transfer, as when the father, singing 'You might learn little save what is bad', echoes the Tempter's intervals. And as we have seen, the servants' sad leavetaking, in wistful little mirror canons (see e.g., fig 28), is coloured with the chromatic inflexions of a world they will never see. A further modification, one which achieves its fullest significance later, is that at the robing of the Younger Son, his symbolic investment with the 'Portion' for which he has appealed, it is the *harp* which rings various changes, chordally decked out, on the father's motive, Ex. 21b. The Tempter's part in the ceremony is made clear when, to the same music, he strips the son of a part of his robe after each act of debauchery is completed (the impoverishment this represents is further underlined in that the first part is stripped to the harp's chords again, the second only to a solo horn, and the third to the meagrest outline of the motive on drums).

497

The symmetrical nature of the action in *The Prodigal Son* (home—the city—home) is made particularly obvious musically by the use of the plainsong, *Jam lucis orto sidere*, not only as the frame of the whole work but as a frame around the central adventure. The Younger Son leaves on his travels to farewells fashioned from the hymn (fig. 32 onwards) in an antiphony of sharp keys (the son) and flat (those he leaves behind). The thought of returning home comes to him with a memory of the hymn's second line (in B flat) at 'While even my father's servants can eat' and he rehearses the confession he will make to the plainsong, but still in a sharp key area, which is then sustained by the alto flute through the journey interlude discussed above, turning towards the B flat area with his last line as the father is seen in the distance. Thus the hymn becomes a symbol of virtue as markedly as (though more schematically than) the plainsong was a symbol of the true faith in *The Burning Fiery Furnace*. Yet in neither parable is it used to celebrate the triumph of that which it symbolizes, for to distend the plainsong melody in climactic textures would be to render anti-climactic its unadorned reappearance at the end of the work. In the previous parable, the canticle *Benedicite* created the climax accompanying the miracle just as *Custodes hominum* had done in *Curlew River*. *The Prodigal Son*, one of the earthiest and most unromantic of parables, has no miracle, yet in his joy the father finds something like one: 'For this son of mine was dead, and is alive again, Was lost, and is found'. And his rejoicing is made corporate in another canticle setting *Cantate Domino*; its presentation over a ground bass makes this as assuredly his victory as the famine ground was the Tempter's. The ostinato (Ex. 22), though it begins on a Lydian E natural (cf. the tailpiece of

Ex.19.22

heavy and sust.

Ex. 21c) delineates a B flat tonality (the upper parts typically introducing a Mixolydian A flat to balance the opening) in grandly swinging phrases of 7 + 6 minims. As well as its straight and inverted forms, a permuted version is used (segments ordered iii–ii–i–iv); each form is repeated and there is a *da capo*. The servants sing variants, florid but rigidly timed, on the ground, and the organ amasses clusters, so that a splendidly elemental ritual of rejoicing is set in motion. But around this father and son continue to marvel at their reunion, with moving recollections of earlier phrases ('the younger son' cf. after fig. 33). The instruments too bring back motives from the first home scene, especially the piccolo (*vice* alto flute), and the piece brightens to become the richest instrumental canvas of the whole work before it is rudely interrupted by the Elder Son's appearance. Though his sour response to his brother's return finally banishes the ensemble, this serves the dramatically necessary purpose of reducing the musical gestures to a level from which a convincing return to the epilogue and final plainsong can be made. The forming and dispersing harmonies to which the voices muse over 'was dead and is alive again . . .' draw us steadily away from the drama to reflect on the wider truth; they are beautifully resolved in a serene C major chord at which, with the beginning of the instruments' quavering plainsong fantasy, we discover ourselves outside the parable.

The Elder Son's music is distinctive enough for its return to contribute to the manifold symmetries of this piece, but it calls for little comment since it is peripheral to the true musical action. He is more given than any other character to throwing phrases across a wide compass (see fig. 31, for example) and the tetchiness of his speech is intensified by the minor ninths of the supporting chords, the off-beat movement of the viola that traverses them, and the ungainly thudding of the pizzicato double bass that punctuates them. Only in the rising of his anger is he distinguished from the team of honest, unimaginative workers he leads. Yet the Prodigal Son himself is far from a fully formed character; indeed, we are clearly to see in him a character still in the making. Since his adolescent fantasy is personified in the Tempter, his music vacillates between echoes of this mentor in evil and of his father's sober influence for good. Only in the torment of the soliloquy (or dialogue with his instrumental personification, the viola) that leads to his return do we glimpse the tempering of his steel, and perhaps the ultimate triumph in him of the values represented by the plainsong is that which the journey interlude so powerfully suggests.

Much has been said about the inevitable symmetries of this enacted parable, and it is easy to draw up a neat table of motivic correspondences across the work. However, Britten has avoided mechanistic exactitude. In the first place the proportions of the piece are not really symmetrical. While the preamble and exposition (the flat serenity of home *versus* the Tempter's promise of excitement) juxtapose rapidly many sections of contrasted material, and the career from pleasure to ruin works out one body of this in a big rondo structure, the reconciliation, rejoicing and moral bring the triumph of the other body of material in a section that, apart from *Cantate Domino*, is relatively short. Secondly, the introduction of the Tempter in the prologue cannot be balanced by the Abbot's reversion to his own *persona* in the epilogue. Instead, Britten contrives an effectively literal recall of the Tempter's introductory promises at the moment of their fulfilment, when the Younger Son collapses to the ground as poverty, hunger and utter desolation face him (fig. 61). If the consequent lack of symmetry in the epilogue gives this parable a less obviously satisfying moral tailpiece than the others, perhaps we are intended to sense more potently in consequence the contrast between an opening with the powers of evil strutting at the centre of the stage and a close where they have been banished. For in this sense, more has been 'achieved' in this parable than in the other two, whatever the relative attractions of their musical means.

With the trilogy completed, Britten was ready to move on to other fields, but the emancipation from strict textural synchronization and orthodox harmonic movement he enjoyed in these parables was clearly destined to outlast that exploration of the Noh-play convention which pointed the way.

20 Owen Wingrave

The three church parables, Britten's chief dramatic music of the sixties, were of the greatest importance for his stylistic development, while their use of rigorous limitations to stimulate expressive precision placed them among his most powerfully cogent works. Yet as the composer returned to the type for a third work, one might have feared that he had abandoned the opera house. One explanation is that these were transitional years at Aldeburgh: once the intention to acquire and convert The Maltings at Snape was formed, there was little point in writing pieces for the minute Jubilee Hall (magically though that had housed even *A Midsummer-Night's Dream*). Orford Church made an excellent setting for *Curlew River* and the succeeding ritual pieces, but a full-scale opera should await the resources of the new stage and auditorium. *Death in Venice* was the work which eventually marked this crowning moment in the festival's development, but meanwhile Britten had already returned to operatic composition in fulfilling a BBC commission, for a full-length opera conceived with the possibilities and limitations of television specifically in mind.

Owen Wingrave was written during 1970 and first transmitted by the BBC on 16 May 1971. When the corporation's sole rights had expired, it was presented for the first time in a stage production, at Covent Garden on 10 May 1973. We may assume that such a transfer was in the composer's mind as he wrote the score, but he and his librettist, Myfanwy Piper, did not therefore avoid those resources of television which cannot convincingly be reproduced in a theatre. At the one extreme is a scene like the opera's prelude, in which the camera lets us move in to see the details of one portrait after another. At the other are cross-cutting scenes like that of Owen in the park, his aunt and Coyle in a room near by, and the passing Horse Guards seen by both. Owen's second interview with his grandfather demands two planes of musical action that the screen can isolate or fuse more selectively than the stage, and the dinner scene, during which each character in turn relapses into private thoughts, almost invites a televisual cliché. Even the device of the ballad, heard out of time, might seem to be prompted by the medium, though in fact its performance to a darkened stage at Covent

Garden created the intended reverberation far more persuasively than did the mimed action of characters in 'historical' dress of the televised production. But this is to touch on a matter well beyond the scope or competence of the present study—the singular disenchantment that the small screen in our drawing-rooms, so often the means of reporting on the most deadeningly 'realistic' of scenes, brings to the creations of fantasy. And that the quality of musical reproduction is so wretched a feature of television receivers provides an even stronger argument for the staging of *Owen Wingrave*: to hear in the theatre a texture like the bi-planar one which accompanies Owen's apostrophe to peace is to recognize under how dark a coat of uniform varnish the opera was first revealed to the world.

Once it became known that Britten was to collaborate for this opera with Myfanwy Piper on the reinterpretation of a ghost story by Henry James, all the signs appeared to suggest that they were intent on providing a companion piece to *The Turn of the Screw*. And when the score revealed (as it does on even the most perfunctory reading) that the opera is unified by methods which owe much to twelve-note principle—though little to any practice other than Britten's own—one might have thought to see a still closer connexion with the earlier James-Piper opera. Yet the two works reveal none of those detailed similarities, of procedure and language, which make the three parables appear facets of a single experience; the sixteen-year interval between them is rarely to be forgotten. Indeed, the discovery of his 'parable' methods was among the vital gains of that period, and *Wingrave* demonstrates some contexts for which Britten was able to retain textural and temporal ideals established in creating an enclosed, ritualized world, while also rounding out musico-dramatic situations and portraying characters that call for the more generous melodic, harmonic and colouristic symbols of his earlier operas. Had *Wingrave* immediately followed the *Screw* (already in some respects a rigorous piece), it might have seemed spare, perhaps even a little dry in flavour; coming after the parables it signals a return to a richer variety of mood and colour. Both its scoring and its vocal phraseology appear sumptuous by contrast, yet sonorous felicities are not indulged for their own sake and, as we shall see, the organization of thematic material is a good deal more pervasive than it was in the scenes (as opposed to the interludes) of *The Turn of the Screw*.

James's *Owen Wingrave* is a shorter and far less suggestive story than his *Turn of the Screw*. Its account of the young descendant of a fanatically military family who refuses to follow a military career is recounted in studiedly prosaic terms, with many a shaft of telling irony but none of those chilling innuendoes that confirmed our visions of another sphere of existence behind the complacent façade of life at Bly. So when Owen, disinherited by his family and scorned by the girl he has loved since childhood, is goaded into proving that his renunciation of war springs from passionate conviction, not from cowardice, the denouement in which he sleeps in the haunted room and is there found dead can appear melodramatic rather than fateful. Whereas Mrs Piper's most hazardous task in the *Screw* must have been the invention of a mode of discourse proper to ghosts who in James are mute, in *Owen Wingrave* she had both to develop characters merely hinted at in James and to protract the action. This she has done not merely to achieve the time-span of a two-act opera, but so as most skilfully to allow Britten to elaborate upon the morbid quality of the Wingrave family tradition and, springing from this, to create a mounting sense of foreboding. Whether this suffices to invest the denouement with as overwhelming a force as that of the *Screw* must, however, be doubted. Two factors seem to militate against that. The first is a miscalculation of a kind rare in Britten: the music at the crucial moment of Kate's discovery of the body is neither as memorable in itself nor so palpably the crisis in a musical conflict waged throughout the work as was the equivalent catastrophe in the *Screw*. The more general point is that Mrs Piper's very adroitness in making three-dimensional characters of the story's other personages tends to make us see Owen's struggle as taking place primarily at the level of human relationships, whether highly-charged or no more than courteous. He has to justify his actions not only to the peppery, if not demented, Wingraves, but to eminently reasonable people like the Coyles and to a pathetic figure like Mrs Julian. The very substantiality of these characters to a considerable extent counteracts the talk of supernatural forces; and even after the apparition of the old man and the boy which invades Owen's soliloquy we do not, as in the *Screw*, weigh every action and word in terms of a substratum of existence that has been not merely glimpsed but explored. So when Owen finally has to settle his score with (we must assume) ghosts as well as men, the shift of dramatic level comes too late, however steady the musical accumulation of tension has been. The end of *Owen Wingrave* shocks, but it leaves questions that are not brushed away by the return of the ballad. The flaw begins in the original story; despite its failure to eradicate it, the opera markedly improves on the shape and power of its source.

The scale of Henry James's story does not permit the creation even of its central character in much depth. Instead of beginning, like James, with Owen's decision to give up his preparation for the army, Myfanwy Piper devised an introductory scene in which we see Mr Coyle's enthusiastic tuition and the contrasted response to it of Owen and his fellow student, Lechmere. Similarly, instead of our arriving at the Wingraves' house, Paramore, after Owen has been interviewed by his grandfather and disinherited, we see him tested in two painful confrontations with his family. No less importantly, we see him constantly set into relief against the background of Wingrave tradition represented by the charmless house and by the gallery in which hang the portraits of his ancestors, soldiers to a man and, as he now sees them, unimaginative gentlemanly brutes too. James's Owen, escaping from Coyle's tutorial to read Goethe in the park, may strike his gesture of revolt, however unflinchingly, largely out of a hazy idealism. The opera's more articulate Owen is steadily plumbed, until we are able to accept as the final illumination of his character the noble *Credo* in which he apostrophizes peace, in all its manifestations, as the supreme human aspiration. The theme was implicit in James, but in refashioning the treatment to admit so explicit a statement, Britten was returning to a preoccupation that had inspired some of his most eloquent music.

Mrs Piper's amplification of some other characters is less directed towards this central issue, though the relentless, clipped phrases of Owen's aunt, Miss Wingrave, and the senile trumpetings of his grandfather, Sir Philip, contribute to a grim picture of the forces against which he rebels. But the character of Mrs Julian, for example, a war widow resident at Paramore, who is sketched by James in a few wry words, has also been defined far more exactly in the opera. Her ready agitation and lachrymose woe provide material for a vivid musical portrait, one that helps us to glimpse the tensions which underlie the behaviour of her daughter, Kate. This is another figure deepened in the operatic treatment: the love she has felt towards an Owen for whom she had always foreseen a battlefield death (like her own father's) is racked but not destroyed by his renunciation of war, yet her pride is too strong to condone his action. Even Coyle, a student of strategy but a wiser student of human motivations than the fanatical Wingraves, Mrs Coyle, his gently shrewd wife, and the impulsive because empty-headed Lechmere, are given rôles substantial enough for this opera to demand one of Britten's most uniformly distinguished teams of singers; there are no minor parts, and the BBC commission allowed each part to be written with a particular artist in mind. Having been granted a cast including many of the finest British singers of the day, Britten took pains to provide each with worthy material. In fact the eight singers are rarely allowed extended set pieces, for the camera (or perhaps only those who control it) becomes uncomfortable in circumstances which call for a renunciation of visual action in favour of the musical intensification of a situation. The quite rapid flux does not reduce the individuality of each musical personality, however, and this is the more remarkable when we consider how very tightly unified is so much of this opera's thematic material. As in all Britten's vocal contexts, his use of accompanying motives and colours contributes much to the exact differentiation of character, but it remains impressive how vocal lines that draw persistently upon a very restricted store of intervals are made apt vehicles for a wide range of emotional nuances. (We shall see that still more restricted motivic sources feed the lines of *Death in Venice*, but there the essential point is that every situation is another manifestation of one complex emotional-cum-physical process—and there is in essence only a single character.)

The primary source of this intervallic material in *Owen Wingrave* is the twelve-note proposition reiterated in the alternations of three clangorous

Ex.20.1 (a)   Ex.20.1 (b)

chords by piano, harp and elaborate percussion with which the opera begins (Ex. 1). These sounds, evoking long-past battles, become a symbol, of war and of the Wingraves' fanatical devotion to it, that is to recur frequently in the opera. Its rhythmic profile is scarcely less important than its pitch content, and either in isolation can make an unambiguous point. At various moments the opening complex is quite literally cited. In the first orchestral interlude, for example, heard against a visual 'sequence of brilliant flags', it follows naturally from Coyle's description of Owen as the presumed successor to the Wingrave tradition. But in Scene 3, as Owen imagines the reception his family will give to the apostate, it sounds muted and chilling; here the pitch set is elaborated by transposition, then by a slight permutation which converts the first two chords into whole-tone clusters; finally, as Owen and Lechmere argue, the initial chord is protracted through an orchestral crescendo into Interlude III (the Paramore music), where it sets off a linear process in the bass. Other literal returns accompany Owen's two approaches to his ancestors' portraits, after Kate has spurned him on his arrival at Paramore in Act I, and when he is left alone after the disinheritance scene in Act II. The first remains distant, but the second swells ominously and recedes again across its three appearances; its rhythms are then transformed into the conflicting element sustained by the percussion throughout Owen's 'Peace' soliloquy, and erupt openly in Ex. 1 terms at his reference to wars; still more tellingly, its initial chord once again makes a transition, but by *acting* for once as a dominant seventh that is ultimately released in the serene B flat chord that opens the celebration of peace. So the one symbol represents that which Owen most abhors and that battle he must wage against the moral pressures of those he most loves. The recognition of this battle is made by Coyle as early as Scene 6, but it comes to Owen most forcefully in the recitative when he resolves to enter the haunted room: 'Not fear but anguish makes me tremble. The anger of the world is locked up there—the horrible power that makes men fight: Now I alone must take it on; I must go in there'. Inevitably the backgrounds to both these contexts are versions of Ex. 1, the second conflating it to a twelve-note mass. Even divorced from its original textural and rhythmic context, the pitch set may usually be apprehended by the listener because of its relationships between very familiar chords, i.e., two dominant sevenths (usually in 6/5 positions) and a minor ninth (in root

505

position), on roots that rise by semitones. This is an even simpler proposition than that set out by the chords in Act II of *A Midsummer-Night's Dream*; because of the uniform density of the *Wingrave* chords, however, they can at times be used less obtrusively than those in the *Dream*, which always exercise their spell openly. Thus, the reference to Ex. 1 (*ii-i-iii*) in Act II, Scene 1, when Mrs Julian describes the legend of the house as 'noble' is plain, but Sir Philip's dangerously quiet 'There's no more to be said' that finally breaks up the wretched dinner party may not at once be heard to contain a dry mockery of the war theme.

As in *A Midsummer-Night's Dream*, the twelve-note harmonic complex generates no definitive linear forms; we are at the furthest remove from the operation of a melodic mechanism that characterized the *Screw* music. We shall see that there are, in fact, a number of twelve-note melodic contexts (independently harmonized) and some passages in which melody-plus-harmony consistently form twelve-note fields. But these do not derive *directly* from Ex. 1. That they invariably have intervallic cells in common with it makes them no more than special examples of a general situation, for the substance of the whole opera is strongly coloured by the dissolution into it of the opening proposition. The dominant sevenths (*i* and *ii* in Ex. 1b) rarely either function as such (the most important exception has been noted already) or take on that poignancy of expression Britten had discovered in the 'natural' sound of the major triad with flat seventh ever since *Peter Grimes*. Instead, its major and diminished triads are separated out and used with great consistency as contradictory elements: to see them as 'peaceful' and 'warlike' in nature may appear unduly schematic but can often be supported by a wealth of detail. The 'peace' symbols, however, must be seen also in relation to another field of intervals—that set up by the ballad, which inflects the major triad with diatonic 'added note' nuances.

How obsessively the diminished triad is laboured in this score is clear already in the sequence of Wingrave family portraits through which we are conducted in the Prelude, immediately following the presentation of the fundamental Ex. 1. The percussion which characterize that motive are now recalled only by tenor-drum rhythms (permuting the Ex. 1 units); these punctuate a series of wind solos, above sustained string harmony, which provide musical profiles for the figures we see in successive portraits (see Ex. 2). It will be obvious from the example that each one of these themes is built around a succession of diminished triads, which may (as in the fourth portrait) closely reflect the pitch content of Ex. 1, but need not (as in, say, the sixth). The fifth portrait requires a duet, of piccolo and trombone, being of two figures, an old general and his young son. The accompanying string harmony has set out from a single pitch for the first portrait and added one for each new figure (two, obviously enough, for the double portrait), so that the eleven-note chord shown in Ex. 2k *ii* accompanies the tenth portrait theme, of which it is in fact a harmonic conflation. The missing pitch class is

Ex.20.2 (a)

Bassoon

pp

Ex.20.2 (b)

Oboe

p

Ex.20.2 (c)

Horn

p

Ex.20.2 (d)

Clarinet

mf

Ex.20.2 (e)

Piccolo

p dolce

etc.

Muted
Tbne.

p

Ex.20.2 (f)

Muted Tpt.

p   *mf*

Ex.20.2 (g)

Unison W.W.

p   etc.

507

Ex.20.2 (h)

Ex.20.2 (j)

Ex.20.2 (k) i

Ex.20.2 (k) ii

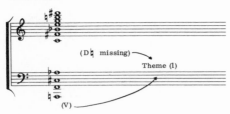

Ex.20.2 (l)

D, to which with its bass A the vast chord is a quasi-dominant, and it is this twelfth pitch which is supplied by the last Wingrave generation, Owen himself, who appears as the chord resolves on to a D luminously coloured across some six octaves. The process as described appears ludicrously mechanical but it operates effectively on the listener, countering the effect of themes that are merely listed with that of harmony which steadily grows. Owen's own theme (Ex. 2 1), played by the horn, is naturally enough of much the same stuff as its precursors, but in two important respects is to be differentiated: triadic arpeggios with the perfect fifth now outnumber

508

diminished triads, and the whole theme is explicable within the single tonal field of D, principally of minor modality though coloured by a whole-tone descent to the final tonic. One wonders whether Britten at some stage had in mind a more central rôle for this theme than he eventually accorded it. It makes some significant reappearances during Act I: as Owen reads in the park of the vile sham that is war, the succession of muted portrait themes, heard against a sequence of flags now 'old, faded, tattered', ends at the words 'Look to thyself . . .' with his own theme forlornly inverted in the tuba; when Coyle recognizes the fighter in Owen (Scene 6), the horn plays his theme with consistently *diminished* triads; and as the party files off from the abortive dinner, Owen brings up the rear, attended by his horn theme in a shortened form, cadencing upwards through whole tones to the D which ends the act. Thereafter, however, the gulf that separates Owen from his family and ancestors is made absolute by various aspects of the war/peace dichotomy noted above, and especially by enhancing the rôle of the ballad theme, with its historical resonances from the one Wingrave who offers a model for Owen, the fated young boy. Once the ballad is brought into the open (its rôle in Act I has been a submerged one), then its influence in opposition to Ex. 1 can be more certainly grasped by the listener than would be a distinction that rested solely on those features we have noted as differentiating Ex. 2 l from Ex. 2a–k. But this may seem to leave Owen in Act II without a clearly defined musical character of his own. This is in a sense true, and no doubt intentional, for only after he has won several stages of the battle against all that he is not does he acquire the strength of purpose to affirm what he is, in the soliloquy to peace.

The other portrait themes commonly recur as a sequence, though not necessarily a complete one: for example, Interludes I and II, the 'brilliant' and the 'tattered' flags, use complementary selections. After Kate's rejection (Act I, Scene 5) Owen appeals to the portraits in a forlorn fantasy of their themes. The most remarkable return of this instrumental material comes, however, not in an orchestral passage, but when Sir Philip delivers his ultimatum to Owen (Act II, Scene 2); backed by the authority of each one of those ancestors, he trumpets his condemnation to a vocal *fioritura* on their themes, ending with a peroration on themes of his own (to be discussed later). The extravagent nature of this, particularly in relation to Sir Philip's terse vocal style elsewhere, conveys a near-madness that could easily topple in performance into the merely ludicrous—perhaps still worse, into the self-consciously virtuoso. Britten avoids these dangers by reinforcing Sir Philip's batteries with warlike signals of horn and percussion, but casting this trio as only one element of a dual texture, its sounds from behind closed doors (so that the wordless vocalise is plausible) being complemented by the foreground comments of the rest of the party; the two planes preserve strict but quite independent tempos. Heard in this interrupted and apparently fortuitous way, Sir Philip's outburst takes on a goaded quality that may even allow us to direct a little of our sympathy towards him, as his most fervent ideals are rejected and his family pride is soured. Among the themes he touches on are those of the old general and the son he killed for refusing to fight (Ex. 2e). These have a more independent rôle than the other portrait themes, appearing with their ghostly visual counterparts at the climax of Owen's soliloquy, just after he has gloried in being 'finished with you all'; the boy's theme, now high in the oboe, has the urgency of an appeal, choked off by the brassy fury his father's theme releases. Less expectedly, Miss Wingrave dismisses Owen from the family record, 'The renegade is now as if he had not ever been . . .' to a recall of the boy's theme, and Owen bitterly echoes this as he reviews his fate. If we care to make the connexion, then we may reflect here just how far outside the family pale was the boy in the simple diatonic scales of his theme, untroubled by a single diminished triad. Much earlier (perhaps too early for the point to go home unless the work is familiar) Mrs Coyle evoked a quotation of the same theme with her 'Had I a son I could not bear to think of his bright life banished to some dreadful battlefield'—followed by the admission that such a son might have had to serve (and the diminished triads roll back into the bass).

To chart all the other contexts in the opera which relate to the Wingraves' military fixations by drawing prominently on diminished triads would be an elaborate but wearying exercise in the obvious; comment on one or two will serve to begin a process of identification the ear will have no difficulty in extending. Passing from the prelude into the opera's opening scene, we find the one chordal shape endlessly circling in the strings' arpeggios; although their warmer sound marks a move to the sphere of Coyle's more civilizing influence, the subject he expounds is still war. And Owen has learnt well: as he enters Paramore to face his family and finds all silent, he recognizes the tactics—'Good soldiers in a mist, we're told, keep silent'—to a hazy orchestral texture that recalls the circling triplet arpeggios of Coyle's lesson. At dinner Mrs Coyle's tactless reference to Owen's 'scruples' is seized on by Sir Philip and his allies, who mull over the word in an ecstasy of scorn, vividly conveyed by the parallel diminished triads (initially with minor ninths reminiscent of chord *iii* in Ex. 1) of their vocal harmony. Other figurations have a more equivocal flavour in playing off diminished against perfect-fifth triads, reflecting Owen's position in terms more cryptic than his theme. Thus his first declaration to Coyle, 'I can't go through with it', exposes a diminished triad in juxtaposing 'purer' triads (see Ex. 3a), and the beautiful texture of muted strings that accompanies his thoughts in the park (Ex. 3b) deflects from unison Gs to sound alternately the diminished triad of war and a major 6/5, a 'peace' symbol deriving from the ballad, as we shall see; similarly in Scene 3 (e.g., at fig. 74) Owen's decision is argued over to orchestral figures that conflate both kinds of triad (Ex. 3c).

Just how prodigally Britten has drawn on certain intervallic characteristics of his twelve-note proposition will be clear, but also how rarely the deriva-

Ex.20.3 (a)

Ex.20.3 (b)

Ex.20.3 (c)

tions contribute to twelve-note situations. Some of the special cases mentioned above, which demonstrate this property, may be noted now. A simple
and memorable instance is the ceremonial theme (tutti but pianissimo for
the most part) to which the Wingraves and their guests enter dinner; its
melodic diminished triads form two complete sets, while its bass (thickened
by triads) ascends the two whole-tone scales in succession to form a third set.
The withdrawal begun by Sir Philip attempts an inversion of this theme, but
in far less orderly array. But the most protracted use of twelve-note organization is to be found in Interlude IV. This is not a purely orchestral piece but
depended originally on a televisual 'abstraction of the four heads' of the
residents of Paramore, whose separate reactions to Owen's defection are
thus fused into a nightmarish résumé of his reception. The familiar initial
chord (Ex. 1 *i*) is already rumbling when Sir Philip's 'Sirrah!' gives it vocal
form, and all Owen's accusers pile up their outraged cries, 'How dare you!'
(Ex. 4a) to complete a declaration of war, i.e., the Ex. 1 set. Their individual

reproaches are supported and punctuated by orchestral details that extend the original chordal principle through a chain of twelve-note sets (every third chord serves as first in the next set), a piece of serial artifice such as Britten had never before employed so consistently. What follows, however, is still more surprising. Leading off from Sir Philip's 'Ha, they'll never stand

Ex. 20.4 (a)

Ex. 20.4 (b)

for it', the orchestral accompaniment continues to create a twelve-note succession (now by inflecting the woodwind notes added to immobile brass perfect fifths), while the voices enter in fugato manner, the three successive entries completing the same set; that one of the regular countersubjects is freely timed adds to the novelty of this context. Its technical device is not a mere conceit: such palpable concentration of the means serves a direct dramatic end, creating a feeling of suffocating pressure brought to bear. And when the mood suddenly changes, after an explosive climax, to sorrow rather than anger, the material is, if anything, further concentrated: the three segments of the set are now delivered ('sweetly') as successive woodwind solos, but the string accompaniment to each oscillates, in four rhythmic strata (see Ex. 4b) between the remaining eight pitches. The maudlin interlude does not last long, and through a succession of brassy rhythms (♩♫♫♩—a key pattern introduced in the Paramore interlude, and discussed below) that build up a linear twelve-note set from the ubiquitous

512

diminished triads, Owen's tormentors outdo the paroxysm of their original 'How dare you!' in repeating it in pure Ex. 1 terms.

The other principal body of interrelated material, it will by now be clear, is that which symbolizes the influences in opposition to the warlike spirit. Their most clarified expression, in the form of rooted triads with perfect fifths, comes in Owen's address to peace, yet the final line of that (quoted below at Ex. 7) memorably closes on an added sixth. The source of the many mild diatonic dissonances of that kind is to be found in the ballad which frames Act II; note especially the bracketed groups in Ex. 5. The effect of this ballad

Ex.20.5

is likely always to depend greatly on the producer's treatment. Unlike 'Malo' in the *Screw*, it can never carry with it the weight of that sympathy, compounded with whatever revulsion, we have experienced for a character whose development has been shown to us at disturbingly various levels. Whether he appeals to us from the portrait (see above) or is described to us in the ballad, the Wingrave boy remains a shadow—however long it is cast over Owen's path. By creating an historical perspective in which we see Owen's action as a rare but recurrent stand against brutish violence, the ballad can add to the opera's expressive reach, yet for this purpose it does not need, I believe, to be at all involved in the opera's action. Its emergence after the 'supernatural' denouement is in danger of falsifying our response: no longer cool and timeless, it can seem too direct an extension of what we have just witnessed. Furthermore, the ballad tune is a good deal more diffuse as a melodic structure than was 'Malo'. In addition to the diatonic characteristics of the first three bars (the chief influence on other material), there is the Mixolydian modality of the refrain and, rather disconcertingly, the sequential semitones of bars 5 to 7. The later stanzas of the first presentation necessarily stave off monotony by their modulations, while the final one is smoothly worked into the substance of the scene, but these very refinements tend to reduce the gulf that would ideally set apart the artless repetition of ballad from the sophisticated nuances through which opera makes its expressive points. The otherness of the ballad is safeguarded mainly by the distance from which it reaches us, and the use of a chorus of trebles that is never heard within the action; to use a tenor familiar from the action, as was done in the original productions (Peter Pears sang the narrative as well as the rôle of Sir Philip), appears needlessly to endanger the intended effect.

However one may respond to the ballad itself, one may find its dissemination through the opera to be put to impressive dramatic ends. Particularly successful is the allocation of an important rôle to its melodic shape x in Ex. 5 during Act I, before we can attach to this the specific meaning that is revealed when it burgeons into the ballad tune, and a new facet of Paramore's history is understood. Such associations as x has are with the house, for the shape was first outlined in the orchestral Interlude III, accompanying our first views of Paramore. As we should expect, our first *musical* impressions of it are grimly charged with the rumblings of war: we noted above how Ex. 1 formed the climax of Owen's argument with Lechmere as he prepared to leave for Paramore, and the interlude unfolds above the heavy irregular tread of the note-row in an expanded linear form. It is also punctuated by a nervous rhythm (see Ex. 6, from bar 7), military enough in its stabbing reiterations on muted brass, but oddly faltering in its deceleration and diminuendo; the dying trumpet calls of the ballad (see above, Ex. 5) are to recall this. But the melodic thread that gives this interlude a warm, fervent tone we cannot yet explain is that drawn by the strings (see Ex. 6), forming great curves from a multiplication of the ballad's opening cells; meanwhile the wind, doubling these notes individually, are sustaining them to form

Ex.20.6

harmonic units (compare the orchestral methods of *Budd*—the mist and the trial shot—but also the textural methods of the parables), and these are the prototypes for those bright added-note-diatonic chords referred to already. The passage is an example of Britten's scoring at its most ardent, so that later our memory can respond keenly to quite minute promptings. Its returns are quite literal as the occupants of Paramore await Owen's arrival, confident that he will 'listen to the house' (ironically, he will listen to the wrong part of its message), and as Owen approaches the music swells and quickens. Thereafter, it is recalled only in fragments and, in particular, harmonies, like the luminous build-up of the *x* figure to which he calls his greeting. Repeated with interpolated notes in the percussion, this exhausts twelve pitches—by 'peaceful' means for the first time. (The context is to have an ironic counterpart in Act II: when Kate wounds Owen with her 'coward that you are', its diminished triads chime on in a twelve-note context directly modelled on this one.) With the Coyles' arrival at Paramore (Scene 6), these harmonies again create one aspect of the house's atmosphere, a wandering cello solo dwelling on the diminished triads of the other aspect.

The ballad having been heard in full, Act II's references to its opening shapes carry more explicit meanings, drawing inescapable parallels between past and present Wingraves; indeed, the immediate sequel to the ballad is permeated by its lingering influence. Less obviously but very affectingly, the shapes of the ballad refrain drift into the still moment when Owen returns from his interview to announce, 'It's over, I'm disinherited. He turns me out for ever'. A bitterly direct reference to the ballad, paraphrasing its text, is made by Owen after the scene in which Lechmere has ingratiated himself with Kate—'And with his friend young Lechmere played'. Of more consequence is the 6/5/3 brass chord that accommodates the reference, for it is the outcome of a wedge-shaped figure heard for the first time at this point (Ex. 7). The figure (passing from unison to added-sixth not without dissonance but with no trace of tritone or diminished triad) seems like a slow breath of an air purified of all the ugly emotions we have been witnessing, and its return to end Owen's soliloquy, when he believes himself to have broken the last tie, is very fitting.

Ex.20.7

The use of the twelve-note material of Ex. 1 was compared with that of the 'Sleep' chords in *A Midsummer-Night's Dream*. In Owen's apostrophe to Peace, the articulation by richly spaced wind triads that cover a span of all twelve roots (and the succession of roots is also triadic; see Ex. 8a) may

515

Ex.20.8 (a)

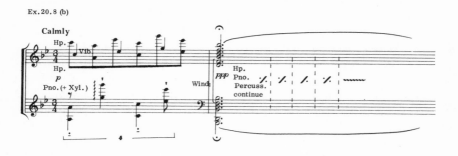

Ex.20.8 (b)

suggest a parallel with the twelve transfigured triads of the lovers' awakening in the same opera. Yet by the end of *Owen Wingrave* it is possible to feel that the triads of the famous interlude in *Billy Budd* offer a closer emotional parallel; in both contexts an innocent victim is vouchsafed a rarefied, even beatific, vision before he faces his ordeal. That Owen's is given articulate form (almost to a fault: one could wish him to avoid the sermonizing tone of so many parallel clauses) and Billy's is mute is an accurate enough reflection of the gulf that separates these two Britten heroes. Whereas the triads in *Budd* seem serenely isolated in musical space, those in *Wingrave* are sustained against flickering rhythms of the percussion instruments (xylophone, glockenspiel, harp and piano) that were predominant in the music of war (i.e., Ex. 1); the pitches create opposition, but no longer of a violent kind; as Ex 8b shows, the percussion's oscillations form extensions of the third-chain, above the basic wind triads. Only at the eruption of the warlike spirit does the percussion harmony form into a diminished seventh (i.e., two diminished triads) and take on the aggressive manner of Ex. 1. The second deflection from the characteristic tone of Owen's soliloquy comes, as we have noted, just after he exults in his freedom from the obligations of his inheritance, whereupon a ghostly transformation of the Paramore interlude music conjures up the apparition of the old man and the boy. Their power over him defied, he arrives again at the clarified stage of Ex. 7; and the final triad, A flat (with sixth) in the strings, is free of the percussion's unrest. To describe the central vocal paragraph of the opera in terms of its accompaniment may seem perverse, yet the crucial musico-dramatic argument is undoubtedly conducted there. Owen's lines are a generous arioso, straightforwardly diatonic within the prevailing triad's tonal field, except at the warlike episode and at the ghosts' appearance, where pitched lines give way to a tense *Sprechstimme*.

But the serenity in which the soliloquy ends is short-lived. The *x* chord (joined by the Ex. 6 rhythm) acquires an unsuspected edge when Kate, during the saddening scene of their attempt to find a reconciliation, challenges Owen to sleep in the room haunted since it witnessed the terrible events of the ballad's story. As he enters the room, the orchestra bursts out triumphantly with a spaciously scored chord, 4/2 on G, to which Owen's defiant note and the brass's Ex. 6 rhythms add the E that completes the characteristic harmonic colour. The reverberations of this climactic moment (within which Lechmere's inane enquiry is felt to be the impudence Kate finds it) take a very long time to clear. And when the last wind chord has faded, the strings keep the sound in our ears as dry pizzicato reiterations of the ballad's first line, overlapped within itself in a nervously stumbing pattern, Ex. 9. (The method derives from the parables, through the last

Ex.20.9

Pushkin song, while the quintuplets and triplets are, of course, offshoots of the Ex. 6 rhythm.) The regular pulse of the upper parts marks the leaden passing of highly charged seconds throughout Scene 5, while echoes of the climactic chord, each a step lower, accompany fade-outs representing longer passages of time as the Coyles, sleepless and uneasy, wait and talk. The ticking sounds are at last suspended, but the added-sixth harmonies, now restored to the pitches of the ballad itself, slowly swell to their last climax as the whole household rushes to join Kate, who has cried from the haunted room. (The echo of 'How dare you!' at their 'What is it?' gives an extra twist to this anguished moment.) Then the ticking resumes blankly as the distraught Kate tells of finding Owen dead within. There remains only Sir Philip's arrival, to his own military signal (see below) that is choked as he opens the door and we see the body; in the macabre tone of the xylophone the Ex. 6 rhythm fades for the last time, and the ballad takes over from the frozen stage action.

In concentrating so far on the behaviour of two bodies of material, this account has ignored many moments of the opera which the listener may find to be among its most immediately attractive. Yet a scheme of relationships as ramified as that just described (far from exhaustively) carries evidently enough the dramatic burden of the entire work: either we accept Britten's

symbols, and experience (consciously or intuitively) the conflict generated
between them, or we must find much of the opera's music an irrelevance, if not
a confusion, thrust between us and the story. However, this does not mean
that we may reverse the argument and view the music motivically furthest
from the central conflict as irrelevant: the more lyrical episodes, for example, even though they may concern the less central characters, never for a
moment allow us to forget the opera's preoccupations. In the sense that
learning geography, going to church, playing the piano, and so on could *seem*
(albeit not for long) diversions in *The Turn of the Screw*, there are no
diversions in *Owen Wingrave*. On the other hand, almost every character has
some individual musical attribute, creating across the whole opera a range of
gesture wide enough to counterbalance the motivic concentration of the
principal dramatic events.

Miss Wingrave, for example, sings almost throughout in the same highly
idiosyncratic manner: her 2/2 metre of clipped rhythms is imposed on
whatever temporal situation prevails around her, and her wide, insistent
intervals, supported by simmering woodwind shakes, discourage contradiction; see Ex. 10a. So her abandonment of this manner when she addresses
the company after Owen's disinheritance suggests how deeply she is
wounded below the stiffly preserved dignity. Even Sir Philip does not exist
for us solely as one further example of the standard Wingrave warrior (i.e.,
one further Ex. 1 derivative). His simple joy in the call to battle is embodied
in a leaping-fourth signal that is often extended into a near-quotation of
'The Minstrel Boy' (see Ex. 10b). Rather oddly, though not at all inexplic-

Ex.20.10 (a)

Ex.20.10 (b) i

Ex.20.10 (b) ii

ably, this echoes exactly the delight young Lechmere has shown at the prospect of action ever since the first scene, during which he actually sang a snatch from the same song and elatedly brandished a weapon. The two men's music finds an unexpected meeting point during Owen's interview with his grandfather: Lechmere, seizing on Kate's talk of her 'rejection' by Owen, questions her eagerly as he sees a chance to leap into a new kind of campaign, and the wind quote 'The Minstrel Boy'; immediately afterwards, Sir Philip, from within, in an incoherent fury that terribly resembles joy, trumpets out the same shape. Little of Lechmere's music calls for notice, since he is so predictable a character, yet the scene in which Kate calculatedly flatters his vanity in order to wound Owen develops a new thematic shape to an edgy rhythm, the opening of woodwind figurations being underlined by brass (from one bar before fig. 228); though the growth of this shape gradually ousts the material of which it was no more than an interruption, it seems to convey as much a growing tension in the amazed spectators (among them Owen) as Lechmere's excitement sweeping him beyond discretion.

In the drooping arpeggios of Kate's lines in these exchanges there is a clearer reflection of the musical character already outlined, notably in the arietta, 'How strange to abandon the dreams of our childhood', through which she is introduced. This comes in Act I, Scene 4, made up of vignettes of Paramore's three women residents; each is seen alone at a different upstairs window, but their burden is cumulative till all three voice their conviction that Owen will 'listen to the house'. Kate's soliloquy begins wistfully with a slowly descending melodic line extended through three octaves (mainly in whole-tone steps) by the strings, but counterpointed in the wind by winding arpeggios (see Ex. 11). The semiquaver rhythm which

Ex.20.11

ends their figure acquires a harder, pizzicato edge in the sequel, 'I'll not allow him his treacherous thoughts', and the steely resolve of which Kate is capable stamps the heroic climax phrase. Yet the use of gentle string triads (*never* diminished) tends in the context of this opera to suggest a 'sympathetic' character, even if the tonal instability no less certainly suggests a deeply troubled one. The recurrent swing is between G flat major and G minor (as in the climax phrase, for example), a trait Kate shares with her mother. But before we consider Mrs Julian's music, we should look at the other extended Kate scene, her duet with Owen; it follows an infinitely sad recall of the Ex. 11 material. The nostalgia they bring to shared childhood memories is released in a long flow of impulsive melody that seems to take us back to an earlier Britten. Like most of *Wingrave*, however, this remains texturally spare—the melodic line doubled (or, as the vocal phrases lose their control, sustained) in the strings and an accompaniment figure of parallel sevenths moving conjunctly in mixed-woodwind colouring (replaced at the second statement by trumpets). Illustrative touches like the xylophone's 'click-click of antlers' are a rare indulgence in this work, but can be accommodated within what is obviously to be one of the opera's most spacious statements—as the beautiful cadence phrase ending a clear first strophe confirms. But in the arrested wind chord, now of a seventh made up of two perfect fourths, Kate's first reproach is voiced, and the second strophe is far less contained: the perfect fourths intrude on the flowing texture as edgy reminders of an earlier Kate rhythm (cf. Ex. 11, bar 2), and this paragraph ends not in sonorous vocal octaves but stridently dissociated sevenths. It is in the following dialogue (tensed always against the sustained wind fourths and/or the timpani's rhythmic ones) that Kate flings her 'coward' jibe, to material noted already; after this the warm flow of the duet can only be recalled in hopeless appeal as the tragic sequence is set into motion. Owen's *tierce de Picardie* to the whole C minor duet is that E which complements the orchestra's blazing chord as he enters the haunted room.

Mrs Julian, discovered at her window in Scene 4, expresses her agitation at Owen's fall from grace in compulsive word repetitions, to a bitonal canon-by-inversion in rapid pizzicato. The self-pity already apparent is given its head after Owen's disinheritance, and the ruin of Kate's marital prospects, when a recall of this music passes into the maudlin aria, 'O, come Kate, come my only child'—to the strains of which Kate is devoting herself to the encouragement of Lechmere. Like Mrs Julian's words, this aria totters on the verge of caricature, though Jennifer Vyvyan's creation of the rôle showed that such extravagant woe can be drawn into a plausible musical character study. The aria is nearer Britten's standard distortion techniques than anything else in the opera, a vocal line in G flat being orchestrally doubled at the sixth below (i.e., in B flat) and at the diminished octave (i.e., in G) and accompanied sonorously in G; the interruptions we have noted above prevent this contrivance from appearing too automatic.

Coyle's lesson in Scene 1 was mentioned as an example of that *idée fixe* of war, the diminished triad, employed in the relatively 'friendly' context of lapping string arpeggios. The music that characterizes the man, still warmer, even fatherly in tone, is given fullest expression in his arioso, 'Straight out of school', at the end of the same scene. Again a reminder of Britten's early style in the melody (its Lydian A opening and the tonal arch from A to E flat and back stir memories back to *Grimes*) is modified by the tenuous accompanying texture—a scalic thread of wind tone; both in the overlaps which occur in this and in its free association of duplet, triplet and quadruplet divisions this owes more to the parables' methods. The recurrence of this music just before the denouement is not contrived, but provides a natural vehicle for Coyle's anxieties for Owen. Mrs Coyle's music is less memorably defined, and she is never heard alone. Her reflections in Scene 3 most nearly approach soliloquy, but the generous lines never acquire accompaniments peculiar to her. She takes on a stronger profile in relation to Kate, whose musical manner she parodies almost as soon as she arrives at Paramore ('Oh what a very important personage'). Her counsel to Kate in Act II, Scene 2, to trust even where she does not understand, subtly smoothes with conjunct lines the tensions of the violas' diminished triads, revealing Kate's angular answers to be a stubborn adherence to the Paramore fixation.

In discussing the opera's thematic material so much, I have referred to its assembly of the larger units only when, as in the 'How dare you' ensemble, a single principle is operating throughout. Elsewhere the juxtaposition of sections that aspire towards (but are not fully granted) 'set piece' status is not dissimilar from that of many other Britten scores; as we have seen in the Owen-Kate duet, the frequent suspension of patterned accompaniment for recitative-like dialogue allows such pieces to pass on naturally into the sequel. The rôle of the interludes is much less schematic than in *The Turn of the Screw*. The early introduction of the first two, the 'brilliant' and the 'tattered' flags, prepares us for a regular articulation of the action by such orchestral paragraphs that withdraw us from it, but the subsequent interludes are far more integrated, the third preparing the Paramore scene and the fourth ('How dare you') being itself essentially a scene, albeit between 'abstractions'. The final interlude prepares for the dinner scene that ends Act I by establishing the three ostinato shapes (chromatically knotted woodwind triplets, brass fourths doubled by harp, and curving string phrases delineating the diminished triad) whose repetitions in so long a scene help us to share the frayed nerves of the guests. The first act feels long and the interludes contribute to this; the second act, dispensing with them altogether, moves on relentlessly until that last scene when the sensation of time ticking endlessly is powerfully evoked, creating a tension that is to be explosively released.

Enough reference has been made to the textural dispositions of *Owen Wingrave* to support the argument that the opera, while in some pieces markedly (and no doubt consciously on the composer's part) recalling Britten's early operas, has profited from the experience of the parables. Where temporal strata are only loosely aligned this is self-evident, but the frequent reliance on a single vocal line and a single accompanying thread confirms how little recourse Britten now has to harmonic mechanisms *per se*; as we have seen, the opera's harmonic phenomena fall into two classes, systematically opposed, and the symbolic intent of a chord is more crucial than its place in an unfolding argument. The orchestra used is bigger than that of the chamber operas, comprising double woodwind, two each of horns, trumpets and trombones, and a tuba, as well as an elaborate array of percussion, with which we might class harp and piano for their important

521

roles in the music of war. Except at a very few moments (Owen's entry into the haunted room is the supreme one), the full force of a tutti is not exploited, but complete sections are restricted to the characterizing colours—dark string undulations with a flutter of harp arabesque (irresistibly recalling the *Lucretia* night music: see Ex. 3b) as Owen reads in the park; violas and flutes (alternating with oboes) in the conversation between Mrs Coyle and Kate; the opposed rôles of string and wind lines in Kate and Owen's duet (described above); or in Coyle's reflective music, and so on. The score thus leaves as many clearly defined sonorous memories as any Britten opera.

The use of a twelve-note source for so much of his material will not in itself lead us to expect any significant departure from the tonal ordering that was so important in Britten's operas before the break during the parables period. *The Turn of the Screw* was at once the score most obviously indebted to a twelve-note principle and the score most fastidiously organized as a long-term tonal argument. *Wingrave* has rather more passages of suspended tonality than earlier Britten, but also many pieces that can be assigned accurately enough (and often on the evidence of their key signatures) to a single point, or two opposed points, of reference. However, it is clear that the composer no longer treats tonal relationships as the fundamental dramatic analogues that they were in *Lucretia* or *Budd* (or even *The Burning Fiery Furnace*). As we have seen, *conflict*, the essence of virtually all Britten's dramatic scores, is now represented by the behaviour between contrasted bodies of motivic material, in particular, cells of intervals. The obsessive proliferation of such cells may often be pursued without the restriction to any given simple or extended tonal field being of the first importance, and thus there is a notable weakening of the buttress-like tonal props that loom so large in earlier scores. Canticle IV shows a highly concentrated form of this new saturation of texture by motivic cells of intervals, but the perfection of the method to an ambitious dramatic end was to be achieved with *Death in Venice*.

21 Death in Venice

It was possible to regret that Britten and Myfanwy Piper returned to Henry James for their second collaboration since they chose to adapt a story that is a good deal less compelling than *The Turn of the Screw*. With their last adaptation of story into opera, however, they showed a daring, and an imaginative power to justify it, fully equal to those exhibited by the first James opera. Britten's *Death in Venice* was completed in short score in December 1972, and in full score early in 1973, for performance at the Aldeburgh Festival of that year. Because of the composer's illness, he was unable to take part in the preparations for this production; Steuart Bedford conducted and Colin Graham produced the opera.

The choice of Thomas Mann's novella as the subject of a Britten opera promised another work in which, as in the first James adaptation, the composer might show his signal ability to illuminate a literary source at a variety of levels—by statement, ironic understatement, allusion, even innuendo. Indeed, Mann's text is more intricately layered than James's, and to preserve its richness of meaning within the constricting shape of a libretto must have been at least as problematic as Mrs Piper's first task. Though she was not called upon here to invent an entire mode of speech, as in the ghosts' scenes of *The Screw*, she was required to put into the direct form of soliloquy much that in Mann is rendered in the impassive third-person form of a delicately ironic narrative. Inevitably, the result, if one simply reads it, lacks both the nuances and the cumulative impact of Mann's magnificently timed paragraphs, yet in the musical context it contributes to a result that is remarkably true to Mann. In place of the verbal subtleties, Britten's characteristic refinements of musical detail afford comparably penetrating insights, while cumulative force is secured by a motivic chain more complex yet less obtrusive than in his previous operas, making of the whole work a sustained study of festering obsession.

Mann's text presents difficult material for a librettist not only because of its narrative form, but because it is so unremittingly concentrated upon one man's thoughts, visions and dreams. 'A solitary', writes Mann, 'unused to speaking of what he sees and feels, has mental experiences which are at once more intense and less articulate than those of a gregarious man'.[1] Granted that the intensity of his experiences must be communicated to us almost solely by musical means, the Aschenbach of the opera must none the less be articulate. Since soliloquy takes the place of narrative, his part is swollen to vast proportions, and the man of letters' tendency to subject his every sensation to an intellectual scrutiny is therefore more pronounced in Britten than in Mann. To convey this process of thought, Britten had to find a musical manner even further from the stylization of song than conventional recitative. But *Sprechgesang*, Schoenberg's most celebrated contribution to the continuum between speech and song, would not ideally answer his purpose since its aim is to suggest in a somewhat musicalized form (and often enough in a form intentionally distorted to Expressionistic ends) the contours and rhythms of natural speech. Britten restricted his notation to exact indications of pitch, and left his singer (Peter Pears in the original production) to find convincing 'thought'- rather than 'speech'-rhythms. In reviving the use of the piano as the only accompaniment of these inward deliberations, Britten was able to underscore that 'literary detachment' upon which Aschenbach's self-esteem is built, and the retention of this convention even when his soliloquies have become a clear-eyed recorder of, but in no sense a control upon, harrowing emotional experiences, makes a wry comment.

There is little in the words given to Aschenbach that cannot be traced back fairly directly to Mann, and even to the standard translation of the story by Mrs Lowe-Porter. For example, the writer's musings after his first glimpse of Tadzio are rendered in the direct speech of operatic recitative as follows:

> How does such beauty come about?
> What mysterious harmony between the individual and the universal law produces that perfection of form?
> Would the child be less good, less valuable as a human being, if he were less beautiful?
> The fact is that, in that disciplined family, beauty dominates.
> The severe plain little girls must be quiet, demure, the elegant boy may show off his grace.
> No doubt Mama with her fabulous pearls indulges herself in a pampering partial love—just as I indulge myself in these novelist's speculations.
> There is indeed in every artist's nature a wanton and treacherous proneness to side with beauty.

This compresses and re-orders passages from a much longer narrative in Mann, of which the first reads:

> Tired, yet mentally alert, he beguiled the long, tedious meal with abstract, even with transcendent matters: pondered the mysterious harmony that must come to subsist between the individual human being and the universal law in order that human beauty may result . . . [2]

[1] T. Mann, *Death in Venice* (transl. H. T. Lowe-Porter), Harmondsworth 1955, p. 29.
[2] Ibid., p. 33.

while the last two of Mrs Piper's sentences are drawn from the following:

> Was he delicate? . . . Or was he simply a pampered darling, the object of a self willed and partial love? Aschenbach inclined to think the latter. For in almost every artist nature is inborn a wanton and treacherous proneness to side with the beauty that breaks hearts, to single out aristocratic pretensions and pay them homage . . .
> This lady's abundant jewels were pearls . . . She might have been, in Germany, the wife of some high official. But there was something faintly fabulous, after all, in her appearance, though lent it solely by the pearls she wore: they were well-nigh priceless, and consisted of ear-rings and a three-stranded necklace, very long, with gems the size of cherries.[3]

Inevitably, one result of Mrs Piper's compression is an impoverishment of style, sometimes needlessly vulgarizing (as here in both the facetious 'Mama' and the term 'fabulous pearls', a less precise use of the epithet than in Mann/Porter), while the amplifications she introduces also threaten to reduce in stature the impressive character painted by Mann. Thus, when Aschenbach of the novella read the texts on the mortuary chapel, 'They enter into the House of the Lord' and 'May Light Everlasting shine upon them', he 'beguiled some minutes of his waiting with reading these formulas and letting his mind's eye lose itself in their mystical meaning', but Aschenbach of the opera has glib responses to each text—'Yes! From the black rectangular hole in the ground' and 'Light everlasting?—Would that the light of inspiration had not left me'. Some of the jarring notes are amplified by the composer's treatment, as in the arch repetitions of 'You notice when you're noticed', a lapse into a *buffo* style that ill suits Aschenbach, at this stage at least. But to carp about particular phrases is an ungenerous response to a libretto that, even though deprived of Mann's spacious paragraphs of carefully wrought prose, conveys so accurately the inner conflict which devours Aschenbach. The abandoning of narrative meant that many other sections of the libretto had to render into plausible speech what Mann could leave to allusive description. The Traveller's long aria, 'Marvels unfold', very directly converts Aschenbach's vision into a verbal appeal to his senses, but characters like the Hotel Manager and the Barber had to be created with far less help from the author, while ensemble scenes like that on board the boat to Venice or those in the city's public places must be almost wholly dependent on librettist and composer for their verisimilitude. Again minor irritations, like the ridiculous convention of requiring foreigners to pepper their speech with familiar native expressions while otherwise using English, can be ignored when these scenes contribute so effectively to the developing predicament of the central character.

Few operas have thrust on to a singer a burden as exclusive as that which Aschenbach carries. He is rarely off the stage, and then for the briefest of

[3] Ibid., pp. 32 and 31.

periods, while no action of any other character has any meaning independently of him. Yet this centrality does not mean that he dominates the events of the opera; rather is he dominated by them. Nothing makes this clearer than one's memories of the recurrent ideas upon which the work's tensions and also its chief beauties depend: the two most pervasive motivic sources (see Exx. 6a and 9a below) symbolize forces to which Aschenbach is helplessly subject, at the simplest level the godlike Tadzio and the plague, and his yearning after the one and uneasy quest for news of the other yield the most memorable shapes (Ex. 5a and b) directly associated with him. Of course, it could be argued that all the Tadzio music is Aschenbach's, his idealization of what attracts him in the boy into a model of that poised beauty towards which he has aspired in his own work. In this sense Aschenbach forges the instrument of his destruction, but his being powerless to act otherwise establishes him as a prey to fate after the manner of many a classical hero; it is appropriate therefore to consider his own *persona* and the agencies of fate as dramatically confronted.

Britten's use of an unmeasured notation for Aschenbach's thought processes has been noted. Across the many scenes of the opera a remarkable number of transitions have to be made by this slender means, on paper as unpromising and artificial as the most secco of recitatives. But no classical opera began with that device. By introducing us immediately to the writer's fretful mental activity, Britten helps us to accept soliloquy as Aschenbach's natural medium. Outside his writings he can communicate only with himself, and from the start we see him isolated from, even while at the mercy of, events around him. In fact, this opening passage is measured in notation, and has an orchestral background richer than the piano, yet the fluttering wind rhythms, elaborately crossed and at different tempos, create an apt sonorous limbo out of which the worn-out yet mentally relentless Aschenbach is heard. Mrs Piper's recurrent phrase, 'My mind beats on', admirably summarizes the situation, and Britten has set it to one of his introverted figures that nag in the memory (Ex. 1). These phrases initiate a complete twelve-note row, duly followed by its inversion, a form so near its retrograde as to suggest careful construction by the composer. Yet, while there can easily enough be found in this row the seeds of later developments (in particular, through the opera's most fateful and ubiquitous motive, x in Ex. 1b), it does not as an entity play at all the dominating rôle which its immediate exposition might lead us to expect—far less for example than the opening proposition of *Owen Wingrave*. Twelve-note fields of other kinds recur in the piano accompaniment to Aschenbach's soliloquies, such as complementary whole-tone scales and 'white-note'-versus-'black-note' contexts, both of which derive quite naturally from the row's own scalic properties. For example, when the writer first takes a book from his pocket as 'the sign of his literary detachment', the gesture is musically identified by Ex. 1c. From the consistency of such usages we might conclude that Britten has chosen to

regard twelve-note ordering as unduly intellectual, a sign of parched creativity, but it is no doubt much too early to consider the autobiographical
implications that would follow. Parenthetically it can be noted that there is,
in any event, one further twelve-note idea in the opera which does not relate

to Aschenbach's intellectualizing propensity, the Bergian series of intervals shown at Ex. 1d. Though its various forms recur at enough decisive moments (most notably when Aschenbach salutes in Tadzio his model) to acquire importance, I find it impossible to assign one cut-and-dried significance to the motive.

Aschenbach's soliloquies range from the most transparent melodic shapes (the fully chromatic descent through a tenth for the sand's passing through the hour glass recovers that boldly obvious originality of early Britten) to lines riddled with passing references to the central motives of the work, the many permutations of the *x* cell (see Ex. 6a, and Exx. 5 and 13 below) that symbolize the plague but also many other aspects of the fateful course to which he is committed. Some are overt, as when Aschenbach admits to 'a sudden desire for the unknown' in precisely the notes of the Traveller's 'Marvels unfold' (cf. Ex. 6a), but many more are hidden in apparently free lines, creating even in the recitatives that impression of a constricting web which the rest of the music more elaborately delineates; a single example must suffice; see Ex. 2. Before we become too inextricably enmeshed in that web, the opera's most remarkable technical (but, of course, ultimately dramatic) feature, we should look further at the musical depiction of its central figure for those details which reveal his character, not only his fate.

It may be that the character that he was is already under attack from his

Ex. 21.2

Ex. 21.3

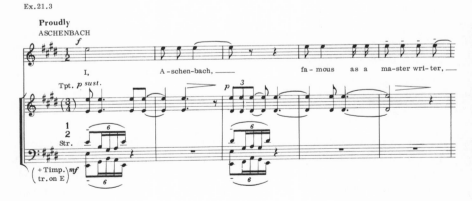

own sense of irony when the opera begins, for the trumpet motive which portrays the distinguished man of letters (Ex. 3) is self-consciously stiff, and when this is evoked by the unctuous address of the hotel manager, Aschenbach is quick to see embodied in it 'the writer who has found a way to reconcile art and honours'; at the last appearance of the motive (Act II, fig. 307), when his emotional and physical collapse is advanced, he spurns fame and self-discipline alike as 'all folly, all pretence'. And from the outset we have known that behind the façade of the public figure there could stir indefinable longings, symbolized in a motive of overlapping string scales, in the same E major as Ex. 3. This scalic texture (Ex. 4) first appears when the

Ex.21.4

Traveller's seductive appeal induces the writer to consider abandoning his habitual routine to journey to the South. Its warm, sweet sound of 'higher diatonic' dissonance recalls early Britten, its rhythmic blurrings are typical of his later manner; we have heard a similar fusion in Coyle's music in the previous opera. In an essentially unchanged form, the motive accompanies Aschenbach's voyage to Venice, but with its emergence at the end of Act I his aspirations have found a new object. Tadzio has smiled at him, and there is released in the orchestra a version of Ex. 4 no longer of limpid diatonic sonority, but racked by chromatic clashes that betoken the emotional conflict precipitating the crucial moment of self-discovery. Other motivic references at work in the passage are discussed below, including the x shape, multiplied here to create the chromatic relationships among the overlapping scales. Whether or not the listener takes the whole point of this at once, he will understand the distortion that has affected the string texture, and the isolation of Ex. 6f that ends the act merely chills into the hackneyed phrase what has burned in this orchestral eruption. On the physical level the plague is at work through the motive x, but now the canker has entered Aschenbach's emotional world; the wider significance of this will be considered later. With the opening of Act II, the music is resumed at the same point (cf. *Wozzeck*, and the original Act III–IV of *Budd*), and an orchestral prelude draws on the love motive to articulate ardent string lines: the connexion with Ex. 4, though tenuous, is not broken. This prelude represents Aschenbach's assimilation of an experience that we soon find him accepting, in a characteristic reversion to self-examination, as 'ridiculous, yet sacred too, but not dishonourable'. Its material makes several apt returns, but in the fevered atmosphere of the second act still more striking is the literal return of Ex. 4. This steals in gently as Aschenbach sleeps, recurring (like the long slow breaths of other Britten sleep music) between the conflicting commands of the priests of Apollo and Dionysus, whose appearance heralds the dream that develops into an orgiastic nightmare. The Ex. 4 recurrences become more animated but retain the 'purity' of their original diatonic form; the dreamer's longings are still fixed upon that Apollonian ideal he has found in Tadzio (in Mann, 'his will was steadfast to preserve and uphold his own god against the stranger'),[4] and so the horror is intensified when Tadzio's music bursts in, hideously bloated and interspersed with grotesque quotations of the plague motive, to envelop the dreamer in the orgy ('the stranger god was his own').

Aschenbach is destroyed physically by the plague, spiritually by an infatuation for the boy Tadzio that is ultimately a betrayal of his lifelong devotion to an ordered beauty, free from the excesses of unbridled passion. The recurrences of two orchestral motives help to chart his pitiable progress towards the abyss. In one (Ex. 5a) we witness his pursuit, to urgent bitonal

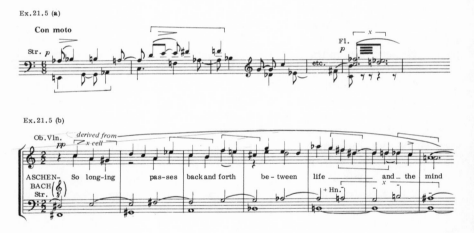

Ex.21.5 (a)

Ex.21.5 (b)

counterpoint, of accurate information about the cholera epidemic, and in the other (Ex. 5b) we see him driven by his yearning for Tadzio to reckless, panic-stricken pursuit of the boy. The one always leads into a form of the 'canker' motive (either in the vocal line or a tremolando chord, as in Ex. 5a), the other is itself branded with that shape (see the *x* markings in Ex. 5b) and is often compounded with Tadzio's motive (see Ex. 9) above, and sometimes with the plague form of *x* below. The means are almost excessively obvious, yet the end is unerringly achieved—the many recurrences of these ideas induce a sense of mounting obsession that is felt very strongly in the theatre.

[4] Ibid., p. 76.

530

Neither theme has a simple tonal basis: Ex. 5a commonly maintains a tritonal tension between its strands, but at no consistent levels, and Ex. 5b twists on a modulatory course but is consistently frustrated when the entire span is repeated as a ground (see after fig. 210 and at 217 and 222 in Act II).

Though they generate considerable orchestral paragraphs and Ex. 5b supports arioso lines, these ideas do not foster the vocal stability of aria. Aschenbach's thoughts are rarely rounded into that mode of expression, and significantly there is no example at all between his Hymn to Apollo, before the close of Act I, and the little setting of Socrates' words to Phaedrus, when Aschenbach's end is already foreshadowed. Earlier in the first act there have been three approaches to the sustained vocal exploration of a mood, but none expands far. As Aschenbach is rowed by gondola on his arrival in Venice, the orchestral barcarolle heard already in an 'Overture to Venice' (quoted at Ex. 6e below) continues while he savours the rediscovery of the city's enchantment in 'Ah Serenissima', a lilting piece in which sequential patterns of thirds show the great man capable of relaxing into a simplicity of style far from the tortuous formulations of his opening soliloquy: only the false relations of 'Ambiguous Venice' (a musical pun Britten must have found irresistible) and some concealed forms of the x motive faintly disturb the serenity of this moment. But x shapes leap to the fore as Aschenbach notices the wrong direction his gondolier has taken; though the journey drifts on smoothly in the orchestra, the altercation between the rower and the rowed overshadows the brief resumption of the aria manner before this is finally cut off by the singers on a passing boat. On shore at the Lido, Aschenbach's mood has darkened in his next expansive paragraph, 'Mysterious gondola'. Its *cantabile* line maintains essentially B flat minor against the A minor of the Stygian string chords. Mediating between such semitonally opposed areas, the harp figuration often suggests x cells (i.e. major containing minor third), and its glimmers of light make the surrounding gloom still blacker. Pondering on the gondola as a symbol of death prompts Aschenbach to review the hazards of his recent adventure in a more animated middle section, the return of the opening material being restricted to a single spacious phrase that at last reaches a consonant relation with the bass harmony. Such a piece, beautiful though its brief span is, might go almost unremarked in some other Britten operatic contexts, but the rarity of Aschenbach's achieving this reflective calm, and the weight of premonition the piece assumes in retrospect, give it an important place in the dramatic structure of Act I. One questions therefore the effectiveness of recalling this music (somewhat refashioned, it is true) for Aschenbach's later arrival at the Lido, when he has resolved to leave Venice: the repeated situation no doubt draws ironic attention to his changed sentiments (the result of some exposure to the city's foul air), and the greater prominence of x shapes, especially in the bass harmony, is to the point, but the garrulous Hotel Manager's speech destroys the earlier impression of this music.

531

The thought of leaving had entered Aschenbach's mind before this, when he sat on the beach below overcast skies and feared for his health. But the rhapsodic *fioritura* of this passage ('The wind is from the West'; before fig. 74), so rare in his part, tells us more of his romanticized attachment to Venice than of his vague apprehensions; his lines convert into scalic form rhythms that have just shaped the thirds of an orchestral theme symbolizing the beauty of the scene (see Ex. 14 below). And another theme at work both in this orchestral interlude (fig. 77) and as he sings is significant—that in which Tadzio's name is called across the beach (see Ex. 9b). Having watched some of the children at their games (even though Tadzio is absent for the moment), he returns to his languorous *fioritura* but to reversed purpose— 'I'll stay'. Rationalizing busily, he hails the restful 'perfection' he finds in the sea, but Tadzio's arrival offers another image, and prompts a reverie (from fig. 91) that perhaps marks Aschenbach's happiest moment, clouded by no nagging self-awareness and by no suspicion of the spreading plague. Now the *fioritura* is spun into orchestral lines that alternate with mysteriously blurred reiterations of Tadzio's name (see Ex. 9b) by an offstage chorus, and the sumptuous Ex. 14 returns to mark the climax. It is interesting that Aschenbach offers no direct comment on this scene, contenting himself with disentangling a shade pedantically the blurred name he has heard. It is only after two momentous decisions, to surrender openly 'to the sun and the feasts of the sun', and, following the visionary Apollonian scene, consciously to observe Tadzio as a model for his own style, that the quiet happiness of this reverie is exchanged for exaltation. Thought is to become feeling, feeling thought, but Aschenbach the observer now becomes a participant, and his Hymn to Apollo cannot bid the intoxication thus far and no further—as the end of the act will demonstrate.

This most expansive of all Aschenbach's statements is more properly discussed in relation to the Tadzio music, on which it is so heavily dependent. There remains, however, the one aria-like statement he makes in the disintegrating sequence of Act II. When degradation is complete and he sits, hideously painted, exhausted from the pursuit of a Tadzio who has now eluded him, and sick, he looks back on the man he was. Mann introduces as follows the recollections of Socrates that then enter his mind: 'His eyelids were closed, there was only a swift sidelong glint of the eyeballs now and again, something between a question and a leer; while the rouged and flabby mouth uttered single words of the sentences shaped in his disordered brain by the fantastic logic that governs our dreams'.[5] In Britten the mood created is not entirely in accordance with this. Partly because Mrs Piper has been compelled to reduce Mann's very substantial paragraph of the address to Phaedrus to a few rather elliptical lines, partly because of the strophic musical plan, but chiefly because of Britten's manner of setting the lines, this

[5] Ibid., p. 80.

little piece seems less a dream than a terrible access of clear-eyed vision as Socrates/Aschenbach uncovers the snare that may lie in wait for the Apollonian disciple, plunging him to that abyss which the follower of Dionysus has known to be his goal. Simple diatonicism makes a startling return here with the C major shape of 'O perilous, perilous sweetness', which becomes the opening phrase of the three stanzas (from fig. 308). The crystalline accompaniment of harp and piano (and there is imagery even in this mixture of a sensuous and a 'detached' colour) is made up of triadic arpeggios operating on diverging planes in the two instruments. The singer's first question and answer, with their accompaniment, embrace all twelve notes (essentially as a white-note/black-note juxtaposition), but the outcome of the two harmonic circuits is C minor versus C major, which is to hold the tensions of x (cf. Ex. 6a) in equipoise. A threefold repetition of the whole pattern throws into relief the valedictory coda, rendering the unaccompanied voice inordinately moving. All that can remain in the drama is the hopeless playing-out of this leave-taking.

Metaphors like 'canker' and 'snare' have been used in an attempt to convey the sensation of hidden undermining forces active in the work. Now that we are to consider the innumerable uses of the motivic cell x, it may be worth emphasizing that the near-ubiquity of shapes drawn from this one source implies that the vast majority are intended by the composer to remain hidden. The listener bent on consciously identifying every derivation would exchange an acute dramatic experience for a fatiguing boredom. This should not prevent our recognizing how potently the restriction of melodic shapes can contribute subconsciously to that experience. Britten had often enough relied on such devices, as many earlier chapters have shown: not all the consequences of Grimes's 'And God have mercy upon me' are apprehended at an immediate level, the masculine conjunct motion and feminine thirds in *Lucretia* help to create cogency rather than ostentatious 'leading-themes'; and so we could go on work by work to the unifying intervals of the parables and *Owen Wingrave*. The diminished triads in the last afford the closest precedent, yet they are more overt, whereas the many hidden derivatives of the one intervallic cell in *Death in Venice* exceed altogether any usage we might consider comparable in Britten's other operas. It might be said that the principle at work, of alternative thirds in close proximity, is so general as to be no more a *motivic* matter than, say, the scales and the triads which permeate any classical score: Britten's addiction to 'mixed modes' has been repeatedly referred to in this study, and the variability of the third degree is one of their most common characteristics. Even so, it remains impossible to find a parallel for the proliferation of the one nucleus of intervals (not necessarily extended to define a whole mode) in this opera. The nucleus itself has its most obvious precursor in the alternative or superimposed thirds of B minor and B flat major of *Billy Budd* (see p. 164, Ex. 8.1b); whereas that important thread was wholly absent from much of the work's

material, here it colours almost everything that is not patently drawn from
Tadzio's theme (to be discussed later).

It will be unnecessary to weary the reader who has persevered thus far in
this book, or the listener who knows a cross-section of the music, with many
examples of the expressive associations that in Britten's work surround the
inflexion to the minor of a major third. They are essentially traditional ones,
familiar to Purcell and to Schubert, of brightness dimmed (*War Requiem*, cf.
p. 462 of this book), the worm in the rose (Serenade, cf. p. 92), man's
destructive intervention in nature (*Our Hunting Fathers*, cf. p. 70), and so
on. Used repeatedly in the modal context 1–2–flat 3–natural 3 so unsubtle a

device would rapidly become intolerably tedious. In fact Britten first throws emphasis on the cell in just such a context, at the opening words of the mysterious Traveller's song in the Munich graveyard, 'Marvels ∙unfold' (a prophetic text to be attached to this shape), Ex. 6a, but elsewhere the interval content is more decisive than the modal context. In Ex. 6b are shown the two basic arrangements of tone and semitone within the major third (the further form t—s—s is simply the retrograde or retrograde inversion of x 1). Ex. 6, c to g shows some of the derivatives that are consistently used in at least one section of the opera, but many pages of examples would be needed to include all the isolated references; yet we have seen already at the end of the 'Phaedrus' aria that these too may be of great significance.

The Traveller who, by conjuring up for Aschenbach a vision of an alluringly exotic swampy landscape, rouses in him the urge to travel is the first of the agencies of fate. Following some clear leads from Mann (compare, for example, his descriptions of the Traveller, the surly gondolier and the leader of the travelling players), Britten assigned many of the rôles to the same bass-baritone singer. This thrusts home by means still more direct than description the single function they all discharge, of conducting Aschenbach towards a preordained end; and the common origin of much of their material in the x shapes heightens the impression of an unfolding myth. But not only human agencies are at work: the irresistible attraction Venice has for Aschenbach openly sways his judgment, and it is the cholera epidemic, lurking in wait throughout the opera, which on the physical level claims him a victim; both are symbolized by x motives. In Britten as in Mann, Aschenbach himself discerns dimly, if at all, the crossing strands of the net that envelops him. Mann's narrative ensures that the reader will interpret retrospectively the Munich vision when the young Englishman at the travel bureau describes the origins of Asiatic cholera in the swampy delta of the Ganges and its subsequent spread to Venice, but offers no evidence that Aschenbach does so too. In the opera even more falls into place with the later scene. The Traveller's principal motive (Ex. 6a) has come into the open as the symbol of the plague early in Act II (at the barber's incautious mention of 'sickness'), but why this should be so is only clarified with the travel agent's words and music. His long explanation, in a parlando style, is delivered above, and given coherence by, a complete return of the Traveller's aria in the orchestral bass. Texturally the two pieces are so contrasted that the correspondence is far from laboured. The Traveller's melodic lines form their own accompaniment by accumulation or dispersal of their pitches in the orchestra after the manner Britten had first practised in *Curlew River*. Here the instruments involved are chiefly wind in low register, the dense clusters of their overlaps serving to depict the 'wilderness swollen with fearful growth', while the parables' methods are further recalled by the rhythms of a variety of drums which constitute the only other textural element. The vocal thread is spaciously planned—in comparison with more typical Britten set pieces it seems a luxuriant growth indeed. But as soon as we admit the principle of octave transposition we find that the greater part of this line consists of *x* cells of one kind or another (sometimes fully semitonal in content). A rough count yields sixteen such groupings, of which six are different permutations of the actual pitches quoted at Ex. 6 a; cf. the treatment of the Father's motive in *The Prodigal Son* (see p. 496). These help to stabilize the piece by setting up a referential pitch area, and ultimately a tonic C, and so they occupy important positions, heading the first two musical sentences, ending the penultimate one and forming the entire final sentence. Each sentence consists of two or three phrases, the last always being given cadential force by the contraction of the texture to a unison. In consequence the impression persists of a traditional tonal arch, (C)–E–A–G–B–C, even though traditional functional harmony is abandoned (not, however, a two-voice framework) and the pitch content at most points is tonally equivocal. Nowhere in *Death in Venice* is the experience of the parables put to more original use than in this sombre fantasy. Inevitably the travel agent's scene cannot reproduce such mystery: explanations require a prosier vocal style than visions. There are no harmonic conflations of the orchestral bass melody, and the young Englishman's words make a very clipped counterpoint to it, but the woodwind add a new element, a descending scale operating at various levels. In its twisting between alternative forms of each scalic degree (e.g., E–D sharp–E–D natural is its mode of progress), it retains a connexion with *x*, recalling a stock 'Oriental' exoticism that is also reflected in its arabesques—an unduly naïve way of representing the plague's insidious invasion from the East, one might think, but its contrast to the studied self-control of the Englishman's account makes this more impressive.

Of the 'plague' form of *x* in other contexts little need be said. From its first open appearance on the tuba in the first scene at the Barber's, it is frequently associated with that baleful instrument, but the listener whose ears have been sharpened by Aschenbach's much earlier misgivings about Venice's rank air (see above, Ex. 5a) will hear the motive at work at innumerable other moments; for instance, its cluster form recurs when Aschenbach questions the leader of the players about the plague. Its outbursts in the orgy scene, noted already, are particularly gross since these pitches (i.e., as in Ex. 6a) invade the A major area of Tadzio's music. And when our attention, with Aschenbach's, is on the last of the children's games (in which Tadzio is cruelly humiliated), the plague motive erupts for the last time as Aschenbach's fears mount.

Scarcely less pervasive is the second form of the *x* cell, shown as *x2* in Ex. 6b and at Ex. 6d in the note-order that characterizes Venice. That unique city has a power of attraction which Mann felt as strongly as his Aschenbach, and one cannot doubt that Britten was equally subject to it. It was an inspired idea (though perhaps also a dangerous one) to represent Venice's compound of the majestic and the seedy by bandying the proud title of the Most Serene Republic within a banal popular song—'Serenissima'. Like so much good bad music, this has one melodic twist (here of a sentimental, because gratuitous, chromaticism) that lodges it unshakably in the memory. But the greater irony in Britten's opera is that this very song, first heard in the rather maudlin rendering of the callow youths who with an elderly fop are Aschenbach's companions on the voyage to Venice, is to give rise to the most hauntingly beautiful orchestral music in the opera—the barcarolle that accompanies his many journeys by gondola. The youths' version emerges out of the brazen major third of the ship's siren, but the later versions too (for example, that sung by the party on the boat that passes Aschenbach's gondola) are idealizations of that mechanical succession of thirds which is the authentic performing style of so many popular songs, not only in Italy. Britten's succession of intervals fluctuates, taking in seconds and fourths (or their compounds) with a curiously rocking effect. This is elaborated in the barcarolles by accompanying figures that set ♪♪♪ against ♪♪♪ (see Ex. 6e), most happily suggesting the gondola's propulsion and the lapping of the water around it. The 'overture' to Venice which marks Aschenbach's arrival has two other elements, a chant-like passage for brass (with built-in reverberations, in the church parable style) and a remarkable evocation of that hectic jangle at which Italian church bells excel. While these return for the scene inside St Mark's, the barcarolle's appearances are so frequent as to act like a ritornello. But it is not a wholly indifferent one. The melody can assume new contours under the influence of events: the *x* shape of 'Foul exhalations rise' (cf. Ex. 5a) is still active as Aschenbach is rowed away from the scene at fig. 115; at fig. 129 the steady scalic ascent reflects his soaring spirits at discovering a justification for abandoning his departure, and so on. As his own decline accelerates, the theme loses its slow, nostalgic mood, becoming more urgent in rhythmic accompaniment and importunate in orchestral sound (see fig. 299).

Of the minor, but never insignificant, figures who carry in their voices the memory of the Traveller, it is the Barber whose material draws most directly on the *x* cell. Punctuated by a mincing orchestral refrain, his solicitude for his clients is expressed over the suavest harmonic accompaniment in the opera, Ex. 7. The repetitions of this figure make for caricature, but once the plague motive has made its open appearance, the Barber's bland reassurances become more sinister, and the later scene, in which he applies literal as well as verbal cosmetics to the demoralized Aschenbach, is as macabre as anything in Britten's operas. In fact, the directly scalic *x* figure shown at Ex. 7 and the rhythm in which it is cast derive from another form that was introduced by the Traveller (see above, Ex. 6c). It framed his aria, orchestrally identifying the foreigner 'from beyond the Alps' and finally carrying his message, 'Go, travel to the South'. The relation of Ex. 7 to this motive is not quite exact (in the size of the seventh) and other characters are related

Ex.21.7

back to the Traveller by modifications of the Ex. 6c shape, not all of which are *x* forms in themselves. The genteel *falsetto* which flavours the Elderly Fop's leering innuendos widens the motive (Ex. 8a), while the surly Gondolier's clipped phrases contract it (Ex. 8b) to a form echoed in the pompous greeting of the Hotel Manager (Ex. 8c). The Leader of the Players, although the most sinister of all the baritone figures, is principally heard in songs that are extraneous to the action (though not to the moods) of the opera, but his brief exchange with Aschenbach on the plague forges a link with *x* material. And one character who is not impersonated by the bass-baritone, the Hotel Porter, is accompanied on his duties (which include the fateful assignment of Aschenbach's luggage to the wrong train) by an orchestral figure made up of *x*'s major/minor thirds (see Ex. 6g).

Ex.21.8 (a)   Ex.21.8 (b)

Ex.21.8 (c)

The last body of material to be considered is Tadzio's, the primary form of which is shown at Ex. 9a. Whereas many manifestations of the *x* shape are not intended to be consciously recognized, either by the audience or by Aschenbach, the whole world of sound in which the boy, his mother and his friends move is so distinctive as to be instantly apparent, and its effect on Aschenbach is equally open. At this point of the discussion, it would be neat to extend the Apollonian/Dionysiac dichotomy, made schematic in the vision by sunlit day of Act I and the dream by night of Act II (in the first

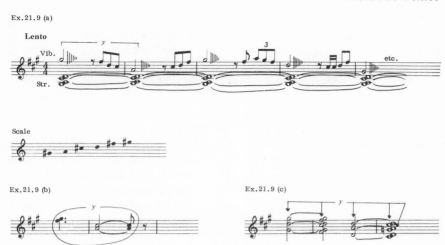

Ex.21.9 (a)

Ex.21.9 (b)

Ex.21.9 (c)

production one was set and costumed in a glowing white, the other in black), by regarding all the *x* material as pertaining to Dionysus and the *y* material (see Ex. 9) to Apollo. T. J. Reed, in a valuable note on Mann's story which appeared in the Aldeburgh programme book for the opera's first performances,[6] reminds us of the link between the cholera epidemic and the 'cult of the alien god Dionysus': both were thought to have their origins in India. So the Traveller's 'marvels' from the swamps can be interpreted on the psychological-cum-mythological level (to retain Reed's argument) as well as on the physical level. It is the orgy scene which seems to falsify this assumption, since Tadzio's music, in a distorted form (and with the intrusions of *x* we have noted), lies at its heart. But surely this is precisely what Socrates expounds to Phaedrus in Aschenbach's last 'aria' in the opera: the way of 'form and pure detachment' that the Apollonian treads can lead to a sensuous response to beauty, to passion, and thus to the Dionysiac abyss. Mann reduces the argument to a single sentence (if we are willing to read it with hindsight) when Aschenbach looks at Tadzio:

> 'Good, oh, very good indeed!', thought Aschenbach, assuming the patronizing air of the connoisseur to hide, as artists will, their ravishment over a masterpiece.[7]

The Dionysiac reaction is suppressed, the Apollonian acknowledged, and

[6] A more accessible form of his argument is Reed's introduction to *Der Tod in Venedig*, Oxford 1971, pp. 31–2. See also T. J. Reed, *Thomas Mann: The uses of tradition*, Oxford 1974, pp. 171–2.

[7] T. Mann, op. cit., p. 35.

The Music of Benjamin Britten

(to return to the musical point at issue) so it is with the *x* and *y* motivic elements. The point was made earlier that it is with an *x* derivative (see Ex. 6f) that Aschenbach recognizes at last his love for Tadzio, though even then, by octave transposition and that vast hesitating rest, the crudest association is averted; following so closely upon the proud artistic manifesto of the Hymn to Apollo (see Ex. 12), this illuminates the paradox that Act II must so painfully work out.

The otherness of Tadzio's world is not created solely by musical means. He and his mother are silent throughout and interpret their rôles through balletic mime. Even Tadzio's companions (his subjects almost) remain within this convention; insulated from the commerce of the hotel, they play out their games with a ritualistic precision that Aschenbach's imagination has no difficulty in translating to the ancient world. The only direct address to the boy we ever hear is that strange incantation to which his name is converted as it is called across the beach (Ex. 9b), a sound which, we have seen, can give rise to the reverie of Act I, Scene 5 or the bestial howls of the orgy in Act II. Its crucial interval is the spanning major seventh, taken from the central Tadzio theme, Ex. 9a. This *y* theme defines a kind of A major that is the opera's most consistently deployed key colour and its eventual goal, yet the prominence given to G sharp and the emphasis on the tritone are so persistent as to suggest less an unstable seventh-degree situation than a Locrian gapped mode, i.e., G sharp as *final* in the 'A major' set of pitches 7–1–3–4–6 (see Ex. 9). As in so much Britten since the parables, melodic and harmonic dimensions are virtually identical except in their timing; and the field of intervals, so far from the introverted *x* shape, soon acquires a highly individual tone. One is encouraged to compare this with that of Quint's motive in *The Screw* (cf. p. 208) though in fact the similarity of usage is immediately striking for other reasons: as consistently as Quint's presence was associated with the cloying timbre of the celesta, Tadzio's is linked to the vibraphone's statement of Ex. 9a. The vibraphone is not a cloying instrument, for it has little pronounced character at all, but its sound is appropriately disembodied, and Britten takes further the process of isolating Tadzio's music from the rest of the work by colouring it all with the delicately bright sounds of a large percussion orchestra. It seems that at one stage the composer even planned to separate spatially the Tadzio percussion from the main band; this would have made an absolute distinction between the two strata on which the music sometimes operates simultaneously, but the fundamental point is not lost even when both sound sources are in the pit.

Taken in conjunction with the oblique modality, the *gamelan*-like scoring creates a markedly oriental effect, comparable in both respects with that of the pagodas music in Act II of Britten's ballet. The parallel goes further in that Tadzio's theme as such is rarely placed in any progressive context: the *y* shape may be elaborated, for example in little vibraphone fantasies, but its movement usually remains within that one petrified modal situation (cf. p.

540

226 on *The Prince of the Pagodas*, but note also contexts like the feast in *The Burning Fiery Furnace*—see p. 487). This is psychologically accurate, since to Aschenbach the presence of the remote yet alluring Tadzio creates a fundamentally different level of experience, while the boy's varying activities and environments affect this only as nuances. However, there remain many contexts in which the *y* theme serves as more than a signal of the boy's presence (and a cue for Aschenbach's responsive *frisson*). Derivatives of it identify the circle around Tadzio, since Aschenbach never considers them in any other relationship. Tadzio's mother, the Polish lady of the pearls, is attended by a more spacious version of the theme (see Ex. 10a), with harmonic units that alternate between perfect and augmented fourths, and an independent bass that marks out similar intervals in linear form. The product of these elements is a mild chromaticism, though wholly without the Romantic stresses of appoggiatura, even when intensified in the sequel; this lends to the boy's pentatonic version by contrast a rather blank innocence. In depicting the children's games on the beach in little ballet scenes, Britten does not hesitate to employ still simpler music. In Act I, the essential shape and often the pentatonicism of *y* are preserved, but in new tonal areas and with a momentum foreign to it. The percussion orchestra's hard clarity emphasizes the repetitive quality of these patterns (Ex. 10b). In Act II this quality is no less obvious in the children's music, but the material has changed (Ex. 10c): it is no longer dominated by motives generated from *y*

Ex. 21.10 (a)

Ex. 21.10 (b)

Ex. 21.10 (c) i

Ex.21.10 (c) ii

and is far more adventurous in pitch relations, so that the revolt of the faithful courtier, Jaschiù, is prepared for.

As well as these scenes in which the children are shown at an ordered play, there is the extended 'Idyll' scene in Act I, in which their activities assume for Aschenbach the nature of a great festival in praise of Apollo. Critics of the opera's first production found this scene too long, and some of them thought the material undernourished, comparing it unfavourably with the choral dances in *Gloriana*. The comparison was bound to be made, not only because this too is a big celebratory tableau in which choral singing and ballet are matched, but also because the bright tone of much of the music recalls earlier Britten more strongly than almost anything (a deliberate exception will be noted shortly) in *Death in Venice*. The spectacle devised by librettist and composer has a rather tenuous foundation in Mann. In a paragraph that opens 'But that day, which began so fierily and festally, was not like other days; it was transmuted and gilded with mythical significance . . .',[8] Mann introduces the legend of Apollo, Hyacinth and Zephyr as an example of 'the most delicate fancies' into which Aschenbach's 'doting heart' converts the actions of Tadzio and his companions. It was essential in the opera to represent more fully this aspect of the writer's intoxicated state, since the means available to Mann cannot be adapted to a musical end: in several paragraphs of over-rich prose, saturated in classical allusions, he created a picture, a sensation even, of hot, timeless days spent in Elysium. Britten offers instead three mimed sequences with choral commentary, of which the Hyacinth legend forms the centrepiece. An orchestral interlude (necessary for the stage preparation of so elaborate a scene) presents in a quiet brass chorale the music that is then sung by the chorus as the brilliantly-lit beach scene is revealed:

> Beneath a dazzling sky
> The sea rolls silver white;
> Calm morning hours drift on
> To scented dusk and melting night.
> Day after carefree day
> The idle minutes run
> While he, transported to the antique world,
> Lives in Elysium.

[8] Ibid., p. 56.

542

Ex.21.11

This is set, inevitably, in Tadzio's A major (Ex. 11), its beautiful effect owing much to the simplicity of means—a descending and ascending chain of thirds, accompanied by the same shape reduced to conjunct motion paralleled in sixths. Formulas of this kind can be found so often in Britten's music of the 'forties that one may wonder whether the composer did not consciously transport himself back to a style that was in some sense more 'carefree' than his later music. The voice of Apollo (counter-tenor), the presiding deity of Aschenbach's vision, is heard between the three sequences, the first of which presents Tadzio as Phoebus. (It could thus be said to be an extrapolation from Mann's first plunge into mythological prose: 'Now daily the naked god with cheeks aflame drove his four fire-breathing steeds through heaven's spaces; and with him streamed the strong east wind that fluttered his yellow locks'[9].) Despite the swing to B flat for this piece, both its melodic line and its orchestral figures clearly reflect y, and Phoebus' zenith (Tadzio at the top of the pyramid formed by his companions) is marked by a quotation literal even to key. In the story of Apollo and Hyacinth the choral texture, still a mildly dissonant homophony, is now essentially in C major; but a strong link with y is preserved in the bass emphasis on the seventh degree, acting like a final and giving the tritone more importance than the perfect intervals. In a section with no action other than Tadzio's idle wandering, a dialogue between women's voices and men's represents Mann's first adaptation of Socrates' words to Phaedrus. The vocal lines are of triadic arpeggios ranging widely in tonality, but this discourse on beauty, 'the only form of spirit that our eyes can see', is underlaid by pure y elements in the fixed accompaniment. Finally the boys enact the pentathlon; classical precedent, in requiring as many as five of their races and trials of strength, leads at this point to the sense of protraction in an already long scene. References to Tadzio are as predictable as is his emergence from each contest as the victor, but the variety of reference is wide; note, for example, the bells' 1.3.4.6.7 (plus a flattened 2) of C sharp in the race, the percussion ostinato adapting y to a Lydian C for the javelin throwing, and the blatant retrograde form, restored to the A major pitch set, at 'Who is the victor?'. Simply to point to these unifying devices is to do scant justice to some highly

[9] Ibid., p. 46.

inventive choral writing in this scene. Since all of the music and action belongs to Aschenbach's fantasy world, it cannot be said to be irrelevant, but his being a silent spectator throughout checks noticeably the rising emotional temperature of the first act.

However, the lengthy silence gives great force to his return from this mythological excursion. As the choral reverberations of 'Tadzio has won' (motive y) continue as though into infinity, the voice of Apollo draws the moral of Aschenbach's vision—'This is the mirror and image of the spirit. Dedicate your prayers to me and to my powers'. Though the vision fades, the figure of Tadzio remains in the foreground, and Aschenbach, vowing to take him as the model that shall form his style, sings his Hymn to Apollo. This begins by echoing Apollo's own lines (cf. the opening phrase of each, at figs. 143 and 178), a melodic shape which Britten has derived from a classical source (the first Delphic Hymn[10]). In one of those glowing wind colourings, of trumpets as well as wood, which Britten has often used at peaks of aspiration, the orchestra develops this into bigger arches between the singer's phrases. But these already rest on a sustained Tadzio chord (harmony of Ex. 9a) and the orchestra soon introduces open references to the associated y shapes. A less rapturous line checks the mounting ecstasy: its text, 'when genius leaves contemplation for one moment of reality', casts less shadow than its very audible derivation from the fateful motive x, almost forgotten at this point in the opera. But the orchestral line mounts again to reach in an incandescent sonority the peak G sharp of Tadzio's theme, and Aschenbach, transfigured in this glow, sings his new artistic credo to a hymnic version of the theme (Ex. 12). The hymn dies and Aschenbach tries

Ex. 21.12

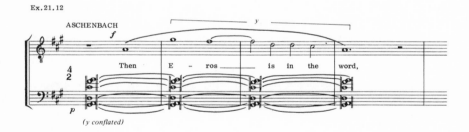

(y conflated)

to face the deity in the colder light of mundane existence, but fails the test utterly, finding himself incapable of speaking to the boy. 'The heat of the sun has made me mad', he explains to himself, in an ominous counterpoint of x references, from which he passes to the first statement of that yearning theme which is to colour his pursuit of the boy in the following act (Ex. 5b above); a cadential phrase, not retained in the later ostinati, is worth quoting

[10] Cf. e.g., A. Davison and W. Apel (eds), *Historical Anthology of Music*, Cambridge, Mass, 1949, I, p. 9.

Ex.21.13

as perhaps the most tortuous cross between *x* motives and the *y* theme in the opera (Ex. 13). The fusion of *x* shapes with Ex. 4 in the closing moments of the act has already been examined; Tadzio's smile has finally broken down Aschenbach's protective idealism and ravishment has openly supplanted connoisseurship. One further element in the elaborate orchestral crescendo should be mentioned, the stammering repetitions in the brass of Aschenbach's 'Don't smile like that', for it is out of this hammering in his brain that he breaks through to the truth: the brass figure begins as a faithful copy of his phrase, tone-semitone, but is converted to semitone-tone. Light dawns fully in the s–t–s of the *x* form, Ex. 6f.

Other music that utilizes the *y* theme derives so evidently as to warrant little comment. For example, the 'yearning' theme just mentioned is often placed below chords that conflate the properties of the whole theme into two moves (see above, Ex. 9c). When Tadzio is at a nearby table in the Piazza, even the café orchestra's waltz and march tell Aschenbach of his presence; this little band within the action (looking back through *Grimes* to *Wozzeck*), of violin, clarinet and double bass, decorously distorts the symbol of immanent beauty into one of trivial prettiness. But the orchestral violins promptly convert the rising seventh A–G sharp back into an aspiring shape, overlapped with itself. Yet this is equivocal: we may hear in it an echo of 'Eros in the word' (Ex. 12) or of the siren song, 'Adjiù' (Ex. 9b). On this point the end of the opera is to turn. After the boy's defeat in the last beach game, the voices call his name in its Ex. 9b form, but Aschenbach, for so long a silent spectator of the beach scenes, gently adds his own appeal in the melodic seventh A–G sharp, a direct approach (not to be found in Mann) that elicits Tadzio's enigmatic beckoning gesture and provokes Aschenbach's fatal collapse. It is in the orchestral postlude that the interval is drawn back into the idealized Apollonian world of the Hymn, which reappears as a fervent string *cantabile*, finally mounting through overlapping segments of Ex. 12 to the last ethereal A. Even at this moment of sublime valediction, the counterpoint provided by Tadzio's theme seems impassive. Though it ultimately achieves a unison with the violins' high A, a shake on G sharp persists at the lowest extreme of this tenuous texture, so that the Locrian slant is never wholly abandoned and 'resolution', if glimpsed, is never savoured.

Only one further motivic shape calls for mention. Tadzio embodies a beauty that Aschenbach finds overwhelming because of its strangeness, and we have seen how certain exotic musical colourings confirm this impression.

But the connoisseur of beauty is susceptible to more familiar manifestations, and he is repeatedly moved by the grand view of the sea that the hotel commands. For this 'conventional' response, Britten creates a musical idea that, albeit strikingly beautiful, appears in terms of his own style to be conventionally, almost out-datedly, so. The drooping third-chains of its juxtaposed triads strike echoes back to the Britten of the forties (Ex. 14) and

Ex.21.14

the textures to which its later developments give rise provide the opera's nearest approach to an indulgence in rich sound for its own sake. One noted already is the opening of the Apollonian choral scene, 'Beneath a dazzling sky' (see Ex. 11), but the various orchestral stretti on the 'view' theme finally achieve a great peak of sonority in the interlude that follows the words of Socrates recalled by Aschenbach when, utterly broken, he looks steadily into the abyss. Ironic though it can seem at this point, the nobility of this last orchestral upsurge is none the less a commemoration of the man that was, able to transform the experience of beauty into the grand designs of art. All the more painful, therefore, is the final return of this theme when Aschenbach surveys the empty beach for the last time: as a lonely flute solo (marked 'cold'), it is heard over the low seconds of two double basses in an amalgam of *x* forms.

Such crossings of motivic references are almost continuous in many of the opera's later scenes. But few require much exposition to the listener familiar with the basic shapes, for in a work characterized by textures that can look dangerously thin on paper, every overt reference can sound through clearly. In fact the textural range is a good deal wider than first appearances suggest. After the opening independently-timed wind rhythms there are far fewer examples of flexible alignment than in the parables, or even *Wingrave*, but the prolongation of melody notes into harmonic support is impressively used in the Traveller's aria and the Act II Prelude, while in Tadzio's music, as we have seen, the vertical and horizontal dimensions can scarcely be considered to have separate existence. Tenuous two-part writing gives the stamp to the music of Aschenbach's pursuit, but distortions of conventional harmonic textures often characterize those who assist his progress. The whole of the players' scene affords a study in this field, apparently so fully explored in earlier Britten scores yet here yielding a dry, cryptic tone that, in a nominally amusing context, creates a very uneasy mood, most plainly in the wheezing concertina accompaniment of the laughing-song; its singer, the players' leader, is the last of the bass-baritone characters.

As with *Owen Wingrave*, so with *Death in Venice* little has been said about tonal schemes by comparison with their discussion in earlier chapters. The Traveller's C major/minor fixes the pitches (Ex. 6a) that most often carry the plague form of *x*, and the Socrates piece shows the end of that line very clearly, yet innumerable *x* contexts cannot be assigned to a single tonal field. Indeed, the proliferation of this motive does not form neat correspondences within the octave but tends to take us into a tonal limbo: to call this 'atonality' would be misleadingly to invite comparison with textures of far more densely 'dissonant' pitch content, but in charting Aschenbach's almost crazed wanderings Britten has moved further than in any other opera score from the demonstrably tonal regulation of events. Only Tadzio's music, essentially immutable amid the turmoil assailing its victim, does set up one fixed pitch area to which an audience must be immediately susceptible. *Death in Venice* reinforces the conclusion arrived at in the commentary on *Wingrave*, that the symbolism of conflict (War-Peace; Dionysiac-Apollonian) has moved from the tonal plane to the motivic, even intervallic. The decline of primarily tonal structuring means that Britten has less recourse than in his earlier operatic style to schematic organization of a kind explicable in isolation from the drama. Ritornellos, whether in the shape of the 'Serenissima' barcarolles or of the 'yearning' theme, help to articulate the succession of short scenes (the formal 'interlude', on the other hand, is almost entirely discarded, so that the pace of events is rapid); but a diagram would reveal few symmetries of more monumental a cast. On the contrary, Act II always represents a decline (in scale, not quality) from what was achieved in Act I: the huge Apollonian idyll is scarcely balanced by a Dionysiac orgy almost too short to shatter us as the dreamer is shattered, and the spacious Hymn to Apollo is countered pathetically by the miniature strophes of the Socrates piece. In that Act II resumes exactly where Act I left us, there is created the impression of a single continuous line of action, whether Aschenbach is subject or object: far less than in *Grimes* or *Lucretia*, less even than in *Budd*, *The Screw* or *Wingrave*, is any diverting element allowed to make an appeal to us independently of the reflection it offers of the central character's condition. The close of *Death in Venice* scarcely invites anything as easy as our compassion, still less the patronage of our pardon, but in no Britten operatic character study have we been taken as fearlessly towards the state of understanding all.

Bibliography

A comprehensive Britten bibliography, such as was provided in the Mitchell-Keller symposium of 1952, would by now be very extensive; it would also include a good deal of ephemeral writing. The select bibliography which follows is an attempt to identify important writings relating to each stage of the composer's output. Articles are therefore listed according to the chronology of the compositions on which they offer comment.

BOOKS AND 'BRITTEN ISSUES' OF PERIODICALS
E. Crozier (ed.), *Peter Grimes*, London 1945.
H. Keller, *The Rape of Lucretia; Albert Herring*, London 1947.
E. Crozier (ed.), *The Rape of Lucretia: a Symposium*, London 1947.
E. W. White, *Benjamin Britten: a Sketch of his Life and Works*, London 1948; German transl., 1948; revised 2nd ed., London 1954.
Music Survey, vol. II, no. 4—Britten issue; 1950.
Opera, vol. II—Britten issue; 1951.
Tempo, no. 21—Britten issue (*Billy Budd*); 1952.
D. Mitchell and H. Keller (eds), *Benjamin Britten: a commentary on his works from a group of specialists*, London 1952.
H. Lindler, *Benjamin Britten: das Opernwerk,* Bonn 1955.
A. Gishford (ed.), *Tribute to Benjamin Britten on his Fiftieth Birthday*, London 1963.
Tempo, no. 66/67—Britten 50th birthday issue; 1963.
I. Holst, *Britten*, London 1966; revised 2nd ed., London 1970.
M. Hurd, *Benjamin Britten*, London 1966.
P. M. Young, *Benjamin Britten*, London 1966.
P. Howard, *The Operas of Benjamin Britten*, London 1969.
E. W. White, *Benjamin Britten: his life and operas*, London 1970.
D. Mitchell and J. Evans (eds), *Benjamin Britten: pictures from a life*, London 1978.

ARTICLES ON THE PERIOD 1932–45
H. Boys, 'Benjamin Britten', *Monthly Musical Record* lxviii, 1938, p. 234.

J. A. Westrup, 'The Virtuosity of Benjamin Britten', *The Listener,* xxviii, 1942, p. 93.

C. Mason, 'Britten: another view', *Monthly Musical Record* lxxiii, 1943, p. 153.

S. Goddard, 'Benjamin Britten' in A. L. Bacharach (ed.), *British Music of our Time*, Harmondsworth 1946, p. 209.

P. Evans, 'Sonata Structures in early Britten', *Tempo* 82, 1967, p. 2.

E. W. White, 'Britten in the Theatre: a provisional catalogue', *Tempo* 107, 1973, p. 2.

P. Le Page, 'Benjamin Britten's *Rejoice in the Lamb*', *Music Review* xxxiii, 1972, p. 122.

ARTICLES ON THE PERIOD 1945–54

E. Stein, 'Opera and *Peter Grimes*', *Tempo* (old series) 12, 1945, p. 2.

A. Payne, 'Dramatic Use of Tonality in *Peter Grimes*', *Tempo* 66/67, 1963, p. 22.

P. Brett, 'Britten and Grimes', *Musical Times* cxviii, 1977, p. 995.

E. Stein, 'Form in Opera: *Albert Herring* examined', *Tempo* 5, 1947, p. 4.

H. Keller, 'Benjamin Britten's Second Quartet', *Tempo* (old series) 18, 1947, p. 6.

I. Holst, 'Britten's *Saint Nicolas*', *Tempo* 10, 1948, p. 23.

D. Mitchell, 'A Note on *St. Nicolas*: some point of Britten's style', *Music Survey* ii, 1950, p. 220.

D. Mitchell, 'Britten's *Let's Make an Opera*, Op. 45', *Music Survey* ii, 1949, p. 86.

E. Stein, 'Benjamin Britten's Operas', *Opera* i. 1950, p. 16.

L. Berkeley, 'Britten's Spring Symphony', *Music and Letters* xxxi, 1950, p. 216.

E. Stein, 'Britten's Spring Symphony', *Tempo* 15, 1950, p. 19.

D. Mitchell, 'More off than on *Billy Budd*', *Music Survey* iv, 1952, p. 386.

A. Porter, 'Britten's *Billy Budd*', *Music and Letters* xxxiii, 1952, p. 111.

E. Stein, 'The Music of *Billy Budd*', *Opera* iii, 1952, p. 206.

A. Porter, 'Britten's *Gloriana*', *Music and Letters* xxxiv, 1953, p. 277.

J. Klein, 'Reflections on *Gloriana*', *Tempo* 29, 1953, p. 16.

ARTICLES ON THE PERIOD 1954–63

E. Stein, '*The Turn of the Screw* and its musical idiom', *Tempo* 34, 1955, p. 6.

D. Brown, 'Britten's Three Canticles', *Music Review* xxi, 1960, p. 55.

J. Noble, Britten's *Songs from the Chinese*; *Tempo* 52, 1959, p. 25.

E. Stein, 'Britten's new opera for children: *Noyes Fludde*', *Tempo* 48, 1958, p. 7.

E. Roseberry, 'The Music of *Noyes Fludde*', *Tempo* 49, 1958, p. 2.

I. Holst, 'Britten's Nocturne', *Tempo* 50, 1958, p. 14.

S. Bradshaw, 'Britten's *Cantata Academica*', *Tempo* 53/54, 1960, p. 22.

549

E. Roseberry, 'Britten's *Missa Brevis'*, *Tempo* 53/54, 1960, p. 11.

P. Evans, 'Britten's new opera: a preview' [of *A Midsummer-Night's Dream*], *Tempo* 53/54, 1960, p. 34.

P. Evans, 'Britten's Cello Sonata', *Tempo* 58, 1961, p. 8.

P. Evans, 'Britten's *War Requiem'*, *Tempo* 61/62, 1962, p. 20.

A. Robertson, 'Britten's *War Requiem'*, *Musical Times* ciii, 1962, p. 308.

A. Whittall, 'Tonal Instability in Britten's *War Requiem'*, *Music Review* xxiv, 1963, p. 201.

M. Boyd, 'Britten, Verdi and the Requiem', *Tempo* 86, 1968, p. 2.

P. Evans, 'Britten's Cello Symphony', *Tempo* 66/67, 1963, p. 2.

J. Warrack, 'Britten's Cello Symphony', *Musical Times* cv, 1964, p. 418.

E. Roseberry, 'Britten's *Cantata Misericordium* and *Psalm 150'*, *Tempo* 66/67, 1963, p. 40.

A. Whittall, 'Tonality in Britten's Song Cycles with Piano'. *Tempo* 96, 1971, p. 2.

ARTICLES ON THE PERIOD 1964–76

P. Evans, 'Britten's Television Opera', *Musical Times* cxii, 1971, p. 425.

P. Evans, 'Britten's *Death in Venice'*, *Opera*, xxiv, 1973, p. 490.

P. Evans, 'Britten's Fourth Creative Decade', *Tempo* 106, 1973, p. 8.

C. Matthews, 'Britten's Indian Summer', *Soundings* vi, 1977, p. 44.

Catalogue of Britten's Published Compositions
and
Index of References in the Text

As the chapters of this book provide in effect an arrangement by genre of the composer's works, the catalogue below is simply a chronological list; the dates given are of composition, though revision or publication dates are added when these are significantly later. The list is based primarily on *Benjamin Britten: A Complete Catalogue of his Published Works*, London 1973, to which reference should be made for further details, e.g., of dedications, scoring, movement titles, first performances and durations.

Publishers are indicated as follows:

BH   Boosey and Hawkes

FM   Faber Music

OUP   Oxford University Press

A page number in italics refers to the principal discussion of that work in this book.

1923–25	*Five Walztes*, waltzes for piano; re-written 1969 (FM), 6
1929	*A Wealden Trio: The Song of the Women*, carol for SSA voices unaccompanied (F. M. Ford); re-written 1967 (FM).
	The Birds, song with piano (Belloc); revised 1934 (BH).
1930	*A Hymn to the Virgin*, unaccompanied anthem (Anon.); revised 1934 (BH).
	The Sycamore Tree, carol for SATB unaccompanied (Trad.); re-written 1967 (FM).
1928–31	*Tit for Tat*, five songs with piano (de la Mare); re-written 1968 (FM), 6
1931	*Sweet was the Song the Virgin Sung*, Carol for SSAA unaccompanied; re-written 1966 (FM).
	String Quartet in D major; revised 1974 (FM), 6, 13, *21–3*, 340

1932		Three two-part songs for boys' or women's voices and piano (de la Mare) (OUP).
	Op. 1	*Sinfonietta* for chamber orchestra (BH), 1, 6, 8, *15–21*, 22, 23, 24, 26, 27, 31, 58, 60, 70, 92, 125, 340
	Op. 2	*Phantasy*, quartet for oboe and strings (BH), 9, 21, *23–6*, 27, 31, 86
1933	Op. 3	*A Boy was Born,* variations for unaccompanied choir (Anon., C. Rossetti, Tusser, Quarles) (OUP), *64–8*, 70, 77, 86, 429, 430, 444, 446, 448
	—	Two part-songs for SATB and piano (Wither, Graves); (BH).
1934	Op. 4	Simple Symphony for string orchestra (OUP), *38–9*, 349
	Op. 5	*Holiday Diary*, suite for piano (BH), 8, *26–7*, 29, 33, 48, 62, 329, 343
	—	*May*, unison song with piano (Anon.); The Year Book Press.
	Op. 7	*Friday Afternoons*, twelve children's songs with piano (Anon., Thackeray, J. Taylor, Udall, I. Walton, E. Farjeon) (BH), *257–8*
	—	*Te Deum* in C major, for choir and organ (OUP), *68*
1935	Op. 6	Suite for violin and piano (BH), 8, *27–30*, 42, 44, 308
1936	Op. 8	*Our Hunting Fathers*, symphonic cycle for high voice and orchestra (devised Auden) (BH), 38, 43, *68–73*, 76, 79, 94, 355, 385, 395, 429, 534
	Op. 9	*Soirées Musicales*, suite after Rossini, for orchestra (BH), *43–4*
1937	—	Two Ballads for two voices and piano (Slater, Auden) (BH).
	Op. 10	Variations on a Theme of Frank Bridge, for string orchestra (BH), 9, 30, 38, *39–43*, 44, 46, 51, 54, 73, 74, 76, 79, 243, 277, 301, 326, 469
	Op. 11	*On this Island,* five songs for high voice and piano (Auden) (BH), 30, *73–5*, 76, 79, 101, 228, 353, 355
	—	*Fish in the Unruffled Lakes*, song for high voice and piano (Auden) (BH).
	Op. 12	*Mont Juic*, suite of Catalan Dances for orchestra, by Lennox Berkeley and Benjamin Britten (BH), *43–4*
	—	Pacifist March, unison song with piano (Duncan); Peace Pledge Union.
1938	Op. 13	Piano Concerto; revised 1945 (BH), 30, *44–7*, 48, 50, 57, 77
	—	*Advance Democracy*, for unaccompanied choir (Swingler) (BH), *76*
1939	Op. 14	*Ballad of Heroes*, for tenor (or soprano), chorus and

1945   Op. 33   *Peter Grimes*, opera in a prologue and three acts (Slater) (BH), 2, 3, 7, 9, 10, 11, 12, 42, 47, 51, 76, 81, 92, 94, 101, 103, *104–23*, 124, 125, 126, 131, 136, 145, 146, 153, 160, 161, 163, 164, 168–9, 176, 216, 242, 243, 303, 308, 315, 319, 349, 355, 368, 373, 394, 414, 443, 448, 450, 462, 491, 506, 520, 533, 545, 547

        Op. 35   *The Holy Sonnets of John Donne*, nine songs for high voice and piano (BH), 10, 47, 262, 294, 300, *349–55*, 356, 370, 377, 388, 392, 473

        Op. 36   String Quartet No. 2 in C major (BH), 10, 35, 47, 58, *294–300*, 303, 308, 340, 349

1946   Op. 37   *The Rape of Lucretia*, opera in two acts (Duncan, after Obey) (BH), 10, 11, 27, *124–43*, 144, 161, 170, 212, 224, 347, 355, 373, 374, 394, 395–6, 398, 399, 400, 405, 414–15, 425, 429, 465, 490, 522, 533, 547

        Op. 34   *The Young Person's Guide to the Orchestra*, variations and fugue on a theme of Purcell, for orchestra (with speaker *ad lib.*; Crozier) (BH), 235, *300–3*, 333, 349

—   Prelude and Fugue on a Theme of Vittoria, for organ (BH), *303*

1947   Op. 39   *Albert Herring*, comic opera in three acts (Crozier, after Maupassant) (BH), 10, 11, 71, 99, 103, 126, 139, *144–62*, 168, 197, 203, 212, 216, 253, 270, 347, 360, 414–15, 435, 475, 485, 490

        Op. 40   Canticle I, 'My beloved is mine', for high voice and piano (Quarles) (BH), 393, *402–4*, 406

        Op. 41   *A Charm of Lullabies*, five songs for mezzo-soprano and piano (Blake, Burns, R. Greene, Randolph, J. Philip) (BH), *355–6*, 376, 392, 401

1948   Op. 42   *Saint Nicolas*, cantata for tenor, choruses, string orchestra, piano duet, percussion and organ (Crozier) (BH), 11, 148, 257, *258–64*, 271–2, 283, 284, 285, 292, 419, 466, 487

      (Op. 43   *The Beggar's Opera*; for details see under 'Arrangements and Realizations'), 6

1949   Op. 44   Spring Symphony, for SAT soloists, chorus, boys' choir and orchestra (Anon., Spenser, Nashe, Peele, Clare, Milton, Herrick, Vaughan, Auden, Barnefield, Blake, Beaumont and Fletcher) (BH), 11, 87, 126, 203, 212, 293, 376, *419–29*, 433, 436, 465

        Op. 45   *The Little Sweep*, opera for young people (Crozier) (BH), 11, 76, 148, 257, *264–71*, 272, 390

        Op. 46   A Wedding Anthem (*Amo ergo sum*), for ST solos, choir and organ (Duncan) (BH), *429–30*

554

PUBLISHED ARRANGEMENTS, REALIZATIONS AND
WRITINGS BY BRITTEN

Although this book examines only the composer's original compositions, a list of his other published work is included here. Some details of unpublished music, including film scores and incidental music, are to be found in the catalogue issued in 1963 by Boosey and Hawkes, but only when the Britten estate is fully explored and documented will a comprehensive list become possible.

Realizations

1948   Op. 43, *The Beggar's Opera*, ballad opera realized from the original airs (BH).

1951   *Dido and Aeneas*, opera by Henry Purcell, realized and edited by Britten and I. Holst (BH).

1967   *The Fairy Queen*, masque by Henry Purcell, concert version edited and realized by Britten, I. Holst and P. Ledger (FM).

At various dates the following works of Henry Purcell:

   Chacony in G minor, for strings (BH).

   The Golden Sonata, for two violins, cello and piano (BH).

   When night her purple veil had softly spread, chamber cantata for baritone, two violins and continuo (FM).

   Orpheus Britannicus, realized and edited by Britten and P. Pears (BH):

       Five Songs for voice and piano

       Six Songs for high (or medium) voice and piano

       Seven Songs for high (or medium) voice and piano

       Six Duets for high and low voices and piano

       Suite of Songs for high voice and orchestra

       Three Songs for high voice and orchestra

   Harmonia Sacra, realized and edited by Britten and P. Pears (BH):

       The Blessed Virgin's Expostulation, for high voice and piano

       Job's Curse, for high voice and piano

       Saul and the Witch at Endor, for STB voices and piano

       Three Divine Hymns for high (or medium) voice and piano

       Two Divine Hymns and Alleluia, for high voice and piano

   Odes and Elegies, realized and edited by Britten and P. Pears (BH):

       The Queen's Epicedium, for high voice and piano.

Arrangements

i) of folk songs, various dates

       Vol. 1, British Isles, for high or medium voice and piano (BH)

       Vol. 2, France, for high or medium voice and piano (BH)

       Vol. 3, British Isles, for high or medium voice and piano (BH)

       Vol. 4, Moore's Irish Melodies, for voice and piano (BH)

Vol. 5, British Isles, for voice and piano (BH)
Vol. 6, England, for high voice and guitar (BH)
The Holly and the Ivy, for unaccompanied chorus (BH)
King Herod and the Cock, for unison voices and piano (BH)
Eight British Folk Songs, for voice and orchestra (BH)
Six French Folk Songs, for voice and orchestra (BH)
Eight British Folk Songs, for voice and harp (FM)

ii) other arrangements
What the wild flowers tell me, second movement of Mahler's Third
Symphony, for reduced orchestra (BH)
The National Anthem, for chorus and orchestra, 1961 (BH)
Five Spiritual Songs by J. S. Bach, for high voice and piano, 1969
(FM)
God save the Queen, for orchestra, 1971 (FM)

Concerto Cadenzas
Cello Concerto in C by Haydn, 1964 (BH)
Piano Concerto in E flat, K. 482, by Mozart, 1966 (FM)

Writings
1940 'An English composer sees America', *Tempo* (New York) i.
1942 'On behalf of Gustav Mahler', *Tempo* (New York) ii.
1958 *The Story of Music*, with I. Holst; London; reissued as *The Wonderful
World of Music*, London, 1968.
1959 'On realizing the continuo in Purcell's songs', in I. Holst (ed.), *Henry
Purcell, 1659–1695*, London.
1964 *On receiving the first Aspen Award*, London.
1966 'Frank Bridge (1879–1941)', *Faber Music News*, Autumn 1966.

Index

Index